BOOK LOVERS'

PARIS

CW01496313

For
The Winslow Boy

Book Lovers'
PARIS

A Guide and Companion

ALLAN FOSTER

Published by Book Lovers' Press

www.edinburghbooktour.com

First published in 2021

ISBN 978-1-5272-7858-5

Cover artwork by Lucy Foster

Cover design by Kit Foster

CONTENTS

CONTENTS

CONTENTS

CONTENTS

PREFACE

I researched and wrote *Book Lovers' Paris* over a seven-year period. The research involved a lot of legwork, usually with Chris, my infinitely patient wife and editor, tracking down and photographing sites, getting lost, and coming up against countless dead ends. On finishing the final entries the exhilaration I felt was palpable. Marcel Proust would have understood. In 1922, the year he completed his seven-volume series of novels, *À la recherche du temps perdu (In Search of Lost Time)*, he remarked to his housekeeper: 'Ah, dear Céleste, I have great news to tell you, something enormous. I wrote the word "end". Now I can die.' On finishing *Book Lovers' Paris*, I understood his sentiment completely, and although I'm not yet ready to die, I got his drift.

By necessity this is a hefty book: it would not have done justice to its subject matter otherwise. That said, no literary guide to Paris can ever be definitive, and this one, although significant in size, makes no claim to be. Surveying the end result I am aware I have given some writers more curt treatment than they perhaps deserve, but the material had just kept growing, and had needed to be reined in. Casualties were inevitable. I tried to restrict each entry to a thousand words, or fewer: not much to sketch out a writer's life, but without this constraint the book would have run out of control. Nevertheless, its synoptic form offers the essential elements, and the footnotes will, I hope, lead you to a more in-depth reading experience. I do not expect the reader to pack sandwiches and a Thermos flask and visit every single address in the book, but many of the sites listed are well worth a visit, depending on where your interests lie.

I decided to self-publish this, my seventh book, because I knew it was unlikely to fit into any of most publishers' standard pigeonholes; and even if it had, it would have ended up a very different publication from the one I envisaged. My intention was not to write this book for academics, or students of literature in the academic sense. Had I done so, to quote Mark Twain in *The Innocents Abroad*, 'it would have about it that gravity, that profundity, and that impressive incomprehensibility which are so proper to works of that kind.' It was written, rather, for the mainstream book lover whom I know very well, having led thousands of book tours over the years for lovers of literature from all over the world. If you fall into this category, then this book was written for you.

In the end one comes to realise that the past being sought is all but invisible, and that the remnants being researched, photographed and, ultimately, described on the page, are only traces, or signposts to the past. Of most significance, of course, is the enduring work of the artist: not the associated buildings, not the photographs, not even the lives of those writers who are no longer with us. All of them became famous – or infamous, some have been neglected, and some forgotten, but in the end their shared heritage is the bricks and mortar they created that built the legend that turned Paris into the literary capital of the world.

Allan Foster
Scotland 2020

NOTES TO THE READER

Layout:

This book has twenty sections, nineteen of which are named by arrondissement. These are Paris's administrative districts, and are encircled by a ring road around the city known as the périphérique. There are no entries for the 19th arrondissement. The last section of the book covers the suburbs, some of which are served by the Métro, and a few outlying areas, which are not.

Paris's present system of twenty arrondissements dates from the late 1850s and was conceived by Napoleon III, and Baron Haussmann, the urban planner responsible for transforming the city with the wide tree-lined boulevards we know today. Arrondissements are arranged in the shape of a clockwork spiral, starting with the 1st arrondissement in the heart of the city. All arrondissements north of the Seine are on the right bank (Rive Droite) and all south of the Seine are on the left bank (Rive Gauche). In French, arrondissements are numbered as 1er (premier), 2e (deuxième), 3e (troisième), up to 20e (vingtième). On street signs the number often appears in Roman numerals. The last two digits of a Paris address denote its arrondissement; for example, 102 blvd. du Montparnasse 75014 is in the 14th.

**Select Bibliography
and Further Reading:**

Most writing on French literature is, naturally, in the French language. The 'Select Bibliography' and 'Further Reading' notes of this book attempt, where possible, to list editions – whether critical, biographical, or works of a specific author – that have been written in or translated into English. English translations are given in brackets immediately after the French title. Where no translation of a publication exists (or where I have been unable to track one down), the bracketed material is purely an English translation of the French title, and is in roman type (i.e., not italicised, or

placed in quote marks, where relevant). Publication dates shown throughout the book are for the French editions unless otherwise stipulated.

Gender Balance:

Male writers are, predictably, predominant throughout the book. Before the Victorian heroine arrived (Charlotte Brontë, Florence Nightingale, etc.) women authors were rarely granted much recognition. There are some pre-nineteenth century exceptions and a few appear here, notably Madame de Sévigné and Madame de Staël, but for the most part they are thin on the ground. Only in the early twentieth century did French and expatriate women in Paris begin to find their artistic voice, with some of those significantly shaping the development of literary modernism.

Cemeteries:

Searching for graves can be a formidable task. Be prepared to spend a much longer time than you bargained for. Some divisions and plots are poorly marked, paths are overgrown, and many tombs are weathered and covered with lichen. A more accurate direction to a grave, other than the plot division number given, would, in many cases, be impractical and complicated. The more famous graves may be signposted, but some are almost impossible to find, buried beneath undergrowth and crumbling masonry. The reader should not be disheartened by this: just enjoy the challenge!

Hotels, etc.:

Any hotels, cafes, restaurants and other watering holes are featured because they have a literary connection, not because they have rooms named after writers or bars that serve up Hemingway's Mojito.

CHRONOLOGY

300 BC
The Gallic tribe known as the Parisii build a settlement on what is now the Ile de la Cité.

52 BC
Julius Caesar writes *Commentarii de Bello Gallico (Commentaries on the Gallic War)*. After conquering the Parisii Roman control of Gaul lasts for five centuries until AD 486.

1078
The French Benedictine monk, Anselm, offers, in his *Proslogion*, his 'ontological argument' for God's existence.

c.1102
Chansons de geste (epic songs and poems) are sung by minstrels, based on legendary and heroic deeds. More than one hundred survive in around three hundred manuscripts. The troubadour tradition of composing and singing courtly love themed lyrics begins in southern France.

c.1130
'La Chanson de Roland' is written, most likely, by the Norman poet Turold, telling the tale of Charlemagne's army fighting the Muslims in Spain, and is the oldest surviving major work of French literature.

c.1160
Best known for his work on the Arthurian legends, Chrétien de Troyes writes some of France's classic medieval literature.

1163–1345
The Cathedral of Notre-Dame de Paris is built on the site of Basilique Saint-Étienne.

1190
The building of the Louvre Palace is begun.

1257
The Collège de Sorbonne is founded.

1337
The Hundred Years War begins between England and France.

1368
Charles V inaugurates the Bibliothèque du Roi (King's Library) at the Louvre Palace.

1415
The English inflict a disastrous defeat on France in battle at Agincourt.

1426
François Villon writes his epitaph, 'Ballade des pendus' (Ballad of the hanged), while imprisoned under sentence of death in the Grand Châtelet.

1431
Joan of Arc is burned at the stake in Rouen.

1453
The Hundred Years War ends.

1469
Thomas Malory writes *Le Morte d'Arthur* in prison. In it he reworks legends of romance, translating from the Arthurian stories of thirteenth century French prose.

1532
French physician and Humanist François Rabelais begins writing his classic *Gargantua* series.

1550
Pierre de Ronsard, known as the 'prince of poets', publishes the first four books of his Odes.

1572
Catholic mob violence erupts killing tens of thousands of Huguenots across France.

1612
Queen Marie de Medici creates the Luxembourg Palace and Gardens.

1631
Théophraste Renaudot publishes of France's first newspaper, *La Gazette de France*.

1635
The Académie française is founded by Cardinal de Richelieu.

1637
Pierre Corneille, one of the chief architects of French classical drama, stages his tragicomedy *Le Cid*, at the Théâtre du Marais in Paris.

1644
René Descartes writes his *Principles of Philosophy* in Latin, in which he sets forth the Laws of Physics.

1648
The École des Beaux Arts is founded by Cardinal Mazarin.

1661
Louis XIV begins the construction of the Palace of Versailles.

1667
Performed before the court of Louis XIV, Jean Racine's tragedy, *Andromaque,* establishes his reputation as one of the great French playwrights.

1673
Molière dies after falling ill while acting in his comédie-ballet, *Le malade imaginaire*.

1680
The Comédie-Française is founded by a decree of Louis XIV.

1686
Café Procope, Paris's first successful coffee house, opens.

1694
François-Marie Arouet, better known by his nom de plume, Voltaire, is born in or near Paris.

1702
Paris is divided into twenty quartiers.

1715–1774
Louis XV's reign.

1721
The Bibliothèque du Roi is moved to the Mazarin Palace in Rue de Richelieu.

1759
Voltaire publishes his philosophical tale, *Candide*.

1762
Jean-Jacques Rousseau's *Émile*, a treatise on the nature of education and the nature of man, is banned and publicly burned.

1768
Chateaubriand, founding father of Romanticism, is born in Saint-Malo.

1772
Denis Diderot completes his epic *Encyclopédie* showcasing the sciences, arts and crafts of the Enlightenment.

1777
Le Journal de Paris, France's first national daily newspaper, is published.

1778

Voltaire dies in Paris. As his body cannot be buried in consecrated ground it is smuggled out by night and interred in Champagne in north-east France.

1789

Fall of the Bastille on 14 July. French Revolution ends rule of monarchy and the First Republic is established.

1790

Political theorist, Edmund Burke, publishes *Reflections on the Revolution in France*, attacking the French Revolution.

1791

Radical political thinker, Thomas Paine, publishes the first part of *The Rights of Man*, in which he supports the French Revolution.

Voltaire's remains are reburied in the Panthéon, the mausoleum for France's national heroes.

1792

Fall of the monarchy. The Assembly of the First Republic declares the Bibliothèque du Roi the property of the French people and renames it the Bibliothèque Nationale.

First public execution by guillotine.

1793

The Reign of Terror.

Thomas Paine is found guilty of treason and condemned to death.

Louis XVI and Marie Antoinette are executed by guillotine.

The Louvre Palace becomes the property of the people and opens as a museum with seized art from the church and monarchy.

1794

Execution of Robespierre, and the end of the Reign of Terror.

1799

Napoleon Bonaparte leads coup to overthrow government.

1804

Napoleon Bonaparte crowns himself Emperor of the First French Empire.

Cimetière du Père Lachaise is established and becomes the first garden cemetery in the world.

Napoleon decrees all brothels to be state controlled and all prostitutes to be registered.

1814

The Bourbon Restoration restores a constitutional monarchy.

1815

Napoleon is defeated at Waterloo.

1824

Cimetière du Montparnasse is established.

1825

Cimetière de Montmartre is established.

1826

Louis Hachette enters the book trade, buying a bookshop near the Sorbonne.

First edition of *Le Figaro* newspaper is published.

1830

The July Revolution brings Louis-Philippe to the throne.

Marie-Henri Beyle (Stendhal), creator of the pyschological novel, publishes *Le Rouge et Le Noir*.

Victor Hugo's romantic drama *Hernani* causes a riot on the first night.

1831

Victor Hugo publishes *Notre-Dame de Paris* (*The Hunchback of Notre-Dame*).

1832

George Sand publishes *Indiana*.

1833

The Guizot Schools Law is passed creating schools in all French communes.

1834–52

Prosper Mérimée tours France as Inspector General of Historic Monuments.

1835

Honoré de Balzac publishes *Le Père Goriot*, set during the Bourbon Restoration.

1836

The Arc de Triomphe is inaugurated at the western end of the Champs-Élysées.

1840

Émile Zola is born in Paris.

1842

Honoré de Balzac begins publishing his series of loosely connected novels and stories entitled *La Comédie Humaine*.
Eugène Sue begins publishing his serial novel *Les Mystères de Paris*.

1844

Alexandre Dumas's *Les Trois Mousquetaires* is first published in serial form.

1848

Fall of King Louis-Philippe. Louis Napoleon is proclaimed President of the Second Republic.

1852

Louis Napoleon takes the title of Napoleon III of the Second Empire.

1853

Baron Haussmann begins his massive renovation of Paris.

1856

Gustave Flaubert's novel *Madame Bovary* is serialised in *La Revue de Paris*.

1857

Gustave Flaubert and Charles Baudelaire are prosecuted for 'offence to public and religious morality': Flaubert for *Madame Bovary*, and Baudelaire for *Les Fleurs du mal (The Flowers of Evil)*.

1859

Stendhal publishes his novel *La Chartreuse de Parme (The Charterhouse of Parma)*, an early example of realism.
Charles Dickens publishes *A Tale of Two Cities*.

1862

Victor Hugo publishes *Les Misérables*.
Restaurant Magny dinners are instituted and attended by Flaubert, Turgenev, the Goncourt brothers, Sainte-Beuve, George Sand and many others.

1863

Jules Verne publishes his first novel, *Cinq Semaines en Ballon (Five Weeks in a Balloon)*.

1866

Pierre Larousse publishes the first part of his *Grand dictionnaire universel du XIXe siècle*.

1867

Paul Verlaine publishes his first collection of poetry, *Poèmes saturniens*.

1869

Alphonse Daudet publishes *Lettres de mon Moulin (Letters from my Windmill)*.

1870

The Third Republic is proclaimed following the defeat of Napoleon III by the Prussians at Sedan.

The Prussians besiege Paris. Food shortages follow and over 40,000 people die.

1871

France surrenders to the Prussians.

The Paris Commune, a revolutionary government, attempts to take control of the city until suppressed by the army.

1873

Paul Verlaine wounds Arthur Rimbaud with a pistol and serves eighteen months in prison.

1874

W. Somerset Maugham is born at the British Embassy in Paris.

1875

Henry James arrives in Paris and begins his first novel, *The American.*

1880

Gustave Flaubert dies. His adventure of two Parisian clerks, *Bouvard et Pécuchet*, remains unfinished.

Émile Zola's *Nana* sells 55,000 copies on its first day of publication.

Guy de Maupassant achieves national fame with his short story 'Boule de suif' ('Ball of Fat').

1881

The artistic cabaret, Le Chat Noir, is founded in Montmartre.

The Law on the Freedom of the Press is passed under The Third Republic, bringing major libertarian reform.

1883

Ivan Turgenev dies at his chalet in the Paris suburb of Bougival.

1889

The Eiffel Tower is inaugurated at Paris's Exposition Universelle and becomes the world's tallest structure.

The Moulin Rouge opens on the Boulevard de Clichy.

1894

George du Maurier creates the legend of Svengali in his novel *Trilby.*

1897

Edmond Rostand's tragi-comedy, *Cyrano de Bergerac*, premieres at Paris's Théâtre de la Porte Saint-Martin.

1898

Émile Zola publishes 'J'Accuse...!', his article condemning the War Office and its generals for suppressing evidence during the trial of Alfred Dreyfus. Zola is sentenced to imprisonment for libel.

1900

Oscar Wilde dies of cerebral meningitis at the Hôtel d'Alsace on the Left Bank.

First Métro line opens between Porte Maillot and Porte de Vincennes.

1901

Sully Prudhomme is awarded the first Nobel Prize in Literature.

1902

Émile Zola dies from carbon monoxide poisoning.

1903

Le Prix Goncourt, France's most celebrated literary prize, is founded.

Gertrude Stein arrives in Paris with her brother Leo.

1905

Maurice Leblanc creates his gentleman thief Arsène Lupin.

1907

Gertrude Stein meets Alice B. Toklas.

1908

Anatole France publishes his novel *L'Ile des pingouins (Penguin Island)*.

1909

American salonnière Natalie Barney launches her famous literary salon on Rue Jacob, which continues for over sixty years.

Louis Blériot flies across the English Channel.

1910

Gaston Leroux publishes *Le Fantôme de l'Opéra (The Phantom of the Opera)*.

T.S. Eliot arrives in Paris in the hope of discovering his own poetic voice.

1913

Alain-Fournier completes his semi-autobiographical novel *Le Grand Meaulnes* (variously translated in English as *The Lost Domain* or *The Wanderer*).

Marcel Proust publishes the first volume of *À la recherche du temps perdu (In Search of Lost Time)* at his own expense.

1914

Germany declares war on France.

Edith Wharton establishes the American Hostels for Refugees in Paris.

Alain-Fournier is killed in action near Verdun and is buried in an unmarked mass grave.

1915

The French Army randomly selects and executes four corporals by firing squad as an example to their companies who ignored orders to attack. These events inspired the 1935 anti-war novel *Paths of Glory* by Humphrey Cobb.

The government bans absinthe.

Romain Rolland is awarded the Nobel Prize in Literature.

1916

Henri Barbusse publishes his classic war novel, *Le Feu (Under Fire)*.

Guillaume Apollinaire suffers a serious head wound and is invalided out of the army.

Adrienne Monnier establishes France's first public lending library at her shop, La Maison des Amis des Livres.

1917

Paul Valéry completes his poem 'La Jeune Parque' ('The Young Fate'), considered one of the greatest French poems of the twentieth century.

The French Army experiences widespread mutinies on the Western Front. A record 27,000 troops desert.

Following the aftermath of the Russian Revolution thousands of refugees flee the former Russian Empire and settle in Paris.

1918

France and its Allies sign an Armistice with Germany in the Forest of Compiègne ending the First World War in which 1.4 million Frenchmen were killed: an average of 893 deaths per day.

Guillaume Apollinaire dies during the influenza pandemic.

1919

Sylvia Beach opens the first Shakespeare and Company bookshop on Rue Dupuytren.

Treaty of Versailles; Alsace-Lorraine is returned to France.

Marcel Proust wins the Prix Goncourt.

1920

The American Library in Paris is founded on Rue de l'Élysée.

James Joyce arrives in Paris.

1921

Anatole France is awarded the Nobel Prize in Literature.

1922

Sylvia Beach publishes James Joyce's *Ulysses*.
Ernest Hemingway arrives in Paris and begins sending feature stories to the *Toronto Star*.
Marcel Proust dies.

1924

André Breton publishes *Le Manifeste du surréalisme*.

1925

Scott and Zelda Fitzgerald arrive in Paris.
Janet Flanner begins writing her fortnightly 'Letter from Paris' for *The New Yorker*.

1927

Henri Bergson is awarded the Nobel Prize in Literature.

1928

George Orwell arrives in Paris, an experience that inspires his first full-length work, *Down and Out in Paris and London*.

1929

Jean Cocteau publishes *Les Enfants Terribles*.
Ernest Hemingway finishes the final draft of *A Farewell to Arms* at his apartment on Rue Ferou.
Children's newspaper *Coeurs Vaillants* (Valiant Hearts) introduces Tintin to France.

1932

Jean Anouilh has his first play, *L'Hermine*, produced and published.
Louis-Ferdinand Céline publishes *Voyage au bout de la nuit (Journey to the End of the Night)*.

1934

The Obelisk Press publishes Henry Miller's *Tropic of Cancer*.

1936

Anaïs Nin publishes her first novel, *The House of Incest*.

1937

Launch of *Marie Claire* magazine.
Roger Martin du Gard is awarded the Nobel Prize in Literature.
Samuel Beckett is stabbed and nearly killed on Avenue d'Orléans.

1938

Jean-Paul Sartre's first novel, *La Nausée (Nausea)* is published.

1940

Fall of France; Nazis invade Paris on 14 June 1940. The Vichy regime remains in the unoccupied south and collaborates. The Germans seize control of the French press and publishing. General de Gaulle establishes a government-in-exile in London.

1942

Round-up of Jews in Paris.
Jewish Ukrainian writer Irène Némirovsky is arrested by French police and deported to Auschwitz where she dies from typhus.
Vercors's novel of French Resistance, *Le Silence de la mer*, is published in occupied France.
Albert Camus publishes *L'Étranger (The Outsider)*.
Jean Genet begins his first novel, *Notre-Dame des Fleurs (Our Lady of the Flowers)*, in Paris's La Santé Prison.

1943

Jean-Paul Sartre presents his theory of

existentialism in *L'Être et le néant (Being and Nothingness)*, and writes his first play, *Les Mouches (The Flies)*.

Antoine de Saint-Exupéry publishes *Le Petit Prince*, which will eventually become one of the world's bestselling books.

1944

The Allies land at Normandy. Hitler orders Paris to be rased to the ground but his general disobeys the order. Paris liberated on 24 August; purges of collaborators.

First edition of *Le Monde* is published.

Antoine de Saint-Exupéry is reported missing over the Mediterranean when his reconnaissance aircraft fails to return to base. His body was never found.

Colette publishes her novella, *Gigi*, about a young Parisian girl being groomed as a courtesan.

Poet Robert Desnos is arrested by the Gestapo and sent to a concentration camp. He dies the following year.

1945

First issue of *Elle* magazine is published.

Women vote for the first time in French elections.

Editor and author Robert Brasillach is executed for treason.

1946

The Fourth Republic is proclaimed.

State-controlled brothels are abolished.

1947

André Gide is awarded the Nobel Prize in Literature.

1949

Simone de Beauvoir publishes *Le Deuxième Sexe (The Second Sex)*.

First edition of *Paris Match* is published.

1950

Eugène Ionesco's play *La Cantatrice chauve (The Bald Soprano)* sets in motion the Theatre of the Absurd.

1951

George Whitman opens his bookstore, Le Mistral. In 1964, in homage to Sylvia Beach, he changes its name to Shakespeare and Company.

1952

François Mauriac is awarded the Nobel Prize in Literature.

1953

Samuel Beckett's play *En attendant Godot (Waiting for Godot)* has its world premiere in the Théâtre de Babylone in Paris.

1954

French colonial influence in Indochina ends after the Vietminh victory at Dien Bien Phu.

18-year-old Françoise Sagan has a major international success with her first novel, *Bonjour Tristesse*.

Colette receives the first state funeral ever given to a woman by the Republic.

1957

Albert Camus is awarded the Nobel Prize in Literature.

Novelist Émile Henriot originates the phrase 'Nouveau Roman' to describe the experimental style of writers who challenge the structure of the traditional novel.

The French courts decide to continue an 1814 ruling banning all the works of the Marquis de Sade.

1958

Charles de Gaulle is elected president and founds the Fifth Republic.

Olympia Press publishes Vladimir Nabokov's controversial novel *Lolita*.

1959
The Astérix series makes its first appearance in *Pilote* magazine, and will eventually become France's most popular comic strip.

1960
Albert Camus dies in a car crash near Petit Villeblevin.
Saint-John Perse is awarded the Nobel Prize in Literature.

1961
Jean-Paul Sartre's flat is bombed by the OAS, the pro-French Algeria terrorist organisation.

1962
Second bomb attack on Jean-Paul Sartre's flat.
France's Algerian war ends with Algerian independence.
Attempted assassination of President de Gaulle, later depicted in Frederick Forsyth's 1971 novel, *The Day of the Jackal*.

1963
Hôtel Rachou, known as The Beat Hotel, closes down.

1964
Jean-Paul Sartre is awarded the Nobel Prize in Literature, but he turns it down on the grounds that he does not want 'to be transformed into an institution'.

1968
Student protests, supported by 10 million striking workers, paralyse all of France.

1969
Georges Pompidou becomes president.
Samuel Beckett is awarded the Nobel Prize.

1970
Charles de Gaulle dies.

1980
50,000 spectators line the streets of Paris to view the funeral cortege of Jean-Paul Sartre.
Novelist Marguerite Yourcenar is elected first female member of the Académie française.

1981
France abolishes the death penalty.

1984
Marguerite Duras wins the Prix Goncourt for *L'Amant (The Lover)*.

1985
Claude Simon is awarded the Nobel Prize in Literature.

1991
Alain-Fournier's body is identified nearly eighty years after his death near Verdun, and is reburied in the military cemetery at Saint-Remy-La-Colonne.

1996
The Bibliothèque Nationale's François-Mitterand Library is opened.

2008
J.M.G. Le Clézio is awarded the Nobel Prize in Literature.

2014
Patrick Modiano is awarded the Nobel Prize in Literature.

2016
The gun with which Verlaine shot Rimbaud in 1873 sells at auction for £368,000.

2020
Allan Foster finishes *Book Lovers' Paris*.

1st

Arrondissement

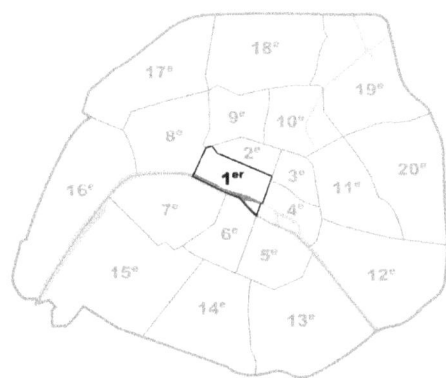

LES BOUQUINISTES

PONT NEUF

(Métro: Pont Neuf)

**BIRTHPLACE OF LES BOUQUINISTES
RIVERSIDE BOOKSELLERS SINCE THE
SIXTEENTH CENTURY**

*The dealers in second-hand books put their
boxes on the parapet. These good retailers
of Mind, who are always in the open air, with
blouses loose to the breeze, have become
so weatherbeaten by the wind, the rain, the
frost, the snow, the fog, and the great sun,
that they end up by looking very much like
the old statues of cathedrals. They are all
friends of mine, and I scarcely ever pass
by their boxes without picking out of one of
them some old book which I had always been
in need of up to that very moment, without
any suspicion of the fact on my part.
Then on my return home I have to endure*
*the outcries of my housekeeper, who accuses
me of bursting all my pockets and filling the
house with waste paper to attract rats. Ther-
ese is wise about that, and it is because she
is wise that I do not listen to her; for in spite
of my tranquil mien, I have always preferred
the folly of the passions to the wisdom of
indifference ... My old books are Me. I am
just as old and thumb-worn as they are.*
Anatole France, *The Crime of Sylvestre
Bonnard* (1881)

Bouquinistes have been trading on the
streets of Paris for over 500 years
and are now a common fixture along
the banks of the Seine, but from their
birth during the sixteenth century until
they were legalised in the late nineteenth
century, they fought a hard battle for
their right to survive. Alongside the *colporteurs*, small-time street hustlers who
sold books and pamphlets from trays
and barrows, the authorities constantly

hounded them for selling banned, seditious or pornographic texts. 'Police spies wage war on the colporteurs' wrote Louis-Sébastien Mercier in *Le Tableau de Paris* (1781),

> a race of men who trade in the only good books one can still read in France, which are consequently banned. They are horribly treated, all the police bloodhounds pursue these poor creatures who do not know what they are selling and would hide the Bible under their cloaks if the Lieutenant of Police took it into his head to ban the Bible. They are put in the Bastille for selling silly pamphlets that will be forgotten tomorrow.

Les Bouquinistes

Boekiniste or *bouquiniste* comes from the Flemish word *boekin*, meaning 'little book'. The stalls first saw the light of day on the bridges of Paris and, notably, from the seventeenth century, on the Pont Neuf, then the widest and busiest thoroughfare in Paris. Gradually they crept along the riverside, and by 1732 there were over 120 bouquinistes along the banks of the Seine all dispensing their own brand of underground literature, from the Marquis de Sade's *The 120 Days of Sodom* to Gustave Flaubert's *Madame Bovary*. Today there are well over 200 of them, and they can be found along the Right Bank from Pont Marie to Quai du Louvre, and on the Left Bank from Quai de la Tournelle to Quai Voltaire. But, alas, what Balzac described as 'catacombs of glory' are now struggling to survive in the modern world, and at some bouquinistes the tourist trinket has eclipsed the book. In the end it's about what keeps the wolf from the door, which has nothing to do with 'glory'.

See Also: Wilkie Collins, Anatole France, Bastille, Marquis de Sade, Gustave Flaubert, Honoré de Balzac.

Further Information: Pont Neuf (New Bridge) took almost thirty years to build and was completed in 1607. In the seventeenth and eighteenth centuries the bridge was the hub of Parisian cultural life and a gathering place for a cross section of its populace, from the respectable bourgeoisie to beggars, prostitutes and criminals. At 28 metres wide it was broader than any other bridge or street in the city, and was packed with market stalls, medicine booths and street theatre. It seethed with anti-establishment and anti-religious flurry on which the bouquinistes thrived.

Pont Neuf

JEAN COCTEAU

36 RUE DE MONTPENSIER
(Métro: Pyramides/Bourse)

FORMER HOME OF JEAN COCTEAU
NOVELIST, POET, PLAYWRIGHT, ARTIST
AND FILM-MAKER
ONE OF THE GREAT FRENCH
MODERNISTS

Asking an artist to talk about his work is like asking a plant to talk about horticulture.
Jean Cocteau

Jean Cocteau in his youth

Versatile is a word that is used often when discussing Jean Cocteau because it was impossible to categorise him. 'People have been looking for me for thirty years,' he wrote, in *Le Cordon Ombilical.* 'The most important grievance fabricated by the witnesses for the prosecution in my Socratic trial is that I dissipate my efforts. Don't they know that an organism is made up of a heart, a liver, a gall bladder, lungs, kidneys, and so on? How could any creation live if it had only one organ?' But in his heart Cocteau was always a poet. Everything he did he classified under its title *poésie* (poetry): '*poésie de roman, poésie critique, poésie graphique, poésie de théâtre*, and *poésie cinématographique*'. Poetry, however, is not what he is remembered for. His ideal mediums were, arguably, the theatre and cinema, but it was his array of talents that made him one of the great French modernists. He was born in 1889 into the Parisian bourgeoisie at Maisons-Laffitte, near Paris, where his family spent their summers away from the city. He described his family as 'artistic', but 'not artistic enough to give me useful advice'. His father, a lawyer, committed suicide

when Cocteau was nine. At fifteen, exasperated, bisexual and expelled from school, he ran away from home to Marseilles where he hoped to become 'a sailor-boy before the mast'. He ended up living under a false name in the Vieux Port, the old quayside quarter where he worked in a Chinese restaurant, smoked opium (which would eventually become an addiction) and experienced the waterfront underworld. 'Marseilles', he said, 'was my real school.' After a year the gendarmes found him and returned him to Paris.
In 1909 he began working for the magazine *Scheherazade*, and in the same year his first anthology of poems, *La Lampe d'Aladin* (Aladdin's Lamp), was published. Two more books of verse followed, and his work was now appearing in major publications. With the outbreak of war in 1914, and having been declared unfit for the military, he joined the Red Cross, serving as an ambulance driver on the Belgian front.

By now Cocteau was having remarkable success in whatever he became involved with in the traditional as well as the avant-garde. He created ballets. Inspired by Diaghilev's famous command, '*étonne-moi!*' ('surprise me!'), he devised *Parade* in 1917 with music by Erik Satie, and was still writing ballets well into the 1950s. He created his first major play, *Orphée* (Orpheus) in 1926, and for prose he will be best remembered for his 1929 novel, *Les Enfants Terribles*. The same year, at the age of forty, Cocteau began his career in film, two of his most memorable being *La Belle et la Bête (Beauty and the Beast)* (1945), and *Orphée* (1950).

Some critics have said it was his life, not his work, that was his masterpiece; but still, there remains a distinctive quality in Cocteau's art that is ambiguous to some, and fascinating to others. He was a drug-addict, a poseur, a socialite and a rebel, and he was tried but acquitted after the war for collaborating with the Germans. Many French people never forgave him. But as Cocteau said, 'what the public criticises in you, cultivate. It is you.' He died of a heart attack in 1963, aged seventy-four, at his home in Milly-la-Forêt near the Forest of Fontainebleau.

See Also: Guillaume Apollinaire, Jean Genet, Ezra Pound, Raymond Radiguet.

Further Information: Cocteau lived at 36 rue de Montpensier from 1940 until his death in 1963. The Cocteau family's town house was at 45 rue la Bruyère in the 9th arrondissement. Milly-la-Forêt is about 60 km from the centre of Paris, where Cocteau is buried under the floor of the town's Chapelle Saint-Blaise-des-Simples. In 1959 Cocteau decorated this once-abandoned chapel with his murals and stained glass designs that can

still be seen today. Cocteau's lover from 1937 until his death was the actor Jean Marais (1913–1998). The Musée Jean Cocteau opened in Menton, on the French Riviera, in 2011.

Select Bibliography: *The Art of the Cinema* (Boyars, 1994); *Five Plays* (Hill & Wang, 1996); *Tempest of Stars: Selected Poems* (Enitharmon, 1997); *Les Enfants Terribles* (Vintage, 2003).

Further Reading: C. Arnaud, *Jean Cocteau: A Life* (Yale University Press, 2016); J. Williams, *Jean Cocteau* (Manchester University Press, 2010); F. Steegmuller, *Cocteau* (Macmillan, 1970); P. Mauries, *Jean Cocteau* (Assouline, 2004).

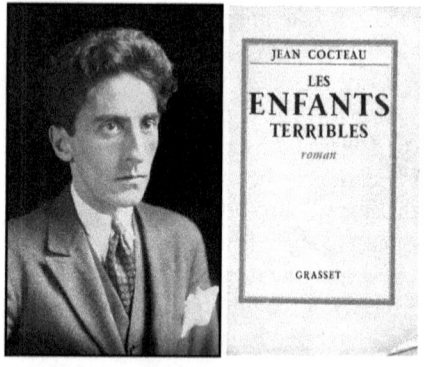

Left: Jean Cocteau in 1923   Right: Éditions Bernard Grasset's first edition of *Les Enfants Terribles*, published in 1929

Chapelle Saint-Blaise-des-Simples
Tomb of Jean Cocteau

COLETTE

9 RUE DE BEAUJOLAIS
(Métro: Bourse/Palais Royal Musée du Louvre)

FORMER HOME OF COLETTE
ONE OF THE MASTERS OF FRENCH
PROSE AND CREATOR
OF *CHÉRI* AND *GIGI*

If we want to be sincere, we must admit that there is a well-nourished love and an ill-nourished love. And the rest is literature.
Colette, *La Fin de Chéri* (1926)

Willy and Colette *c.*1902

9 rue de Beaujolais

Colette achieved fame as a writer with her semi-autobiographical 'Claudine' novels about an irreverent country schoolgirl, but the bedrock of her writing reputation was the Bohemian Paris of her youth. She never failed to shock her readers with her relaxed outlook on morality, yet although her books were often regarded as scandalous, her exploration of sexual and emotional relationships was always highly perceptive. She wrote over forty books, of which *Chéri* (1920) and *Gigi* (1944) were amongst her most widely known. After her first divorce in the early 1900s she embarked on a lively stage career as a dancer and actor, often in plays adapted from her own novels. But whether as a writer, theatrical performer or sexual icon, she consistently challenged the conventions of her day, and notoriety always followed in her wake.

She was born Sidonie-Gabrielle Colette, in the Burgundian village of Saint-Sauveur-en-Puisaye in 1873. At twenty, she married her first husband, novelist and music critic, Henry Gauthier-Villars, known by his pen name Willy, who was fourteen years her senior. He brought her to Paris where she collaborated with him on a series of works that became known as the 'Claudine' novels. Sensuous and titillating, they became bestsellers. The first four were published under the pen name Willy. By 1906, weary of her lack of recognition and her husband's constant infidelities, Colette divorced Willy and launched her career as a music-hall artiste. She took a lover, an aristocratic lesbian transvestite known as Missy, and became a leading light of the demi-monde.

25

The curtain came down on her bohemian life in 1912 when she married Baron Henry de Jouvenel, editor of the daily newspaper, *Le Matin*, with whom she had a daughter – her only, and neglected, child – in 1913. A decade later, and a year before the collapse of the marriage, Jouvenel serialised Colette's *Le Blé en herbe (Ripening Seed)* in *Le Matin*, but he was compelled to stop printing it before the story's completion as the readers were finding it too shocking. In 1935 she married the prosperous and debonair Maurice de Goudeket, with whom she lived for the rest of her life.

Crippled by arthritis in old age, Colette died in 1954 surrounded by her troupe of cats at Rue de Beaujolais, aged eighty-one. Her notoriety did not end with her death, however, as the Catholic Church refused her a religious burial. Ironically, the Republic awarded her a state funeral, the first ever granted to a woman.

'On every storm-tossed vessel filled with retching bodies', wrote Colette's biographer, Judith Thurman, 'there is usually one passenger, freakishly sound, who strolls the pitching deck on steady feet while insolently eating a ham sandwich. Colette was that sort of freak at the fin de siècle.'

See Also: Colette (Père Lachaise), Renée Vivien, Le Prix Goncourt.

Further Information: Built for Cardinal Richelieu in 1663 as his personal residence, the Palais Royal and its gardens have had many occupiers over the centuries, from royal families to theatres and shopping arcades. Apartment blocks with galleries underneath were constructed in three new streets – Rue de Montpensier, Rue de Beaujolais and Rue de Valois – which were built around the three sides of the gardens in 1780. Colette first lived in Rue de Beaujolais from 1927 to 1929, in a small mezzanine apartment she called 'the tunnel', later moving to a larger apartment from 1938 until her death in 1954. Colette finally established the literary rights to her early 'Claudine' books in 1926, a quarter of a century after they were published under the pen name Willy. In 1949 she became the first woman President of the Académie Goncourt. Musée Colette is located at 10 rue Colette, Saint-Sauveur-en-Puisaye.

Select Bibliography: *Claudine à l'école (Claudine at School)* (1900); *La Vagabonde (The Vagabond)* (1910); *L'Enfant et les sortilèges: Fantaisie lyrique en deux parties (The Child and the Spells: A Lyric Fantasy in Two Parts)* (1917–1925); an opera with music by Ravel to a libretto by Colette); *Mitsou* (1919); *Chéri* (1920); *Le Blé en herbe (Ripening Seed)* (1923); *La Fin de Chéri (The Last of Chéri)* (1926); *Sido* (1929); *Ces Plaisirs (These Pleasures)* (1932), later published as *Le Pur et l'impur (The Pure and the Impure)* (1941); *Duo* (1934); *Gigi* (1944).

Further Reading: Judith Thurman, *Secrets of the Flesh: A Life of Colette* (Bloomsbury, 1999).

Colette overlooking the Palais Royal from her apartment in 1941

PIERRE CORNEILLE

296 RUE SAINT-HONORÉ
(Métro: Pyramides/Tuileries)

ÉGLISE SAINT-ROCH

TOMB OF PIERRE CORNEILLE

DRAMATIST WHO WAS ONE OF

THE CHIEF ARCHITECTS

OF FRENCH CLASSICAL DRAMA

Yesterday, I saw our friend [Corneille] and relation. He's not doing badly for his age. We went out together after dinner and as we passed along the rue de la Parcheminerie, he went into a shop to have his shoe repaired; it had come unstitched. He sat down on a bench with me beside him and paid out the three coins that were left in his pocket. When we got home, I offered him my purse, but he would not accept it, nor any part of it. I cried to see so great a genius in this extremity of wretchedness.
Quoted in Jacques Hillairet, *Dictionnaire historique des rues de Paris* (1963)

Église Saint-Roch

Pierre Corneille was born in Rouen to a middle-class Norman family of lawyers and churchmen in 1606. Educated by Jesuits, he went on to study law, eventually practising in Rouen for many years. He married a local girl and they had seven children together. From 1628 to 1650 he held the position of King's Counsellor in the local office of the department of waterways and forests.

His poetical gift surfaced in 1629 when he wrote the comedy *Mélite*, a production which was subsequently performed at Paris's Théâtre du Marais. This was followed in 1632 by the tragi-comedy *Clitandre*. These works constituted the start of a series of comedies which brought his rising talent to the attention of Cardinal Richelieu, who invited Corneille to join his personal group of playwrights, formed to write plays based on Richelieu's own ideas. Corneille agreed and the group became known as *La Société des cinq auteurs* (the society of the five authors). However, Corneille, being fiercely independent and unsuited to a collective undertaking, soon parted company with the group, much to Richelieu's annoyance. In the years following the break-up he would create the first masterpiece of French classical theatre, *Le Cid*.

Corneille was a genius at creating grand theatre in which heroic characters, such as those in *Le Cid*, struggle through events of epic proportions. First performed in early 1637, *Le Cid* was an immediate success, playing to packed houses nightly. Set in medieval Spain, it tells the story of a young heroic knight who is torn between avenging his wronged father, and his passionate love for Ximena, daughter of a sworn enemy. Although the public loved it, Cardinal Richelieu – predictably – suppressed it, ensuring the continuation of a troubled relationship with Corneille that would last until Richelieu's death in 1642.

The early 1640s saw the appearance of Corneille's great tragedies, *Horace, Cinna, Polyeucte,* and *Rodogune,* and although by now he was taking his place alongside Molière and Racine, the greats of seventeenth-century drama, his plays brought him more fame than money. Corneille retired shortly after the failure of his last tragedy, *Suréna* (1674) and died a neglected legend, aged seventy-eight, at his house on Rue d'Argenteuil in 1684.

See Also: Jean Racine, Molière, Marquis de Sade, Denis Diderot, Académie française.

Further Information: Corneille was admitted to the Académie française in 1647. Église Saint-Roch was completed in 1740, but Corneille's final resting place lay unmarked until 1821. The church is dedicated to Saint Roch, patron of dogs, and against the plague, which eventually killed him. The Marquis de Sade was married at the church in 1763. Philosopher and writer, Denis Diderot, was buried there in 1784.

Select Bibliography: *The Cid, Cinna, The Theatrical Illusion* (Penguin, 1975); *Polyeuctus, The Liar, Nicomedes* (Penguin, 1980).

Further Reading: P. Yarrow, *Corneille* (Macmillan, 1963); C. Carlin, *Pierre Corneille Revisited* (Twayne, 1998); F. Guizot, *Corneille and His Times* (Kennikat, 1972).

HENRY JAMES

29 RUE CAMBON

(Métro: Madeleine)

LODGINGS OF HENRY JAMES
AMERICAN NOVELIST AND MAJOR
FIGURE OF NINETEENTH-CENTURY
LITERARY REALISM

At various times during the latter half of the eighteenth century there crossed the Atlantic two Protestant Irishmen, a Lowland Scotsman, and an Englishman, and thereby they fixed the character of Mr. Henry James' genius. For the essential thing about Mr. James was that he was an American; and that meant, for his type and generation, that he could never feel at home until he was in exile.

Rebecca West, *Henry James: A Critical Biography* (1916)

Young Henry James *c.*1863

H enry James (1843–1916) arrived in Paris on 11 November 1875, aged thirty-two. He rented a furnished apartment at 29 rue de Luxembourg (now Rue Cambon), and had come to Paris for the same reasons all young, promising, ex-patriate writers had: to be inspired and, he hoped, to live by his pen. The child of a wealthy American family, he was the second eldest of five siblings who were brought up in a world of governesses, private tutors, European travel and, fun-damentally, books. In 1875, after years of writing stories and articles, his first novel, *Roderick Hudson*, was serialised in *The Atlantic Monthly*. That same year he left America behind and sailed for Europe, sowing the seeds of what would become his ultimate exile.

'If you were to see me,' he wrote to his father shortly after his arrival, 'I think you would pronounce me well off: a snug little *troisième* with the eastern sun, two bedrooms, a parlor, an antechamber and a kitchen. Furniture clean and pretty, house irreproachable, and a gem of a *portier*, who waits upon me.' A 'pretty house', however, was one thing, but his social life was at an all-time low. 'I shall eat my Xmas dinner in a lonely restau-rant,' he wrote to his sister. 'Nothing happens to me worth relating; & I see no one of consequence. I do a good deal of work, which is the principal thing; but outside of this my days are a blank.'

Before long he encountered the Amer-ican expatriate community, which he loathed; but he soon made contact with the literary world, notably with Russian expatriate Ivan Turgenev, who intro-duced him to Gustave Flaubert and the French literary elite. 'I am in the council of the gods,' he wrote to a friend. But his real 'god' was Turgenev. After their first meeting he wrote that 'he is a magnifi-cent creature, and much handsomer than his portraits. ... He seemed very simple and kind etc; his face and shoulders are hugely broad, his stature very high, and his whole aspect and temperament of a larger and manlier kind than I have ever yet encountered in a scribbler.' James also fell in love with young Russian aesthete and amateur painter, Pavel Zhukovsky, whom he described as 'very sweet and *distingué*'. And so his life improved. 'I feel quite Parisianized', he wrote to a friend. 'I have taken root.'

The 'roots' would prove to be shallow, and his initial enchantment with the city turned to disillusionment. 'I remember how Paris had, in a hundred ways', he wrote in his journal, 'come to displease me', and soon he began to realise that he would always be 'an eternal outsider'. Paris may have been the literary capital of the world, but it was also provincial, and he knew his cosmopolitan writings were doomed to sink like a stone. His former literary idols fell well below his expectations and Impressionist art defeated him. After a viewing of the works of Degas, Renoir and Monet, he wrote, 'None of its members show signs of possessing first-rate talent, and indeed the 'Impressionist' doctrines strike me as incompatible, in an artist's mind, with the existence of first-rate talent.' On 10 December 1876, almost thirteen months after his arrival, he packed his bags, crossed the Channel, and headed for England, where he would spend most of his writing career, eventually becoming a British citizen in 1915.

James's fiction, which is often described as Anglo-American, attempts to capture a world between the values of two cultures. 'I have not the least hesitation in saying', he wrote to his brother, 'that I aspire to write in such a way that it would be impossible to an outsider to say whether I am at a given moment an American writing about England, or an Englishman writing about America (dealing as I do with both countries), and so far from being ashamed of such an ambiguity I should be extremely proud of it, for it would be highly civilized.'

See Also: Ivan Turgenev, Gustave Flaubert, James Baldwin, Edith Wharton.

Further Information: Henry James wrote twenty novels during his life, as well as short stories, plays, travelogues and criticism. During his 1875–76 stay in Paris he wrote a regular column for the *New-York Tribune*, and began his novel, *The American*. He died from a stroke, aged seventy-two, on 28 February 1916, at his London home, and is buried in Cambridge, Massachusetts, where the epitaph on his tombstone reads: *Novelist – Citizen of two countries – Interpreter of his Generation on both sides of the sea.*

Select Bibliography: *The American* (1877); *Daisy Miller* (1879); *Washington Square* (1880); *The Portrait of a Lady* (1881); *The Bostonians* (1886); *The Aspern Papers* (1888); *What Maisie Knew* (1897); *The Turn of the Screw* (1898); *The Awkward Age* (1899); *The Wings of a Dove* (1902); *The Ambassadors* (1903); *The Golden Bowl* (1904).

Further Reading: P. Brooks, *Henry James Goes To Paris* (Princeton, 2007); C. Tóibín, *The Master* (Picador, 2004); L. Gordon, *Henry James: His Women and His Art* (Chatto & Windus, 1998); F. Kaplan, *Henry James: The Imagination of Genius* (Morrow, 1992); J. Henry, *Henry James: A Life in Letters* (Penguin, 2001).

MUSÉE DU LOUVRE
RUE DE RIVOLI
(Métro: Palais Royal–Musée du Louvre)

INSPIRATION FOR GENERATIONS OF WRITERS FROM BALZAC TO THE PRESENT DAY

On a brilliant day in May, in the year 1868, a gentleman was reclining at his ease on the great circular divan which at that period occupied the centre of the Salon Carré, in the Museum of the Louvre. This commodious ottoman has since been removed, to the extreme regret of all weak-kneed lovers of the fine arts, but the gentleman in question had taken serene possession of its softest spot, and, with his head thrown back and his legs outstretched, was staring at Murillo's beautiful moon-borne Madonna in profound enjoyment of his posture.
Henry James, from *The American* (1877)

The Louvre was first opened to the public by the Revolutionary government, during the Reign of Terror, on 10 August 1793. Once the residence of kings, it was now ruled the property of the French people, and was filled with the confiscated art of the church and monarchy. Before the Revolution the main repositories of art were to be found in the chateaux and palaces of the aristocracy, to which only the privileged had access. The only place the people had been able to admire works of art was in the gloom of a badly-lit church. The opening of the Louvre, therefore, liberated and transformed the world of art for Everyman, and over the next twenty years its collections increased dramatically through the pillaging armies of the French Empire, ending with the fall of Napoleon in 1815. But art, looted or not, was now available to all.

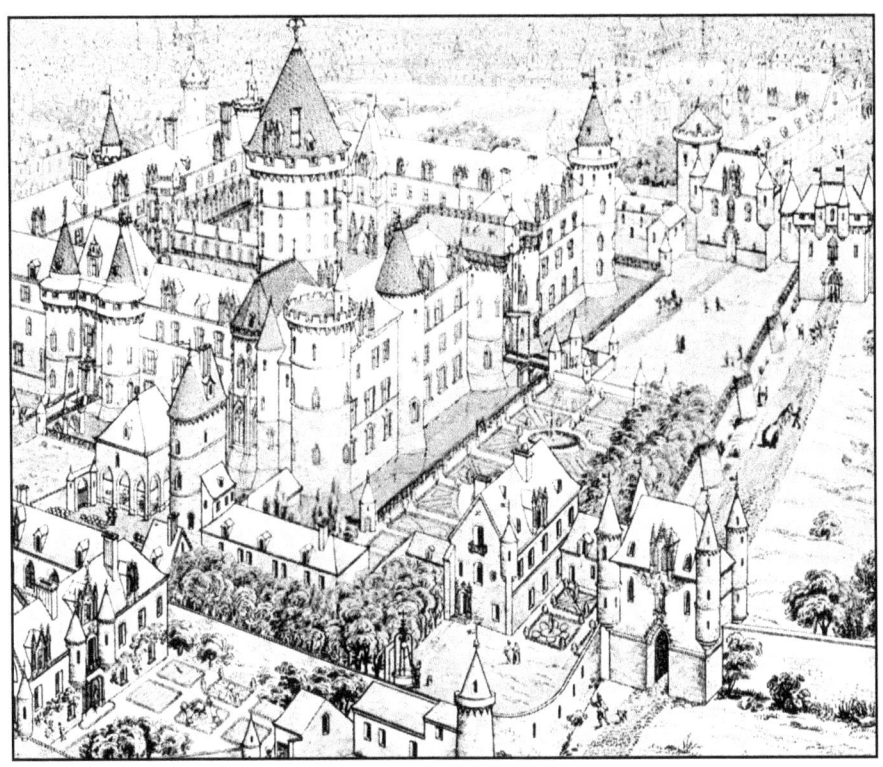

A bird's-eye view of the medieval Louvre after the modifications made during the reign of Charles V, drawn by French artist, Charles de Clarac, in 1826

Many writers were also being exposed to great art for the first time at the Louvre and an endless procession of nineteenth century wordsmiths poured through its portals. For many, it had an enormous influence on their literature, inspiring and developing in them the painter's eye for looking at the world anew. Honoré de Balzac, who visited the Louvre regularly when he was a young law clerk, described himself as a 'literary painter', referring to his novel, *Eugénie Grandet*, as a painting on an easel. Other regular visitors were Théophile Gautier, who only turned to writing after he despaired of becoming a painter, and the Goncourt brothers, who, at one time, believed their entwined

destiny would be as artists. Émile Zola, who was acquainted with most of the Impressionist painters of the day, set the famous wedding scene at the Louvre in his novel, *L'Assommoir*. D'Artagnan and his faithful musketeers met Louis XIII there in Alexandre Dumas's *The Three Musketeers,* and the opening scene of Henry James's first novel, *The American*, begins at the Louvre. Marcel Proust was another dedicated visitor, whose 3000-page novel, *In Search of Lost Time*, mentions over 100 painters from the Middle Ages to the early twentieth century, making it among one of the most visual works of literature ever written, and a supreme example of how writing was the way Proust painted. 'I shall not find a painting more beautiful because the artist has painted a hawthorn in the foreground,' he wrote in his preface to *La Bible d'Amiens* (1904), 'though I know of nothing more beautiful than the hawthorn, for I wish to remain sincere and because I know that the beauty of a painting does not depend on the things represented in it. I shall not collect images of hawthorn. I do not venerate hawthorn, I go to see and smell it.'

Mark Twain, whose writing was definitely not influenced by the Louvre, wrote about his experience there in *The Innocents Abroad* (1869). He was no Proust. He could not 'see and smell' art; however, he did have a flair for demolishing it: 'I will drop the subject', he wrote, 'lest I say something about the old masters that might as well be left unsaid.'

See Also: Honoré de Balzac, Théophile Gautier, Goncourt brothers, Émile Zola, Alexandre Dumas, Henry James, Marcel Proust, Charles Baudelaire, Mark Twain.

Further Information: The Louvre was first built around 1190 as a garrison fortress to protect the city. Following its becoming the official residence of the monarchy in 1528, successive architects rebuilt and developed it over the centuries, according to the taste and fashions of the day. The controversial Louvre Pyramid was completed in 1989. Memorable incidents over the years include the purchase of the Tiara of Saitaphernes in 1896, which proved to be a fake, and the theft of the Mona Lisa in 1911.

Further Reading: E. Karpeles, *Paintings in Proust: A Visual Companion to 'In Search of Lost Time'* (Thames and Hudson, 2008); A. Muhlstein, *The Pen and the Brush* (Other Press, 2017).

MARK TWAIN

PLACE DU PALAIS ROYAL

(Métro: Palais Royal–Musée du Louvre)

FORMER SITE OF THE

GRAND HÔTEL DU LOUVRE;

RESIDENCE OF MARK TWAIN

DURING HIS 'PLEASURE TRIP' ABOARD

THE *QUAKER CITY*; INSPIRATION FOR

THE INNOCENTS ABROAD

Travel is fatal to prejudice, bigotry, and narrow-mindedness, and many of our people need it sorely on these accounts. Broad, wholesome, charitable views of men and things cannot be acquired by vegetating in one little corner of the earth all one's lifetime.
Mark Twain, *The Innocents Abroad* (1869)

Mark Twain in 1882

Irreverent, witty and master at deflating the opulence and romance of antiquity wherever he encountered it, Mark Twain was a comic writer of genius. His quirky humour, combined with his irascible character, persuaded the San Francisco newspaper, the *Daily Alta California*, to pay his passage of

Passengers aboard the *Quaker City* in 1867. Twain's face is just visible to the right of the man holding the hat

$1250, on the *Quaker City*, a ship that was sailing from New York in 1867 on a five-month cruise to Europe, North Africa, and the Holy Land. In return, he would send weekly reports of the voyage. The resulting book, *The Innocents Abroad or, The New Pilgrims' Progress*, became the most popular American travel book of all time.

In July 1867, the *Quaker City* docked in Marseille, where Twain and a few fellow passengers boarded the train for Paris. On arrival, they checked into the Grand Hôtel du Louvre, one of the city's top hotels and, the men having attended to the immediate priority of tracking down a barber for a shave, made ready to see the sites with a hired local guide, whom Twain described as 'a born pirate' and a 'treacherous miscreant'.

They visited the International Exposition, 'a wonderful show, but the moving masses of people of all nations we saw there were still a more wonderful show'. They mingled with the crowds and saw the passing spectacle of a parade of cavalrymen escorting Napoleon III and Abdul-Aziz, ruler of the Ottoman Empire, 'whose Three Graces are Tyranny, Rapacity, Blood ... the First Century greets the Nineteenth!' Next was 'the Cathedral of Notre Dame – We had heard of it before', and later the nearby Morgue, where, 'On a slanting stone lay a drowned man, naked, swollen, purple; clasping the fragment of a broken bush with a grip which death had so petrified that human strength could not unloose it.' One evening they went to the Jardin Mabille, and the next, to another 'great garden in the suburb of Asnières', both famous places for their performances of the notorious cancan. 'I placed my hands before my face for very shame. But I looked through my fingers.' They visited the Louvre, 'and looked at its miles of paintings by the old masters. Some of them were beautiful, but at the same time they carried such evidences about them of the cringing spirit of those great men that we found small pleasure in examining them.' Other excursions included a drive in the Bois de Boulogne, a visit to the tomb of Abélard and Héloïse in Père Lachaise Cemetery, and finally the giddy wonders of Versailles.

'This book is a record of a pleasure-trip,' wrote Twain in the preface of *The Innocents Abroad.*

If it were a record of a solemn scientific expedition, it would have about it that gravity, that profundity, and that impressive incomprehensibility which are so proper to works of that kind, and withal so attractive. Yet notwithstanding it is only a record of a pic-nic, it has a purpose, which is, to suggest to the reader how he would be likely to see Europe and the East if he looked at them with his own eyes instead of the eyes of those who travelled in those countries before him.

After his five-month cruise, Twain set about trying to find a publisher for the book. This proved a hard task, but eventually, the American Publishing Company of Hartford agreed to take it on. Its success was immediate and went through edition after edition, turning Twain into a bestselling author virtually overnight. Throughout his life, he always had a love–hate relationship with France. 'We shall remember something of pleasant France; and something also of Paris,' he wrote, 'though it flashed upon us a splendid meteor, and was gone again, we hardly knew how or where.'

See Also: La Morgue, Cathédrale Notre-Dame de Paris, Père Lachaise, Abélard and Héloïse.

Further Information: Mark Twain stayed in the original Grand Hôtel du Louvre on the Place du Palais Royal in July 1867. Designed by Alfred Armand, it opened in 1855. With 700 suites and 1250 staff, it was the largest hotel in Europe. In 1877, the Galeries du Louvre, the department store next door, purchased the hotel and relocated it in a building nearby on Place André Malreaux. Jardin Mabille, or Bal Mabille, was an open-air space for dancing which opened in 1831 where Nos. 49 to 53 avenue Montaigne stand today. Allegedly the birthplace of the polka and the cancan, and referred to by Balzac in *La Comédie humaine*, it became a tourist trap and the haunt of prostitutes. Mark Twain and his family returned to Europe in 1891, where they lived for nine years. In 1895 they rented a 'charming mansion' at No. 169 rue de l'Université, and with the typical Twain dry sense of humour, he observed that, 'In Paris they just simply opened their eyes and stared when we spoke to them in French! We never did succeed in making those idiots understand their own language.'

MOLIÈRE

28 RUE MOLIÈRE

(Métro: Pyramides)

FONTAINE MOLIÈRE

DEDICATED TO THE COMIC

DRAMATIST MOLIÈRE

Disquietingly off-centre, as though the designer had a squint, Molière is enthroned, dead serious, above a pair of languid nymphs who couldn't care less. The playwright did in fact die near here: but if he hadn't, then something would have had to be invented to be an excuse for this preposterous and enchanting public gesture.
Ian Nairn, *Nairn's Paris* (1968)

Fontaine Molière

Molière wrote: 'It's an odd job, making decent people laugh.' But when he started out acting in plays, and later writing them, laughter was not on his agenda. Molière believed his talents lay in tragedy; however, his attempts at it were a total failure. Fortunately for the world of drama, he soon realised he had a gift for comic roles and a taste for farce. Today, his masterly social comedies, which satirised the manners and fashions of his time, are among the most frequently performed of all French plays. Many playwrights, including English dramatists John Dryden and William Wycherley, borrowed freely from him, making Molière the chief influence on the Restoration Comedy of seventeenth-century England. Nonetheless, although he may have won the hearts of fellow playwrights, he failed to gain the approval of the Church and was denied a Christian burial with the pomp and circumstance he most assuredly deserved.

Molière was the stage name of Jean-Baptiste Poquelin, who was born in Paris in 1622. He was the first son of Marie Cressé, and Jean Poquelin, an upholsterer and draper to the Royal Court. Jean's intention was that his son would follow in his footsteps, but Molière broke with tradition and sought out a precarious career on the stage, a career that would last thirty years and change the face of French comedy.

His first attempt at creating a theatre caused him to accrue massive debts, for which Molière was briefly jailed in 1645. Thereafter, Molière and his troupe left Paris to tour the provinces, where they would remain for thirteen long years, performing all over the French countryside in village squares, tented theatres and local halls, or from their horse-drawn caravan. It was a lengthy sojourn that polished their performances, rewarded them with a modicum of success, and gave them the confidence to return to Paris where they eventually found their holy grail: royal patronage.

In 1658 Molière's company performed before Louis XIV. The Louvre Palace, however, had no theatre, and the King had to make do with a temporary stage

Etching of Molière by Adolphe Lalauze

erected in a room on the Louvre's ground floor known today as the Salle des Caryatides. The main performance was Corneille's tragedy, *Nicomède*, which seemed to stupefy the audience, but when the stage was hastily reset for Molière's farce, *The Amorous Doctor*, the spectators were soon rolling in the aisles and the King shedding tears of laughter. Afterwards, the King decreed that Molière's troupe should have a permanent home in Paris at the Théâtre du Petit Bourbon. From that day, Molière realised his future lay in comedy.

After the patronage of the King, his path to fame was assured, but his life was still plagued by scandal and harassment from the authorities, particularly the Roman Catholic Church. Every year until his death, Molière produced at least one comic masterpiece, usually receiving condemnation by the authorities.

Notable among these were *Les Précieuses ridicules* (1659) (The Affected Young Ladies), *Le Misanthrope* (1666), *Tartuffe* (1667) and *Amphitryon* (1668). He was a great comic dramatist, but sometimes he wrote hastily, and his plots could be trivial, descending into buffoonery.

Yet, when all is said and done, no one can deny Molière recognition as father of modern French comedy.

See Also: Tomb of Molière, Jean Racine, Pierre Corneille, Basilica of Sainte-Jeanne-d'Arc.

Further Information: Molière married in 1662. The marriage was not a happy one, but it produced three children; only a daughter survived to adulthood. Molière died from a massive haemorrhage at his home, aged fifty-one, in 1673, shortly after performing in his three-act comédie-ballet, *Le Malade imaginaire*.

The Louvre's Salle des Caryatides is located on the ground floor of Pierre Lescot's sixteenth-century Renaissance wing, and takes its name from the four female figures sculpted by Jean Goujon in 1550 to support the musician's gallery. Today it exhibits classical antiquities and a plaque commemorates Molière's royal debut.

The Théâtre du Petit Bourbon was located in the grand hall of the Hôtel du Petit Bourbon that stood adjacent to the Louvre and was demolished in 1660. Thereafter, the King gave Molière the use of the Théâtre du Palais-Royal on Rue Saint-Honoré, a theatre located in the east wing of the Palais-Royal. Molière's troupe was resident there from 1660 to 1673. It was destroyed by fire in 1763, rebuilt in 1770, and again destroyed by fire in 1781.

Select Bibliography: *The Misanthrope, Tartuffe, and Other Plays* (Oxford Classics, 2008); *Don Juan and Other Plays* (Oxford Classics, 2008); *The Miser and Other Plays* (Penguin Classics, 2000).

Further Reading: V. Scott, *Molière: A Theatrical Life* (Cambridge University Press, 2002); M. Bulgakov, *The Life of Monsieur de Molière* (Alma Books, 2009); J. Gaines (ed.), *The Molière Encyclopedia* (Greenwood, 2002).

OBELISK PRESS

16 PLACE VENDÔME

(Métro: Opéra/Tuileries)

FORMER OFFICES OF

OBELISK PRESS

ENGLISH-LANGUAGE PUBLISHER

OF RISQUÉ BOOKS

FOUNDED BY JACK KAHANE

Tropic of Cancer, 1st edition, 1934

'At last!' I murmured to myself. I had read the most terrible, the most sordid, the most magnificent manuscript that had ever fallen into my hands; nothing I had yet received was comparable to it for the splendor of its writing, the fathomless depth of its despair, the savour of its portraiture, the boisterousness of its humour... I was exalted by the triumphant sensation of all explorers who have at last fallen upon the object of their years of search. I had in my hands a work of genius and it had been offered to me for publication.

Jack Kahane rhapsodising after reading the manuscript of Henry Miller's *Tropic of Cancer* in 1932.

The black phallic obelisk, logo of Jack Kahane's Obelisk Press, was an appropriate symbol for a publisher whose main goal was to publish controversial books no other publisher would dare to publish for fear of prosecution. If it was illegal to publish books elsewhere in the world, reasoned Kahane, 'it was not so in France, and if the law was respected as it should be, many fine books which would therefore be lost to the world might be saved by the creation of a vehicle for their publication in a country where it was legal'. Kahane's noble, yet money-spinning logic – i.e. if it was banned in England and the USA it could still be published in Paris – went on to benefit many writers who had witnessed the heel of censorship, including Henry Miller, D.H. Lawrence, James Hanley, Radclyffe Hall, James Joyce, Anaïs Nin, Lawrence Durrell, Frank Harris and Cyril Connolly.

Born in Manchester, the son of Romanian immigrants, Kahane's early years were spent in the Lancashire textile industry. During the First World War he was badly gassed and contracted tuberculosis. Convalescing in the French countryside he began writing novels, which after a few years he regarded as a 'fruitless occupation', and he became partners in a small Paris publishing house, eventually founding his own company, the Obelisk Press, in the summer of 1931. Publishing everything from cheap erotica to the novels of those who have become literary legends, Obelisk's greatest triumph was publishing Henry Miller's *Tropic of Cancer* in 1934, which was only declared a non-obscene book by the US Supreme Court thirty years later in 1964, and is now frequently listed among the 100 best English-language novels of the twentieth century. The moral to be taken here is that genius flourishes in all environments no matter its reputation or its reasoning.

See Also: Henry Miller, Anaïs Nin, Olympia Press, Eric Losfeld.

Further Information: In 1937 the Obelisk Press moved from 338 rue Saint-Honoré to more upmarket premises at 16 place Vendôme, opposite the Ritz, although Kahane conducted most of his business from the nearby Castiglione Café. Kahane married a French girl named Marcelle Eugenie Girodias. Their son, Maurice, who took his mother's surname and followed in his father's footsteps, founded Olympia Press in 1953. Jack Kahane died in September 1939, a few days after the outbreak of World War II.

Further Reading: J. Kahane, *Memoirs of a Booklegger* (Michael Joseph, 1939); N. Pearson, *Obelisk: A History of Jack Kahane and the Obelisk Press* (Liverpool University Press, 2007); G. Miers, *Of Obelisks and Daffodils: The Publishing History of the Obelisk Press (1929–1939)* (Handsack Press, 2011); H. Ford, *Published in Paris* (Garnstone Press, 1975).

Jack Kahane

PALAIS DE JUSTICE

4 BOULEVARD DU PALAIS

(Métro: Cité)

**WHERE FLAUBERT AND BAUDELAIRE
WERE INDICTED FOR 'OFFENCE TO
PUBLIC AND RELIGIOUS MORALITY'
AND EDMOND DANTÈS WAS
CONDEMNED TO THE CHÂTEAU D'IF
IN *THE COUNT OF MONTE CRISTO***

A door that communicated with the Palais de Justice was opened, and they went through a long range of gloomy corridors, whose appearance might have made even the boldest shudder.
Alexandre Dumas, *The Count of Monte Cristo* (1844)

Ernest Pinard (1822–1909)

The Palais de Justice was once part of the royal Palace de la Cité, which also consisted of the Saint-Chapelle and the Conciergerie, the prison which held hundreds of prisoners, including Marie Antoinette and Dickens's fictional hero Sidney Carton in *A Tale of Two Cities*, prior to their execution by guillotine during the Reign of Terror.

Justice has been dispensed from this imposing and majestic spot since the Middle Ages, and French writers of literature have been indicted here throughout history, usually as a warning to put their house in order. Émile Zola was found guilty of libel here in February 1898 and sentenced to one year's imprisonment and a fine of 3000 francs during the Dreyfus Affair for writing 'J'Accuse...!', his 'Open Letter to the President of the Republic'. In January and August of 1857 Gustave Flaubert and Charles Baudelaire, respectively, were prosecuted at the Palais de Justice for 'offence to public and religious morality and to good morals': Flaubert for *Madame Bovary*, and Baudelaire for *Les Fleurs du mal*.

Public Prosecutor, Ernest Pinard, declared that *Madame Bovary* was 'an affront to decent comportment and religious morality', and the trial, which evolved into a debate about art and morality, created a furore in Paris. The novel was the artistic sensation of its day when it was first serialised in the literary magazine, *La Revue de Paris*, in 1856. Set in Normandy, the narrative explores the frustrations and doomed romances of Emma Bovary, a farmer's daughter who is married to a provincial doctor. Often described as the world's first 'Shopping and Fucking' novel, the prosecution claimed that the book made adultery look attractive to women. This shocked Flaubert, who believed he had written a very moral book. 'The novel *Madame Bovary* reveals a true talent,'

The Palais de Justice

wrote Prosecutor Pinard, 'but the descriptions of certain scenes goes beyond all bounds; if we close our eyes, Flaubert will have many imitators, who will go even further in the same direction.' Flaubert's 'direction', however, was not to make Emma Bovary an object to be admired by women, but was a moral warning to them and to the social hypocrisy of the day, which condemned adultery for women, but turned a blind eye to men, who could frequent prostitutes and keep mistresses. The novel, understandably, had a huge female readership. After Flaubert's acquittal on 7 February 1857, *Madame Bovary* became a bestseller when it was published a few weeks later.

Baudelaire was not so fortunate. *Les Fleurs du mal (The Flowers of Evil)*, his collection of lyric poems, was published in 1857, and its sacrilegious themes almost immediately aroused the scrutiny of the authorities. Baudelaire and his publishers were summarily investigated by the Public Prosecutor, Ernest Pinard, and all copies of the book ordered to be confiscated. On 20 August 1857 Baudelaire was fined 300 francs for '*outrage à la morale publique*', and six poems from the book ordered to be suppressed because of their lesbian and sadomasochistic themes, a ban that remained technically in place until 1949. The formidable Ernest Pinard went on to become Minister of the Interior in 1866, but today his political career is all but forgotten and he is remembered chiefly for his indictments against Flaubert and Baudelaire. 'Art that observes no rule is no longer art,' he said. 'It is like a woman who disrobes completely. To impose the one rule of public decency on art is not to subjugate it but to honour it'.

The Palais de Justice was also where Edmond Dantès was sentenced to imprisonment in the Château d'If in Alexandre Dumas's *The Count of Monte Cristo*:

Château d'If in the Bay of Marseille

> The Palais de Justice communicated with the prison, – a sombre edifice ... After numberless windings, Dantès saw a door with an iron wicket. The commissary took up an iron mallet and knocked thrice, every blow seeming to Dantès as if struck on his heart. The door opened, the two gendarmes gently pushed him forward, and the door closed with a loud sound behind him. The air he inhaled was no longer pure, but thick and mephitic, – he was in prison.

The Count of Monte Cristo remains one of the greatest thrillers ever written, and Dumas's tale of treachery and vengeance has never lost its appeal since it was first serialised in 1844. Those who ostensibly called themselves his friends, and the scheming prosecutor, Villefort, wrongly accuse innocent victim, Edmond Dantès, a young sea captain, of treason. While imprisoned in the notorious Château d'If, he befriends a fellow prisoner, the Abbé Faria, who educates him and tells him of a vast treasure hidden on the Island of Monte Cristo. Dantès eventually escapes captivity, discovers the treasure, and returns to Paris where he plots revenge on those who imprisoned him.

Dumas's main plot structure, culminating in Dantès's long-awaited retribution, was based on the true story of a nineteenth century shoemaker in Nîmes named Pierre Picaud. Dumas discovered his story in a book written by police archivist, Jacques Peuchet, published in 1838. Jealous friends falsely accused Picaud, who was engaged to marry a wealthy woman, of treason, and he was imprisoned in Fenestrelle Fort in Northern Italy for seven years. While there, he tunnelled into the neighbouring cell of a wealthy Italian priest named Father Torri who, on his deathbed, bequeathed his fortune to Picaud. On his release Picaud tracked down those who were responsible for his imprisonment and embarked on a grisly killing spree that ended with his own death. Peuchet's story was the basic framework of the plot, but the foundations of Dantès's character were based on Dumas's father, Alexandre Davy de la Pailleterie (aka Alex Dumas): a legendary general, a dashing swordsman and a hero of the French Revolution who was imprisoned on an island fortress and forgotten by the country he fought for, his memory all but eradicated by Napoleon.

Alex Dumas was born in the French sugar colony of Saint-Domingue (now Haiti) in 1762 to French nobleman, Alexandre Antoine Davy, the Marquis de la Pailleterie and Marie Cessette Dumas, a black African slave. The Marquis eventually returned to France with his son, but after an estrangement, Alex spurned his father's name and title, and took his mother's slave name of Dumas. He enlisted in the revolutionary army and quickly rose through the ranks, becoming, by the time he was thirty-one, a fully-fledged general and national hero whose exploits were legendary. This would have been an extraordinary feat for a white soldier, but for a soldier of mixed race it was unheard of.

His downfall came during Napoleon's failed attempt to conquer Egypt and the Levant (1798–1801), where Dumas commanded the French cavalry. When concern in the ranks over the stagnation of the campaign caused Dumas to challenge Napoleon, his grievances were interpreted as mutinous and Dumas was threatened with being shot for sedition. For health reasons Dumas sailed for France in March 1799, along with other military personnel. The ship, an old hulk, started sinking almost immediately, and a storm shipwrecked the vessel at Taranto in the Kingdom of Naples, then an enemy of France. Dumas was confined in the fortress of Taranto for two years. On his release he was a broken man. Partially blind and deaf, malnourished and walking with a limp, his military career was over. All revolutionary generals received the Legion of Honour, but Dumas never did. Nor did he receive the military pension that was due him. Ignored by the French authorities, his memory erased by Napoleon, he died in poverty, aged forty, in 1806.

See Also: Gustave Flaubert, Les Bouquinistes, Charles Baudelaire, Louise Colet, Alexandre Dumas, Émile Zola.

Further Information: The four towers of the Palais de Justice, which face on to the quays, date from the reign of Philip IV (1268–1314). The two central towers stand on either side of the entrance of the Conciergerie, which is now a museum. On the Boulevard du Palais is the iron gateway of the Cour du Mai (May Courtyard), the main entrance to the Palais de Justice. The Saint-Chapelle was King Louis IX's private chapel and is located in the courtyard. Château d'If was built between 1524 and 1531 as a strategic fortress on the Île d'If, a mile offshore in the Bay of Marseille. It ceased to be used as a prison in the late nineteenth century and is now a local tourist attraction. Alexandre Dumas's grandfather is said to have smuggled slaves and sugar to the Caribbean island of Monte Cristo.

Further Reading: D. LaCapra, 'Madame Bovary' on Trial (Cornell, 1986); T. Reiss, The Black Count: Glory, Revolution, Betrayal, and the Real Count of Monte Cristo (Harvill Secker, 2012).

Alex Dumas: inspiration for the Count of Monte Cristo

CHARLES PERRAULT

JARDIN DES TUILERIES

(Métro: Tuileries)

MONUMENT TO CHARLES PERRAULT
FRENCH FABULIST WHO TRANSFORMED
SIMPLE FAIRY TALES
INTO LITERARY CLASSICS

I call them wolves, but you will find
That some are not the savage kind,
Not howling, ravening or raging;
Their manners seem, instead, engaging,
They're softly-spoken and discreet.
Young ladies whom they talk to on the street
They follow to their homes and through the
hall,
And upstairs to their rooms; when they're
there
They're not as friendly as they might appear:
These are the most dangerous wolves of all.

Charles Perrault, The Moral of This Tale,
from 'Little Red Riding Hood' (1695)

Sculptor Gabriel Pech's monument to
Charles Perrault. Erected in 1908

The origins of 'Little Red Riding
Hood', 'Cinderella', 'Sleeping
Beauty' and all the other stories from our
childhood that terrified and enchanted
us are buried deep in history, but the
man who gave us the classic versions
we know today was Charles Perrault
(1628–1703). Written in Paris at the
end of the seventeenth century, Perrault
reshaped these old folk tales, paying
great attention to detail. He invented the
glass slipper, the cat's boots and the red
hood, and, using his fertile imagination,
created the stories that have been read
to generations of children for over three
hundred years.

He was born in Paris, the seventh child
of a wealthy bourgeois family. He
studied law and embarked on a career
in government service, but throughout
his life he was a determined writer, publishing his first work in 1653. In 1665
he was appointed First Commissioner
of Royal Buildings under the monarchy
of Louis XIV, and in 1671 he became
a member of the French Academy. His
writing was eclectic, covering varying
subjects from poetry to biography, but
in his sixties, and for no known reason,
he turned to the world of fairy tale. In
1695, aged sixty-seven, and now retired,
he published *Histoires ou Contes du
temps passé. Avec des moralités* (Stories
or Tales of Bygone Times. With their
Morals), including 'Little Red Riding
Hood', 'Cinderella' and 'Bluebeard'.

Shortly after publication of the *Contes*,
an anonymous article, probably written
by Perrault, appeared in the French
literary magazine, *Mercure galant*,
arguing that the origins of the folk tale
were rooted in the oral tradition rather
than being the inventions of their present-day authors: 'an infinite number of
fathers and mothers, grandmothers, governesses and much-loved nannies, who

for perhaps as long as a thousand years have contributed, each one improving on the one before, many entertaining circumstantial details which have been preserved, while anything ill-conceived has been forgotten.'

Ironically, Perrault's other writings have been all but forgotten, but his fairy tales live on, happily ever after, and are now the most widely read French works ever written.

See Also: La Fontaine.

Further Information: As a result of Charles Perrault's successful campaign against proposals to reserve the Jardin des Tuileries for royal use and their subsequent opening to the public in 1667, a monument was erected to him in 1908, created by sculptor Gabriel Pech. The French word *tuilerie* means tilery or tile-kiln, and the gardens were named after the tile factories that stood on the site before Queen Catherine de Medici built the Palais des Tuileries in 1564. Louis XIV's gardener, André Le Nôtre, landscaped the gardens in 1664 to create the gardens that lie today between the Louvre and Place de la Concorde.

Further Reading: C. Perrault, *The Complete Fairy Tales* (Oxford, 2009); I. & P. Opie, *The Classic Fairy Tales* (Oxford, 1974).

Perrault by Gérard Edelinck

JEAN-JACQUES ROUSSEAU

52–54 RUE JEAN-JACQUES ROUSSEAU

(Formerly Rue Plâtrière)

(Métro: Louvre–Rivoli/Les Halles/Palais Royal–Musée du Louvre)

FORMER HOME OF

JEAN-JACQUES ROUSSEAU

WRITER, PHILOSOPHER, POLITICAL

THEORIST AND MAJOR FIGURE OF THE

FRENCH ENLIGHTENMENT

To live is not to breathe; it is to act; it is to make use of our organs, our senses, our faculties, of all the parts of ourselves, which give us the sentiment of our existence. The man who has lived the most is not he who has counted the most years but he who has most felt life. Men have been buried at one hundred who died at their birth. They would have gained from dying young; at least they would have lived up to that time.
Jean-Jacques Rousseau, *Émile, or On Education* (1762)

Samuel Johnson thought him 'one of the worst of men, a rascal, who ought to be hunted out of society.' Johnson was not alone in his loathing of Rousseau; however, any man who sets out to reshape and build the foundations of modern political and social thought, as Rousseau did, will not pass through life without enemies. And Rousseau's enemies were amongst the finest, from David Hume to Voltaire. Rousseau can also lay claim to being the father of the modern autobiography after the posthumous publication of his *Confessions* (1782), full of self-revelatory experiences that inspired many autobiographies and autobiographical novels thereafter. He also composed a one-act opera that was performed before the royal court at

Fontainebleau. Although Rousseau was a man of many parts, he is best remembered today, together with Denis Diderot and Voltaire, as one of the major figures of the French Enlightenment, and it is his works of political philosophy that have made the greatest impact on the world's stage.

He was born in Geneva in 1712 to Isaac Rousseau, a watchmaker, and Suzanne

A 1753 portrait of Rousseau by Maurice Quentin de La Tour

Bernard, who died a few days after her son's birth. Rousseau had no formal schooling, and at thirteen he became apprenticed to a notary, then later to an engraver. At sixteen he journeyed to the kingdom of Savoy (now part of north-west Italy) where he befriended Madame de Warens, a noblewoman who took him under her wing. She became his surrogate mother and, later, his lover. She was a woman of intelligence and taste with a large library in which Rousseau immersed himself. In 1741 he moved to Paris where he hoped to make a living from his new system of numbered musi-

cal notation, and although it was a failed endeavour, music always remained the love of his life. Other jobs followed, notably working as a secretary for the French Embassy in Venice, and writing articles for Diderot's *Encyclopédie*.

In 1745 he met laundress and chambermaid, Thérèse Levasseur, who became his lifelong partner. They had five children together, all of whom were given up to a foundlings' home. Up until this time Rousseau had written nothing of major significance, but in 1751 his *Discours sur les arts et sciences (A Discourse on the Arts and Sciences)* won the Académie de Dijon prize with its condemnation of intellectual and technical progress, a literary debut that brought him prestige and celebrity. Rousseau's most prolific period, however, was between 1756 and 1762, during which time he wrote *Du Contrat Social (The Social Contract)* and *Émile, ou De l'éducation (Émile, or On Education)*. *Social Contract* was almost immediately banned in Paris and burnt in Geneva, and *Émile* was castigated for its religious unorthodoxy. Rousseau fled to Switzerland and at the invitation of David Hume in 1765 he sought refuge in England. Relations soon soured with Hume and by 1770 he was back in Paris, where he lodged with Thérèse in Rue Plâtrière, supporting himself by copying music notation. In 1765 he had begun writing his *Confessions*, mostly to protect his reputation against malicious hearsay. He completed it in 1770, but it was not published until 1782, four years after his death.

Rousseau and Thérèse left Rue Plâtrière in the summer of 1778 at the invitation of his admirer the Marquis René de Girardin who offered them a house on his estate at Ermenonville, north-east of Paris. Six weeks after their arrival, Rousseau died of a stroke. He was sixty-six years old. The Marquis buried him in a mock-Roman sarcophagus on the Île des Peupliers (Isle of Poplars), a small island on his Ermenonville estate. Here Rousseau lay entombed until 1794 when the leaders of the Revolution had his remains transferred to the Panthéon, France's mausoleum for national heroes. Praised and also decried during his lifetime, and leaving a substantial imprint on French literature that still survives today, Rousseau was, without doubt, one of the most important writers and thinkers of his time. A precursor of the Romantic movement, he influenced many, from Shelley to Emerson. 'At the age of sixteen', commented Leo Tolstoy, 'I wore a medallion with a portrait of Rousseau instead of a cross on my neck.'

See Also: Voltaire, Samuel Johnson, Denis Diderot.

Further Information: In honour of Rousseau, Rue Plâtrière was changed to Rue Jean-Jacques Rousseau in 1791, during the early days of the French Revolution.

Select Bibliography: *Discours sur les sciences et les arts* (1750) *(A Discourse on the Arts and Sciences)* (1751); *Discours sur l'origine et les fondements de l'inégalité parmi les hommes (Discourse on the Origin and Basis of Inequality Among Men)* (1754); *Émile, ou De l'éducation (Émile, or On Education)* (1762); *Du Contrat Social (The Social Contract)* (1762); *Les Confessions* (1782–1789).

Further Reading: N. Dent, *Rousseau* (Routledge, 2005); L. Damrosch, *Jean-Jacques Rousseau: Restless Genius* (Mariner, 2007); R. Wokler, *Rousseau: A Very Short Introduction* (Oxford University Press, 2001); C. Spector, *Rousseau* (Polity Press, 2019).

GEORGES SIMENON

36 QUAI DES ORFÈVRES

(Métro: St-Michel/Cité)

OFFICE OF SIMENON'S
CHIEF INSPECTOR MAIGRET

I was born in the dark and in the rain, and I got away. The crimes I write about are the crimes I would have committed if I had not got away. I am one of the lucky ones. What is there to say about the lucky ones except that they got away?

Georges Simenon, *The New Yorker* (1953)

André Gide described Simenon as 'the greatest novelist we have had this century'. He also won praise from Colette, T.S. Eliot, W. Somerset Maugham, Henry Miller and Céline. But Simenon tells us he could easily have become a criminal and held a gun rather than a pen. He also tells us that chance, that mysterious twist of fate, mercifully intervened, and he 'got away', to become one of the most widely published authors of the twentieth century, writing over four hundred books that sold more than five hundred million copies worldwide in fifty-five languages. But Simenon was an enigma, who loved laying false trails about his life and works. Few, if any, of the world's Simenon experts agree about the facts of his life, and Simenon's twenty volumes of autobiography, a supreme exercise in contradiction, defeat anyone's attempt to try. His life, therefore, was a succession of deceptions and eventual exile.

He was born in 1903 in Liège, Belgium, to Henriette Brüll, and Désiré Simenon, an accountant in an insurance office. During his troubled childhood, which would scar him for the rest of his life,

Quai des Orfèvres

his mother rejected him and his father smothered him with love. His father died aged only forty-four from heart disease, but Simenon alleged his mother hounded him to death. When Simenon's brother was killed, his mother lamented, 'Why did it have to be him? Why couldn't it have been you?' Simenon's life of petty crime began in 1914, when he was eleven, during the German occupation of Liège. When he was sixteen he began working on a local newspaper, first as an office boy and later as a reporter. At the age of nineteen, in 1922, he left for Paris where he matured into a prolific writer of popular fiction. Between 1923 and 1933, he wrote over two hundred books under sixteen different pseudonyms, and was by then well on his way to fame and fortune.

Pietr-le-Letton (1929) *(The Strange Case of Peter the Lett)* was the first novel published under his own name, and it introduced the cool-headed, pipe-smoking Parisian police inspector Jules Maigret, the most famous fictional detective after Sherlock Holmes. Unlike Holmes, however, Maigret insists he 'has no method', but simply tries to put himself inside the head of a criminal. Maigret featured in over eighty novels, and is probably the character for which his creator is most remembered.

Simenon also revolutionised the crime novel by exploring the psychological depths of his characters, once commenting, 'I have no imagination; I take everything from life.' Most of his books were written in less than two weeks, and up until his retirement from fiction writing in 1972, he had produced an average of four to five titles a year over a period

Georges Simenon in 1965

of forty-four years. He was a colossus in the world of crime and thriller fiction, raising the genre to a literary level, but he never escaped his past. He was also a womaniser, claiming he had had sex with 10,000 women. His new wealth and independence made it possible for him to travel the world, living in various places in France and the USA before settling in Switzerland in the late 1950s. He married twice and had four children. His only daughter committed suicide in 1978 aged only twenty-five. Simenon died in 1989, aged eighty-six, after a fall from his bed at his home in Lausanne. 'The artist', he once wrote, 'is above all else a sick person, in any case an unstable one – if the doctors are to be believed ... Why see in that some form of superiority? I would do better to ask people's forgiveness.'

See Also: Eugène Vidocq, André Gide, Colette, T.S. Eliot, Somerset Maugham, Henry Miller, Céline, Émile Gaboriau, Eugène Sue, Fantômas, Maurice Leblanc.

Further Information: 36 quai des Orfèvres was the former headquarters of the criminal investigation unit of the French national police, known as *La direction régionale de la police judiciaire*, and the direct successor of the *Sûreté*, founded in 1812 by Eugène Vidocq. It was the inspiration behind the FBI, Scotland Yard and other criminal investigation departments around the world. Since September 2017, the *DRPJ* have new headquarters at 36 rue du Bastion. At the time of writing, 36 quai des Orfèvres is occupied by the *Brigade de Recherche et d'Intervention*, a research and intervention organisation known as the 'Anti-Gang Brigade'.

Select Bibliography: *The Crime at Lock 14* (1931); *Maigret and the Yellow Dog* (1931); *The Engagement* (1933); *The Man Who Watched the Trains Go By* (1938); *The Strangers in the House* (1940); *The Widow* (1942); *Pedigree* (1948); *The Stain on the Snow* (1948); *My Friend Maigret* (1949); *Red Lights* (1953); *The Watchmaker of Everton* (1955); *Maigret in Court* (1960); *African Trio* (1979); *Intimate Memoirs* (1981).

Further Reading: P. Marnham, *The Man Who Wasn't Maigret: A Portait of Georges Simenon* (Bloomsbury, 1992); P. Assouline, *Simenon: A Biography* (Vintage, 1997).

Maigret's Citroën Light 15/6H Traction Avant that featured in the 1960s TV series

HÔTEL RITZ

15 PLACE VENDÔME

*(Métro: Madeleine/Opéra/Pyramides/
Tuileries)*

WATERING HOLE AND
SETTING FOR WRITERS SINCE 1898

*Abe North was still in the Ritz bar, where he
had been since nine in the morning. When he
arrived seeking sanctuary the windows were
open and great beams were busy at pulling
up the dust from smoky carpets and cushions. Chasseurs tore through the corridors,
liberated and disembodied, moving for the
moment in pure space.*
F. Scott Fitzgerald, *Tender is the Night* (1934)

César and Marie-Louise Ritz in 1888

The antithesis of Left Bank bohemia, Hôtel Ritz has enticed and enchant-ed writers over the years like a moth to a flame. From the well-heeled, to those who just wanted to be swathed in its grandeur, Hôtel Ritz catered for them all, including Marcel Proust, Noël Cow-ard, Djuna Barnes, Somerset Maugham, Janet Flanner, Ernest Hemingway, F. Scott Fitzgerald, Jean Cocteau, Jean-Paul Sartre and Simone de Beauvoir. It has been used as an opulent backdrop for countless novels, from Hemingway's *The Sun Also Rises* to Ian Fleming's *From Russia, with Love*. For those with delusions of grandeur Hôtel Ritz was the place to rub shoulders with their fanta-sies. And for those who simply wanted the best food and drink in Paris, none could surpass it.

Probably the most retold folk tale con-nected to Hôtel Ritz is associated with its most famous barfly, Ernest Hemingway, who used the Ritz as a watering hole before and after World War II. Sylvia Beach, founder of Shakespeare and Company recalled in her memoirs that on 26 August 1944 Hemingway arrived outside her shop in Rue de l'Odéon amongst an armada of jeeps:

[He] was in battle dress, grimy and bloody. A machine gun clanked on the floor … He wanted to know if there was anything he could do for us. We asked him if he could do something about the Nazi snipers on the rooftops in our street, particularly on Adrienne's rooftop. He got his company out of the jeeps and took them up on the roof. We heard firing for the last time in the rue de l'Odéon. Hemingway and his men came down again and rode off in their jeeps – 'to liberate,' according to Hemingway 'the cellar at the Ritz.' He led several soldiers through the place Vendôme and into the chic hotel, where he proceeded to order seventy-three dry martinis.

Hôtel Ritz, Place Vendôme

During World War II the hotel's standards never dropped; even the Nazis treated it with respect, although they claimed ninety per cent discount as they were 'guests of the French people'. Weapons were checked into a kiosk before entering the hotel, and the luxurious Imperial Suite was occupied by Luftwaffe commander, Reichsmarschall Hermann Göring.

In 1921 Hôtel Ritz created a large art deco bar in the Cambon Wing called Le Café Parisien. Opposite the bar was a small wood-lined room called the salon de correspondance, where ladies, who were not allowed in bars, wrote letters while they waited for their inebriated husbands. In 1936 the bar finally opened its doors to women, and was redesigned to accommodate them. This included creating a second, smaller bar, called Le Petit Bar. And it was this smaller bar that Hemingway frequented, often being seen there drinking Bloody Marys while studying the racing form at Auteuil. In the mid 1980s Le Petit Bar was closed and became used for private functions only. In 1994, fifty years after Hemingway's liberation of 'the cellar at the Ritz', the Hotel transformed the former Le Petit Bar into Bar Hemingway, dedicated to its most legendary elbow-bender.

Hemingway often drank at Hôtel Ritz with fellow expatriate writers, including Scott Fitzgerald. In his posthumous, and often scathing memoir, *A Moveable Feast* (1964), Hemingway wrote:

Many years later at the Ritz bar, long after the end of World War II, Georges, who is the bar chief now and was a chasseur when Scott and I lived in Paris, asked me, 'Papa, who was this Monsieur Fitzgerald that everyone asks me about?' ...

'He was an American writer of the early Twenties and later who lived some time in Paris and abroad ...'

'It is strange that I have no memory of him,' Georges said.

'All those people are dead.'

'Still one does not forget people because they are dead. '

See Also: Harry's New York Bar, Dingo Bar, Marcel Proust, Somerset Maugham, Ernest Hemingway, F. Scott Fitzgerald, Janet Flanner, Djuna Barnes, Jean Cocteau, Jean-Paul Sartre, Simone de Beauvoir.

Further Information: Hôtel Ritz was founded by Swiss-born hotelier, César Ritz (1850–1918), in collaboration with legendary French chef Auguste Escoffier (1846–1935) in 1898. Ritz worked his way up from porter, barman and assistant waiter to maître d' in various European hotels. He met Escoffier at the Hotel National in Lucerne where they formed a partnership. In 1890 they were invited to oversee London's Savoy Hotel, from where they were both sacked in 1897, Ritz having been implicated in the disappearance of wine and spirits, and backhander payments. This misconduct was, however, never proven. The following year Ritz created the Hôtel Ritz on Place Vendôme. It soon became one of the most elegant and exclusive hotels in the world, and his name today is synonymous with ostentatious luxury and glamour. In the early 1900s, his health failing, Ritz handed over the management of his hotel empire to his wife, Marie-Louise Ritz.

Further Reading: M. Boxer, *The Paris Ritz* (Thames & Hudson, 1991); T.J. Mazzeo, *The Hotel on Place Vendôme* (Harper, 2014); C.P. Field, *The Cocktails of the Ritz Paris* (Scribner, 2005).

FRANÇOIS VILLON

PLACE DU CHÂTELET

(Métro: Châtelet)

SITE OF LE GRAND CHÂTELET

STRONGHOLD OF THE ANCIEN RÉGIME

WHERE MEDIEVAL POET FRANÇOIS

VILLON WAS IMPRISONED UNDER

SENTENCE OF DEATH

O brother men who after us remain,
Do not look coldly on the scene you view,
For if you pity wretchedness and pain,
God will the more incline to pity you.
You see us hang here, half a dozen who
Indulged the flesh in every liberty
Till it was pecked and rotted, as you see,
And these our bones to dust and ashes fall.
Let no one mock our sorry company,
But pray to God that He forgive us all ...

Prince Jesus, we implore Your Majesty
To spare us Hell's distress and obloquy;
We want no part of what may there befall.
And, mortal men, let's have no mockery,
But pray to God that He forgive us all.

François Villon, from the *Ballade of the Hanged Men (Ballade des pendus)*

A woodcut image of
François Villon in 1489

Le Grand Châtelet *c.*1780

François Villon's brief and squandered life (*c.*1431–*c.*1463) was draped in shadows and mystery, and what little biographical information we do have is thin. His surviving work amounts to a mere 3000 lines, but its mastery of form and technical style place his poetry among the most memorable of the medieval age. Nonetheless, we know little about his ill-fated existence. Villon was the 'accursed poet', wrote Arthur Rimbaud – a characterisation as accurate as it is tragic. His father died when he was still a child, and he was brought up by his uncle, who was an affluent cleric. Under his uncle's patronage, Villon began an academic career at the Sorbonne where records reveal he received the degree of bachelor, and later of master. But what should have been an encouraging start towards a sober and rewarding life soon began to wither.

Villon appeared to have a standing feud with a priest named Chermoye, and court records reveal that on the evening of *La Feste-Dieu* (The Feast of Corpus Christi), on 5 June 1455, Villon was seated on a stone bench in Rue Saint-Jacques when he was approached by an incensed Chermoye, who uttered 'By God! I have found you!' and who then proceeded to draw a dagger from beneath his gown with which he struck Villon. 'The first blow,' writes his biographer, Wyndham Lewis, 'a downward slash, has left Villon's upper lip gashed and bleeding profusely. Villon recoils, and groping under his cloak whips out the dagger at his belt and returns the slash, wounding the priest in the groin.' The priest later died from his wounds and the motive for the fight remains a mystery. Villon went into hiding, but was ultimately absolved of any crime. It was his first clash with justice, but it was not to be his last. The following year, in November 1456, he was imprisoned in the Châtelet on charges of theft. A few weeks later he broke into the College of Navarre with three companions and stole a treasure-chest of five hundred gold crowns. Thus began a miserable life of exile, theft, deceit, brawling, frequenting the tavern and the brothel – and prison.

Villon's reputation essentially rests on two poems, *Le Lais (The Legacy)*, aka *Le Petit Testament*, and his longest work, *Le Testament* aka *Le Grand Testament. Le Lais*, which he claimed was written while in hiding in 1456, after the College of Navarre robbery, takes the form of a mock will made out to friends and acquaintances, and in *Le Testament* he assesses and regrets his wasted life and talent. In 1462 he was arrested again and imprisoned in the Châtelet, where he was sentenced to be hanged for an affray in which a papal notary was injured. In his cell, he was inspired to write what he believed would be his epitaph, *Ballade des pendus (Ballade of the Hanged Men)*. Fortunately for Villon he never swung from the end of a rope as his sentence was quashed on appeal, but the court exiled him from Paris for ten years 'in view of his evil life'.

After his banishment he disappeared from history. 'It seems most likely of all, since there was the faint legend of him years after in Poitou,' wrote Wyndham Lewis, that,

> he found his way there in the end and later died; whether among the Franciscans of St. Maixent, shriven and houselled by his protector, the good honest Abbot of that place, whether in a village tavern-brawl, whether alone, in some obscure hovel far from friends, whether in the arms of a wench, whether hanged from a country gibbet, will never be known until the Day.

Further Information: Le Grand Châtelet, which was built in 1130 by Louis VI as a defensive castle, later housed police headquarters, courts and prison cells. It was demolished in the early 1800s to make way for the present Place du Châtelet.

Select Bibliography: *François Villon – Selected Poems* (Penguin Classics, 1978).

Further Reading: D.B. Wyndham Lewis, *François Villon: A Documented Survey* (Sheed & Ward, 1945).

2nd

Arrondissement

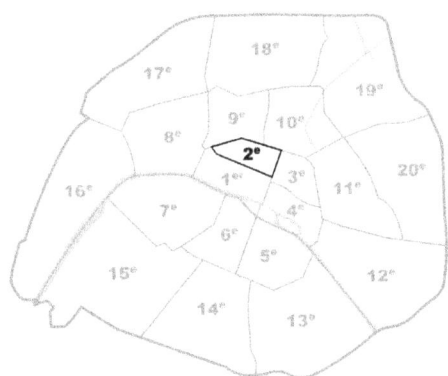

ASTÉRIX

31 RUE DU LOUVRE

(Métro: Sentier)

**FORMER OFFICES OF
DARGAUD ÉDITEUR
PUBLISHER OF *PILOTE* MAGAZINE
WHERE *ASTÉRIX* MADE ITS FIRST
APPEARANCE IN 1959**

These Romans are crazy!
René Goscinny, *Astérix le Gaulois*

Today *Astérix* is one of the most popular European comic books in the world. It has been translated into over a hundred languages, adapted for film and merchandising, and even has its own theme park. Set during the Roman invasion of Gaul, the books follow the adventures of a village of stalwart natives who refuse to accept the might of the invader. The main protagonists are Astérix and his simple-minded friend, Obélix, whose quirky sense of humour, full of puns, stereotypes and cultural jibes, appeals to adults and children of all nationalities.

In 1956 writer René Goscinny (1926–1977), illustrator Albert Uderzo (1927–2020), writer Jean-Michel Charlier and publicist Jean Hébrad founded the comic book syndicate Édipresse/Édifrance. On 29 October 1959 the syndicate launched the weekly magazine *Pilote* in cooperation with Radio Luxembourg, and its first issue introduced its readers to *Astérix le Gaulois (Asterix the Gaul)*, written by Goscinny and illustrated by Uderzo.

Born in Paris, Goscinny moved to Argentina at the age of two where his

(1911–1990), the French publisher of *Journal de Tintin*. The final issue of *Pilote* appeared in 1989. *Pilote* magazine is also where Jacques Tardi (1946–), one of the masters of comic book art, known as the father of 'new realism', launched his career. After studying art in Lyon and Paris, Tardi joined *Pilote* magazine in 1970 where he began his career as a writer and illustrator in many different genres. In 1976 he began his epic serial *Adèle Blanc-Sec*, set in turn-of-the-century Paris, and filmed by Luc Besson in 2010. Unlike many comic book artists, Tardi dislikes illustrating the modern world, and much of his work is set in the nineteenth and twentieth centuries, depicting the underworld of Paris and the horrors of war. In 2013 he refused the Légion d'honneur, stating that he would rather 'remain a free man and not be held hostage by any power whatsoever'.

father worked as a mathematics teacher. In Buenos Aires Goscinny graduated in Fine Arts, and after the death of his father he moved to New York with his mother in 1945. Following army service in France he joined a small illustrator's studio in Brooklyn and began writing for comic books. Here he met Georges Troisfontaines, head of an agency that packaged comics for the Belgian magazine *Spirou*. Troisfontaines made Goscinny head of his Paris office in 1951, and it was there he first met his long-term collaborator, Albert Uderzo. The son of Italian immigrants, Uderzo was already a successful comic book artist by the time he met Goscinny. They collaborated on various comic strips together, but it was *Astérix* that would become timeless and immortalise them both.

Above: 31 rue du Louvre. Below: Albert Uderzo (left), René Goscinny (right)

See Also: Hergé.

Further Information: Following financial difficulties in 1960 *Pilote* was rescued by the comic publisher, Georges Dargaud

ALBERT CAMUS

**CORNER OF RUE RÉAUMUR &
BOULEVARD DE SÉBASTOPOL**
(Métro: Réaumur–Sébastopol)

**WHERE ALBERT CAMUS AND MARIA
CASARES EVADED A NAZI SECURITY
BLOCKADE**

*What's true of all the evils in the world is true
of plague as well. It helps men to rise above
themselves.*
Albert Camus, *The Plague* (1947)

Following the occupation of Paris by the Germans in 1940, author, journalist and philosopher, Albert Camus (1913–1960), joined the Resistance movement, where he edited and contributed to their clandestine newspaper, *Combat*. Created during the Second World War to sabotage the Nazi war effort, *Combat* was a merging of two earlier publications, *Liberty* and *Truth*, and Camus became head of the writers' division. Other contributors included Jean-Paul Sartre and André Malraux. Many of Camus's associates were captured and tortured by the Gestapo or sent to concentration camps. *Combat*'s printer, André Bollier, shot himself through the head rather than face capture when he was surrounded by the Gestapo.

In 1944 Camus came dangerously close to being caught by the Nazis. He was with his actress girlfriend, Maria Casares (1922–96), outside the Réaumur-Sébastopol Métro station when he realised the French police and the Germans had blocked off the street for a random security check. He was carrying forged identity documents under the name of Albert Mathé, his resistance pseudonym, and in his briefcase was a proof copy of the next issue of *Combat*. As they stood in the queue waiting to be searched, Camus observed that the police were only searching the men. The women only had to show their identity papers. He passed the *Combat* issue to Casares who slipped it into her coat pocket. The security duly searched Camus, but not Casares, and they both passed through undetected. It was a close call, and a very brave act on the part of Casares, who, if she had been caught, would have faced torture and execution by the Gestapo.

Maria Casares and Albert Camus

55

NIKOLAI GOGOL

12 PLACE DE LA BOURSE

(Métro: Bourse)

**FORMER LODGINGS OF UKRAINIAN
DRAMATIST AND NOVELIST
NIKOLAI GOGOL
WHERE HE WROTE PART OF HIS
MASTERPIECE, *DEAD SOULS***

Well, so that's the prosecutor! He lived and lived, and then died! And they will say in the papers that he died to the regret of his staff and all mankind, a respected citizen, a rare father, a model husband, and they will write a lot more stuff and nonsense about him; they will add, maybe, that he was mourned by widows and orphans; but if one were to investigate the matter thoroughly, it will emerge that he had nothing to him except his bushy eyebrows.

Nikolai Gogol, *Dead Souls* (1842)

See Also: Albert Camus, Jean-Paul Sartre, André Malraux, Samuel Beckett.

Further Information: *Combat* was one of eight French Resistance movements during WWII and was created in 1940 by French army captain, Henri Frenay. The first issue of the *Combat* newspaper was published in late 1941 with a print run of 10,000, increasing to 250,000 in 1944. After liberation it set up its offices at 100 rue de Réaumur, the former offices of the collaborationist press.

Maria Casares was the daughter of a wealthy Spanish Republican, a refugee from Franco's fascist regime. She was already an established actress when she met Camus and would go on to star in Marcel Carné's *Les Enfants du Paradis* in 1945. Her liaison with Camus lasted for sixteen years.

Further Reading: A. Mitchell, *Nazi Paris: The History of an Occupation 1940–1944* (Berghahn Books, 2010); A. Beevor, A. Cooper, *Paris After the Liberation 1944–1949* (Penguin, 1994).

Gogol was Russia's greatest satirist and the first outstanding realist of the Russian theatre. He influenced all Russian satirists and humorous writers from the mid nineteenth century to the present day. He has had many imitators, none less than Dostoevsky; but few, if any, were his equal. Born on his parents' country estate in Ukraine in 1809, he settled in St Petersburg in 1829. In 1831–1832 he published his first major work, *Evenings on a Farm Near Dikanka*, followed by two short story collections, *Mirgorod* (1835), and *Arabesques* (1835), which contained some of his greatest stories, including 'The Overcoat' and 'The Diary of a Madman'. In 1836 the premiere of his play *The Government Inspector* was staged to great critical acclaim in Moscow. That same year, he left Russia for

An 1840 portrait of Gogol by F. Möller

Europe, arriving in Paris in November. Initially he lodged in a cold, damp hotel room that utterly destroyed his creative spirit, impelling him to move to an apartment on the corner of Place de la Bourse and Rue Vivienne. 'God has stretched out his protection over me and performed a miracle by pointing out to me a warm apartment in the sun with a stove,' he wrote to a friend. 'My good humour is back. I write the Dead Souls with more enthusiasm and courage.'

Dead Souls, the novel for which he is best remembered, is primarily a satire about serfdom, read by many at the time as an indictment against tsarism and a rousing summons to abolish the slavery of serfs. This interpretation shocked Gogol who was a lifelong supporter of the tsarist regime and its patriarchal system. 'It is no use to blame the looking glass', he wrote, 'if your face is awry.'

Like most of Paris's expatriates that came before and after him, Gogol seemed more in touch with his homeland when he was away from it, than when he

was in it. He enjoyed taking long walks, visiting the Louvre, Versailles and the opera, and playing endless games of billiards in cafes, where his love of French food frequently gave him indigestion. 'A rather good place to live, this Paris,' he remarked. He finally departed in March 1837, with fond memories, and died in his Moscow apartment in 1852. His remains are buried in the city's Novodevichy Cemetery. A fitting epitaph for him would surely have been the oft-quoted testimonial attributed to Dostoevsky: 'We all came out of Gogol's overcoat.'

See Also: Ivan Turgenev, Alexander Nevsky Cathedral, Henry Miller.

Further information: Serfdom was eventually abolished throughout the Russian Empire in 1861, nine years after Gogol's death.

Further Reading: H. Troyat, *Gogol: The Biography of a Divided Soul* (Allen & Unwin, 1975).

Place de la Bourse

HARRY'S NEW YORK BAR

5 RUE DAUNOU

(Métro: Opéra)

EXPATRIATE WATERING HOLE

SINCE 1911

When Bond was in Paris he invariably stuck to the same addresses ... If he wanted a solid drink he had it at Harry's Bar, both because of the solidity of the drinks and because, on his first ignorant visit to Paris at the age of sixteen, he had done what Harry's advertisement in the Continental Daily Mail *had told him to do and had said to his taxi-driver 'Sank Roo Doe Noo'. That had started one of the memorable evenings of his life, culminating in the loss, almost simultaneous, of his virginity and his notecase.*

Ian Fleming, 'From a View to a Kill' (*For Your Eyes Only*, 1960)

The New York Bar was Paris's first American bar that was not located in a hotel, and for over a hundred years it has been a refuge for the homesick exile. The bar opened on Thanksgiving Day, 26 November 1911. Its interior came from a Seventh Avenue bar in Manhattan, where it was dismantled, shipped to Paris, and re-erected on Rue Daunou by its owner, a former American jockey named Tod Sloan. One of Sloan's early bartenders was a Scot from Dundee named Harry MacElhone who had already amassed a wealth of bartending experience in hotels and casinos on the French Riviera. Harry didn't settle in Paris, however, and he moved to America. After WWI he worked in bars in London, principally at The Savoy Hotel and Ciro's. In 1919 he published his famous bartender's bible, the *ABC of Mixing Cocktails*, containing over 300 classic recipes.

Gambling debts eventually forced Tod Sloan to sell the the New York Bar in 1913 and, after passing through the hands of various owners, it was put on the market once again in 1923 and purchased by Harry MacElhone, who afterwards added his now-famous prefix and changed it to Harry's New York Bar. With the change of ownership came a change of clientele. Harry was a sports fan who enjoyed the racetrack, but his real love was boxing, and soon the bar became a regular watering hole of the boxing fraternity. And wherever boxers congregated, Ernest Hemingway was never far away. Harry, who was a good friend of Hemingway, often acted as his towel-holder at Hemingway's 'friendly' boxing bouts, and later had a metal plaque engraved with his name and fixed to the famous barfly's stool.

American journalists based in Paris also became regular patrons. These, Sinclair Lewis summed up in his 1929 novel, *Dodsworth*: 'His longing for low and intelligent company could not be denied. He went to the New York Bar ... Sam had met a dozen journalists there, and he felt at home with them.' Over the years the famous and the infamous were drawn to this little piece of Manhattan in Paris, celebrated for its cocktails and hot-dogs; but it was for its clientele of writers that it is remembered in literary history today, a list of which reads like a who's who of literature: Brendan Behan, Sinclair Lewis, Ring Lardner, William Saroyan, Marguerite Duras, Thornton Wilder, Simone de Beauvoir, Jean-Paul Sartre, Gertrude Stein, John Dos Passos, John Steinbeck and F. Scott Fitzgerald. Some of them actually stayed sober long enough to write about it, notably Ernest Hemingway in his *The Sun Also Rises* (1926), Wythe Williams's *Dusk of Empire* (1937), Samuel

Putnam's *Paris Was Our Mistress* (1947), and Budd Schulberg's *The Disenchanted* (1950). Harry MacElhone died of a heart attack in 1958, aged sixty-seven. 'Scotsman by birth,' read the *Daily Mail*'s obituary, 'American by mistaken identity, bar-tender by dedication.' Harry's Bar is still owned by the MacElhone family.

See Also: Ernest Hemingway, Sinclair Lewis, William Saroyan, Marguerite Duras, Thornton Wilder, Simone de Beauvoir, Jean-Paul Sartre, John Dos Passos, John Steinbeck, F. Scott Fitzgerald, Gertrude Stein, Ian Fleming.

Further Reading: I. MacElhone, *Harry's Bar* (Stewart, Tabori & Chang, 2012).

NADAR

35 BOULEVARD DES CAPUCINES

(Métro: Opéra)

FORMER ATELIER OF NADAR
LEGENDARY NINETEENTH–CENTURY
PHOTOGRAPHER WHO CAPTURED
THE DEFINITIVE IMAGE OF THE
LEGENDS OF LITERARY PARIS

Nadar in 1854

Photography is a fantastic discovery: a science which engages the most advanced intellects, and an art which provokes the most profound minds: and yet its use lies within the capacity of the shallowest idiot.

Felix Nadar

Nadar was one of the most celebrated portrait photographers of the late nineteenth century. His legacy to French literature was his contemporary portraits of its literary giants. Naturally posed, like a painter's model, and in stark contrast to the reserved and formal portraits of the day, they included the Goncourt brothers, George Sand, Victor Hugo, Alexandre Dumas, Charles Baudelaire, Alphonse Daudet, Jules Verne, Charles Sainte-Beuve, Théophile Gautier, Gérard de Nerval and many more. In Paris during the 1860s there were more than 200 professional photography studios, and hundreds of photographers, but Nadar was the undisputed master of them all.

He was born Félix Tournachon in 1820, the eldest son of a printer and publisher from Lyon. After his father's attempts to establish a business in Paris ended in bankruptcy and death in an asylum in 1837, the teenaged Félix was forced to abandon his medical studies in Lyon and earn a livelihood to support his mother and younger brother. The following year the family returned to Paris, and after a succession of uninspiring jobs he began working as a journalist and caricaturist for various newspapers. Known for his sarcastic wit, his bohemian friends twisted Tournachon into the nickname Tournadard (*dard* meaning sting), which was eventually truncated to Nadar. In 1849 his caricatures began appearing regularly in the new illustrated magazine, *Le Journal Pour Rire*, and he was soon producing around a hundred caricatures a month. It was supply and demand, therefore, that forced Nadar to create his first atelier with a dozen craftsmen transplanting his art on to wooden printing blocks for the tabloids of Paris.

But caricatures were only a means to an end. What Nadar yearned for was a technique that would unmask a subject and reproduce their inner, spiritual being. 'How to draw out, for example,' he wrote, 'in the wonderfully sympathetic face of Dumas *père*, the hints of exotic blood, how to press the simian analogy in a profile which seems a living proof of Darwin, and yet to emphasize above all the predominant note in his

35 boulevard des Capucines, formerly Atelier Nadar

character, his extreme and inexhaustible generosity … without ever forgetting, as a final detail, the increased reduction of the conch of his already microscopic ear.'

In 1854, and now married, Nadar moved into a house at 113 rue Saint-Lazare where his real destiny awaited him. A friend had left behind some photographic equipment and Nadar's interest was aroused. From that moment he began religiously to learn the rudiments of the photographic world, preparing wet-collodion glass negatives, experimenting with exposures and fitting out his attic with glass tiles. He tried to get subjects, usually his friends, to sit motionless in all conditions. He learned fast, and had a natural talent that won him the *grande medaille d'or* for photography at the Brussels Exhibition. He became the first person to take photographs from a balloon, and in 1855 he patented the idea of using aerial photographs for map-making and surveying. In 1858 he started experimenting with electric flash photography in the Paris sewers and catacombs.

In 1860 he moved to his atelier on the Boulevard des Capucines. The top two floors, which caught the most sun, were the studios, where cleverly designed plate-glass windows on iron trellises manipulated the light. The exterior of the building was painted bright red and, three storeys up, across the facade of the entire building, ten-foot high and fifty-foot long gas-tubes spelled out in red the name NADAR.

By now the public's initial misgivings and aversion to photography was waning. The ancient art of the painter had survived its onslaught, and few people still believed the camera had the power to steal souls – although Balzac was never convinced. But to Baudelaire the art of photography was doomed: 'A revengeful God has answered the supplications of the multitude. His Messiah was Monsieur Daguerre. And the multitude said: "Art means Photography". From this moment forth, our vile society, like some Narcissus, rushed to contemplate its own trivial image in the metal plate. A madness, an extraordinary zealotry seized these new worshippers of sunlight. And strange abominations were brought forth.'

Baudelaire by Nadar, 1885

Nadar died in 1910, aged eighty-nine, and is buried in Père Lachaise Cemetery (Division 36). His vast legacy of 'strange abominations' still survives today, and amongst the best, ironically, are those of Baudelaire.

See Also: The Goncourt brothers, George Sand, Victor Hugo, Alexandre Dumas, Charles Baudelaire, Alphonse Daudet, Jules Verne, Charles Sainte-Beuve, Théophile Gautier, Gérard de Nerval.

Further Information: In 1874 Nadar hired his studio on the Boulevard des Capucines to the Société Anonyme des Artistes Peintres, Sculpteurs et Graveurs, etc., for the world's first Impressionist exhibition, led by Monet, Degas, Renoir, Pissarro and Morisot.

Select Bibliography: F. Nadar, *When I Was a Photographer* (MIT Press, 2015).

Further Reading: R. Holmes, *Sidetracks* (HarperCollins, 2000); A. Begley, *The Great Nadar: The Man Behind the Camera* (Tim Duggan Books, 2017).

Atelier Nadar in 1860

LE PRIX GONCOURT

16–18 RUE GAILLON

(Métro: Quatre-Septembre)

RESTAURANT DROUANT

HOME OF LE PRIX GONCOURT

FRANCE'S MOST PRESTIGIOUS

LITERARY AWARD

What I want from a literary critic – and what is rarely given – is for the critic to tell me, better than I could do myself, why reading a book gives me pleasure that cannot be replaced ... what it has exclusively is all that matters to me.
Julien Gracq, the only writer to refuse the Prix Goncourt.

Edmond de Goncourt by Nadar

Following the death in 1896 of novelist and man of letters, Edmond de Goncourt, his entire estate was bequeathed to create l'académie Goncourt, a foundation to promote French literature and honour the memory of his brother Jules (1830–1870). Since 1903 the académie has awarded Le Prix Goncourt, France's most celebrated literary prize, to the writer of 'the best and most imaginative prose work of the year'. The académie originally met at the Café de Paris, but after its closure it transferred to Restaurant Drouant, a former haunt of Edmond de Goncourt, in 1914. For more than a hundred years the jury has been meeting here to determine the winner of Le Prix Goncourt.

Past prizewinners for the best novel have included Henri Barbusse in 1916 for *Le Feu (Under Fire)*, Marcel Proust in 1919 for *A l'ombre des jeunes filles en fleurs (Within a Budding Grove)*, André Malraux in 1933 for *La Condition humaine (Man's Fate)*, Maurice Druon in 1948 for *Les Grandes Familles*, Simone de Beauvoir in 1954 for *Les Mandarins (The Mandarins)*, and Marguerite Duras in 1984 for *L'Amant (The Lover)*. The académie Goncourt also awards prizes for the best first novel, short story, biography and poetry.

The rules distinctly state that an author can only be awarded the prize once, but Romain Gary (1914–1980) managed to win it twice: the first time for his novel *Les racines du ciel (The Roots of Heaven)* in 1956, and the second time for his novel *La vie devant soi (The Life Before Us)* in 1975. Unbeknown to the jury of the académie, his second novel was published under the name Émile Ajar, and it was not until the posthumous publication of Romain Gary's *Vie et mort d'Émile Ajar*, in 1981, that Émile Ajar was revealed as his pseudonym.

The only novelist to refuse the Prix Goncourt was Julien Gracq (1910–2007) in 1951. Julien Gracq was the pseudonym of Louis Poirier, a very private man and an astute critic, who was a teacher at the lycée Claude-Bernard in Paris. He refused the prize because of his concern over the increasing amount of publicity attaching itself to literature in the 1950s. Poirier never appeared on radio or television and refused several invitations to dine with President Mitterrand. 'A writer', he once said, 'is one who writes instead of talking, who reads rather than making public appearances, who meditates at home rather than droning away about himself on T.V.'

See Also: Edmond and Jules de Goncourt, Henri Barbusse, Marcel Proust, André Malraux, Maurice Druon, Simone de Beauvoir, Marguerite Duras.

Further Information: Restaurant Drouant was founded in 1880. It is also home to the Renaudot literary prize, which was created in 1926 by a group of critics who were awaiting the deliberations of the Prix Goncourt jury. Although not officially associated with the Prix Goncourt, it takes place on the same day. The prize was named after French physician, Théophraste Renaudot (1586–1653), who founded France's first newspaper, *La Gazette de France*, in 1631, and is revered as the father of French journalism. Other major French literary awards include the Prix Femina, the Prix Médicis, the Prix Interallié, and the Grand Prix du Roman de l'Académie Française.

Restaurant Drouant

GEORGE W.M. REYNOLDS

RUE SAINT-AUGUSTIN

Formerly Rue Neuve Saint-Augustin

(Métro: Quatre-Septembre)

LIBRAIRIE DES ÉTRANGERS

BOOKSHOP OF ENGLISH WRITER

GEORGE W.M. REYNOLDS,

THE MAN WHO OUTSOLD DICKENS

But on the very summit of the hill whence a pleasing view of Porte Saint Denis is afforded to the spectator who may happen to be on that eminence, the sledge encountered a ponderous omnibus, and immediately overturned, the traces snapping in halves, and the unfortunate trio of great men being precipitated into the quiet and undisputed seclusion of a large heap of snow that had accumulated by drifting on one side of the road. As is usual in such cases, the horse stood perfectly still, and doubtless pondered on the ruins he had caused.
A crowd was immediately collected on the spot; and most exhilarating were the loud peals of laughter that welcomed Mr. Pickwick, Mr. Winkle, and Mr. Weller, as those gentlemen emerged, each like 'a sea Cybele fresh from the ocean', from the heap of snow into which they had fallen.

George W. Reynolds, *Pickwick Abroad: Or the Tour in France* (1839)

For a writer who outsold Charles Dickens in his heyday, George W.M. Reynolds (1814–1879) is today little known and rarely read. His most popular work, first published in weekly instalments, was his vast, sprawling blockbuster, *The Mysteries of London* (1844–1848), which sold over a million copies prior to being published as a novel. In the story Reynolds unashamedly caters for the 'penny dreadful'

Rue Neuve Saint-Augustin, *c.*1866

audience, fuelling its taste for sensation and exposure. With over fifty different plots running concurrently, it predated the modern soap opera by a hundred years. Reynolds was a rebel, an extrovert, a plagiarist and an opportunist, but he understood exactly what his audience wanted. *The Mysteries of London* had been inspired by the success of *Les Mystères de Paris*, written by French writer, Eugène Sue (1804–57), and although both books were serialised and had similar themes, they were very different books, written by very different writers. Reynolds was born in Kent in 1814, the son of a naval officer. His father sent him to Sandhurst Military College, but in 1830 he resigned his commission and journeyed to Paris in the aftermath of the July Revolution. Little is known about his time in Paris, but we do know he immersed himself in journalism, and edited an English language newspaper. He also opened a bookshop, ventured into publishing, and married. He eventually became bankrupt, returning to England in 1836 virtually penniless.

Back in London, Reynolds now had to survive by his pen, where he contributed to magazines and began writing novels; but his first great success was a novel inspired by Dickens's *The Pickwick Papers*, entitled *Pickwick Abroad: Or the Tour in France*, originally serialised in *The Monthly Magazine* in 1837. Reynolds was not the first Dickens imitator, but he was undoubtedly the best, and in *Pickwick Abroad* he takes Mr Pickwick and friends to Paris, a city with which Reynolds was far more familiar than Dickens was. Like most plagiarised authors, Dickens loathed all his imitators, but he had a special abhorrence for Reynolds. In his preface to *Household Words*, on 30 March 1850, Dickens attacks Reynolds, without naming him:

> We aspire to live in the Household affections, and to be numbered among the Household thoughts, of our readers … But, there are others here – Bastards of the Mountain, draggled fringe on the Red Cap, Panders to the basest passions of the lowest natures – whose existence is a national reproach. And these, we should consider it our highest service to displace.

Reynolds never forgot Dickens's abusive remarks and, soon after launching his own newspaper, *Reynolds's Weekly Newspaper*, in 1850, he would frequently use it as a platform to assail the great Boz, describing him in the June 1851 issue as 'that lickspittle hanger-on to the skirts of Aristocracy's robe'.

Dickens's forte was character. With Reynolds it was plot, and Dickens probably discreetly admired the skill of this 'Bastard of the Mountain'. Had they been friends they might have learned a lot from each other, but Reynolds was cast from a different die. He was anti-establishment, infused with radical politics, and an adherent of Chartism, a movement demanding parliamentary reform, whose fringes verged on the revolutionary. And although Dickens was a social commentator and critic who exposed appalling abuse in his novels, he never trod the radical and revolutionary paths of Reynolds. No doubt they shared many ideals, but essentially they were polar opposites. Dickens's memory has survived because his books never lost their universal, timeless appeal, but that of Reynolds has been effaced, perhaps because his appeal was too sensational, too seditious, and too much of the moment – now forgotten – to survive.

George W.M. Reynolds, *c.*1846

See Also: Eugène Sue, Charles Dickens, William Thackeray.

Further Information: Reynolds's bookshop was located at 55 rue Neuve Saint-Augustin, but in the late nineteenth century the street was renamed Rue Saint-Augustin, and possibly renumbered, making the exact location uncertain. Reynolds employed a young William Makepeace Thackeray here in 1836, who claimed Reynolds was the first publisher to pay him for his writing. *Reynolds's Weekly Newspaper* continued publishing under various titles until the early 1960s.

Select Bibliography: *The Youthful Imposter* (1835); *Pickwick Abroad: Or the Tour in France* (1837–38); *The Mysteries of London* (1844–48); *The Mysteries of the Court of London* (1848–56).

ÉMILE ZOLA

10 RUE SAINT-JOSEPH

(Métro: Bourse)

BIRTHPLACE OF ÉMILE ZOLA
ONE OF THE GIANTS OF
FRENCH LITERATURE

If you ask me what I came to do in this world, I, an artist, will answer you: I am here to live out loud.
Émile Zola

Émile Zola was born at number 10 on the third storey of this narrow street, on the evening of 2 April 1840 to Émilie Aubert (1819–1880), and Francesco Zola (1796–1847), an Italian engineer. Émilie had just turned twenty-one and her newborn son was to be her only child. Her family originated from Dourdan, about 60 kilometres south of Paris, where her mother was a seamstress and her father a glazier. In the 1830s her family moved to Paris where she met her future husband, Francesco Zola, a man twenty-three years her senior. Born in Venice, Francesco became a civil engineer who planned and supervised many enterprising projects, including railways, canals, tunnels and dockyards. His financial affairs, however, were often in a precarious state. During the 1840s he was involved in negotiations to build a dam in the mountains above Aix-en-Provence to supply water to the city. Operations began on the project in the summer of 1846, but while supervising the workmen he caught a chill, and when journeying to Marseille on business, he fell seriously ill with pleurisy, dying in a hotel room with Émilie at his bedside. Francesco's death left his wife in straitened circumstances, and with a seven-year-old son to support, and only a meagre pension, the penny-pinching life of a single mother seemed her only prospect. Zola would remark in later life that, after eleven years in Aix 'with nothing to commend it but the beauty of its skies', he and his mother wisely cut their ties with Provence in 1858 and decamped to Paris.

See Also: Médan Museum (Émile Zola House), Dreyfus Affair.

Further Information: Rue Saint-Joseph was named after the Chapel of Saint-Joseph that once stood on the corner of Rue Saint-Joseph and Rue Montmartre. Mysteriously, it was historically known as La rue du Temps Perdu (The street of Time Lost). A plaque marks Zola's birthplace.

10 rue Saint-Joseph

THE DREYFUS AFFAIR

144 RUE MONTMARTRE

(Métro: Sentier/Grands Boulevards)

FORMER OFFICES OF *L'AURORE*
PUBLISHER OF ÉMILE ZOLA'S
ARTICLE *J'ACCUSE…!*
AN 'OPEN LETTER TO THE PRESIDENT
OF THE REPUBLIC' IN WHICH ZOLA
ACCUSED THE GOVERNMENT OF
ANTI-SEMITISM AND THE UNLAWFUL
IMPRISONMENT OF ALFRED DREYFUS

Dreyfus himself was not the cause. Zola met Dreyfus only years later and was unimpressed; if all his sacrifices had been made merely in order to rehabilitate this small-minded professional soldier, he might have wondered if the struggle had been worth it … What he was really fighting for was neither a man, however unjustly used, nor an abstraction, however noble, but a principle.
F. W. J. Hemmings, *The Life and Times of Émile Zola* (1977)

Towards the close of the nineteenth century, those old enemies, the French and German Empires, comprised a hotbed of cloak-and-dagger activities, constantly on the alert for the warlike preparations of the other. In September 1894 a cleaning lady at the German Embassy in Paris, in the employ of French intelligence, discovered documents written in French in the wastepaper basket of the German military attaché. These documents offered confidential military information. A French officer, Captain Alfred Dreyfus, was subsequently arrested and charged with treason, but he persistently proclaimed his innocence. Dreyfus was a member of the General

67

144 rue Montmartre, former offices of the newspaper *L'Aurore*

Infantry Regiment, whose handwriting turned out to be identical to that found on the documents discovered in the German military attaché's wastepaper basket. Searching through the records of the Dreyfus case, Picquart found that all the evidence used to convict Dreyfus could equally have been used to convict Esterhazy. The army, however, took no action against Esterhazy because, had they done so, it would have been tantamount to admitting that Dreyfus had been framed and that the entire General Staff was guilty. Picquart's 'reward' for exposing a traitor was to be relieved of his job in intelligence, posted to French Tunisia, and later imprisoned. Prior to his imprisonment, Picquart had confided his misgivings to a solicitor friend, who in turn contacted officials in the government; nonetheless, this only resulted in the army General Staff closing ranks and shielding Esterhazy, whom they knew to be the real traitor.

By now, July 1897, Émile Zola began to get involved. 'No one denies', he wrote, 'there is a traitor, all we ask is that the guilty man, not the innocent, should expiate the crime. You will still have your traitor, but it must be the real traitor, that's all.' Esterhazy was eventually tried by a military court, but found not guilty. Sympathisers of Dreyfus were dumbstruck. Zola said he felt 'sick with rage', and in exasperation he wrote his 'Open Letter to the President of the Republic', printed in the newspaper *L'Aurore* on 13 January 1898 under the headline *J'Accuse...!*, which charged the generals and the War Office with negligence and suppressing evidence. Zola knew he was committing libel, and was effectively challenging the generals to put him on trial, which, had they refused to do so, would have brought them dishonour.

Staff who had access to confidential information, and his handwriting was said to be similar to that on the discovered documents. The evidence against him was misleading. He was, however, a Jew; a birthright that sealed his fate in the eyes of those baying for a scapegoat, and the ensuing court martial sentenced him to banishment for life on Devil's Island, the notorious penal colony off the coast of French Guiana.

Eighteen months later fresh evidence was discovered by a Colonel Picquart, the new head of French military security, in the form of a torn-up telegram addressed to a Major Esterhazy of the 74th

Zola was duly brought to trial at the Palais de Justice on 7 February 1898, and amid cries from the hostile crowds of 'Down with Zola! Down with the Jews!' Zola was found guilty and sentenced to one year's imprisonment and a fine of three thousand francs. After an appeal failed to overturn his sentence Zola fled to England where he lived in exile for almost a year. In June 1899, after the Court of Appeals eventually overturned the verdict against Dreyfus and granted him a retrial, Zola returned to France and his conviction was annulled. But despite the evidence of Dreyfus's innocence, the military court again found him guilty of treason and once again the verdict caused an outcry, until the President of the Republic stepped in and signed Dreyfus's pardon. After six years of solitary confinement Dreyfus was now free, but he was not officially exonerated until September 1995, when the French Army admitted that Dreyfus had been framed. On the centennial anniversary of *J'Accuse...!*, 13 January 1998, French President Jacques Chirac answered Zola's 'Open Letter to the President of the Republic', formally apologising to the Dreyfus and Zola families: 'In spite of the unyielding efforts by Captain Dreyfus' family,' said Chirac,

> his case could have been filed away forever. A dark stain, unworthy of our country and our history, a colossal judicial error and a shameful state compromise! But a man stood up against lies, malice and cowardice. Outraged by the injustice against Dreyfus, whose only crime was to be a Jew, Émile Zola cried out his famous "I Accuse...!". Published on January 13, 1898 by *L'Aurore*, this text struck minds like lightning and changed the fate of the Affair within a few hours. Truth was on the march.

See Also: Émile Zola, Palais de Justice.

Further Information: Alfred Dreyfus (1859–1935) is buried in the Cimetière du Montparnasse; Plot: Division 28. Ferdinand Esterhazy (1847–1923) fled to England and lived the rest of his days on a military pension in the village of Harpenden in Hertfordshire where he is buried in St Nicholas churchyard under the alias Jean de Voilemont.

Further Reading: F. W. J. Hemmings, *The Life and Times of Émile Zola* (Scribner, 1977); G. Whyte, *The Dreyfus Affair: A Chronological History* (Palgrave Macmillan, 2005); R. Harris, *The Man on Devil's Island* (Penguin, 2011); P. Read, *The Dreyfus Affair* (Bloomsbury, 2013).

Major Esterhazy of the 74th Infantry Regiment: the real traitor

BROTHELS AND COURTESANS

12 RUE CHABANAIS

(Métro: Quatre-Septembre/Pyramides)

LE CHABANAIS

FAMOUS PARISIAN BROTHEL

HAUNT AND INSPIRATION FOR WRITERS

FROM GUY DE MAUPASSANT TO

ALPHONSE DAUDET

12 rue Chabanais

Nana was left alone, with upturned face in the light cast by the candle. She was fruit of the charnel-house, a heap of matter and blood, a shovelful of corrupted flesh thrown down on the pillow. The pustules had evaded the whole of the face, so that each touched its neighbour. Fading and sunken, they had assumed the greyish hue of mud, and on that formless pulp, where the features had ceased to be traceable, they already resembled some decaying damp from the grave. ... And over this loathsome and grotesque mask of death, the hair, the beautiful hair, still blazed like sunlight and flowed downwards in rippling gold. Venus was rotting.

Émile Zola describing the death of his eponymous heroine from smallpox in *Nana* (1880)

Émile Zola's *Nana* is arguably the most celebrated novel ever written about the harlot, which narrates the life of Nana Coupeau's transformation from street whore to high-class fashionable prostitute. In just a few months it went through fifty editions, having sold out of its first edition print run of 55,000 copies on the first day. 'Nana turns into myth', wrote Flaubert, 'without ceasing to be real.'

From streetwalkers to elite courtesans, the nineteenth century Parisian prostitute was all things to all men, from the tart with a heart to American critic Henri Peyre's classification of the 'romantic notion of woman as a demon'.

Writers, of course, were not immune to their allure, but many of them lacked the courage and foresight to see beyond the prostitute's negative stereotype. The few that did, notably Michel de Montaigne (*On Some Lines of Virgil*), Alexandre Dumas *fils* (*La dame aux camélias*) and Guy de Maupassant (*Boule de Suif*), criticised the hypocrisy of it all. The medieval poet, François Villon ('Ballade de la Grosse Margot'), who led a life of criminal excess, stood all but alone when he wrote about *filles de joie* unsentimentally, portraying them exactly as they were and without moral judgement.

Alphonse Daudet, Gustave Flaubert, Guy de Maupassant and Charles Baudelaire all wrote about their own sexual experiences with prostitutes, and all of them died from the consequences of sexually transmitted infections. The fates of the harlot and the client, however, were often intertwined, with both parties dying a miserable death. Balzac's somewhat callous description of the whore's fate in *Splendeurs et misères des courtisanes (Scenes from a*

70

Salon de la rue des Moulins (1894),
Toulouse-Lautrec

Courtesan's Life) (1847) holds nothing back:

> The daughters of pleasure are essentially unstable beings, changing without reason from bewildered suspicion to absolute trust. In this respect they are lower than the animals. Extreme in everything, in their joys, their despairs, their religion, their irreligion; most of them would go mad if they were not decimated by an unusual rate of mortality, and if accidents of fortune did not raise some of them out of the mire in which they live.

In 1804 Napoleon Bonaparte decreed that all brothels should be state controlled and all prostitutes registered and given twice-weekly medical inspections. The brothels were known as *maisons de tolerance* or *maisons closes*, and by the end of the Second World War France had over 1500 legal brothels – 177 of which were located in Paris – catering for all sexual and gender identities, including *goûts spéciaux* (special tastes). One of the city's most famous and luxurious was Le Chabanais, which opened in 1878 at 12 rue Chabanais, near the Louvre. Founded by the Irish-born Madame Kelly (Alexandrine Joannet), its clients ranged from Guy de Maupassant to Albert, Prince of Wales, heir apparent to the British throne. Other establishments included One-Two-Two at 122 rue de Provence, which opened in 1924 and could process up to three hundred clients a day; La Fleur blanche at 6 rue des Moulins was frequented by Toulouse-Lautrec ('I may only be a small coffee-pot, but I have a big spout!') and was the inspiration for over forty of his paintings, notably *Salon de la rue des Moulins* (1894); Le Sphinx, at 31 boulevard Edgar-Quinet opened in 1931 and during the 1937 Exposition welcomed more than a thousand customers a night; and Miss Betty's, at 36 rue Saint-Sulpice, which specialised in sadomasochistic sex and had its own 'crucifixion parlour'.

French state-controlled brothels were abolished in 1946, and as a result all brothels became illegal, along with procuring, pimping and soliciting. Prostitution, however, providing it was done in private, remained legal.

See Also: Émile Zola, Honoré de Balzac, Alexandre Dumas *fils*, Guy de Maupassant, François Villon, Michel de Montaigne, Gustave Flaubert, Marie Duplessis, Charles Baudelaire, Alphonse Daudet.

Further Reading: M. Seymour-Smith, *Fallen Women: A controversial look at prostitutes and prostitution in literature* (Panther Books, 1971).

Nana by Édouard Manet (1877)

3rd

Arrondissement

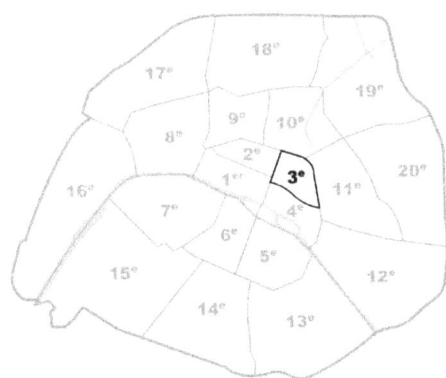

MADAME DE SÉVIGNÉ

16 RUE DES FRANCS BOURGEOIS

(Métro: Chemin Vert/Saint-Paul)

LE MUSÉE CARNAVALET

FORMER HOME OF

MADAME DE SÉVIGNÉ

FRENCH ARISTOCRAT REMEMBERED

FOR HER LETTER WRITING

But what do you think I learned when I came here? I am not yet recovered, and hardly know what I write. Vatel, the great Vatel, late maître-d'hotel to M. Fouquet, and in that capacity with the prince, a man so eminently distinguished for taste, and whose abilities were equal to the government of a state – this man, whom I knew so well, finding, at eight o'clock this morning, that the fish he had sent for did not come at the time he expected it, and unable to bear the disgrace that he thought would inevitably attach to him, ran

himself through with his own sword. Guess what confusion so shocking an accident must have occasioned. Think, too, that perhaps the fish might come in just as he was expiring. I know no more of the affair at present, and I suppose you think this enough. I make no doubt the consternation was general; it must be very disagreeable to have so fatal an event break in upon an entertainment that cost fifty thousand crowns.

Marquise de Sévigné, writing to her daughter from the residence of Monsieur de La Rochefoucauld, 24 April 1671

In French literature, from the late sixteenth century to the end of the eighteenth century, letter writing was very much in vogue. Whether it was the popular format of the epistolary novel or the everyday correspondence of a mother writing to her daughter, its immediacy brought the events of the time to life. In Madame de Sévigné's case, her writing mostly took the form of correspondence

relationship, often simply discussing the book she was currently reading or how late in the year it was to hear a nightingale, her letters on controversial subjects about parliament or the court politics of the day had to adopt a more cautious tone, as Louis XIV's police were prone to intercepting private correspondences. Regardless of whether she was writing about hairstyles or politics, her letters remain a unique window into the world of seventeenth-century France.

Further Information: Madame de Sévigné was born in February 1626 in Place Royale, now Place des Vosges. She lived at the Hôtel Carnavalet from 1677 to 1696, and a gallery of exhibits in the museum is dedicated to her memory. More than a thousand of her letters have been recovered to date, but what proportion this represents of her total output during her life remains unknown.

with her daughter, and with French court society in the time of Louis XIV, a series of letters lasting nearly fifty years.

Marie de Rabutin-Chantal (1626–1696), who was born into an old aristocratic family, was orphaned at an early age and brought up by her uncle, the abbot of Livry. In 1644 she married the marquis de Sévigné, a womaniser who frittered away their fortune and who was killed in a duel over another woman in 1651, leaving his widow, Marie, with their son and daughter.

Many of her letters, written in her racy, colloquial style, were full of the gossip and scandals of court life. In others she acquaints us with interesting people and events of the day, such as a performance of Racine's *Esther* at Versailles, or the trial of her friend Fouquet, Louis XIV's Superintendent of Finances, for embezzlement. Much of her correspondence was with her daughter, who had moved to Provence following her marriage – a separation that caused Marie much sadness. While letters to her daughter were fairly typical of a mother–daughter

The Hôtel Carnavalet is one of Paris's few remaining examples of Renaissance architecture. It was built between 1548 and 1560 for Jacques des Ligneris, president of the Parliament of Paris, and was originally called the Hôtel des Ligneris. Various owners over the years have altered and expanded it, changing its appearance dramatically. Its current name dates from 1578 and is a distortion of the name of its then owner, Mme de Kernevenoy.

Select Bibliography: *Selected Letters* (Penguin, 1982).

Hôtel Carnavalet

MARY WOLLSTONECRAFT

22 RUE MESLAY

(Metro: République)

FORMER LODGINGS OF

MARY WOLLSTONECRAFT

AUTHOR OF *A VINDICATION OF THE*

RIGHTS OF WOMAN (1792)

But how quickly vanishes the prospect of delights! of delights such as man ought to taste! – The cavalcade of death moves along, shedding mildew over all the beauties of the scene, and blasting every joy! The elegance of the palaces and buildings is revolting, when they are viewed as prisons, and the sprightliness of the people disgusting, when they are hastening to view the operations of the guillotine, or carelessly passing over the earth stained with blood.
Mary Wollstonecraft, *An Historical and Moral View of the Origin and Progress of the French Revolution* (1794)

Mary Wollstonecraft from the title page of William Godwin's *Memoirs* (1798)

Radical English feminist, freethinker and advocate of women's rights, Mary Wollstonecraft shocked her contemporaries when she published her *A Vindication of the Rights of Woman*, in which she argued that women had the same fundamental rights as men. Horace Walpole may have described her as 'a hyena in petticoats', but today she is rightly acknowledged as the mother of modern feminism. By the time *A Vindication of the Rights of Woman* was published in 1792 she had already published four books and was earning her living by writing and reviewing: a remarkable achievement for a woman of her time.

In December 1792, she travelled alone to France to experience and to write about the impact of its Revolution. Initially, her plan was to spend six weeks in France, but she ended up staying for nearly two years, all the time writing articles and letters, and the first volume of her *Historical and Moral View of the French Revolution* for her London publisher. Her *Rights of Woman* had been translated in France under the title *Défense des droits des femmes* and was admired by the Girondists, the Revolutionary faction that predominantly seemed to encourage social reform, and who introduced her to like-minded campaigners and reformers. She also witnessed the power struggles, the Reign of Terror, and Louis XVI being escorted through the streets to the trial that would condemn him to death, an incident she later related in a letter to a friend:

About nine o'clock this morning, the king passed by my window, moving silently along (excepting now and then a few strokes on the drum, which rendered the stillness more awful) through empty streets, surrounded by the national guards, who, clustering round the carriage, seemed to deserve their name. The inhabitants flocked to their windows, but the casements were all shut, not a voice was heard, nor did I see any thing like an insulting gesture. For the first time since I entered France, I bowed to the majesty of the people, and respected the propriety of behaviour so perfectly in unison with my own feelings. I can scarcely tell you why, but an association of ideas made the tears flow insensibly from my eyes, when I saw Louis sitting, with more dignity than I expected from his character, in a hackney coach going to meet his death, where so many of his race have triumphed.

While in France she also met and fell in love with American writer and businessman, Gilbert Imlay, with whom she had a daughter. They never married; however, Imlay secured her safety when Britain declared war on France, by registering her as his wife at the American embassy, thus giving her the protection of US citizenship.

Nonetheless, the affair was short-lived. When Wollstonecraft returned to London in April 1795 with Fanny, her baby daughter, she learned of Imlay's infidelity, and a few weeks later attempted suicide with an overdose of laudanum. After returning from a summer trip to Scandinavia on business for Imlay, she attempted suicide for a second time by jumping off Putney Bridge into the River Thames. In 1797 she became the wife of journalist William Godwin, with whom she had a daughter, Mary, the future creator of the novel *Frankenstein*. Ten days after giving birth Mary Wollstonecraft Godwin died from septicaemia, aged thirty-eight. Fanny Imlay died at the age of twenty, following an opium overdose.

See Also: Guillotine.

Select Bibliography: *Thoughts on the Education of Daughters* (1787); *Mary: A Fiction* (1788); *Original Stories from Real Life* (1788); *A Vindication of the Rights of Woman* (1792); *An Historical and Moral View of the Origin and Progress of the French Revolution* (1794); *Letters written in Sweden* (1796); *Posthumous Works*, ed. W. Godwin (1798).

Further Reading: C. Tomalin, *The Life and Death of Mary Wollstonecraft* (Weidenfeld & Nicolson, 1974); R. Holmes, *Footsteps* (Hodder & Stoughton, 1985); W. Godwin, *Memoirs of the Author of A Vindication of the Rights of Woman* [1798], (Kessinger, 2009); J. Todd, *Mary Wollstonecraft: A Revolutionary Life* (Orion, 2001).

Title page of the first American edition of *A Vindication of the Rights of Woman* (1792)

4th Arrondissement

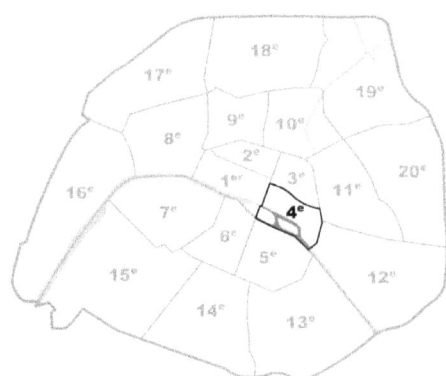

PIERRE BEAUMARCHAIS

JUNCTION OF RUE SAINT-ANTOINE AND
RUE DES TOURNELLES

(Métro: Bastille)

STATUE OF PIERRE BEAUMARCHAIS
FRENCH PLAYWRIGHT AND AUTHOR OF
THE BARBER OF SEVILLE AND
THE MARRIAGE OF FIGARO

Drinking when we are not thirsty and making love all year round, madam: that is all there is to distinguish us from other animals.
Pierre Beaumarchais, *The Marriage of Figaro* (1785)

Beaumarchais's most famous plays, and ultimately the ones that were to have the most lasting success, are his comedies, *Le Barbier de Séville (The Barber of Seville)* (1775) and his masterpiece *Le Mariage de Figaro (The Marriage of Figaro)* (1785) , adapted for the operatic stage by Rossini and Mozart respectively. Both plays are filled with adventure, intrigue and inventiveness of plot, but they pale into insignificance beside Beaumarchais's real life.

Pierre-Augustin Caron was born in Paris in 1732, the son of a clockmaker, and the title Beaumarchais was later taken from a property owned by his first wife. His education was scant and at the age of twelve he trained as an apprentice clockmaker under his father. Although seemingly indifferent to the craft, he had a definite talent for it, inventing, when he was twenty-one, a mechanism that made clocks and watches significantly more accurate, an idea that was promptly stolen by André Lepaute, clockmaker to Louis XV. Beaumarchais took Lepaute to court and won his case, which brought him to the attention of the King who duly appointed Beaumarchais clockmaker to the royal court.

Beaumarchais seemed able to turn his hand to anything. He was a talented harpist, and soon he became music-master to the daughters of Louis XV. His business acumen in the financial world later brought him considerable wealth, but also a succession of enemies. As a financial speculator and entrepreneur he was ideally qualified to join the King's secret service as a spy, and was subsequently sent on various missions. In 1776 he helped convince the French government to enter the American War of Independence against the British, and later sold arms to the American colonists. Amidst all this intrigue and high adventure, Beaumarchais still found time to write memoirs and plays.

As a dramatist, he is little remembered today, but what Beaumarchais should really be celebrated for is his revival of the comedy of intrigue, which had lain dormant in French drama since the time of Molière, over a hundred years previously. Jack of all trades, and also master of many, he made a fortune, and lost a fortune. After the Revolution he was imprisoned and narrowly escaped death. Yet, out of the adventure and turmoil of his life he still managed to create masterpieces of comic theatre. 'I make myself laugh at everything', he wrote in *The Barber of Seville*, 'for fear of having to weep at it.'

See Also: Molière, Voltaire, Cimetière Père Lachaise.

Further Information: After the death of Voltaire in 1778 Beaumarchais bought the rights to most of his works, many of which were banned in France, and published them in Germany, saving many manuscripts from oblivion. Beaumarchais's statue (below), created by French sculptor Louis Clausade (1862–1899), was inaugurated in 1897. Beaumarchais died from apoplexy in 1799, aged sixty-seven, and is buried in Père Lachaise Cemetery, Division 28.

Select Bibliography: *The Barber of Seville and The Marriage of Figaro* (Penguin Classics, 1976).

MAISON DE VICTOR HUGO

6 PLACE DES VOSGES

(Métro: Saint-Paul/Chemin-Vert/Bastille)

MAISON DE VICTOR HUGO

THE HUGO FAMILY HOME

FROM 1832 TO 1848

Victor Hugo in later life

Poet, novelist and dramatist, Victor Hugo (1802–1885) was much more than the sum of his talents. He was a gargantuan figure who overshadowed nineteenth-century French literature and his characters and stories are now part of popular legend. He was also a painter, a politician, a revolutionary and a womaniser. He influenced many artists and writers, including Charles Dickens, Fyodor Dostoevsky, Paul Verlaine and Albert Camus. Rodin sculpted his head. To the French he became a kind of heroic deity, a living symbol of Romanticism and the French patriot. At his funeral two million people lined the streets to bid him farewell, before he was laid to rest at the Panthéon alongside France's great men.

Hugo was born in Besançon in eastern France, the third son of Joseph Hugo, one of Napoleon's generals, and Sophie Trébuchet. The birth of Victor-Marie was complicated and the midwife did not expect him to live. Despite her prediction, however, the puny infant survived. Unfortunately, Joseph and Sophie's marriage did not. A combination of conflicting political views (Joseph was a republican; Sophie, a Catholic Royalist), a peripatetic army life in Italy and Spain, Joseph's womanising and a general incompatibility all took their toll, resulting in a separation which endured, on and off, until Sophie's death in 1821.

Sophie settled in Paris with her children, and from 1815 to 1818 Victor studied at the Pension Cordier and the Lycée Louis-le-Grand, after which he graduated from the law faculty in Paris. Writing, however, eclipsed his law ambitions, and verses and translations began to flow from his pen. In 1822, his collection of poems, *Odes et poésies diverses*, was published. Its royal sentiments were greatly admired by Louis XVIII, to the extent that he awarded Hugo a pension of a thousand francs. This gesture, which boosted Hugo's marriage prospects, resulted in his marriage later in the year to his childhood sweetheart, Adèle Foucher, with whom he had five children. In 1823 he published his first novel, *Han d'Islande*, which, in 1825, appeared in an English translation as *Hans of Iceland*. Throughout the 1820s and 1830s he produced further poetry and drama, confirming his place in the vanguard of the Romantic movement. Notable in this respect was his play *Hernani* (1830), remembered more today for the riots it incited between Romanticists and Classicists than for its merits as a dramatic work. The following year he published, to great public acclaim, his epic historical romance, *Notre-Dame de Paris (The Hunchback of Notre-Dame)*. Throughout his life Hugo had been a passionate Royalist, but during the 1840s he became a fierce supporter of republicanism, and in 1848 he was elected to the Constituent Assembly. Following Napoleon III's coup d'état at the end of 1851, Hugo, who opposed the coup, went into exile, briefly to Brussels, and then to the Channel Islands where he remained for nineteen years. In 1862, while still in exile, he published *Les Misérables*. When he returned to Paris in 1870 he was hailed as a national hero.

Victor and Adèle's marriage was not a happy one, with both guilty of infidelity. In 1833, Hugo fell in love with the actress Juliette Drouet; however, although the relationship developed into a long-standing attachment, it did not prevent him from having other extramarital liaisons, including one with French actress Sarah Bernhardt. Despite their affairs, Hugo and his wife continued to live together until Adèle's death in 1868. In 1878 Victor Hugo moved into his last home, with Juliette Drouet, at 130 avenue d'Eylau. Three years later, on 27 February, Hugo was paid the greatest public tribute ever given to a living writer, when a procession to mark him 'entering his eightieth year' stretched from Avenue d'Eylau to the centre of Paris. Hugo watched from his window as half a million people took six hours to pass in what was one of the largest parades in French history since the days of Napoleon Bonaparte. The following day the city of Paris changed the street name to Avenue Victor-Hugo. Hugo outlived four of his five children, his wife, and his faithful mistress Juliette, dying from pneumonia on 22 May 1885, aged 83.

See Also: Panthéon, Arc de Triomphe, Cathédrale Notre-Dame de Paris, The Bastille, Père Lachaise, Le Musée des Égouts de Paris, Eugène Vidocq, Charles Dickens, Paul Verlaine, Albert Camus.

Further Information: Place des Vosges dates back to 1604 when King Henry IV built a royal pavilion designed by Baptiste du Cerceau at the southern end of the square. The square, which was officially inaugurated in 1612 as Place Royale, became a favourite place for duels. In 1800 Napoleon changed the name of the square from Place Royale to Place des Vosges to demonstrate his gratitude towards the Vosges department, the first department in France to pay taxes. The Maison de Victor Hugo, in the south-east corner of the square, was inaugurated as a museum during the celebrations of Hugo's centenary in 1902. Victor and Adèle lived there with their children, on the second floor of house number 6, within the central body of the mansion, the Hôtel de Rohan-Guémené, from 1832 to 1848.

Further Reading: G. Robb, *Victor Hugo* (Picador, 1997).

Place des Vosges

THE HUNCHBACK OF NOTRE-DAME

PARVIS NOTRE-NAME

PLACE JEAN-PAUL-II

(Métro: Cité)

CATHÉDRALE NOTRE-DAME DE PARIS

SETTING FOR VICTOR HUGO'S CLASSIC NOVEL

His cathedral was enough for him. ... The saints were his friends and blessed him; the monsters were his friends and kept watch over him. He would sometimes spend whole hours crouched before one of the statues in solitary conversation with it. If anyone came upon him then he would run away like a lover surprised during a serenade.
Victor Hugo, *The Hunchback of Notre-Dame (Notre-Dame de Paris)* (1831)

In 1828 Victor Hugo (1802–1885) convinced his publisher, Gosselin, to commission a historical epic set during the Middle Ages. It was to be Hugo's first full-length novel, but it had such an abundance of plots that the scale of it almost defeated him. He eventually finished it on 15 January 1831. The cult of Victor Hugo was beginning.

Set in the teeming bustle of fifteenth-century Paris, *Notre-Dame de Paris* revolves around the pitiful life of Quasimodo, the hunchback bell-ringer of the cathedral, and his love for Esméralda, a Gypsy dancer.

In 1999 the handwritten memoirs of a nineteenth-century English sculptor named Henry Sibson were found in an attic in Cornwall, England. The seven-volume memoirs record Sibson's time in Paris in the 1820s when he was employed by French contractors to do repair work to Notre Dame Cathedral. 'The [French] Government', wrote Sibson, 'had given orders for the repairing of the Cathedral of Notre Dame. ... here I met with a M. Trajan, a most worthy, fatherly and amiable man as ever existed – he was the carver under the Government sculptor whose name I forget as I had no intercourse with him, all that I know is that he was humpbacked and he did not like to mix with carvers.' In another entry, Sibson mentions working with the same sculptors on another project outside Paris, and he again mentions the 'humpbacked' sculptor, remembering his nickname was Monsieur Le Bossu, (Mr Hunchback).

For his research when writing *Notre-Dame de Paris*, Hugo visited the Cathedral many times. It is therefore distinctly possible that Hugo knew, or knew of the existence of, 'Le Bossu', and perhaps had a sudden inspiration.

Further Information: The landscape around Notre Dame was very different during the Middle Ages. Buildings were closely packed with narrow, interweaving streets, which were insanitary and disease-ridden. Baron Haussmann's nineteenth-century modernisation programme cleared most of it away, but Victor Hugo, always the romantic, valued the city's lost past. In the novel Quasimodo is the sole bell-ringer, but in the fifteenth century the job would have required sixteen men.

ALPHONSE DAUDET

CORNER OF RUE PAVÉE AND RUE DES FRANCS BOURGEOIS

(Métro: Saint-Paul)

HÔTEL LAMOIGNON
FORMER HOME OF
ALPHONSE DAUDET
NOVELIST, DRAMATIST AND
SHORT-STORY WRITER
REMEMBERED FOR HIS HUMOROUS
SKETCHES OF PROVENÇAL LIFE

Alphonse Daudet, *c.*1860

We lived in the hotel Lamoignon at 24 rue Pavée in the Marais ... Almost every Wednesday evening Flaubert, Zola, Turgenev and Edmond de Goncourt used to meet in our modest dining room. I called them 'the giants', because Flaubert and Goncourt were so tall: 'Mummy, is it the day the giants come?' Flaubert and my father brought everything to life with their jokes, their laughter, their stories. Regularly, as soon as he arrived, Flaubert would say to my father: 'Good day, Alphonse, how do I look? ... Young as ever I trust?' This 'young as ever' sent the giants off into roars of laughter, which I joined in with a will.

Léon Daudet, from *Paris vécu* (1928)

Today Alphonse Daudet is a forgotten writer and his books remain, for the most part, unread outside France. In his heyday, however, between 1875 and 1890, he was deemed one of the foremost novelists in France with a huge international reputation. Charles Dickens referred to him as his 'little brother in France'. But after his death in 1897, Daudet's spinner-of-yarns style of storytelling became outmoded and his star began to wane. He is chiefly remembered today for his sentimental and humorous stories of life in rural Provence, particularly in *Lettres de mon moulin (Letters from my Windmill)*, and although he is still read in France, the rest of the world has regrettably consigned him to literary oblivion.

Daudet was born in Nîmes, Provence, in 1840, where his father was a silk manufacturer. His early years were happy ones that instilled in him his lifelong love of the Provençal culture and countryside, however in 1849 his father's business failed and the family moved from the rural bliss of Provence to the depressing gloom of the city of Lyon. In 1856, his parents' desperate financial circumstances forced him to leave school at sixteen to become a pupil-teacher in the Cévennes, a job which he hated. After a year of academic misery he resigned his post and set out for Paris to join his elder brother, Ernest, where he hoped to launch his career as a writer and a poet. A few months later he found a publisher for his book of poems, *Les Amoureuses*, and, although sales were poor, it opened the doors of the Paris literary salons where his poems charmed the Empress Eugénie, wife of Napoleon III, and it was due to her influence that he was appointed secretary to the Duc de Morny, President of

Bibliothèque Historique, formerly Hôtel Lamoignon

the Corps Législatif. This immediately made him self-sufficient, and no longer a financial burden to his brother. But it also enabled him, as his brother wrote, 'to enter every low haunt of Bohemia', and it was most likely during these dissolute years that he contracted the then incurable (and unmentionable) disease of syphilis that was to give him so much pain and distress in later life.

Although much of Daudet's early literary career was concentrated on the stage, none of the handful of plays he wrote made any great impact. In the early 1860s his health was starting to decline and he took leave of absence from the Duc de Morny's employment, wintering at various times in the healthier climes of Algeria and Corsica. Here he gathered much of the material and inspiration for *Lettres de mon moulin*, the book he is primarily remembered for, first published as a series of stories in *Le Figaro* in 1866. He will also be remembered for his semi-autobiographical tale *Le Petit Chose (Little Good-For-Nothing)* (1868), and his *Tartarin* parodies, notably *Tartarin de Tarascon* (1872). But of all the genres in which he wrote, it was his novels, notably *Fromont jeune et Risler aîné (Fromont the Younger and Risler the Elder)* (1872), now largely forgotten, that established his fame.

In 1867 Daudet married author Julia Allard, with whom he had three children, his sons Léon and Lucien both also becoming writers. The marriage was a happy one; nonetheless, Daudet was a long-standing womaniser who reputedly lost his virginity at the age of twelve. It was his promiscuousness that would eventually kill him, when, in the mid 1880s, he was diagnosed with tabes dorsalis, a strain of neurosyphilis which, as Julian Barnes notes in the introduction to his translation of Daudet's *La Doulou* (*In the Land of Pain*), is 'literally, wasting of the back. Its chief manifestations in his [Daudet's] case were locomotor ataxia (the progressive inability to control one's movements) and, eventually, paralysis. He died twelve years later, in 1897, after years of pain, morphine and failed experimental treatments, aged fifty-seven.

See Also: Alphonse Daudet (Père Lachaise), Gustave Flaubert, Émile Zola, Ivan Turgenev, Edmond and Jules de Goncourt, Charles Dickens.

Further Information: The Hotel Lamoignon now houses the Bibliothèque historique de la Ville de Paris, a library specialising in the history of Paris. When Daudet first arrived in Paris he lived with his brother at the Hôtel du Sénat, 7 rue de Tournon. The old windmill referred to in *Lettres de mon moulin*, at Fontvieille, near Arles, was built in 1814 for grinding wheat and ceased operation in 1915. In 1935 it was restored and is now a museum dedicated to Alphonse Daudet. It is open from April to September. Daudet's self-examination of his terminal illness in *La Doulou*, published by his widow in 1930, was translated by Julian Barnes (*In the Land of Pain*) and published in 2002 by Jonathan Cape. Alphonce Daudet is buried in Père Lachaise (Division 26).

Select Bibliography: *Lettres de mon moulin (Letters from my Windmill)*, (1869); *Le Petit Chose* (1868), *(Little Good-For-Nothing* (1878))*; Tartarin de Tarascon* (1872); *Fromont jeune et Risler aîné* (1872), *(Fromont the Younger and Risler the Elder* (1874)*); Robert Helmont (Robert Helmont: Diary of a Recluse)* (1874); *Jack* (1876); *Le Nabab* (1877); *Sapho* (1874); *La Doulou (In the Land of Pain)* (1930).

Further Reading: L. Daudet, *Alphonse Daudet* (Ulan Press, 2012); R.H. Sherard, *Alphonse Daudet: A Biographical and Critical Study*, (Read Books, 2008); E. & J. Goncourt, *Pages From The Goncourt Journals* (NYRB, 2007).

LA GUILLOTINE

PLACE DE L'HÔTEL-DE-VILLE
(formerly Place de Grève)
(Métro: Hôtel-de-Ville)

LOCATION OF THE FIRST PARIS GUILLOTINE

ICONIC IMAGE OF FRENCH REVOLUTIONARY HISTORICAL FICTION

One by one, all the pieces of [the death penalty's] dread panoply: its multiplicity of executions, its fantastically cruel sentences, its rack at the Grand Châtelet ... is to-day well-nigh banished from our laws and our cities, tracked from code to code, hunted from place to place, till in all great Paris it has but one dishonoured corner it can call its own—in the Place de Grève; but one wretched guillotine, furtive, craven, shameful, that always seems to fear being caught red-handed, so quickly does it vanish after dealing its fatal blow.
Victor Hugo,
Notre-Dame de Paris (1831)

Today the guillotine is remembered as the prime instrument of terror during the bloody aftermath of the French Revolution: a class struggle turned public spectacle. Volumes have been written about The Reign of Terror, and the Revolutionaries' ideas of liberty and equality still dominate the modern world. Literature recorded both its tyranny and its romance, usually with the guillotine looming in the shadows.

Wealthy English baronet and master of disguise, Sir Percy Blakeney, rescued condemned aristocrats in Baroness Orczy's 1905 novel, *The Scarlet Pimpernel*. Charles Dickens immortalised the Terror in *A Tale of Two Cities* (1859), one of the bestselling works of historical fiction ever written, in which Sydney Carton, a cynical alcoholic lawyer, redeems his wasted life with his own sacrifice on the guillotine, uttering the immortal lines: *It is a far, far better thing that I do, than I have ever done; it is a far, far better rest that I go to than I have ever known.* Dickens's novel is highly romanticised, but he did actually witness an execution by guillotine in Rome in 1845, which he described as 'an ugly careless sickening spectacle meaning nothing but butchery'.

Writing in 'Reflections on the Guillotine' (1957) Albert Camus recalled his father, before the war of 1914, rising early in the dark to see the public execution in Algiers of a man who had killed a family of farmers and their children. 'What he saw that morning he never told anyone,' wrote Camus.

Dr Joseph-Ignace Guillotin

> My mother relates merely that he came rushing home, his face distorted, refused to talk, lay down for a moment on the bed, and suddenly began to vomit. He had just discovered the reality hidden under the noble phrases with which it was masked. Instead of thinking of the slaughtered children, he could think of nothing but that quivering body that had just been dropped onto a board to have its head cut off.

In pre-Revolutionary France there were more than a hundred offences liable to the death penalty. Beheading by broadsword was the privilege of the aristocracy. Lesser mortals could expect to be broken on the wheel, burned alive, or hanged, which, at a time before trap-door neck-breaking techniques had been invented, meant slow strangulation. Nonetheless, France in the late eighteenth century was trying to reform its feudal penal code, and one

man who was actively involved in that was physician Dr Joseph-Ignace Guillotin (1738–1814). Pacifist, reformer, champion of the poor, advocate for the abolition of capital punishment and deputy of the Assemblée Nationale (the French parliament), Dr Guillotin was a humanitarian of the first order. In 1789 he submitted his plans for a new penal code to the Assemblée Nationale, which included a 'simple device' to decapitate criminals sentenced to death. Three years later, in 1792, the Assemblée approved his proposal. Decapitation machines had been around in various primitive guises for at least eight hundred years, so, as such, were not an original idea; however, 'With my machine,' Dr Guillotin declared, 'at worst, the patient will feel no more than a breath on the back of his neck!' A prototype had to be built and Dr Guillotin recruited the expertise of surgeon, Antoine Louis, and German harpsichord-maker, Tobias Schmidt. After various experiments, which included

Hôtel-de-Ville in the late nineteenth century

decapitating sheep, and fresh corpses from a local hospital, the machine, painted bright red, was mounted on to a high scaffold in the Place de Grève on 25 April 1792, for its public inauguration, where a large crowd had gathered to watch the execution of convicted murderer Nicolas Jacques Pelletier. The guillotine took over two hours to assemble; the execution was over in a minute. 'The people were not satisfied at all', proclaimed the newspaper *Chronique de Paris*. 'There was nothing to be seen. Everything happened too fast. They dispersed with disappointment, consoling themselves for their disillusionment by singing, *Give me back my wooden gallows ...* '

Public despondency with the guillotine did not last long. The following year, in September 1793, there began a period of violence in France that became known as The Reign of Terror, when conflict between rival political factions incited mass executions of all 'enemies of the Revolution'. In contrast to the guillotine's first execution, which lasted a minute, crowds could now wallow in a daily parade of death. The guillotine, by a twist of fate, had arrived at exactly the right time in history and ironically, though born out of purely philanthropic motives, it became an iconic symbol of terror and revolution. It was used for 188 years in France with the last State execution in 1977. Only the Nazis exceeded the mass executions of Revolutionary France when the Third Reich guillotined 16,000 political prisoners between 1933 and the end of the Second World War. Capital punishment was abolished in France in 1981.

See Also: Alfred Dreyfus, Victor Hugo, Charles Dickens, Albert Camus.

Further Information: The Paris guillotine has been located at various sites around the city, the most famous being on the Place de la Révolution (now Place de la Concorde), site of the execution of Louis XVI. The Terror (5 September 1793 to 28 July 1794) claimed the lives of over 2500 people, a feat only made possible by the guillotine. The name Place de Grève refers to its situation as a sandy area on the bank of the river. In 1830 its name was changed to Place de l'Hôtel-de-Ville in tribute to Paris's City Hall which borders the square.

Further Reading: R. Opie, *Guillotine* (Sutton Publishing, 2003).

LA MORGUE

SQUARE DE L'ÎLE DE FRANCE

(Métro: Pont Marie)

FORMER SITE OF LA MORGUE

GRUESOME INSPIRATION FOR

NINETEENTH-CENTURY WRITERS

The Morgue is a spectacle within the reach of all pockets, free for all, the poor and the rich. The door is open, anyone who wishes enters. There are fans who make detours so as not to miss a single representation of death. When the slabs are empty, people leave disappointed, robbed, mumbling under their breath. When the slabs are well furnished, when there is a good display of human flesh, the visitors crowd each other, they provide cheap emotions, they scare one another, they chat, applaud or sniffle, as at the theatre, and then they leave satisfied, declaring that the Morgue was a success, that day.
Émile Zola, *Thérèse Raquin* (1867)

A nineteenth-century etching of the viewing gallery at the Morgue

Many nineteenth-century writers visited the Paris Morgue for research, and no doubt from straightforward morbid curiosity. Some included it in their narratives, but most were shocked and disgusted by its brutal pageant. Zola used it to great effect in *Thérèse Raquin*, Frances Trollope put on record her experiences in *Paris and the Parisians* and Robert Browning mentions it in his poem 'Apparent Failure'. Wilkie Collins, in a letter to his mother, refers to having 'looked in at the Morgue', and Charles Dickens was a frequent visitor, 'dragged by an invisible force', an obsession he describes as 'the attraction of repulsion'.

Every major city in the world now has a morgue, but it was Paris that turned the storing of corpses into spectacle. The city's first official morgue was built in 1804 on the Quai du Marché Neuf, but the Morgue that so often features in nineteenth-century literature was built in 1864 as part of Napoleon III's urban planning that transformed the entire city. The new Morgue was streamlined and modernised, and situated directly behind Notre-Dame Cathedral, a city centre location strategically chosen because of the number of bodies washed up here from the river. It also needed to be centrally situated to give the public easy access to view, and hopefully identify, the bodies, many of them suicides, that were exhibited on marble slabs behind a glass screen. This sounds like a practical and efficient method of establishing identity, but it also turned the Morgue into a bizarre circus of the macabre. The 1869 guidebook *Paris Partout!* made this report :

In 1866 the Morgue received a record 733 corpses – 486 men, 86 women, 161 infants. Of these 445 were identified; 285 had committed suicide by drowning, 19 were homicidal victims, 36 were hanged, 5 had shot themselves, 3 had been knifed, 6 charcoaled, 6 poisoned,

3 starved, and 82 had died suddenly in the street. Failed speculation on the Stock Exchange is said to be the greatest cause of suicide.

One of the most mysterious cadavers to end up on the marble slabs of the Morgue, that would cast a strange enchantment over many people all around the world, was the body of a young woman who became known as L'Inconnue de la Seine (the unknown woman of the Seine). Her unmarked body was fished out of the river, a suspected suicide, in the late 1880s. When her body was delivered to the Morgue, a pathologist was so struck by her beauty that he had a plaster cast made of her face. The girl's identity was never discovered, but copies of her death mask soon became a popular wall decoration all over Europe. L'Inconnue de la Seine's allure and mystique penetrated all levels of society, seeming to have a particular attraction to artists and writers.

She made her first literary appearance in *The Worshipper of the Image*, a 1900 novella by English writer Richard le Gallienne, who owned a copy of the mask. Vladimir Nabokov wrote his poem 'L'Inconnue de la Seine' in 1934, in which a man sits on the edge of his bed staring hypnotically at 'the white mask'. Anaïs Nin mentions her in her 1944 story 'The Houseboat', Albert Camus had the mask among his collection of sculptures, and the mask featured in Louis Aragon's 1944 novel *Aurélien*.

Ironically, for a young woman who probably took her own life when it was at its lowest ebb, her image has since helped to save countless lives all around the world. In 1958, after discovering her mask hanging on the wall of a relative's house in Stavanger, Norwegian toy maker Asmund Laerdal made her the face of the world's first rescue dummy, Resusci Anne, a lifelike mannequin used to train people in mouth-to-mouth resuscitation.

See Also: Émile Zola, Charles Dickens, Anaïs Nin, Louis Aragon, Albert Camus, Vladimir Nabokov.

Further Information: In 1907, the Morgue was closed to the public due to concerns for 'morality', but it survived behind closed doors on the Île de la Cité until 1921. The site is now occupied by the Mémorial des Martyrs de la Déportation, a memorial to the 200,000 people deported from France to the Nazi extermination camps. Excerpts from poems by Robert Desnos, Louis Aragon, Paul Éluard, Jean-Paul Sartre and Antoine de Saint-Exupéry are inscribed on the walls. The Paris Morgue today is located on the Quai de la Rapée in the 12th arrondissement and is known as the IML (Institut médico-légal). It is not open to the public.

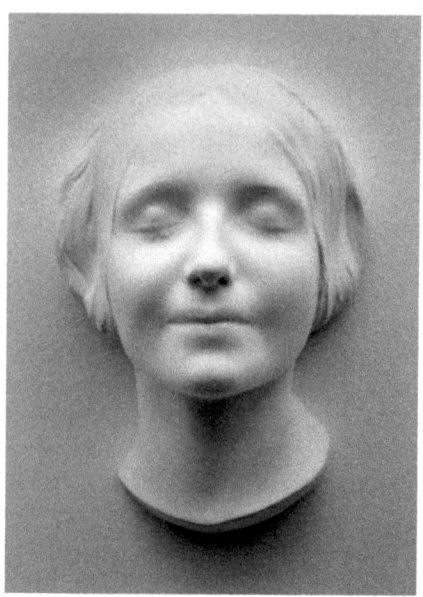

L'Inconnue de la Seine (the unknown woman of the Seine)

FRANÇOIS RABELAIS

RUE DES JARDINS SAINT-PAUL

(Métro: Saint-Paul)

WHERE HUMANIST, SATIRIST

AND PHYSICIAN

FRANÇOIS RABELAIS LIVED AND DIED

Rabelais.

The people so pestered him, in fact, that he was compelled to take a rest on the towers of Notre-Dame; and when from there he saw so many, pressing all around him, he said in a clear voice: 'I think these clodhoppers want me to pay for my kind reception and offer them a solatium ...' Then, with a smile, he undid his magnificent codpiece and, bringing out his john-thomas, pissed on them so fiercely that he drowned two hundred and sixty thousand, four hundred and eighteen persons, not counting the women and small children.

François Rabelais, *The Histories of Gargantua and Pantagruel*

Rabelais (*c*.1495–*c*.1553) is best remembered today for his outrageously inventive prose satires, *Pantagruel* and *Gargantua*, both classics of Renaissance literature. Written in the vernacular, they were filled with bawdy songs, crude jokes and sexual innuendo, works the Sorbonne added to their list of prohibited books in 1542. He was also a humanist who opposed authority and the senseless dogma of his day, arousing the anger of theologians and politicians, and making himself many enemies. The adjective 'Rabelaisian' is still used today when referring to bawdy or earthy humour, but it would be wrong to caricature Rabelais as just an uncouth comic writer. His satirical humour was a burlesque device used to create an extravagant and imaginative world in which he challenges and attempts to transform the problems of the world he himself is living in and, in so doing, rise above them. His comic masterpieces influenced many writers, including Jonathan Swift, Thomas Love Peacock, John Donne, Francis Bacon, Laurence Sterne and Samuel Butler. Molière borrowed Rabelais's inventiveness, and Voltaire and Balzac emulated him. George Orwell thought him 'a case for psychoanalysis'.

Rabelais's birth date is undetermined. He was born near Chinon in the Loire Valley, the son of a prominent lawyer, but virtually nothing is known of his early life. He studied law in his youth, but in 1510–11 he entered a Franciscan monastery at Fontenay-le-Comte in the Vendée where he took holy orders. Here he studied Greek, which was regarded as suspect and heretical by his superiors, prompting him to change course and join the Benedictines. By 1526 he had, without permission, renounced his holy orders and begun studying medicine.

Church of Saint-Paul-Saint-Louis at the northern end of Rue des Jardins Saint-Paul

Some six years later, he was appointed physician to the hospital of Lyon. Around this time, he was beginning to flourish as a writer, publishing, to great acclaim, his first novel, *Pantagruel*, in 1532. *Gargantua* followed two years later. Both novels were published under the name of Alcofribas Nasier, an anagram of François Rabelais. In 1546 he published *Tiers Livre (The Third Book)* under his own name, and *Quart Livre (The Fourth Book)* appeared in 1552–53. In 1535 he gave up medicine, acquired papal absolution for leaving holy orders without permission, and became a priest. In later life he lived on Rue des Jardins Saint-Paul, where his house faced the ancient thirteenth-century wall of Paris, the remains of which are still standing. On his deathbed his last words were reputedly, 'I am going to seek a great perhaps … Bring down the curtain, the farce is played out.'

See Also: Molière, Voltaire, Honoré de Balzac, George Orwell, Gustave Doré.

Further Information: Rabelais was buried in the nearby cemetery of Saint-Eloi, which was closed at the end of the eighteenth century and cleared for development. The burial grounds, which were once a monastic cemetery, attached to the chapel of Saint-Paul. The existing church of Saint-Paul-Saint-Louis, which was built on the original site, can be seen at the northern end of Rue des Jardins Saint-Paul and dates from 1641. A plaque erected to the memory of François Rabelais can be seen on the corner of Rue des Jardins Saint-Paul and Quai des Célestins.

Further Reading: M. Bakhtin, *Rabelais and His World* (John Wiley, 1984); B. Bowen, *Enter Rabelais, Laughing* (Vanderbilt University Press, 1998); D. Frame, *François Rabelais: A Study* (Harcourt Brace, 1977); G. Doré, *Doré's Illustration for Rabelais* (Dover, 1979).

EUGÈNE SUE

RUE DES URSINS

(Métro: Hôtel de Ville)

ONE OF THE FEW SURVIVING MEDIEVAL
STREETS THAT INSPIRED EUGÈNE SUE'S
LES MYSTÈRES DE PARIS

Eugène Sue, *c.* 1844

It was on a cold and rainy night, towards the end of October, 1838, that a tall and powerful man, with an old broad-brimmed straw hat upon his head, and clad in a blue cotton carter's frock, which hung loosely over trousers of the same material, crossed the Pont au Change, and darted with a hasty step into the Cité, that labyrinth of obscure, narrow, and winding streets which extends from the Palais de Justice to Notre Dame ... The murky-coloured houses, which were lighted within by a few panes of glass in the worm-eaten casements, overhung each other so closely that the eaves of each almost touched its opposite neighbour, so narrow were the streets. Dark and noisome alleys led to staircases still more black and foul, and so perpendicular that they could hardly be ascended by the help of a cord fixed to the dank and humid walls by holdfasts of iron.
Eugène Sue, *Les Mystères de Paris* (1842–43)

In the early 1840's Eugène Sue's novel, *Les Mystères de Paris (The Mysteries of Paris)*, was a literary phenomenon without precedent and for a short period of time the most widely read novel in the western world. Published in 90 parts in *Journal des débats* (Journal of Debates) from 19 June 1842 until 15 October 1843, it was one of the first serial novels to be published in France. It was a haunted house novel, in which Sue substitutes the menacing underbelly of the city for the house. The story begins in the dark warren of streets in the Île de la Cité, where we meet the novel's mysterious hero, Rodolphe, a nobleman disguised as a workman, who, like all superheroes, has exceptional strength and compassion for the underdog, and who battles against injustice. With its vast patchwork of loosely connected episodes resembling the script of a modern-day soap opera, the novel enthralled all levels of society, its portrayal of social misery and corruption giving rise to an acute public awareness comparable to that which the novels of Dickens had achieved for Victorian England.

Sue was born in Paris into a family of surgeons in 1804. Following in the footsteps of his father and grandfather, he joined the navy as ship's surgeon; however, after the death of his father, from whom he inherited a sizeable fortune, he retired from the navy in 1830, settled in Paris, and began his literary career. His early novels were inspired by his naval experiences, and had great success, which provoked the critic Sainte-Beuve to describe Sue as the first French writer to have 'risked taking the French novel to sea'. Sue later wrote a five-volume history of the French Navy and some

Charles Marville, Rue des Ursins *c*.1853–70

historical romances, but his talents for melodrama and romance, mixed with a growing socialistic doctrine, reached its zenith with the serialised publication of *Les Mystères de Paris* in 1842–43.

Sue's inspiration for the novel came partly from the Natty Bumppo novels of James Fenimore Cooper, and the *Memoirs* (1828) of the French former criminal turned private detective, Eugène Vidocq. In the wake of the publication of *Les Mystères de Paris*, imitations quickly followed, notably G.W. Reynolds's *The Mysteries of London* (1844) and George Lippard's *The Quaker City* (1844), inspiring a new worldwide category of novels that became known as the city-mysteries genre. In the United States over fifty novels in this format were published between 1844 and 1850. After taking part in the 1848 Revolution, which brought down the monarchy of King Louis Philippe and led to the creation of France's Second Republic, Sue was elected to the Legislative Assembly. But following Louis-Napoléon's coup d'état in 1851, which Sue opposed, he was forced into exile at Annecy in south-eastern France, where he died in 1857, aged fifty-three.

See Also: Eugène Vidocq, George W.M. Reynolds, Charles Sainte-Beuve, Charles Dickens.

Further Information: Eugène Sue is buried in the non-Catholic section of Loverchy Cemetery, Annecy, Department of Haute-Savoie.

Select Bibliography: *Plik et Plok* (1831), *Arthur* (1838); *Mathilde* (1834); *Les Mystères de Paris* (1842–43); *Le Juif errant (The Wandering Jew)* (1844–45); *Les Mystères du peuple (Mysteries of the People)* (1849–56).

THREE MOUNTAINS PRESS

29 QUAI D'ANJOU

(Métro: Pont Marie/Sully-Morland)

FORMER PRINT SHOP AND OFFICES
OF THE THREE MOUNTAINS PRESS,
CONTACT EDITIONS AND
TRANSATLANTIC REVIEW

I'd sit out in front of the Café de la Paix and watch the people go by. [There was] one old wormy-looking guy that went by with post-cards of Paris, showing them to everybody, and, of course, nobody ever bought any, and then he would come back and show the under side of the pack and they would all be smutty post-cards and lots of people would dig down and buy them.
Ernest Hemingway, 'My Old Man', from *In Our Time* (Three Mountains Press, 1924)

Hemingway and McAlmon in Spain, 1923

In 1922 American journalist Bill Bird (1888–1963) purchased a seventeenth century Belgian Mathieu printing press and started a small printery, named the Three Mountains Press (the three mountains being Montmartre, Montparnasse and the Montagne Sainte-Geneviève), in the former wine cellar of an ancient house at 29 quai d'Anjou on the Île Saint-Louis. With minimal experience and no specific agenda, he began looking for manuscripts to publish. Had it not been for a chance meeting with the correspondent of the *Toronto Star*, while covering a conference in Genoa, he would very likely have spent his days publishing mediocre and forgettable books. The young reporter he met was the 23-year-old Ernest Hemingway, whose advice to Bird was to approach poet and critic Ezra Pound for potential manuscripts on his return to Paris. Bird not only consulted Pound, he also appointed him general editor, and on Pound's recommendation Bird launched his publishing enterprise with a series of six books, including Pound's own short autobiography, *Indiscretions*. Other books in the series included works by Ford Madox Ford, William Carlos Williams, and Hemingway's collection of stories and sketches, *In Our Time*. Hemingway also introduced Bird to American essayist, poet and fledgling publisher, Robert McAlmon (1896–1956), who had founded Contact Editions in 1923, a peripatetic publishing concern with no fixed abode. McAlmon proposed to Bird that they join forces. Bird could see the advantages, especially for book distribution, and Contact Editions moved to Quai d'Anjou. Today, Robert McAlmon is best remembered, if at all, for one book: his contemptuously titled, yet absorbing memoir of expatriate Paris, *Being Geniuses Together*, written in 1934. Alongside Hemingway's *A Moveable Feast*, it is probably one of the greatest hatchet jobs on 1920s literary Paris ever written. McAlmon had married Bryher (the pen name of

English writer Winifred Ellerman) in 1921. Bryher, who was lesbian, arranged the marriage with McAlmon to escape her overbearing but enormously wealthy father, whose generous allowance to McAlmon gave birth to Contact Editions. By 1925, McAlmon had published Ezra Pound, Djuna Barnes, Mina Loy, Edith Sitwell, Havelock Ellis, William Carlos Williams, James Joyce, H.D., Gertrude Stein, Marianne Moore, Kay Boyle, and Ernest Hemingway's first book, *Three Stories and Ten Poems*. His own writing career, however, never prospered, and most of what was published was published by himself at Contact. Bryher's family fortune became a bed of roses that defeated him in the end, where struggle and restraint may have achieved so much more. McAlmon spent eight years in Paris, returning to America in 1929 a resentful, dissatisfied man, dying in obscurity in California from tuberculosis in 1956. 'But I knew all too well that Paris is a bitch', wrote McAlmon, 'and that one shouldn't become infatuated with bitches, particularly when they have wit, imagination, experience, and tradition behind their ruthlessness.'

In January 1924, another literary luminary joined the Quai d'Anjou community. English writer and editor, Ford Madox Ford (1873–1939), had agreed to edit a new literary magazine entitled *The Transatlantic Review*, but he had no office space. Bird offered him the mezzanine at the back of the print shop, and for a year Ford edited the magazine's monthly issues from cramped quarters at the Quai d'Anjou. Although the *Review* only published twelve issues it was enormously influential, publishing James Joyce's *Finnegans Wake*, as well as works by Gertrude Stein, Hilda Doolittle, Djuna Barnes, Jean Rhys, and Ernest Hemingway, who, for a short time, was assistant editor. 'I do not think', Ford wrote, 'that there could ever have been an artistic atmosphere younger and more pleasurable or more cordial than that which surrounded the *Review* offices and Thursday teas.'

See Also: Ezra Pound, Robert McAlmon, Ford Madox Ford, James Joyce, Gertrude Stein, Djuna Barnes, Jean Rhys, Ernest Hemingway, James Joyce, Kay Boyle, Nancy Cunard.

Further Information: In 1928 Bill Bird sold his ancient printing press to Nancy Cunard who founded the Hours Press.

Select Bibliography: Robert McAlmon – *Explorations* (1921); *A Hasty Bunch* (1922); *Village: As It Happened Through a Fifteen Year Period* (1924); *The Infinite Huntress and Other Stories* (1932); *Being Geniuses Together* (1938); Ford Madox Ford – *The Good Soldier* (1915); *Parade's End* (1924–28); *The Fifth Queen* (1906–08).

LOUIS ARAGON

PLACE LOUIS-ARAGON

(Métro: Cité/Saint-Paul/Hôtel-de-Ville)

DEDICATED TO NOVELIST AND POET

LOUIS ARAGON

FOUNDING MEMBER OF

THE SURREALIST MOVEMENT

Old men, garbage of a world; young men, tragic in their unfulfilment; equivocal shadows of the lowest kind of prostitution; the sudden apparition of a little old woman, neat with the neatness of the provinces, her black hat and folding chair ... Each of these figures represents the conclusion of a long story of common life which takes on the note of grandeur at just the moment when it reaches the last act. Like iron hands, the arches of the bridges join their dark fingers over the tempting water.

Louis Aragon, *Les beaux quartiers* (1936)

Louis Aragon in 1981

Writer and political activist, Louis Aragon (1897–1982) was one of the leading surrealists of the 1920s, and his 1926 hallucinatory novel, *Paris Peasant*, is arguably one of the most important pieces of prose fiction to come out of the surrealist movement. From being an *enfant terrible*, he evolved via Dadaist experiments to become a writer of social-realistic novels. The outbreak of the Second World War saw him lead the literary resistance and, through his poetry, he became the voice of France.

He was born in Paris in 1897, the illegitimate son of Marguerite Toucas and Louis Andrieux. A former ambassador to Spain, Andrieux named his son after the medieval Spanish Kingdom of Aragon. Married to a woman other than his son's mother, however, he disowned him. Marguerite, who was thirty years younger than Andrieux, only revealed the true identity of the boy's father when he was nineteen. Consequently, the pursuit of legitimacy and identity became important themes in Aragon's work throughout his life.

He became one of the founding members of surrealism along with André Breton and Philippe Soupault, and in 1919 they co-founded the short-lived, but influential surrealist journal, *Littérature*. Following a visit to Russia in 1930 Aragon became a committed communist and broke with surrealism, turning his talents to socialist realism, writing a series of novels entitled *Le monde réel* (The Real World) (1933–1951). In 1939 he married Russian-born writer Elsa Triolet, and during the Nazi occupation of France, they both fought with the French Resistance. During the war, Aragon wrote for the underground press Les Éditions de Minuit, and throughout this period he created some of his finest poetry that would keep up France's morale against the Nazis, notably, 'Le Crève-coeur' ('Heartbreak') (1941), 'Les Yeux d'Elsa' ('The Eyes of Elsa') (1942), 'Liberté' (1942), and 'La Diane

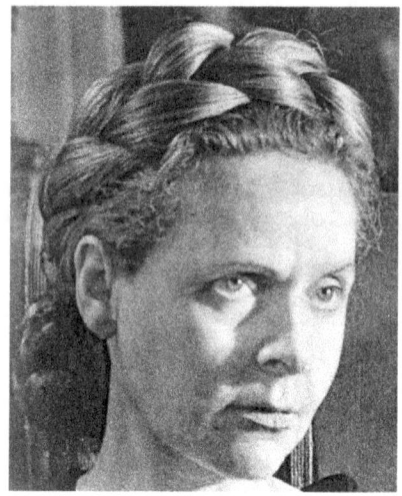

Elsa Triolet (1896–1970)

française' ('The French Diana') (1944). In the post-war years he became one of France's foremost communist writers, continuing to publish poetry throughout the 1950s and 1960s. He strenuously defended Stalinism, but was later 'overwhelmed' by the 1956 revelations of Stalin's crimes. He denounced the Soviet persecution of writers and he condemned the Soviet invasion of Czechoslovakia in 1968; and following the death of Elsa in 1970, he distanced himself from communism.

In spite of his political views, which many were unsympathetic towards, Aragon's reputation as a poet and novelist is secure in the annals of French literature.

See Also: Tristan Tzara, André Breton, Les Éditions de Minuit, Le Prix Goncourt.

Further Information: Place Louis Aragon was inaugurated on 27 March 2012, the thirtieth anniversary of Aragon's death, and is located at the western tip of Île Saint-Louis, close to the apartment of Aurélien, eponymous hero of Aragon's 1944 novel.

In 1951 Louis Aragon and his wife Elsa Triolet moved to the Moulin de Villeneuve in Saint-Arnoult-en-Yvelines, about 60 kilometres south-west of Paris. Aragon and Triolet are both buried in the grounds, and the mill is now a museum dedicated to their memory. In 1944 Elsa Triolet was the first woman to be awarded the Prix Goncourt for her novel *Le premier accroc coûte deux cent francs (A Fine of Two Hundred Francs).*

Select Bibliography: *The Adventures of Telemachus* (1922); *Paris Peasant* (1926); *The Bells of Basel* (1933); *Heartbreak* (1941); *The Eyes of Elsa* (1942); *Aurélien* (1944); *The French Diana* (1944); *The Unfinished Roman* (1956).

5th

Arrondissement

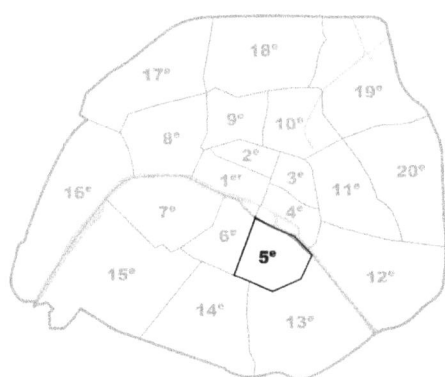

BIBLIOTHÈQUE SAINTE-GENEVIÈVE
10 PLACE DU PANTHÉON
(Métro: Cardinal Lemoine)

This is just about the perfect French building: if I had to choose one thing from which to deduce the French virtues it might well be this. Intelligent, adaptable, concise and well ahead of its time ... Nothing is overstated; there is no attempt at tickling up emotion by association, which was the besetting fault of the nineteenth century and the reason why the [London] Houses of Parliament are no more than a shattering coup de théâtre instead of an international masterpiece.
It is not surprising that with this wisdom the staircase has a free and easy feeling utterly unlike the British Museum; or that the main reading room under its frilly, double-naved iron roof feels relaxed as well as serious. At the British Museum the readers exist to fill the structure. Here and at the Bibliothèque

[Sainte-Geneviève], the room exists to enhance each person's study. The roof itself resembles nothing so much as a salad of that spiky kind of French lettuce that discharges all other tastes without imposition and without losing its own identity.
Ian Nairn, *Nairn's Paris* (1968)

The Bibliothèque Sainte-Geneviève was built in 1851 and designed by the architect Henri Labrouste (1801–1875), who is remembered for his unique use of iron-frame construction in public buildings, a technique normally used for industrial buildings, giving a calm yet substantial quality to his overall design, a technique that imbues the reading room, Salle Labrouste, with light. Its three main departments are the *Fonds général* (documents and books published after 1821), *La Réserve* (collections of old and rare books) and the *Bibliothèque Nordique* (documents and

Salle Labrouste, Bibliothèque Sainte-Geneviève

books in Scandinavian, and Finno-Ugric, the languages of north-east Europe and north Asia).

The Bibliothèque Sainte-Geneviève inherited its early collections from the nearby Abbaye-Sainte-Geneviève, once a celebrated seat of learning containing a vast medieval library. In AD 507 the Frankish Merovingian King Clovis chose the site for a basilica in which to bury himself and his wife Clotilde. In AD 512 Sainte-Geneviève, patroness of Paris was buried here; and in 1774, when King Louis XV was seriously ill, he vowed to build a church to replace the ruined abbey if he survived his illness. He did survive and the remodelled Abbey of Sainte-Geneviève was completed in 1791. Following the French Revolution the church was deconsecrated and reconsecrated several times, and today it serves as the Panthéon, a secular mausoleum containing the remains of eminent French figures.

See Also: Bibliothèque Nationale de France, Bibliothèque Mazarine, Bibliothèque de l'Institut, Académie des Inscriptions et Belles-lettres, The American Library in Paris, Panthéon.

Further Information: In 1851, the physicist Jean Bernard Léon Foucault first held his pendulum experiment, proving that the world spins around its axis, at the Abbaye-Sainte-Geneviève.

Bibliothèque Sainte-Geneviève

PANTHÉON

PLACE DU PANTHÉON

(Métro: Cardinal Lemoine)

**MAUSOLEUM FOR FRANCE'S
NATIONAL HEROES**

*The Panthéon was built as a church, became
a pantheon at the Revolution, and thereafter
seesawed twice between God and the Légion
d'Honneur.*
Ian Nairn, *Nairn's Paris* (1968)

Panthéon

Originally a church dedicated to Sainte-Geneviève, the Panthéon is now a secular mausoleum containing the remains of France's national figures. An early example of neoclassicism, its exterior was modelled on the Panthéon in Rome. It was deconsecrated during the Revolution into a temple to inter the remains of the great men of France, but was reconsecrated several times during the nineteenth century, before being secularised once again in 1885 to receive the remains of Victor Hugo, who had asked that there be no religious rites at his funeral. The inscription above the entrance reads *Aux Grands Hommes La Patrie Reconnaissante* (To the great men, the grateful homeland). Legends entombed here include Voltaire, Jean-Jacques Rousseau, Victor Hugo, Émile Zola, Alexandre Dumas *père*, and André Malraux. In 1899 the poet Georges Rodenbach descended into the vaults of the Panthéon where, behind a huge door, he found himself

> opposite the place where Victor Hugo's coffin rests, just as it was brought there, the day of his unforgettable funeral. That is to say that no one has since been concerned with building him a tomb.

> He is still in a provisional situation; he is lingering on some trestles. …
> And, all around, are the old wreaths, the flowers, the bouquets, all wrinkled, shrivelled, withered, discoloured; faded ribbons, inscriptions with letters going awry, cardboard lyres crumbling away, spectres of roses, corpses of flowers which are themselves decomposing.

In 2002 the coffin of Alexandre Dumas (1802–1870) was transferred from its original grave in Picardy to the Panthéon. Six Republican Guards carried the coffin which was draped with a velvet cloth inscribed with 'Un pour tous, tous pour un' ('One for all, all for one'). In the past two hundred years 74 people have been entombed at the Panthéon, but only two of them were women: Marie Curie, and Sophie Berthelot, the wife of nineteenth-century chemist, Marcellin Berthelot.

99

Today there is a growing consensus that more women should be recognised, and suggestions so far, amongst others, have included George Sand, Simone de Beauvoir and Marguerite Duras. Hopefully, in the near future the gold lettering on the Panthéon's facade will read 'To the great men and women, the grateful homeland'.

See Also: Voltaire, Jean-Jacques Rousseau, Victor Hugo, Émile Zola, Alexandre Dumas *père*, André Malraux, George Sand, Simone de Beauvoir, Marguerite Duras, Denis Diderot.

Further Information: In AD 507 the Frankish Merovingian King Clovis chose the site for a basilica in which to bury himself and his wife Clotilde. In AD 512, patroness of Paris Sainte-Geneviève was buried here; and in 1774, the seriously ill King Louis XV vowed to build a church dedicated to Sainte-Geneviève if he survived his illness. He did survive and the Abbaye-Sainte-Geneviève was duly built. It took 34 years to build and was finished in 1791. In 1851, the physicist Jean Bernard Léon Foucault first held his experiment here, proving that the world spins around its axis.

Tomb of Voltaire

JEAN RACINE

PLACE SAINTE-GENEVIÈVE

(Métro: Cardinal Lemoine)

ÉGLISE SAINT-ÉTIENNE-DU-MONT

TOMB OF JEAN RACINE

CLASSICAL DRAMATIST AND POET

In the opinion of devout people, the qualities of a novelist and a playwright are not very honourable; indeed, judged by the standards of the Christian religion, they are abominable. A man who writes novels and plays is a public poisoner – not of the bodies but of the souls of the faithful. He must be considered guilty of an infinite number of spiritual homicides, which he has either caused in reality or which he may have caused by his pernicious writings.
Extract from a pamphlet published *c.*1665 by Jean Racine's former school.

Jean Racine was an unconvincing candidate for the career of playwright. His first choice had been an ecclesiastical vocation, but he ended up becoming one of France's chief classical dramatists at a time when the Church considered a playwright to be a moral outcast, and that an actor could only be buried in consecrated ground if he renounced the stage before dying. It was a time when the Church and the theatre were at war, and Racine was ripe for purgatory.
The first child of Jean Racine the elder, a local official in the salt-tax office, and Jeanne Sconin, he was born in 1639 in La Ferté-Milon, a small town fifty miles north-east of Paris. When Racine was thirteen months old his mother died giving birth to his sister, and when his father died two years later the two young orphans were sent to live with their grandparents.

Église Saint-Étienne-du-Mont

affiliations. He lodged with his cousin's family, the Vitarts, and it was through their contacts that Racine started to climb the literary ladder towards success. The only way to survive financially as a poet in the seventeenth century was through patronage. A sonnet he sent to Cardinal Mazarin failed to awaken any response, but an ode, *La Nymphe de la Seine*, composed on the occasion of the marriage of Louis XIV, was rewarded with a grant of one hundred *Louis D'or*. The theatre, however, did not depend on patronage: a playwright was paid a percentage of the receipts. Racine's career as a dramatist began with his play *La Thébaide*, which, after many rejections, was eventually produced by Molière's troupe in 1664, although it made little impression. Molière also produced Racine's second tragedy, *Alexandre*, but after Racine seduced Molière's leading actress then offered his play to a rival troupe the relationship between the two men became somewhat estranged. By 1667 Racine had become a dramatist of considerable stature, and in 1673 he was admitted to the Académie française. He had written ten plays and was popular with both the court and the public, but suddenly he abandoned it all. The King had offered him the appointment of Historiographer Royal, a position that involved accompanying the King and chronicling his exploits, and one that came with an annual pension of 6000 *livres*. One of the conditions of the post, however, was that he ceased writing for the theatre.

At the age of sixteen Racine entered the Jansenist school at Port-Royal, south of Paris, peopled mainly by nuns and novices. Jansenism was a doctrine within the Catholic Church, an austere interpretation of Christianity that spread through France and the Low countries in the seventeenth and eighteenth centuries, which condemned most pleasures, including the theatre. It was at Port-Royal that Racine composed his first poems: seven odes, written in Latin, called *Promenades de Port-Royal*. They did not constitute a love song to Jansenism as one might assume from the title, but were primarily a tribute to the natural beauty of his surroundings.

In the autumn of 1658 he left Port-Royal and went to Paris to study at the Collège d'Harcourt (now the lycée Saint-Louis). Although it was not a Jansenist establishment, many of the staff had Jansenist

Around this time Racine married the pious Catherine de Romanet, a woman who was ignorant of drama and poetry, but who was, nonetheless, well aware of the prestige of her husband's royal post. They had two children.

Racine's last two plays, written after a silence of twelve years, were *Esther* and *Athaliah*, both religious subjects. In 1699 Racine finally made his peace with God, and died from a liver abscess in the early morning of 21 April. 'My tragedy is done,' he once remarked. 'Now I have only to write it.'

See Also: Molière, Académie française, Panthéon, Bibliothèque Sainte-Geneviève.

Further Information: Église Saint-Étienne-du-Mont is located in the Latin Quarter, on the Montagne Sainte-Geneviève, to the rear of the Panthéon. Its origins date back to the thirteenth century, but it was completely re-built during the sixteenth century, and finally dedicated by the archbishop of Paris in 1626. It contains the shrine of Sainte-Geneviève, the patron saint of Paris, and the tombs of Jean Racine and the mathematician and physicist, Blaise Pascall (1623–1662).

Select Bibliography: *Iphigenia, Phaedra and Athalia* (Penguin, 2004); *Andromache, Britannicus, Berenice* (Penguin, 1974).

Further Reading: J. Sayer, *Jean Racine: Life and Legend* (Peter Lang, 2006); R. Knight, *Racine* (Aurora, 1972); C. Abraham, *Jean Racine* (Twayne, 1978); L. Goldmann, *Racine* (Writers and Readers, 1981); G. Brereton, *Jean Racine* (Cassell, 1951).

Jean Racine by Gérard Edelinck

ALBERT CAMUS

13 RUE DES ÉCOLES

(Métro: Cardinal Lemoine)

HÔTEL MINERVE
FORMER RESIDENCE OF
ALBERT CAMUS
NOBEL PRIZE–WINNING AUTHOR,
JOURNALIST AND PHILOSOPHER

The Arab drew his knife and held it out towards me in the sun. The light leapt up off the steel and it was like a long, flashing sword lunging at my forehead. ... All I could feel were the cymbals the sun was clashing against my forehead and, indistinctly, the dazzling spear still leaping up off the knife in front of me. ... The sky seemed to be splitting from end to end and raining down sheets of flame. My whole being went tense and I tightened my grip on the gun.
Albert Camus, *L'Étranger* (1942)

Albert Camus's rise from a poverty-stricken childhood in Algiers to the life of an internationally celebrated writer was an extraordinary feat. When his mother received a telegram in 1957 informing her that her son had been awarded the Nobel Prize in Literature she was unable to read it because she was illiterate. Today Camus is the French writer most widely translated into English and, though his reputation firmly rests on his fiction: *L'Etranger (The Outsider)* (1942), *La Peste (The Plague)* (1947), *La Chute (The Fall)* (1956), he was also an acknowledged master of the philosophical essay. His was a new voice in literature, his concise, unsentimental writing reaching out to the subversive anti-hero in us all. He made his fame in the 1940s and 1950s, capturing the spirit of those decades, and after his untimely death in 1960 Jean-Paul Sartre summed him up in a sentence: 'Camus could never cease to be one of the principal forces in our cultural domain, nor to represent, in his own way, the history of France and of this century.'

He was born in Mondovi (now called Dréan), Algeria, in 1913, the second son of Lucien Camus, a farm labourer who died from his wounds after the Battle of the Marne in 1914 during World War I. His mother Catherine was a cleaner, who, with her two sons, shared a small apartment with the family of her domineering mother-in-law in the Belcourt suburb of Algiers. In 1923 Camus was accepted into the lycée and later to the University of Algiers where he studied philosophy, interrupted by long spells of illness with tuberculosis. Camus always maintained that what little morality he learned was through playing football and in the theatre. 'It was only when playing for a team as a young man', he wrote, 'that I experienced that powerful sense of hope and exaltation which used to accompany long days of training before a match. And really, what little morality I have learned I have learnt in the theatre or the football pitch, both of which remain my true universities.' In 1934 he married Simone Hié, a drug addict. The marriage was a disaster and they separated in 1936. In 1940 he married Francine Faure, with whom he had two children, but marriage was never a stabilising influence for Camus and throughout his life he was an inveterate womaniser.

He arrived in Paris as a journalist in 1940 and briefly joined the staff of the newspaper *Paris-Soir* before returning to Algeria in 1941, the year of the German occupation of France. By this time

Albert Camus

Hôtel Minerve

Camus was working on his first novel, *L'Étranger*. The following year it was published by Gallimard, and has been translated into English variously as *The Stranger, The Foreigner* and *The Outsider*. The story is of a murder, written in a seemingly simple style, but its ideas are complex. Meursault, a French-Algerian, shoots an Arab just because he feels like it, and Camus attempts to make the reader understand his state of mind and behaviour. '[It's] the study of an absurd man in an absurd world,' wrote Camus.

The same year he also published his philosophical essay, *Le Mythe de Sisyphe (The Myth of Sisyphus)*, in which Camus introduced his philosophy of the absurd. 'Man alone is not absurd,' he said, 'and the world itself is not absurd, but it is the clash between the two that gives rise to the absurd.'

In 1943 Camus took up residence in the Hôtel Minerve on the Rue des Écoles because of its close proximity to his new job as a manuscript reader with Gallimard. Unlike the luxury of today's hotel, Camus's room had no toilet, no bath and no heating, but the owner supported the Resistance movement of the Second World War and its members occupied much of the building. During the war Camus joined the Resistance and became editor of their covert newspaper, *Combat*.

His next novel, *La Peste (The Plague)*, published in 1947, was inspired by the war, and the rats that carry the plague are a metaphor for the human rats that were the Nazis. Paris in the 1940s was the cradle of a new philosophic trend called existentialism, and the cafes of the Left Bank were full of people proclaiming that life had no meaning. Its gurus were Jean-Paul Sartre, Simone de Beauvoir and Albert Camus, although Camus always refused to be defined as an existentialist. The famous threesome became firm friends, but Camus's and Sartre's conflicting ideologies eventually severed their friendship. Camus's writings began to achieve international acclaim, and when Camus spoke the world listened.

Since 1954 Algerian nationalists had been waging war against the French in a fight for independence, and it was a conflict that devastated Camus. He was one of the first French intellectuals to denounce the use of torture in Algeria, but he never took sides.

From his diaries we know he was tempted several times by suicide and he was very unhappy in later life. On hearing he had been awarded the Nobel Prize in Literature in 1957 his immediate reaction was to remark that it should have gone to André Malraux. The prize money, however, did allow him to buy a house in the village of Lourmarin in Provence, deep in the south of France, set in a landscape reminiscent of his beloved Algeria.

On Monday 4 January 1960, Camus was driving from Lourmarin to Paris with his publisher and friend, Michel Gallimard, together with Gallimard's wife and daughter, and their dog. Gallimard was driving, and in the early afternoon, on a plane tree-lined road near Petit Villeblevin, the car swerved and smashed into a tree. Camus died instantly, his neck broken. Gallimard died later in hospital, but his wife and daughter survived virtually unscathed. The dog, strangely, disappeared without trace. Amongst the wreckage the police found the handwritten manuscript of Camus's unfinished partly autobiographical novel, *Le Premier Homme (The First Man)*, which would be published thirty-five years later, in 1995.

See Also: *Combat*, Jean-Paul Sartre, Simone de Beauvoir, André Malraux, Gaston Gallimard, Guillotine.

Further Information: Albert Camus is buried in Lourmarin Cemetery, Vaucluse.

Further Reading: O. Todd, *Albert Camus: A Life* (Carroll & Graf, 2000); A. Martin, *The Boxer and The Goal Keeper: Sartre versus Camus* (Simon & Schuster, 2013); E. Hawes, *Camus, A Romance* (Grove, 2010).

LA SORBONNE: UNIVERSITY OF PARIS

CORNER OF RUE DES ÉCOLES
AND RUE SAINT-JACQUES
(Metro: Cluny – La Sorbonne)

ALMA MATER OF HONORÉ DE BALZAC,
VICTOR HUGO AND OTHERS

Works of literature could be studied, not for their cargo of imperishable truths, but as an expression of society. Romanticism had entered academe and, most exotic of all, so had works from other European countries: Goethe, Byron, Walter Scott, and that playwright who until then had been considered too vulgar to be placed on any syllabus – William Shakespeare.
Graham Robb, *Balzac* (1994)

The inner courtyard of the Sorbonne

From the early thirteenth century schools began to appear on the slopes of this quarter, which a thousand years before had been the site of a Roman town. These schools were the genesis of the University of Paris and their standards and reputation spread throughout Europe. It became known as the Latin Quarter, since Latin was the language of learning institutions in the Middle Ages.

The name Sorbonne is derived from Robert de Sorbon (1201–1274), a French theologian, who founded the Collège de Sorbonne in 1257. It evolved into an important centre of learning and eventually became the heart of what would become the University of Paris, known today as Paris-Sorbonne University, a group of several colleges.

Sorbonne literary alumni include Thomas Aquinas, François Villon, Honoré de Balzac, Victor Hugo, Simone de Beauvoir, Roland Barthes, Françoise Sagan, Lawrence Ferlinghetti, Norman Mailer, Raymond Queneau, Pauline Réage and Susan Sontag. The oldest building connected to the Sorbonne is the seventeenth-century chapel on Rue de la Sorbonne, built in 1635 and housing the white marble tomb of Cardinal Richelieu ('If you give me six lines written by the hand of the most honest of men, I will find something in them which will hang him.'). Richelieu was interred in 1642 and would later be immortalised as one of literature's greatest villains in Alexandre Dumas's *The Three Musketeers* (1844).

In 1968 students occupied the Sorbonne protesting against the university system, a rebellion that turned into a mass uprising throughout the nation, paralysing the entire country. Riots, strikes and protests brought President de Gaulle's government to near collapse, setting in motion a cultural and social revolution that changed the face of French society.

See Also: Alexandre Dumas, Honoré de Balzac, Victor Hugo, Simone de Beauvoir, Roland Barthes, Françoise Sagan, Académie française.

SAMUEL JOHNSON

269 RUE SAINT-JACQUES

(Métro: Censier-Daubenton/Place Monge)

SITE OF THE ENGLISH

BENEDICTINE MONASTERY

WHERE SAMUEL JOHNSON

HAD A CELL 'APPROPRIATED' TO HIM

To James Boswell, Esq.

My Dear Sir,
... I now write to tell you that I shall not very soon write again, for I am to set out tomorrow on another journey. ... I am, Sir, &c. September 14, 1775.

Sam. Johnson.

Boswell later discovered that Samuel Johnson's journey 'was no less than a tour to France ... the only time in his life that he went upon the Continent'. Johnson (1709–1784) was always like a duck out of water whenever he was parted from his beloved London for any length of time and a visit to France was no exception. His appearance and his manner were obstinately predictable: he dressed in his customary brown garb, with plain shirt and black stockings, while cynically scrutinising the French. The following year Johnson gave Boswell an account of his tour:

Sir, I have seen all the visibilities of Paris, and around it; but to have formed an acquaintance with the people there, would have required more time than I could stay. ... And, Sir, I was very kindly treated by the English Benedictines, and have a cell appropriated to me in their convent. The great in France live very magnificently, but the rest very miserably. There is no happy middle state as in England. The shops of Paris are mean; the meat in the markets is such as would be sent to a gaol in England ... The French are an indelicate people; they will spit upon any place. At Madame [du Boccage]'s, a literary lady of rank, the footman took the sugar in his fingers, and threw it into my coffee. I was going to put it aside; but hearing it was made on purpose for me, I e'en tasted Tom's fingers. The same lady would needs make tea *à l'Angloise*. The spout of the tea-pot did not pour freely; she bade the footman blow into it. France is worse than Scotland in every thing but climate. Nature has done more for the French; but they have done less for themselves than the Scotch have done.'

Although Johnson understood French perfectly, he refused to speak it. 'It was a maxim with him', wrote Boswell, 'that a man should not let himself down, by speaking a language which he speaks imperfectly.' In France, therefore, Johnson conversed solely in Latin; but alas, combined with his English accent, not many understood him. His dislike of the French was well known, and he even begrudged them their literature, as Boswell records in his *The Life of Samuel Johnson*:

No, Sir, if literature be in its spring in France, it is a second spring; it is after a winter. We are now before the French in literature; but we had it long after them. In England, any man who wears a sword and a powdered wig is ashamed to be illiterate. I believe it is not so in France. Yet there is, probably, a great deal of learning in France, because they have such a number of religious establishments; so many men who have nothing else to do but study. I do not know this; but I take it upon the common principles of chance. Where there are many shooters, some will hit.

106

T.S. ELIOT

151 *BIS* RUE SAINT-JACQUES

(Métro: Luxembourg)

FORMER LODGINGS OF

AMERICAN POET T.S. ELIOT

WINNER OF THE NOBEL PRIZE

IN LITERATURE

I have rather hoped you would not specialize later on French literature… I cannot bear to think of your being alone in Paris, the very words give me a chill. English speaking countries seem so different from foreign. I do not admire the French nation.
Charlotte Champe Eliot (1843–1929), mother of T.S. Eliot.

Schola Cantorum, formerly the site of the English Benedictine Monastery

Further Information: Although now consigned to the status of a back street in the Latin Quarter after Baron Haussmann's renovations, the Rue Saint-Jacques was once one of the main arteries of medieval Paris, which explains its plethora of monasteries, convents, institutes and schools, notably the Sorbonne, sited here throughout history. King James II, and VII (of England and Ireland, and Scotland, respectively) died in exile in France and was interred in the Chapel of Saint Edmund in the Church of the English Benedictines in Rue Saint-Jacques. His tomb was later desecrated during the Revolution. No. 269 rue Saint-Jacques, which is now a music school, is near the junction of Rue Saint-Jacques and Rue des Feuillantines.

Further Reading: J. Boswell, *The Life of Samuel Johnson* (Penguin, 2008).

Despite his family's misgivings, young American student Thomas Stearns Eliot (1888–1965) was determined to visit Paris after graduating from Harvard in 1909, and two main catalysts spurred him in this endeavour. The first was a book: *The Symbolist Movement in Literature* (1899) by Arthur Symons, which was, Eliot wrote, 'an introduction to wholly new feelings, as a revelation'. The second was Irving Babbitt, literary critic and professor of French literature at Harvard, who deeply influenced him. With the Gallic seed firmly planted he sailed for France in early October 1910. He took a room with the Casaubons at their pension in the Rue Saint-Jacques, close to the Sorbonne where he attended lectures on literature and philosophy. And although the expatriates of the Lost Generation were yet to arrive, the belle époque was still alive and kicking, and Eliot balanced his academic pursuits with the stimulus of Parisian life, from the opera to the boxing match. But his main reason for coming to Paris was to find his own poetic voice. Rimbaud, Baudelaire, Laforgue and Mallarmé had all inspired him, and he believed that 'the use of my own voice … was only to be found in French'. He even had 'the idea of giving up English and trying to settle down and scrape along in Paris and gradually write in French'.

His 'idea' came to nothing and he never did settle in Paris, returning instead to the United States in late September 1911; but his year in the city was a crucial stepping stone towards becoming one of the most influential poets of the twentieth century. 'On the one hand', he wrote, 'Paris was completely the past; on the other hand, it was completely the future; and these two aspects combined to form a perfect present.'

See Also: Alain-Fournier, Arthur Rimbaud, Charles Baudelaire, Jules Laforgue, Stéphane Mallarmé, James Joyce.

Further Information: Eliot's pension at No. 151 *bis* rue Saint-Jacques was designed in the early eighteenth century by architect Lepas-Dubuisson and is now a registered historic monument. Arthur Symons's *The Symbolist Movement in Literature* was a 'revelation' not only to Eliot: it also inspired James Joyce to visit Paris in 1902, and Ezra Pound described Symons as one of his 'gods'. While in Paris, Eliot practised French conversation with Alain-Fournier, who went on to write *Le Grand Meaulnes* (1913), one of the great masterpieces of French literature. T.S. Eliot became a British citizen in 1927 and was awarded the Nobel Prize in Literature in 1948. He died from emphysema at his London home in 1965.

Select Bibliography: *Prufrock and Other Observations* (1917); *The Waste Land* (1922); *The Hollow Men* (1925); *Four Quartets* (1945); *Murder in the Cathedral* (1935); *The Cocktail Party* (1949).

Further Reading: A. Symons, *The Symbolist Movement in Literature* (Fyfield, 2014); N. Duvall, *T.S. Eliot's Parisian Year* (University Press of Florida, 2009); R. Crawford, *Young Eliot: From St Louis to The Waste Land* (Jonathan Cape, 2015); H. Haughton, V. Eliot (Eds.), *The Letters of T.S. Eliot Volume One: 1898–1922* (Faber & Faber, 2009); G. Panichas, *The Critical Legacy of Irving Babbitt* (ISI Books, 1999).

Top: T.S. Eliot
Above: 151 *bis* rue Saint-Jacques

JOHN DOS PASSOS

45 QUAI DE LA TOURNELLE

(Métro: Maubert-Mutualité)

FORMER APARTMENT OF
JOHN DOS PASSOS
AMERICAN NOVELIST OF
THE POST-WORLD WAR I
'LOST GENERATION'

I want to swallow the oyster of the world. I want to peel the rind of the orange. I want to drink the cup to the dregs – no – I want to swallow it and still have it to look at. I want to peel off the rind in patterns of my own making. I want to paint with the dregs pictures of gods and demons on the great white curtains of eternity.
John Dos Passos

John Dos Passos was never one of the legendary Paris expatriates like his fellow countrymen Hemingway and Fitzgerald, but after the war he did live and study there. Like many others, he suffered from the trauma and shattered illusions of World War I. Shy and softly spoken, Dos Passos went on to become a major American novelist and social historian, writing about twentieth-century American life – of which he was a fierce critic – and the roots of American tradition. He is best known for his *USA* trilogy: *The 42nd Parallel, 1919* and *The Big Money.*

Dos Passos was born in a Chicago hotel room in 1896, the son of a wealthy lawyer, John Randolph Dos Passos, whose father had been an immigrant from the Portuguese island of Madeira. When he was fifteen, Dos Passos embarked on a grand tour of Europe, and visited Paris for the first time. In 1912 he enrolled at Harvard where he became friends with E.E. Cummings. After his graduation in 1916 he was keen to join a volunteer ambulance unit on the Western Front, but submitting to his father's objections he journeyed to Spain to learn the language and study art instead. A few months after his father's death in 1917, the United States entered World War I, and Dos Passos sailed to France to join an Ambulance Corps. Members of the Corps were known as 'gentlemen volunteers', mostly recruited from the Ivy League universities and prep schools of New England, who agreed to serve for a minimum of six months and pay for their own uniforms and passage overseas.

In France, he was posted to the Western Front where he witnessed the Verdun offensive, a slaughter in which six hundred Frenchmen died in one day. It was this experience that inspired his scathing anti-war novel *Three Soldiers*. 'As for the troops,' he recalled in an interview, 'they had an ambivalent feeling about the

[Ambulance] corps. Where they saw us in greatest volume was where an attack had been planned and was going to be mounted and a lot of people were going to be killed. They must have thought us a collection of scavenger crows.' Three months later, in October 1917, the Ambulance Corps had been taken over by the United States Army, so to avoid being drafted Dos Passos signed up for the newly formed American Red Cross on the Italian front. In 1920 he published his first book, *One Man's Initiation*, a memoir of his wartime experiences, which sold just 63 copies in the first six months.

When the war was over, Dos Passos decided to stay on in France and study. The Army Overseas Educational Commission (similar to the 1940s GI Bill) accepted his application to study anthropology at the Sorbonne, and on his arrival in the spring of 1919 he rented a room on Rue de la Montagne-Sainte-Geneviève close to the university. Shortly afterwards, he moved into rooms at 45 quai de la Tournelle overlooking the Seine, which had recently been vacated by a friend. It was here he began writing his second novel, *Three Soldiers*. After many rejections it was eventually published in 1921 to great critical acclaim. F. Scott Fitzgerald described it as 'the first war book by an American worthy of serious notice'.

In the early post-war years he worked as a newspaper correspondent and travelled extensively, later reporting on the Spanish Civil War and World War II. By the end of his life he had written over forty books, working both in fiction and non-fiction, including plays, poetry, novels, biographies, travelogues, histories and memoirs. Always an outsider, he championed the radical Left, the

John Dos Passos

communist revolution and the labour movements of the twenties and thirties. In his maturity, however, he retreated into political conservatism and, to a certain extent, this is the reason why he is largely forgotten today. Nevertheless, his contribution to the American novel was undoubtedly considerable. Dos Passos died of heart failure in 1970, aged 74, and is buried near his Virginia farm.

See Also: American Ambulance, E.E. Cummings, Jean-Paul Sartre, Ernest Hemingway, F. Scott Fitzgerald, The American Hospital in Paris, Harry Crosby, Robert Service.

Select Bibliography: *Three Soldiers* (1921); *Manhattan Transfer* (1925); *Orient Express* (1927); *The 42nd Parallel* (1930); *Nineteen Nineteen* (1932); *The Big Money* (1936); *Adventures of a Young Ma*n (1939); *Chosen Country* (1951); *The Best Times: An Informal Memoir* (1966).

Further Reading: V. Carr, *Dos Passos: A Life* (Northwestern University Press, 2004).

ERNEST HEMINGWAY

74 RUE DU CARDINAL LEMOINE

(Métro: Cardinal Lemoine)

FIRST PARIS APARTMENT

OF ERNEST HEMINGWAY

AND HIS WIFE HADLEY RICHARDSON

They did not need Hemingway's income from Star feature stories, for Hadley's several trust funds provided them with almost $3000 a year, more than enough money to live well in Paris. Their first apartment came furnished for only 250 francs a month, or less than $20. If he wished, Hemingway could have spent the entire year working on his fiction without selling a single line to the Star.
Michael Reynolds, *Hemingway: The Paris Years* (1989)

Hemingway with his son John, nicknamed Bumby

Ernest Hemingway (1899–1961) became famous for his tough, scant, hard-edged prose, his macho sporting bravado and his four marriages. His style, at least in his early writings, had a clean, crisp simplicity, without a trace of sentimentality – characteristics that, regrettably, he lost with maturity. Paris was his rite of passage, where he progressed from the spare news article to the complexity of his first novel, *The Sun Also Rises*. During this apprenticeship he met, and was given the support of, Gertrude Stein, Ford Madox Ford and Ezra Pound, and he became part of the disillusioned band of young expatriate writers known as The Lost Generation, a label Hemingway sneered at. He later recalled this period of time in his rose-tinted memoir, *A Moveable Feast*, published posthumously in 1964.

The son of an Illinois doctor, Hemingway was born in a Chicago suburb in 1899. His working life began as a reporter in Kansas City. In 1918 he volunteered as an ambulance driver for the Red Cross in Italy and was wounded the following year. Discharged, he returned to America and two years later, after a whirlwind romance, he married his first wife, Hadley Richardson. In December 1921 they arrived in Paris, where Hemingway planned to send feature stories to the *Toronto Star* and establish his reputation as a writer.

They had both been to Paris before – Hemingway during the war, and Hadley as a teenager in 1910. Hadley had passable schoolgirl French, but Hemingway's knowledge was limited. On arrival they headed for a Left Bank hotel recommended by Sherwood Anderson, the Hôtel Jacob on Rue Jacob in the heart of St-Germain-des-Prés. In January 1922 they found permanent accommodation in the Latin Quarter: a fourth floor apartment at 74 rue du Cardinal Lemoine with two rooms, a tiny

111

kitchen and a squat toilet on the landing. Writing to his parents he described it as 'the jolliest place you ever saw':

> We rented it furnished for 250 francs a month, about 18 dollars ... Bones [Hadley] has a piano and we have all our pictures up on the walls and an open fire place and a peach of a kitchen and a dining room and big bed room and dressing room and plenty of space. It is on top of a high hill in the very oldest part of Paris. The nicest part of the Latin Quarter.

The 'peach of a kitchen' had a two-burner stove, and there was room for only one person. There was no hot water. After Hadley's rental piano was delivered into the dining room, they had to eat off a table in the bedroom. The 'dressing room' was a cupboard where the water pitcher, bowl and slop jar were stored. They humped their rubbish down four flights of stairs, where drunks often urinated and slept in the doorway. But Hemingway was doing what he did best: writing fiction.

See Also: La Closerie des Lilas, Harry's New York Bar, American Hospital in Paris, American Ambulance Field Service, Dingo Bar, Hotel Ritz, Gare de Lyon, F. Scott Fitzgerald, Sylvia Beach, Gertrude Stein, Alice B. Toklas, Sherwood Anderson, Ford Madox Ford, Ezra Pound, Three Mountains Press.

Further Information: During his time at 74 rue du Cardinal Lemoine Hemingway also rented a top floor garret at nearby 39 rue Descartes, where he could write without distraction. This was also the building where poet Paul Verlaine died in 1896. Plaques mark both these addresses, the latter commemorating the sojourns of both Hemingway and Verlaine. In 1923 Hemingway's first book, *Three Stories & Ten Poems*, was published

privately by Robert McAlmon's Contact Editions. During the autumn of 1923, Ernest and Hadley Hemingway moved to Toronto where Hemingway worked on assignments for the *Toronto Daily Star*, and where their only child John was born on 10 October. They had planned to stay a year, but realising their mistake, they returned, homesick for their lifestyle in Paris, after only four months. On 8 February 1924, the Hemingways signed the lease for an apartment at 113 rue Notre-Dame-des-Champs (now demolished) in Montparnasse. In 1925 Hôtel Jacob became Hôtel Jacob et d'Angleterre, changing again a few years later to Hôtel d'Angleterre. At 71 rue du Cardinal Lemoine James Joyce finished *Ulysses* in September 1921.

Select Bibliography: *Three Stories & Ten Poems* (1923); *In our time* (1924); *The Sun Also Rises* (1926); *The Torrents of Spring* (1926); *A Moveable Feast* (Restored Edition, 2009); *Ernest Hemingway on Paris* (2010, first published in *The Toronto Star*, 1922–23).

Further Reading: M. Reynolds, *Hemingway: The Paris Years* (Norton, 1999).

Ernest and Hadley's wedding day at Horton Bay, Michigan, 1921

MICHEL DE MONTAIGNE

PLACE PAUL PAINLEVÉ

(Métro: Cluny – La Sorbonne)

STATUE OF MONTAIGNE

ESSAYIST AND MORALIST

FIRST OF THE GREAT

CONFESSIONAL WRITERS

The twenty-first century is full of people who are full of themselves. A half-hour's trawl through the online ocean of blogs, tweets, tubes, spaces, faces, pages and pods brings up thousands of individuals, fascinated by their own personalities and shouting for attention. They go on about themselves; they diarise, and chat, and upload photographs of everything they do. ... This idea – writing about oneself to create a mirror in which other people recognise their own humanity – has not existed forever. It had to be invented. And, unlike many cultural inventions, it can be traced to a single person: Michel Eyquem de Montaigne.
Sarah Bakewell, *How to Live: A Life of Montaigne in one question and twenty attempts at an answer* (2011)

Detail from the statue of Montaigne in Place Paul Painlevé

It was not until he reached his mid-thirties that Montaigne (1533–1592) metamorphosed into the man we think of today. In his early adulthood he was simply a minor magistrate at the *parlement de Bordeaux*, and a young nobleman who looked after his family's estates in the Dordogne. But in 1569 or early 1570 – the date is uncertain – he almost died in a riding accident. One of his servants had ploughed his horse into him from behind, which struck 'like a thunderbolt' and knocked Montaigne to the ground where he lay unconscious. His servants carried him home on horseback as he vomited and coughed up blood. Back home at his château he slipped in and out of consciousness. 'It seemed to me', he wrote, 'that my life was hanging only by the tip of my lips.' He described this as 'an idea that was only floating on the surface of my soul ... in truth not only free from distress but mingled with that sweet feeling that people have who let themselves slide into sleep.' He was convinced he was going to have 'a very happy death'. But Montaigne didn't die. He had touched death and tasted it in a near death experience, but it changed his life completely.

He renounced his post at the *parlement* where he had worked for thirteen years. Shortly afterwards, around 1572, he began writing his *Essays*. For his writing retreat he chose one of the towers of his château complete with toilet, bedroom and his library with more than a thousand volumes. On the roof beams of the main chamber he painted classical quotations such as Pliny the Elder's 'Only one thing is certain: that nothing is certain | And nothing is more wretched or arrogant than man.' On a wall in the side chamber to his library he had a Latin inscription painted:

> In the year of Christ 1571, at the age of thirty-eight, on the last day of February, anniversary of his birth, Michel de Montaigne, long weary of the servitude of the court and of public employments, while still entire, retired to the bosom of the learned Virgins [the Muses], where in calm and freedom from all cares he will spend what little remains of his life now more than half run out. If the fates permit he will complete this abode, this sweet ancestral retreat; and he has consecrated it to his freedom, tranquillity, and leisure.

And so Montaigne turned his life around, living only for himself as much as was possible, and recording his personal insight on humanity through his *Essays*, works that would leave an indelible impression on readers and writers throughout history. His subjects ranged from drunkenness to smells and odours, from friendship to cruelty, from the art of conversation to the way his dog's ears twitched when it was dreaming. Today he is rightly acknowledged as the creator of the modern essay form. 'Don't read him as children do, for amusement,' wrote Flaubert, 'nor as the ambitious do, to be instructed. No, read him *in order to live*.'

Montaigne suffered from kidney-stone attacks and, after an attack in 1592 that left him with a serious throat infection, he died, aged fifty-nine, from a stroke or suffocation.

See Also: Gustave Flaubert.

Further Information: Montaigne was born at the Château de Montaigne in the Dordogne in 1533 where he spoke only Latin until he was six. He was sent to college in Bordeaux where he studied under Scottish humanist scholar, George Buchanan. He went on to study law, obtained a post at the *parlement de Bordeaux*, and married in 1565. He was elected Mayor of Bordeaux in 1581. Château de Montaigne is situated in the commune of Saint-Michel-de-Montaigne in the Dordogne. The original fourteenth-century château was destroyed by fire in 1885, but it has been completely rebuilt. Montaigne's original tower survived the fire and is open to the public. His statue in Place Paul Painlevé was sculpted in white marble by Paul Landowski (1896–1961) in 1934, but was replaced in 1988 with a bronze copy.

Select Bibliography: *The Complete Works: Essays, Travel Journal, Letters* (Everyman, 2003).

Further Reading: S. Bakewell, *How to Live: A Life of Montaigne in one question and twenty attempts at an answer* (Vintage, 2011).

Tour de Montaigne at Saint-Michel-de-Montaigne in the Dordogne

ELLIOT PAUL

5 RUE DE LA HUCHETTE

(Métro: St-Michel)

LE CAVEAU DE LA HUCHETTE

FORMERLY HÔTEL DU CAVEAU

FORMER RESIDENCE OF ELLIOT PAUL

AMERICAN JOURNALIST AND

CO-EDITOR OF *TRANSITION*

It was on a narrow side street on the way to the Bastille quarter where I found the laundry for men with only one shirt.
One winter week-end, Georges, the garçon, always depressed by stretches of bad weather, got boiled on Saturday night, and in attempting to cut his throat spilled blood all over my laundry ... Monsieur Léonard [the accordion player] then led me to the Blanchisserie des Imprévoyants (Laundry for the Non-foresighted), where conversing or reading, naked from the waist up, on crude benches placed around the wall, about a dozen men were waiting unhurriedly. ... Some looked wasted, a few depraved, others thoughtful and resentful, one or two philosophic. ... A small old man with stained silver beard was murmuring over a volume of Verlaine. Four tramps were playing belotte with greasy cards. ...
The other occupants of the room had gathered around Monsieur Léonard and his accordion. Their desire for music was too insistent to be denied; so Léonard unslung his instrument ...
I went out for liquor and brought back a bottle of cognac and a gallon of red wine. At seven o'clock that evening, four of the tramps were still standing.
Elliot Paul, *The Last Time I Saw Paris* (1942)

First edition, 1942

the Paris street where he lived in the twenties and thirties. In the summer of 1923 he moved into two rooms on the top floor of the Hôtel du Caveau and stayed there for eighteen years. 'There', he wrote, 'I found Paris.'
Paul had already published three novels by the time he arrived in Paris to start work as a journalist on the Paris editions of the *Chicago Tribune* and later the *New York Herald*. One of the literary critics on the *Tribune* was Eugene Jolas (1894–1952), who left the paper in 1927 and, together with his wife Maria, founded the literary magazine *transition*. Paul joined them as co-editor and helped in the running of it, a move that brought him in close contact with *transition*'s contributors, including James Joyce and Gertrude Stein.
According to Stein, Paul wrote the 'first seriously popular estimation of her work'. Needless to say she was very fond of him, and often reminisced about the evenings when he would take up his

E lliot Paul (1891–1958) was a journalist and author best remembered today for his book *The Last Time I Saw Paris*, a memoir about the daily life and characters on Rue de la Huchette,

accordion and play her 'favourite ditty', 'The Trail of the Lonesome Pine'.
'Elliot Paul was a new englander', she wrote in *The Autobiography of Alice B. Toklas,*

> but he was a saracen, a saracen such as you sometimes see in the villages of France where the strain from some Crusading ancestor's dependents still survives. Elliot Paul was such a one. He had an element not of mystery but of evanescence, actually little by little he appeared and then as slowly he disappeared.

Above: Le Caveau de la Huchette (Photo: Celette)
Below: Rue de la Huchette, late 19th century

According to Paul's friends, he had a tendency to suddenly disappear from the city without warning, these disappearances possibly coinciding with the arrival of his royalty cheques. In 1931 he took flight to Ibiza, where he lived until 1936 during what he described as 'the most soul-stirring adventure of my disorderly life'. Forced to flee during the Spanish Civil War he later wrote about his experience in *The Life and Death of a Spanish Town.*

With the outbreak of World War II Paul returned to America where he continued to write books and screenplays. The film rights of *The Last Time I Saw Paris* were sold to Hollywood, but sadly it was only the title that made it onto the screen for a film loosely based on F. Scott Fitzgerald's 'Babylon Revisited'. Elliot Paul married five times and had one son. When he died in 1958 aged sixty-seven, he had published over thirty books.

See Also: *Paris Tribune, transition,* Eugene Jolas, Gertrude Stein, F. Scott Fitzgerald, James Joyce.

Further Information: The building that once housed the Hôtel du Caveau dates back

to the sixteenth century and has a labyrinth of cellars and subterranean passages. During the French Revolution it was known as 'Caveau de la Terreur' because of the trials and executions that took place there. After World War II it became a celebrated jazz venue said to have inspired Liverpool's famous Cavern Club.

Select Bibliography: *The Life and Death of a Spanish Town* (1937); *The Last Time I Saw Paris* (1942); *Summer in December* (1945); *Linden on the Saugus Branch* (1946).

SHAKESPEARE AND COMPANY

37 RUE DE LA BÛCHERIE

(Métro: St-Michel)

ENGLISH-LANGUAGE BOOKSHOP

FOUNDED BY GEORGE WHITMAN

I live for the day when I'll have a bookstore to embellish this workaday world. I now own one of the best private libraries in the Latin Quarter and, living as I do on less than a dollar a day, I have accumulated a small capital augmented by English lessons and occasional book sales. I've talked with Sylvia Beach, the daughter of a minister from Princeton, New Jersey, who started a bookstore in Paris that became the rendezvous of André Gide, James Joyce, and the most famous writers of Europe. There is a possibility that she would consent to go into business with me – although I've been avoiding offers of partnership, it would be an honor and a privilege to work with Sylvia Beach, should she decide to re-open Shakespeare and Company.
George Whitman, Journal entry,
Spring 1950.

Since its birth in 1951, this bookshop has held a prominent place in the Parisian literary world, with a peculiar mindset all of its own, an eccentricity it owes solely to the free spirit of its late founder, George Whitman. Born in East Orange, New Jersey, in 1913, Whitman grew up in Salem, Massachusetts, and he opened his first second-hand bookshop in Taunton, Massachusetts. During WWII he worked as an army medical technician, which involved a posting to the Arctic Circle for almost two years. In 1946, having sold his bookshop, he sailed to Europe and settled in Paris where he began studying at the Sorbonne under the GI Bill. 'For the first time since the War,' he wrote in his journal, 'life has regained its colors of romance.'

In June 1947 he opened a lending library called the Librairie Franco-Américaine on Boulevard de Courcelles. The following year he opened another from his room at the Hôtel de Suez on Boulevard Saint-Michel, where he first met American poet Lawrence Ferlinghetti, who remembered George 'seated in an armchair in the middle of his tiny room in this third-rate hotel. Books were piled from floor to ceiling on all four sides.'

In 1951 Whitman acquired the premises of a former grocery shop, with a clear view of Notre Dame, on Rue de la Bûcherie. 'I almost didn't take it when I learned that the building had been condemned,' reflected George. 'But then I found out it had been condemned in 1870, so I decided to take a chance on its holding up for a few more decades.' He named his bookshop Le Mistral. The bookshop prospered and also evolved

117

into a meeting place for Paris anglophones and literary exiles. In 1964, after the death of Sylvia Beach, Whitman changed the name of the shop to Shakespeare and Company in homage to her legendary shop that closed on Rue de l'Odéon in 1941.

Paris publisher John Calder recalls in *The Garden of Eros* that:

> Sylvia had visited Whitman on previous occasions and once gifted him a brass plaque reading 'Shakespeare & Company – Writers' Guest House', giving him permission to use the name for his shop. Although the locations of the old and the new Shakespeare bookshops are about a mile apart, George Whitman never did anything to reduce the impression visitors got that the two bookshops were one and the same. If directly challenged, he would admit the truth. … There was much mythomania in George Whitman, but with time he has become enough of a myth himself, and a famous Parisian character … He nevertheless gave his life to books and bookselling and, after a little carping, is due much credit for it.'

Today Shakespeare and Company, apart from its name, has no supposed connection with the literary world of Sylvia Beach. It is solely the post-war creation of George Whitman and, latterly, his only daughter, Sylvia (named after Sylvia Beach). George Whitman died a literary legend in 2011, at the age of ninety-eight, at his apartment above the shop. He is buried in Paris's Cimetière du Père Lachaise.

See Also: Sylvia Beach.

Further Information: George Whitman always encouraged aspiring writers to live

and work among his books, and since 1951 over 30,000 fledgling writers have taken up his offer. Lawrence Ferlinghetti went on to co-found the City Lights bookstore in San Francisco in 1953.

Further Reading: K. Halverson (ed.), *Shakespeare and Company, Paris: A History of the Rag & Bone Shop of the Heart* (Distributed Art Publishers, 2016); J. Calder, *The Garden of Eros: The Story of the Paris Expatriates and the Post-War Literary Scene* (Alma Books Ltd., 2014).

Above: A photo-booth picture of a young George Whitman. Below: George outside his bookshop in the mid-1950s

GEORGE ORWELL

6 RUE DU POT DE FER

(Métro: Place Monge)

FORMER LODGINGS OF

GEORGE ORWELL

A SOJOURN THAT INSPIRED

DOWN AND OUT IN PARIS AND LONDON,

HIS FIRST FULL-LENGTH WORK

George Orwell

Writing is bosh. There is only one way to make money at writing, and that is to marry a publisher's daughter. But you would make a good waiter if you shaved that moustache off.
George Orwell, *Down and Out in Paris and London* (1933)

Today George Orwell (1903–1950) can be ranked among the world's great essayists. He was amusing, engaging and disturbing, with journalistic values reminiscent of Daniel Defoe and William Cobbett, and is chiefly remembered today for his two political allegories of the 1940s: *Animal Farm* and *Nineteen Eighty-Four*. The latter is a book whose impact on modern culture was so great that its phrases and terminology have passed into the English language. Born Eric Blair, in Bengal, in 1903, Orwell was a complex and enigmatic man. Educated at Eton, he joined the Indian Imperial Police when he was just nineteen years old. After a five-year tour of duty in Burma he returned home on leave a thoroughly discontented young man; but with aspirations of becoming a writer, he headed – like many literary hopefuls before him – for Paris in the spring of 1928 where he rented a shabby little room in the Latin Quarter. However, few of his articles and stories were published in Paris, and with his

writing career virtually at a standstill, and most of his possessions pawned, his Russian friend Boris, a former waiter, found him a job in the kitchens of a large hotel. It was a miserable and poorly paid job, but one that would eventually find its way into the pages of *Down and Out in Paris and London*:

It was amusing to look round the filthy little scullery and think that only a double door was between us and the dining-room. There sat the customers in all their splendour – spotless table-cloths, bowls of flowers, mirrors and gilt cornices and painted cherubim; and here, just a few feet away, we in our disgusting filth. For it really was disgusting filth. There was no time to sweep the floor till evening, and we slithered about in a compound of soapy water, lettuce-leaves, torn paper and trampled food. A dozen waiters with their coats off, showing their sweaty armpits, sat at the table mixing salads and sticking their thumbs into the cream pots. The room had a dirty, mixed smell of food and sweat. ... In the kitchen the dirt was worse. ... [A French cook] is an artist, but his art is not cleanliness. To a certain extent he is even dirty because he is an artist, for food, to look smart, needs dirty treatment. When a steak, for instance, is brought up for the head cook's inspection, he does not handle it with a fork. He picks it up in his fingers and slaps it down, runs his thumb round the dish and licks it to taste the gravy… In very cheap restaurants it is different; there, the same trouble is not taken over the food, and it is just forked out of the pan and flung on to a plate, without handling. Roughly speaking, the more one pays for food, the more sweat and spittle one is obliged to eat with it.

Orwell returned to England in December 1929 where, assuming the garb of a tramp, he studied the conditions of the lowest levels of society. This was a spell of misery that would also find its way into *Down and Out in Paris and London*. A signed first edition sold for £86,000 in 2010.

Further Information: In his book Orwell gave Rue du Pot de Fer the fictional name of Rue du Coq d'Or. 'Hotel X', Orwell's place of employment in the novel, was Hôtel Lottie, No 7 rue Castiglione.

Rue du Pot de Fer

PROSPER MÉRIMÉE

25 RUE TOURNEFORT

(Métro: Place Monge)

**FORMER HOME OF
PROSPER MÉRIMÉE
NOVELIST AND PLAYWRIGHT
AND AUTHOR OF THE NOVELLA
*CARMEN***

She was wearing a very short skirt, below which her white silk stockings – with more than one hole in them – and her dainty red morocco shoes, fastened with flame-coloured ribbons, were clearly seen. She had thrown her mantilla back, to show her shoulders, and a great bunch of acacia that was thrust into her chemise. She had another acacia blossom in the corner of her mouth, and she walked along, swaying her hips, like a filly from the Cordova stud farm. In my country anybody who had seen a woman dressed in that fashion would have crossed himself.
Prosper Mérimée, *Carmen* (1845)

Prosper Mérimée (1803–1870) is famous for three things: his novella, *Carmen*; proposing marriage to Mary Shelley while she was recovering from smallpox in Paris; and being appointed the second Inspector General of Historic Monuments, a job he described as 'a voice crying in the wilderness.'
His greatest literary achievements were his novellas *Colomba* (1840) and *Carmen* (1845), Bizet's opera of which, according to Mérimée's biographer, Alan Raitt, is 'no more than an emasculated and prettified version of Mérimée's tale'. He was also a dramatist, translator, short story writer, historian and passionate letter writer, whose surviving correspondence totals over 5000 letters, including the famous *Lettres à*

Carmen – illustration by Luc for *Journal Amusant*, 1875

une inconnue (Letters to an Unknown) which were published posthumously in 1873. He was also an Anglophile, an experienced traveller who travelled widely in England and Spain, an early translator of Russian literature in France, a lover of George Sand and a man with a wide range of friends, including Charles Sainte-Beuve, Ivan Turgenev, Adolphe Thiers, Napoleon III, and Stendhal, whose first impression of Mérimée was:

a young man in a grey frock-coat, very ugly, and with a turned-up nose ... This young man had something insolent and extremely unpleasant about him. His eyes, small and without expression, had always the same look, and this look was ill-natured. ... Such was my first impression of the best of my present friends. I am not too sure of his heart, but I am sure of his talents. ... His mother has a good deal of French wit and a superior intelligence. Like her son, it seems to me that she might give way to emotion once a year.

Mérimée, the son of a painter, was born in Paris. Although he studied law, he never practised, becoming more inclined towards a literary career. It was a career that began with a hoax – *Le Théâtre de Clara Gazul* (1825) – comprising six short plays, which purported to be translations from the writings of 'Clara Gazul', a fictitious Spanish actress. These were followed by another hoax entitled *La Guzla* (1827), supposedly translations of ancient Illyrian ballads of murder, revenge and vampires, written under the pseudonym of Hyacinthe Maglanowich. His only novel, *Chronique du règne de Charles IX* (1829), was largely inspired by the popularity at that time of Sir Walter Scott, whose works fostered Mérimée's enthusiasm for mysticism and historical fiction. The remainder of his writings were mostly short stories and novellas, many of which were masterpieces of the genre. However, his biographer Alan Raitt observes that:

Mérimée's place in the history of French culture is a lonely one. ... none of [his] works has quite the spark of genius to lift Mérimée into the first rank of authors. ... Only in the evolution of the short story can he be said to occupy a key position, since he not only developed a new technique of concision and concentration, copied by most subsequent practitioners of the art, but also produced some of the finest tales in any language. ... Today Mérimée is as much a living force as any writer of his time.

See Also: George Sand, Charles Sainte-Beuve, Ivan Turgenev, Stendhal.

Further Information: Prosper Mérimée died in 1870, aged sixty-six. His achievements in literature were considerable, but his capability as an inspector of monuments should not be forgotten. Poitou's Abbey Church of Saint-Savin, Burgundy's Vézelay Abbey and Picardy's Laon Cathedral are only standing today because of Mérimée's efforts. He was also instrumental in saving much of the architectural heritage of Avignon, Caen, Cunault, Narbonne and Saulieu. 'Modern tourists,' wrote Julian Barnes,

> seeing a distant spire pointing to the heavens, spotting the glisten of pepper-pot towers half-lost in woodland, or gazing up at the ribbed vaulting of an airy abbey, should pause and give thanks to the man without whom one French town after another might have ended up looking like Carpentras. And yes, I have been to Carpentras. All I can remember is the pizza I ate there.

Select Bibliography: *Le Théâtre de Clara Gazul* (1825); *La Guzla* (1827); *Chronique du règne de Charles IX* (1829); *Mateo Falcone* (1829); *Mosaïque* (1833); *La Vénus d'Ille* (1837); *Colomba* (1840); *Carmen* (1845); *Lokis* (1869).

Further Reading: A. Raitt, *Prosper Mérimée* (Eyre & Spottiswoode, 1970); A. Symons, *The Symbolist Movement in Literature* (Fyfield, 2014).

Prosper Mérimée in 1829

BERNARDIN DE SAINT-PIERRE

57 RUE CUVIER

(Métro: Jussieu/Place Monge)

JARDIN DES PLANTES

STATUE OF BERNARDIN DE

SAINT-PIERRE

WRITER AND NATURALIST

REMEMBERED FOR HIS NOVEL

OF INNOCENT LOVE,

PAUL ET VIRGINIE

> *They believed the world ended at the shores of their own island, and all their ideas and all their affections were confined within its limits. Their mutual tenderness, and that of their mothers, employed all the energies of their minds. Their tears had never been called forth by tedious application to useless sciences. Their minds had never been wearied by lessons of morality, superfluous to bosoms unconscious of ill. They had never been taught to steal, because every thing with them was in common: or not to be intemperate, because their simple food was left to their own discretion; or not to lie, because they had nothing to conceal ...*
> Bernardin de Saint-Pierre, *Paul et Virginie* (1788)

Bernardin Saint-Pierre's novel, *Paul et Virginie*, tells the story of two children brought up by their mothers on the tropical island paradise of Île de France. They fall in love and intend to marry, but when Virginie reaches puberty she is sent to France to live with her great-aunt and to be educated. On her return to the island her ship is wrecked off the coast in a storm. A sailor offers to carry her ashore to safety, but he insists she must first remove her cumbersome clothes. Virginie's newfound Western

modesty forbids her exposure in her undergarments, whereupon she drowns. Paul dies later from grief.

First published in 1788 *Paul et Virginie* went straight to the hearts of the public and became a bestseller. Readers, novelists and critics alike were enraptured by this idyllic tale of childhood innocence in an earthly paradise corrupted and destroyed by the moral values of Western civilisation. Today it may seem overly didactic and sentimental, but since the captivation of its eighteenth-century audience there have been hundreds of editions published and it has been translated into dozens of languages. Honoré de Balzac mentions the novel in *Old Goriot*, as does Gustave Flaubert in *A Simple Soul*, Guy de Maupassant in *Bel Ami*, Maria Edgeworth in *Belinda*, Thomas Hardy in *Jude the Obscure* and Charles Dickens in *Little Dorritt*. It has inspired poems, songs, ballets, operas and plays, as well as igniting a fashion for naming children Paul and Virginie.

Jacques-Henri Bernardin de Saint-Pierre (1737–1814) was born into a middle-class family in Le Havre. When he was twelve, his schooling, which had always been troublesome, ended abruptly, and he joined his uncle's ship which was setting sail for the Caribbean island of Martinique. It was his first taste of an island paradise, but he returned from the voyage 'more disgusted with my uncle, with the vessel and with trade than with my teacher and his college'. On his return he trained as an engineer and joined the army, seeing action in Germany during the Seven Years War. While in Germany, he was punished for insubordination and he returned to France – a move that marked the beginning of a peripatetic existence throughout Europe – becoming a geographer in Malta, a journalist in Holland and an engineer in Russia.

In 1768 he joined an expedition to Madagascar but abandoned it at Île de France, the French colonial name for today's Mauritius. On the island he worked as an engineer, but he also catalogued its geology, flora and fauna, making a detailed survey of the countryside, which included recording its brutal treatment of slaves and the corruption of its white settlers. He returned to France in 1770, publishing *Voyage à l'Île de France* three years later. *Études de la nature (Studies of Nature)* followed in 1788, but it was with *Paul et Virginie* that he gained celebrity, prestige and wealth. He later made friends with Rousseau, whose doctrines had a considerable influence on him, and whose biography he wrote in 1820.

Today Bernardin de Saint-Pierre is chiefly remembered for *Paul et Virginie*, but during his later life he was recognised as a celebrated naturalist and philosopher. Literary history will always equate him with paradise and a style that he believed should be 'simple' and 'naïve', and 'have no other eloquence than the eloquence of the heart'.

See Also: Jean-Jacques Rousseau.

Further Information: Bernardin de Saint-Pierre's statue is near entrance No. 57, off Rue Cuvier. Turn left off the cobbled courtyard and follow the path running behind the Grand Amphithéâtre du Muséum National d'Histoire Naturelle. The statue is across a grassy area at eleven o'clock from the rear door of the Amphitheatre. Jardin des Plantes is one of the seven departments of the Muséum National d'Histoire Naturelle (National Museum of Natural History). In 1625 Guy de la Brosse, physician to Louis XIII, founded a garden for the cultivation of medicinal herbs. It was opened to the public in 1640 and became known as the Jardin du Roi (King's Garden). During the Revolution the Jardin became the property of the people and acquired its present name. Bernardin de Saint-Pierre became its director in 1792, and the following year he was involved in the creation of the Muséum National d'Histoire

Bernardin de Saint-Pierre

Naturelle as a centre for scientific study. He also added a menagerie to exhibit wild animals, most of which were killed for the pot to feed starving Parisians during the Prussian siege of Paris in 1870–1871. Bernardin de Saint-Pierre is buried in Père Lachaise, Division 11.

Select Bibliography: *Paul and Virginia* (Peter Owen, 2005).

6th

Arrondissement

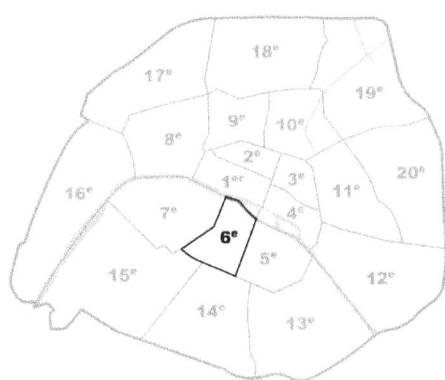

GEORGE DU MAURIER

PLACE SAINT-ANDRÉ-DES-ARTS

(Métro: St-Michel)

SETTING FOR THE FICTIONAL
PLACE SAINT-ANATOLE-DES-ARTS
IN GEORGE DU MAURIER'S
NOVEL *TRILBY*, WHICH CREATED
THE LEGEND OF SVENGALI

[He was] a tall, bony individual of any age between thirty and forty-five, of Jewish aspect, well-featured but sinister. He was very shabby and dirty, and wore a red beret and a large velveteen cloak, with a big metal clasp at the collar. His thick, heavy, languid, lusterless black hair fell down behind his ears on to his shoulders, in that musician-like way that is so offensive to the normal Englishman. He had bold, brilliant black eyes, with long, heavy lids, a thin, sallow face, and a beard of burnt-up black, which grew almost from
his under eyelids; and over it his moustache, a shade lighter, fell in two long spiral twists. He went by the name of Svengali.
George du Maurier, *Trilby* (1894)

Many of us are familiar with the Trilby hat, but fewer recall the novel that inspired its name. When it was first published in 1894 *Trilby* had everything the reading public desired: the myth of bohemia, scandal, nudity, promiscuity, unrequited love, ambiguous morality, mesmerism, and the sinister Jew, Svengali. It also introduced the phrase 'in the altogether'. Despite its anti-Semitic overtones, in its first year of publication it sold over 200,000 copies in America alone. It was adapted for the stage and by 1896 there were more than twenty different productions running around the globe. Trilbyana, or Trilby-Mania, went berserk and made George du Maurier rich. There were Trilby sweets

Place Saint André-des-Arts. *c.*1866 by Charles Marville (1813–1879)

and lozenges, Trilby sausages, Trilby hams, Trilby high-heeled shoes, Trilby hearth-brushes, Trilby sheet music, Trilby soap, Trilby toothpaste and, most famously, the Trilby hat. 'The phenomenon grew and grew,' remarked du Maurier's friend, Henry James.

The novel is set in the Latin Quarter where Trilby O'Ferrall works as an artist's model and where she befriends three bohemian painters in their studio at the Place Saint-Anatole-des-Arts, the setting for the first half. Trilby is beautiful, innocent and charming, and everybody falls in love with her. Their daily lives together, surrounded by the colourful characters of the Latin Quarter, epitomise the myth of bohemian Paris. But before long Trilby falls under the spell of the mysterious Svengali, whose hypnotic powers shape her into a

virtuoso singer destined for a tragic end. George du Maurier was born in Paris in 1834, the eldest son of French scientist and inventor, Louis Mathurin, and Ellen Clarke, daughter of a former actress and mistress of the Duke of York. George was encouraged to study chemistry, but after his father's death in 1856 he decided to study art in Paris. Throughout his life he was primarily an artist who became an illustrator after losing the sight of an eye due to a detached retina. He contributed caricatures and illustrations regularly to *Punch* and illustrated many of the books of the Victorian masters, including Thomas Hardy, Elizabeth Gaskell and Henry James. In the 1890s, when he was in his late fifties, he began writing novels, the most acclaimed of which, in 1894, was *Trilby*. Inspired by Henri Murger's *Scènes de la vie de bohème*,

A 1902 advertising poster for *Trilby*

George du Maurier

John Barrymore in the title role of the
1931 screen adaptation of the novel *Trilby,*
renamed *Svengali,* directed by Archie Mayo

it recalls his own experiences as an art
student in bohemian Paris in the 1850s.
In 1896, aged sixty-two, he suffered the
same fate as Svengali, dying from heart
failure.

His memorial in London's St John-at-
Hampstead churchyard is inscribed with
the last two lines of *Trilby*:
A little trust that when we die,
We reap our sowing! And so – goodbye!

See Also: Henry James, Henri Murger.

Further Information: George du Maurier
was the grandfather of the English novelist
Daphne du Maurier (1907–1989). The name
'du Maurier' was an invention of George du
Maurier's grandfather, Robert Mathurin, a
convicted fraudster with delusions of grandeur who wanted to give his family name an
aristocratic image.

Select Bibliography: *Peter Ibbetson* (1891),
Trilby (1894), *The Martian* (1897).

Further Reading: D. du Maurier, *The du
Mauriers* (Virago, 2004); R. Kelly, *The Art of
George du Maurier* (Scolar Press, 1996); E.
Rosenberg, *From Shylock to Svengali: Jew-
ish Stereotypes in English Fiction* (Stanford
University Press, 1960).

THE BEAT HOTEL

9 RUE GÎT–LE–COEUR

(Métro: St-Michel)

SITE OF HÔTEL RACHOU

ALSO KNOWN AS THE BEAT HOTEL

Chester Himes with Jemima, his 1934 Fiat roadster, in Paris, 1963

We got a front room on the second floor, above the proprietors, an elderly couple from the provinces with an old-fashioned, passé awe and respect for writers and artists and a genuine sympathy and admiration for any young woman who had dedicated her body to their support. Monsieur M. L. Rachou, the proprietor, was a mountain of a man who performed the duties of a chambermaid, janitor and porter in a silent, slow and patient manner, never getting upset if roomers wet their beds, painted on the floor and walls, defecated on the stairs or were late with their rent. Mme. Rachou, a small, gray-haired, pleasant woman who had obviously been the belle of her village, took care of the tiny bistro on the ground floor, registered the guests and fed her man.

Chester Himes, from *My Life of Absurdity*

The Hôtel Rachou was a dosshouse for the creative mind, a cheap, run-down rooming house that became popular with writers and artists in the fifties and early sixties. There were nine categories of hotel in Paris and Hôtel Rachou was in the lowest: squat toilets with newspaper for toilet paper, ancient plumbing, a solitary bath, leaking roofs, perilous electrics and subsiding floors. But it was dirt cheap; each room had a gas ring to cook on, and Madame Rachou, who had a penchant for artists, ran a small bistro on the ground floor where everyone could hang out. African American writer Chester Himes and his girlfriend lived there from spring 1956 until their departure for Majorca the

following year, missing the advent of the Beats by just a few weeks. Had they met, one wonders what they would have made of each other.

Himes was born in Missouri in 1909, and began his writing career in the Ohio Penitentiary where he spent nearly nine years for armed robbery. His first novel, *If He Hollers Let Him Go* (1945), explored racial prejudice in California, and *Cast the First Stone* (1952) recalled his prison experiences. He first arrived in Paris in 1953 with four respectable novels under his belt, but none had brought him recognition or financial security. In Paris he started writing hard-boiled detective novels, which in Europe were classed as important existential fiction, and had a wide audience. But it was his Harlem thrillers, written between 1957 and 1969, featuring two black detectives, Grave Digger Johnson and Coffin Ed Jones, which were to eclipse all his earlier work. In 1958, *La reine des pommes* (republished as *A Rage in Harlem*, 1957) gained him the Grand Prix de Littérature Policière, France's most prestigious award for crime and detective fiction. Himes never returned to settle in America. 'Now I was a French writer', he wrote in his autobi-

In the bar of the Beat Hotel (photo Harold Chapman)

ography, 'the United States of America could kiss my ass.' He died on Spain's Costa Blanca in 1984.

Shortly after Himes's departure from the Hôtel Rachou in September 1957, most of the founding members of the Beat movement began staying there on and off until 1963, notable among these being Allen Ginsberg, William Burroughs, Peter Orlovsky and Gregory Corso. Ginsberg would write some of his best work there, including 'To Aunt Rose', 'At Apollinaire's Grave' and sections of 'Kaddish'. Corso wrote 'Bomb' there, and Burroughs finished *Naked Lunch*.

Ginsberg arrived in November 1957, after six months of travels in Europe, including Tangier, Barcelona, Florence, and Ischia in the Gulf of Naples where he met W.H. Auden and his friends, whom he described, after being insulted by Auden, as 'a bunch of shits'. Ginsberg and his lover, Peter Orlovsky, together with the poet Gregory Corso, stayed at the Hôtel Rachou for ten months, all living in the same room and sleeping in the same bed on the third floor overlooking the street. At this time Ginsberg had written only one book, *Howl and other poems*, but it had made him famous, at least in America, because its San Francisco publisher, Lawrence Ferlinghetti, had been arrested on charges of obscenity. The court finally ruled that *Howl* was not an obscene book, but the publicity was priceless.

In Paris, like poets that had gone before him, Ginsberg wrote in cafes such as Le Select on Boulevard du Montparnasse, where he worked on one of his finest poems, 'Kaddish', in which he mourns his mother Naomi. He also carried with him the manuscript that would eventually become *Naked Lunch*, written by his friend and former lover, William Burroughs, who was still an unknown living in Tangier. Ginsberg had tried in vain to get Maurice Girodias's Olympia Press to publish *Naked Lunch*, but the manuscript was in such a mess, 'just fragment after fragment strung together', wrote Ginsberg, that Girodias rejected it.

Born into a wealthy Missouri family, Burroughs spent his errant youth evading work and using his family's allowance to buy drugs and sex. In 1953, when he was in his late thirties, he published his first novel, *Junkie: Confessions of an Unredeemed Drug Addict*, under the pen name William Lee. That same year he spent several months in Tangier, returning to settle there in November 1954, where, with his family's financial support, he worked on the manuscript of *Naked Lunch*. 'Compared to Tangier', writes writer Robert Ruark, 'Sodom was a church picnic', and for Burroughs, it offered a hedonistic excess like no other picnic on the planet. However, after three years of living in Tangier Burroughs had finally had enough. He wrote to Ginsberg asking him to reserve a room at the Hôtel Rachou. 'Must absolutely get out of here for my health,' he wrote. 'The place is plague-ridden … ' He arrived in Paris in early January of 1958.

Burroughs didn't really fit the template for the Beat Generation in appearance. He was older by about ten years, and wore a suit, a shirt and tie, steel-rimmed glasses and a grey felt hat, more reminiscent of an FBI agent than a Beat. Following Girodias's rejection of *Naked Lunch*, Burroughs sent the manuscript to Lawrence Ferlinghetti in San Francisco. Ferlinghetti also rejected it, but in the spring of 1959, a handful of its chapters were published in the American magazine, *Big Table*. They were declared obscene by the US Post Office, and promptly banned. The ensuing public outrage triggered scandalmonger Maurice Girodias into action. 'Dear Mr Bur-

Site of the Beat Hotel today

roughs,' he wrote, 'what about letting me have another look at *Naked Lunch*?' The manuscript was duly resubmitted and in July 1959 Girodias published the book. Ginsberg returned to America early that year.

Burroughs remained at Hôtel Rachou with his fellow Beats, including Englishman Brion Gysin, who introduced Burroughs to the cut-up technique, where text is cut up and rearranged, a practice that dates back to the 1920s when French poet Tristan Tzara pulled random words out of a hat to create poetry. Burroughs embraced the method, resulting in *The Soft Machine* and *The Ticket that Exploded* published by Olympia Press in 1961 and 1962 respectively. Burroughs and Gysin also spent many hours sitting with eyes closed in front of the Dreamachine, a device created by technician Ian Sommerville, which consists of a spinning, light-emitting cylinder that, it is claimed, alters consciousness. The Dreamachine is referred to by Burroughs in *The Ticket that Exploded* and *Nova Express*.

The Hôtel Rachou closed down in 1963 and the Beats moved on to new mind altering pastures. It has since been completely modernised and refurbished, and is now the Relais Hôtel du Vieux Paris. A plaque was unveiled outside the entrance in 2009, the fiftieth anniversary of *Naked Lunch*, commemorating the Beat Hotel and its clientele, whose anti-authoritarian vision went on to revolutionise American literature.

See Also: Café de Tournon, Olympia Press.

Further Information: Jack Kerouac never stayed at Hôtel Rachou, but he did visit Paris in April 1957. After sailing on a cargo ship from New York to Tangier, he travelled north through Spain and France and checked in to 'a dismal dirty cold hovel run by two Turkish pimps but the kindest fellows I'd met yet in Paris'. He visited all the usual tourist sites then caught the ferry from Dieppe to Newhaven, England, where immigration officers treated him with suspicion. 'I told them my story – I was going to London to pick up a royalty check from an English publisher and then on to New York on the *Île de France* – They didn't believe my story – I wasn't shaved, I had a pack on my back, I looked like a bum.' Luckily for Kerouac he had a magazine in his pack with an article about himself and Henry Miller. Immigration knew Miller as they had 'stopped him several years ago'. Kerouac was released with the provision that he leave the UK after one month.

In *The Old Patagonian Express*, Paul Theroux writes:

> At the age of fifty, with *On the Road* well behind him, [Jack Kerouac] decided to hitch-hike across America again. He was fatter now, and felt defeated, but he was convinced he could repeat his cross-country epic. So he left New York, seeking California. His menacing features were ineradicable, and times had changed. The lugubrious man reached New Jersey; there he stood for hours in the rain, trying to thumb a ride until, at last, he gave up and took a bus home.

Select Bibliography: Chester Himes: *If He Hollers Let Him Go* (1945); *A Rage in Harlem* (1957); *The Crazy Kill* (1959); *Pinktoes* (1961); *Cotton Comes to Harlem* (1965); *Blind Man with a Pistol* (1969); *Black on Black (1973).*

Allen Ginsberg: *Kaddish and Other Poems* (1961); *Reality Sandwiches* (1963); *The Yage Letters* (with William Burroughs, 1963); *Planet News* (1968); *Iron Horse* (1973); *Mind Breaths* (1978); *Deliberate Prose 1952–1995* (2000).

Gregory Corso: *The Vestal Lady on Brattle* (1955); *Bomb* (1958); *Gasoline* (1958); *The Happy Birthday of Death* (1960); *The American Express* (1961); *Mindfield* (1989).

William Burroughs: *Junkie* (1953); *Naked Lunch* (1959); *The Soft Machine* (1961); *The Wild Boys* (1971); *Exterminator!* (1973); *Cities of the Red Night* (1981); *Place of Dead Roads* (1983); *Queer* (1985).

Further Reading: B. Miles, *The Beat Hotel* (Grove Press, 2001), *Allen Ginsberg: Beat Poet* (Virgin, 2010); *William S. Burroughs: A Life* (Weidenfeld & Nicolson, 2014); H. Chapman, *The Beat Hotel* (Gris Banal, 1984); C. Himes, *My Life of Absurdity* (Doubleday, 1976).

JULES SANDEAU

21 RUE DES GRANDS-AUGUSTINS

(Métro: Odéon/St-Michel)

**FORMER HOME OF WRITER
JULES SANDEAU
COLLABORATOR AND LOVER
OF GEORGE SAND**

[He was] as adorable as a hummingbird from the perfumed savannahs ... If you only knew how much I love him, the poor child! How, from the first day, his expressive look, his sudden and candid movements, his timid gaucheness with me, made me want to see him, to examine him. I do not know the nature of my curiosity, but each day it became greater.
George Sand describing Jules Sandeau

Although Jules Sandeau (1811–1883) wrote novels and plays for almost half a century, his work today is overshadowed by his brief love affair with Aurore Dupin (later known as George Sand), with whom he co-authored the novel *Rose et Blanche*, published under the pseudonym Jules Sand in 1831. Dupin later took the first syllable of his surname for her *nom de plume*. Had she chosen another, history may well have overlooked him.

Aurore Dupin met Sandeau in July 1830, at Le Coudray, in northern France, during the turmoil and political unrest of the July Revolution. He was nineteen, and she was twenty-six. With her marriage heading for the rocks, the two lovers moved to Paris. Here they mingled with the literati and collaborated on a few stories, including their novel *Rose et Blanche*. At first, Aurore lived in her brother's apartment on Rue de Seine, later moving in with Sandeau to his apartment on Rue des Grands-Au-gustins. In her novel *Horace* (1840) she described it as 'made up of three rooms ... My balcony crowns the final storey of the house ... We could see, with one glance, the best part of the Seine's course, the length of the Louvre, yellow in the sun and sharp-edged against the blue sky.'

Towards the end of 1832 the relationship ended and Aurore Dupin's life as George Sand began. Although he is now remembered more for a love affair than for his writing, Jules Sandeau did have a fair amount of success with the dramatisations of his novels, the most successful of which was *Mademoiselle de la Seiglière* (1848).

See Also: George Sand.

Further Reading: A. Faktorovich, *The Romances of George Sand* (Anaphora, 2014).

21 rue des Grands-Augustins

GERTRUDE STEIN
AND ALICE B. TOKLAS

5 RUE CHRISTINE

(Métro: Mabillon/Odéon/St-Michel)

LAST PARIS HOME AND SALON

OF GERTRUDE STEIN AND

ALICE B. TOKLAS

She was slight and dark, with beautiful gray eyes hung with black lashes – and she had a drooping Jewish nose, and her eyelids drooped, and the corners of her mouth, and the lobes of her ears drooped under the black, folded Hebraic hair, weighted down as they were with long, heavy oriental earrings ... She looked like Leah, out of the Old Testament, in her half-Oriental get-up – her black hair – her barbaric chains and jewels – and her melancholy nose.

Mabel Dodge describing Alice B. Toklas in *Intimate Memories* (1933)

The Alice B. Toklas Cook Book, (1954)

In 1907 Gertrude Stein met and fell in love with San Francisco-born Alice B. Toklas who, before long, moved into the apartment and atelier Gertrude shared with her brother Leo at No. 27 rue de Fleurus. A few years later, Leo, who loathed Alice, left Paris in a fit of pique and returned to America. In 1937 the lease on the apartment expired, and Gertrude and Alice moved to a new apartment at No. 5 rue Christine. It was the last Paris home they would share together. During World War II they lived in their villa in Bilignin in the Rhône-Alpes region of Vichy France, and after the liberation of Paris they returned once more to Rue Christine. In 1945 Gertrude published *Wars I Have Seen*, an account of her wartime experiences, the following year dying suddenly after an unsuccessful operation for stomach cancer. Alice found herself alone after a relationship of nearly forty years.

In her widowhood, Alice steadfastly dealt with all Gertrude-related correspondence in her old-fashioned, spidery handwriting, scrupulously guarding her lover's literary reputation. Gertrude's will decreed that her art collection be left in trust with Alice until her death, with provision for the sale of some of the collection for her support and to fund the publication of Gertrude's unpublished manuscripts. Gertrude had never insured her art collection, claiming it was too expensive, but Alice did, although far below its value. With justification, Stein's heirs were concerned for their legacy, and when Alice sold some Picasso drawings at a bargain-basement price without consulting them, the collection was impounded in a bank vault by court order.

Alice's own career as a writer began when she became the author of two cookbooks and a memoir, the most successful of which was *The Alice B. Toklas Cookbook*, a combination of recipes

133

and reminiscences, published in 1954, containing her famous recipe for fudge made with hashish, which 'anyone could whip up on a rainy day'. By this time, she was growing old and frail, and was increasingly troubled by arthritis.

In 1954 the apartments on her block in Rue Christine were offered for sale to the tenants, but as Alice could not afford to buy, eviction proceedings were started, which ended up lasting for ten years. In 1964 an officer of the court finally arrived at Rue Christine to read out the eviction order. Alice was bedridden at the time, recovering from a broken hip. 'I was born in 1877,' she told the officer. 'If I leave this apartment it will be to go to Père Lachaise.'

She wasn't quite ready for Père Lachaise yet, though; and friends found her an apartment on Rue de la Convention, contributing what funds they could spare for her support. She died on 7 March 1967, just a few weeks short of her ninetieth birthday and is buried beside Gertrude Stein in Père Lachaise.

See Also: The American Hospital in Paris, No. 27 rue de Fleurus, Jardin du Luxembourg, Cimetière du Père Lachaise.

Further Information: Alice Toklas left her book royalties to her priest, but both Toklas and Stein were born Jewish. Stein was a non-practising Jew, and Toklas converted to Catholicism after Stein's death. During World War II they both supported Marshal Pétain, chief of Vichy France, the puppet-controlled government of Nazi Germany. Stein also produced some of Pétain's propaganda, which goes some way towards explaining why two Jewish Americans survived living in Nazi-occupied France. 'Gertrude was a real fascist,' said Picasso. 'She always had a weakness for Franco ... You know she wrote speeches for Pétain. Can you imagine it? An American, a Jewess, what's more.' After the war Pétain was condemned to death, a sentence which was later commuted to solitary confinement for life.

Further Reading: E. Burns (ed.), *Staying on Alone: Letters of Alice B. Toklas* (Norton, 1973); B. Will, *Unlikely Collaboration* (Columbia U.P., 2011); D. Souhami, *Gertrude and Alice* (Pandora, 1991); J. Malcolm, *Two Lives: Gertrude and Alice* (Yale, 2007).

5 Rue Christine

BORIS VIAN

33 RUE DAUPHINE

(Métro: Odéon/Mabillon)

HÔTEL D'AUBUSSON

FORMER CELLAR LOCALE OF

CLUB LE TABOU

JAZZ VENUE AND STAMPING GROUND

OF BORIS VIAN

JAZZ TRUMPETER, NOVELIST, POET

AND PLAYWRIGHT

On June 23, 1959, at ten in the morning, a black American author sneaked uninvited into a small cinema near the Champs-Elysées to watch the preview of a film made from one of his novels. ... In the darkened theatre, as the projector whirred, he had a heart attack and died.

The author was Boris Vian. He was thirty-nine and had long since been exposed as 'Vernon Sullivan', who wrote J'irai cracher sur vos tombes [I Shall Spit on Your Graves] in 1946. The first white Negro came from St-Germain-des-Prés.

James Campbell, *Paris Interzone* (1994)

The writings of Boris Vian (1920–1959), most of which went unrecognised during his short life, ranged from fantasy to realism, often with a snappy, hard-boiled and provocative dialogue. Also a jazz trumpeter, he epitomised the post-war generation of Parisian writers who clustered in the cafes and smoke-filled cellar clubs of Saint-Germain-des-Prés, whom he satirically portrayed in his novel, *L'Écume des jours (Froth on the Daydream)*. He wrote in many genres, from jazz journalism to drama, but he is best remembered today for his four controversial novels that were parodies of American-style popular fiction. They were written in the patois of an African American, and published under the pseudonym Vernon Sullivan.

Vian was born in 1920, the second of four children, in the well-heeled Paris suburb of Ville-d'Avray. As a child he developed rheumatic fever that left him suffering from a heart disease that would eventually kill him before he reached forty. He trained as an engineer, a career he eventually cast aside in favour of

Boris Vian

135

writing, and the jazz trumpet. In the early 1940s, together with his brothers and clarinettist Claude Abadie, he formed a semi-professional jazz orchestra known as 'Abadie-Vian', and began playing in the clubs of Saint-Germain-des-Prés. In 1943, by now an accomplished jazz trumpeter, he wrote his first novel, *Trouble dans les andains (Turmoil in the Swaths)*, which was not published until after his death. In 1947 he had several works published by Gallimard, including his tragic love story, *L'Écume des jours*. None of these sold well, however, but in 1947 his fortunes improved when he changed tack and set out to write a novel in the American style of popular fiction.

J'irai cracher sur vos tombes (I Shall Spit on Your Graves), a novel of sexual and racial conflict set in the United States, was written under the pseudonym of Vernon Sullivan, an ostensible African American writer, with Vian claiming to be the translator. The deception paid off and the book entered the bestseller list for 1947. The book went on to sell more than 100,000 copies and was eventually banned, but the hoax achieved its objective and three more Vernon Sullivan novels followed. In 1959 Vian entered a Paris cinema screening an adaptation of *I Shall Spit on Your Graves*, a film he had publicly denounced and the credits of which he wanted his name removed from. During the screening the Frenchman who had fantasised of being an African American died of a heart attack. He was thirty-nine years old.

See Also: Gaston Gallimard.

Further Information: Boris Vian is buried in an unmarked grave in the cemetery at Ville-d'Avray, Vian's birthplace.

Select Bibliography: Plays: *L'Équarrissage pour tous (The Knacker's ABC)* (1950); *Les Bâtisseurs d'empire (The Empire Builders)* (1959); Novels: *J'irai cracher sur vos tombes (I Shall Spit on Your Graves)* (1946); *L'Écume des jours (Froth on the Daydream)* (1947); *L'automne à Pékin (Autumn in Peking)* (1947); *Les morts ont tous la même peau (The Dead All Have the Same Skin)* (1947); Journalism: *Round About Close to Midnight: Selected Jazz Writings of Boris Vian* (1988).

Further Reading: J. Campbell, *Paris Interzone* (Minerva, 1995).

33 Rue Dauphine

SITE OF THE RESTAURANT MAGNY

3 RUE ANDRÉ MAZET

(Métro: Odéon)

HOME OF THE FAMOUS
MAGNY DINNERS
LEGENDARY NINETEENTH-CENTURY
LITERARY GATHERINGS

Dinner at Magny's ...
Edmond and Jules de Goncourt, *Journal des Goncourt* (1851–1896)

Charles Augustin Sainte-Beuve

The Magny dinners began on Saturday, 22 November 1862, and took place fortnightly until their demise in 1870. The dinners were an informal dining club founded by the critic Sainte-Beuve and his physician friend, Doctor Veyne. Initially they were instituted to raise the spirits of their depressive friend, caricaturist and illustrator, Paul Gavarni, but they soon evolved into one of the most celebrated literary gatherings Paris has ever known, attended by Flaubert, Turgenev, Gautier, the Goncourt brothers, George Sand and many others. The dinner-table conversation was recorded by most of them in their letters, diaries and memoirs, and aphorisms and anecdotes flourished, notably from the pen of those masters of gossip, the Goncourt brothers:

9 May 1865: As we were leaving Magny's Flaubert said to us: 'When I was young my vanity was such that when I went to a brothel with my friends I always picked the ugliest girl and insisted on making love to her in front of them all without taking my cigar out of my mouth. It wasn't any fun for me: I just did it for the gallery.' Flaubert still has a little of this vanity left, which explains why, though perfectly frank by nature, he is never wholly sincere in what he says he feels or suffers or loves.

12 February 1866: Mme Sand dined today at Magny's. She sat beside me, with her beautiful, charming face, in which, as she grows older, the characteristics of the half-caste become daily more visible. She looked shyly at the assembled company and whispered into Flaubert's ear: 'You are the only person here who doesn't frighten me.' She listened, said nothing, and shed a tear over a piece of poetry by Hugo, just at the sentimental point. She has wonderfully delicate little hands, almost entirely hidden in lace cuffs.

Restaurant Magny was named after its proprietor, Modeste Magny, who was born at Montmort in north-eastern France in 1812. When he first arrived in Paris as a young man he was employed as a dishwasher, but steadily worked his way up through the restaurant trade's pecking order to become a chef. In 1842 he bought a small down-at-heel tavern at No. 3 rue Contrescarpe-Dauphine (now Rue André Mazet), which, over the years, he converted into a first-class restaurant. Business began to thrive, as the moneyed bourgeois became his clientele. The composer Rossini, the novelist George Sand and the critic Sainte-Beuve became regular guests. 'He was adored by his clientele,' wrote poet and writer, Théodore de Banville, 'which was uniquely composed of those perceptive Parisians who can discover good restaurants as unerringly as pigs discover truffles.' But Magny's greatest accolade came in 1862 when the Restaurant Magny was listed in the acclaimed *Guide Joanne*: 'Magny's cuisine', wrote Joanne, 'is reputed to be one of the best in Paris, and behind its rather humble exterior, his establishment occupies one of the highest ranks in the hierarchy of Parisian restaurants.'

Today in the Rue André Mazet there is nothing to remind the passer-by that the Restaurant Magny ever existed. 'But if nothing now remains of the most famous literary restaurant in Paris,' writes Robert Baldick in *Dinner at Magny's*, 'any lover of nineteenth-century France who stands in the Rue Mazet late at night can still hear in imagination Flaubert's guffaw, Turgenev's deep bass, Sainte-Beuve's piping treble, and the angry, shouting, laughing voices of the illustrious company which used to gather there for dinner at Magny's.'

See Also: Gustave Flaubert, Ivan Turgenev, Théophile Gautier, Charles Sainte-Beuve, the Goncourt brothers, George Sand.

Further Information: Modeste Magny (1812–1879) is buried in the Cimetière Montparnasse (6th Division, 3rd line East, No. 3 North). The tombstone does not bear his name, but those of family members Charles and Louis Magny. When the Restaurant Magny first opened in 1842, Rue André Mazet was then named Rue Contrescarpe-Dauphine. It was renamed Rue Mazet in 1867 in homage to the French doctor, André Mazet (1793–1821), and became Rue André Mazet in 1994.

Further Reading: R. Baldick, *Dinner at Magny's* (Gollancz, 1971); R. Baldick (ed. & trans.) *Pages From The Goncourt Journals* (NYRB Classics, 2007).

NANCY CUNARD

15 RUE GUÉNÉGAUD

(Métro: Pont Neuf)

FORMER LOCATION OF

THE HOURS PRESS

FOUNDED BY NANCY CUNARD

WRITER, PUBLISHER, POLITICAL

ACTIVIST AND JOURNALIST

I am an exiled king without his crown,
A dying poet with a tattered mask,
A starving beggar who may nothing ask,
And a religion that has been cast down.
Nancy Cunard, from 'Lament'

Portrait of Nancy Cunard by Daniel Garbade

English heiress Nancy Cunard (1896–1965) was the sole heir to the Cunard shipping fortune. An unwanted, only child, who was acutely neglected by her parents, Nancy grew into a rebel, despising everything her parents and their class represented. She fought racism, fascism and poverty. She championed humanitarian causes. She wrote poetry. She founded a small press, and she sent dispatches from the Spanish Civil War. Nancy Cunard became one of the most celebrated socialites of the twentieth century.

Before her family eventually disinherited her, Cunard could afford to take financial risks, and in 1928 she set up a hand press in the Normandy countryside where she lived, naming it the Hours Press. In 1925, the Hogarth Press, run by Leonard and Virginia Woolf, had published Cunard's book of poems entitled *Parallax*, and she wrote to them for practical advice on running a press. 'Your hands will always be covered with ink!' declared the Woolfs. But Cunard was not to be discouraged. 'The smell of printer's ink pleased me greatly,' she wrote, 'as did the beautiful freshness of the glistening pigment.' She soon mastered the technical side of things and gradually became seasoned at book design and typefaces. Her main goal in launching the Hours Press was to publish experimental poetry by young contemporary writers, 'in a manner more generous than to which they were accustomed'. Although Cunard never used the press to publish her own works, the Hours went on to publish not only fledgling poets, but many prominent writers, including Louis Aragon, Ezra Pound, Samuel Beckett, George Moore, Robert Graves, Laura Riding, Richard Aldington and Havelock Ellis.

In 1930, to be closer to the hub of literary life, Cunard relocated the press from her Normandy farmhouse to a small shop at 15 rue Guénégaud in Saint-Germain-des-Prés. 'The clock did not exist for her,' wrote Harold Acton. 'In town she dashed in and out of taxis clutching an attaché-case crammed with letters, manifestoes, estimates, circulars and her latest African bangle, and she was always several hours late for any appointment. A snack now and then but seldom a regular meal; she looked famished and quenched her hunger with harsh white wine and gusty talk.'

Cunard's lovers were many, and included Ezra Pound, Louis Aragon and T.S. Eliot, but the love of her life was Henry Crowder, a black American jazz pianist. In 1931 she handed over the management of the press in order to concentrate on the research of a new publishing project inspired by Crowder, who had opened her eyes to the racial injustices of black America. The resulting book, published in 1934, was a nine-hundred-page anthology of black politics and culture called *Negro*, for which, perhaps unsurprisingly, she received death threats. Meanwhile, the press reviews appeared more concerned with her relationship with a black man than with racial injustice.

In the mid 1930s she joined the fight against fascism and reported for the British press on the brutality of the Spanish Civil War. She organised refugee relief efforts and soup kitchens, and experienced the appalling conditions encountered across the French border where thousands of refugees were housed in concentration camps, and where many starved to death.

In later life her ideals and crusades all but consumed her, and her rebellious, altruistic lifestyle eventually took its toll in illness, alcoholism and poverty. Declared insane in 1960, she was by now physically and mentally destroyed. When crossing a Paris street in 1965 to visit her friend, Janet Flanner, she collapsed and lay face down in the street, weighing no more than sixty pounds. The police took her to Hôpital Cochin in Rue du Faubourg-Saint-Jacques where she died a few days later. 'Her body had wasted away', wrote her friend Pablo Neruda, 'in a long battle against injustice in the world. Her reward was a life that had become progressively lonelier, and a god-forsaken death.'

See Also: Père Lachaise, Janet Flanner, Louis Aragon, Ezra Pound, Samuel Beckett, Three Mountains Press, Pablo Neruda.

Further Information: Nancy Cunard's ashes rest in Père Lachaise, Division 87, Columbarium, urn 9016.

Select Bibliography: *Outlaws* (1921); *Sublunary* (1923); *Parallax* (1925); *Poems* (1930); *Negro: an Anthology* (1934); *These Were the Hours: Memories of my Hours Press, Reanville and Paris, 1928–1931* (1969); *Selected Poems* (2016).

Further Reading: H. Ford, ed., *Nancy Cunard, Brave Poet, Indomitable Rebel* (Chilton, 1968); A. Chisholm, *Nancy Cunard: A Biography* (Random House, 1979); L. Gordon, *Nancy Cunard: Heiress, Muse, Political Idealist* (Columbia University Press, 2007); H. Crowder & H. Speck, *As Wonderful as All That* (Wild Trees Press, 1987); S. Benstock, *Women of the Left Bank* (University of Texas Press, 1986).

15 rue Guénégaud

LA PALETTE

43 RUE DE SEINE

(Métro: Mabillon/St-Germain-des-Prés)

CAFE FAMOUS OVER THE YEARS
FOR ITS CLIENTELE OF WRITERS
AND ARTISTS

He walks into La Palette at twenty-five past four, almost half an hour late. He would not be surprised if Cécile has already left, storming out in a huff and vowing to rain down a thousand curses on him if he should ever cross her path again. But no, she is still there, sitting calmly at a table in the back room, reading a book, a half-finished bottle of Orangina in front of her, wearing glasses this time, and a fetching little dark blue hat that resembles a beret.
Paul Auster, *Invisible* (2009)

Established in 1913, La Palette is located at the intersection of Rue de Seine and Rue Jacques-Callot. It was originally situated beneath a *passage couvert*: a covered passageway that was part of a nineteenth-century shopping arcade, now long gone. The cafe consists of two salons: a small one with a bar, and a larger one to the rear. This rearmost room, which is now listed as a historic monument, is decorated with ceramics from the 1930s and 1940s. La Palette's name derives from the artists and gallery owners who have frequented it, notably Cézanne, Braque and Picasso, and the staff and students from the nearby École Nationale Supérieure des Beaux-Arts. It boasts a collection of painters' palettes that can be seen hanging on its walls. Writers also attracted to La Palette included Ernest Hemingway, Apollinaire, Alfred Jarry, Harry Crosby, Paul Auster and Djuna Barnes.

See Also: Walter Benjamin, Ernest Hemingway, Malcolm Cowley, Harry Crosby, Djuna Barnes, Apollinaire, École des Beaux-Arts.

Further Information: By the mid nineteenth century there were around 150 *passages couverts* in Paris, but many of them disappeared under the demolition hammer of Baron Haussmann's renovations. Today only a couple of dozen remain on the Right Bank. German literary critic, Walter Benjamin, documented most of them in his unfinished magnum opus, *Passagenwerk (Arcades Project)*, posthumously published in 1999.

INSTITUT DE FRANCE

23 QUAI DE CONTI

(Métro: Palais Royal – Musée du Louvre)

Established in 1795, the Institut de France describes itself as the 'Protector of Arts, Literature and Science'. Built between 1662 and 1688 by Cardinal Mazarin, it was initially a school: the Collège des Quatre-Nations. Since 1795 it has housed a collection of academies and libraries, notably the Académie des Sciences, the Académie des Beaux-arts and the Académie des Sciences Morales et Politiques. Of particular interest to the book lover are the Académie française, the Académie des Inscriptions et Belles-lettres, the Bibliothèque Mazarine and the Bibliothèque de l'institut.

ACADÉMIE FRANÇAISE

CUSTODIANS OF THE FRENCH

LANGUAGE SINCE 1635

Those who have been persuaded to think well of my design, require that it should fix our language, and put a stop to those alterations which time and chance have hitherto been suffered to make in it without opposition. With this consequence I will confess that I flattered myself for a while; but now begin to fear that I have indulged expectation which neither reason nor experience can justify.
Dr Samuel Johnson writing on the futility of attempting to 'secure it [the English language] from corruption and decay' in his *Preface to a Dictionary of the English Language* (1755)

The Académie française has been the guardian of the French language for nearly four centuries, advising successive governments on usage, vocabulary and grammar, while at the same time trying to keep their language as uncorrupted as possible, especially by anglicisation. French novelist and Académie member Dominique Fernandez suggested that if the French were taught English properly from the very beginning, then they could ignore it and 'leave it where it ought to be, in the English language, and not in anglicisms, that hybrid ruse of ignoramuses'.
France was not alone in trying to fix language, and many countries throughout history have taken measures to attempt to prevent their language suffering from what they saw as decay and debasement. A standard dictionary was seen to be the remedy, and the exemplars of the Italian Accademia della Crusca and the French Académie française were the target sought by many for imitation. Early advocates of an English Academy, using that of the French as an example, were John Dryden, Daniel Defoe and Jonathan Swift. The idea came to nothing; but, although doubts also began to be cast upon the value of results achieved by the French Academy, the notion of a standardising dictionary remained.

Cardinal Richelieu

Since 1694 the French Academy has been publishing successive editions of the *Dictionnaire de l'Académie française*, and at the time of writing is working on its ninth edition.

Established by Cardinal Richelieu in 1635, suppressed during the French Revolution in 1793, and restored to its glory by Napoleon in 1803, the Académie française is the oldest of the five academies of the Institut de France. It came into being through a small literary society that Cardinal Richelieu took under his wing with the idea of turning it into a formal academy. In 1635 Louis XIII granted the society the authority to initiate the Académie française, which was 'to labour with all the care and diligence possible, to give exact rules to our language'. Today it has a membership limit of forty, with the first woman being elected in 1980. Members are usually made up of writers and artists, notably Victor Hugo and Voltaire, known as *les Immortels*, who are required to wear a gold and green uniform known as *l'habit vert*, topped with a feathered hat. Imposing in their pageantry, they regularly meet to defend the purity of the French language. But their recommendations to the French government, much to their annoyance, are not legally binding, and are often ignored.

Charles Dickens unwittingly summed up the Académie's philosophy in *Dombey and Son* (1847–1848): 'There was no light nonsense about Miss Blimber … She was dry and sandy with working the graves of deceased languages. None of your live languages for Miss Blimber. They must be dead – stone dead – and then Miss Blimber dug them up like a Ghoul.'

See Also: Dr Samuel Johnson, Maurice Druon, Victor Hugo, Voltaire.

ACADÉMIE DES INSCRIPTIONS
ET BELLES-LETTRES
A SOCIETY DEDICATED TO THE
STUDY OF THE HUMANITIES
HOUSING PAPYRUS SCROLLS
FROM HERCULANEUM

O ye, who patiently explore
The wreck of Herculanean lore,
What rapture! could ye seize
Some Theban fragment, or unroll
One precious, tender-hearted scroll
Of pure Simonides.
William Wordsworth, from
'September, 1819'

Founded in 1663, the Académie's charter states that it is 'primarily concerned with the study of the monuments, the documents, the languages, and the cultures of the civilisations of antiquity, the Middle Ages, and the classical period, as well as those of non-European civilisations.' Pride of place in its collection of antiquities are six charred papyrus scrolls from Herculaneum, the Roman town destroyed along with neighbouring Pompeii in the eruption of Mount Vesuvius in AD 79. The scrolls were discovered in 1752 in a villa buried almost 90 feet deep by the volcano, which became known as the Villa dei Papiri. The library of the villa was the only library of any size from the ancient world known to have survived intact. It survived because the intense heat dried out the moisture and carbonised its scrolls; however, because the scrolls are so dry, and literally resemble a lump of black mud, attempts to unfurl them risk turning them to dust. Eight hundred scrolls were discovered there, many of which are now housed in institutions around the world; equally, many were destroyed through inept attempts to read them. Modern technology is slowly unwrapping their secrets, but the lost masterpieces of Sophocles and Aristotle have yet to surface. Napoleon Bonaparte donated six scrolls, which had been gifted to him by King Ferdinand of Naples in a politically judicious move, to the Institut de France in 1802.

Further Reading: D. Sider, *The Library of the Villa Dei Papiri at Herculaneum* (Getty Publications, 2005); A. Wallace, *Herculaneum: Past and Future* (Frances Lincoln, 2012).

BIBLIOTHÈQUE MAZARINE

THE OLDEST PUBLIC LIBRARY

IN FRANCE

Those who create a library defy mortality, they transmit to us a lively portrait of what was most noble in themselves.
Gabriel Naudé

The Bibliothèque Mazarine was the personal library of Cardinal Jules Mazarin (1602–1661), whose enlightened librarian, Gabriel Naudé (1600–1653), filled its shelves with thousands of rare books and manuscripts, transforming it into one of the finest European libraries of its day. Naudé, a French physician and librarian, is regarded today as the first significant theoretician of modern library organisation, and his book, *Advis pour dresser une bibliothèque (Advice on Establishing a Library)*, published in 1627, is the first substantial study of library science. His talents first came to the attention of Cardinal Richelieu who hired him as his personal librarian, and when Mazarin succeeded Richelieu as first minister, Naudé came under his patronage, a partnership through which both patron and scholar would reap great rewards. During the 1640s Naudé collected over 40,000 books for Mazarin from all over Europe, and his philosophy that a good library should inform and give pleasure to all was somewhat unorthodox.

Bibliothèque Mazarine

We should 'not neglect all the works', he wrote, in *Advice on Establishing a Library*,

of the principal heretics or adherents of religions that are new and differ from the one most commonly revered among ourselves as being more sound and true … it is necessary that our scholars should find these authors somewhere available in order to refute them. … There are no scruples about having a Talmud or a Koran, which belch forth against Jesus Christ and our religion a thousand blasphemies infinitely more dangerous than those of the heretics; since God permits us to profit from our enemies … I think it neither an absurdity nor a danger to have in a library all the works of the most learned and famous heretics.

Naudé's 'famous heretics' included Calvin, Luther, Melanchthon and Beza. Naudé also advocated that libraries should collect dissertations, pamphlets and manuscripts. He even advised on a library's location in *Advice*: 'between some spacious court and a pleasant garden, from which it may enjoy good light, a wide and agreeable prospect, and pure air, unpolluted by marshes, sinks, or dunghills'. He also recommended providing 'feather dusters, clocks, pens, paper, ink, penknife, sand, a calendar, and other small items and suchlike instruments, which cost so little and are yet so necessary.'

The Mazarin Library was opened to the public for the first time on 30 January 1644 becoming France's first public library. Scholars came from all over Europe describing it as 'une bibliothèque vivante', a living library. Mazarin, however, had his enemies at court, and many resented his influence on the young Lou-is XIV who was still a minor. Between 1648 and 1653 the Fronde, a series of civil wars and uprisings, forced Mazarin to flee into exile, and Parliament decreed that the library should be divided and sold. Naudé left for Sweden where he was appointed royal librarian to Queen Christina. Mazarin returned to power in 1653 and asked Naudé to return to Paris and reassemble the library. Naudé agreed, but died en route from Sweden.

See Also: Académie des Inscriptions et Belles-lettres, Bibliothèque de l'institut, Bibliothèque Nationale, The American Library in Paris.

Further Information: The Bibliothèque Mazarine's collection includes a copy of the *Gutenberg Bible*, one of the earliest books printed using movable metal type, a system invented *c.*1455 by Johann Gutenberg. This three-volume work, also known as the *Forty-two-line Bible* due to its being printed in 42-line columns, is sometimes referred to as the *Mazarin Bible* because the first copy is thought to have been located in the library of Cardinal Mazarin. The original is kept in a vault, but a facsimile copy can be viewed in the reading room.

Further Reading: G. Naudé, *Advice on Establishing a Library* (University of California Press, 1950).

BIBLIOTHÈQUE DE L'INSTITUT
LIBRARY OF THE
INSTITUTE OF FRANCE
CUSTODIANS OF THE WORLD'S
LARGEST COLLECTION OF
LEONARDO DA VINCI'S NOTEBOOKS

The heavens often rain down the richest gifts on human beings, but sometimes they bestow with lavish abundance upon a single individual beauty, grace and ability, so that

whatever he does, every action is so divine that he distances all other men, and clearly displays how his greatness is a gift of God and not an acquirement of human art. Men saw this in Leonardo.
Giorgio Vasari, *The Lives of the Artists* (1550)

Housed in a wing of the Palais de l'Institut this library contains manuscripts, prints and books on French constitutional, political, diplomatic and cultural history from the late Middle Ages to the present day. Among its many treasures are the manuscripts of Leonardo da Vinci (1452–1519). Leonardo is rarely thought of as a writer, but over 7000 pages of manuscripts written by him still survive today; perhaps thousands more existed in history, and are now lost to posterity. His surviving manuscripts come in three different categories: bound collections compiled after his death, single sheets and notebooks. The largest collection of notebooks – Napoleonic plunder from the historic library of the Biblioteca Ambrosiana in Milan – is housed in the Bibliothèque de l'Institut de France. A fusion of art, science and technology, the notebooks record Leonardo's observations on anatomy, flight, optics, geology, architecture, sculpture and painting, and are sprinkled with letters, epigrams, formulas and fables: a unique window into the mind of a Renaissance genius.

In 1516 Leonardo was invited to France as court painter to King Francis, who gave him the Château du Cloux on the banks of the Loire near Amboise for his official residence. Here Leonardo died in 1519, aged sixty-seven, and legend has it that he died cradled in the arms of the King. A nice story, but the King was actually at Saint-Germain-en-Laye that day, two days travel away by horseback. Leonardo's remains are supposedly buried in the Chapel of Saint-Hubert adjacent to the nearby Château d'Amboise. The Church Saint-Florentin, where he was originally buried, was desecrated during the French Revolution, and demolished in 1802. The stones from the church and graveyard were used to repair the chateau and, it is said, all the scattered bones in the graveyard were piled in a heap by a gardener named Goujon. In 1863 the site of Saint-Florentin was excavated, and when a skeleton with an extraordinary skull size was found, the excavators were convinced they had found the remains of Leonardo. These questionable remains now lie buried in the Chapel of Saint-Hubert in the grounds of the Château d'Amboise. 'It is just possible', wrote Charles Nicholl in *Leonardo da Vinci: The Flights of the Mind*, 'that the capacious skull interred at St Hubert once housed the mind of Leonardo da Vinci, but one certainty, at least, is that it does so no longer. The cage is empty; the mind has flown.'

Leonardo da Vinci

OSCAR WILDE

13 RUE DES BEAUX-ARTS

(Métro: St-Germain-des-Prés)

SITE OF HÔTEL D'ALSACE

WHERE OSCAR WILDE DIED

IN NOVEMBER, 1900

So with curious eyes and sick surmise
We watched him day by day,
And wondered if each one of us
Would end the self-same way,
For none can tell to what red Hell
His sightless soul may stray.
Oscar Wilde, from *The Ballad of Reading Gaol* (1897)

Dramatist and poet Oscar Wilde (1854–1900) bedazzled Victorian society with his wit and charisma. He will be best remembered for his peerless comedy *The Importance of Being Earnest* and his novel of artistic decadence, *The Picture of Dorian Gray*; but in 1895 his remarkable success ended abruptly in personal disaster. Encouraged by his lover Lord Alfred Douglas, Wilde brought a libel action against Lord Alfred's father, the Marquess of Queensberry, who had accused Wilde of being a sodomite. The resulting trial backfired on Wilde with the court convicting him of gross indecency. He was sentenced to two years' imprisonment with hard labour, serving the majority of his sentence at Reading Gaol. At his release on 19 May 1897 he left immediately for France where he adopted the alias Sebastian Melmoth to avoid attracting publicity. 'How grateful I was and am to France', he wrote, 'for their recognition of me as an artist in the day of my humiliation.' He eventually settled in Paris, the city where he had spent his honeymoon, and where he had

startled the Parisian literary salons with his wit in the winter of 1891. This time, however, he was a tragic figure, almost broken by a brutal penal system. And except amongst his closest friends, he was *persona non grata* and shunned by those who had once courted him. He had little money (he was declared bankrupt in prison), little energy and little hope for the future. His friend André Gide, and others, observed that his appearance was slowly descending to the shabby and threadbare. 'I don't think I shall ever write again,' he told a friend. 'Something is killed in me. I feel no desire to write. I am unconscious of power. Of course my first year in prison destroyed me body and soul. It could not have been otherwise.' He survived on money from his sporadic royalties, gifts and loans from friends, and a small monthly allowance from his estranged wife. Wilde's last literary effort, *The Ballad of Reading Gaol*, was written in France during the summer of 1897, and gives stark and sombre emphasis to the brutality of a prisoner's life. The press offered him

147

money to write about his prison experiences, but he always refused. 'I wish to be read for Art's sake,' he said, 'not for my notoriety.'

Sliding inevitably towards lower and lower classes of accommodation, by the summer of 1899 he was staying at the Hôtel d'Alsace on the Left Bank. His room was on the first floor and was reached by a spiral staircase. It overlooked a courtyard to the rear of the hotel, where Wilde would sometimes sit sipping absinthe and reading Balzac. 'I fear you would not like my hotel,' he wrote to a friend. 'I live here because I have no money. It is an absurd place.' It was his good fortune, however, to have met and made friends with its proprietor, Jean Dupoirier, who gave him credit, loaned him money, and generally ensured he ate and drank well.

While in prison Wilde had fallen in his cell and injured his middle ear, and by October 1900, his ear was so painful it had to be operated on. Unable to afford the operation, he joked, 'I fear I shall die beyond my means.' Following the unsuccessful operation, which was complicated by an abscess in the left lobe, he was diagnosed with cerebral meningitis. On the morning of 29 November, his friend Robbie Ross, realising the end was not far away, sent for a priest, remembering Wilde's quip that 'Catholicism is the only religion to die in.' Wilde died the following day and Ross described the scene:

In the morning a complete change came over him, the lines of the face altered, and I believe what is called the death rattle began, but I had never heard anything like it before, it sounded like the horrible turning of a crank, and it never ceased until the end. His eyes did not respond to the light test any longer. Foam and blood came from his mouth … I went to the bed side and held his hand, his pulse began to flutter. He heaved a deep sigh, the only natural one I heard since I arrived, the limbs seemed to stretch involuntarily, the breathing came fainter, he passed at 10 minutes to 2 p.m.

Oscar Wilde died disgraced, impoverished and in exile. Victorian society had all but eradicated his memory. His friends, however, especially his literary executor and former lover, Robbie Ross, worked for years successfully restoring and rebuilding his reputation. Today, thanks to those friends, his place among the giants of literature is assured.

'I made art a philosophy, and philosophy an art,' he wrote. 'I altered the minds of men, and the colour of things. I awoke the imagination of my century so that it created myth and legend around me: I summed up all things in a phrase, all existence in an epigram: whatever I touched I made beautiful.'

See Also: Oscar Wilde (Père Lachaise), André Gide, Honoré de Balzac.

Further Information: Hôtel d'Alsace is now a boutique luxury hotel. A plaque above the left-hand side of the entrance marks it as the site of Wilde's death. On the right-hand side a plaque commemorates Argentinian poet, essayist and short story writer, Jorge Luis Borges's (1899–1986) sojourns there in 1977 and 1984. By staying here, Borges was paying homage to Wilde, his boyhood hero. In 1909, aged nine, Borges published his first work in a Buenos Aires newspaper. It was a Spanish translation of Wilde's *The Happy Prince*.

Further Reading: R. Ellmann, *Oscar Wilde* (Penguin, 1988).

ÉCOLE DES BEAUX-ARTS

14 RUE BONAPARTE

(Métro: St-Germain-des-Prés)

THE ART SCHOOL THAT PRODUCED
SOME OF THE WORLD'S
LEGENDARY BOOK ILLUSTRATORS

Nothing is a waste of time if you use the experience wisely.
Auguste Rodin (1840–1917), who failed to gain admittance to the École des Beaux-Arts, despite applying three times.

Louis-Maurice Boutet de Monvel

École des Beaux-Arts (School of Fine Arts) is the title given to a number of top art schools in France, the most prestigious of which is located in Paris and is today known as the Ecole Nationale Supérieure des Beaux-Arts. It was established in 1648 as the teaching wing of the French Academy of Fine Arts by Cardinal Mazarin to instruct students of prodigious talent in life drawing, painting, sculpture, engraving and architecture. The curriculum was later divided into the 'Academy of Painting and Sculpture' and the 'Academy of Architecture', with emphasis on the arts and architecture of classical antiquity. In 1663 the École des Beaux-Arts created the Grand Prix de Rome, a scholarship award for students to study in Rome. Appraisals for the award lasted three months, and competition was stiff. Édouard Manet and Edgar Degas both entered the competition, but failed to win.

The École des Beaux-Arts was originally inspired by the great Italian academies of Florence and Rome, which demanded extremely high standards, and today its list of alumni reads like an Encyclopedia of European Art. It is now the largest

Monvel's cover design for La Fontaine's *Fables* (1888)

art school in France, but throughout history the Academy and the School both courted controversy for their rigid following of the principles and styles of ancient Greek and Roman art, refusing to recognise anything other than the idealised form. Today, though, the old masters mix with the new and the school incorporates all forms of art, teaching students from all over the world.

Many of its students went on to become

Students of the École des Beaux-Arts with life model *c.*1900

influential exponents of book illustration, notably Edmund Dulac (1882–1953), best known for his illustrations of the classics, including the *Arabian Nights* (1907), the *Rubáiyát of Omar Khayyám* (1909), and *The Sleeping Beauty and Other Tales* (1910); George Barbier (1882–1932), one of the leading artists of art deco book illustration; André Castaigne (1861–1929), illustrator of the first edition of *Phantom of the Opera* (1910); and Louis-Maurice Boutet de Monvel (1850–1913), best remembered as one of the nineteenth century's leading figures of the golden age of children's book illustration.

See Also: Gustave Doré, Gaston Leroux, Cardinal Mazarin, La Palette, La Fontaine.

Further Information: Other alumni of the École des Beaux-Arts are Pierre-Auguste Renoir, Édouard Manet, Henri Matisse, Eugène Delacroix, Georges Seurat, François Boucher, Jean-Auguste-Dominique Ingres, Jean-Honoré Fragonard, Théodore Gericault, Claude Monet, Mary Cassatt, Jean-François Millet, Alfred Sisley and Pierre Bonnard. The first woman to be enrolled was Julia Morgan, in 1898, an architecture student from San Francisco, who became the first woman architect licensed in California.

The inner courtyard of the École des Beaux-Arts

RENÉ DESCARTES

3 PLACE SAINT-GERMAIN-DES-PRÉS

(Métro: St-Germain-des-Prés)

ÉGLISE SAINT-GERMAIN-DES-PRÉS

TOMB OF RENÉ DESCARTES

FATHER OF MODERN

WESTERN PHILOSOPHY

His true monument is the modern world, of which he is one of the founders. Every philosophy student reads him, and his is a household name. That is fame. Fame is acquired in many ways, not all of them involving merit; Descartes' fame rests on great merit, and is unlikely ever to fade so long as people read history and think about philosophy, and contemplate the lifetimes of those who made a difference to both.
A.C. Grayling, *Descartes* (2006)

René Descartes

The works of René Descartes have been in print for nearly four hundred years. His contributions to science, mathematics, modern thought, and a wide range of other fields and disciplines make him the embodiment of the Renaissance world.

He was born in 1596 at La Haye (now Descartes) in the Loire Valley, the son of a lawyer and magistrate. His mother died fourteen months after his birth and René was raised, together with his two siblings, by their grandmother. He went on to study law, and in his early twenties he joined the army. Later, he lived in the Netherlands, working in seclusion and devoting himself to the study of science and philosophy for over twenty years, publishing many works during this time. By the mid seventeenth century Descartes was one of Europe's most famous philosophers.

In 1649 he was invited to come and live

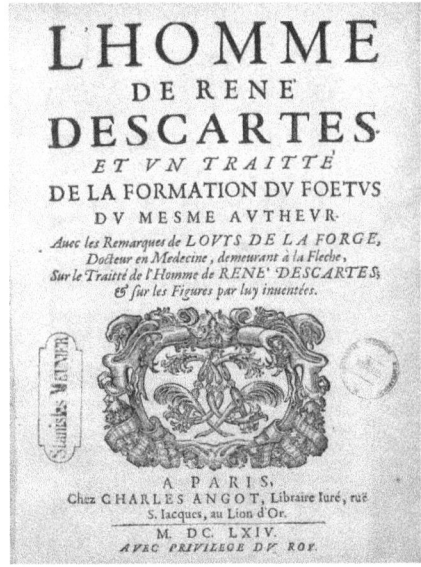

L'homme (1664)

at the court of Sweden's ruler, Queen Christina. She was eager to make her court a centre of learning, and the presence of a renowned thinker like Descartes would give it prestige. Des-

The church of Saint-Germain-des-Prés

alien land wasn't enough, what happened next was pitiable and humiliating. Christina decided Descartes must have a state funeral and be interred in a marble tomb beside her ancestors. All this was going to take time to organise, so, as a temporary measure he was buried in a cemetery for the 'unbaptised', with a makeshift wooden marker over his grave. Christina soon forgot about her grandiose plans, and Descartes lay buried and ignored for seventeen years until his body was exhumed in 1667 and transported back to France. Several burial places later, his remains finally came to rest in Saint-Germain-des-Prés, but without his skull, which had been removed during the original exhumation and had subsequently been sold and resold over the centuries. The skull of Descartes is now held at Musée de l'Homme.

Further Information: The church of Saint-Germain-des-Prés once belonged to an eighth-century Benedictine abbey located in the middle of meadows (*prés*). Plundered several times throughout history by the Vikings, it was rebuilt between AD 990 and 1201 from which parts of the present church date. Descartes's tomb is beneath the side chapel of Saint-Benoît inside Saint-Germain-des-Prés. It has been alleged over the centuries that Descartes did not die from pneumonia, but was poisoned by rivals at Christina's court, but no evidence exists to justify these claims.

cartes also became her teacher, but her insistence on beginning lessons at five o'clock in the morning during the winter months in the land of 'bears, rocks and ice' took its toll on his health. Descartes soon fell ill with pneumonia and died on 11 February 1650, six weeks short of his fifty-fourth birthday.

As if dying far from home in a cold,

Select Bibliography: *Meditations and Other Metaphysical Writings* (Penguin, 1998); *Discourse on Method and The Meditations* (Penguin, 2005).

Further Reading: A. Grayling, *Descartes* (Pocket Books, 2006); S. Gaukroger, *Descartes: An Intellectual Biography* (OUP, 2002).

DENIS DIDEROT

BOULEVARD SAINT-GERMAIN

(Métro: Mabillon)

**STATUE OF DENIS DIDEROT
PHILOSOPHER, ART CRITIC AND
MAJOR FRENCH WRITER OF THE
EIGHTEENTH CENTURY**

Denis Diderot

There are two sorts of laws, those of absolute equity and universality, and the bizarre ones which owe their autonomy only to blindness or to the force of circumstance. The latter merely cover the man who is breaking them with a passing disgrace, which time then transfers to the judges and the nations, on whom it remains forever.
Denis Diderot, *Oeuvres romanesques* (1762)

Denis Diderot (1713–1784) was a leading figure of the Enlightenment of the eighteenth century, whose works ranged through innovative drama, philosophical writings, essays on religion, art criticism and political thought, to his celebrated philosophical novels, notably *Rameau's Nephew* (1761) and *Jacques the Fatalist* (1773). He spent the first part of his life on the work for which he is most remembered today: the monumental *Encyclopédie*, which showcased the achievements of the Enlightenment. Many of his works outwith the *Encyclopédie*, including his masterpiece, *Rameau's Nephew*, were not published until many years after his death; and some of his minor works were still only surfacing two centuries later. Diderot was always deemed a threat to the status quo, a committed atheist of subversive activities, and was continually under threat of exile throughout his life. His *Pensées philosophiques (Philosophical Thoughts)* was burned by the authori-

ties in 1746 because of its scepticism towards religion, and in 1749 he was imprisoned in the Château de Vincennes for three months for publishing his *Lettre sur les aveugles (Letter on the Blind)*, a proposal to teach the blind to read through the sense of touch, which was also a discourse on materialist atheism. Excluded from many histories of philosophy, his original and liberating precepts were considered too dangerous for the proletariat. He was never awarded the customary posts given to the men of letters of his day and, since his death in 1784, his remains have consistently been refused burial in the Panthéon, the

153

mausoleum for France's national heroes. Diderot was born in 1713 in Langres, a commune in the north-east of France, where his father was a master cutler. His mother died when he was very young, leaving him two sisters and a brother. One sister died, mad, in a convent, and his younger brother became a priest, a vocation the teenage Denis rejected, along with that of physician and lawyer, working, from choice, as a tutor and publisher's hack in Paris. In 1742 he married the penniless Nanette Champion with whom he had several children, only one of whom lived to adulthood. Several affairs would follow, but his marriage appeared to remain intact until the day he died.

In 1745 he became editor of the *Encyclopédie*, which was published over a period of almost thirty years, in 28 volumes, containing 71,818 articles and 3129 illustrations on the sciences, arts and crafts of the Enlightenment. Its contributors included Voltaire and Rousseau, and according to Diderot it would 'change the way people think'. Threatened with censorship and criticised by conservatives, the *Encyclopédie* was eventually completed in 1772, but left Diderot with no income and mounting financial worries. Help came from an unexpected source when Catherine the Great, Empress of Russia, purchased his library and appointed him her librarian with an annual salary for the rest of his life. Diderot died from a coronary thrombosis on 31 July 1784, aged seventy, in a house on Rue Richelieu bestowed on him by the Empress. He was buried in the Chapelle de la Vierge (Chapel of the Virgin) at the church of Saint-Roch on Rue Saint-Honoré and, although his remains disappeared long ago, his works and influence still flourish today.

See Also: Voltaire, Jean-Jacques Rousseau, Panthéon, Château de Vincennes.

Further Information: Sculptor Jean Gautherin's (1840–1890) bronze statue of Diderot on Boulevard Saint-Germain was erected in 1884 across from the church of Saint-Germain-des-Prés, near the junction of Boulevard Saint-Germain and Rue Bonaparte.

Select Bibliography: *Essay on Merit and Virtue* (1745); *Letter on the Blind* (1749); *Letter on the Deaf and Dumb* (1751); *The Nun* (1796); *Jacques the Fatalist* (1796); *Rameau's Nephew* (1805).

Further Reading: A. Wilson, *Diderot* (Oxford University Press, 1972); L. Crocker, *The Embattled Philosopher – a Life of Denis Diderot* (Neville Spearman, 1955); P. Furbank, *Diderot* (Secker & Warburg, 1992); P. Blom, *Wicked Company: Freethinkers and Friendship in pre-Revolutionary Paris* (W&N, 2011); R. Zaretsky, *Catherine & Diderot* (Harvard University Press, 2019).

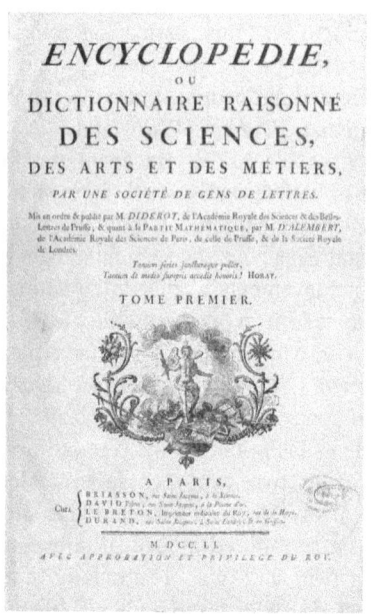

Title page of the first volume of the *Encyclopédie,* dated 1751

LES ÉDITIONS DE MINUIT

7 RUE BERNARD-PALISSY

(Métro: St-Germain-des-Prés)

CLANDESTINE PUBLISHING HOUSE

DURING WORLD WAR II

PUBLISHER OF VERCORS'S NOVEL OF

FRENCH RESISTANCE,

LE SILENCE DE LA MER

Authors assemble outside the offices of Les Éditions de Minuit in the 1950s. Left to right: Claude Simon, Alain Robbe-Grillet, Robert Pinget, Jérôme Lindon, Samuel Beckett, Nathalie Sarraute

There was a time when people were exiled for preferring Euripides's Phaedra to Racine's. The glory of France was at stake, claimed the tyrant of the day. Today Einstein's physics, Freud's psychology, Isaiah's laments are all banned. It is forbidden to reprint Meredith, Thomas Hardy, Katherine Mansfield, Virginia Woolf, Henry James, Faulkner, all the others whom we love. 'Do not display in your shop-windows Shakespeare, Milton, Keats, Shelley, the English poets and novelists of all time,' commands the Booksellers' Association, acting on instructions from German Propaganda ...
Propaganda is not our [Les Éditions de Minuit's] domain. We mean to safeguard our inner life and freely serve our art. The names matter little. It is no longer a question of petty personal fame. Nor does it matter if the road is beset with difficulties. What is in question is man's spiritual purity.
From the manifesto of Les Éditions de Minuit, slipped into each of their published volumes during the Nazi occupation of France.

L es Éditions de Minuit (The Midnight Press) began as an underground press in Nazi-occupied France in 1941. Founded by Jean Bruller (1902–1991), novelist and graphic artist, and Pierre Lescure, novelist and bookseller, it was essentially created to prove to the world at large that in the midst of the brutalities and censorship of the Nazi occupation intellectual life in France was still alive and kicking. Clandestine broadsheets and newspapers existed during the occupation, but there was no underground publishing house previous to Les Éditions de Minuit that had the capacity to publish full-length books of any scope and quality. Firstly, Bruller and Lescure had to find suitable undercover authors, but secondly – and more importantly – they had to find someone courageous enough to print the books. This was a task that was fraught with danger, as many printers were pro-German, and many of those who were not

155

had already lost their lives working for the Resistance. After tentative enquiries, George Oudeville, the owner of a small printing works, was finally chosen. Oudeville, who printed wedding invitations and funeral cards, worked alone, and had premises across the street from a German military hospital. 'Who would imagine', wrote Bruller, 'anybody crazy enough to print subversive material under the enemy's very nose?'

The first book chosen for publication was Bruller's own novella, *Le Silence de la mer (The Silence of the Sea)*, a tale of passive resistance over evil, whose message to the French people was to refuse to communicate with the Germans. The story tells of the moral resistance, through silence, of an old man and his niece, which eventually psychologically disturbs a German officer billeted in their house. 'I took a long time trying to find a title which would fit the hidden violence of this tale without sound or fury,' wrote Bruller in *The Battle of Silence*. ' Every day I lined up scores of them but found none to my liking. Then there came to my mind a wild and poetic image which had often haunted me: beneath the deceptively calm surface of the sea, the ceaseless, cruel battles of the beasts of the deep. And I called my story *The Silence of the Sea*.'

Bruller published the novella under the pseudonym Vercors, named after the Vercors Massif near Grenoble, where he had been demobilised after the French army's defeat in 1940. His childhood friend, Yvonne Paraf, turned her apartment into a workshop, and, with a few female volunteers, they folded, collated, and stitched the pages into books, hiding them in cupboards until ready for distribution. The appearance of the book was delayed for several months for security reasons, but it was finally released in the early autumn of 1942. The book, the first to appear in France for two years without the stamp of the German censor, was a triumph. Soon parachute drops all over France were distributing it, and any profits from the book were earmarked for the families of printers who had been executed or imprisoned. Today, *The Silence of the Sea* remains an outstanding tribute to what a tenacious group of people can achieve under tyranny.

See Also: Paul Éluard, François Mauriac, André Gide, John Steinbeck, Louis Aragon, Samuel Beckett, Marguerite Duras, Claude Simon, Alain Robbe-Grillet.

Further Information: Les Éditions de Minuit is still publishing books from Rue Bernard-Palissy. As a wartime press, it published Paul Éluard, François Mauriac, André Gide, John Steinbeck and Louis Aragon. After the war, its stable of authors included Samuel Beckett, Marguerite Duras, Claude Simon and Alain Robbe-Grillet.

Further Reading: Vercors, *The Silence of the Sea* (Berg, 1991); *The Battle of Silence* (Collins, 1968).

Jean Bruller

BRASSERIE LIPP

151 BOULEVARD SAINT-GERMAIN

(Métro: St-Germain-des-Prés)

The influx of people who came to be called 'expatriates'... hung out in Montparnasse ... At the time I was doing Lipps ... I was hardly aware of Montparnasse, even as a legend, and Sylvia Beach informed me it was ghastly, a hangout for pederasts.
Robert McAlmon, *Being Geniuses Together* (1938)

Originally called the Brasserie des bords du Rhin (Brasserie on the Banks of the Rhine), it was opened by its owner, Léonard Lipp, in 1880. Lipp was a native of Alsace, but following its annexation by Otto von Bismark after France's defeat in the Franco-Prussian war in 1871, Lipp made his way back to his native France, eventually settling in Paris.

His brasserie prospered, and became affectionately known as 'chez Lipp'. With its art nouveau decor, fine wines and food, it attracted the beau monde of Parisian society including various French presidents from Charles de Gaulle to Jacques Chirac. Its clientele over the years has also included Left Bank Americans and writers, notably Albert Camus, Jean-Paul Sartre, Simone de Beauvoir, and Ernest Hemingway, who remembers Lipps serving 'a sausage like a heavy, wide frankfurter split in two and covered with a special mustard sauce', typical of the Alsace region. Lipps was also the scene of the famous confrontation between Richard Wright and James Baldwin in 1949, when Wright accused Baldwin of trying to demolish his reputation after the publication of Baldwin's essay 'Everybody's Protest Novel' in the magazine *Zero*, which savagely criticised Wright's novel *Native Son*.

Following the publication of Hemingway's *The Sun Also Rises* in 1926 – a *roman-à-clef* novel, in which the characters are based on real people – some of his friends and associates strongly objected to his portrayal of them. Hemingway's response was typically macho: anyone with a bone to pick could find him at the Brasserie Lipp most afternoons. It appears no one showed.

See Also: Robert McAlmon, Sylvia Beach, Albert Camus, Jean-Paul Sartre, Ernest Hemingway, Richard Wright, James Baldwin.

LES DEUX MAGOTS
6 PLACE SAINT-GERMAIN-DES-PRÉS
(Métro: St-Germain-des-Prés)

The Deux Magots is the modest inheritor of a silk lingerie store of that name that stood on the spot for decades, until the 1860s, when the growth of the big department stores across the river drove it out of business. The owners eventually rented out the space to a café liquoriste, which kept the name and started selling coffee. No one knows exactly when the two famous statues of Chinese mandarins – the Deux Magots – were installed; Anatole France, in his memoirs, written at the turn of the century, speaks of a big picture of three magots that used to hang in the lingerie store.
Adam Gopnik, *Paris to the Moon* (2000)

L es Deux Magots has always been a popular cafe with Americans, from the time of the belle époque to the present day. It was once the home of the beau monde and the cream of the literary and artistic world. Its patrons over the years have included Albert Camus, James Joyce, Bertolt Brecht, Ernest Hemingway, Richard Wright and Pablo Picasso. In literature it has featured in dozens of novels, including Vladimir Nabokov's *Lolita*, and Jean Rhys's *Good Morning Midnight*. The surrealists also favoured Les Deux Magots, and according to Janet Flanner they 'had their own club table facing the door ... from which vantage point a seated surrealist could conveniently insult any newcomer'.
In the late twenties, Flanner and Hemingway became aware that each other's father had committed suicide: 'a piece of personal duplicate history', wrote Flanner, 'that he and I discovered one day at a quiet back table in the Deux Magots café, which he always favoured for serious talk, such as his reading aloud in a

Janet Flanner and Ernest Hemingway at Les Deux Magots in 1944

rumbling whisper the first poetry he had written after the war.'
The main competitor of Les Deux Magots has always been its neighbour, Café de Flore: frequenting one cafe would be de rigueur while the other was out of vogue, both at the mercy of the passing fancy of the day. In the words of Yves Saint Laurent, 'Fashions fade, style is eternal.' And 'style' is something both these cafes will surely always have.

See Also: Anatole France, Janet Flanner, Ernest Hemingway, Jean Rhys, James Joyce, Albert Camus, Richard Wright.

CAFÉ DE FLORE

172 BOULEVARD SAINT-GERMAIN

(Métro: St-Germain-des-Prés)

The practice of café-writing did not begin and end with Sartre, though, and less conspicuous writers continued to make an office out of a quiet table in a corner. It was a pleasant way of being both outdoors – at play – and indoors – working – at once. In the café, the solitary writer could be writing and yet socializing at the same time. A good café was like a ship at sea: a closed society, of varied parts and activities. Friends, acquaintances, enemies were all within shouting distance, but there was no obligation to talk to them.
James Campbell, *Paris Interzone* (1994)

When Jean-Paul Sartre moved from Montparnasse to a hotel in Saint-Germain-des-Prés, the Flore became his favoured cafe to write in. 'He came from opening time until midday and from the afternoon until closing,' commented the proprietor. 'I didn't know him by name, and he usually came with a woman [Simone de Beauvoir] who sat at another table in the corner.'

Café de Flore, along with Les Deux Magots, became the nerve centre of the post-war Parisian avant-garde. Sartre held court at the Flore in a downstairs room, and among his inner circle were his lover Simone de Beauvoir, Albert Camus, Boris Vian, Jean Genet, Raymond Aron, and Maurice Merleau-Ponty, editor of *Les Temps Modernes*, the journal founded by Sartre in 1945. 'It may seem strange,' wrote Sartre, 'but the Flore was like home to us: even when the air raid alarm went off, we would merely feign leaving and then climb up to the first floor and go on working.'

In those far-off post-war days, the Flore proudly advertised itself as 'Le rendez-vous des existentialistes'. Inevitably Sartre and Beauvoir became tourist exhibits, and eventually they escaped to quieter cafes. 'When they die,' remarked Flore proprietor Paul Bourla, 'you'll have to dig them a grave under the floor.'

See Also: Jean-Paul Sartre, Simone de Beauvoir, Albert Camus, Boris Vian, Jean Genet, Maurice Merleau-Ponty.

Further Information: Café de Flore, named after Flora, the Roman goddess of flowers, opened in 1880, and its art deco interior has changed little since World War II. Paul Bourla was the Flore's owner from 1939 until his retirement in 1983.

JEAN-PAUL SARTRE

42 RUE BONAPARTE

(Métro: St-Germain-des-Prés)

FORMER APARTMENT OF

JEAN-PAUL SARTRE

EXISTENTIALIST PHILOSOPHER,

DRAMATIST AND NOVELIST

Jean-Paul Sartre in 1965

He is a philosopher (but in the French, not the British sense: professional British philosophers shudder at his name and think of bedrooms, spit and semen; they only read him on holiday).

Martin Seymour-Smith, *Guide to Modern World Literature* (1973)

Jean-Paul Sartre was one of the leading intellectual figures of his generation and the principal exponent of existentialism, a movement in philosophy and literature that is based on the view that, as there is no God, the only way to oppose nothingness is to embrace one's individual existence and seek out the true meaning of life. Sartre is also remembered for refusing the Nobel Prize in Literature in 1964 on the grounds that he did not want 'to be transformed into an institution', and, famously, for his relationship with the celebrated feminist, Simone de Beauvoir, who remained loyal to him for over fifty years, despite his many affairs with other women.

Sartre was born in Paris on 21 June 1905 in the 16th arrondissement, the only child of French naval officer, Jean-Baptiste Sartre (1874–1906), and Anne-Marie Schweitzer (1882–1969). His father died from a fever contracted while serving in Cochinchina (now part of Vietnam) when his son was only fifteen months old. Anne-Marie, at that time a 24-year-old widowed mother

with no means of support, moved in with her parents near Versailles, where Sartre's maternal grandparents undertook, albeit reluctantly, the role of parents to the boy. In 1911 they all moved to a top floor flat at No. 1 rue Le Goff, near the Luxembourg Gardens. This was the house Sartre reminisces about in *Les Mots (Words)*: 'Up till the age of ten, I lived alone with an old man and two women.' Sartre's overbearing grandfather, Charles Schweitzer, was a teacher of German with an extensive library that was to spark Sartre's love of literature. 'I had found my religion,' he wrote, 'nothing seemed more important to me than a book. I saw the library as a temple.'

His 'temple', along with his idyllic life, was shattered in 1917 when his mother decided to remarry. 'My mother certainly didn't marry my stepfather out of love,' he recalled in 1972. 'In any case, he wasn't very lovable.' Sartre later studied at the Sorbonne and taught philosophy at Le Havre, Paris and Berlin. Despite poor eyesight from birth (he lost the use of his right eye when he was a child) he was called up in 1939 and later imprisoned by the Nazis in a prisoner of war camp. Shortly after his release in 1941 he joined an intellectual resistance group. Following the end of the war in 1945, financial success from his writings enabled him to buy an apartment for his mother and himself at 42 rue Bonaparte (third floor), overlooking Place Saint-Germain-des-Prés.

By that time he was achieving fame not only through his writings, but also as a political activist. During his life Sartre issued the clarion call for many causes, notably the struggle for Algerian independence from France in the 1950s and early 1960s. He flirted with communism, but never joined the Communist Party. He became the leading hate figure for the French Right and in 1960 ten thousand French army veterans marched through the streets chanting 'Shoot Sartre!' In 1961, and again in 1962, the right-wing terrorist group OAS bombed Sartre's Rue Bonaparte flat. But nothing could halt Sartre's campaigning. After signing an illegal petition calling on French soldiers to disobey orders, an act for which he could have been imprisoned, President de Gaulle allegedly remarked, 'One does not imprison Voltaire.'

Sartre's novels belong to the earlier part of his writing life. *Nausea* (1938), his first published novel, is about a man struggling to restore meaning to his life, while *The Roads to Freedom* trilogy (1945–1949) is a chronicle of his war years. *In Camera* (1944) was his most successful dramatic work, and among his philosophical writings it is *Being and Nothingness* (1943), which became the core of existentialism, that is regarded as his most important non-fiction work.

During the 1970s his ideas became more extreme, and he became an exponent of social violence. Today Sartre is appreciated more outside France than in it, and he is distinctly unfashionable among modern contemporary French thinkers; but when all is said and done, it was from Sartre's radicalism and confrontations during the fifties and sixties that many of these thinkers were spawned. He died in April 1980, a few weeks short of his seventy-fifth birthday, after being rushed to hospital with a pulmonary oedema, and is buried in Montparnasse Cemetery (Division 20) beside Simone de Beauvoir.

See Also: Simone de Beauvoir, Café de Flore, Sorbonne, Voltaire, Cimetière du Montparnasse.

Select Bibliography: Fiction: *Nausea* (1938); *The Age of Reason* (1947); *The Reprieve* (1947); *Intimacy* (1949); *Iron in the Soul* (1950). Biography & Autobiography: *Baudelaire* (1950); *Words* (1964). Plays: *The Flies* (1946); *In Camera* (1944). Philosophical Works: *Existentialism* (1948); *Being and Nothingness* (1957).

Further Reading: D. Drake, *Sartre* (Haus, 2005); C. Seymour-Jones, *A Dangerous Liaison* (Century, 2008); S. Bakewell, *At The Existentialist Café* (Chatto & Windus, 2016).

42 rue Bonaparte

EZRA POUND

70 *BIS* RUE NOTRE-DAME-DES-CHAMPS

(Métro: Vavin/Notre-Dame-des-Champs)

FORMER HOME AND STUDIO OF
AMERICAN POET EZRA POUND
ONE OF THE FOUNDING FATHERS
OF MODERNISM

The apparition of these faces in a crowd;
Petals on a wet, black bough.
Ezra Pound, 'In a Station of the Metro'
(1913)

Pound in the courtyard of his Paris studio in 1923

Arguably, no twentieth-century writer has had more influence on modern literature than Ezra Pound (1885–1976). He was one of the motivating forces behind the imagist and Vorticist movements, and he supported and encouraged W.B. Yeats, T.S. Eliot, James Joyce, Hilda Doolittle (H.D.), Ernest Hemingway and many others. He was one of the most controversial writers of his time, but his own individual achievements have become obscured over the years, mainly due to his political and racist preoccupations with fascism and anti-Semitism during the Second World War, which led to his incarceration in later life in an asylum for the insane.

An only child, he was born in Idaho of Quaker ancestry. In 1908 he sailed to Europe on a cattle boat, eventually arriving in London towards the end of that year. He knew virtually nobody, but he soon started to gather the modernists around him, including Wyndham Lewis, Richard Aldington, H.D., and T.S. Eliot, who described Pound as 'more responsible for the twentieth century revolution in poetry than any other individual'. He met and married English artist Dorothy Shakespear, and began publishing early parts of *The Cantos*, his epic poem written between 1915 and 1962. In December 1920, Pound and Dorothy left for Paris, where they hoped a new literary powerhouse and 'paradise for artists' beckoned. They moved into 70 *bis* rue Notre-Dame-des-Champs, near the Jardin du Luxembourg, which Pound filled with his own hand-made furniture. Paris invigorated him and gave him a new lease of life, immersing him in new crusades and writers. He met Cocteau, Tzara and Aragon, and embraced Dadaism. He gave advice to James Joyce on *Ulysses*, and to T.S. Eliot on the then incomplete *The Waste Land*, helping transform it into one of the landmarks of modernism. He developed a friendship with Hemingway, who, somewhat predictably, taught him to box. Gertrude Stein, however, 'did not find him amusing'.

In 1922 Pound met young concert violinist, Olga Rudge, and the two became lovers, embarking on an infidelity that lasted, and was endured by Dorothy, until Pound's death. One of his final artistic involvements in Paris was helping Ford Madox Ford launch his short-lived, but hugely influential, *The Transatlantic Review* in 1924. Ultimately, however, Paris did not live up to his expectations. His reputation, and also his health, began to wane, and in October of 1924 the Pounds, with Olga in pursuit, arrived in Rapallo, Italy, in search of new horizons. During the 1930s it became evident that Pound's mind was becoming unsound, and during the war years he began broadcasting on Italian radio unintelligible and technically subversive programmes on fascist ideas. In 1945 he was indicted for treason, but was declared insane, and placed in an asylum until 1958. There was a terrible poignancy to his latter years, and although his flame has dimmed today, at his zenith Ezra Pound changed the way poets used poetic language. He died in Venice in 1972.

See Also: James Joyce, T.S. Eliot, Ernest Hemingway, Ford Madox Ford, Three Mountains Press, Jean Cocteau, Tristan Tzara, Louis Aragon, Djuna Barnes.

Further Information: The imagist movement of English and American poets was a revolt against romanticism and Victorian verse, focusing on simplicity and the use of visual imagery, that lasted from around 1910 until 1917. Vorticism (the vortex being the point of maximum energy) was a literary and artistic movement that flourished from 1912 until 1915. It attempted to connect art to industrialisation, rejecting sentimentality and celebrating the violent energy of the machine age.

Select Bibliography: The majority of work on which Pound's renown now rests can be found in *Personae* (Faber & Faber, 1952) and *The Cantos* (Faber & Faber, 1975).

Further Reading: N. Stock, *The Life of Ezra Pound* (Penguin, 1974); P. Ackroyd, *Ezra Pound and his world* (Thames and Hudson, 1980); F.M. Ford, *Return to Yesterday* (Carcanet, 1999).

Left to right: Ford Madox Ford, James Joyce, Ezra Pound, and patron of the arts John Quinn in Pound's Paris studio in 1923

MARGUERITE DURAS

5 RUE SAINT-BENOÎT

(Métro: St-Germain-des-Prés)

FORMER HOME OF

MARGUERITE DURAS

CELEBRATED AND CONTROVERSIAL

NOVELIST OF POST-WAR FRANCE

I've known you for years. Everyone says you were beautiful when you were young, but I want to tell you I think you're more beautiful now than then. Rather than your face as a young woman, I prefer your face as it is now. Ravaged.

Marguerite Duras, *The Lover*

Marguerite Duras in 1955

In 1984, 70-year-old Marguerite Duras won the Prix Goncourt, France's most prestigious literary award, for her semi-autobiographical novel *L'Amant (The Lover)*, an erotic tale of lost innocence set against the backdrop of Cochinchina (now part of South Vietnam) during the time of the French colonial empire. It tells the story of a 15-year-old French girl who becomes the lover of a 27-year-old Chinese man, and who discovers she wants to be a writer. After *The Lover* became a worldwide bestseller Duras's readership reached a mass audience around the globe, and was perhaps the icing on the cake for a writing career that had often been at odds with the literary vogues of the day. She was also a prolific playwright, filmmaker and screenwriter, but despite the success of her screenplay for Alain Resnais's *Hiroshima, Mon Amour* (1960), her film career was relatively undistinguished.

She was a woman with a strong sense of character, who was overbearingly narcissistic and determined to have her own way. She had many lovers, most of whom appear in her novels, and she could write about eroticism and pubescent passion almost instinctually, a gift that surfaces in many of her works, notably in *The Lover*. '[It] is an important book,' remarked Alain Robbe-Grillet, 'even though it has sold two million copies: let's not be petty here … Marguerite Duras is a fool, but she's a great writer.' Marguerite Duras was born Marguerite Donnadieu in 1914 in Gia Dinh, a suburb of Saigon in French Indochina. Her parents were teachers, and her pseudonym, Duras, was taken from her father's village in Aquitaine. Her father died in 1918, leaving Marguerite, her two brothers and mother in straitened circumstances. At the age of eighteen she moved to France where she graduated in political sciences at the Sorbonne. Her first job was with the French Colonial Office, where she promoted French bananas. At this time, she also co-wrote a book in praise of the virtues of colonialism, which she spent most of the rest of her life trying to forget. In 1939 she married fellow writer, Robert Antelme, and in 1942 they moved into a third floor flat in Rue Saint-Benoît, where they were later joined by her lover, Dionys Mascolo. Here Duras would live for the rest of her life in the heart of her beloved Saint-Germain-des-Prés. In 1942, during the Nazi occupation, she worked as a secretary to the agency in charge of allocating paper to publishers, which was created by Marshal Pétain, and under direct control of the Vichy government. In later years, when questioned about this involvement, which could be deemed collaborationist, she shrugged it off with a resentful wave of her hand. In 1943 Antelme and Duras joined a Resistance cell, which included France's future president, François Mitterand, an experience she wrote about in *La Douleur (The War)* (1985). In June 1944 Antelme was arrested by the Gestapo and sent to Dachau where he barely survived. In April 1947 Duras divorced Antelme, and a few months later she gave birth to a son, her only child, by her lover Dionys Mascolo.

Her first novel, *Les impudents*, was published in 1943, followed by *La Vie tranquille* (1944), both family sagas set in the French provinces. In 1950 she published *Un Barrage contre le Pacifique (The Sea Wall)* (1950), a semi-autobiographical novel recalling her adolescence in Cochinchina and Cambodia. Her later works, however, show a gradual change in writing style, in which she abandons a realist framework and, moving towards the margins of the *nouveau roman*, challenges the traditional conceptions of the novel. This is notable in *Le Marin de Gibraltar* (1952), *Les Petits Chevaux de Tarquinia*

(1953), *Le Square* (1955) and *Moderato cantabile* (1958).

Her last years were dogged by ill health, due largely to her long struggle with alcoholism. In the 1980s she had a loving relationship with Yann Andréa Steiner, a young homosexual writer who shared her life until her death. Marguerite Duras was a difficult woman who trod her own path, but she was a skilled and intelligent writer whose place in literature is secure. On 3 March 1996, a month short of her eighty-second birthday, she died from throat cancer at 5 rue Saint-Benoît. She is buried in Montparnasse Cemetery, Division 21.

See Also: Le Prix Goncourt, Les Éditions de Minuit, Alain Robbe-Grillet, Gallimard, American Hospital in Paris.

Further Reading: L. Adler, *Marguerite Duras: A Life* (University of Chicago Press, 2000); L. Hill, *Marguerite Duras: Apocalyptic Desires* (Routledge, 1993); A. Vircondelet, *Duras* (Dalkey, 1994).

5 rue Saint-Benoît

JANET FLANNER

36 RUE BONAPARTE

(Métro: St-Germain-des-Prés)

**HÔTEL SAINT-GERMAIN-DES-PRÉS
FORMER HOME OF JANET FLANNER
WRITER, JOURNALIST AND PARIS
CORRESPONDENT OF *THE NEW YORKER***

Genius is immediate, but talent takes time.
Janet Flanner

Janet Flanner and Solita Solano

Although born an American, Janet Flanner (1892–1978) spent most of her life in Europe, predominantly in Paris, as foreign correspondent of *The New Yorker*. She began dispatching her now legendary 'Letter from Paris' in 1925, under the nom de plume Genêt and, apart from an interlude during the war years, she continued writing her 'Letters' for fifty years. 'I act as a sponge,' she wrote. 'I soak it up and squeeze it out in ink every two weeks.'

Flanner was from a Quaker background in Indianapolis where her father ran a mortuary. After a two-year stint at the University of Chicago, from 1912 until 1914, one of her jobs was on a local Indianapolis newspaper as their very first movie critic. In 1919, after a failed marriage, she met her long-term lover, the writer and journalist, Solita Solano, in Greenwich Village. They travelled to Europe together, finally settling in Paris in 1922. 'Paris then seemed immutably French,' Flanner wrote. 'The quasi-American atmosphere which we had tentatively established around Saint-Germain had not yet infringed onto the rest of the city. In the early twenties, when I was new there, Paris was still yesterday.'

In early December 1923, Flanner and Solano moved into the Hôtel St-Germain-des-Prés where they would live in four rooms on the fourth floor for the next sixteen years. The bathroom, 'barely containing a tub and chair,' remarked Solano, was on the fifth floor, 'The bath mat was five attached wooden slats. To have a bath, it was necessary to notify well in advance the one and only servitor – there was no maid – the *garcon de tous les étages*; he drew the water, laid one towel, small, on the chair, and marked down the equivalent of 20 cents in his little black book.' Nearby were the now-famous cafes, Les Deux Magots (where they breakfasted) and the Café de Flore, 'rapidly filling with the accents we hoped to leave behind,' observed Solano.

In her letters home Flanner wrote to her mother, her estranged husband, and her old New York friend, Jane Grant, who had married journalist Harold Ross. Around this time Ross was in the throes of founding *The New Yorker*, a weekly cosmopolitan magazine of reportage and humour, with a strong literary bent. A few months after its launch in 1925, Harold Ross, inspired by Flanner's witty and incisive letters to his wife, hired Flanner to write for *The New Yorker*. 'In

September 1925, I started the fortnightly "Letter from Paris"' wrote Flanner. 'The only specific guidance I had received from the editor, Harold Ross, was his statement that he wanted to know what the French thought was going on in France, not what I thought was going on. This was a new type of journalistic foreign correspondence, which I had to integrate and develop, since there was no antecedent for it. *The New Yorker*, at its beginnings, was also like an over-sized minnow learning to swim. It had not yet found its style, and it was to take me some time before I began to find my own, which instinctively leaned toward comments with a critical edge, indeed a double edge, if possible.'

Flanner kept up her 'double edge' eloquence for over fifty years, writing about everything from Josephine Baker's 'stomach dance' to the execution of Mata Hari, shot by a firing squad in the Paris suburb of Vincennes 'wearing a neat Amazonian tailored suit, specially made for the occasion, and a pair of new white gloves.'

Janet Flanner was a good friend of Sylvia Beach, who had published James Joyce's *Ulysses* in 1922. Thirteen years later, when Beach's finances were at a low ebb, she planned to sell off some of the manuscripts and rare editions in her possession. These included: her own first edition of Ulysses in blue morocco binding; the second volume off the press in a print run of two hundred, containing a poem that Joyce had written for her; and the original *Ulysses* proofs. To drum up interest among American bibliophiles Flanner announced the sale in the Paris Letter in *The New Yorker*. As a thank-you for her efforts, Beach gave Flanner a numbered uncut first edition of *Ulysses* on vergé d'Arches paper,

which contained an original page of the manuscript. In 1950, when Beach was still experiencing hard times, Flanner sold the book to the Pierpont Morgan Library and gave the proceeds to Beach. 'Publishing *Ulysses*', Flanner wrote, 'was her greatest act of generosity.'

See Also: Hôtel Scribe, Hôtel Ritz, Sylvia Beach, James Joyce, Café de Flore, Les Deux Magots.

Further Information: Flanner wrote one novel, *The Cubical City*, in 1926. Flanner returned to New York in 1975, where she lived with her partner, Natalia Danesi Murray, until her death in 1978.

Select Bibliography: *An American in Paris: Profile of an interlude between two wars* (1940); *Conversation Pieces* (1942); *Paris Journal: 1944–1955* (1965); *Paris Was Yesterday 1925–1939* (1972).

Further Reading: B. Wineapple, *Genêt: A biography of Janet Flanner* (University of Nebraska, 1992); W. Murray, *Janet, My Mother, and Me: A Memoir of Growing Up with Janet Flanner and Natalia Danesi Murray* (Simon & Schuster, 2000).

SHERWOOD ANDERSON

44 RUE JACOB

(Métro: St-Germain-des-Prés)

HÔTEL D'ANGLETERRE,
FORMERLY HÔTEL JACOB
RESIDENCE OF NOVELIST
AND SHORT-STORY WRITER
SHERWOOD ANDERSON IN 1921

Paris must be a marvelous place. I imagine it full of great wide avenues, and palaces, and beautiful women, and then, right alongside the palaces and the avenues, streets filled with dark tenements, strangled women, men with knives, poor dirty children, thousands of simple people wondering what it's all about – and not realizing at all that they're living in a place most of us would give our eye-teeth to get to.
Sherwood Anderson

Sherwood Anderson

Thomas Wolfe declared that he was 'the only man in America who ever taught me anything'. 'Sherwood Anderson was the father of all my works', wrote William Faulkner, ' — and those of Hemingway, Fitzgerald, etc. We were influenced by him. He showed us the way.' Anderson's influence can also be found in the style of William Saroyan, Henry Miller, Taylor Caldwell, John Steinbeck and others. But, alas, the writer who influenced so many of our literary legends has today himself drifted into obscurity, and is remembered in the main for one book of short stories, his nervous breakdown in 1912, and being famously parodied by Hemingway in *The Torrents of Spring*. However, although overlooked and underrated, Anderson's writing left an indelible imprint on a generation of twentieth-century writers who remain forever in his debt.

Born in 1876, the third of seven children, he spent his youth in Ohio, and later worked as an advertising copywriter in Chicago while writing in his spare time. In 1906 he returned to Ohio where he became a paint manufacturer; but in 1912, following a breakdown, he walked away from the pressures of the business world and returned to Chicago and his old advertising job, until such times as – he hoped – he could earn enough money to survive as a writer. Essentially a storyteller in the oral tradition, Anderson published several novels, notably *Dark Laughter* (1925), his only bestseller; but his most celebrated work, and the one for which he is remembered today, was his book of short stories, *Winesburg, Ohio*, written in 1919 and set in a small town in the American Midwest.

One of Anderson's own major literary influences was Gertrude Stein, whom he had never met. In 1921, however, on his first visit to Paris, a meeting was arranged, as bookseller Sylvia Beach relates in her memoir, *Shakespeare and Company*:

One day I noticed an interesting-looking man lingering on the doorstep, his eye caught by a book in the window. The book was *Winesburg, Ohio*, which had recently been published in the United States. Presently he came in and introduced himself as the author. He said he hadn't seen another copy of his book in Paris. I was not surprised, as I had looked everywhere for it myself – in one place they had said, "Anderson, Anderson? Oh, sorry, we have only the Fairy Tales. … Sherwood told me that Gertrude Stein's writing had influenced him. He admired her immensely, and asked me if I would introduce him to her. I knew he needed no introduction, but I gladly consented to conduct him to the rue de Fleurus.

This meeting was something of an event. Sherwood's deference and the admiration he expressed for her writing pleased Gertrude immensely. She was visibly touched. Sherwood's wife, Tennessee, who had accompanied us, didn't fare so well. She tried in vain to take part in the interesting conversation between the two writers, but Alice held her off.

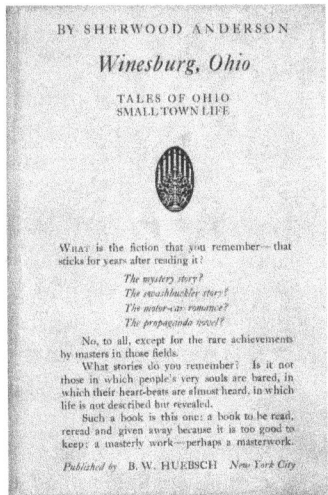

First edition of *Winesburg, Ohio*, published in 1919

Anderson also met James Joyce and André Gide in Paris, but importantly his time in the city itself influenced his thoughts and his writings as it had for so many before him. 'Everyone is settled down here,' he wrote. 'Men stay in the place to which fate has assigned them. A certain freedom of action and living is achieved. We at home have all been fed upon the notion that it is our individual duty to rise in the world. … it may have much to do with our national weariness.' Anderson was en route to South America when he died of peritonitis in Colon, Panama, on 8 March 1941.

See Also: Gertrude Stein, Sylvia Beach, Djuna Barnes, F. Scott Fitzgerald, Ernest Hemingway, Hart Crane, William Saroyan, Henry Miller, John Steinbeck.

Further Information: During the eighteenth century the building now occupied by the Hôtel d'Angleterre housed the British Embassy. In 1783 the Treaty of Paris, which formally ended the American War of Independence, was to have been signed at the Embassy, but Benjamin Franklin, one of the American signees, refused to enter the building as it was British territory. The Treaty was eventually signed at a hotel further along the street, at 56 rue Jacob. In 1925 the Hôtel Jacob became Hôtel Jacob et d'Angleterre, and a few years later it changed again to the Hôtel d'Angleterre. It was a popular haunt for American writers, notably Washington Irvine in 1805; poet Alan Seeger in 1913, who was killed at the Somme the following year; Djuna Barnes; newly-weds Ernest and Hadley Hemingway in 1921, and Hart Crane in 1929.

Select Bibliography: *Winesburg, Ohio* (1919); *Poor White* (1920); *The Triumph of the Egg* (1921); *A Story Teller's Story (1922) Dark Laughter* (1925); *Tar: A Midwest Childhood* (1926); *Death in the Woods and Other Stories* (1933).

OLYMPIA PRESS

13 RUE JACOB

(Métro: St-Germain-des-Prés)

FORMER OFFICES OF OLYMPIA PRESS
ENGLISH LANGUAGE PUBLISHER
OF EROTIC AND RISQUÉ BOOKS
FOUNDED BY MAURICE GIRODIAS

Lolita, light of my life, fire of my loins. My sin, my soul. Lo-lee-ta: the tip of the tongue taking a trip of three steps down the palate to tap, at three, on the teeth. Lo. Lee. Ta. She was Lo, plain Lo, in the morning, standing four feet ten in one sock. She was Lola in slacks. She was Dolly at school. She was Dolores on the dotted line. But in my arms she was always Lolita.
Vladimir Nabokov, *Lolita* (1955)

Front cover of the 1959
Olympia first edition

It's easy to discount Maurice Girodias as solely a publisher of dirty books, with titles such as *Hell and the Whore* and *There's a Whip in My Valise*, but, like his father before him, he was an opportunist with a deep respect for literature, yet who also knew how to turn a buck. He began his apprenticeship working for his father Jack Kahane's Paris-based Obelisk Press in the 1930s. During the Nazi occupation of France, Maurice took the maiden surname of his French mother, Marcelle Girodias, to disguise his Jewish roots. After the war, his father dead, he briefly resurrected Obelisk before launching Olympia Press in 1953, following Kahane's model of publishing the erotic, avant-garde and sexually explicit fiction most publishers were afraid to publish for fear of prosecution. In an age when it was forbidden to print the word 'bugger' without the threat of imprisonment, books were being published by Olympia that today are considered classics of contemporary literature, notably Vladimir Nabokov's *Lolita*; J.P. Donleavy's *The Ginger Man*; Samuel Beckett's trilogy *Molloy*, *Malone Dies*, and *The Unnamable*; Henry Miller's *Sexus, Nexus* and *Plexus*, and William Burroughs's *Naked Lunch*.

Olympia Press was born in the back room of a bookshop that traded from the courtyard at No. 13 rue Jacob. 'My staff', wrote Girodias, 'included an ex-sailor with a gift for picturesque swearwords, and a very small secretary who had for a chair the back seat of a Delahaye automobile. We used the same rickety table, behind which I sat on a couch which my friend the bookseller also used as a bed.' By the mid 1960s Olympia had moved its offices to New York, where Girodias continued his life of pornography and lawsuits. While in his youth he liked to say, 'It is my job to deprave and corrupt', in later life he would write 'I accepted in principle my unworthiness, my image as a publisher of the scandalous, the clandestine.'

Whatever Maurice Girodias thought his purpose was, by publishing some of the great works of contemporary literature that pushed the boundaries of respectability he helped break down the walls of censorship.

See Also: The Obelisk Press, Samuel Beckett, William Burroughs, Jean Genet, Henry Miller, Eric Losfeld.

Further Information: Scottish-born writer Alexander Trocchi (1925–1984) began his writing career in the early 1950s penning erotica for Olympia Press. After graduating at Glasgow University he was awarded a travelling scholarship whereupon he toured Europe with his wife and two daughters before choosing to settle in Paris. Abandoning his family, he found a new lover in Jane Lougee, the daughter of an American banker who financed the Paris literary magazine *Merlin*, which was edited by Trocchi. *Merlin* lasted for five years, publishing Samuel Beckett, Jean Genet, Henry Miller, Eugène Ionesco and other greats of modernism. *Merlin* ceased publication when Trocchi's relationship with Lougee ended in 1955.

Further Reading: M. Girodias, *The Frog Prince: An Autobiography* (Crown, 1980); J. Campbell, *Paris Interzone* (Secker & Warburg, 1994).

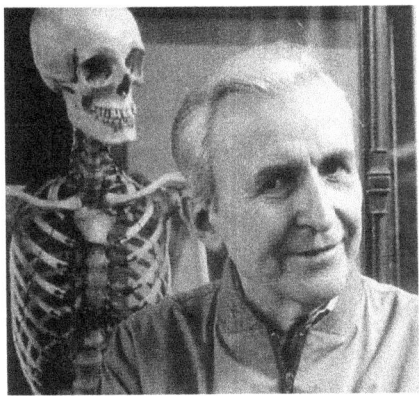

Maurice Girodias

JULES VERNE

18 RUE JACOB

(Métro: Mabillon/St-Germain-des-Prés)

**FORMER OFFICES OF HETZEL & CO.,
PUBLISHERS OF JULES VERNE'S
FIRST NOVEL**
FIVE WEEKS IN A BALLOON

If men go on inventing machinery they'll end up by being swallowed by their own machines. I've always thought that the last day will be brought about by some colossal boiler heated to three thousand atmospheres blowing up the world.
Jules Verne, *Five Weeks in a Balloon* (1863)

One of the world's most translated authors, Jules Verne (1828–1905) is best known for his adventure novels, notably *20,000 Leagues Under the Sea* and *Around the World in Eighty Days*. Verne's fantastic stories, intertwined with newly discovered technologies, gave birth to an original kind of novel in which scientific fact meets scientific fiction, forming the bedrock of the modern science fiction genre. It was a formula that made him a wealthy man and also earned him the much-lauded, though ambiguous, title, the 'Father of Science Fiction'.

Born in Nantes on 8 February 1828, Jules Gabriel Verne was the eldest of five children of Pierre Verne, a lawyer, and his wife Sophie. In 1847, aged nineteen, he was sent to Paris to study law, and although he obtained his licence, he never practised. Verne's real love was the world of theatre and literature. Since his early youth he had been writing poems, essays and plays, many of which were later published in the juvenile periodical *Musée des familles*. He tried a career as a

171

An 1870 engraving of Captain Nemo viewing a giant squid from his submarine *Nautilus*, in *20,000 Leagues Under the Sea*

playwright, but his success was modest; and when he married in 1857, he took up employment as a stockbroker in order to support his wife.

Success as a writer eventually arrived in his thirty-fifth year, with *Cinq semaines en ballon (Five Weeks in a Balloon)*, published by Pierre-Jules Hetzel (1814–1886), in which the protagonists set out to explore darkest Africa in a hot-air balloon. The far-sighted, yet canny, Hetzel went on to publish fifty-four of Verne's novels between 1863 and Verne's death in 1905 under the collective title *Voyages Extraordinaires*, a forty-year partnership almost unique in the annals of publishing. Verne, through his imagination and inventiveness, became one of the first to prosper as a science fiction writer; but he was no scientist, he just observed what was happening in the world around him. He made no predictions, but described things based on his own knowledge. And although he never claimed to be a prophet, he certainly inspired those who came after him, and left a legacy without equal for them all. Jules Verne suffered from chronic diabetes and died at his home at Amiens in 1905 aged seventy-seven.

Further Information: Most of Verne's novels were initially serialised in Pierre-Jules Hetzel's periodical, *Magasin d'éducation et de récréation*, before appearing as book editions; and although Hetzel also published Balzac, Hugo and Zola, he is best remembered today for his editions of Verne's *Voyages Extraordinaires*. Verne's second novel, the dystopian tale, *Paris in the Twentieth Century*, was rejected by Hetzel for being too bleak and likely to damage his career. Filed away by Verne, the manuscript was discovered 130 years later and eventually published in 1994.

Select Bibliography: *Five Weeks in a Balloon* (1863); *Journey to the Centre of the Earth* (1864); *20,000 Leagues Under the Sea* (1870); *Around the World in Eighty Days* (1873); *The Mysterious Island* (1874); *Michael Strogoff* (1876); *Robur the Conqueror* (1886); *Master of the World* (1904).

Further Reading: H. Lottman, *Jules Verne: An Exploratory Biography* (St. Martins, 1997).

Jules Verne by Nadar

NATALIE BARNEY

20 RUE JACOB

(Métro: Mabillon/St-Germain-des-Prés)

**FORMER HOME AND LITERARY SALON
OF NATALIE BARNEY
AMERICAN PLAYWRIGHT, POET,
NOVELIST AND SALONNIÈRE**

*A double being needs no other mate –
So seraphita-seraphitas lives;
Self-wedded angel, armed in self-delight,
Hermaphrodite of heaven, looking down
On the defeat of our divided love.*
Natalie Barney, *The One Who Is Legion,* or
A.D.'s After-Life (1930)

The Temple of Friendship at 20 rue Jacob

Writer Natalie Barney (1876–1972) is remembered more today for her lesbian relationships and her famous literary salon on Rue Jacob, where a coterie of artists, writers and sycophants, including Colette, Mata Hari, Radclyffe Hall, Ezra Pound and Gertrude Stein gathered every week for over half a century. It was a dazzling sixty-year-long party, but it tended to overshadow her writing. A contributory factor in this eclipsing was that her work was written in French and published infrequently in limited editions by small publishing houses. Even today much of her work still remains in its original manuscript state. She wrote twelve books across various genres, mostly about the nature of womanhood, stamped with her own individual feminism. Courtesan Liane de Pougy, with whom she had a love affair in 1899, later turned the story of their relationship into a best-selling novel, immediately establishing Barney's notoriety within Parisian high society. Her lovers included British poets Olive Custance and Renée Vivien; French writers Elisabeth de Gramont, Lucie Delarue-Mardrus and Colette; American painter Romaine Brooks; and Oscar Wilde's niece, Dolly Wilde. Her life and love affairs also inspired many novels, notably salonnière Valérie Seymour in Radclyffe Hall's *The Well of Loneliness.* Natalie Barney, however, was much more than a salonnière and notorious lesbian celebrity. She was a literary rebel.

Her staggeringly wealthy parents, Albert Clifford Barney, a railroad car manufacturer, and painter Alice Pike, from Dayton, Ohio, endured a desperately unhappy union that would cast a pall over Natalie throughout her life. By the age of twelve she knew she was lesbian, and was determined to 'live openly, without hiding anything'. In 1900 she published her first book, *Quelques portraits: sonnets de femmes* in which she wrote about lesbian love. The book outraged her father so much he bought all the copies including the printer's plates, which he subsequently destroyed. Her other works included: *Cinq petits dialogues*

173

grecs (1901), *Pensées d'une amazone* (1929), *The One Who Is Legion* (1930), *Souvenirs indiscrets* (1960) and *Selected Writings* (1963). Due mainly to its inaccessibility, Barney's writing has drifted into obscurity, and her legacy today rests on scandalous love affairs and her reputation as a flamboyant and avant-garde salonnière. Nonetheless, although her writing is now mostly unread and forgotten, her impact, inspiration and influence on literature should not be underestimated.

See Also: Colette, Ezra Pound, Gertrude Stein, Renée Vivien.

Further Information: The vast majority of Natalie Barney's papers can be found at the Bibliothèque Littéraire Jacques Doucet, 10 place de Panthéon, Paris, and at the Beinecke Rare Book and Manuscript Library, Yale University. In addition, the McFarlin Library Department of Special Collections at the University of Tulsa holds hundreds of letters exchanged between Barney and Romaine Brooks.

Further Reading: S. Benstock, *Women of the Left Bank* (University of Texas Press, 1986); G. Wickes, *The Amazon of Letters: Life and Loves of Natalie Barney* (W.H. Allen, 1977); J. Chalon, *Portrait of a Seductress: The World of Natalie Barney* (Crown, 1979).

Natalie Barney

BLACK SUN PRESS

2 RUE CARDINALE

(Métro: Mabillon/St-Germain-des-Prés)

**SITE OF THE PRINTERY AND OFFICE
OF BLACK SUN PRESS
PUBLISHING HOUSE OF HARRY AND
CARESSE CROSBY**

*You come to feel that his strength was what
killed him: a weaker man would have been
prudent enough to survive. He had gifts that
would have made him an explorer, a soldier
of fortune, a revolutionist: they were qualities fatal to a poet.*
Malcolm Cowley, *Exile's Return* (1934)

Rue Cardinale in 1922 (photo: Eugène
Atget)

In December 1929, 31-year-old Harry Crosby and a young woman were found dead in a New York apartment. Harry was holding a gun in his right hand and had a bullet hole in his right temple. The girl had a bullet hole in her left temple. Facing each other, his arm was curled around her neck. Their left hands were clasped. Their double suicide was headline news, but there was no suicide note, no explanation and no clues.

The nephew of banker J.P. Morgan, Harry Crosby was rich, Harvard educated, and a budding poet who was earmarked for a career in banking. During World War I he volunteered for the Ambulance Service in France. At Verdun he survived a German artillery shell that should have killed him, but the experience, 'the violent metamorphose from boy to man', severely traumatised and haunted him for the rest of his short life. On his return from the war he drank, gambled and worked half-heartedly for a bank. At this time he also met Polly Peabody, who later became known as Caresse, and when Crosby's family se-cured him a position in a bank in Paris, the newly married couple sailed together for France in September 1922.

The Paris bank job was short-lived, but through the haze of their extravagant alcohol and party-fuelled expatriate living, they both managed to write poetry and self-publish some of their work. In 1927 they founded their own publishing company, Éditions Narcisse, later renamed Black Sun Press, in a room above Roger Lescaret's printery at 2 rue Cardinale. Begun primarily as a non-profit venture and outlet for their own work, Black Sun Press soon began publishing limited runs of the early modernists, notably Hart Crane, Kay Boyle, D.H. Lawrence, Ernest Hemingway, Archibald MacLeish, Eugene Jolas, James Joyce and Laurence Sterne, establishing itself as one of the major small presses of the 1920s. They were also gaining a reputation for the quality of their editions, which were handsomely bound and printed on the finest paper. It seemed that Harry Crosby had finally found his place in the world. He loved, and lived for, books. He was at the heart of Parisian literary life. He had achieved great things in the world of art.

But to him, was it all just a void that gradually melted away in that New York apartment in December 1929, leaving him standing alone in a shell crater at Verdun? He had certainly lost his innocence during the war, as all young men did. Harry Crosby believed in an afterlife but he nurtured a death wish, and suicide was never far from his thoughts.

He collected news clippings about suicide, wrote out suicide pacts, purchased his own headstone, and made friends with the staff of the cemetery where he had arranged to be buried. Harry was always planning his adventure into the great unknown. 'It was not so much that he had chosen the moment for suicide', wrote Malcolm Cowley, 'as rather that in his disorganized frenzy the moment had chosen him.'

See Also: The American Hospital in Paris, Hart Crane, Kay Boyle, Ernest Hemingway, Archibald MacLeish, Eugene Jolas, James Joyce, Laurence Sterne.

Select Bibliography: H. Crosby, *Shadows of the Sun: The Diaries of Harry Crosby* (Black Sparrow, 1977); *Ladders to the Sun: Poems of Harry Crosby with Extracts from His Diaries* (Soul Bay Press, 2013).

Further Reading: G. Wolff, *Black Sun: The Brief Transit and Violent Eclipse of Harry Crosby* (Random House, 1985); M. Cowley, *Exile's Return: A Literary Odyssey of the 1920s* (Norton, 1934); H. Ford, *Published in Paris* (Garnstone, 1975); C. Crosby, *The Passionate Years* (LLC, 2012).

Harry Crosby (second from left) and friends, shortly before Verdun, 22 November 1917

DJUNA BARNES

PLACE SAINT-SULPICE

(Métro: St-Sulpice)

ÉGLISE SAINT-SULPICE

SETTING FOR THE NOVEL

NIGHTWOOD BY DJUNA BARNES

AMERICAN NOVELIST, POET AND

ILLUSTRATOR

Djuna Barnes

Sometimes, late at night, before turning into the Café de la Mairie de VIe, he would be observed staring up at the huge towers of the church which rose into the sky, unlovely but reassuring, running a thick warm finger around his throat, where, in spite of its custom, his hair surprised him, lifting along his back and creeping up over his collar. Standing small and insubordinate, he would watch the basins of the fountain loosing their skirts of water in a ragged and flowing hem, sometimes crying to a man's departing shadow: 'Aren't you the beauty!'

Djuna Barnes, *Nightwood* (1936)

Modernist writer Djuna Barnes is mostly remembered today for one book: her poetic novel, *Nightwood*, a surrealist study of Americans and Europeans living in Paris in the 1920s. T.S. Eliot, in his glowing 1937 preface to the novel, wrote that it was 'a quality of horror and doom very nearly related to that of Elizabethan tragedy'. But although a book may shine, its creator can linger in its shadow. Writing to Natalie Barney in 1963, a concerned Djuna Barnes summed up her fading recognition: 'There is not a person in the literary world who has not heard of, read and some stolen from *Nightwood*. The paradox that in spite of all the critical work flooding the press since 1936, not more than three or four have mentioned my name. I am the most famous unknown of the century!'

Djuna Barnes was born in Cornwall-on-Hudson on the west bank of the Hudson River in 1892 to Elizabeth Barnes, and Wald Barnes, a failed artist. Her father practised polygamy, and his mistress joined the family a few years after Djuna's birth. It was a *ménage à trois* that produced eight children. At the age of sixteen, Djuna was reportedly raped, either by her father or a neighbour. Two years later she married the fifty-two-year-old brother of her father's mistress. In 1912, together with her mother and her three brothers, she fled to New York, where her mother filed for divorce, and Djuna began a career as a reporter and illustrator. By 1915 she was living in Greenwich Village where she published her first book of poetry, *The Book of Repulsive Women*.

In 1920 she left for Paris on a magazine assignment to portray the world of the expatriate writer and artist, a world she would live in, on and off, for the next ten years. Dressed in her iconic cloak and hat, she soon became a well-known figure around the bohemian haunts and habitats of Paris's expatriates. Djuna Barnes was bisexual and most of her close relationships in Paris were with women. In 1921 she met and fell in love with the artist Thelma Wood; it was a volatile relationship, which lasted until 1928. During her Paris years Barnes met most of the literary high priesthood, including T.S. Eliot, Ezra Pound (who tried to seduce her), James Joyce (who became a friend and allowed her to call him Jim), Natalie Barney, and Gertrude Stein, whom she detested. 'I couldn't stand her,' she wrote. 'She had to be the centre of everything. A monstrous ego.'

In Paris, in 1923, she wrote and published *A Book*, a collection of poems, stories, plays and drawings. Five years later, in 1928, she published *Ryder*, a fictionalised history of the Barnes family in mock-Elizabethan style, and the *Ladies Almanack,* a *roman-à-clef* novel about Paris lesbians. *Nightwood* (1936), set in the homosexual underworld of Paris, was mostly written in England at the home of her friend, the art collector Peggy Guggenheim.

Djuna Barnes left Paris in 1931, eventually returning to New York's Greenwich Village ten years later, where she lived out her life in seclusion. Plagued by asthma, arthritis and emphysema, she died there in 1982, aged ninety.

See Also: Natalie Barney, T.S. Eliot, Ezra Pound, James Joyce, Gertrude Stein, Charles Baudelaire, Victor Hugo, Joris-Karl Huysmans, Marquis de Sade.

Further Information: For most of her time in Paris Djuna Barnes lived with Thelma Wood, first at 173 boulevard Saint-Germain, and a few years later at 9 rue Saint-Romain. The Roman Catholic Church of Saint-Sulpice is the second largest church in Paris after Notre Dame Cathedral. Founded in 1646 and dedicated to the seventh-century bishop, Sulpitius the Pious, it can lay claim to several literary connections. Madame de La Fayette, author of *La Princesse de Clèves* (1678), reputedly France's first psychological novel, was baptised and married, and, eventually, in 1693, buried here. The Marquis de Sade and Charles Baudelaire were also baptised here, in 1740 and 1821 respectively. It was here that Victor Hugo married Adèle Foucher in 1822, and Durtal, Joris-Karl Huysmans's hero in his 1891 novel, *Là-bas (The Damned)*, decried its architecture when he declared that it had taken five or six architects to raise its 'pitiful pile of stones!'

Select Bibliography: *The Book of Repulsive Women* (1915); *A Book* (1923); *Ryder* (1928); *Ladies Almanack* (1928); *A Night Among the Horses* (1929); *Nightwood* (1936); *The Antiphon* (1958); *Collected Stories of Djuna Barnes* (1996).

Further Reading: J. Scott, *Djuna Barnes* (Twayne, 1976); A. Field, *Djuna* (G.P. Putnam's Sons, 1983); P. Herring, *Djuna* (Penguin, 1997).

Église Saint-Sulpice

ERNEST HEMINGWAY

6 RUE FEROU

(Métro: St-Sulpice)

HÔTEL DE LUZY

WHERE HEMINGWAY LIVED WITH HIS

SECOND WIFE, PAULINE PFEIFFER, AND

WHERE HE WROTE THE BEGINNING

AND THE END OF

A FAREWELL TO ARMS

I ate the end of my piece of cheese and took a swallow of wine. Through the other noise I heard a cough, then came the chuh-chuh-chuh-chuh – then there was a flash, as when a blast-furnace door is swung open, and a roar that started white and went red and on and on in a rushing wind. I tried to breathe but my breath would not come and I felt myself rush bodily out of myself and out and out and out and all the time bodily in the wind. I went out swiftly, all of myself, and I knew I was dead and that it had all been a mistake to think you just died. Then I floated, and instead of going on I felt myself slide back. I breathed and I was back ...

Ernest Hemingway, *A Farewell to Arms* (1929)

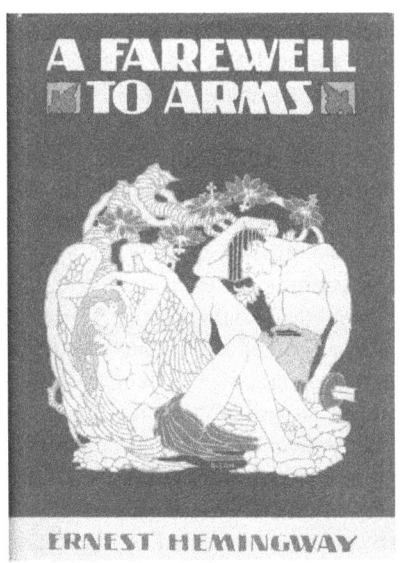

First edition (Scribner's, September 1929)

Pauline Pfeiffer (1895–1951) was the second of Hemingway's four wives, and the mother of two of his three children. She was from a wealthy family in the Midwest of America, where she majored in journalism. In the early 1920s, while she was working as a journalist for the French edition of *Vogue* magazine in Paris, she met Hemingway through Kitty Cannell, Paris fashion editor for *The New York Times*, who was a friend of Hemingway's wife, Hadley. Following Hemingway's ensuing affair with Pfeiffer, and subsequent divorce from Hadley, they married in May

1927. After a honeymoon in the south of France, they moved into a luxurious flat, paid for by Pfeiffer's rich uncle, in the eighteenth-century Hôtel de Luzy, imposingly situated behind a high gate guarded by stone sphinxes on Rue Ferou. They lived here, on and off, between trips back to the USA, until January 1930, when they returned to America and settled in Key West – where Pfeiffer would live for the rest of her life. The marriage produced two sons and ended in divorce in 1940, but Pfeiffer was the wife who was with Hemingway throughout the time of his most creative period, when she played an often unsung but essentially crucial role in his development as a writer. When Pfeiffer first met Hemingway he had yet to achieve fame, but the publication of *A Farewell to Arms* in 1929 changed everything, bringing him the public and critical acclaim he had yearned for.

Before *A Farewell to Arms*, Hemingway had published two slender volumes of

179

stories with small Paris presses, and four books in the USA, one of which was *The Sun Also Rises*, in 1926. It was, according to his mother, 'one the filthiest books of the year'. In 1924 he began an autobiographical novel about his war experiences, but later abandoned it. It was not until March 1928, at the Rue Ferou apartment, that he made a start on the novel that would become *A Farewell to Arms*. Set on the Austrian front during the Italian campaign of World War I, it was not an autobiographical work, but Hemingway's clear-sighted descriptions of war, courage, comradeship and love. Over the next fifteen months it was written in America, at Key West, their home in Florida; in Arkansas, where Pfeiffer's parents lived; in Kansas City, where their son was born (a difficult delivery, elements of which Hemingway fictionalised for the concluding pages of the novel); and Wyoming. The last draft was finally completed back in Paris, in the Rue Ferou apartment, on June 24, 1929. Hemingway rewrote the last page thirty-nine times before he was satisfied. He called it 'getting the words right'.

See Also: Ernest Hemingway, Harry's New York Bar, American Hospital in Paris, American Ambulance Field Service, Dingo Bar, The Ritz, Gare de Lyon, F. Scott Fitzgerald, Sylvia Beach, Gertrude Stein, Sherwood Anderson, Ford Madox Ford, Ezra Pound, Café Le Sélect, Les Deux Magots.

Further Information: Scribner's wanted to serialise *A Farewell to Arms* in its magazine in the May to October 1929 issues, and had offered Hemingway $16,000, their largest payout at that time, but were concerned about its language. Hemingway agreed to cuts, but even with cuts Boston's police chief banned the June issue of *Scribner's Magazine* because it was deemed indecent – good

publicity that helped boost the sales of the novel published a few months later. It was at his Rue Ferou flat that Hemingway, returning from a drunken night out with poet Archibald MacLeish, mistook a skylight cord for the lavatory chain, crashing the skylight onto his forehead, resulting in a gash that would require several stitches and leave a lifelong scar (see The American Hospital in Paris). Hemingway and Pfeiffer were married on 10 May 1927 in the Saint-Honoré-d'Eylau Church in Place Victor-Hugo.

Select Bibliography: *The Sun Also Rises* (1926); *The Torrents of Spring* (1926); *Men Without Women* (1927); *A Farewell to Arms* (1929).

Further Reading: S. Donaldson (ed.), *New Essays on A Farewell to Arms* (Cambridge University Press, 1991); R. Hawkins, *Unbelievable Happiness and Final Sorrow: The Hemingway-Pfeiffer Marriage* (University of Arkansas Press, 2012); M. Reynolds, *Hemingway: The Paris Years* (Norton, 1999); R. McAlmon, *Being Geniuses Together*, revised by Kay Boyle, (Michael Joseph, 1968).

6 rue Ferou

THE PARIS REVIEW

8 RUE GARANCIÈRE

(Métro: Odéon/Mabillon/St-Sulpice)

SITE OF *THE PARIS REVIEW*'S

FIRST OFFICE, FOUNDED IN 1953

Dear reader,
The Paris Review *hopes to emphasize creative work—fiction and poetry—not to the exclusion of criticism, but with the aim in mind of merely removing criticism from the dominating place it holds in most literary magazines and putting it pretty much where it belongs, i.e., somewhere near the back of the book. I think The Paris Review should welcome these people into its pages: the good writers and good poets, the non-drum-beaters and non-axe-grinders. So long as they're good.*
William Styron, letter in the inaugural issue of *The Paris Review* (1953)

Many literary magazines have been launched with bold statements of intent, and later sunk without trace. *The Paris Review* not only still survives today, but it has clung to its 1950s principles, boldly espoused by novelist William Styron. Based in New York since 1973, it was founded in Paris twenty years earlier by Harold Humes and Peter Matthiessen, with George Plimpton as editor. Its first office was in the basement boardroom of the publisher Les Éditions de la Table Ronde in Rue Garancière, with the terrasse of the nearby Café de Tournon being a regular meeting place for staff and contributors.

Over the years the *Review* has promoted writers who were relatively unknown, but who are today household names, notably: Adrienne Rich, Philip Roth, V.S. Naipaul, T. Coraghessan Boyle, Mona Simpson, Edward P. Jones and Rick Moody. Selections from Samuel Beckett's novel *Molloy*, one of his first publications in English, appeared in the fifth issue. It also acknowledged the talent of Jack Kerouac, with the publication of his short story 'The Mexican Girl', in 1955. Other significant works that made their first appearance in *The Paris Review* were, Italo Calvino's *Last Comes the Raven*, Philip Roth's *Goodbye Columbus*, Donald Barthelme's 'Alice', Jim Carroll's *Basketball Diaries*, Peter Matthiessen's *Far Tortuga*, Jeffrey Eugenides's *The Virgin Suicides* and Jonathan Franzen's *The Corrections*.

But the *Review's* icing on the cake has always been its author interviews, known as Writers at Work, described by one critic as 'one of the single most persistent acts of cultural conservation in the history of the world'. The first interview was with E.M. Forster in 1953,

George Plimpton with writers outside Café Tournon, Paris, 1950s. Front row, from left: Vilma Howard, Jane Lougee, Muffy Wainhouse, Jean Garrigue. Second row: Christopher Logue, Richard Seaver, Evan Connell, Niccolò Tucci, Eugene Walter, unidentified, Peter Hyun, Alfred Chester, Austryn Wainhouse. Back row: George Plimpton, Michel van der Plas, James Broughton, William Gardner Smith, Harold Witt

and since then other interviewees have included William Faulkner, Dorothy Parker, Simone de Beauvoir, Vladimir Nabokov, Isak Dinesen, Graham Greene, Marianne Moore, Ernest Hemingway, Truman Capote, T.S. Eliot, Françoise Sagan, James Thurber, Thornton Wilder, and Katherine Anne Porter, who made it very clear in her 1963 interview that 1920s expatriate Paris was not her idea of paradise:

I think it was a horrible time: shallow and trivial and silly. The remarkable thing is that anybody survived in such an atmosphere—in a place where they could call F. Scott Fitzgerald a great writer! ... I couldn't read him then and I can't read him now. There was just one passage in a book called *Tender Is the Night*—I read that and thought, 'Now I

will read this again,' because I couldn't be sure. Not only didn't I like his writing, but I didn't like the people he wrote about. I thought they weren't worth thinking about, and I still think so. It seems to me that your human beings have to have some kind of meaning. I just can't be interested in those perfectly stupid meaningless lives.

See Also: Samuel Beckett, Simone de Beauvoir, F. Scott Fitzgerald, Jack Kerouac, Ernest Hemingway, T.S. Eliot, Françoise Sagan, James Thurber, Thornton Wilder, Katherine Anne Porter, Café de Tournon.

Further Information: George Plimpton (1927–2003), who became a well known sports writer, edited the *Review* from its founding until his death in 2003. Peter Matthiessen (1927–2014), co-founder of the *Review*, who became a successful writer and environmental activist, was recruited by the CIA when he was a student at Yale, and sent to Paris as a spy during the Cold War. In 1953, the *Review*, along with the novel he was writing, became a cover for his CIA activities. He soon realised, however, that he was on 'the wrong side'. In later life he claimed his two years with the CIA 'was the one adventure he regretted'.

8 rue Garancière

182

CAFÉ DE TOURNON

18 RUE DE TOURNON

(Métro: Odéon)

1950S EXPATRIATE WATERING HOLE

FOR AFRICAN AMERICAN WRITERS AND

ARTISTS

During that spring the Café Tournon became the most celebrated cafe in all of Europe, and from there one could select entertainments of all types. All of us vocal blacks collected there to choose our white woman for each night, and the white women gathered about us and waited our selection. White women love an absurd black, especially if he's funny ... I was intrigued by these women, many of whom were beautiful and intelligent, competing to sleep with us blacks. But I didn't let them confuse me.
Chester Himes, *My Life of Absurdity* (1976)

Café de Tournon's artistic heyday was the 1950s, and, through the rose-tinted, misogynist spectacles of Chester Himes at least, it 'became the most celebrated cafe in all of Europe'. But what makes a cafe become a gathering place for writers, artists and expatriate bohemians? In Café de Tournon's case it may have been because the management were happy to turn a blind eye to the drugs that were always easy to obtain there; additionally, they were not averse to giving an impoverished writer credit or a small loan. Its proprietor, Mme Alazar, had been accused of collaborating with the Nazis during the war, a disgrace that might explain the lack of Parisian natives queuing at its doors. 'Behind the counter, for all to see,' wrote journalist and Tournon regular Danny Halperin, 'was a large photograph of her walking

down the street in Paris, followed by a jeering crowd, with not a hair on her head. She had had a Gestapo lover, but she didn't try to hide it, unlike a lot of people who had collaborated and then became *résistants* overnight.'

Café de Tournon is best remembered in literary history as a rendezvous for African American writers, notably Richard Wright, William Gardner Smith, Chester Himes and, occasionally, James Baldwin. For the first time in their lives they were very likely experiencing life without racial prejudice, in a country where a black man could kiss a white woman and not be hanged from a tree. Paris was no ethnic paradise in the 1950s: racism did exist; but it wasn't Mississippi by a long chalk. Racial equality made the FBI and the CIA jumpy and agents were planted in Café de Tournon to spy on this supposed left wing, communist-fuelled emancipation. The extent of these intelligence operations, which were substantial, only became public knowledge with the Freedom of Information Act in the late 1960s.

The staff of *The Paris Review*, whose offices were on nearby Rue Garancière, were Café de Tournon regulars in the 1950s. It was also a regular watering hole for the staff of the literary magazine *Merlin*, founded by Jane Lougee and her lover, the novelist and heroin addict, Alexander Trocchi. Other regulars mostly consisted of American writers, journalists and jazz musicians.

Writer, critic and journalist, Joseph Roth (1894–1939) is commemorated by a plaque on the wall opposite the bar. Roth, an alcoholic, lived above the cafe in the late 1930s and it became a regular refuge for him. Born in Galicia, in the Austro-Hungarian Empire (now Ukraine), Roth had Jewish heritage.

He served in the Austrian army during WWI, then after the war he worked as a journalist in Vienna and Berlin, while also writing novels. He became part of the intellectual opposition to Nazism and wisely fled Germany for Paris when Hitler came to power in 1933. 'I won't bet a penny on our lives,' he wrote to a friend. 'They have succeeded in establishing a reign of barbarity. Do not fool yourself. Hell reigns.' His wife, who was schizophrenic, spent many years in sanatoriums and was later murdered by the Nazis. Roth's semi-autobiographical fiction is greatly undervalued today, but he will be remembered for *The Radetzky March* (1932), the story of three generations of the Trotta family in the years preceding the 1918 collapse of the Austro-Hungarian Empire. Roth died in poverty in 1939 aged forty-four.

See Also: Richard Wright, James Baldwin, Chester Himes, *The Paris Review*, Alexander Trocchi.

Chester Himes

184

JARDIN DU LUXEMBOURG

PLACE PAUL CLAUDEL

(Métro: Odéon)

A UNIQUE SENSE OF PLACE FOR WRITERS, FEATURING IN MANY NOVELS

Then Gertrude Stein and I took our first walk. In the nearby Luxembourg Gardens she called my attention. Alice, she said, look at the autumn herbaceous border. But I did not propose to reciprocate the familiarity.
The Luxembourg was filled with children around the artificial lake floating their boats; others were rolling hoops with bells ... The nurses were still wearing their long capes and starched white caps with long broad streamers. Through the gardens into the Petit Luxembourg and down the boulevard Saint-Michel Gertrude Stein led me.
Alice B. Toklas, *What is Remembered* (1963)

At the Luxembourg Gardens, by Renoir (1883)

Situated between Saint-Germain-des-Prés and the Latin Quarter, the Luxembourg Gardens have always been a kind of inner sanctum for writers throughout history, a brief asylum from the urban chaos and daily struggle, a place where writers sought refuge and inspiration while sketching out settings for their novels. 'It is a garden I have always loved,' wrote Robert Louis Stevenson in *The Wrecker* (1892). 'You sit there in a public place of history and fiction ... The city tramples by without the railings to lively measure; and within and about you, trees rustle, children and sparrows utter their small cries and the statues look on forever.' William Makepeace Thackeray, in his *Paris Sketch Book* (1840) remembers walking to the Luxembourg, 'where bonnes, students, grisettes, and old gentlemen with pigtails love to wander in the melancholy, quaint old gardens.' Irish novelist, George Moore, recalls in *Memoirs of My Dead Life* (1906) that after breakfast one morning in the 1870s 'I threw myself on a bench, and began to wonder if there was anything better in the world worth doing than to sit in an alley of clipped limes smoking, thinking of Paris and of myself.' In Henry James's *The Ambassadors* (1903), the protagonist, Lambert Strether, has a moment of sudden revelation in the Gardens about his identity, and in William Faulkner's 1931 novel *Sanctuary*, the final scene is set in the Gardens, when Temple Drake and her father finally find sanctuary in Paris. In Dumas's *The Three Musketeers* (1844), d'Artagnan, Athos, Porthos, and Aramis play tennis at a *jeu de paume* court in the Gardens. And in a scarcely credible recollection, Ernest Hemingway reminisced about

185

strangling the Luxembourg's pigeons for the pot: 'There was always a *gendarme* on duty,' he wrote,

> but I knew that about four o'clock he would go to a bar across from the park to have a glass of wine. That's when I would appear with Mr. Bumby [Hemingway's son] – and a pocketful of corn for the pigeons. I would sit on a bench, in my guise of buggy-pushing pigeon-lover, casing the flock for clarity of eye and plumpness.

French novelist, Alfred de Musset, was more sympathetic to the Gardens' feathered friends and remembers 'throwing bread to a few poor birds that were numb and cold' in his novel *La Confession d'un enfant du siècle (The Confession of a Child of the Century)* (1836) which recounts his love affair with George Sand. Marius first laid eyes on Cosette when 'she was about thirteen or fourteen' in the Luxembourg in Victor Hugo's sprawling masterpiece, *Les Miserables* (1862). A year later Marius returns to the Luxembourg and once again beholds Cosette. This time, however, he is smitten: 'The person he now saw was a tall and lovely creature, possessing the charming outlines of a woman, at the precise moment when they are still combined with the most simple graces of the child – a fugitive and gracious moment which can alone be rendered by the two words "fifteen years".'

See Also: Thomas Paine, Gertrude Stein, Alice B. Toklas, Victor Hugo, Robert Louis Stevenson, Alfred de Musset, George Sand, Henry James, Ernest Hemingway, Stendhal, Gustave Flaubert, Alexandre Dumas, d'Artagnan, Charles Baudelaire, Paul Verlaine, W.M. Thackeray.

Further Information: The Luxembourg Palace and Gardens were created by Queen Marie de Medici in 1612. Inspired by the Pitti Palace and Boboli Gardens in Florence, they encompass an area of more than 50 acres split into French and English gardens. As well as the Medici Fountain, the Orangerie, the Pavillon Davioud, and a memorial to Stendhal, the Gardens also feature more than 100 statues, which include sculptures of Flaubert, Sand, Stendhal, Sainte-Beuve, Murger, de Banville, Baudelaire, and Verlaine, who described de Banville's sculpture as 'the one with the tits'.

Top: Paul Verlaine
Above: Charles Baudelaire

THOMAS PAINE

15 RUE DE VAUGIRARD

(Métro: Odéon/St. Sulpice)

PALAIS DU LUXEMBOURG
WHERE RADICAL POLITICAL WRITER
THOMAS PAINE WAS IMPRISONED
DURING THE FRENCH REVOLUTION

But such is the irresistible nature of truth, that all it asks, and all it wants, is the liberty of appearing.
Thomas Paine,
The Rights of Man (1791–1792)

Thomas Paine

On 26 December 1793, Thomas Paine was found guilty of treason and condemned to death by the French Revolution's Committee of Public Safety for having allegedly 'conspired against the interests of France', and was removed to the Luxembourg Prison to await execution. Ironically, when he had arrived in Paris a few months previously he was hailed as a hero and elected to the French Convention, the Revolutionary government; but his opinions so infuriated Robespierre, one of the most influential figures of the Revolution, that he was sentenced to death by guillotine, a fate he narrowly escaped only when Robespierre himself was assassinated.

The son of an English Quaker, Thomas Paine was born in Thetford, Norfolk, in 1736. At the age of thirteen his schooling ended when his family was unable to afford his continuing education, and he was apprenticed to his father's corset-making business. From then on he began to educate himself whenever he could. In 1762, through his father's influence, he gained a job as an excise officer, a job that gave birth to his first political work: a pamphlet demanding better pay and conditions for his fellow workers. His campaigning pamphlets came to the attention of the Anglo-Irish writer, Oliver Goldsmith, and through Goldsmith he became acquainted with Benjamin Franklin, one of the founding fathers of the United States, the man who would change the course of Paine's life. Franklin was the first to realise Paine's potential as a political writer, and, after many meetings, he convinced Paine his talents were needed in the North American colonies. Following his advice Paine landed on the shores of America in November 1774.

In the beginning, Paine did not see himself as any kind of freedom fighter to aid the colonists in their struggle, but rather as someone who simply wanted to make himself a new life and improve his circumstances. He ended up in Philadelphia where he turned his hand to journalism, but it wasn't long before he became a champion of liberty.

Maximilien Robespierre (1758–94)

In January 1776 he published a short pamphlet entitled *Common Sense*, which stated the case for democracy over monarchy, and independence over British rule. The pamphlet was a great success; it sold thousands of copies, it captured the imagination of the people, and it was hugely influential towards the United States Declaration of Independence in 1776. Paine went on to publish many more pro-revolutionary pamphlets (later published as *The American Crisis*) and to work in a variety of posts in the revolutionary government until, in 1787, his work done, he sailed for Europe where another revolution was on the horizon.

Arriving in Paris, a city on the brink of revolution, in the summer of 1787, he was given a hero's welcome. In September of the same year, he returned to England for the first time in thirteen years. It was a country where he now had many enemies, following the American Revolution. The British establishment had not forgiven him, and news of the burgeoning French Revolution had them extremely unnerved. Anglo-Irish

politician, Edmund Burke, who fiercely opposed the Revolution, responded with a pamphlet entitled *Reflexions on the Revolution in France*. Paine's reply, and challenge to Burke, was in publishing *The Rights of Man*, a groundbreaking assault on the status quo and a defence of man's inviolable rights. Conditions in England steadily deteriorated for Paine, and in September 1792 he fled to France. In his absence he was convicted for seditious libel against the Crown.

In France, Paine was honoured with citizenship and was elected to the National Convention, but his opposition to Louis XVI's execution had him denounced as a traitor to the Revolution for which he was imprisoned and sentenced to death. During his imprisonment, France descended into the Reign of Terror, witnessing the mass executions of the enemies of the Revolution. Paine escaped execution by a quirk of fate. Prisoners to be executed had their door marked with chalk. 'But it happened', wrote Paine, 'that the mark was put on when the door was open, and flat against the wall, and thereby came on the inside when we shut it at night, and the destroying angel passed us by.'

Paine returned to the United States in 1802 where he published his magnum opus, much of which he had written while in prison, the anti-Church *The Age of Reason*, a work for which he was widely condemned. Although Paine wrote nothing more of consequence he did not retire quietly into old age, but remained a radical to the end. He died in his sleep on 8 June 1809, aged seventy-two, and was buried on his farm at New Rochelle, New York State. Four months later his remains were illegally exhumed by newspaperman, William Cobbett, and shipped back to England, where Cobbett hoped people would pay for the privilege of viewing them. The public, however, chose to stay away. Today the location of his remains is unknown, but an old rhyming verse still survives:

Poor Tom Paine! Here he lies,
Nobody laughs and nobody cries;
Where he's gone and how he fares,
Nobody knows and nobody cares.

See Also: Jardin du Luxembourg, Guillotine, Louis XVI.

Select Bibliography: *Common Sense* (1776); *The American Crisis* (1776–83); *The Rights of Man* (1791–92); *The Age of Reason* (1796).

Further Reading: J. Keane, *Tom Paine: A Political Life* (Bloomsbury, 1995); C. Hitchens, *Thomas Paine's 'Rights of Man'* (Atlantic, 2007).

Further Information: The Palais du Luxembourg was built in the early 1600s for Marie de Médicis, wife of Henry IV of France. Little remains of the original interior, but the exterior is still intact. It was used briefly as a prison during the Revolution, and since 1879 it has been the home of the Senate, the upper house of the Parliament of France.

The Palais du Luxembourg

RACHILDE
26 RUE DE CONDÉ
(Métro: Odéon)

FORMER RESIDENCE OF RACHILDE
FRENCH WRITER WHO CHALLENGED
PATRIARCHAL RULES
AND OFFICES OF THE LITERARY
REVIEW *MERCURE DE FRANCE*

A few years more, and that pretty creature who you love too much, I think, will, without ever loving them, have known as many men as there are beads on her aunt's rosary. No happy medium! Either a nun or a monster! God's bosom or sensual passions! It would, perhaps, be better to put her in a convent, since we put hysterical women in the Salt-petriere! She does not know vice, she invents it!
Rachilde, *Monsieur Vénus* (1884)

To be a young, single, female writer in late nineteenth-century Paris was to be regarded, if not as a woman of loose morals, then certainly as one whose morals were under suspicion. But cross-dressing author Marguerite Eymery (pen name Rachilde), who cared nothing for morality codes, rebelled against the patriarchal protocols of her day, and made a scandalous debut into the French literary world with her novel *Monsieur Vénus* in 1884. Judged pornographic with its themes of sadomasochism, transvestism and necrophilia, it was published in Belgium and promptly banned, whereupon Rachilde was sentenced, in absentia, to two years imprisonment. Paul Verlaine congratulated her on the invention of a new vice, and *Rachilde, Homme de Lettres* (Rachilde, Man of Letters), as she was styled on her visiting cards, took her place alongside

189

Marguerite Eymery (pen name Rachilde)

Arthur Rimbaud, Charles Baudelaire and other fellow Decadents of French literature.

Marguerite Eymery was born in 1860 near Périgueux, south-western France, the only child of army officer, Joseph Eymery, and his wife Gabrielle. 'My father, magnificent brute that he was,' she wrote, 'could not forgive me for being a little girl.' After a peripatetic army childhood with minimal schooling, she discovered writing when she was twelve, later claiming to have invented the name Rachilde during a seance when she was sixteen. Her parents, who were devout followers of spiritism, regularly sat round the table communicating with the spirits of the dead. One evening, Marguerite decided to play a hoax on them by faking the sound of a spirit knocking on the table. The spirit had, she maintained, designated her as his medium and, through Marguerite, revealed

he was a sixteenth-century Swedish nobleman named Rachilde. The family was absolutely convinced Marguerite had been possessed, and from that day forth, conveniently indeterminate of sex and class, Rachilde became the pen name of Marguerite Eymery.

In 1878, chaperoned by her mother, she arrived in Paris to work on her cousin's magazine for women, *L'École des femmes,* for which she wrote everything from the fashion page to its serialised novel. It was a good training ground for the world of the Parisian press, and soon she discovered the cafes of the Latin Quarter, inhabited by like-minded writers and artists of the avant-garde. Rachilde's first novel, *Monsieur de la Nouveauté*, was published in 1880, but it was her next novel, in 1884, that brought her unexpected celebrity. Living in 'absolute poverty', she wrote, she could either 'throw herself into the gutter or … write within a fortnight that truly shocking work'. The end result was *Monsieur Vénus*. 'A new era began for the little bohemian', she wrote of herself in the preface to her 1886 novel *À Mort*, 'who was still, at this point, a society woman. She finally understood what sort of place literary Paris allotted to young women without a big house, or a protector – and also without prejudices. She threw good manners to the winds … started to wear men's clothing, did the rounds of public balls in the company of heroic decadents.'

In June 1889 she married printer Alfred Vallette, giving birth six months later to their daughter, Gabrielle. The following year Vallette launched the literary journal, *Mercure de France*, with Rachilde as resident fiction reviewer and member of the editorial staff. The journal's home was the family home, at first in

Rue de l'Échaudé, and later in Rue de Condé, where it became very much a family business. The journal prospered, and although its finances were shaky, its contributors, notably Remy de Gourmont, Stéphane Mallarmé, Villiers de l'Isle-Adam, André Gide, and Guillaume Apollinaire were proficient and dependable. Rachilde dubbed herself 'patronne du *Mercure*'. As well as her intensive journal work and hosting a weekly literary salon, she continued her own writing, which, by the end of her life, amounted to over sixty novels, many of which dealt with sexual identity. She was an impassioned writer who consistently confronted the hierarchies of the state. She was anti-Semitic and anti-feminist. She was bisexual, and she defended homosexual love. The French expression *enfant terrible* is a suitable appraisal of her enormously creative and scandalous life, which ended at the age of ninety-three in 1953.

See Also: Marquis de Sade, Pierre Beaumarchais, Paul Verlaine, Arthur Rimbaud, Charles Baudelaire, Remy de Gourmont, Stéphane Mallarmé, André Gide, Guillaume Apollinaire, Gaston Gallimard.

Further Information: *Mercure de France* was purchased by Gallimard in 1958, and at the time of writing is still based at 26 rue de Condé. Rue de Condé is named after Henry II of Bourbon, Prince de Condé, who purchased a mansion there in 1612, located at Nos. 9 to 15, and where, on 2 June 1740, the Marquis de Sade was born. Rachilde's seventeenth-century house at No. 26 was also where French playwright Pierre Beaumarchais (1732–1799) lived from 1763, and where he wrote *The Barber of Seville*.

Select Bibliography: *Monsieur Vénus* (1884); *À Mort* (1886); *La Marquise de Sade*

(1887); *Madame Adonis* (1888); *Le mordu* (1889); *La Jongleuse* (1900); *Pourquoi je ne suis pas féministe* (1928); *Quand j'étais jeune* (1948).

Further Reading: D. Holmes, *Rachilde: Decadence, Gender and the Woman Writer* (Berg, 2001); *French Women's Writing 1848–1994* (Athlone, 2000); E. Showalter, *Sexual Anarchy: Gender and Culture at the Fin de Siècle* (Virago, 1992).

26 rue de Condé

SHAKESPEARE
AND COMPANY

8 RUE DUPUYTREN

(Métro: Odéon)

SITE OF THE FIRST

SHAKESPEARE AND COMPANY

NOVEMBER 1919 TO JULY 1921

We hurried to the rue Dupuytren, where, at No. 8 – there were only about ten numbers on this hilly little street – was a shop with the shutters up and a sign saying Boutique à louer [shop for rent]. It had once been a laundry, said Adrienne, pointing to the words 'gros' and 'fin' on either side of the door, meaning they did up both sheets and fine linen. Adrienne, who was rather plump, placed herself under the 'gros' and told me to stand under the 'fin'. 'That's you and me,' she said.
Sylvia Beach, *Shakespeare and Company* (1959)

Sylvia Beach visited Paris many times in her youth, but in 1916, aged 29, she arrived in the city to stay, perchance to study literature, and also, she hoped, to start a career. She tried her hand – to no avail – at journalism, but in a letter to her mother the future was clearly beckoning when she wrote: 'I must get something profitable. My uselessness utterly depresses me … As for a business, when the war is over, if I'm not old and buried by that time, I must have a bookstore, I must.' She did not have long to wait.

One day at the Bibliothèque Nationale, the National Library of France, while looking in a book for a particular review of symbolist poetry, a note inside informed her that the book could be purchased at Adrienne Monnier's bookshop, 7 rue de l'Odéon. 'I had not heard of it before,' she wrote, 'nor was the Odéon quarter familiar to me, but

suddenly something drew me irresistibly to the spot where such important things in my life were about to happen.' She was welcomed into the shop by Monnier, and from that day their friendship blossomed. In the weeks that followed, Monnier gave Beach the advice and the opinions of an experienced Parisian bookseller. Beach had toyed with the idea of opening a French bookshop in New York or London, but Monnier suggested a complete reversal: an American bookshop in Paris. And in November 1919, financed by the Beach family and with Adrienne Monnier's help, an obscure little bookshop on Rue Dupuytren – a former laundry – opened its doors for business. With its brightly painted walls, 'flea-market' furniture, and a sign suspended over the door portraying the 'Bard of Avon', Shakespeare and Company was born.

One of the first books she sold, which from then on she prominently displayed a copy of in the window as a lucky talisman, was Jerome K. Jerome's *Three Men in a Boat* (1889). The shop soon became 'like a house with the members of the family growing up in it', and subscribers to its lending library during that first year included Aldous Huxley, Edith Sitwell, Nancy Cunard, Roger Fry, Walter de la Mare, Gertrude Stein, André Gide, Louis Aragon and Paul Valéry: her 'bunnies' (from *les abonnés*, French for 'subscribers'), as she called them. But although it was an impressive coterie, literary celebrities don't pay bills, and Shakespeare and Company wasn't making enough to survive. Without funds sent from home the shop would certainly have gone under. This rocky apprenticeship, however, was to pass, and in July 1920, at an afternoon tea party on the second floor of 34 rue du Bois de Boulogne, Sylvia Beach met the man that would make her and her bookshop immortal. 'I worshipped James Joyce', she later wrote, 'and on hearing the unexpected news that he was present, I was so frightened I wanted to run away.' Beach encountered Joyce alone in the apartment's library slumped in an armchair wearing tennis shoes and an old jacket. 'Is this the great James Joyce?' she exclaimed. 'James Joyce,' he replied, and they shook hands. Their destiny was sealed.

Joyce began writing his vast novel *Ulysses* in 1914. Parts of it had been serialised in the American journal *The Little Review,* but in 1920 its editors were found guilty, as a consequence of *Ulysses* instalments, of publishing obscenity. The English periodical, *The Egoist*, had also already published some sections of *Ulysses*, and its editors predicted the same fate in England, so were forced to drop it. Depressed, and with all bridges seemingly burned for his novel's publication, Joyce wandered into Shakespeare and Company the day after his meeting with Beach and poured his heart out to her. 'It occurred to me', wrote Beach, 'that something might be done, and I asked, "Would you let Shakespeare and Company have the honor of bringing out your *Ulysses*?"' Joyce probably laughed from the effects of shock; after all, how could this little-known bookshop with its feisty, but grossly inexperienced proprietor possibly think she could pull it off? But Joyce's back was against the wall. To wait for the bans to be lifted in America and Britain could mean waiting forever. He therefore had no alternative but to accept Beach's proposal. He 'seemed delighted', wrote Beach, and they took their leave of each other 'very much moved'. In July 1921 Sylvia Beach relocated Shakespeare and Company to more spacious premises at 12 rue de l'Odéon, across the street from Adrienne Monnier's bookshop, La Maison des Amis des Livres.

See Also: Shakespeare and Company (Rue de l'Odéon), Adrienne Monnier, Gare de Lyon, Bibliothèque Nationale, Nancy Cunard, Gertrude Stein, André Gide, Louis Aragon, Paul Valéry, Sherwood Anderson, Shakespeare and Company (Rue de la Bûcherie).

Further Information: Sylvia Beach was born Nancy Woodbridge Beach in Baltimore, Maryland, in 1887, the second of three daughters of Eleanor, and Sylvester Beach, a Presbyterian minister. She first visited Paris with her family in 1901, when her father was appointed assistant minister at the American Church. In 1905 the family moved to Princeton, New Jersey, where her father became minister of the First Presbyterian Church. In later life she lived for two years in Spain, and during World War I she became a volunteer farm labourer in France and a Red Cross worker in Serbia, settling in Paris in 1916.

ADRIENNE MONNIER

7 RUE DE L'ODÉON

(Métro: Odéon)

SITE OF LA MAISON

DES AMIS DES LIVRES

BOOKSHOP OF ADRIENNE MONNIER

BOOKSELLER, POET, PUBLISHER AND

TRANSLATOR

I saw in front of me a girl with a round, rosy face, with blue eyes, with blond hair, who, it appeared all at once, had just entered the service of literature as others decide to enter the service of religion.

Jules Romains on Adrienne Monnier

Adrienne Monnier's (1892–1955) bookshop, La Maison des Amis des Livres, stood opposite Sylvia Beach's Shakespeare and Company on the Rue de l'Odéon, but although Beach and her shop achieved global fame, Monnier has remained, outside France at least, very much in the shadows. Yet, had it not been for Monnier's experience, advice and inspiration it is unlikely that Shakespeare and Company would ever have been born.

Beach's vision had initially been a French bookshop in London or New York. Monnier turned the idea on its head and suggested an American bookstore in Paris. Beach was financed by her family in America, but Monnier had little money other than a small settlement her father received after an accident. She had no literary contacts, advisors or credentials other than her innate love of literature. In 1916 she opened for business knowing very little about the book trade and at a time when it was unheard of for a woman to advertise herself as a bookseller. 'The truth is that only one of our walls was furnished with books,' she wrote.

The others were decorated with pictures, with a large old desk, and with a chest of drawers in which we kept wrapping paper, string, and everything we did not know where to put; our chairs were old chairs from the country that we still have. This bookshop hardly had the look of a shop, and that was not on purpose: we were far from suspecting that people would congratulate us so much in the future for what seemed to us as an unfortunate makeshift.

Monnier's 'makeshift' approach to bookselling, which also became Beach's, gave their shops an almost anti-business atmosphere, a 'place of transition between street and house' as Monnier called it. This was one of the main ingredients of their success. However, while Beach's customers were mostly Americans, looking for English-language books, Monnier's were mainly Parisian; and 'a French person', wrote Monnier, 'does not lightly engage in the purchase of a book'. And so, from the very beginning, Monnier created a lending library, as Beach would do a few years later. Her shop also became a salon where writers, including Eliot, Joyce, Larbaud, Hemingway and Gide would come to read. In 1925 she launched the French language review, *Le Navire d'Argent,* also translating many works, notably those of Hemingway and Eliot, into French. The two bookshops were a hive of literary life and gossip, whimsically referred to by Monnier as the entrance to a country called 'Odéonia'.

Sylvia Beach closed Shakespeare and Company shortly after the start of the German occupation of Paris, but

Monnier kept La Maison des Amis des Livres open into the early 1950s, when her health started to decline. Suffering from Ménière's disease, a disorder of the inner ear, and distressed with her life, she died from a sleeping pill overdose in 1955. After Monnier's death, Beach wrote, 'I've a queer feeling about Adrienne – that not only is she gone but I've gone away myself somewhere'.

See Also: Sylvia Beach, Shakespeare and Company (Rue Dupuytren), Shakespeare and Company (Rue de l'Odéon), Ernest Hemingway, James Joyce, André Gide.

Further Information: Adrienne Monnier's apartment, which she shared with Sylvia Beach for almost seventeen years, was at No. 18 rue de l'Odéon. Public lending libraries, although in existence in Britain and America, were completely unknown in France before the arrival of La Maison des Amis des Livres.

Further Reading: A. Monnier, *The Very Rich Hours of Adrienne Monnier* (Scribner, 1976); S. Beach, *Shakespeare and Company* (Harcourt, Brace, 1959).

7 rue de l'Odéon

SHAKESPEARE AND COMPANY

12 RUE DE L'ODÉON

(Métro: Odéon)

SITE OF THE SECOND SHAKESPEARE AND COMPANY, JULY 1921 TO DECEMBER 1941

Then to Silvia let us sing,
That Silvia is excelling;
She excels each mortal thing
Upon the dull earth dwelling;
To her let us garlands bring
William Shakespeare 'Who is Silvia?'
From *Two Gentlemen of Verona*
(*c.*1590–1594)

During the 1920s and 1930s Sylvia Beach's Shakespeare and Company was the most famous bookshop in the world. Author Morrill Cody described it as the 'cradle of postwar American literature'. In its early days it was not only a bookshop, but a lending library, post office, salon, and ad hoc bank to the expatriate writing community, notably Ezra Pound, Robert McAlmon, and Ernest Hemingway, who became Shakespeare and Company's 'best customer'. But more importantly, at least by the mid 1920s, Shakespeare and Company started to get what it desperately needed to survive: English and American tourists eager to visit the shop, buy books, and meet the woman responsible for publishing James Joyce's *Ulysses*, one of the most important books of the twentieth century.

Sylvia Beach initially opened Shakespeare and Company on the nearby Rue Dupuytren in November 1919, and it was here that she suggested to Joyce that Shakespeare and Company

195

Sylvia Beach

Darantière, a Dijon printer who slavishly waded through manuscripts and proofs totalling over 250,000 words. He grappled with Joyce's almost illegible handwritten proof corrections, which expanded the size of the book by a third. He tolerated Joyce's demands about paper, binding and typeface, as well as his unyielding insistence that the book's cover be coloured the cobalt blue of the Greek flag, a demand that sent Darantière to Germany and Holland in search of elusive inks. Who could blame Darantière for cursing himself for getting involved with this eccentric Irishman?

Typists were needed to copy the manuscripts, but most did not last the course, and replacements were always being sought. Among those who volunteered their services were Robert McAlmon, Beach's sister Cyprian, and a Mrs Harrison, whose husband, a British Embassy official, was so scandalised by what his wife was copying that he threw it into the fire. But Beach never ceased to be supportive of Joyce. 'He was never a slacker,' she wrote. 'If he was, I would never have helped him. He did great work. He gave himself to his work and expected you to do the same.' In keeping with his superstitious nature, Joyce wanted the book to be published on his fortieth birthday, and the long-suffering Darantière was pleaded with to do his best to meet this deadline. Miraculously, he completed two copies and dispatched them on the Dijon–Paris express, due to arrive in Paris at seven o'clock in the morning on 2 February 1922, the day of Joyce's birthday. Joyce signed his copy to his wife Nora, who read twenty-seven pages then sold it to a visiting friend from Dublin. Sylvia Beach's copy was proudly displayed

publish *Ulysses*. As the content had been deemed obscene in America and England, no printer would touch it and Joyce, with few alternatives, gladly accepted Beach's offer. From that day, in the summer of 1921, she became Joyce's unofficial private secretary and publisher of what she claimed was 'the most difficult book in the world'. The first priority was to find subscribers who would help fund the initial print run. These included Hemingway, Winston Churchill, W.B. Yeats and André Gide. Beach also decided to limit the first printing to a thousand copies, a number Joyce thought far too high for a limited edition. At first he suggested printing a dozen, but changed that to perhaps only two copies, still worrying that some might be left unsold. But Beach was not so despondent and announced that *Ulysses* would be printed in three impressions: 100 signed copies on Holland paper, 150 copies on Vergè d'Arches paper, and the cheapest edition, on plain linen paper, 750 copies. Joyce would receive 66 per cent of the net profits.

The printer she chose was Maurice

in the window of Shakespeare and Company.

By this time the book's print run was fully subscribed, and demand was beginning to exceed supply. The next gargantuan task was to get copies into America and England before the postal authorities realised what was happening, although large numbers were still confiscated or destroyed. Some were sent to American subscribers via Canada where there was no embargo on the book, but, in the end, copies reached the four corners of the earth and *Ulysses* caused a worldwide literary explosion.

Joyce and Beach's business partnership lasted until 1939, and although it had its share of problems, it spawned ten editions of *Ulysses*, totalling around 28,000 copies. Over the years Shakespeare and Company sold many of these copies through subscription and to visiting tourists, for whom Sylvia Beach would covertly wrap them in dummy book jackets suggesting contents such as *Shakespeare's Complete Works in One Volume* and *Merry Tales for Little Folks.*

See Also: Sylvia Beach, Shakespeare and Company (Rue Dupuytren), James Joyce, Adrienne Monnier, Gare de Lyon, Hôtel Ritz, Shakespeare and Company (Rue de la Bûcherie).

Further Information: Paris surrendered to the Nazis in 1940, and by the end of 1941 Shakespeare and Company was forced to close. Beach was interned for six months, but her stock of 5000 books was safely hidden in an empty fourth-floor apartment at 12 rue de l'Odéon. The shop never reopened. On 6 October 1962, Sylvia Beach was found dead in her Paris apartment having suffered a heart attack. Her ashes are buried in Princeton Cemetery, New Jersey.

Further Reading: S. Beach, *Shakespeare and Company* (Harcourt, Brace, 1959); N.R. Fitch, *Sylvia Beach and the Lost Generation* (Norton, 1985); K. Walsh (ed.), *The Letters of Sylvia Beach* (Columbia University Press, 2010).

Sylvia Beach and James Joyce with early reviews of *Ulysses* in 1922

RICHARD WRIGHT

14 RUE MONSIEUR-LE-PRINCE

(Métro: Odéon)

FORMER HOME OF RICHARD WRIGHT

MAJOR AFRICAN AMERICAN WRITER

AND AUTHOR OF *NATIVE SON*

Our too-young and too-new America, lusty because it is lonely, aggressive because it is afraid, insists upon seeing the world in terms of good and bad, the holy and the evil, the high and the low, the white and the black; our America is frightened of fact, of history, of processes, of necessity. It hugs the easy way of damning those whom it cannot understand, of excluding those who look different, and it salves its conscience with a self-draped cloak of righteousness.
Richard Wright, *Black Boy* (1945)

Richard Wright

Richard Nathaniel Wright was born in 1908 in Roxie, a small town two miles east of Natchez, Mississippi. He was the eldest son of Ella Wilson and Nathan Wright, a sharecropper. It was not a happy marriage, and in 1916, Nathan abandoned his wife and children and left them without support. From then on the family stayed with various relations, including Richard's Uncle Silas, who was murdered by a white man during their stay. By the early 1920s Richard was forced to leave school to find work, eventually moving to Chicago in 1927 where he worked at various unskilled jobs, including a spell as a post office worker. In 1932 he became a member of the Communist Party (which he would eventually reject) and in 1937 he went to New York where he became the Harlem editor of the communist newspaper, *Daily Worker*.

Having failed to find a publisher for his first novel, he continued to submit essays and poems to magazines; then in 1938 he had his first real success with a collection of novellas entitled *Uncle Tom's Children*, work that not only brought him national attention, but its critical and commercial success gave him the financial security to write his bestseller, *Native Son*, later staged on Broadway by Orson Welles. In 1945, now married with a child, Wright published *Black Boy*, a partially auto-biographical account of a young boy growing up in a white-dominated black culture. A bestseller, it was translated into many languages, and hailed as a major contribution to African American literature.

Following a visit to France in 1946 as a guest of the French government, he wrote to his publishers about his visit: 'there is such an absence of race hatred, that it seems a little unreal'. He became so enthralled with France, and disgusted with America, that he returned in August 1947 to settle permanently with his family in Paris. They stayed at first with friends, before buying an apartment on Rue Monsieur-le-Prince in 1948. Had he delayed his departure from America, the surging rise of McCarthyism and its fanatical fear of communism would probably have made writing and travel impossible for him. And had he returned to America during the height of the witch-hunts, which lasted from the late 1940s through the 1950s, he would, no doubt, have been subpoenaed.

One of the few people who understood Wright's passion with France was his friend and fellow writer, Dorothy Norman, who wrote: 'Several people who knew both of us begged me to try to change his mind. "Why doesn't he accept his place in America and write as a black man about the Negro? He will kill himself as an author, as a creative force, if he goes abroad to live." I understood the argument, but couldn't agree with it.' Nonetheless, Wright settled comfortably into Paris, and was soon acquainted with its writers, notably Albert Camus, Simone de Beauvoir, Jean-Paul Sartre, Chester Himes, William Gardner Smith, Boris Vian, André Gide, Gertrude Stein and his occasional nemesis, James Baldwin. Surprisingly, Wright had shipped his large American Oldsmobile car to Europe, a rare sight in the Paris streets, and guaranteed to be gaped at. 'I don't know whether to feel proud or ashamed,' he confessed. 'I'm ashamed most of the time.'

Richard Wright lived out the rest of his days in Paris, dying there in 1960 from a heart attack, aged only fifty-two. He was always an outsider, but he rightly deserves to be at the forefront of modern

14 rue Monsieur-le-Prince

American writers of fiction. 'Writing', he once said, 'is my way of being a free man'.

See Also: Café de Tournon, Albert Camus, Simone de Beauvoir, Jean-Paul Sartre, Chester Himes, Boris Vian, André Gide, James Baldwin, Gertrude Stein, Père Lachaise.

Further Information: Richard Wright never returned to America save for a short stopover in the late 1940s on his way to Argentina to make a film adaptation of *Native Son*. His funeral was held at Père Lachaise on the morning of Saturday, 3 December 1960, where he was cremated and his ashes interred in the columbarium, Division 87, urn 848. Ironically, Richard Wright's papers are in the Beinecke Rare Book and Manuscript Library at Yale University, which in his day would have been a bastion of white privilege.

Select Bibliography: *Uncle Tom's Children: Four Novellas* (1938); *Native Son* (1940); *12 Million Black Voices: A Folk History of the Negro in the United States* (1941); *Black Boy* (1945); *The Outsider* (1953); *Savage Holiday* (1954); *The Color Curtain* (1956); *Lawd Today!* (1963).

Further Reading: A. Gayle, *Richard Wright: Ordeal of a Native Son* (Doubleday, 1980); J. Baldwin, 'Everybody's Protest Novel' and 'Many Thousands Gone', in *Notes of a Native Son* (Beacon, 1955).

LE POLIDOR

41 RUE MONSIEUR-LE-PRINCE

(Métro: Odéon/Cluny – La Sorbonne)

HISTORIC BISTRO

HAUNT OF LITERARY LEGENDS

Le Polidor n'accepte plus les cartes de crédit depuis 1845.
Sign hanging in Le Polidor

The above quote states that Le Polidor has not been accepting credit since 1845, and this is just one of this restaurant's conspicuously old-fashioned traits. A throwback to the days when it first opened its doors in the mid-nineteenth century, Le Polidor today is more a historic monument than a modern restaurant, with a decor that has remained virtually unchanged for a hundred years. During its golden age it was a cheap, communal eating house, where its long, shared tables attracted the likes of Arthur Rimbaud, Paul Verlaine, André Gide, James Joyce, Ernest Hemingway, Henry Miller, and Paul Valéry. In the 1950s it was nicknamed le Collège de Pataphysique by a collective of avant-garde regulars, including Boris Vian, Max Ernst, and Eugène Ionesco, after pataphysics, the science of reasoned anti-reason introduced by French writer of the Absurd, Alfred Jarry.

Thankfully Le Polidor has failed miserably to keep up with the passage of time and is still stuck in its own celebrated time warp.

See Also: Arthur Rimbaud, Paul Verlaine, André Gide, James Joyce, Henry Miller, Paul Valéry, Boris Vian, Eugène Ionesco, Alfred Jarry, Ernest Hemingway.

KATHERINE ANNE PORTER

20 *BIS* RUE NOTRE-DAME-DES-CHAMPS

(Métro: St-Placide/N-D-des-Champs)

FORMER RESIDENCE OF

KATHERINE ANNE PORTER

PULITZER PRIZE-WINNING

SHORT-STORY WRITER AND NOVELIST

Over the course of more than forty years, even while Katherine Anne Porter was being praised as the First Lady of American Letters (a title she abhorred as patronizing sexism), she also was summed up as an FBI informant, a poseur, an alcoholic, a racist, and a hate-filled monster. Her life has been portrayed as one of deception and betrayal as well as artistic success, and she has been painted as a brilliant writer but a class-conscious, compulsive liar who was capricious, vain, and disloyal to friends and political ideals.
Darlene Harbour Unrue, *Katherine Anne Porter: The Life of an Artist* (2005)

Katherine Anne Porter in 1933

Katherine Anne Porter's portrayal of her life was without doubt her greatest work of fiction. But in the end, what does it really matter? It was, after all, from the drama of her nomadic life – factual or fictitious – that her masterful stories were created, and without that life American literature would be worse off. Born Callie Russell Porter in rural Texas in 1890, the fourth of five children, she later took her maternal grandmother's name and created an ancestry that recast her as a high-born daughter of the Old South's plantation-owning aristocracy, a myth she maintained all her life, carrying it off to perfection. 'I shall try to tell the truth', she wrote in her essay, 'My First Speech', 'but the result will be fiction. And with such a talent for invention, where else could her destiny lie but as a great storyteller?

By the time she settled in Paris in 1932, a city she fell in love with 'on sight and without reservation', Porter was in her early forties and in her third marriage, to Eugene Pressly, a minor employee of the diplomatic corps. Her short stories and essays were receiving great acclaim. 'The Jilting of Granny Weatherall' appeared in the February issue of the literary journal *transition*, and 'Flowering Judas' had secured her place in the annals of American literature.

Shortly after her arrival in Paris she visited Shakespeare and Company, becoming good friends with Sylvia Beach and her friend Adrienne Monnier. After Monnier's death, Porter recalled in a letter to Beach their Paris days together and 'the sparkle of life in *everybody* present, which you two could always bring out'. She also described, in her *Collected Essays*, a meeting at the bookstore with Ernest Hemingway when both writers, who were not acquainted, unexpectedly came face-to-face, a situation made uneasy by Beach declaring she wanted the two best writers in America to meet:

> Hemingway and I stood and gazed unwinkingly at each other with poker faces for all of ten seconds, in silence. Hemingway then turned in one wide swing and hurled himself into the rainy darkness as he had hurled himself out of it, and that was all. I am sorry if you are disappointed. All personal and lack of sympathy and attraction aside, and they were real in us, it must have been galling to this most famous young man to have his name pronounced in the same breath as writer with someone he had never heard of, and a woman at that. I nearly felt sorry for him.

In the spring of 1936 Porter returned to America and divorced Pressly. In later life she taught and became a writer in residence at various universities, gaining a reputation as a political activist. But personally and creatively, Paris was deemed by Porter to have given her one of the best times, if not the best, of her life: a time when *Katherine Anne Porter's French Song-Book* was published, also 'The Witness', 'The Last Leaf', 'The Grave', 'The Circus' and *Flowering Judas and Other Stories*, essential reading for all college campuses. In 1962 she published her only novel, *Ship of Fools*, an allegorical narrative about Nazi Germany, and in 1966 she was awarded the Pulitzer Prize. She died in Maryland at the age of ninety in 1980.

See Also: Ernest Hemingway, transition, Sylvia Beach, Adrienne Monnier.

Select Bibliography: 'Flowering Judas' (1930); 'Pale Horse, Pale Rider' (1939); 'The Leaning Tower' (1944); 'The Days

Before' (1952); '*Ship of Fools*' (1962); 'The Never-Ending Wrong' (1977).

Further Reading: J. Givner, *The Life of Katherine Anne Porter* (Jonathan Cape, 1983); D. Unrue (ed.), *Letters of Katherine Anne Porter* (Atlantic Monthly Press, 1990); D. Unrue, *Katherine Anne Porter: The Life of an Artist* (University Press of Mississippi, 2006; D. Unrue (ed.), *Katherine Anne Porter Remembered* (University of Alabama Press, 2010).

Top: Rue Notre-Dame-des-Champs
Above: Poster for the 1965 screen adaptation of Porter's novel, *Ship of Fools*

GERTRUDE STEIN
27 RUE DE FLEURUS
(Métro: St-Placide)

FORMER HOME AND ATELIER OF GERTRUDE STEIN AMERICAN WRITER AND PARIS'S MOST FAMOUS SALONNIÈRE

Gertrude Stein projected a remarkable power, possibly due to the atmosphere of adulation that surrounded her. A rhomboidal woman dressed in a floor-length gown apparently made of some kind of burlap, she gave the impression of absolute irrefragability; her ankles, almost concealed by the hieratic folds of her dress, were like the pillars of a temple: it was impossible to conceive of her lying down. Her fine close-cropped head was in the style of the late Roman Empire, but unfortunately it merged into broad peasant shoulders without the aesthetic assistance of a neck; her eyes were large and much too piercing. I had a peculiar sense of mingled attraction and repulsion towards her. She awakened in me a feeling of instinctive hostility coupled with a grudging veneration, as if she were a pagan idol in whom I was unable to believe. John Glassco, *Memoirs of Montparnasse* (1970)

Ridiculed, satirised and rarely published unless at her own expense, Gertrude Stein's writings have always had a reputation for being incomprehensible, abstract and read only by a few. Sinclair Lewis claimed she was 'conducting a racket'. *The New York Times* compared her to 'the Chinese water torture', and Virginia Woolf described her practice of repeating a word '100 times over' as a 'dodge'. Despite her critics, however, much of Stein's writing was intelligible and extremely entertaining,

Gertrude Stein

home at 27 rue de Fleurus', she wrote in her *Autobiography of Alice B. Toklas*, 'consisted then as it does now of a tiny pavillon of two stories with four small rooms, a kitchen and bath, and a very large atelier adjoining.'

Existing solely on their private incomes they began collecting the art of the avant-garde, which they hung from floor to ceiling on the whitewashed walls of their new studio. And before long, a steady stream of visitors began to visit Rue de Fleurus to praise, puzzle over and deride the works of Cézanne, Matisse, Picasso and others. Their Saturday evening salons, dominated by Leo, with Gertrude in support, became an event in the social calendar, and whether they knew it or not, the Steins were creating the world's first museum of modern art. In the autumn of 1907 Gertrude Stein met Alice Toklas, who became a regular visitor to the Stein salon, soon becoming Stein's lover and an integral part of the household. 'Alice was making herself indispensable,' wrote their friend Mabel Dodge.

though she was certainly eccentric, conceited and wholly convinced that her destiny was to 'create the twentieth century'. Today, she is remembered more for her famous salon than for her books. And although her writings should not be dismissed, her real legacy was that of an experimentalist who gave a much-needed self-confidence and vitality to modern art and literature at a time when it needed it most.

She was born in Pennsylvania, the youngest of five children, to a wealthy Jewish family in 1874, and spent her childhood, outwith family sojourns to Europe, in Oakland, California. She studied psychology and medicine, but in 1902 she left medical school without her degree to join her elder brother Leo in London. The following year they decamped to Paris together where Leo had hopes of becoming an art critic, and by the autumn of 1903 they had taken up residence on the Left Bank. 'The

> She did everything to save Gertrude a movement – all the housekeeping, the typing, seeing people who called, and getting rid of the undesirables, answering letters – really providing all the motor force of the ménage. ... And Gertrude was growing helpless and foolish from it and less and less inclined to do anything herself, Leo said; he had seen trees strangled by vines in the same way.

After Alice's arrival into their sibling world, Leo became increasingly despondent and was very much in the shadow of his sister. Gertrude Stein's literary star was on the rise, and more and more salon visitors were coming solely for her. Leo could never abide her books and thought them 'abominable'. He also resented his sister's relationship with Alice, whom he described as 'a kind of abnormal vampire'. Understandably, Leo departed for good in 1912.

In the early 1900s the Steins' salon nurtured the world of art, but in the 1920s Gertrude concentrated more and more on the Paris literary community and the young Americans who remained after the war, becoming, for many, their counsellor and guru. Notable among these were Sherwood Anderson, Janet Flanner, Ezra Pound, Thornton Wilder, Scott Fitzgerald, Ernest Hemingway, Sinclair Lewis and Paul Bowles. It was to Ernest Hemingway that Stein is said to have made her famous comment about the 'lost generation', which he recounts in *A Moveable Feast*. A young mechanic had not repaired Stein's Model T Ford on time, for which he was severely reprimanded by the garage's exasperated patron, who declared to the mechanic, 'You are all a *génération perdue*.' 'That's what you are,' Stein later said to Hemingway. 'That's what you all are. All of you young people who served in the war. You are a lost generation.'

In later life many of her disciples wrote about her. Some in praise, some for revenge, some just for the memory. But whatever their hindsight, she remained embedded in their memory, like a world preserved in aspic. And her advice, whether embraced or rejected, was never forgotten. She once said, 'There ain't no answer. There ain't gonna be any answer. There never has been an answer. There's your answer.'

See Also: The American Hospital in Paris, Père Lachaise, 5 rue Christine, Jardin du Luxembourg, Alice B. Toklas, Ernest Hemingway, Sherwood Anderson, Janet Flanner, Ezra Pound, Thornton Wilder, Scott Fitzgerald, Sinclair Lewis, Paul Bowles, *transition*, Bateau Lavoir.

Further Information: Gertrude Stein died from stomach cancer in 1946, at The American Hospital in Paris, aged 72. Alice Toklas died twenty years later, aged 89. They are buried beside each other in Père Lachaise Cemetery. Leo Stein returned to America where he became a journalist, eventually settling in Italy with his wife, and where he died in 1947, aged 75.

Select Bibliography: *Three Lives* (1909); *Tender Buttons* (1914); *The Making of Americans* (1925); *The Autobiography of Alice B. Toklas* (1933); *Everybody's Autobiography* (1937); *Paris France* (1940); *Ida: A Novel* (1941).

Further Reading: J. Hobhouse, *Everybody Who Was Anybody: A Biography of Gertrude Stein* (Putnam, 1975); J. Mellow, *Charmed Circle: Gertrude Stein & Company* (Phaidon, 1974).

27 rue de Fleurus

Picasso's portrait of Gertrude Stein hangs to Stein's left as she relaxes on a sofa in her Rue de Fleurus studio. According to Stein she sat for him 'some eighty or ninety' times at his Bateau Lavoir studio. Picasso recalled that Stein sat on 'a large broken armchair' and he 'sat very tight' on 'a little kitchen chair … very close to his canvas', clasping 'a very small palette'. But Picasso couldn't capture the Stein he was seeking and finally abandoned the painting. He eventually finished it in the autumn of 1905, famously remarking afterwards, 'Everybody says that she does not look like it but that does not make any difference, she will.'

Alice B. Toklas in 1949 (photo Carl Van Vechten)

Gertrude and Alice with their beloved poodle, Basket

Gertrude Stein and Alice B. Toklas, Aix-les-Bains *c.*1927

CAFÉ LE SÉLECT

99 BOULEVARD DU MONTPARNASSE

(Métro: Vavin)

'Where do you want to go?' I asked. Brett
turned her head away.
'Oh, go to the Select.'
'Café Select,' I told the driver. 'Boulevard
Montparnasse.'
We drove straight down, turning around
the Lion de Belfort that guards the passing
Montrouge trams. Brett looked straight
ahead. On the Boulevard Raspail, with the
lights of Montparnasse in sight, Brett said:
'Would you mind very much if I asked you to
do something?'
'Don't be silly.'
'Kiss me just once more before we get there.'
Ernest Hemingway, *The Sun Also Rises*
(1927)

Monsieur and Madame Jalbert first
opened Le Sélect in 1925. Monsieur was famous for his moustache, and
Madame for her no-nonsense demeanour and profound dislike of Americans.
'Madame had a high colour,' wrote John
Glassco, 'shrewd eyes, and a bosom like
a shelf; she wore little black fingerless
mittens that kept her hands warm without preventing her from counting the
francs and centimes. Monsieur Select,
who made the Welsh rarebit on a little
stove behind the bar, had long melancholy moustaches like Flaubert's.'
Le Sélect was the first cafe in Paris to
stay open 24 hours a day, and, before
the other Montparnasse cafes followed
suit, it attracted its fair share of night
owl regulars, including Henry Miller,

Simone de Beauvoir, Anaïs Nin, André Breton, Jean Cocteau, Samuel Beckett, and Chester Himes, who wrote much of his 1959 novel *The Crazy Kill* at its tables. It has also been patronised by characters from fiction: Jake Barnes in Hemingway's *The Sun Also Rises*, Marya and her lover, Heidler, in Jean Rhys's *Quartet*, and David, who falls in love with a handsome Italian waiter in James Baldwin's *Giovanni's Room*.

But Le Sélect was primarily a cafe for local office workers and students pouring out of the Vavin Métro across the street. On the small side in comparison to neighbouring cafes, it is unpretentious and has changed little over the years, remaining much the same as when Hemingway breakfasted there when he lived nearby in Rue Notre-Dame-des-Champs, and when the photographer Brassaï lived above the cafe in the 1930s.

Le Sélect's most memorable American customer has to be the poet Hart Crane, who arrived in Paris in January 1929. In late June of the same year, he stopped one evening at Le Sélect and had a few drinks. When the waiter presented him with the bill, and Crane realised he had next to nothing in his wallet, several waiters attempted to remove him from the premises. Other American customers offered to settle his bill, but Madame Jalbert was having none of it and refused their gesture. A brawl ensued, the gendarmes arrived, and Crane was thrown into a rat-infested cell in Paris's La Santé prison. When the judge declared that it had taken ten gendarmes to hold him, the court burst into laughter. After questioning, he was fined eight hundred francs and threatened with eight days in prison should he ever be arrested again. Immediately afterwards, Crane booked a passage on a ship bound for New York, and safely put 3500 miles between himself and the redoubtable Madame Jalbert.

See Also: Henry Miller, Samuel Beckett, Ernest Hemingway, Simone de Beauvoir, Anaïs Nin, André Breton, Jean Cocteau, Chester Himes, Jean Rhys, James Baldwin.

Further Information: On 27 April 1932, three years after his Paris sojourn, Hart Crane committed suicide at the age of thirty-two by jumping from the stern of a ship en route from Mexico to New York.

Further Reading: John Glassco, *Memoirs of Montparnasse* (Oxford University Press, 1970); N. Fitch, *Paris Café: The Sélect Crowd* (Soft Skull Press, 2007); P. Mariani, *The Broken Tower: The Life of Hart Crane* (Norton, 1999).

Hart Crane

SIMONE DE BEAUVOIR

103 BOULEVARD DU MONTPARNASSE

(Métro: Vavin)

BIRTHPLACE OF SIMONE DE BEAUVOIR
WRITER, EXISTENTIALIST, FEMINIST
AND AUTHOR OF *THE SECOND SEX*

I was born at four o'clock in the morning on the 9th of January 1908 in a room fitted with white-enamelled furniture and overlooking the boulevard Raspail. In the family photographs taken the following summer can be seen ladies in long dresses and ostrich-feather hats and gentlemen wearing boaters and panamas, all smiling at a baby: they are my parents, my grandfather, uncles, aunts; and the baby is me.

Simone de Beauvoir, *Memoirs of a Dutiful Daughter* (1958)

Simone de Beauvoir

Simone de Beauvoir's magnum opus was *The Second Sex*, a groundbreaking and controversial work tracing the misrepresentation of women throughout history from biological, historical, psychoanalytic and mythological viewpoints. It was a landmark in modern feminist writing and has since influenced countless feminist works. But Beauvoir's greatest achievement was, possibly, her lifelong relationship with philosopher Jean-Paul Sartre, a man who was her intellectual equal, but whose shadow pursued her until his death over fifty years later. 'I could not help but comment to my distinguished audience', she wrote in *The Second Sex*, 'that every question asked about Sartre concerned his work, while all those asked about Beauvoir concerned her personal life.' But Beauvoir's devotion to Sartre was no hindrance to her career, and no doubt enhanced it. She became a committed socialist, a leading member of the existentialist movement, a brilliant novelist, and a shrewd chronicler of the social and political mutations of modern France, inspiring a generation of women to question their secondary place in a patriarchal system.

Simone de Beauvoir was born into a bourgeois family in 1908 in a flat above the Café de la Rotonde in Montparnasse. Two years later, her only sibling, Hélène, was born. Simone learned to read at the age of three, and was writing stories by the time she was seven. She embraced Catholicism and yearned to be a nun; however, in her teenage years she lost her faith and remained a committed atheist for the rest of her life. Her father, Georges, was a legal secretary, and in his male-dominated world he famously remarked, 'Simone thinks like a man!' Although brought up in an atmosphere of almost stifling gentility, her early years were extremely happy, but as her teens approached she began to fiercely reject her parents' conventional values. She excelled at school, and in 1928 she began her studies at the Sorbonne and the École Normale Supérieure where she studied for a postgraduate *agrégation* in philosophy.

The following year she met fellow student, Jean-Paul Sartre, and they soon became lovers. Sartre appears to have seduced her intellectually, more than physically, as he had done with other women, but there were rules to be followed: 'What we have,' he said to Beauvoir, 'is an *essential* love; but it is a good idea for us to experience contingent love affairs.' Throughout their fifty-year relationship Simone appeared to consent to this, but although Sartre had numerous other women, and she, a few men, the arrangement did deeply trouble her. They never married and never lived together.

After her graduation various teaching posts followed, and in 1943 her debut novel, *She came to stay*, about a *ménage à trois* loosely based on a real-life experience with Sartre, was published to critical acclaim. Her second novel, *The Blood of Others*, published two years later, is a study of a young girl who initially accepts Nazi ideology, but ends up fighting for the Resistance. Following the liberation of Paris, Sartre and

Beauvoir founded the literary journal, *Les Temps Modernes* (Modern Times) in 1945. The journal was a flagship for existentialism, but it also published early extracts from *The Second Sex* in 1948. Beauvoir wrote energetically all her life, but none of her later fiction would equal her first two novels. In the late 1950s she began writing her volumes of autobiography, the first of which was *Memoirs of a Dutiful Daughter.*

She is remembered today as the mother of modern feminism and a crusader for sexual freedom, and for being one half of one of France's most celebrated intellectual couples. In March 1986 she was admitted to hospital where she drifted into a coma and died from pneumonia on 14 April, aged seventy-eight. Her body was buried beside Sartre's in Montparnasse Cemetery. 'I am too intelligent, too demanding, and too resourceful', she wrote in *The Second Sex*, 'for anyone to be able to take charge of me entirely. No one knows me or loves me completely. I have only myself.'

See Also: Jean-Paul Sartre, Grave of Sartre and Beauvoir, Café de la Rotonde, Bibliothèque Nationale.

Select Bibliography: *L'Invitée (She Came to Stay)* (1943); *Le sang des autres (The Blood of Others)* (1945); *Le deuxième sexe (The Second Sex)* (1949); *Les Mandarins (The Mandarins)* (1954); *Memoires d'une jeune fille rangée (Memoirs of a Dutiful Daughter)* (1958); *Tout compte fait (All Said and Done)* (1972).

Further Reading: L. Appignanesi, *Simone de Beauvoir* (Penguin, 1988); C. Seymour-Jones, *A Dangerous Liaison* (Century, 2008); S. Bakewell, *At The Existentialist Café* (Chatto & Windus, 2016).

CAFÉ DE LA ROTONDE

105 BOULEVARD DU MONTPARNASSE

(Métro: Vavin)

The scum of Greenwich Village, New York, has been skimmed off and deposited in large ladles on that section of Paris adjacent to the Café Rotonde. New scum, of course, has risen to take the place of the old, but the oldest scum, the thickest scum and the scummiest scum has come across the ocean, somehow, and with its afternoon and evening levees has made the Rotonde the leading Latin Quarter showplace for tourists in search of atmosphere.

It is a strange-acting and strange-looking breed that crowd the tables of the Café Rotonde. ... A first look into the smoky, high ceilinged, table-crammed interior of the Rotonde gives you the same feeling that hits you as you step into the bird-house at the zoo.
Ernest Hemingway, 'American Bohemians in Paris', *The Toronto Star Weekly*, 25 March 1922

After the First World War, La Rotonde had an almost exclusive monopoly on the artistic and literary scene of Montparnasse, holding on to it until the early 1920s when other cafes, notably the Dôme, lured its clientele to new pastures. Victor Libion opened Café Rotonde in 1911. Libion was an entrepreneur, but he was also a friend to the struggling artist, allowing many of them to clear their tabs with one of their paintings, which in those days littered the walls of the cafe. With Picasso and Modigliani among his customers, Libion – had he known the future value of these – could have built a nice little nest egg. In 1918, after charges of drug trafficking, Libion sold Café Rotonde and moved on. What became of his art collection is unknown.

With the end of the war, the so-called 'expatriates', including Ernest Hemingway, began to arrive in Paris.

Hemingway hated Café Rotonde and the general sentiment at the time was one of agreement. In 1919, Thora Klinkow-ström, wife of the painter Nils Dardel, found La Rotonde 'a dirty stinking dive with sawdust on the floor and the worst kind of characters at every table'. Robert McAlmon, in his 1938 memoir, *Being Geniuses Together*, also recalled a Rotonde experience during the 1920s:

In the Quarter, foreigners of many nationalities collected daily about the Rotonde, then in bad favour with Americans, for its patron was a bastard. ...

As I wandered toward the Dôme I met an excited group of Americans, headed by Peggy and Laurence Vail. It appeared that Malcolm Cowley had taken a sock at the *patron* of the Rotonde and the cops had arrested him. ... [In court] Kitty Cannell testified that the *patron* had caught her arm brutally and pushed her, without reason. Naturally Cowley, as a gentleman, was angry and protested. The *patron* had then shoved Cowley aside, whereupon Cowley hit. I swore

that the *patron* was noted for his evil disposition and lack of manners; that, although never involved in a scandal there, I had refused since some months to enter the Rotonde. ... The judge told the *patron* that he had no case, with only employees as witnesses ... and the police of the Quarter admitted that the Rotonde *patron* was known as mauvais [nasty].

But what of the literature and poetry written on the Rotonde's wine stained tables? Did it leave any masterpieces for posterity? Hemingway was not convinced: 'Since the good old days when Charles Baudelaire led a purple lobster on a leash through the same old Latin Quarter, there has not been much good poetry written in cafés.'

See Also: Ernest Hemingway, Charles Baudelaire, Robert McAlmon, Simone de Beauvoir.

Further Information: Simone de Beauvoir was born above the Café de la Rotonde in 1908.

Left to right: Polish-born French painter, Moise Kisling (1891–1953), French actress, Pâquerette (1876–1965), and Pablo Picasso (1881–1973) at Café de la Rotonde in 1916

LA CLOSERIE DES LILAS

171 BOULEVARD DU MONTPARNASSE

(Métro: Raspail/Vavin)

Sitting out on the terraces of the Lilas Brett ordered whisky and soda, and I took one, too, and Bill took another pernod ... Brett looked at me. 'I was a fool to go away,' she said. 'One's an ass to leave Paris.'
Ernest Hemingway, *The Sun Also Rises* (1926)

La Closerie des Lilas began life in 1847 as a coaching inn on the road to Fontainebleau. Built amid a garden of lilacs (*lilas*) it attracted all classes of Parisians, but it was also a gathering place for writers and artists, including Émile Zola, Théophile Gautier, the Goncourt brothers, Paul Cézanne, Paul Verlaine and André Breton. In 1924 it became one of Hemingway's favourite watering holes. Contrary to myth, he did not write his first novel, *The Sun Also Rises*, at one of the Lilas's tables. It was written over a period of two months while Hemingway travelled in Spain and on his return to Paris in August 1925. He worked on his revisions during the winter of 1926. But no doubt some of it was written or revised at Lilas, along with parts of his short story 'Big Two-Hearted River'.

In February 1924, Ernest and Hadley Hemingway and their four-month-old son moved from their first Paris flat in the Latin Quarter to more spacious accommodation close to La Closerie des Lilas at 113 rue Notre-Dame-des-Champs (now demolished) in Montparnasse. 'We have the whole second story,' wrote Hadley to her mother-in-law, 'tiny kitchen, small dining room, toilet, small bedroom, medium size sitting room with stove, dining room ... you're conscious all the time from 7 a.m. to 5 p.m. of a very gentle buzzing noise. They make door and window frames and picture frames. The yard is full of dogs and workmen and rammed right up against the funny front door covered with tarpaulin is the baby's buggy.'

Listening to a circular saw all day no doubt tried the Hemingways' patience, but their new location did have its advantages. It was close to the Métro and the Luxembourg Gardens. Ezra Pound lived nearby at 70 *bis* rue Notre-Dame-des-Champs and also, within walking distance, were Gertrude Stein's studio and Sylvia Beach's bookshop, Shakespeare and Company.

But a circular saw and a baby, however convenient one's location, are not conducive to the demands of creative writing, and for five months Hemingway had written no new fiction. 'Don't know when or where able to write,' he wrote to Ezra Pound. But Hemingway did what he always did when he needed peace. He headed for a cafe with a pencil and a notebook, and 'the nearest good cafe' to his flat was La Closerie des Lilas.

Stories and anecdotes abound about Lilas during its artistic heyday, but a favourite concerns the French symbolist writer Alfred Jarry, who once sat next to a beautiful woman in the cafe who wore a haughty expression and who seemed intent on ignoring him. Jarry, tired of being snubbed, made a pun using the word *'glace'* (meaning both 'ice' and 'mirror'). He pulled out a revolver and fired it at a mirror, commenting, *'Madame, maintenant que la glace est rompue, causons!'* ('Madam, now that the ice is broken, let's talk!')

See Also: Ernest Hemingway, Pauline Pfeiffer, Blaise Cendrars, Ford Madox Ford, Ezra Pound, Gertrude Stein, Sylvia Beach,

Thornton Wilder, Émile Zola, Théophile Gautier, the Goncourt brothers, Paul Verlaine, André Breton, Alfred Jarry.

Further Information: Hemingway's marriage had begun to collapse by the time his first novel, *The Sun Also Rises*, was published in 1926. Aware of his affair with journalist Pauline Pfeiffer, Hadley divorced Hemingway in January 1927 and, in the ensuing legal severance, the royalties of *The Sun Also Rises* were transferred to her name. Hemingway and Pfeiffer married a few months after the divorce, in May 1927.

Select Bibliography: *Three Stories & Ten Poems* (1923); *In Our Time* (1924); *The Sun Also Rises* (1926); *The Torrents of Spring* (1926); *A Moveable Feast* (1964); *Ernest Hemingway on Paris* (2010, first published in *The Toronto Star*, 1922–23).

Further Reading: M. Reynolds, *Hemingway: The Paris Years* (Norton, 1999); R. McAlmon, *Being Geniuses Together* (Michael Joseph, 1968); A. Sokoloff, *Hadley, the First Mrs. Hemingway* (Dodd, Mead, 1973); N. Fitch, *Sylvia Beach and the Lost Generation* (Norton, 1985).

SIMONE WEIL

3 RUE AUGUSTE COMTE

(Métro: Vavin/Notre-Dame-des-Champs)

FORMER HOME OF SIMONE WEIL
WRITER, PHILOSOPHER AND POLITICAL
ACTIVIST, WHOSE MORAL IDEALISM
INFLUENCED WESTERN THOUGHT

Simone Weil, I still know this now, is the only great spirit of our times ... For my part, I would be satisfied if one could say that in my place, with the humble means at my disposal, I served to make known and disseminate her work whose full impact we have yet to measure.
Albert Camus, extract of a letter to Simone Weil's mother (1951)

Simone Weil during the Spanish Civil War

Simone Weil (1909–1943) was one of the great European moralists and thinkers. As a writer she is best described as an essayist with a masterly and unpretentious prose style. Most of her work consisted of articles written over a period of fifteen years, and collected into book form after her death. Her work was little known during her lifetime, but shortly after her death her writings began to gain acclaim and influence in the fields of philosophy, sociology, and, especially, religion, where she became one of the key Christian apologists. Unlike most left-wing intellectuals she did not reject religion, but was attracted to it. Marxism also fascinated her, but given her religious inclination, which leaned to Catholicism, she never fully tethered herself to either. This objectivity is probably one of the main reasons why the clarity of her subject analysis can still arouse intense interest today.

Weil, born in Paris to Jewish parentage, was intellectually way ahead of her peers as a child. She was reading the evening newspaper aloud to her family at the age of five. She refused to eat sugar because the troops on the Western Front had none. From reciting Racine at six, she became proficient in classical Greek by her early teens. As an adult she had a dazzling academic career and went on to teach philosophy in schools, where her radical politics and writing for leftist journals frequently antagonised her employers. She worked for a year on the factory floor of the Renault car plant in Paris, experiencing workers' conditions at first hand, and in 1936 she joined the International Brigade during the Spanish Civil War. After the German occupation of Paris in 1940, she moved to the south of France where she worked as a farm hand, eventually escaping with her family to the United States in 1942.

A few months later she returned to England where she worked for the Free French in London. By this time she was eating very little, and when reproached, she would reply that she did not have the right to eat more than the official ration of her fellow countrymen in occupied France. Malnourished and overworked, she collapsed and was admitted to hospital, and later to a sanatorium, where she died a few days later in August 1943, aged only thirty-four. The coroner's report read: 'Cardiac failure due to myocardial degeneration of the heart muscles due to starvation and pulmonary tuberculosis … the deceased did kill and slay herself by refusing to eat whilst the balance of her mind was disturbed.'

In T.S. Eliot's preface to Weil's *The Need for Roots*, he wrote that she had 'an almost superhuman humility and what appears to be an almost outrageous arrogance … a kind of genius akin to that of the saints.'

See Also: Albert Camus, Jean Racine, T.S. Eliot.

Further Information: Simone Weil is buried in Bybrook Cemetery in Ashford, Kent. The Weil family moved to their new apartment on the sixth and seventh floors at No. 3 rue Auguste Comte in May 1929, and it remained in Simone's brother André's family until the late 1990s.

Select Bibliography: *Gravity and Grace* (1947); *The Need for Roots* (1949); *Waiting for God* (1951); *Notebooks* (1956); *Oppression and Liberty* (1958).

Further Reading: D. McLellan, *Simone Weil: Utopian Pessimist* (Macmillan, 1989); F. du Plessix Gray, *Simone Weil* (Weidenfeld & Nicolson, 2001).

Top: 3 rue Auguste Comte
Bottom: Plaque to the right of the entrance

215

Chapter Eleven

7th

Arrondissement

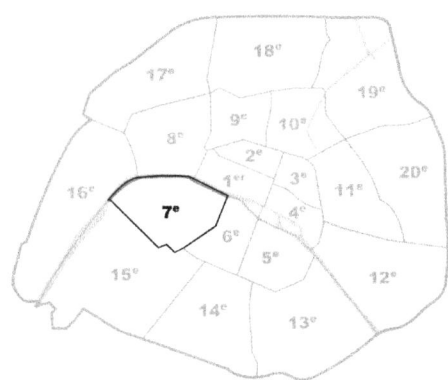

THE EIFFEL TOWER

CHAMP DE MARS

(Métro: Bir-Hakeim, Trocadéro)

ICONIC SYMBOL OF PARIS

LOVED AND LOATHED IN LITERATURE

I left Paris and even France because of the Eiffel Tower. Not only is it visible from every point in the city, but it is to be found everywhere, made of every known material, exhibited in every shop window, an unavoidable and tormenting nightmare ... I wonder what will be thought of our generation if, in some future riot, we do not unbolt this tall, skinny pyramid of iron ladders, this giant and disgraceful skeleton with a base that seems made to support a formidable monument of Cyclops and which aborts into the thin, ridiculous profile of a factory chimney.
Guy de Maupassant, *La Vie Errante* (1890)

All things considered, it's in the eye of the beholder. Many Parisians were outraged at 10,000 tons of metal being dumped in the heart of their city to construct a tower, the main exhibit of the 1889 Exposition Universelle (World's Fair). To others, the world's tallest man-made structure represented a beacon of the machine age proclaiming the birth of modernity. Writers were among the Tower's fiercest critics, and Guy de Maupassant's no doubt apocryphal anecdote about dining regularly at the tower's restaurant because it was the only place in Paris he could not see it, is the one most often repeated. In 1887 forty-seven writers and artists signed their name to the *protestation des artistes*, a letter of protest to the minister of public works spelling out clearly their indignation at the erection of the

La Tour Eiffel surrounded by the bustle of the Exposition Universelle in 1889

proposed monstrosity: 'For the Eiffel Tower … is without a doubt the dishonor of Paris. Everyone feels it, everyone says it, everyone is profoundly saddened by it, and we are only a weak echo of public opinion so legitimately alarmed.' Among the signees were Alexandre Dumas *fils*, François Coppée, Leconte de Lisle, Sully Prudhomme, Guy de Maupassant and Paris Opera architect Charles Garnier. Léon Bloy, a writer famous for his personal attacks, wrote, 'I love Paris, the city of intelligence, and I feel Paris threatened by this truly tragic lamppost to which it has given birth, and which will be seen at night from 20 leagues … as a distress signal of shipwreck and despair.'

But not all writers were prophets of doom. Some were actually excited and inspired by the Tower. One such writer was Guillaume Apollinaire, who composed his 1918 pioneering *Calligrammes: Poems of Peace and War* (1913–1916) with text arranged in the shape of objects, which included the Eiffel Tower. Other Tower enthusiasts included Jean Giraudoux, with his 1923 essay, *Prayer on the Eiffel Tower*; Roland Barthes, who produced an essay collection entitled *The Eiffel Tower and Other Mythologies*; and the inimitable Blaise Cendrars, who remarked, 'I like legends, dialects, mistakes of language, detective novels, the flesh of girls, the sun, the Eiffel Tower.'

The origins of the Tower grew out of defeatism. In the late 1800s France desperately needed to revitalise its nation after its 1870 defeat in the Franco-Prussian War, and the bloody uprising of the Commune that followed in its wake. An Exposition Universelle was the perfect antidote to restore the confidence of the people and their country's stature. In 1884 it was announced that a contest would be held for a fitting centrepiece. The winning design was Gustave Eiffel's one-thousand-foot iron tower. Fifty of Eiffel's engineers and designers produced 5300 drawings, and more than 100 workers built more than 18,000 different parts of the tower in workshops. Another 132 workers assembled the parts on site, where the tower was inaugurated on 31 March 1889, initially conceived as a temporary structure with a proposed life of twenty years. The Exposition Universelle was held from 6 May until 31 October 1889, the hundreth anniversary of the storming of the Bastille, and, like all world fairs, its purpose was to showcase the achievements of the world's nations. It was held on the Champ de Mars, the traditional site for all Paris's Expositions. Attractions for the 1889 fair included a 'Negro Village' and Buffalo Bill's Wild West Show; but the centrepiece that dwarfed everything was the Eiffel Tower.

The Tower ceased to be the world's tallest structure long ago, but Gustave Eiffel's colossal engineering feat has survived its criticisms, revulsions, political intrigues, lawsuits, safety disputes, extremes of weather, millions of tourists, daring stunts and even the tacky souvenir, to become the iconic symbol of Paris.

'Wherever you are [in Paris] ... *the Tower is there*,' observed Roland Barthes; 'incorporated into daily life until you can no longer grant it any specific attribute, determined merely to persist, like a rock or the river, it is as literal as a phenomenon of nature whose meaning can be questioned to infinity but whose existence is incontestable.'

See Also: Blaise Cendrars, Alexandre Dumas *fils*, Leconte de Lisle, Guy de Maupassant, Guillaume Apollinaire, Roland Barthes.

Further Information: In May 1925, in a hotel room at the Hôtel de Crillon on the Place de la Concorde, master con man Victor Lustig, posing as a government official, met with a group of scrap metal merchants and informed them that the government was prepared to sell the Eiffel Tower for scrap. Engineering faults and costly repairs were given as the reasons, but on the pretext of fearing a public outcry he stipulated it must be kept secret. Lustig sold the Tower to the highest bidder and walked away a rich man.

Further Reading: J. Jonnes, *Eiffel's Tower* (Penguin, 2010); D. Harvie, *Eiffel: The Genius Who Reinvented Himself* (History Press, 2004); J. Harriss, *The Tallest Tower: Eiffel and the Belle Époque* (Unlimited, 2008); J. Johnson, *The Man Who Sold the Eiffel Tower* (Doubleday, 1961).

Gustave Eiffel (1832–1923)

219

THE AMERICAN LIBRARY IN PARIS

10 RUE DU GÉNÉRAL CAMOU

(Métro: École Militaire/La Tour-Maubourg)

**LARGEST ENGLISH-LANGUAGE
LENDING LIBRARY IN EUROPE**

Dear Miss Reeder,   *Nov. 21st, 1938*

*... Have you copies of any of the following
books in your library?*

*1) The Secret Doctrine - Madame Blavatsky
2) The Tibetan Book of the Dead
3) Esoteric Buddhism - A.P. Sinnett
4) Seraphita - Balzac (in English)
5) Walt Whitman's Prose works
6) Any book on Zen Buddhism*

Sincerely yours,

Henry Miller

American Library, Rue du Général Camou

In 1917 American libraries shipped one and a half million books to US service personnel fighting in the trenches and war zones of Europe through the Library War Service, which was founded by the American Library Association. American citizens were asked to donate books, magazines and newspapers to their local libraries, which were then shipped to the front and to camps and hospitals behind the front line. Books were also provided on troop ships, trains, in prisoner of war camps, and to barracks and hospitals. The US American Library Association records show that in one camp alone 1050 books were borrowed in a week.

In 1920 the Association used many of these books to lay the foundation that established The American Library in Paris, originally located at No. 10 rue de l'Élysée, which promised to bring the best of American culture and literature to France. Its charter was encapsulated in their motto: *Atrum post bellum, ex libris lux* (After the darkness of war, the light of books), and one of its early trustees was American novelist, Edith Wharton. In 1923 it launched its monthly review, entitled *Ex Libris*, whose contributors included Ernest Hemingway and Gertrude Stein. The 1930s saw the advent of literary evenings with Colette, André Gide, Ford Madox Ford and many other guest authors.

In 1936 the library moved its by then 60,000 volumes to new premises at No. 9 rue de Téhéran, and with the outbreak of war in 1939 the Library began circulating books to French and British troops. Under the Nazi occupation in 1940 all

220

French libraries were forced to close, but The American Library remained open, gaining hundreds of French patrons. The Nazis barred Jewish members from the Library, but the director Dorothy Reeder and her staff operated a perilous underground book-lending service to the Jewish community in Paris. On one occasion the Gestapo arrived for a surprise inspection and shot senior librarian, Boris Netchaeff, in the chest, but luckily he survived. Dorothy Reeder was later sent home to the US for her own safety.

In 1953, Senator Joseph McCarthy's anti-communist investigators arrived outside the Library in their search for subversive and communist-inspired 'red' literature, but were turned away at the front door by its then director, Ian Forbes Fraser. The post-war era also brought a new expatriate community to Paris, which encompassed many writers who all used the Library, the list of whom includes Richard Wright, Irwin Shaw, Mary McCarthy, James Jones, Art Buchwald, and Samuel Beckett. The Library moved to its current premises at No. 10 rue du Général Camou in the mid 1960s. Today its book collection exceeds 120,000, and a quarter of its 2500 members are French.

See Also: Edith Wharton, Ernest Hemingway, Gertrude Stein, Colette, André Gide, Ford Madox Ford, Richard Wright, Irwin Shaw, James Jones, Samuel Beckett, Henry Miller.

Further Information: The American Library in Paris also has twelve provincial branches. The American Library Association, founded in 1876, is the oldest and largest library association in the world with over 60,000 members. Their efforts through the Library War Service led to the creation of permanent library departments in the US Army and Navy.

Further Reading: T.W. Koch, *Books in the War: The Romance of Library War Service* (Houghton Mifflin, 1919); J. Skeslien Charles, *The Paris Library* (John Murray, 2021).

Top: Librarian Dorothy Reeder at The American Library in 1936
Above: 10 rue de l'Élysée, the original location of The American Library

LES MISÉRABLES

ESPLANADE HABIB-BOURGUIBA

(Métro: Alma–Marceau)

LE MUSÉE DES ÉGOUTS DE PARIS
(MUSEUM OF THE SEWERS OF PARIS)
JEAN VALJEAN'S ESCAPE ROUTE
IN VICTOR HUGO'S *LES MISÉRABLES*

The history of men is reflected in the history of sewers. ... The sewer of Paris has been an ancient and formidable thing. It has been a sepulchre, it has served as an asylum. Crime, intelligence, social protest, liberty of conscience, thought, theft, all that human laws persecute or have persecuted, is hidden in that hole ... A hundred years ago, the nocturnal blow of the dagger emerged thence, the pickpocket in danger slipped thither; the forest had its cave, Paris had its sewer. ... The sewer is the conscience of the city. Everything there converges and confronts everything else. In that livid spot there are shades, but there are no longer any secrets. ... All which was formerly rouged, is washed free. The last veil is torn away. A sewer is a cynic. It tells everything.
Victor Hugo, *Les Misérables* (1862)

Illustration of Inspector Javert, nemesis of Jean Valjean, from the original publication of *Les Misérables* in 1862, after a painting by Gustave Brion (1824–1877)

Set in post-Waterloo France, *Les Misérables* revolves around ex-convict Jean Valjean, who is released in 1815 from nineteen years' imprisonment in the galleys and who, throughout the vast panorama of the novel, struggles to become an honourable human being. Valjean, the character of whom was inspired by criminal, turned criminalist, Eugène Vidocq, rescues Cosette's wounded and hunted revolutionary lover, Marius, using the sewer as an escape route, ultimately saving his life.

One of the greatest French Romantics, Victor Hugo had a passion for social justice; yet, perhaps as it took nearly twenty years to write, the book is burdened with digressions, moralising and elaborate essays. Hugo's first attempt was the unfinished *Les Misères* written between 1845 and 1848. Abandoned for twelve years, it was completed from 1860 to 1862 as *Les Misérables*. American author Upton Sinclair (1878–1968) described the book as 'one of the half-dozen greatest novels of the world'. Charles Baudelaire (1821–1867) described it as 'tasteless and inept'. Whatever your opinion, it cannot be denied that it's one of the world's longest, originally totalling around 3000 pages in five volumes. About a quarter of the book is taken up with Hugo's digressions on subjects such as enclosed religious orders, the Battle of Waterloo, street urchins and sewers. In so doing, Hugo totally ignores the accepted discipline of novel writing and does not advance the plot. Some would argue this deviates from the story; others might contend that these deflections enrich it. But, depending on which translation you read, *Les Misérables* is far from tedious, and despite its monumental length and exaggerated coincidences, it is still an awe-inspiring work, and the reader, apart from being made aware of the injustices of French society, the wretchedness of the poor, and the plight of the repressed, will also come away with a comprehensive knowledge of the Paris sewers. If you can set aside the novel's gargantuan size, Hugo's sprawling digressions, and its unremarkable plot, you will find buried deep in its pages a simple, but classic novel about destiny and chance.

See Also: Victor Hugo, Notre Dame de Paris, Arc de Triomphe, Panthéon, The Bastille, Père Lachaise, Eugène Vidocq, Charles Baudelaire.

Further Information: Paris's first underground sewer was built in 1370 beneath Rue Montmartre. In 1805 Napoleon Bonaparte commissioned the engineer Bruneseau to build 182 miles of sewer. 'The complete visitation of the subterranean sewer system of Paris occupied seven years, from 1805 to 1812,' wrote Hugo in *Les Misérables*. 'Bruneseau laid out, directed and brought to an end some considerable works ... At the same time he disinfected and purified the whole network.' In 1850 Baron Haussmann began modernising and enlarging the sewer system, which by 1878 was 360 miles long. Tours of the Paris sewer system began in 1889 and are still running today through Le Musée des Égouts de Paris.

Further Reading: D. Reid, *Paris Sewers and Sewermen* (Harvard University, 1993).

A tour of the Paris sewers in 1920

PABLO NERUDA

2 AVENUE DE LA MOTTE-PICQUET

(Métro: La Tour-Maubourg)

THE CHILEAN EMBASSY
FORMER OFFICIAL RESIDENCE OF
LATIN AMERICAN POET
PABLO NERUDA,
CHILE'S AMBASSADOR TO FRANCE
AWARDED THE NOBEL PRIZE
IN LITERATURE IN 1971

Paris is beautiful, but it is like a suit a few sizes too big for me. It is winter here as well, and the wind is like a flour mill stirring up the snow. The snow rises and rises; it crawls up my skin. I become a sad king in a white cloak. Then it rises to my mouth, covers my lips, and the words no longer come.
Pablo Neruda lamenting his time as Chile's ambassador to France in Antonio Skármeta's novel, *Burning Patience* (1985)

Pablo Neruda in 1971

Pablo Neruda was the pseudonym of Ricardo Elécer Neftalí Reyes Basoalto, who published his first collection of poems in his early teens and grew to become one of the most important Latin American poets of the twentieth century. His politics and political allegiances were often controversial, notably his praise of the Stalinist dictatorship, but it is his commitment to social justice and his spirited poetry that remain his lasting legacy.

He was born in 1904 in Parral, Chile's wine country, where his father, José, was a railway employee. His mother, Rosa, a schoolteacher, tragically died shortly after her son's birth. Never overawed by his son's talent for poetry, his father once threw his notebooks out of a window. This hostile reaction was one of many that persuaded young Ricardo – or

Neftali, as he was known – to change his name unofficially to Pablo Neruda in an attempt to disguise his writings from his father: an identity, no doubt, prompted by his admiration for Czech writer, Jan Neruda, and a name he would officially adopt by deed poll in 1946.

In 1920 he studied French in Santiago, intent on becoming a teacher. His first book of poems, *Crepusculario*, was published in 1923 to critical acclaim; but his first really original collection, published in 1924, was *Veinte poemas de amor y una canción desesperada (Twenty Love Poems and a Song of Despair)*. Inspired by an unhappy love affair, it remains today one of his most popular books.

In 1926 he began a career as a diplomat and travelled extensively throughout the Far East, becoming Chilean consul for Madrid in 1935. Neruda was by now a passionate communist and when Spain became engulfed in civil war he supported the Spanish Republic. After the murder by Franco's fascists of his friend, García Lorca, he immersed himself with

224

a vengeance in the Republican cause through his speeches and writings, publishing *España en el corazón (Spain in Our Hearts)* in 1937, printed by Republican troops on a dilapidated press on the eastern front. He also worked alongside poet and activist Nancy Cunard in the squalid refugee camps of the Pyrenees, and on Cunard's own printing press, they published the magazine *The Poets of the World Defend the Spanish People* to raise funds for the Republican cause. Chile's government found Neruda's actions unacceptable and ordered him to return home. The following year, however, Chile's new president Pedro Aguirre Cerda appointed Neruda special consul for Spanish emigrants in Paris. In this capacity, he supervised the migration to Chile of hundreds of defeated Spanish Republicans, notably transporting 2000 of them in an old cargo ship from the wretchedness of their refugee camps in France to safety in Chile.

After serving as Consul General in Mexico during World War II, during which time he wrote his epic poem, *Canto general*, he joined the Communist Party of Chile. Threatened by the Chilean government with prosecution as a subversive, he went into exile in 1948, travelling extensively in Europe, China and the Soviet Union, returning to Chile's more favourable political climate in 1952.

In 1970 Salvador Allende won the presidency of Chile, and appointed Neruda ambassador to France. By now Neruda was ill with prostate cancer and this would be his final diplomatic posting, lasting from 1970 to 1972. It was in Paris that Neruda was officially awarded the Nobel Prize in Literature in 1971, the year of his sixty-seventh birthday. In November the following year, and with deteriorating health, Pablo Neruda returned home to Chile to die. Augusto Pinochet assumed power in Chile in 1973 following a United States-backed coup d'état overthrowing Allende's democratically elected government. Neruda died a few days later, reportedly of heart failure, his dream of a socialist future in ruins.

Some still find it hard to separate Neruda's poetry from his intense devotion to communism, but, as Argentinian writer, Jorge Luis Borges, Neruda's political opposite, once commented: 'I do not think it is fair that a writer is judged by his political ideas. It's true that Rudyard Kipling defended the British Empire. But we must also recognise that he was a great writer.'

See Also: Nancy Cunard, Jorge Luis Borges.

Further Information: Pablo Neruda married three times, and had one daughter. In 1966 he married his third wife, Matilde Urrutia, who lived with him until his death in 1973. In 1985, Chilean writer, Antonio Skármeta, published his novel *Ardiente Paciencia (Burning Patience),* which told the fictional story of Mario Jiménez, a postman who has only one client, Pablo Neruda, and their resulting friendship in a small Chilean fishing village. The novel was translated into more than twenty languages and has twice been adapted for the screen, the most celebrated adaptation being Michael Radford's 1994 Italian tragi-comedy, *Il Postino,* starring Massimo Troisi.

Select Bibliography: *Twenty Love Poems and a Song of Despair* (Jonathan Cape, 1969); *Love Poems* (New Directions, 2008); *The Essential Neruda: Selected Poems* (City Lights, 2004).

Further Reading: A. Feinstein, *Pablo Neruda* (Bloomsbury, 2005).

ANTOINE DE SAINT-EXUPÉRY

PLACE SANTIAGO-DU-CHILI

(Métro: La Tour-Maubourg)

BUST OF ANTOINE DE SAINT-EXUPÉRY
PIONEERING AVIATOR AND AUTHOR OF
LE PETIT PRINCE

'What makes the desert beautiful,' said the little prince, 'is that somewhere it hides a well ...'
Antoine de Saint-Exupéry, *The Little Prince*

Antoine de Saint-Exupéry

Saint-Exupéry, who, through his love of flying, injected a unique sense of wonder and mystique into his writing, is mainly remembered today for his 1943 novella, *Le Petit Prince (The Little Prince)*, a work which has been translated into more than 250 languages and dialects, with sales totalling in excess of 140 million. *Le Petit Prince*, and his two other books, the novel *Vol de Nuit (Night Flight)* and the non-fictional *Terre des hommes (Wind, Sand and Stars)*, are among the bestselling French books of the twentieth century. Fame in his lifetime, however, was but a shadow compared to the heights to which his reputation would soar after his untimely and mysterious death in a plane crash in 1944, earning him commemoration with an inscription in the Panthéon, an honour only awarded to national heroes. He was born in 1900 into a French aristocratic family in Lyon, the third of five children of the Countess Marie de Fonscolombe and Count Jean de Saint-Exupéry. Following the death of his father from a stroke, when he was three, his early childhood was spent at the family château at Saint-Maurice-de-Rémens in the foothills of the Jura mountains, which he called 'the country of my childhood'. His interest in flying began in 1910 when a local cycling champion, Louis Mouthier, bought a Blériot XI monoplane, the aircraft that made the first successful flight across the English Channel in 1909. Mouthier started a flying school at Ambérieu-en-Bugey, close to Saint-Exupéry's home, and it was soon to become a place of pilgrimage for him.

After various jobs and career blind alleys, Saint-Exupéry finally found his destiny when he was posted to the 37th Fighter Regiment in Morocco in 1921, and awarded his pilot's wings. By 1926 he had become one of the pioneers of early airmail flights operating in West Africa and South America. A high-risk and often perilous experience, it gave him much material for his writings, notably his second novel, *Vol de Nuit*,

226

which describes a postal flight in South America, and was his first major work to attract a widespread readership in 1931. With the outbreak of WWII Saint-Exupéry joined a French reconnaissance squadron, but after the fall of France in 1940 he and his Salvadoran wife, Consuelo Suncín, went into exile in New York, where he would eventually write and illustrate *The Little Prince* in 1942. On his return to France he again joined a reconnaissance squadron flying high-altitude, twin-boomed, unarmed Lockheed Lightnings. On the last day of July 1944, he was returning from a long-distance photographic mission over the Rhône Valley to his base in Corsica when his plane disappeared over the Mediterranean west of Nice. The unidentifiable body of a Frenchman in uniform was discovered south of Marseille shortly after the disappearance of the plane, however it remains inconclusive that it was the body of Saint-Exupéry. It is possible that the Luftwaffe shot down his plane, but this, too, is still the subject of speculation.

Pilote de Guerre (Flight to Arras), published in 1942, about a reconnaissance flight over enemy-occupied France, was written with an apparent awareness that Saint-Exupéry already knew the fate that lay in store for him:

The fighters came down on you like lightning. Having spotted you from fifteen hundred feet above you, they take their time. They weave, they orient themselves, take careful aim. ... You are the mouse lying in the shadow of the bird of prey. The mouse fancies that it is alive. It goes on frisking in the wheat. But already it is the prisoner of the retina of the hawk, glued tighter to that retina than to any glue, for the hawk will never leave it now.

Further Information: In 2000 remains of his aircraft were discovered on the seabed off the coast of Marseille, but they revealed no clues as to the cause of the crash. Shortly after Saint-Exupéry's death, his wife Consuelo wrote a memoir of their life together, called *The Tale of the Rose*. The manuscript was discovered in a trunk long after her death, and the subsequent book, published in 2000, became a bestseller and was translated into sixteen languages. The Madeleine Tézenas du Montcel bust of Antoine de Saint-Exupéry was erected in 1989 in Place Santiago-du-Chili, near where Saint-Exupéry lived, on Rue de Chanaleilles. He later lived at No. 15 place Vauban, which is marked by a plaque.

Select Bibliography: *Courrier sud (Southern Mail)* (1929); *Vol de nuit (Night flight)* (1931); *Terre des hommes (Wind, Sand and Stars)* (1939); *Pilote de guerre (Flight to Arras)* (1942); *Le Petit Prince (The Little Prince)* (1943); *Citadelle (The Wisdom of the Sands)* (1948).

Further Reading: P. Webster, *Antoine de Saint-Exupéry, The Life and Death of the Little Prince* (MacMillan, 1993).

A Lockheed P-38 Lightning similar to the one in which Saint-Exupéry died. His aircraft was unarmed

transition

40 RUE FABERT

(Métro: La Tour-Maubourg)

FORMER HOME OF *transition*
AVANT-GARDE LITERARY JOURNAL
OF MODERNIST AND SURREALIST
WRITING

Then Nuvoletta reflected for the last time in her little long life and she made up all her myriads of drifting minds in one. She cancelled all her engauzements. She climbed over the bannistars; she gave a childy cloudy cry: Nuee! Nuee! A lightdress fluttered. She was gone. And into the river that had been a stream ... there fell a tear, a singult tear, the loveliest of all tears ... for it was a leaptear. But the river tripped on her by and by, lapping as though her heart was brook: Why, why, why! Weh, O weh! I'se so silly to be flowing but I no canna stay!

James Joyce, *Finnegans Wake* (1939)

The innovative literary journal, *transition*, was founded by American expatriates Eugene and Maria Jolas in 1927 in a small, family hotel on Rue Fabert. 'The hotel faced the Place des Invalides,' wrote Maria,

with a wide, unhampered view – and our fourth-floor 'office', erstwhile bedroom, of course, eventually became known to initiates from near and far. I recall that on the occasion of Marshal Foch's *funérailles nationales*, Joyce followed the long ceremony through a telescope, from the *transition* 'office' windows. He did not miss a trick as readers of *Finnegans Wake* will have noticed.

In the third issue of *transition* published in 1927, Eugene Jolas printed a manifesto entitled *The Revolution of the Word*, proclaiming: 'We need new words, new abstractions, new hieroglyphics, new symbols, new myths.' And this is exactly what he got. Distributed principally through Sylvia Beach's bookshop, Shakespeare and Company, *transition* featured writers such as Samuel Beckett, Ernest Hemingway, Paul Bowles, Gertrude Stein, Hart Crane, Dylan Thomas and James Joyce. 'But we clung to our principle,' wrote Maria, 'which had been accepted by all our contributors: 20 francs a page to all alike and the authors retained the copyright.'

The journal's most famous published work was James Joyce's 'Work in Progress', written over a period of seventeen years and finally published in book form as *Finnegans Wake* in 1939, two years before his death. The Jolases became great friends with Joyce, but Gertrude Stein never qualified: 'I did not like Miss Stein,' wrote Maria, 'nor do I think that her talent was an important one; it was too artificial, too blatantly self-conscious and malicious for my taste.'

See Also: Samuel Beckett, Ernest Hemingway, Paul Bowles, Gertrude Stein, Hart Crane, James Joyce, Shakespeare and Company (Rue de l'Odéon).

Further Information: Eugene Jolas (1894–1952) was born in New Jersey. His parents, who were immigrants from Alsace-Lorraine, returned to Germany in 1897 with the young Eugene, who was raised in a bilingual family. As an adult, he began a career as a journalist, at first in the USA, then for the Paris edition of the *Chicago Tribune* in the 1920s. His wife, Maria McDonald Jolas (1893–1987) was born in Kentucky and was a skilled translator who became a well-known peace campaigner in later life. The name 'transition' was inspired by Edwin Muir's volume of essays of the same name, published in 1926.

Further Reading: N. Fitch (ed.), *In Transition: A Paris Anthology: Writing and Art from Transition Magazine 1927–30* (Anchor, 1990); D. McMillan, *transition: The History of a Literary Era* (Calder, 1975); E. Jolas, *Man from Babel* (Yale U.P., 1998); M. Jolas, *Woman of Action* (S. Carolina U.P., 2004).

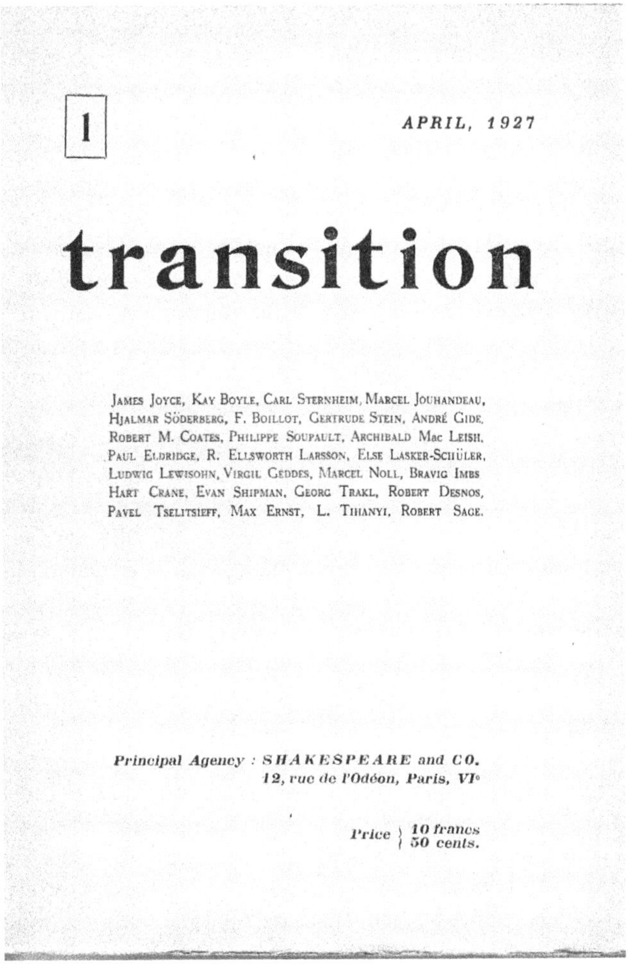

1

APRIL, 1927

transition

JAMES JOYCE, KAY BOYLE, CARL STERNHEIM, MARCEL JOUHANDEAU, HJALMAR SÖDERBERG, F. BOILLOT, GERTRUDE STEIN, ANDRÉ GIDE, ROBERT M. COATES, PHILIPPE SOUPAULT, ARCHIBALD MacLEISH, PAUL ELDRIDGE, R. ELLSWORTH LARSSON, ELSE LASKER-SCHÜLER, LUDWIG LEWISOHN, VIRGIL GEDDES, MARCEL NOLL, BRAVIG IMBS HART CRANE, EVAN SHIPMAN, GEORG TRAKL, ROBERT DESNOS, PAVEL TSELITSIEFF, MAX ERNST, L. TIHANYI, ROBERT SAGE.

Principal Agency : SHAKESPEARE and CO.
12, rue de l'Odéon, Paris, VI⁰

Price } 10 francs
} 50 cents.

229

JULIA CHILD

81 RUE DE L'UNIVERSITÉ

(Métro: Assemblée Nationale)

FORMER HOME OF JULIA CHILD
PIONEERING AMERICAN CHEF
AND CO-AUTHOR OF *MASTERING*
THE ART OF FRENCH COOKING

I think every woman should have a blowtorch.
Julia Child

Julia Child

Such was Julia Child's (1912–2004) impact on American cookery culture that when she moved from her 'big, old, gray clapboard three-storey house' in Cambridge, Massachusetts, to a retirement complex in California in 2001, her entire kitchen was taken apart and reassembled in Washington at the National Museum of American History. From pots and pans to scribbled notes under fridge magnets, nothing was left behind: a unique culinary world preserved in aspic to inspire and remind future generations of a woman who turned cooking into a great adventure. But an appreciation of good food came quite late in Julia Child's life. 'I was 32 when I started cooking,' she once said, 'up until then, I just ate.'

Her father, John McWilliams, worked in real estate and her mother Caroline was a housewife who spent little time in the kitchen. 'I had zero interest in the stove,' Julia wrote of her girlhood in Pasadena, California, in *My Life in France*. 'I was never encouraged to cook and just didn't see the point in it. Our family had a series of hired cooks, and they'd produce heaping portions of typical American fare … It was delicious, but not refined food.' She met her husband, Paul Child, during the Second World War in Ceylon (now Sri Lanka), where they were both working for the OSS (Office of Strategic Services), and they married in 1946. 'The first meal I ever cooked for Paul … ' she wrote, 'was brains simmered in red wine! … In fact the dinner was a disaster. … I was annoyed with myself, and I grew more determined than ever to learn how to cook well.'

Her opportunity came in 1948 when Paul was offered a job at the American Embassy in Paris, and they moved into an apartment on Rue de l'Université on the Left Bank of the Seine. Her first months were spent studying French at the Berlitz School and familiarising herself with the city's streets and markets. In the autumn of 1949 she enrolled at the prestigious Cordon Bleu cookery school on Rue du Faubourg Saint-Honoré, where she was to learn her craft working with many of Paris's professional chefs. However, she did not gel with its proprietress, Madame Brassart, who 'seemed to think', Julia reflected, 'that awarding a student a diploma was like inducting them into some kind of secret society; as a result the school's hallways were filled with an air of petty jealousy and distrust.'

During her intensive and frustrating time at Le Cordon Bleu a friend introduced her to another gastronome named Simone 'Simca' Beck, who was a member of Le Cercle des Gourmettes, a women's gastronomical society founded in 1927. When Julia joined the group, their lunches, she later recalled, were 'the real beginning of French gastronomical life for me.' Simca introduced Julia to her friend and fellow 'gourmette', Louisette Bertholle, and together the three of them came up with the idea of opening a school to teach cooking to Americans. L'École des Trois Gourmandes was thus born, catering for a maximum of five pupils, usually in Julia's kitchen.

Simca and Louisette had also been working on a French cookbook for many years, which was primarily aimed at Americans. The manuscript, however, was a mess. The English translation was inept and the recipes suspect. Julia suggested rewriting the entire book from scratch using what she called 'the informal human approach' as opposed to the pretentious tones and mystique often used in many French cookbooks aimed at the English-speaking market. With Julia heading the project, the 726-page book, *Mastering the Art of French Cooking*, was eventually published in 1961 by Alfred A. Knopf, and became a bestseller. To this day it is considered a groundbreaking work. Julia went on to write a profusion of cookery books both under her own name and with others, and as a result of a television appearance in 1962 she was asked to host her very own cooking show which debuted as *The French Chef* in 1963. The show ran on national television for ten years, and received many awards, turning Julia into a household name. In 1966 she was featured on the cover of *Time* magazine with the heading 'Our Lady of the Ladle'.

See Also: Brillat-Savarin.

Further Information: The French *Ordre du Saint-Esprit* was an elite order of chivalry created by Henri III in 1578. The order hung from a blue ribbon and the knights who wore it became known as les Cordons Bleus. By the eighteenth century, the term Cordon Bleu was applied to anyone who excelled in a particular field, principally celebrated cooks. In the late nineteenth century the name was appropriated by journalist Marthe Distel for her culinary magazine *La Cuisinière Cordon Bleu*. The magazine offered its readership cooking lessons with professional chefs, and it was these lessons which eventually led to the founding of the school known today as Le Cordon Bleu. There is now a network of Cordon Bleu schools around the world.

Select Bibliography: J. Child, S. Beck, L. Bertholle, *Mastering the Art of French Cooking* (1961); J. Child, *My Life in France* (2006).

81 rue de l'Université

GUSTAVE DORÉ

27 RUE DE BELLECHASSE

(Métro: Solférino)

STUDIO OF GUSTAVE DORÉ

NINETEENTH–CENTURY ILLUSTRATOR

OF CLASSIC WORKS OF LITERATURE

Never did an artist show less concern than he does for reality ... He lodges at the hostelry of the fairies, deep in the land of dreams.
Émile Zola

Gustave Doré by Nadar *c.*1855

Gustave Doré was an artistic genius who was self-taught, drew fast, and produced thousands of illustrations during his relatively short life. It was a mass of creativity that many believed diminished his worth. But Doré's world was reproduction, and although he always wanted to be recognised as a painter, and felt embittered throughout his life by his lack of success, his real skills lay elsewhere. Doré was essentially a decorator, a set designer and a stylist whose illustrations leapt to great heights, depths and distance, and which were often dark, sadistic and grotesque. His Gothic wood-engraved visions rank him today among the great artists of the illustrated book.

Doré was born in 1832, the second of three brothers, into a bourgeois family in Strasbourg where his father was an engineer. Throughout his school years, where he was commended for his drawing skills, he developed an early interest in reproduction. In 1847, a Paris company published Doré's first collection of lithographs, *Les Travaux d'Hercule*, and later that year he visited the city that would determine his future. With samples of his work, he visited the Place de la Bourse print shop of journalist and caricaturist Charles Philipon, who promptly contracted him to produce weekly cartoons for his journal. Thus Doré was able to pay his tuition fees at the Lycée Charlemagne.

In 1849, when Doré was seventeen, his father died of pleurisy. For the rest of his days he lived at No. 73 rue Saint-Dominique, in a house his mother had inherited. His mother lived there with him until her death.

Doré was the favoured child of his mother, and it was said that her overbearing love for him hindered his maturity into adulthood. Like a child, he slept in a room with an adjoining door to his mother's bedroom, conversing with her before he fell asleep. 'The profound love they bore one another', observed the novelist Paul Lacroix, 'filled up every other void in their lives ... His adoration for her reached a point which made him indifferent to everything and everybody else.'

Following his move to Rue Saint-Dominique, Doré built a studio on nearby Rue de Bellechasse and soon commissions began to pour in. His first successful foray into the world of classic literature came in 1854 when he illustrated Rabelais's sixteenth-century tales, *Gargantua* and *Pantagruel*, which enjoyed a huge success. Other works followed, notably those of Balzac, Perrault, Cervantes, Chateaubriand, Milton, Hugo, Tennyson, Dante, La Fontaine, Poe, the Bible, and many lesser-known works, establishing Doré as one of the most popular literary artists of his day.

Doré's fame also followed him to England where he had a major exhibition in 1867 that led to the foundation of a permanent Doré Gallery in London. Together with English journalist Blanchard Jerrold he worked on a project exploring the extremes of life in Victorian London. The commission lasted four years, for which Doré was paid a fee of ten thousand pounds per year, a colossal sum for its time. The end result was *London: A Pilgrimage*, published in 1872, which contained one hundred and eighty of Doré's engravings.

After his mother died in 1881 Doré was alone and inconsolable. 'He had always been his mother's child,' wrote his biographer Joanna Richardson, 'Mme Doré had denied him his emotional freedom, the experience of life which is, above all, essential to the creative artist. In doing this, she had largely destroyed him. Her selfishness (and perhaps his weakness) left him an unhappy bachelor, childless, and condemned to solitude.' Doré died following a severe stroke on the morning of 23 January 1883, aged fifty-one,

Doré's engraving for Edgar Allan Poe's narrative poem, 'The Raven' (1884)

and is buried beside his mother in Père Lachaise Cemetery, Division 22.

See Also: Cimetière du Père Lachaise, Charles Perrault, François Rabelais, Honoré de Balzac, Émile Zola, Jean de La Fontaine, René de Chateaubriand.

Further Information: The facade of Doré's former studio, which can be seen from Rue de Bellechasse, has two casts from fragments of the eastern frieze of the Parthenon, originally sculpted between *c*.443 BC and *c*.438 BC.

Further Reading: J. Richardson, *Gustave Doré: a Biography* (Cassell, 1980); B. Jerrold & G. Doré, *London: A Pilgrimage* (Anthem, 2005).

TINTIN

82 RUE DE L'UNIVERSITÉ

(Métro: Solférino)

FORMER EDITORIAL OFFICES OF
COEURS VAILLANTS
THE FIRST CHILDREN'S NEWSPAPER TO
INTRODUCE HERGÉ'S TINTIN
TO FRANCE, IN 1929

I was young then, of course, and I intended to keep my own name for the great, serious painting I was going to do later on. 'Hergé' was just for a laugh, on the side.
Hergé, *Sunday Times* 1968

Hergé

Hergé, the pseudonym of Belgian-born artist Georges Remi (1907–1983), was an alias he adopted in 1924 by reversing his initials G.R. to R.G. Since his first appearance in black and white in a Catholic newspaper in 1929, Hergé's comic strip creation of the boy reporter Tintin has sold more than a hundred million books and been translated into more than forty languages. Tintin's success was in his universal appeal, and even allowing for his strange trousers and permanent quiff, he has stood the test of time and is little dated today.

Georges Remi was born in the Brussels suburb of Etterbeek on 22 May 1907. As a young teenager he attended Saint Boniface's Catholic school where he excelled in most subjects, but not in art. He joined the school's Boy Scout troop, where his artwork was first published in the troop's newsletter, and later in Belgium's national Scouting magazine. In 1925 he joined the newspaper *Le Vingtième Siècle* (The Twentieth Century), a 'Catholic Newspaper for Doctrine and Information', hoping to become an illustrator; however, he was mostly relegated to doing odd jobs. In his spare time he worked on the character he devised for the national Scouting magazine, a Boy Scout called Totor: a brave, quick-witted lad with a quiff and baggy trousers who toured the world fighting against injustice. Totor would eventually metamorphose into Tintin.

In 1926 Hergé was called up for a year's military service. When demobbed in October 1927 he returned to *Le Vingtième Siècle*, but this time as an illustrator. A few weeks later the newspaper decided to launch *Le Petit Vingtième* (The Little Twentieth) for younger readers, and Hergé was appointed editor. Towards the end of 1928, after struggling with various cartoon characters, Hergé introduced a new American-style comic strip without the usual heavy text captions, instead using speech bubbles. Its new hero, Hergé wrote, would be 'a reporter with the spirit of a Boy Scout', named Tintin. The first strip, *Tintin au Pays des Soviets (Tintin in the Land of the Soviets)*, appeared in the eleventh issue of *Le Petit Vingtième*, in January 1929. *Tintin* was first published in France the

234

same year by the children's newspaper, *Cœurs Vaillants*, founded in 1929 by Catholic priests belonging to l'Union des œuvres catholiques de France (The Union of Catholic Works of France). The priests, initially bewildered by *Tintin*'s speech bubbles, introduced their own text captions but later relented, following Hergé's strong objections. *Cœurs Vaillants* went on to publish *Tintin* until 1946.

See Also: Jules Verne, *Astérix*.

Further Information: When Belgium was occupied during the Second World War, Hergé created 'Tintin' serial strips for the Belgian daily *Le Soir*, a newspaper that continued to publish and collaborate under German censorship. When the Allies entered Brussels in September 1944 the staff were sacked and banned from working. Hergé's career came to an abrupt end and he did not work again until the end of 1945 when the Belgian publisher Raymond Leblanc contacted him with the idea of launching a *Tintin* magazine. Leblanc obtained Hergé a 'certificate of good citizenship' enabling him to legally work again. Launched on 26 September 1946, *Tintin* magazine sold 60,000 copies in its first week.

Hergé no doubt drew on many sources to find his inspiration for Tintin, but when quizzed about his creation he would remain enigmatic. Hergé researchers in recent years, however, have detected many similarities with Palle Huld, a fifteen-year-old Danish boy who, in 1928, won a Danish newspaper competition to try to surpass the exploits of Phileas Fogg, the protagonist in Jules Verne's *Around the World In Eighty Days*. With his quiff of red hair, snub nose, freckles, plus fours and Boy Scout background, Huld circumnavigated the world in forty-four days. Having overcome many dangers, including travelling through war-torn Manchuria and Russia, Huld returned home with all the traits of a future Tintin.

In 1980 Hergé was diagnosed with leukaemia and died on 3 March 1983 at a clinic in Brussels. He is buried in the city's Uccle Dieweg Cemetery. The Musée Hergé opened in 2009 and is located at 'Rue du Labrador 26' (the address of Tintin's first home), in Louvain-la-Neuve, Belgium.

Select Bibliography: *Tintin au Pays des Soviets (Tintin in the Land of the Soviets)* (1930); *Tintin au Congo (Tintin in the Congo)* (1931); *Tintin en Amérique (Tintin in America)* (1932); *Les Cigares du pharaon (Cigars of the Pharaoh)* (1934); *Le Lotus Bleu (The Blue Lotus)* (1936); *L'Île Noire (The Black Island)* (1938); *L'Affaire Tournesol (The Calculus Affair)* (1956); *Tintin au Tibet (Tintin in Tibet)* (1960); *Les Bijoux de la Castafiore (The Castafiore Emerald)* (1963).

Further Reading: P. Assouline, *Hergé: The Man Who Created Tintin* (OUP USA, 2009); H. Thompson, *Tintin: Hergé & His Creation* (Hodder & Stoughton, 1991); M. Farr, *Tintin: The Complete Companion* (Egmont, 2011); M. Daubert, *Tintin: The Art of Hergé* (Abrams ComicArts, 2013).

82 rue de l'Université

Top left: Tintin personified: Danish teenager, Palle Huld (1912–2010) in 1928, during his trip around the world. Top right: The Danish 2012 reprint cover of *Jorden Rundt i 44 dage* (Around the World in 44 Days) by Palle Huld, first published in 1928, and subsequently translated into several languages. Above left: Palle Huld in old age. Above right: A 1940 edition of *Cœurs Vaillants*

VOLTAIRE

27 QUAI VOLTAIRE

(Métro: Rue du Bac/St-Germain-des-Prés)

WHERE VOLTAIRE DIED IN 1778

WRITER, PHILOSOPHER AND VOICE OF
THE FRENCH ENLIGHTENMENT

If God did not exist, it would be necessary to invent him.
Voltaire, from *Epistle to the author of The Three Imposters* (1770)

Voltaire was a writer of manifold talents who wrote in many literary genres: poetry, prose, theatre, history and criticism. He even penned a scientific treatise. He was famous for his wit and he argued for freedom of religion and expression, attacking the Catholic Church, as well as anything else society deemed sacred – from censorship to patriotism. He also had many enemies, who played their part in his imprisonment and exile. But Voltaire was a survivor, and although he is best remembered for his philosophical work *Candide*, he was a master of his trade, and as a fountainhead of wit and satire he still endures today, while his enemies and opponents are naught but dust.

Voltaire was the nom de plume of François-Marie Arouet, born on the Île de la Cité, Paris, on 21 November 1694. He was the youngest child of François Arouet, a lawyer, and Marie Daumard, who died when he was only six. From 1704 to 1711 he attended the prestigious Jesuit College, Lycée Louis-le-Grand, where his antics drove his teachers to despair. After college, under the pretence of studying law, he began publishing satirical, often political, verse. One such composition, which accused the Regent of France of incest, led to his first spell of imprisonment in the Bastille in 1717. During his 11-month confinement he wrote his verse tragedy *Oedipe* (an adaptation of Sophocles's *Oedipus the King*), which was premiered shortly after his release, at the Comédie-Française. Ironically, the premiere was attended by the Regent of France, who congratulated its author, now calling himself Voltaire, as a talent to be reckoned with. The play was a great success and its creator acclaimed as the successor of Racine.

With his newfound fame he began to frequent high society and he briefly became a favourite at court. After the political lampooning of the Chevalier de Rohan-Chabot in 1726 he was imprisoned once again in the Bastille. When he was released a month later, it was on the condition that he leave Paris. Wisely, he fled to London, returning to Paris in

1729, but no longer was he the apple of its eye. The sceptical and often bewildered authorities were now growing suspicious of this enlightened individual prone to political revolt.

In 1731 he published his first history, *Histoire de Charles XII*, and the following year saw the overwhelming success of his verse tragedy, *Zaïre*. In 1734, however, after the publication of *Lettres philosophiques*, ('the first bomb thrown at the *ancien régime*', wrote Gustave Lanson), a warrant was issued for his arrest. Rather than face the Bastille again, he went into hiding and took refuge in the château of his mistress, Émilie du Châtelet, in the Lorraine. Here, until Émilie's death in 1749, Voltaire wrote methodically across a number of genres, notably science (*Eléments de la philosophie de Newton*, 1738), poetry (*Le Mondain*, 1736), drama (*Mahomet*, 1741) and prose (*Zadig*, 1747). In 1759 Voltaire purchased Ferney, an estate near the Swiss border, which would remain his home for the rest of his life. It was here he wrote *Candide* in just three days, savagely criticising the arrogance of the aristocracy and the power of the Church. In 1778, aged eighty-four and in poor health, he returned to Paris to attend a performance of his tragedy, *Irène*, at the Comédie-Française, no doubt aware it would be his last visit to his native city. The performance was a great success, and a torchlight parade accompanied the coach back to his lodgings at 27 quai Voltaire. In his bedroom that night, in great pain and coughing up blood, he received a Jesuit priest who pleaded with him to renounce the Devil. 'This is no time for making new enemies,' Voltaire replied.

Refused a burial in consecrated ground, his body was smuggled out of Paris by night and interred secretly at the Abbey of Scellières in the province of Champagne. In Paris, all newspapers were forbidden to print his obituary. In July 1791, two years after the Revolution, Voltaire's remains were reburied in the Panthéon, the mausoleum for France's national heroes.

See Also: Bastille, Panthéon, Académie française, Comédie-Française.

Further Information: Voltaire died in the first-floor apartment that overlooks the courtyard, facing the door to Rue de Beaune. The Lycée Louis-le-Grand is located in the heart of the Latin Quarter at No. 123 rue Saint-Jacques.

Select Bibliography: Poetry: *La Henriade* (1723); *The Maid of Orleans* (1730). Prose: *Zadig* (1747); *Candide* (1759). Drama: *Oedipe* (1718); *Zaïre* (1732); *Mahomet* (1741); *Irène* (1778).

Further Reading: R. Holmes, *Sidetracks* (HarperCollins, 2000); N. Mitford, *Voltaire in Love* (Vintage Classics, 2011); N. Cronk (ed.), *The Cambridge Companion to Voltaire* (Cambridge University Press, 2009).

27 quai Voltaire

ROBERT SERVICE

17 QUAI VOLTAIRE

(Métro: St-Germain-des-Prés/Solférino)

FORMER HOME OF ROBERT SERVICE
KNOWN AS THE 'BARD OF THE YUKON'
THE WORLD'S FIRST MILLION-COPY
SELLING POET

The Northern Lights have seen queer sights,
But the queerest they ever did see
Was that night on the marge of Lake Lebarge
I cremated Sam McGee.
Robert Service,
from 'The Cremation of Sam McGee'

Robert Service

Robert Service once described his role in life as 'writing verse for those who wouldn't be seen dead reading poetry'. His descriptions of the sub-Arctic landscapes of the Yukon and its wild, lawless characters during the gold rush are now part of literary legend. He captured the imagination of millions writing about gold fever, barroom brawls, shoot-outs and mining camps, and dance halls peopled with characters with names like the Ragtime Kid, Klondike Kate, and the lady that's known as Lou. Born in Lancashire in 1874, he was brought up in Scotland where he became a bank clerk. At the age of twenty-one he emigrated to Canada where he joined a bank that sent him to their Yukon branch, and in 1907 his first collection of verse was published under the title *Songs of a Sourdough*, 'sourdough' being the historical term for a prospector in Yukon and Alaska. It brought him wealth for the first time in his life, and within two years he had resigned from the bank.

In the spring of 1913 he arrived in Paris and moved into lodgings on the Quai Voltaire. During World War I he failed a medical for the army, but at the Hôtel Meurice on Rue de Rivoli he met the men who were creating an American Ambulance Corps. By the time he joined them, the Corps had sixty ambulances in the field. 'I loved those trips to the firing trench,' he wrote, 'or even into No Man's Land. We made them during the day when we had cover, but when we were exposed we took the wounded after dark. The danger enhanced the heartening feeling of saving life.' Service also became a correspondent for the *Toronto Daily Star*, and began writing a series of articles entitled 'Records of a Red Cross Man'. In 1916 he was invalided out of the ambulance service and sent home to Paris suffering from the indignity of boils. That same year he published his book of war poetry, *Rhymes of a Red Cross Man*, which outsold Wilfred Owen and Siegfried Sassoon.

Service lived in Paris for sixteen years, but his later life was spent at his house in Brittany, where he died at the age of eighty-four in 1958.

See Also: The American Hospital in Paris, American Ambulance, Café de la Paix.

JAMES BALDWIN

8 RUE DE VERNEUIL

(Métro: St-Germain-des-Prés/Rue du Bac)

HÔTEL VERNEUIL

FORMER LODGINGS OF

JAMES BALDWIN

AMERICAN NOVELIST, ESSAYIST

AND CIVIL RIGHTS ACTIVIST

The country [USA] still thinks I'm a water-melon-eating darkie.
James Baldwin speaking at the University of British Columbia, Vancouver, in 1964

James Baldwin

James Baldwin (1924–1987) emerged from the ghetto to achieve global fame with the publication of his mostly autobiographical novels and provocative essays. Exposing US society and its malignant racism to the world, he established himself as one of the prominent literary voices for civil rights in 1950s and 1960s America. He was born in Harlem and never knew his real father, whom his mother never married. Spurned by his stepfather, who was a preacher, and who died insane, he grew up in an atmosphere of bigotry and holy roller religion. Floating from one down-at-heel job to another he struggled to support his widowed mother and his eight half-siblings. Black, homosexual, and an outsider who had parted ways from the church, he spent most of his relatively unhappy life in France, in exile. He arrived in Paris in November 1948, with forty dollars in his pocket and not a word of French. 'I had to get out of New York,' he said. 'My luck was running out.' That same day he was taken to meet Richard Wright, one of the major black writers of his day, at Les Deux Magots cafe. They had first met in New York, but Wright, the elder of the two, was a success story after publication of his social protest novel, *Native Son*, in 1940. Baldwin was an unknown, his first novel just a jumble of pages in his suitcase. But the joining of minds that was expected turned into a rift after Baldwin savagely criticised Wright's image of African American life in his essay 'Everybody's Protest Novel'. 'All literature is protest!' growled Wright over a table at the Brasserie Lipp. 'But not all protest is literature,' replied Baldwin. The rift widened into an abyss. After borrowing money from friends he ended up at the Hôtel Verneuil, owned by a venerable Corsican lady named Mme Dumont; but shortly after moving in, he became ill. 'To my surprise I wasn't thrown out of the hotel. ... An old, old lady, a great old matriarch, nursed me back to health after three months; she used old folk remedies. And she had to climb five flights of stairs every morning to make sure I was kept alive.' Hôtel Verneuil was not the Ritz, but it was welcoming, and thanks to Mme Dumont's relaxed attitude to her tenants, which included tolerating overdue rent and eccentric behaviour, it soon became popular lodgings for the struggling bohemian expatriate. But Madame was no pushover; if a party got too boisterous or went on too long, she simply switched off the electricity.

After his return to health, Baldwin got down to the serious business of writing, sometimes at the Verneuil, but often he could be seen with his notebook in the warmth of Les Deux Magots, Brasserie Lipp, or his favourite refuge upstairs at the Café de Flore. As well as trying to finish his first novel, *Go Tell it on the Mountain*, he wrote book reviews and numerous essays about life in Paris. In the evenings, if he had money, he would frequent the homosexual bars and jazz clubs of Saint-Germain, haunts that would eventually inspire the setting for Guillaume's bar in Baldwin's second novel, *Giovanni's Room*.

In the spring of 1949 he visited the south of France with friends. It was an ill-fated sojourn during which time he ended up being hospitalised in Aix-en-Provence. On his return to Paris at the end of November, there were no vacancies at the Verneuil and he was forced to check in to the nearby Hôtel du Bac: 'one of those enormous, dark, cold, and hideous establishments in which Paris abounds,' he wrote. A friend had brought him a bed sheet he had pilfered from another hotel. Shortly afterwards, the police arrived and arrested Baldwin for receiving stolen goods, whereupon he spent Christmas 1949 in prison with vagrants and thieves.

Although he began his life in exile in Paris, he never lost touch with his roots and family; nor did his commitment to civil rights falter. He returned to the US frequently for long periods to write, to research, and to support the movement back home, becoming the leading black novelist of his generation. In 1970 he set up home in a Provençal farmhouse in Saint-Paul-de-Vence on the French Riviera where he lived for the rest of his life. He died from cancer in 1987.

His all-time literary hero was fellow New Yorker and exile, Henry James, whom he called 'the Master' – not just for James's discipline, style and technique, but because of their shared understanding of 'the failure of Americans to see through to the reality of others'.

See Also: Richard Wright, Chester Himes, Langston Hughes, Ted Joans, Bricktop's, Henry James, Café de Tournon, Les Deux Magots, Brasserie Lipp, Café de Flore.

Select Bibliography: *Go Tell it on the Mountain* (1953); *Notes of a Native Son* (1955); *Giovanni's Room* (1956); *Another Country* (1962); *The Fire Next Time* (1963). Plays: *The Amen Corner* (1954); *Blues for Mr Charlie* (1964).

Further Reading: J. Campbell, *Talking at the Gates: A Life of James Baldwin* (Faber & Faber, 1991).

Hôtel Verneuil, 8 rue de Verneuil

JAMES JOYCE
9 RUE DE L'UNIVERSITÉ
(Métro: Rue du Bac)

FORMER LODGINGS OF JAMES JOYCE AND WHERE HE RECEIVED THE FIRST EDITION OF *ULYSSES* FROM SYLVIA BEACH ON HIS FORTIETH BIRTHDAY, IN 1922

9 rue de l'Université

James Joyce (1882–1941) was without doubt the most significant experimental writer in the English language of his time. Most of his life – from 1904 until his death in Zurich in 1941 – was spent in exile from his native Ireland, and, like many writers, he brought out the best and the worst of a country deep-rooted in its politics and religion because of his separation from it. He wrote about 'ordinary' and 'vulgar' people, notably in and around Dublin, of which *Ulysses* (1922) is a monumental celebration. 'For myself,' he observed, 'I always write about Dublin, because if I can get to the heart of Dublin I can get to the heart of all the cities of the world. In the particular is contained the universal.'

The eldest of ten children, Joyce came from a middle-class family whose finances were steadily dwindling. Following his Jesuit schooling, he left for Paris in 1902 to study medicine; however, after a few months he abandoned the idea and returned to Dublin. While he was a struggling 22-year-old writer, he met chambermaid Nora Barnacle, with whom he became infatuated. She was twenty, unreserved, lewd, and didn't give a tinker's curse for the written word, but she would become the catalyst for James Joyce's future.

In October of the same year they went into voluntary exile in Zurich, where Joyce sought a teaching post. There was no vacancy, but they eventually settled in Trieste where they remained, on and off, for the next ten years. It was here their two children, Giorgio (1905–1976) and Lucia (1907–1982), were born, and where Joyce was writing the early drafts of *Ulysses*, trying to get his work published in an endless struggle with censors and printers. Ezra Pound, the 'King Lear' of modernism, recognised Joyce's talent and published him in the London literary magazine, *The Egoist*. In 1914 he began serialising Joyce's semi-autobiographical novel, *A Portrait of the Artist as a Young Man*, which led, eventually, to his work being published in novel form. *Dubliners,* his collection of short stories, was published in 1914, followed two years later by *A Portrait*. Nevertheless, the censors, who were always waiting in the wings, took the American literary magazine, *The Little Review*, to court on charges of obscenity after they serialised *Ulysses* in America in 1918.

Joyce's reputation as a key literary modernist was growing, but with mouths to feed, rent to pay, recurring eye problems and medical bills, Joyce needed money more than praise, and in 1917 it landed unexpectedly in his lap. Harriet Weaver (1876–1961), wealthy heiress, political activist and editor of *The Egoist*, believed strongly in Joyce's genius and became his benefactress for the rest of his life, placing large sums of money in trust on his behalf, the interest from which guaranteed him an income for the remainder of his days. It didn't end his money problems, but it made life a lot easier.

In July 1920, at the suggestion of Ezra Pound, Joyce arrived in Paris with his family for a week. They overstayed their visit by twenty years, and it was here that Joyce finished his seven-year labour on that 'bitch-of-mother book', *Ulysses*. The family stayed at a private hotel at No. 9 rue de l'Université, temporary accommodation they would return to several times while flat-hunting in the city. After numerous rejections he found a publisher for *Ulysses* in the unlikely Sylvia Beach, the young American proprietor of the bookshop Shakespeare and Company, on Rue de l'Odéon. Beach had no experience of publishing, but she did have a love of the printed word and a blind faith in the genius of James Joyce. The resulting enterprise is now literary legend, but it was a perilous undertaking that could easily have failed. On the morning of Joyce's fortieth birthday – Thursday, 2 February 1922 – Beach placed in his hands the first copy of *Ulysses* at No. 9 rue de l'Université. With a dust cover of cobalt blue, and littered with thousands of errors, it was an extraordinary achievement. Beach gave her own copy pride of place in the window of Shakespeare and Company. Joyce signed his copy to Nora, who, it is claimed, demanded of him, 'Why don't you write books people can read?' Nora sold the book to a friend.

See Also: Shakespeare and Company (Rue Dupuytren and Rue de l'Odéon), Gare de Lyon, Samuel Beckett, Ezra Pound.

Further Information: Fleeing the Nazi occupation of France, the Joyces settled in Zurich in late 1940, where Joyce died on 13 January 1941 following surgery for a perforated duodenal ulcer. A few weeks short of his fifty-ninth birthday, he was buried in Zurich's Fluntern Cemetery. Harriet Weaver heard of his death on the radio, whereupon she sent money to Nora, and acted as his executrix. Nora died of acute renal failure in 1951, aged 67, and is buried beside Joyce and their son Giorgio. Lucia Joyce, who was diagnosed with schizophrenia in her twenties, died from a stroke in 1982, and is buried in Northampton, England. At the time of writing, No. 9 rue de l'Université is the location of the Hôtel Lenox.

Select Bibliography: *Chamber Music* (1907); *Dubliners* (1914); *A Portrait of the Artist as a Young Man* (1916); *Exiles: A Play in Three Acts* (1918); *Ulysses* (1922); *Finnegans Wake* (1939).

Joyce and his family in Paris, 1924

TRUMAN CAPOTE

5–7 RUE MONTALEMBERT

(Métro: Rue du Bac)

HÔTEL PONT ROYAL

FORMER ABODE OF TRUMAN CAPOTE

BEST REMEMBERED FOR HIS NOVELLA

BREAKFAST AT TIFFANY'S

Truman Capote

[Capote] can give a sense of a perverse boy liking to annoy his reader by being sick and crippled; but that is only one side of the picture. Capote is a consummate artist, a writer very serious about his craft, who, no matter whether his reader likes it or not, does create a world of his own. Things are seen by Capote not with an innocent but with the goblin eye of a self-retarded soul.
Martin Seymour-Smith, *Guide to Modern World Literature* (1973)

In 1948 Truman Capote (1924–1984) had published the American edition of his first novel *Other Voices, Other Rooms* to great critical acclaim. In need of a change of scene he sailed to Europe in May aboard the *Queen Elizabeth*. Although not yet published outside America, his reputation as a promising young writer had gone before him, and Truman Capote was becoming the literary rage of Europe. In London he stayed at Claridge's, and was photographed by Cecil Beaton. He met Somerset Maugham, Evelyn Waugh, Noël Coward, and Harold Nicolson, who attempted to seduce him. But after two weeks he left the drab post-war depression of London and boarded the boat train to Paris.

Compared to London Paris really was a city of light. The Nazi occupation was over, monuments were floodlit, fountains spouted water again, the exchange rate favoured the dollar, life was cheap, and the food and wine were the best in the world. Capote checked into the Hôtel Pont Royal and Paris seemed to fall at his feet. One interviewer described him as 'Small, bordering on the fragile, precious, he's a literary seraph with heavy-lidded eyes ... Disheveled blond locks cover, or uncover, the forehead of a thinker.' French publisher Gallimard was launching his first novel, *Other Voices, Other Rooms*, and through them and his French agent he was introduced to the literary celebrities of Paris, including Colette, Jean Cocteau, Alice B. Toklas, Natalie Barney, and Albert Camus, with whom Capote claimed to have had a brief affair. 'He was a homely little thing,' wrote Capote,

but attractive, with sensitive eyes and a compassionate face. He was my editor at Gallimard, and he took me to dinner. One thing led to another, and one afternoon he came to my room and we just went to bed. It was as simple as that. I don't think he was homosexual in any way. But that was the period when I looked my best. When he met me, he was sort of startled. I must have touched some nostalgic nerve in him, reminded him of something that happened in adolescence.

Capote sailed home from his three-month-long sojourn in Europe on the

Queen Mary on 7 August 1948. It would remain an unforgettable period of his life that found its way into many of the characters and plots of his stories. 'It was right that I had gone to Europe,' he wrote,

> if only because I could look again with wonder. Past certain ages or certain wisdoms it is very difficult to look with wonder; it is best done when one is a child; after that, and if you are lucky, you will find a bridge of childhood and walk across it. Going to Europe was like that. It was a bridge of childhood, one that led over the seas and through the forests straight into my imagination's earliest landscapes.'

See Also: Gallimard, Somerset Maugham, Colette, Jean Cocteau, Alice B. Toklas, Natalie Barney, Albert Camus.

Further Information: Truman Capote was born Truman Streckfus Persons in 1924 in New Orleans, Louisiana. Following the divorce of his parents when he was four, he grew up with relatives in Monroeville, Alabama, where his childhood friend was Harper Lee. In 1933 he moved to New York to live with his mother and her second husband, Cuban-born Joseph Capote, who adopted him and gave him the name Truman García Capote. After years of alcohol and drug abuse Truman Capote died in Los Angeles in 1984, aged fifty-nine. His long-time nemesis, Gore Vidal, described Capote's death as 'a good career move'.

Select Bibliography: *Other Voices, Other Rooms* (1948); *The Grass Harp* (1951); *Breakfast at Tiffany's* (1958); *In Cold Blood* (1965); *Music for Chameleons* (1980).

Further Reading: G. Clarke, *Capote* (Hamish Hamilton, 1988); *Too Brief a Treat: The Letters of Truman Capote* (Vintage, 2005).

TED JOANS

188 BOULEVARD SAINT-GERMAIN

(Métro: St-Germain-des-Prés/Rue du Bac)

LE ROUQUET

ADOPTED CAFE OF TED JOANS

AFRICAN AMERICAN JAZZ POET,

MUSICIAN AND PAINTER

> *I am going back*
> *I am black   but I'm going back*
> *A young Russian poet I once read;*
> *'a poet should be where the action is'*
> *thats what he said*
> *I am going back*
> *I'm going to   r e t u r n*
> *to the land of   Burn,Baby,B u r n !*
> *I am going back*
> *I'm going back and play real dumb*
> *join hands with Whitey and sing*
> *'We Shall Overcome'*

Ted Joans, from 'Believe You Me!' *Black Pow-Wow* (1969)

Born Theodore Jones (1928–2003) in America's Midwest, Ted Joans's poetry flows with the rhythms of jazz, surrealist humour and a dynamic awareness of black culture. He travelled all over Europe in the 1950s and 1960s, reading his poetry and playing his jazz trumpet. He often wintered in Africa, but it was Paris that became his home. In his 1961 book, *All of Ted Joans and No More*, Joans spelled out why he decided to leave the United States: 'I hate cold weather, and they will not let me live democratically in the warm states of the United States, so I'm splitting and letting America perish.'

He earned a BA in Fine Arts from Indiana University in 1951 before moving to New York, where he described himself as a 'jazz poet'. He served his literary apprenticeship in Greenwich Village in the 1950s, becoming a leading member of the beat generation. His lifelong mentor was poet Langston Hughes (1902–1967), who encouraged him to delve deep into his own black heritage, and to whom Joans dedicated his poem 'Passed on Blues: Homage to a Poet'. Joans was unique in bringing jazz and the spoken word together on stage, and his slogan became 'Jazz is my religion, and surrealism is my point of view': a viewpoint that made an impression on French poet André Breton, who once described Joans as 'the only Afro-American surrealist'.

Le Rouquet on Boulevard Saint-Germain became his adopted cafe, postal address and general home from home where staff would take messages for him. Thus – although Le Rouquet was never the haunt of writers, which was probably why Joans chose it – he carried on a long-established literary tradition.

In the late 1990s he was living in Vancouver, in the straitened circumstances he had become accustomed to, and this was where he died, on 25 April 2003, due to complications from diabetes. He is survived by ten children. 'So in my rather sorrowful impecunious state', he wrote shortly before his death, 'I find myself filled to the beautiful brim with love and with this shared love I continue to live my poem-life.'

See Also: Langston Hughes, André Breton.

Further Information: Ted Joans's abstract painting of his former friend, jazz legend Charlie 'Bird' Parker (1920–1955), can be seen at the de Young Museum in San Francisco. After Parker's death, Joans was said to have scrawled 'Bird Lives!' graffiti all over the walls of Lower Manhattan. Ted Joans was the recipient of the American Book Awards Lifetime Achievement Award in 2001.

Select Bibliography: *Jazz Poems* (1959); *The Hipsters* (1961); *Black Pow-Wow: Jazz Poems* (1969); *Afrodisia: New Poems* (1970); *A Black Manifesto in Jazz Poetry and Prose* (1971); *Teducation: Selected Poems 1949–1999* (1999).

CHATEAUBRIAND

120 RUE DU BAC

(Métro: Sèvres–Babylone)

FORMER HOME OF CHATEAUBRIAND
WRITER, DIPLOMAT AND THE MOST
CELEBRATED FIGURE IN FRENCH LITER-
ATURE DURING THE FIRST EMPIRE

Chateaubriand cannot be loved, and his character cannot be admired without grave reserves. But an unique genius, developed at a fortunate time, enabled him to play a most significant part in the history of literature.
Edward Dowden, *A History of French Literature* (1897)

François-René Chateaubriand

Today Chateaubriand is considered the founding father of Romanticism who had a deep-rooted impact on French literature. According to *The Oxford Companion to French Literature* he 'was, by all accounts, a sublime poseur, a sublime egotist, and a sublime day-dreamer, seeing the world in and through himself'. Apart from the beef steak that was named after him, he is remembered today mostly for his sweeping *Mémoires d'outre-tombe (Memoirs from Beyond the Tomb)*, published posthumously in 1849 and 1850, which covers the key events of his life through the French Revolution and the Napoleonic era to the Revolution of 1830.

He was born in 1768 at Saint-Malo in Brittany, the tenth child of René Chateaubriand, a former sea captain with close links to the slave trade, and Apolline de Bedée. He spent his childhood at the family's medieval château in Combourg. At seventeen he gained a commission in the army, and with the outbreak of the Revolution he quit France and sailed to America with a starry-eyed notion of

discovering the North-West Passage. He never found the Passage, but his experiences did inspire him to write his prose epic, *Les Natchez* (1826), about the adventures of a Frenchman in the French and Indian wars.

After receiving news of the execution of Louis XVI he returned to France, married an heiress of seventeen, and joined the Armée des Emigrés, a counter-revolutionary force whose aim was to overthrow the French Revolution. Wounded in battle, he escaped and took refuge in London in 1793 where he supported himself by translating and teaching. It was here that he published his first work, the *Essai sur les révolutions (Essay on Revolutions)* (1797), his attempt to unravel the causes of the French Revolution. In 1800 he returned to France where he worked as a freelance journalist, and wrote *Atala* (1801), the novella that secured his fame. It is an exotic tale that tells the story of a Christian girl torn between love and religion in Louisiana. In 1798, after the death of his mother and sister, Chateaubriand regained the Catholic faith of his childhood, and resolved to write a book describing the hope and joy he had found in religion. The resulting *Génie du christianisme*, which was begun in London, and included his novella *René*, was finally completed four years later in 1802, adding to his fame and coinciding with France's return to Catholicism as the official religion. Napoleon liked it so much he gave Chateaubriand an appointment as first secretary at the French Embassy in Rome, a post he soon resigned from, over internal politics and a growing hostility to the Napoleonic leadership. After Rome he moved to his country house in La Vallée aux Loups, in the Paris suburbs, and in 1806 he set off on a pilgrimage to Jerusalem, taking in Constantinople, Egypt, Carthage and Spain, which resulted in his *Itinéraire de Paris à Jérusalem* (1811). On his return he concentrated on literature and journalism, and became a regular contributor to the literary magazine, *Mercure de France*. With the downfall of Napoleon in 1814, the Bourbon Restoration took power and France was ruled by a constitutional monarchy, but unlike the Ancien Régime, it had limited powers. Chateaubriand was made a peer and a minister, but his political ambitions were open to question, and his competence often in doubt.

After the July Revolution of 1830 that brought Louis-Philippe to the throne, Chateaubriand retired to his Paris apartment and began writing his *Histoire de France* (1831). In 1838 he and his wife moved from their home in Rue d'Enfer to 120 rue du Bac where he would finish writing his *Mémoires d'outre-tombe* in 1847. Chateaubriand's marriage had been a failure from the outset and throughout his life he had many love affairs. In 1801 he had met salonnière Juliette Récamier (1777–1849), who recharged his loveless life. 'As I draw near my end,' he wrote in his *Mémoires*, 'it seems to me that everything I love I have loved in Mme Récamier, and that she was the hidden source of my affections.' Mme Récamier's salon was one of the most prestigious literary salons in Paris, where she cultivated the writers and intellectuals of her day, including Hugo, Balzac, and Sainte-Beuve. It was situated just a few streets away from Rue du Bac at 7 rue de la Chaise, and the devoted Chateaubriand made it his daily pilgrimage. He was once described as 'wearing his heart in a sling': what better place for the founding father of the Romantics?

Further Information: Chateaubriand died on 4 July 1848, and he is buried on the tidal island of Grand-Bé, off the coast of Brittany. 120 rue du Bac is marked by a plaque and his apartment was on the ground floor to the rear of the courtyard. A bust of Chateaubriand can be seen opposite in the Square des Missions-Étrangères.

Select Bibliography: *Memoirs from Beyond the Tomb* (Penguin, 2014); *Atala & René* (Signet, 1962).

120 rue du Bac

MADAME DE STAËL

97 RUE DU BAC

(Métro: Rue du Bac/Sèvres–Babylone)

FORMER RESIDENCE AND SALON OF
MADAME DE STAËL
NOVELIST, ESSAYIST AND CRITIC
DURING REVOLUTIONARY AND
NAPOLEONIC FRANCE

Madame de Staël in 1812 by Vladimir Borovikovsky (1757–1825)

Far from recovering my confidence by seeing Bonaparte more frequently, he constantly intimidated me more and more. I had a confused feeling that no emotion of the heart could act upon him. He regards a human being as an action or a thing, not as a fellow creature. He does not hate more than he loves; for him nothing exists but himself; all other creatures are ciphers. The force of his will consists in the impossibility of disturbing the calculations of his egoism; he is an able chess-player, and the human race is the opponent to whom he proposes to give checkmate. His successes depend as much on the qualities in which he is deficient as on the talents which he possesses. Neither pity, nor allurement, nor religion, nor attachment to any idea whatsoever could turn him aside from his principal direction. He is for his self-interest what the just man should be for virtue; if the end were good, his perseverance would be noble.

Germaine de Staël, *Considerations on the Principal Events of the French Revolution* (1818)

Madame de Staël (1766–1817) was a formidable intellectual in the fields of literature and politics in an age when women were expected to be neither clever nor controversial. Along with Chateaubriand she was one of the great forerunners of romanticism and modern criticism. With a readership that stretched throughout all of Europe, she was the most famous woman of her time, influencing many of her contemporaries, including Byron, who called her 'the first female writer of this, or perhaps any, age'. Her novel *Corinne, or Italy* (1807) outsold the works of Sir Walter Scott, and has never been out of print. She is credited with the birth of the French Romantic movement and was one of the first to use the term romanticism, spreading it throughout France by her repeated use of it. If she is remembered at all today, it is for advancing the philosophical ideas of her time, and for her celebrated novel, *Corinne, or Italy*. She also had a curious penchant for spectacular, kaleidoscopic turbans.

Born Anne-Louise-Germaine Necker in Paris in 1766, she was the only child of Swiss banker Jacques Necker and

Suzanne Curchod. Much of her childhood was spent immersed in the world of her mother's acclaimed literary salon where she was surrounded by the intellectual aesthetes of her day. Her first marriage, in 1785, was to Baron de Staël, Swedish ambassador to Paris. A loveless union, it nevertheless produced three children.

Her hostility to the military dictatorship of Napoleon Bonaparte reached its climax after the publication of her controversial novel *Delphine* (1802), which explores the limits of women's freedom. After publication, an incensed Bonaparte banned her from living in Paris. Her vendetta with Bonaparte and their intense dislike of each other, which continued for several years, was not just political, but also personal: eyeing up her ample cleavage, he once commented: 'No doubt, Madame, you breastfed your children.' Napoleon regularly censored her books and exiled her from France several times between 1803 and 1812.

From her home at 97 rue du Bac, de Staël established her legendary salon which became a renowned centre for political discussion. During the Revolution she saved many of her friends from the guillotine, and contrived a plan of escape for the royal family, which Marie Antoinette rejected. In 1810 her famous work, *De l'Allemagne*, was seized and pulped on Napoleon's orders, and she herself was exiled. She escaped France secretly and eventually arrived in England in 1813, where John Murray in London published *De l'Allemagne* to great acclaim, in both French and English. After Napoleon's defeat at Leipzig she returned to Paris and reopened her salon, but after Napoleon's escape from Elba, she wisely left for her family's estate in Switzerland. Finally, after Napoleon's defeat at Waterloo, she returned once again to Paris. It was here that a stroke ended her life on 14 July 1817. She was fifty-one years old.

In 1814 the French memoirist, Madame de Chastenay, summed her up in a memorable epigram. There were, she wrote, three great powers struggling against Napoleon for the soul of Europe: 'England, Russia, and Madame de Staël'.

See Also: François-René Chateaubriand.

Further Information: Madame de Staël is buried in the family mausoleum at the Château de Coppet, near Nyon in Switzerland. A few months before her death in October 1816, she secretly married a young hussar officer some thirty years her junior.

Select Bibliography: *Corinne, or Italy* (2008); *Major Writings of Germaine de Staël* (1992); *Germany* (*De l'Allemagne*), (2011).

Further Reading: M. Fairweather, *Madame de Staël* (Constable, 2005); J.C. Herold, *Mistress to an Age: A Life of Madame de Staël* (Hamish Hamilton, 1959).

97 rue du Bac

EDITH WHARTON

53 RUE DE VARENNE

(Métro: Rue du Bac/Varenne)

FORMER APARTMENT OF

EDITH WHARTON

AMERICAN NOVELIST

AND SHORT-STORY WRITER

She drew a deep sigh that ended in another laugh. 'Oh, my dear – where is that country? Have you ever been there? ... I know so many who've tried to find it; and, believe me, they all got out by mistake at wayside stations: at places like Boulogne, or Pisa, or Monte Carlo – and it wasn't at all different from the old world they'd left, but only rather smaller and dingier and more promiscuous.'
Edith Wharton, *The Age of Innocence* (1920)

Edith Wharton, *c.*1895

Edith Wharton is all too often given the brush-off as an ageing, blue-blooded aristocrat of old New York high society who fled to the Continent to escape it all, yet still held on to its splendour. But her affluent background gave her a kind of inner perception to the subtleties, the selfishness, and the heartlessness of the social hierarchy in the so-called Gilded Age of the late nineteenth century. Although fatalistic in her view of life, she wrote of a world she knew, and the originality of her observations, her shrewd understanding of the plight of women, are often unrecognised and her talent as a writer underestimated.

Edith Newbold Jones was born in New York in 1862 into a wealthy and aristocratic family, and she received a private education. Her family introduced her to Europe as a child, where the family travelled widely. In 1885 she married Teddy Wharton; it was a troubled union that would end in divorce. After their marriage they visited Paris frequently, and in 1907 they decided to settle in France, renting a first floor furnished apartment at 58 rue de Varenne, in the Faubourg district.

In January 1910 they moved across the street to 53 rue de Varenne. Teddy would leave Rue de Varenne in 1912 for good, but Edith lived on there, in between visits back to America, until 1919. The move to No. 53 was problematic: the Seine had burst its banks and created one of the worst floods in the city's history, with locals rowing along Rue de Varenne while others lowered baskets from their windows for basic supplies. The Whartons' unfurnished apartment was on the

251

second floor, fortunately untouched by the flooding, and eventually they settled comfortably into the apartment. It was a time she summed up fondly in her autobiography, *A Backward Glance*:

> When we finally settled in the rue de Varenne 'The House of Mirth', then appearing in the *Revue de Paris*, was attracting attention in its French dress, partly because few modern English and American novels had as yet been translated, but chiefly because it depicted a society utterly unknown to French readers …
>
> Henry James's visits to the rue de Varenne were always a busy time for me. He had been much in Paris in his youth, had frequented the great generation of the Goncourt 'garret', met Flaubert frequently, and been intimate with Turgeniev, and later with Alphonse Daudet … His description of taking Daudet down to Box Hill to see Meredith, and of the two great writers, both stricken with the same fatal malady [syphilis], advancing painfully toward each other across the platform of the little country station, was one of the most moving things I ever heard him relate.

53 rue de Varenne

Much of Wharton's writing at the Rue de Varenne apartment was set in America, notably the novella *Ethan Frome* (1911), one of only two works Edith Wharton set outside genteel society. By now Wharton's marriage was deteriorating rapidly. She had begun an affair in 1909, and the same year Teddy admitted to embezzling $50,000 from her trust funds. Henry James summed up Teddy's behaviour in a letter to her as 'off his poor little head'. Teddy, who had bipolar disorder, and Edith were finally divorced in 1913.

With the outbreak of the First World War Wharton established the American Hostels for Refugees, and raised $100,000 in the first year. She made frequent visits to the front at Ypres and Verdun, visiting hospitals and doing everything she could to help the war effort on the home front.

After the horrors of the war, in a Paris that was tarnished with jumbled memories, Wharton urgently needed somewhere to retreat to. 'Paris is simply awful,' she wrote to friend, 'a kind of continuous earth-quake of motor-busses, trams, lorries, taxis & other howling & swooping & colliding engines, with hundreds & thousands of US citizens rushing about in them & tumbling out of them at one's door – &, through it all, the same people placidly telephoning one to come to tea.' In 1918 she escaped and purchased Le Pavillon Colombe, a rambling house with expansive grounds in Saint-Brice-sous-Forêt, a village close to Paris. Nineteen years later, on 11 August 1937, she died there, aged seventy-five, of a stroke.

See Also: Edith Wharton (Le Pavillon Colombe), Henry James, Alphonse Daudet, The Goncourt brothers, Gustave Flaubert, Ivan Turgenev.

Select Bibliography: Novels: *The House of Mirth* (1905); *The Reef* (1912); *The Custom of the Country* (1913); *The Age of Innocence* (1920); *The Children* (1928). Novella: *Ethan Frome* (1911). Short story collections: *The Greater Inclination* (1899); *Crucial Instances* (1901). Non-fiction: *The Decoration of Houses* (1897); *Fighting France: from Dunkerque to Belfort* (1915). Autobiography: *A Backward Glance* (1934).

Further Reading: H. Lee, *Edith Wharton* (Chatto & Windus, 2007); R. and N. Lewis, *The Letters of Edith Wharton* (Simon & Schuster, 1988).

Poster advertising the serialisation of *The House of Mirth* in 1905

ANDRÉ GIDE

1 *BIS* RUE VANEAU

(Métro: Varenne/Solférino)

FORMER HOME OF ANDRÉ GIDE

NOVELIST, CRITIC AND DRAMATIST

AWARDED THE NOBEL PRIZE

IN LITERATURE IN 1947

Do not do what someone else could do as well as you. Do not say, do not write what someone else could say, could write as well as you. Care for nothing in yourself but what you feel exists nowhere else. And, out of yourself create, impatiently or patiently, the most irreplaceable of beings.
André Gide

André Gide wrote more than fifty books, but he is best remembered today for his controversial views more than his written works. By the end of the First World War his unorthodox opinions, tinged with his characteristic subversive edge, were moulding Gide into a prophet for French youth. The Soviet government, along with the Communist Party – with whom he had a brief commitment – banned his books in the late 1930s, and during the German occupation of Paris the Nazis followed suit. But the best publicity he could have wished for came a year after his death in 1952 when the Vatican placed his works on their *Index librorum prohibitorum* (Index of prohibited works), forbidding all Catholics to read his books under pain of mortal sin. But despite his celebrity as an agent provocateur, his views on the morals, politics and religion of his time rightly gained him the reputation of a learned sage, a status that won him the Nobel Prize in Literature in 1947.

A 1925 portrait of André Gide by Polish artist, Leopold Gottlieb (1883–1934)

Gide was born in 1869 into a middle-class family at 19 rue de Médicis (now No. 2 place Edmond Rostand), the only child of Juliette Rondeaux and Paul Gide, a law professor. He attended the Protestant *École alsacienne* in Paris, but as a child he suffered from spells of ill health and was often kept at home and taught by private tutors. His father died in 1890 of intestinal tuberculosis when Gide was only eleven, and his upbringing from then on was almost exclusively in a female environment, where his mother was excessively protective of him. In spite of being a self-confessed 'pederast', Gide married his cousin Madeleine in 1892, although it was unconsummated. He did, however, have a daughter from a brief sexual liaison in 1923 with Elisabeth van Rysselberghe. Gide also befriended Oscar Wilde in 1891, but although Gide had several male lovers, there is no evidence that Wilde was one of them.

He published his first novel, *Les cahiers d'André Walter (The Notebooks of André Walter)*, in 1891, a literary debut that appeared at the height of the Symbolist movement, a movement Gide had an affinity with. Symbolism was in essence a reaction against naturalism and realism, and was greatly developed by the poet Stéphane Mallarmé, whose weekly literary salons Gide regularly attended. But Gide experimented with many forms: allegory, lyricism, satire, parody, and especially his own acerbic form of first-person narrative, notably in *L'immoraliste, La porte étroite,* and *La Symphonie Pastorale.* In 1908 he co-founded the literary magazine *La Nouvelle Revue Française.* The *NRF*, as it was known, would later spawn the publishing house *Les Éditions de la NRF*, which famously rejected the first volume of Marcel Proust's masterpiece, *À la recherche du temps perdu (In Search of Lost Time)* in 1913. Gide was also a relentless critic of French bureaucracy, especially in its African colonies, and, following a journey to French Equatorial Africa, he severely criticised colonial policies in his 1927 exposé, *Voyage au Congo.* But the book Gide considered to be his most important work, and one of his most controversial, was *Corydon* (1920), his defence of pederasty. Since his death from pneumonia in 1951, André Gide's reputation and works have waned. But Gide was nothing if not honest about his life, and was openly gay. 'It is better to be hated for what you are', he wrote, 'than to be loved for what you are not.'

See Also: Stéphane Mallarmé, Oscar Wilde, Gaston Gallimard, Marcel Proust, Arthur Symons.

Further Information: André Gide lived on Rue Vaneau from 1926 until his death, aged eighty-one, in 1951. He is buried in the Cimetière de Cuverville, in Calvados, Normandy.

Select Bibliography: *L'immoraliste (The Immoralist)* (1902); *Le retour de l'enfant prodigue (The Return of the Prodigal Son)* (1907); *La porte étroite (Strait is the Gate)* (1909); *Isabelle* (1911); *La Symphonie Pastorale (The Pastoral Symphony)* (1919); *Les faux-monnayeurs (The Counterfeiters)* (1925); *Voyage au Congo (Travels in the Congo)* (1927); *Journals 1889–1949* (Penguin Classics, 1978).

Further Reading: G. Painter, *André Gide* (New York Atheneum, 1968); A. Sheridan, *André Gide: A Life in the Present* (Penguin, 2000); J. Fryer, *André & Oscar: Gide, Wilde and the Gay Art of Living* (Thistle, 2013); N. Segal, *André Gide: Pederasty and Pedagogy* (Clarendon Press, 1998).

1 *bis* rue Vaneau

NANCY MITFORD

7 RUE MONSIEUR

(Métro: St-François-Xavier)

FORMER HOME OF NANCY MITFORD
ENGLISH NOVELIST, BIOGRAPHER
AND JOURNALIST
BEST KNOWN FOR HER NOVELS DEPICT-
ING UPPER-CLASS LIFE IN ENGLAND
AND FRANCE

[The nurse] went away and presently returned carrying a Moses basket full of wails ... and deep down among the frills and lace, there was the usual horrid sight of a howling orange in a fine black wig ... I know it's dreadful of me, but I don't much like them as small as that; I'm sure she'll be divine in a year or two.
Nancy Mitford, *The Pursuit of Love* (1945)

David Freeman-Mitford, 2nd Baron Redesdale, and father of the Mitford girls, once remarked, 'I am normal, my wife [Sydney] is normal, but my daughters are each more foolish than the other,' he lamented. David and Sydney Mitford had six daughters who became known as the 'mad, mad Mitfords'. The eldest and most talented of them was Nancy (1904–1973), whose semi-autobiographical novels depicted the world of pre- and post-war upper-class English eccentricity with a piercing dialogue and wit that turned her into a household name. She started writing for magazines in the late 1920s and although her debut novel, *Highland Fling*, made little impact, her fifth novel, *The Pursuit of Love*, published in 1945, sold 200,000 copies in its first year, establishing her as a bestselling author and literary celebrity.

Top: Nancy Mitford
Above: Unity, Diana and Nancy in 1932

The Mitford sisters were all educated at home, and grew into the Bright Young Things of the twenties. But by the 1930s and 1940s the sisters were progressing towards their destiny. Diana went on to marry Oswald Mosley, founder of the British Union of Fascists, and Unity became besotted with Hitler and shot herself in a botched suicide attempt in 1939. Left-wing Jessica ran off to fight in the Spanish Civil War, Deborah mar-

ried a lord, and Pamela lived quietly in the country.

After the war, with a broken marriage behind her, Nancy Mitford moved to Paris to be near her lover, Free French Officer, Gaston Palewski. She would never return to England again, settling with her maid in an apartment on Rue Monsieur where she lived for more than twenty years. 'One's emotions are intensified in Paris,' she wrote in *The Pursuit of Love*, 'one can be more happy and also more unhappy here than in any other place.'

In the late 1950s she began writing biographies that had all the excitement of a novel, notably *The Sun King*, about the life of Louis XIV, which became an international bestseller. Her novels are often accused of being all diamonds and debutantes, but Nancy Mitford simply wrote about what she knew best; and whether that was eccentric family life in the early twentieth century, or historical France, she wrote it with honesty and without sentiment.

Further Information: In 1969 Nancy Mitford moved to a house at No. 4 rue d'Artois in Versailles where she died on 30 June 1973 from Hodgkin's lymphoma. She is buried at St. Mary's Church in Swinbrook, Oxfordshire.

Select Bibliography: *Wigs on the Green* (1935); *The Pursuit of Love* (1945); *Love in a Cold Climate* (1949); *The Blessing* (1951); *Madame de Pompadour* (1954); *Voltaire in Love* (1957); *The Sun King* (1966).

Further Reading: H. Acton, *Nancy Mitford: A Memoir* (Harper & Row, 1975); S. Hastings, *Nancy Mitford* (Hamish Hamilton, 1985); M. Lovell, *The Mitford Girls* (Abacus, 2002); C. Mosley (ed.), *Love from Nancy: The Letters of Nancy Mitford* (Hodder & Stoughton, 1993).

IRÈNE NÉMIROVSKY

8 AVENUE DANIEL-LESUEUR

(Métro: Duroc)

FORMER HOME OF IRÈNE NÉMIROVSKY
JEWISH UKRAINIAN WRITER, HOLO-
CAUST VICTIM AND AUTHOR OF
SUITE FRANÇAISE

Irène Némirovsky *c.*1919

The stars were coming out, springtime stars with a silvery glow. Paris had its sweetest smell, the smell of chestnut trees in bloom and of petrol with a few grains of dust that crack under your teeth like pepper. In the darkness the danger seemed to grow. You could smell the suffering in the air, in the silence. Even people who were normally calm and controlled were overwhelmed by anxiety and fear. Everyone looked at their house and thought, 'Tomorrow it will be in ruins, tomorrow I'll have nothing left. We haven't hurt anyone. Why?' ... Rare was the person who cared about their possessions; everyone wrapped their arms tightly round their wife or child and nothing else mattered; the rest could go up in flames.

Irène Némirovsky, *Suite française* (2004)

Irène Némirovsky wrote sixteen novels, a biography of Chekhov and several short stories during her short life, but she would probably have been little remembered today had it not been for the posthumous publication of her unfinished novel *Suite française* in 2004. Written in the village of Issy-l'Évêque in eastern France during the 1941–1942 Nazi occupation, the first part of the book portrays a group of Parisians fleeing the city and the second observes a rural community under occupation. The final parts were never written because Irène Némirovsky was arrested by police on 13 July 1942 and transported to the German concentration camp at Auschwitz.

The only child of financier Léon Némirovsky, and Anna Margoulis, Irène was born in Kiev in 1903. Her father, who had his finger in many pies, was a gambler and a womaniser. Her mother, remembered by the family as 'refined and authoritarian', denied her age and her Jewish roots; she resented her child, and had numerous affairs. It was a fusing of character, morals and enormous wealth, which resulted in a lonely and unhappy childhood for their daughter Irène who, in adulthood, paraphrased this misery in her novels. In 1917, when Irène was fourteen, the family fled the Bolshevik Revolution and escaped to Finland, eventually settling in Paris in July 1919. She had begun writing in earnest – mainly out of boredom – in Finland in her early teens. She was writing 'all kinds of stories,' she explained, 'which gave me great pleasure and which I returned to day after day. I began to write them, and ever since, I've always continued.' Her early novels were favourably received, but it was her 1929 novel, *David Golder,*

Avenue Daniel-Lesueur

that would establish her reputation as a writer of exceptional talent. In 1926 she married Michel Epstein, a Russian Jew from Moscow, with whom she had two daughters: Denise, born in 1929 and Elisabeth, in 1937. In 1940, following the Nazi invasion of France, all Jews had to wear the mandatory yellow Star of David, and laws were passed giving Jews threadbare legal and social standing. Michel, who worked in a bank, lost his right to work, and it became no longer possible for Irène to be published, as publishing houses were 'Aryanising' staff and authors. For safety, their daughters were baptised into the Catholic Church and sent to the village of Issy-l'Évêque where their nanny's

parents lived. Shortly afterwards Irène (also recently baptised into the Catholic faith) and Michel followed, and it was in Issy L'Évêque that Irène began writing *Suite française*. Of the five sections, 'Storm in June', 'Dolce', 'Captivity', 'Battle' and 'Peace', only the first two were completed as she was arrested on 13 July 1942 and taken to the Pithiviers transit camp in the Loiret. A few days later Irène was deported to Auschwitz, where she died on 17 August of typhus. She was thirty-nine years old. Her husband was deported to Auschwitz a few months later and was put to death in a gas chamber. After Michel's arrest the police returned to the village school for his daughters, but their schoolteacher had them hidden; it was to be the first of a succession of hiding places, in convents, cellars and safe houses throughout the war. After the war the children returned to Paris seeking their grandmother Anna's help. But she refused them entry, shouting through the closed door that if their parents were dead they should go to an orphanage. Eventually the children reached a refugee reception centre.

Throughout the war, the children had carried their mother's papers along with their own belongings from hiding place to hiding place. These papers included a large leather-bound notebook, which was the unfinished manuscript of *Suite française*. It was finally published in 2004 to great international acclaim. That it should have survived at all was little less than a miracle.

Further Information: Irène and Michel moved into the flat at No. 8 avenue Daniel-Lesueur after their marriage on 31 July 1926. In 1935 they moved round the corner to a more spacious flat on the top floor of No. 10 avenue Constant-Coquelin, and it was from here that the family left for Issy L'Évêque. In 2004 Irène Némirovsky became the first posthumous recipient of the prestigious French literary award, Le Prix Renaudot, for *Suite française.* The Mémorial des Martyrs de la Déportation, a memorial to the 200,000 people deported from Vichy France to the Nazi extermination camps, can be visited at Square de l'Île de France, on the Île de la Cité.

Select Bibliography: *Le Malentendu (The Misunderstanding)* (1926); *L'Ennemie* (Enemy) (1928); *Le bal (The Ball)* (1930); *Les mouches d'automne (Autumn Flies)* (1931); *L'Affaire Courilof (The Courilof Affair)* (1933); *Le vin de solitude (The Wine of Solitude)* (1935); *Jézabel (A Modern Jezabel)* (1936); *Les Chiens et le loups (The Dogs and the Wolves)* (1940); *La vie de Tchekhov (Life of Chekhov)* (1946); *Les Biens de ce monde (All Our Worldly Goods)* (1947); *Les feux de l'automne (The Fires of Autumn)* (1957); *Destinées et autres nouvelles (Destinies and other Novellas)* (2004).

Further Reading: O. Philipponnat & P. Lienhardt, *The Life of Irène Némirovsky* (Chatto & Windus, 2010); E. Gille, *The Mirador: Dreamed Memories of Irène Némirovsky By Her Daughter* (NYRB Classics, 2011); E. Gille, *Shadows of a Childhood: A Novel of War and Friendship* (New Press, 2008); A. Kershaw, *Before Auschwitz: Irène Némirovsky and the Cultural Landscape of Inter-war France* (Routledge, 2011); J. Weiss, *Irène Némirovsky* (Stanford, 2007).

8th

Arrondissement

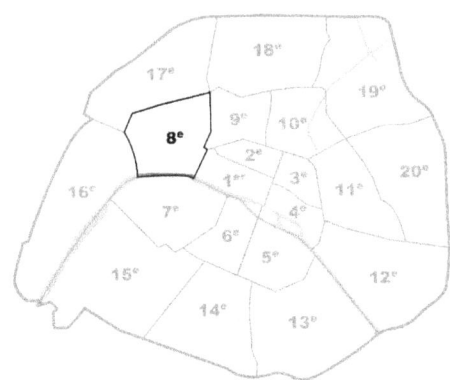

VICTOR HUGO

PLACE CHARLES DE GAULLE

(Métro: Charles de Gaulle-Étoile)

ARC DE TRIOMPHE: 31 MAY 1885
SCENE OF THE CEREMONIAL LYING IN
STATE OF VICTOR HUGO'S COFFIN

Do you hear the people sing
Lost in the valley of the night?
It is the music of a people
Who are climbing to the light.

For the wretched of the earth
There is a flame that never dies.
Even the darkest night will end
And the sun will rise.
Victor Hugo, *Les Misérables* (1862)

Victor Hugo died from pneumonia on 22 May 1885, aged eighty-three, and is buried in the vaults of the Panthéon beside France's national heroes. But Hugo was much more than a national hero to the French. He was immortal; he was a god. When his family tried to remove a journalist from around his deathbed, the reporter exclaimed vehemently, 'Victor Hugo's death belongs to France!' On the last day of May his coffin was taken to lie in state under the Arc de Triomphe. Maurice Barrès described the scene in his 1901 novel, *Les Déracinés*:

> Throughout the day there followed the file past of Paris. Dense crowds formed in the avenue Hoche, and flowed down the avenue du Bois. Raised up, on a double pedestal of violet velvet, a vast urn soared to the centre of the arch and indicated the coffin to the most distant eyes. Everywhere there were shields in trophies of flags, proclaiming the titles

of his works like glorious mottoes. ... A vast crêpe veil, with which they had tried to drape the right angle of the Arc de Triomphe, appeared, from the Champs-Elysées, a small and displaced thing on this triumphal colossus. The bodyguard, entrusted to battalions of schoolchildren, was relieved every half-hour so that a greater number might share in an honour which could leave its mark upon their souls. ...

This corpse had been given twelve young men, poets and fanatics, to honour and serve it. [They] kept watch in a terrible wind which brought them Quasimodo, Hernani, Ruy Blas, the Burgraves, Monseigneur Myriel, Fantine and dear Gavroche, and thousands of rustling lines of poetry, and above all words, words, words! For there was his title, there was his strength, he was the master of French words.

The following day the hearse, carrying Hugo's body in a pauper's coffin, followed behind a procession of eleven wagons draped with wreaths. It threaded its way for hours through two million spectators towards the Latin Quarter and the Panthéon, where Victor Hugo was laid to rest.

See Also: Victor Hugo, Panthéon, *Les Misérables*, Napoleon Bonaparte.

Further Information: The Arc de Triomphe honours those who fought and died for France in the French Revolutionary and Napoleonic Wars. Beneath the Arc lies *La tombe du soldat inconnu* (The tomb of the unknown soldier). Commissioned by Napoleon Bonaparte in 1806 after his victory at Austerlitz, it took thirty years to complete, and was officially inaugurated in 1836. Inspired by the Roman Arch of Titus, it is 50 metres high, 48 metres wide, and 22 metres deep.

Further Reading: D. Rowell, *Paris: The 'New Rome' of Napoleon* (Bloomsbury, 2014).

The Arc de Triomphe in its 'vast crêpe veil', on the morning of 31 May 1885

F. SCOTT FITZGERALD

14 RUE DE TILSITT

(Métro: Charles de Gaulle–Étoile)

**FORMER FIFTH-FLOOR APARTMENT
OF SCOTT AND ZELDA FITZGERALD
EPITOME OF THE JAZZ-AGE COUPLE**

Now the standard cure for one who is sunk is to consider those in actual destitution or physical suffering – this is an all-weather beatitude for gloom in general and fairly salutary daytime advice for everyone. But at three o'clock in the morning ... the cure doesn't work – and in a real dark night of the soul it is always three o'clock in the morning, day after day. At that hour the tendency is to refuse to face things as long as possible by retiring into an infantile dream ... But as the withdrawal persists there is less and less chance of the bonanza – one is not waiting for the fade-out of a single sorrow, but rather being an unwilling witness of an execution, the disintegration of one's own personality.
F. Scott Fitzgerald, *Esquire* (1936)

Scott Fitzgerald in 1937

Sadly, Scott Fitzgerald's playboy image of the extravagant, wasteful, self-indulgent man who defined the Jazz Age generation, and whose alcoholism fuelled his early demise, too often belittles, if not conceals, his achievement as a great writer. His output was small compared to many of his contemporaries, but his fiction, a great deal of which is a scathing critique of the American dream, still endures today. He will be best remembered for his 1925 masterpiece of obsessional love, *The Great Gatsby*, but the quality of much of his other prose leaves us with an abiding image of a writer who expressed an elegiac, and often mythical understanding of the human condition. The tragedy is that it didn't extend to understanding his own.

Francis Scott Key Fitzgerald (1896–1940) was born into an upper-middle-class family in Minnesota and started writing at an early age. When he was a student at Princeton University he submitted a novel to Scribner the publisher, and although it was rejected, his writing was greatly admired. He volunteered as a soldier in the First World War, but never saw active service, and in 1920 he married 'golden' Alabama society girl, Zelda Sayre (1900–1948). The following year, their daughter, nicknamed Scottie, was born. A few months later, Fitzgerald published his first novel, *This Side of Paradise*, about the self-indulgent life of Princeton undergraduates, which met with great critical success. Although Fitzgerald was now forging his reputation as a writer he was also becoming a celebrity known more for his opulent lifestyle, his frenzied behaviour, and his drunkenness, than for his writing.

After a sojourn on the Côte d'Azur, the Fitzgeralds arrived in Paris in the spring of 1925 and rented an apartment at 14 rue de Tilsitt, close to the Arc de Triomphe. 'We were going to the Old World', wrote Fitzgerald, 'to find a new rhythm for our lives.' It was an attempt to restructure his career, and like many writers he was attracted by the city's freedom of expression, energy and frivolity, although Left Bank bohemian life was never on his agenda. *The Great Gatsby* had already been published and sales were poor, but he hoped that Paris would offer a new beginning. In reality it would only serve up an erratic life of alcoholism and depression, and it heralded the onset of his wife's schizophrenia. It was a chapter in his life he described as '1000 parties and no work'. Diminishing royalties required him to write short stories for magazines, and in between time spent working on his new novel, *Tender Is the Night*, Scott and Zelda's existence became one long drunken spree. He met most of the American expatriates, whom he described as 'mostly junk dealers' – almost all of whom finally distanced themselves from him.

On and off, the Fitzgeralds spent around five years in Paris, with intermittent trips to the Riviera and the USA. In 1930, Zelda had a breakdown and they left Paris for a clinic in Switzerland. On her release in September 1931 they returned to Paris for a few days, staying at the Majestic Hôtel on Rue La Pérouse. It would be their last visit to the city. 'I spoiled this city for myself,' he wrote in 'Babylon Revisited', 'I didn't realize it, but the days came along one after another, and then two years were gone, and everything was gone, and I was gone.' Scott Fitzgerald died of a heart attack in Hollywood in 1940, aged forty-four. Zelda died in a hospital fire in North Carolina along with eight other women in 1948. She was forty-seven years old.

See Also: Harry's Bar, The Dingo Bar, Ernest Hemingway, Hôtel Ritz, Bricktop's.

Further Information: In 1928 the Fitzgeralds stayed for a few months in a fourth-floor apartment at No. 58 rue de Vaugirard, overlooking the Luxembourg Gardens. It was the setting for the Paris home 'high above the green mass of leaves' of Dick and Nicole Diver in *Tender Is the Night*. In 1929 the Fitzgeralds briefly resided at No. 6 rue Palatine, a location used in 'Babylon Revisited', and in October of the same year they rented an apartment at No. 10 rue Pergolèse in Neuilly, their final residence in Paris.

Select Bibliography: *This Side of Paradise* (1920); *The Beautiful and the Damned* (1922); *Tales of the Jazz Age* (1922); *The Great Gatsby* (1925); *Babylon Revisited and Other Stories* (1931); *Tender is the Night* (1934); *The Last Tycoon* (1941).

Further Reading: J. Mellow, *Invented Lives, Scott and Zelda Fitzgerald* (Ballantine, 1986); F. Scott Fitzgerald, *A Life in Letters* (Penguin, 1998).

14 rue de Tilsitt

ALEXANDER NEVSKY CATHEDRAL

12 RUE DARU

(Métro: Courcelles/Ternes)

FOCAL POINT FOR RUSSIAN WRITERS IN PARIS FOLLOWING THE 1917 BOLSHEVIK REVOLUTION

In Russia there is an emigration of intelligence: émigrés cross the frontier in order to read and to write good books. But in doing so they contribute to making their fatherland, abandoned by spirit, into the gaping jaws of Asia that would like to swallow our little Europe.
Friedrich Nietzsche

Alexander Nevsky Cathedral

In the bleak aftermath of the Russian Revolution in 1917 around a million and a half people were deported from, or fled, the former Russian Empire. The resulting diaspora, an ethnic mix of Russians, Ukrainians, Poles, Balts, Jews and others found its way to Western Europe, the Slavic states, the USA, Canada and the Far East, but the cultural nucleus for many Russians was France, and predominantly Paris. Before the Revolution, Russian émigrés were mainly peasants heading for a new life in America, but after it a large percentage of them were educated professionals from the middle and upper classes, attracted by France's culture, its language, and its existing colonies of Russian intellectuals. Most of them had opposed the tsarist government, and its overthrow in March 1917 had been welcomed, but the Bolshevik or 'Red' forces' seizure of power in November 1917 was unacceptable to them and they were forced into exile. These émigrés became known as White Russians.

This dispossessed community, for the most part, was close to the poverty line. Imperial Russia's former aristocrats and petty gentry could be found working as waiters, doormen and seamstresses. Former officers of the White Guard who had fought against the Bolsheviks were now driving taxis or working in factories. Among the many Russian writers who had also made Paris their new home, and who faced the same unpredictable future, were Ivan Bunin (the first Russian writer to win the Nobel Prize in Literature), Aleksey Tolstoy, Alexander Yablonovsky, Konstantin Balmont, Aleksandr Kuprin, Valentin Bulgakov, Mark Slonim, Sergei Efron, Ivan Shmelyov, Mark Aldanov, Teffi, and Sasha Chorny. In 1920 'The Union of Russian Writers and Journalists in Paris' was formed, with Ivan Bunin as its first elected chairman. The organisation published many of its members' prose and poetry until the Nazi occupation some twenty years later.

The Alexander Nevsky Cathedral, along

with other Orthodox churches, provided not only spiritual support for these émigrés, but a doorway to a past life. 'The Russian Church', wrote one émigré journalist, 'is the emigration centre for preservation and passing on of Russian culture. Around it group a Russian library, school, theatre, club. It again takes up its medieval role – the provider of enlightenment.'

Some writers eventually returned to their homeland, but others lived the rest of their days in Paris, ending up in the Russian cemetery in Sainte-Geneviève-des-Bois. It was Ivan Bunin (1870–1953) who became the spokesman for Paris's Russian émigré writers, and when he was awarded the Nobel Prize in Literature in 1933 he raised the hearts of the Russian community. 'You see, up until then we, émigrés, felt like we were at the bottom there,' wrote Russian writer Boris Zaitsev.

> Then all of a sudden our writer received an internationally acclaimed prize! And not for some political scribblings, but for real prose! After having been asked to write a first page column for the Paris *Revival* newspaper, I stepped out in the middle of the night onto the Place d'Italie and toured the local bistros on my way home, drinking in each and every one of them to the health of Ivan Bunin!

The USSR's response was not so ecstatic, describing Bunin's award as 'an imperialist intrigue'.

See Also: Nikolai Gogol, Ivan Turgenev.

Further Information: The Alexander Nevsky Cathedral was built during the 1850s with donations from Tsar Alexander II. Initially it was the only Russian church in exile

in Paris, but by the 1860s more than thirty Russian Orthodox churches had been erected around the city. Holy Trinity Cathedral, a new Russian Orthodox place of worship, opened in 2016 close to the Eiffel Tower. Ivan Bunin is buried in the Russian Orthodox cemetery at Rue Léo Lagrange in Sainte-Geneviève-des-Bois, about 25 kilometres south of Paris. The cemetery is part of the Cimetière de Liers, and was set up in 1927 to accommodate the burials of the White Russians who had arrived in Paris after the Bolshevik revolution. Many Russian émigré writers are buried here, including Alexander Galich, Gaito Gazdanov, Zinaida Gippius, Georgy Ivanov, Teffi, Aleksey Remizov, and writer and filmmaker Andrei Tarkovsky.

Further Reading: I. Bunin, *Cursed Days: A Diary of a Revolution* (Dee Inc., 1998), L. Livak, *How It Was Done in Paris: Russian Emigré Literature and French Modernism* (University of Wisconsin Press, 2003).

Top: Ivan Bunin (1870–1953) in 1933
Above: Teffi (1872–1952)

GUSTAVE FLAUBERT

240 RUE DU FAUBOURG-ST-HONORÉ

(Métro: Ternes)

HOME OF GUSTAVE FLAUBERT

LAST OF THE GREAT ROMANTICS

One of the uncontested masters of the contemporary novel, perhaps the only one who owes nothing to anyone, and whom everyone else has more or less imitated.
From a press clipping discovered on Flaubert's desk after his death in 1880.

Gustave Flaubert

One of the greatest writers of his age, Flaubert was the last of the great Romantics who, by the time of his death, was firmly embedded in the realist school of French literature. A romanticist and a realist who remains distinctly modern today, Flaubert was a writer's writer who was always striving for consummate expression.

He was born in 1821, the fifth child of Achille-Cléophas Flaubert, chief surgeon at the Hôtel-Dieu, Rouen, in Normandy, and Anne-Justine-Caroline Flaubert, née Fleuriot. In 1831 he attended the Collège de Rouen where he proved himself an able student, excelling in history and literature. His earliest known writing was a college essay on the French tragedian, Corneille, and during his teenage years he wrote copious amounts of fiction and drama. In the early 1840s he studied law in Paris; however, failure to pass his exams, then his first epileptic attack in 1844 put an end to his future law career. 'Each attack', wrote Flaubert, 'was like a haemorrhage of the nervous system … It was a snatching of the soul from the body, excruciating.' After the first attack he returned to the family home at Croisset, near Rouen, where he was confined

and put on a strict medical and dietary regime. Here he remained with his family, a virtual recluse. Flaubert's father died in January 1846, and a few weeks later his sister Caroline died following childbirth. With his father's substantial inheritance came the financial security that enabled him to concentrate on writing, and the remote Normandy countryside provided the backdrop. Writing abysmally slowly, often at the rate of five words an hour, dressed in long hooded garments, and shut away from society, Flaubert's ascetic lifestyle gave birth to rumours of a hermit-like existence. But Flaubert was no hermit, and as well as lengthy sojourns to Paris, he did in fact journey extensively throughout Europe, North Africa and the Middle East during his life. Following his initiation with one of the family's maids when he was fourteen or fifteen years old, Flaubert led an active sex life, which included the use of prostitutes and the young bath-house boys of the Mediterranean. In 1846 he met the poet Louise Colet and began a long but turbulent relationship with her, much of it conducted by letters that were full of knowledge and insight about his writing.

His first novel, *Madame Bovary*, was published in 1857, a few weeks after Flaubert's acquittal in a trial over the book's morality. Literary and social success followed, and Flaubert was introduced to the writers and royalty of the day. Paris became his home from home, where he met the Goncourt brothers, Baudelaire, Gautier and Sainte-Beuve, and where he became close friends with George Sand. In 1862 he published his most romantic novel, *Salammbô*, set in the First Punic War when Carthage is under siege. That same year, the famous literary male-only (with the exception of George Sand) dinners at Magny's were instituted, and Flaubert began to attend the salon of Princess Mathilde, niece of Napoleon I. In 1864 he was presented to the Emperor Napoleon III; and two years later, at the pinnacle of his success, he was created *Chevalier de la Légion d'honneur*.

But Flaubert's remaining years were a mix of loneliness, weariness and financial privation. He claimed he was 'three-quarters ruined' when he was forced to save his niece's husband from insolvency, a consequence of which was an enforced move, due to cutbacks, to more humble lodgings at 240 rue du Faubourg-St-Honoré in May 1875. The flat famously became one of the regular meeting places of the 'hissed authors': writers, notably Alphonse Daudet, Gustave Flaubert, Ivan Turgenev, Émile Zola and Edmond de Goncourt, who had incurred public ignominy at some time during their career. 'It was at this period', wrote Alphonse Daudet, 'that we conceived the idea of a monthly gathering at which we friends should meet; it was to be called "the Flaubert dinner", or "the dinner of hissed authors", Flaubert belonged to it by

right of his *Candidat*, I by that of my *Arlesienne*, Zola with *Bouton de Rose*, de Goncourt with *Henriette Maréchal*.' A few years after Flaubert's move in more restricted financial circumstances to his new dwelling, his friends arranged a state pension for him.

Flaubert died at Croisset in 1880 at the age of fifty-eight. The cause of his death remains unknown, but on the morning of his funeral Edmond de Goncourt spoke with Flaubert's friend Georges Pouchet:

This morning Pouchet took me down a deserted path and said: 'He didn't die from a stroke, he died from an epileptic fit … In his youth, you know, he had had several fits … His travels in the Middle East had so to speak cured him … He didn't have any more for sixteen years. But the worry over his niece's affairs brought the trouble back … And on Saturday he died from an epileptic fit … Yes, with all the symptoms, foam on his lips, and so on … And then his niece wanted to have a cast taken of his hand, but it couldn't be done, the hand was so tightly clenched … Perhaps if I'd been there to give him half an hour's artificial respiration, I could have saved him.

Flaubert is buried in Rouen Cemetery in the family vault.

See Also: Palais de Justice, Louise Colet, Magny's, Alphonse Daudet.

Select Bibliography: *Madame Bovary* (1857); *Salammbô* (1862); *Sentimental Education* (1869); *Le Candidat* (1874); *The Temptation of Saint Anthony* (1874); *Three Tales* (1877); *Le Château des cœurs* (1880).

Further Reading: J. Barnes, *Flaubert's Parrot* (Jonathan Cape, 1984); *The Selected Letters of Gustave Flaubert* (Hamish Hamilton, 1954).

FANTÔMAS

33 AVENUE DE FRIEDLAND

(Métro: Charles de Gaulle–Étoile)

ROYAL HÔTEL

SITE OF THE FIRST APPEARANCE OF FRENCH CRIME FICTION LEGEND *FANTÔMAS*, **THE LORD OF EVIL**

Poster for the first *Fantômas* film adaptation in 1913 by Louis Feuillade, produced by Gaumont Studios

From the moment it was published in February 1911, Fantômas *(and the thirty-one sequels which immediately followed it) was a phenomenon: a work of fiction whose popularity cut across all social and cultural strata. Countesses and concierges; poets and proletarians; cubists, nascent Dadaists, soon-to-be surrealists: Everyone who could read, and even those who could not, shivered at posters of a masked man in impeccable evening clothes, dagger in hand,* looming over Paris like a somber Gulliver, contemplating hideous misdeeds from which no citizen was safe.
John Ashbery, from his introduction to the 1986 reprint of *Fantômas*.

Fantômas was a peculiarly French publishing phenomenon that was little known outside of France, but still remains embedded in the Gallic psyche today. He was the creation of two enterprising writers: Pierre Souvestre (1874–1914) and Marcel Allain (1885–1969), both of whom were qualified lawyers who ditched their professions for the world of the literary hack. Souvestre entered the early pioneering world of automotive journalism, writing for *L'Auto* and *Poids Lourds* (Heavy Trucks). While he was looking for a secretary he met Allain, and being so impressed with Allain's talent for waffle (he had produced a seventeen-page article on a new truck he knew next to nothing about) promptly hired Allain as his ghostwriter and managing editor of *Poids Lourds*. Their collaboration began in earnest after a sizeable advertiser withdrew from *L'Auto*, leaving the magazine with several blank pages to fill. Ingeniously they filled the gap with their own pulp serial, which they later parodied in another journal, *Le Vélo* (The Bike). The Paris-based publishing house, Arthème Fayard, spotted the parody and commissioned them to write a series of five novels with a common theme. After much brainstorming, they came up with the concept of a mysterious arch-criminal who dressed in a dinner jacket and who was capable of anything from serial killings to spreading plague through the streets of Paris. This character would be relentlessly pursued by his arch-enemy, the undaunted Inspector Juve, and the forces of authority. Allain created the title *Fantômus* (with a 'u') one day in the Métro, but when Souvestre wrote it down in a notebook and showed it to Fayard, it was misread – thankfully, for literary history – as *Fantômas*. The Lord of Evil was born.

After a huge publicity campaign the book was a runaway success. Souvestre and Allain went on to pen a further thirty-one sequels, some produced in just a couple of days, until Souvestre died suddenly of Spanish influenza in 1914. After surviving the trenches, Allain wrote a further eleven *Fantômas* novels on his own. By the time he died in 1969 at the age of eighty-three, he had written more than 600 novels.

Over the years Fantômas caught the imagination of readers from all walks of life, making him one of the most popular characters in the history of French crime fiction. He also made a profound impression on many writers and painters, including Guillaume Apollinaire, Jean Cocteau, Max Jacob, Blaise Cendrars, Louis Aragon, Colette, Pablo Neruda, Raymond Queneau, Juan Gris, Picasso and Magritte. Some even immortalised him in their poetry or on their canvases. Never had a pulp fiction hero had such an illustrious fan base. Many of these writers and artists were surrealists, exponents of the avant-garde: who better to appreciate Fantômas wearing gloves of human skin to leave a deceased man's fingerprints on his victims?

Further Information: Fantômas made his first appearance in the early chapters of the 1911 first edition when he robbed the Russian Princess Sonia Danidoff while she was taking a bath in her suite of rooms on the third floor of the Royal Hôtel.

PARIS HERALD

21 RUE DE BERRI

(Métro: George V)

**FORMER OFFICES OF THE PARIS
EDITION OF THE *NEW YORK HERALD***

*I want you fellows to remember that I am
the only reader of this paper. I am the only
one to be pleased. If I want it to be turned
upside down, it must be turned upside down.
I consider a dead dog in the Rue du Louvre
more interesting than a devastating flood in
China. ... If I say the feature is to be Black
Beetles, Black Beetles it's going to be.*
From Gordon Bennett's inaugural speech to
the staff of the *Paris Herald*

James Gordon Bennett Junior in 1904

In 1835 Scotsman James Gordon Bennett Senior founded the *New York Herald*. When, over fifty years later in 1886, he passed control of the paper to his son James Gordon Bennett Junior, it had the highest circulation in America. The younger Bennett became a skilled editor and entrepreneur, but he was also the archetypal playboy. After scandalising New York society by drunkenly urinating in public at his fiancée's family mansion (into the grand piano, some sources cite; others, into the fireplace), for which he was horsewhipped by her brother, Bennett wisely departed for Paris in 1877. In Europe he was still in full control of the *New York Herald* via cable, but he yearned for a more hands-on experience, and in 1887 he bought the English edition of the *Morning News*, a Paris daily which he renamed the *Paris Herald*.

Its editorial offices were initially located in Les Halles on the corner of Rue du Louvre and Rue Berger, but by 1930 the paper had outgrown its premises and

moved to a nine-storey building on Rue de Berri. Most of the staff in the early years were British, and were in plentiful supply just across the Channel. The paper's persona, unlike that of its rival, the *Paris Tribune*, had always been one of caution and conservatism: right bank rather than left bank. By 1931 Ezra Pound was describing it as a 'daily insult … to every yankee in Europe. … run by englishmen all over eighty… Apart from its telegraphic service, the Herald ought to go die.' Pound was playing devil's advocate, as was his wont, but during the 1920s and 1930s 'yankees' were working in the editorial offices, many of them gifted and inventive writers.

The *Herald*'s first society editor was a Missouri seamstress named May Birkhead. She had been on board the *Carpathia* when it rescued survivors from the *Titanic* in 1912. Birkhead was unknown to Bennett, but she had appeared in a recent *Herald* feature about sewing, and, finding her name on the passenger list of the *Carpathia*, Bennett radioed her the message, 'Wireless every possible detail of sinking and rescue.' Birkhead made such a professional job of her unsolicited assignment that Bennett hired her forthwith as the *Paris Herald*'s society correspondent. One of the paper's most popular columns in the 1920s was 'Sporting Gossip' by William 'Sparrow' Robertson, whose column was more gossip than sport, and to which readers turned 'to savor the mayhem it inflicted on the English language'. Martha Foley and Whit Burnett joined the *Herald* in the late 1920s and organised a strike for better wages. During the strike the *Herald*'s printers refused to cross the picket line. 'Thanks to those wonderful printers,' recalled Foley, 'the first American newspaper editorial strike was won. Another experienced newsman on the staff was Elliot Paul, remembered today for his memoir *The Last Time I Saw Paris*. Paul had previously worked for the *Tribune*, which he left in 1926 to co-edit the literary magazine *transition*, before returning to the newspaper business in 1929 to rejoin the *Tribune*. He was a newspaperman of the old school who could drink all night, party all night, get little sleep and yet still seemed to have boundless energy next day to write copy. The *Herald* also hired another writer in 1929: not on the news or features desk, but as a telephone switchboard operator. Paul Bowles was only nineteen at the time, and very much in awe of the literary talent in the *Herald* building. Elliot Paul 'worked upstairs in the editorial department', Bowles wrote,

I would see him, complete with beard and cane, going in and out, since everyone had to pass by the telephonist's cage in the entrance hall. I used to imagine ways in which I might get to speak to him, merely to let him know I was there.

Paul Bowles

They were all impracticable. One day after lunch he appeared from the street and walked straight to the cage. 'Come outside,' he told me. There was a taxi at the curb, in front of the entrance, and its door was open. 'Look inside,' he said. I did. The interior of the cab was entirely upholstered in false boa-constrictor skin. 'Do you see what I see?' he demanded. 'Just tell me that.'
'You mean the snakeskin?'
'Ah!' He was satisfied; slamming the door and with a wave to the driver, he went inside and climbed the stairs, staggering a bit. It seemed like a poor occasion for trying to talk with him.'

See Also: Paris *Tribune*, Ezra Pound, Elliot Paul, *transition*.

Further Information: When Gordon Bennett Jr died in 1918, the trustees of his estate sold the *New York Herald* and the *Paris Herald* to Frank A. Munsey, publisher of the *New York Sun*, which in turn was bought out in 1924 by Ogden Reid, owner of the *New York Tribune*. Reid changed the name of the *New York Herald* to the *Herald-Tribune*, but the *Paris Herald* kept its name to avoid confusion with its competitor, the *Paris Tribune*, only changing its name to the *Paris Herald-Tribune* in 1934 when the *Herald* bought the ailing *Paris Tribune*.

KAY BOYLE

26 RUE DU FAUBOURG-ST-HONORÉ
(Métro: Madeleine/Concorde)

**FORMER LOCATION OF
GALERIE ARTISTE ET ARTISAN
'FOLK ART' SHOP OF RAYMOND DUNCAN,
WHERE WRITER KAY BOYLE WORKED IN
1928**

There is nothing left of the stairway up to the loft in back, nor the beams, nor the bell that rang upstairs whenever the door opened in from the street below. People walked close to the shop-window's glass, handsomely dressed because of the quarter, and the traffic passed one way in endless dignity and hush because of the embassy on the other side. But behind in the alley, set in green stone and slime as rich as a jungle pool's, stood the depths of the beauteous cabinay. Once in a while a wagon drove down the street in the early morning, and the boa-constrictor it carried was uncoiled to suck out the mysteries of that dark, unfathomed cave.
Kay Boyle, *My Next Bride* (1934)

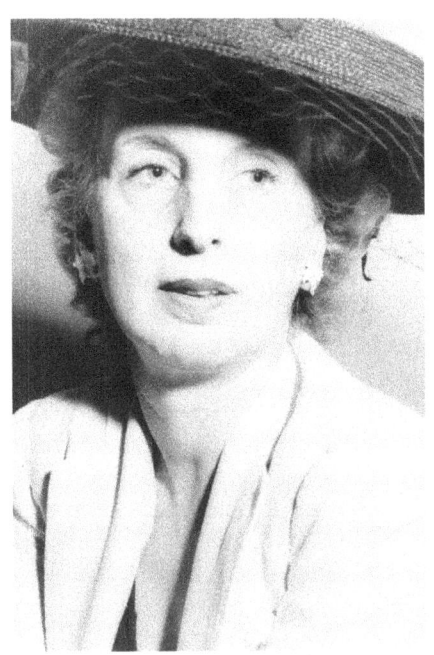

Kay Boyle

K ay Boyle is a writer that is often overlooked today. She is probably best remembered for *Being Geniuses Together*, her joint memoir, with Robert McAlmon, of 1920s Paris. McAlmon first published the book in 1938, and thirty years later, after McAlmon's death, Boyle added additional chapters, turning a book which had gone virtually unnoticed in its day into one of the most memorable chronicles of expatriate Paris. Boyle lived in Europe for thirty years, much of it spent in Paris among the expatriate community and to a great extent her fiction, which delves deep into the complexities of relationships, has its roots in her Parisian past.

Born in Minnesota in 1902 she grew up in Cincinnati where, aged nineteen, she met her first husband, French engineer Richard Brault. Following a year of working on the New York literary magazine *Broom*, she and her husband sailed for France in 1923. It was a move that would give Boyle not only another life, but a source of inspiration for much of her writing: *Plagued by the Nightingale* recounted her life with her husband's family in Brittany; *Year Before Last* described her affair with editor-poet Ernest Walsh; and *My Next Bride*, Boyle's portrait of a utopian artist's colony, was inspired by her own experience.

In 1925, when Boyle and her husband were living in Normandy, she received a letter from Ernest Walsh asking her to contribute to the first issue of *This Quarter*, a literary magazine to be edited by himself and his wife, Ethel Moorhead. Boyle posted off poems and prose and a regular correspondence began between

273

the two. Around this time Boyle's health deteriorated due to a lung ailment and, desperately needing to escape the Normandy winter, she accepted Walsh's invitation to stay near his home in the South of France. A love affair ensued between the pair, and Boyle became pregnant. Walsh died the following year from tuberculosis, and after a brief, albeit platonic, reconciliation with her husband, Boyle and her daughter headed for Paris in the spring of 1928, where a friend had invited her to ghostwrite the memoirs of his cousin, the Dayang Muda of Sarawak.

The so-called Dayang Muda (Princess) of Sarawak was Gladys Palmer of Huntly and Palmer biscuit fame, wife of the brother of the white rajah of the British Crown Colony of Sarawak. For two months Boyle and her daughter lived in luxury with Palmer at her Paris apartment, but the project was exasperating due to Palmer's inability to articulate anything about her life. During this fraught time, Boyle met Raymond Duncan, brother of the dancer Isadora Duncan, a bohemian eccentric who had founded an 'artist's colony' in the Paris suburb of Neuilly. Doubtful about finding a job that would support herself and her daughter after the Palmer assignment ended, Boyle saw the colony as a way out of her difficulties. 'My social conscience was in such a bad way', she wrote, 'that I decided to join Raymond Duncan's colony.' The colony provided food, lodging and childcare, and in return she worked six days a week at the commune's 'folk art' shops. It was a convenient blend of bohemian ideology and practical decision-making. 'For a time she was saleswoman for the Raymond Duncan shops', wrote Robert McAlmon, '... and she managed to sell quantities of hand-woven rugs, tunics, draperies ... She didn't get a percentage, however; only a small salary, but then Raymond Duncan was never a practical man. What could money mean to him when it was Kay who needed it?' Boyle stayed with the colony for six months, but became steadily disillusioned with its deceit and pretensions, especially after Duncan purchased a large American car with the shop's proceeds. Her main fear, however, was that the colony would claim custody of her daughter, so with the help of friends she smuggled her to safety and left the colony for good.

Boyle continued to live in Europe until her return to the United States in the early 1940s where, when she was blacklisted during the McCarthy years, she became a strong political activist. Her years in Paris during the 1920s were relatively few in number in a life of writing that produced over forty books, including fourteen novels and five volumes of poetry, but they had a significant influence on her writing. She had three husbands, a great many lovers and six children, and died aged ninety in 1992.

See Also: Robert McAlmon.

Select Bibliography: Novels – *Plagued by the Nightingale* (1931); *Year Before Last* (1932); *My Next Bride* (1934); *Generation Without Farewell* (1960). Short story collections – *The White Horses of Vienna* (1935); *Fifty Stories* (1980). Poetry – *Collected Poems of Kay Boyle* (1991).

Further Reading: J. Mellen, *Kay Boyle: Author of Herself* (Farrar Straus & Giroux, 1994); S. Spanier, *Kay Boyle: Artist & Activist* (Southern Illinois University Press, 1986).

MARCEL PROUST

102 BOULEVARD HAUSSMANN

(Métro: Saint-Augustin)

THE APARTMENT IN WHICH
MARCEL PROUST
WROTE MOST OF
IN SEARCH OF LOST TIME

My great adventure is really Proust. Well – what remains to be written after that? I'm only in the first volume, and there are, I suppose, faults to be found, but I am in a state of amazement; as if a miracle were being done before my eyes. ... One has to put the book down and gasp.
Virginia Woolf writing to Roger Fry in 1922

Marcel Proust in 1895

Marcel Proust (1871–1922) is often regarded as the greatest writer of the twentieth century. His fame today rests on his seven-volume series of novels, *À la recherche du temps perdu (In Search of Lost Time)*, published between 1913 and 1927. Most of the novels were written in his apartment on the second floor of 102 boulevard Haussmann, a building once owned by his Great-Uncle Louis. Proust inherited a quarter of the building on his uncle's death, but later sold it to an aunt, and ended up renting his apartment. In 1910, Proust had its walls sheathed in cork to shut out noise. His main concern, however, was dust and pollen, which floated up from the tree-lined, traffic-strewn boulevard, and could flare up his asthma. He had the windows hung with heavy curtains that were never opened to the light, and he kept furniture to a minimum. When he had the apartment as hermetically sealed as was possible, and filled with thick asthma-relieving inhalants, he effectively isolated himself from a world that threatened to kill him. 'Every speck of dust suffocates me,' he wrote. 'Every piece of furniture gathers dust. And in a house where it's difficult to beat or clean, because of the hours at which I sleep and my fear of noise, because of my sensitivity to the cold and my fear of open windows, an apartment like a hospital would be the ideal.' Proust was also neurotic from his youth, no doubt exacerbated by his asthma, but caused largely by his suppressed homosexuality. Much of his time at Boulevard Haussmann was spent in bed writing, attended by his devoted housekeeper, Céleste, who would arrange the delivery of his meals and ice-cold beer from the Ritz. If he ever went out, it was usually at night.

The first volume, *Du côté de chez Swann*, appeared in 1913, but as it was rejected by several publishers, Proust decided to publish the novel at his own expense. André Gide, an editor of *Les Éditions de*

275

la NRF, one of the publishers who turned the manuscript down, deeply regretted the decision: 'The rejection of this book will remain the most serious mistake ever made by the NRF and (since I bear the shame of being very much responsible for it) one of the most stinging and remorseful regrets of my life.' Proust later agreed to *Les Éditions de la NRF* publishing it, but only on the condition that they publish it in its entirety.

Few had taken him seriously as a writer, but in 1920 he was awarded *Le Prix Goncourt*, France's highest literary honour, and it became clear to all that Proust was one of the great novelists of the twentieth century. In 1922, the year Proust completed *À la recherche du temps perdu*, he exclaimed to his housekeeper: 'Ah, dear Céleste, I have great news to tell you, something enormous. I wrote the word "end". Now I can die.' True to his word, he died later that year on 18 November 1922, aged fifty-one.

See Also: Marcel Proust (grave), *Prix Goncourt*, André Gide, Gaston Gallimard, Hôtel Ritz.

Further Information: At the time of writing, Proust's Boulevard Haussmann apartment is owned by a bank. Public access is limited. A reconstruction of Proust's cork-lined bedchamber can be seen at the Musée Carnavalet, 16 rue des Francs-Bourgeois. On the death of his mother in 1906, Proust moved from his family home at 45 rue de Courcelles to 102 boulevard Haussmann. In 1919 he moved to a fifth-floor apartment at 44 rue Hamelin. In recognition of Proust's masterpiece, Combray, the fictional name Proust gave to the town of Illiers, near Chartres, was combined with Illiers on the centenary of his birth in 1971. The town is now known officially as Illiers-Combray. *In Search of Lost Time* is also known as *Remembrance of Things Past*, a title Proust never liked.

Marcel Proust in 1887

Select Bibliography: *By Way of Sainte-Beuve* (tr. S. Townsend, Chatto & Windus, 1958); *In Search of Lost Time* (tr. C.K. Scott-Moncrieff, T. Kilmartin, A. Mayor, revised by D.J. Enright, Chatto & Windus, 1992); *Jean Santeuil* (tr. G. Hopkins, Weidenfeld & Nicolson, 1955); *Marcel Proust: Letters to his Mother* (tr. and edited by G. Painter, Rider & Co., 1956); *On Reading* (tr. and edited by J. Autret and W. Burford, Souvenir Press, 1972).

Further Reading: G.D. Painter, *Marcel Proust: A Biography* (Chatto & Windus, 1989); J. Tadié, *Marcel Proust: A Life* (Penguin, 2001); J.E. Rivers, *Proust and the Art of Love* (Columbia, 1980); E. White, *Proust* (Weidenfeld & Nicolson, 1999); C. Albaret, *Monsieur Proust* (New York Review of Books, 2003); S. Beckett, *Proust* (Chatto & Windus, 1931).

Boulevard Haussmann *c.*1853–1870, 2.53 km (1.57 mi.) long. In Ian Fleming's James Bond thriller, *Thunderball* (1961), it is the headquarters of SPECTRE

Marcel PROUST
1871 - 1922
habita cet immeuble
de 1907 à 1919

SOMERSET MAUGHAM

39 RUE DU FAUBOURG SAINT-HONORÉ

(Métro: Concorde/Madeleine)

HÔTEL DE CHAROST

THE BRITISH EMBASSY

BIRTHPLACE OF SOMERSET MAUGHAM

Somerset Maugham in 1934

For men and women are not only themselves; they are also the region in which they are born, the city apartment or the farm in which they learnt to walk, the games they played as children, the old wives' tales they overheard, the food they ate, the schools they attended, the sports they followed, the poets they read, and the God they believed in.

Somerset Maugham, *The Razor's Edge* (1944)

It has been a tradition ever since permanent foreign diplomatic missions became the norm in the late sixteenth century that ambassadors have large and impressive residencies. They are, of course, for status, but also for hosting grand events, and for partaking in the court life of the host nation. The Hôtel de Charost was no exception. Built in 1720, and designed by King Louis XV's own architect, it had various owners until Pauline Borghese, sister of Napoleon Bonaparte, purchased it in 1803. Following her brother's exile on Elba, she sold the property to the British government in 1814 and used the money to aid her brother's plight. The building has since remained the official residence of the British Ambassador and Embassy in France. One of its many roles is looking after the interests of British nationals, which in 1873 the Embassy took to inventive extremes.

Most diplomatic missions are exempted from the jurisdiction of local laws; this is known as extraterritoriality. In 1873, shortly after the siege of Paris by the Prussians, and the fall of the Commune, the French government was threatening to introduce legislation imposing French nationality on all male children born in France to foreign parents, which would have made them eligible for military service. But the British Ambassador of the day, Lord Lyons, cleverly sidestepped the legislation by turning the second floor of the Embassy into a maternity ward, allowing British wives – or, at least, well connected wives – to give birth on British territory. And that is why Somerset Maugham came to be born there in 1874. Had Lord Lyons not circumvented the French legislation Maugham could well have been born a French citizen, joined the French Foreign Legion, and died in a flyblown outpost before he had written his first creative sentence.

His father, Robert Maugham (1823– 1884), was a solicitor who moved to Paris from London in the 1840s to open a branch of his legal practice on Rue du Faubourg Saint-Honoré, opposite the British Embassy. Business prospered

278

and his practice was appointed legal advisor to the Embassy. In 1863, aged thirty-nine, he married Edith Snell, who was sixteen years his junior. They were married at the British Embassy and moved into a third-floor apartment at 25 avenue d'Antin, producing three sons within as many years. By 1870 the Prussians were advancing on Paris and the Maughams wisely draped a Union Jack over their balcony and decamped to England, leaving their apartment in the care of servants. After the Prussians' five-month siege of Paris and the bloody civil war that followed, the Maughams returned to Paris in August 1872 to find, miraculously, their apartment unscathed. In January 1874 their fourth son, christened William Somerset, was born at the British Embassy. W. Somerset Maugham would go on to become one of the most popular writers of his era, dying in France ninety-one years later in 1965.

Another writer who used the locale and services of the Paris Embassy was William Makepeace Thackeray, who was married there in 1836. Best remembered today for his comic masterpiece, *Vanity Fair* (1847), Thackeray was born into affluence in Calcutta in 1811, but after his father died and his mother remarried, he was packed off to England, where he had a miserable stint at boarding school, followed by an idle one at university, squandering most of his inheritance on gambling and failed investments. His talents, however, were writing and drawing, and in 1834 he left for Paris to study art, where he became a caricaturist contributing to various magazines. While in Paris he met and married seventeen-year-old Isabella Shawe, and when the honeymoon months were over, in the summer of 1837, they moved to London. Here Isabella gave birth to three daughters, one of whom died at eight months. After the birth of their third daughter in 1840, Isabella suffered a serious mental breakdown, eventually becoming incurably insane. Thackeray sent his children to live with his mother in Paris, and after years of hack journalism, he began to write in earnest the novels for which posterity remembers him. He died in 1863, aged fifty-two. Isabella, who required constant care for her illness, outlived him by thirty years, dying in 1894 at the age of seventy-seven.

See Also: George W.M. Reynolds, Arnold Bennett.

Further Reading: S. Hastings, *The Secret Lives of Somerset Maugham* (John Murray, 2009); C. Peters, *Thackeray: A Writer's Life* (Sutton, 1999).

Hôtel de Charost

LOUISE COLET

PLACE DE LA CONCORDE

(Métro: Concorde)

STATUE REPRESENTING STRASBOURG

MODELLED BY LOUISE COLET

MUSE AND LOVER OF

GUSTAVE FLAUBERT

AND ONE OF THE MODELS FOR

MADAME BOVARY

He used to send me flowers. Special flowers; the convention of an unconventional lover. He sent me a rose once. He gathered it one Sunday morning at Croisset, from a hedge in his garden. 'I kiss it,' he wrote, 'Put it quickly to your mouth, and then – you know where... Adieu! A thousand kisses. I am yours from night to day, from day to night.'
Julian Barnes, *Flaubert's Parrot* (1984)

Louise Colet's image representing Strasbourg on Place de la Concorde

Flaubert's first meeting with Louise Colet was in 1846 at the studio of his sculptor friend, James Pradier, where Colet was posing for a sculpture. 'Your curls touching your white shoulders,' Flaubert recalled, 'your blue dress [...] the light falling on you from one side, I was gazing at you and you were gazing back at me'. Thus began the tempestuous love affair that would last from 1846 until 1854. Colet was thirty-five, and Flaubert was twenty-four.

Regrettably, history has more or less consigned Colet to the role of mistress and muse to famous men, notably Gustave Flaubert, Victor Hugo, Alfred de Musset, Alfred de Vigny and Leconte de Lisle, yet she was a prolific author in her own right, who won the Académie française grand prix de poésie (poetry prize) no fewer than four times. She was also a feminist and a socialist, as well as host at a popular salon frequented by the writers of her day in the Rue de Sèvres. She exchanged letters with many of them, and it is through her correspondence, particularly that with Flaubert, that her memory survives today.

Her affair with Flaubert was a stormy one, often conducted from a distance, entailing copious epistles of love and rejection. But these provide an invaluable insight into Flaubert as writer and lover, as well as Colet's battle to be recognised and loved. That battle, however, was doomed from the start, as Flaubert was devoted to another woman: his formidable widowed mother. 'The two women I love the most have fitted a bridle to my heart,' wrote Flaubert, 'and they hold it on a double rein. They take it in turns to pluck at me with love and pain.' Flaubert made it abundantly clear to Colet that he would never leave his mother, and he never did. When their affair was coming to an end, one of Flaubert's last letters to her proposed that she pretend he had gone off on a long journey, just as the wily and cynical Rodolphe, one of the main protagonists in Flaubert's novel *Madame Bovary* had done. Rodolphe had no misgivings about seducing and abandoning Emma Bovary.

See Also: Gustave Flaubert, Victor Hugo, Alfred de Musset, École des Beaux-Arts, Académie française.

Further Information: The sculptor James Pradier (1790–1852) was born in Geneva and arrived in Paris in 1807 to work with his elder brother who was an engraver. He attended the École des Beaux-Arts, where he won the prestigious Prix de Rome, enabling him to study in Rome from 1814–1818. He became a popular sculptor of the pre-Romantic period, when his neoclassical works were often deemed scandalous because of their erotic overtones. There are eight statues representing French cities around the perimeter of Place de la Concorde. 'Lille' and 'Strasbourg' are situated near Rue de Rivoli, and were sculpted by Pradier between 1836 and 1838. Following France's defeat after the Franco-Prussian War (1870–1871), Alsace-Lorraine was annexed by Germany, and the 'Strasbourg' statue was draped in mourning black, a practice that only ended when France regained sovereignty after World War One. Pradier is buried in Père Lachaise, Division 24.

Select Bibliography: *Fleurs du midi* (1836); *Poésies* (1844); *Une histoire de soldat* (1856); *Lui, roman contemporain* (1860).

Further Reading: F. Gray, *Rage and Fire: A Life of Louise Colet* (Penguin, 1995); J. Barnes, *Flaubert's Parrot* (J. Cape, 1984).

Alsatians decorate the 'Strasbourg' statue, *c*.1910

ALAIN-FOURNIER

COURS-LA-REINE

(Métro: Champs-Élysées–Clemenceau)

STEPS OF THE GRAND PALAIS
WHERE ALAIN-FOURNIER FIRST SAW
YVONNE DE QUIÉVRECOURT
MUSE FOR *LE GRAND MEAULNES*

Alain-Fournier at Caylus in 1913

Disconcerted, Meaulnes stood and watched her move away. A little later, when he too had reached the shore, he saw her turn, before losing herself in the distant throng, to look back at him. For the first time her eyes rested on him in a steady regard. Was it meant as a final farewell? Was she forbidding him to accompany her? Or was there perhaps something more she would have liked to say?
Alain-Fournier, *Le Grand Meaulnes* (1913)

Published in 1913, *Le Grand Meaulnes* was the only novel Alain-Fournier ever completed as he was killed a year later in action, in the early weeks of the First World War. A tale of the passage from adolescence into adulthood, it tells the story of a young man who accidentally discovers an enchanted world where he finds the love of his life, Yvonne de Galais, and where his quest to return to this world takes him on a mysterious journey. Not read widely, although much loved by its devotees, the novel, variously translated in English as *The Lost Domain* or *The Wanderer*, is now considered one of the masterpieces of French literature.
Alain-Fournier's adolescent obsession with Yvonne de Quiévrecourt (1885–1964), his muse for Yvonne de Galais in *Le Grand Meaulnes*, is one of the world's most passionate tales of unrequited love. Fournier first saw her when he was descending the twin stone stairways of the Grand Palais towards the Cours-la-Reine on Ascension Day, 1 June 1905, where he had been to see an art exhibition. He was 18 years old. Ten days later he saw her again walking to Mass. He introduced himself and told her he was still at school, but hoped to be a writer one day. She explained she was living with relatives and would be leaving Paris the next day. They parted soon afterwards. Eight years later, in October 1913, Fournier sent Yvonne – now married with two children – an inscribed advance copy of *Le Grand Meaulnes*. The dedication inside was dated 1 June 1905 (the date he first saw her) to 25 October 1913.

The son of schoolteachers, Henri-Alban Fournier, better known by his pseudonym Alain-Fournier, was born in 1886 at La Chapelle-d'Angillon, in the Cher department. In 1891 his father was appointed headmaster of a boy's school in the Cher village of Épineuil-le-Fleuriel, where Fournier would spend much of his childhood, and where the school and the surrounding countryside would form the backdrop for *Le Grand Meaulnes*. When the First World War began in August 1914, Fournier was mobilised and given the rank of lieutenant. He was killed in action a few weeks later fighting near

Verdun on 22 September 1914. He was posted as missing, but had been buried in an unrecorded mass grave. His body was not discovered until 1991, nearly eighty years after his death. Yvonne Brochet, née de Quiévrecourt, died on 29 December 1964, aged seventy-nine, and is buried beside her husband and son in Père Lachaise Cemetery (Division 42). Her son, an army officer, was killed during the Algerian conflict in 1957, and her daughter, Marie-Yvonne, who died aged eighty-nine in 1999, became a nun. 'I'm now convinced', Marie-Yvonne once said, 'that my mother was deeply troubled by those conversations with a man who had loved her in silence for eight years. But which woman wouldn't have been? That's probably why she never talked about it.'

See Also: T.S. Eliot, Les Éditions Émile-Paul Frères, Père Lachaise.

Further Information: Alain-Fournier's body was reburied in the military cemetery at Saint-Rémy-La-Colonne, Département de la Meuse, Lorraine. He wrote much of *Le Grand Meaulnes* at his parents' house at 2 rue Cassini, in Montparnasse, which is now marked by a plaque. Most of Fournier's writing was published posthumously: *Miracles*, a book of poems and essays in 1924, various correspondences and family letters, and his unfinished novel *Colombe Blanchet*. The literary archives of Alain-Fournier are held at Bourges Municipal Library, and include correspondence, personal papers, and drafts of *Le Grand Meaulnes*. Museums dedicated to Alain-Fournier can be visited at La Chapelle-d'Angillon and Épineuil-le-Fleuriel. The Grand Palais was built for the Universal Exposition of 1900 as a museum and exhibition complex.

Further Reading: D. Arkell, *Alain-Fournier: A Brief Life* (Carcanet, 1986); R. Gibson,

The End of Youth, The Life and Work of Alain-Fournier (Impress Books, 2005); M. Maitron-Jodogne, *Alain-Fournier et Yvonne de Quiévrecourt* (PIE – Peter Lang, 2000).

Top: Steps of the Grand Palais
Above: Alain-Fournier's grave in the military cemetery at Saint-Rémy-La-Colonne

E.E. CUMMINGS

7 RUE FRANÇOIS PREMIER

*(Métro: Champs Elysées Clemenceau/
Franklin D. Roosevelt/Alma–Marceau)*

**FORMER OFFICES OF THE
NORTON–HARJES AMBULANCE CORPS
WHERE AMERICAN POET
E.E. CUMMINGS
REPORTED FOR DUTY IN 1917**

We were in fundamental disagreement as to the attitude which we, Americans, should uphold toward the poilus [French infantry] in whose behalf we had volunteered assistance, Mr. A. maintaining 'You boys want to keep away from those dirty Frenchmen' and 'We're here to show those bastards how they do things in America', to which we answered by seizing every opportunity for fraternization.

E.E. Cummings, *The Enormous Room* (1922)

E.E. Cummings

Cummings discarded the principles of syntax and punctuation, changed the rules of the game and reinvented poetic form. A radical path, with no known habitat, it was so far-reaching in its literary experimentation that it would eventually influence all modern poetry and establish Cummings as one of the great American poets.

Born Edward Estlin Cummings in 1894 in Cambridge, Massachusetts, he was named after his father, Edward, a Harvard professor, and his father's British friend, J. Estlin Carpenter. Following his education at Harvard he joined the Norton-Harjes Ambulance Corps in 1917 to avoid being enlisted as a regular soldier. Norton-Harjes was a private ambulance corps started by American archaeologist Richard Norton, and French banker Henry Harjes, to aid allied troops on the Western Front. *The Harvard Crimson*, the daily college newspaper, proclaimed that 'for those who wish to go over …, the requirements are briefly these: A man should pay his way over and back, and have at least $150 in spending money. His uniform will be furnished him in Paris. He should have considerable driving experience, but not necessarily mechanical experience. His physical and nervous condition must be good.'

During the Atlantic crossing to France Cummings made friends with William Slater Brown, a graduate in journalism from Columbia and a fellow Norton-Harjes volunteer. After docking in France in April 1917 they both boarded a train for Paris with other ambulance corps volunteers, but for no known reason they got off the train at a different station from the other recruits. When they eventually arrived at the Norton-Harjes office it was closed. It was also closed the next day. For five weeks, due to a misunderstanding or an oversight, Cummings and Brown were able to soak up the pleasures of Paris, from breakfast at Les Deux Magots to the treasures of the Louvre. When they finally did register with the Norton-Harjes office – amid the scorn of its officials – they were posted for duties to a Casualty Clearing Station on the Western Front near the Somme.

All they experienced at the Front, however, was boredom, mixed with terrible food and the endless maintenance of ambulances while waiting for action that never arrived. Much of their tedium and restlessness was poured out into the letters they wrote back home, all of which were read by military censors. 'I hope M. le Censor won't mind my saying that nothing exciting is going on where I am,' Cummings wrote to his mother. 'Every day French aeroplanes are shot at by German anti-aircraft guns, without the slightest effect.' They also wrote about the low morale of French troops and how the Germans might conceivably win the war. All of which, in the eyes of the censors, would have come under the axiom of *careless talk costs lives* and could well have been interpreted as treason.

On 21 September 1917, Cummings and Brown were arrested on suspicion of espionage and undesirable activities, and imprisoned in a military detention camp in Normandy, an experience Cummings later wrote about in *The Enormous Room*. But with the war to end all wars still raging and thousands being slaughtered daily, two interred and forgotten Americans meant little to the authorities. Cummings may well have remained incarcerated until the Armistice if his father had not taken decisive action and written an impassioned letter to President Woodrow Wilson. 'Pardon me, Mr. President,' he wrote, 'but if I were

President and your son were suffering such prolonged injustice at the hands of France, and your son's mother had been needlessly kept in Hell as many weeks as my boy's mother has, – I would do something to make American citizenship as sacred in the eyes of Frenchmen as Roman citizenship was in the eyes of the ancient world.'

Cummings was eventually released on 19 December 1917, and Brown was released a month later, but bleak as their incarceration was, it had sheltered them from the carnage of the Somme, and may well have saved their lives. Cummings returned to America where he lived in New York's Greenwich Village for most of the rest of his life. *The Enormous Room* became one of the classic American chronicles of World War I.

See Also: American Ambulance Field Service, Robert Service.

Further Information: In May 1921 Cummings returned to Paris for his first prolonged visit since being released from his Normandy detention camp in 1917, and stayed for a few months at the Hôtel Marignan at 13 rue du Sommerard. It was here that he learned that his autobiographical narrative, *The Enormous Room*, had found a publisher. E.E. Cummings died aged sixty-seven of a cerebral haemorrhage in 1962.

Select Bibliography: *The Enormous Room* (1922); *Tulips and Chimneys* (1923); *&* (1925); *XLI Poems* (1925); *is 5* (1926); *EIMI* (1933); *No Thanks* (1935); *Santa Claus: A Morality* (1946); *Fairy Tales* (1965); *Complete Poems, 1904–1962* (2008).

Further Reading: S. Cheever, *E.E. Cummings: A Life* (Pantheon, 2014); R. Kennedy, *Dreams in the Mirror* (Liveright, 1994); C. Sawyer-Lauçanno, *E.E. Cummings: A Biography* (Methuen, 2005).

THE TARTAN PIMPERNEL

17 RUE BAYARD

(Métro: Franklin D. Roosevelt/Champs Elysées–Clemenceau)

THE SCOTS KIRK

CHURCH OF WARTIME MINISTER

DONALD CASKIE, AUTHOR OF

THE TARTAN PIMPERNEL

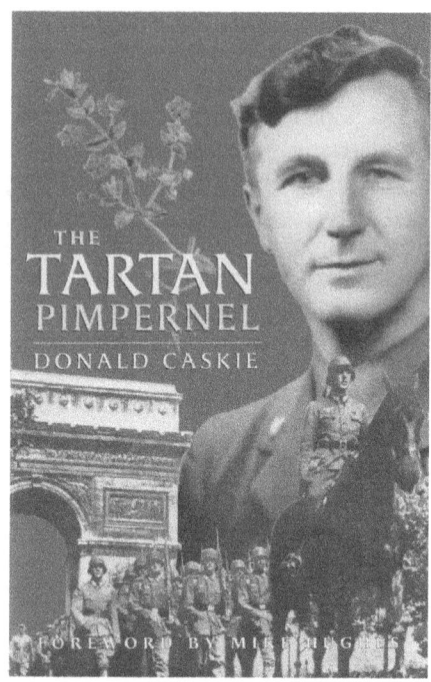

I found myself in a medieval 'bottle' cell. ... [It is] ingenious, easy for the torturer to operate and guaranteed in time to drive the strongest victim insane. Shaped like a man, it is a bottle-shaped cell of stone big enough to contain one human being but short enough not to permit him to stand upright and narrow enough to restrain him from lying down. It tapers at the top so that the face is never more than two inches from the walls that encase his head. ... He cannot move his knees more than a few inches. If he rests on his shoulders the strain on his legs becomes agonising. ... His own stench fills his lungs for there are no facilities for physical relief in the 'bottle'. It is, I conjecture, the most vile instrument of torture ever devised by men.
Donald Caskie, *The Tartan Pimpernel* (1957)

Donald Caskie was minister of the Scots Kirk when the Nazis were marching towards Paris in 1940. With the Germans only days away, thousands of Parisians were evacuating the city, including Caskie, who had openly denounced Hitler from his pulpit. Closing his church he headed south following the trail of bewildered and panic-stricken refugees. Declining passage on one of the last ships to Britain, he ended up in the Mediterranean port of Marseilles where, he wrote: 'The streets around the docks were crowded with British soldiers and airmen, the remnants of Dunkirk ... merchant seamen who had been torpedoed in the Atlantic and escaped while on the way to prison camps in Germany. The plight of these men was pitiable. ... My new vocation came with the clarity of crystal.' Near the old harbour he commandeered a deserted British Seaman's Mission and pinned a notice over the door which read: 'Now open to British civilians and seamen ONLY.'

Marseilles was in Vichy France, which was controlled by a puppet French government directed by the Gestapo. In a city full of spies, black marketeers and hard-boiled crooks, hundreds of exhausted allied soldiers and airmen ended their flight through war-torn France at what they hoped would be their salvation: Donald Caskie's Seamen's Mission, which doubled as a clandestine clearing house for escaping allied forces. Here Caskie fed and clothed these worn-out men, issued them with non-combatant papers and endeavoured to dispatch them safely across the frontier to Spain, and it was by these covert escape routes that Caskie earned the nickname Tartan Pimpernel. Supported by the British Secret Service and the French Resistance, Caskie was eventually betrayed by a British double agent and consequently arrested and expelled from Marseilles. Undaunted, Caskie continued his activities until he was finally arrested and imprisoned under sentence of death, his life only saved through the mediation of a German pastor. It was later estimated that Donald Caskie had been involved in the safe return of approximately 2000 men.

After the liberation of Paris Caskie returned to the Scots Kirk, eventually leaving France in 1960 to work in a parish on Scotland's Firth of Clyde, retiring through ill health in 1968. He died in 1983, aged eighty-one, and is buried on his native island of Islay in the Inner Hebrides of Scotland. The Church of Scotland's Fasti Ecclesiae Scoticanae (lists of the succession of ministers in the parish churches of Scotland) modestly states that he was 'engaged in church and patriotic duties in France, 1939–45'.

See Also: Nazi occupation of Paris.

Further Information: The Scots congregation of Paris was established in 1858, and services were held at the Oratoire du Louvre. In 1885 the congregation moved to the former American Episcopal church in Rue Bayard, but after World War II, due to war damage, the building had to be demolished. Caskie wrote *The Tartan Pimpernel* to raise funds for a new church, which replaced the old building in the late 1950s, but due to structural problems it, too, was eventually demolished and superseded by the present building in 2002.

IRWIN SHAW

24 RUE DU BOCCADOR

(Métro: Alma-Marceau)

FORMER HOME OF IRWIN Sнaw
AMERICAN NOVELIST,
PLAYWRIGHT AND SCREENWRITER
BEST KNOWN FOR HIS NOVEL
THE YOUNG LIONS

He loved the legend of the city and the fact that it was one place on the face of the earth that lived up to the legend it had established in the hearts of men. He loved the fact that he had fought on the road to the city and had killed to get there and he loved the little shabby Frenchman he had killed and he loved Corporal Kraus, lying dead beside him, far from the farm in Silesia, with cherry stains on his lips. He loved the fact that he had been tested on the road and in the forest, that death had whistled past him, and he loved the war because in no other way could a man be truly tested, and he loved it that the war was going to end soon, because he did not want to die.
Irwin Shaw, *The Young Lions* (1949)

With his thick Brooklyn accent and stocky build, Irwin Shaw looked as if he belonged more on the football field or the boxing ring than in front of a typewriter. Ernest Hemingway once said that the only way to tackle Irwin Shaw in a boxing match was to 'rip off your glove and sink your fingers deep into the bulge of his forearm, severing a few of the muscles there and rendering the arm more or less useless'. But despite his uncharacteristic appearance and Long Island drawl, Shaw was a talented and compelling writer who enjoyed universal critical esteem. From Depression-era Brooklyn to Broadway and Hollywood he became one of America's celebrated

Pan Books edition, 1977

storytellers; ultimately, however, he was one of its most underrated.

Irwin Shamforoff was born to Russian Jewish immigrants in the Bronx, New York City, in 1913. The family moved to Brooklyn, and upon entering college he changed his name to Shaw. In his first job as a writer, at the age of 21, he was creating fifteen-minute long Dick Tracy radio scripts for $25 an episode. He was also writing short stories and trying to write plays. In 1936 he wrote *Bury the Dead*, a play full of passion and energy about the spirit of dead soldiers killed in battle that return to confront the living. The play was a Broadway hit and Shaw became one of the most talked about young contemporary writers. By this time he was also publishing stories in *The New Yorker*, and the motion picture company RKO had hired him as

screenwriter. It was an upward spiral of success that was to be derailed by WWII. In 1942 Shaw, along with other writers and artists, was drafted into the Signal Corps's film unit to create documentary and print productions for the war effort. He was posted to the Middle East and later covered the Allied invasion of Normandy, eventually ending up on the outskirts of Paris on the eve of its liberation. Shaw was one of the first Americans to enter the city, which still had pockets of German snipers. 'The first time I saw Paris', wrote Shaw,

was on the day of its liberation, August 25, 1944. I was in a Signal Corps camera unit that was attached to the Twelfth Regiment of the Fourth Division. The unit was made up of two cameramen, a driver, and myself. ... Our jeep was banked with flowers, a gift from the people in the little towns on our route to Paris, and we had a small store of tomatoes and apples and bottles of wine that had been tossed to us as we slowly made our way through the crowds that tore down barricades in our path.

In 1951 Shaw moved to Paris with his wife and young son to an apartment on Rue du Boccador near the Eiffel Tower. He stayed at various addresses in the city, on and off, for almost twenty-five years. 'But I was never a Parisian,' he wrote. 'I was always an American. ... Somehow, all during the period when almost every wall was decorated with the sign, "Americans Go Home", it never occurred to me that they meant me.'

Drawing on his wartime experiences, Shaw published his first novel in 1948 to great acclaim. *The Young Lions* is about a German and two American soldiers during the war. 'What I was trying to do in *The Young Lions*', he explained,

was to show the world at a certain point in its history, its good and evil, and as many people as I could crowd into the book struggling through that world, trying to find some reason for trying to stay alive in it... I wanted to show how a man [the German soldier in the novel] can start out decent, intelligent, well meaning, as so many people in Germany must have been, even in the greatest days of Nazism – and wind up bestialized, almost bereft of humanity, almost dead to the instincts of survival even, as the Germans finally were, by believing in one false thing, which spreads and spreads and finally corrupts them entirely.

He went on to write a dozen novels in all, half of them between the late 1940s and the early 1960s, but by the end of the sixties his career was in free fall. In 1970 this downward trajectory was dramatically reversed when he published his bestseller, *Rich Man, Poor Man*. The resulting television miniseries made Shaw a household name and, in so doing, introduced his books to a much younger generation, revitalising his book sales. But rediscovery by television had its price: critics and the media began to pigeonhole him as a commercial writer and, ironically, his newfound fame and success – although very lucrative – finally sold him short. Had he died in the early 1950s, before the real onslaught of mass television, he would probably be recognised today as one of the most important writers of his generation.

See Also: Hôtel Scribe, Ernest Hemingway, Joseph Kessel, William Saroyan.

Further Information: Irwin Shaw died on 16 May 1984 from prostate cancer and its complications at a hospital in Davos, Switzerland, near his home.

Selected Bibliography: *Bury the Dead* (1936); *Quiet City* (1939); *The Young Lions* (1948); *Report on Israel* (1950); *Lucy Crown* (1956); *Rich Man, Poor Man* (1970); *Evening in Byzantium* (1973); *Paris! Paris!* (1976); *Beggarman, Thief* (1977).

Further Reading: M. Shnayerson, *Irwin Shaw, A Biography* (Putnam's, 1989).

Irwin Shaw in Paris in the 1950s

289

9th

Arrondissement

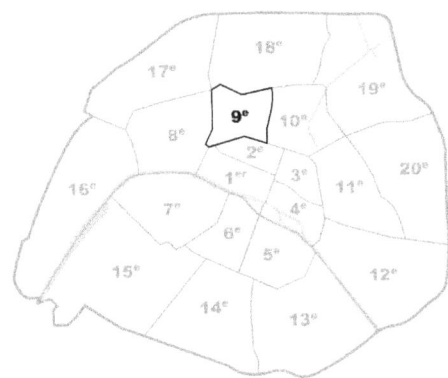

LE FANTÔME DE L'OPÉRA

PLACE DE L'OPÉRA

(Métro: Opéra)

THE PALAIS GARNIER

FORMERLY L'OPÉRA DE PARIS

SETTING FOR GASTON LEROUX'S

THE PHANTOM OF THE OPERA

If I am the phantom, it is because man's hatred has made me so. If I am to be saved it is because your love redeems me.
Gaston Leroux, *The Phantom of the Opera*

The Phantom of the Opera, like many other celebrated fiends of literature, arouses the reader's revulsion as well as their sympathy. And it is this balance of compassion and loathing that enabled Gaston Leroux to create one of the greatest psychological suspense dramas

ever to come out of French literature. A simple *Beauty and the Beast* story, it is set in the romantic world of the Opéra de Paris where the glamour of *Don Giovanni* and *Faust* are juxtaposed with the dark mystery of its rat-ridden secret passages below. It has been adapted for cinema, television, theatre and ballet, and like Dracula and Frankenstein's creature before him, the Phantom has become one of literature's timeless masters of the macabre.

Leroux was born in 1868 at No. 66 rue Faubourg Saint-Martin, the eldest of four children of Dominique Leroux, a public works contractor, and Marie Bidault, the daughter of a Normandy bailiff. When he was twelve he was sent to boarding school in Normandy, and as a young man he pursued a brief career in law before taking up journalism. Initially, his legal training found him jobs as a law

Gaston Leroux

Poster for the 1925 silent film adaptation
directed by Rupert Julian

correspondent, but in 1893, when he
was hired by *Le Matin*, he reported on
everything from polar exploration to
the Russian Revolution. He published

his first novel, *The Double Life of
Théophraste Longuet*, in 1903, but his
most memorable were the five novels
featuring master criminal, Chéri-Bibi,
and the seven with detective Joseph
Rouletabille, most notably in the 1908
locked room mystery, *Le mystère de la
chambre jaune (The Mystery of the Yellow Room)*, described by John Dickson
Carr as 'the best detective tale ever written'. He wrote over thirty novels, as well
as short stories and screenplays. Most of
them are immersed in mystery and the
grotesque, none more so than 'Le dîner
des bustes' ('A Terrible Tale'), which
tells the story of an annual gathering of
limbless men who survive a shipwreck
by eating each other's arms and legs.

'You want the secret of my success; my
recipe?' wrote Leroux. 'I'm happy to
give it to you. I have always brought
the same care to making an adventure
novel, a serialized novel, that others
would bring to the making of a poem.
My ambition was to raise the level of
this much maligned genre.'

Leroux's son, Jules, observed that his
father only worked in the early morning,
between five and eight, and that the entire household would be hushed during
this time, especially when the story he
was working on was reaching its climax.
'The more the minutes passed by,' wrote
Jules,

the more we were on tenterhooks. My
father, revolver lying on his bureau, was
finishing the epilogue. When he wrote
the word 'end' he squeezed off a shot
in the direction of the balcony window.
It was the signal so long awaited. From
then on bells rang, drums and trumpets
were unleashed, as well as iron pot
covers, pots, hammers, and any other
utensil capable of making a noise ... until we were breathless, and in Indian file,

a howling mob we would run through the garden and the house.

Gaston Leroux, master of the macabre, died suddenly of uremic poisoning on 27 April 1927, aged fifty-eight, and is buried at the Cimetière du Château in Nice. When asked where he got his strange ideas from, Leroux once replied, 'Ah well, I'll tell you: It's not by listening to the song of the nightingale.'

Further Information: In 1861 Emperor Napoleon III commissioned architect Charles Garnier (1825–1898) to build a new Paris opera house. Completed in 1875 it was then the largest opera house in the world, with 17 storeys (7 beneath the stage), an audience capacity of 2200, a stage measuring 11,000 square metres capable of holding 450 performers, a treadmill floor for herds of galloping horses, and a staff of 1500 employees. In 1896, one of the counterweights holding the seven-ton chandelier above the auditorium accidently crashed through the ceiling killing a member of the audience, an incident which inspired one of the scenes in *The Phantom of the Opera*. Leroux visited the cellars of the Opera when he was a journalist, where, in 1871, prisoners were held captive during the Commune. In 1990, the Paris Opera moved to new premises on Place de la Bastille. Garnier's opera house, re-named the Palais Garnier, is the headquarters of the Ballet de l'Opéra national de Paris.

Further Reading: L. Wolf, *The Essential Phantom of the Opera* (Plume, 1996); G. Perry, *The Complete Phantom of the Opera* (H. Holt, 1988); V. Johnson, *Backstage at the Revolution: How the Royal Paris Opera Survived the End of the Old Regime* (University of Chicago Press, 2009).

Palais Garnier

CAFÉ DE LA PAIX

5 PLACE DE L'OPÉRA

(Métro: Opéra)

Now yonder like a blot of ink
he sits across the way,
Upon the smiling terrace of the
Cafe de la Paix;
That little wizened Spanish man,
his face is ghastly white,
His eyes are staring,
staring like a tiger's in the night.
I know within his evil heart
the fires of hate are fanned,
I know his automatic's ready
waiting to his hand.
I know a tragedy is near.
I dread, I have no peace ...
Oh, don't you think I ought to go
and call upon the police?
Look there ... he's rising up ... my God!
He leaps from out his place ...
Yon millionaire from Argentine ...
the two are face to face ...
A shot! A shriek! A heavy fall!
A huddled heap! Oh, see
The little wizened Spanish man
is dancing in his glee. ...
I'm sick ... I'm faint ... I'm going mad. ...
Oh, please take me away ...
There's BLOOD upon the terrace
of the Cafe de la Paix. ...
Robert Service,
from 'The Absinthe Drinkers'

Detail from János Vaszary's *Terrace of the Café de la Paix* (1925)

Named after the nearby Rue de la Paix, and located on the ground floor of the Grand Hotel, the Café de la Paix opened on 5 May 1862, and the frescoes and lavish gilding of the Second Empire that embellished it then still adorn it as elegantly today. It was certainly no place for the bohemian writer, but for those who had made their mark in the literary world, notably Oscar Wilde, Émile Zola, Gustave Flaubert, Victor Hugo and Guy de Maupassant, it became part of their fashionable and opulent world.

In the summer of 1923 American novelist Kay Boyle (1902–1992) arrived in Paris with her French husband, Richard Brault, a former exchange student. Boyle, then unpublished, and virtually reduced to penury, desperately needed a job. Initially they had both planned a three-month visit to Brault's parents in Brittany, but Boyle ended up staying in Europe for eighteen years. She had considered working in Sylvia Beach's bookshop on Rue de l'Odéon, but she could not muster the courage to go inside. She did, however, resolve to look up American writer and publisher, Harold Loeb, whose magazine *Broom* she had worked for, briefly, in New York. She met him one afternoon at the Café de la Paix along with the author Robert McAlmon. Over forty years later, in the late 1960s, Kay Boyle would edit and revise McAlmon's long-out-of-print memoirs, *Being Geniuses Together*

(1920–1930) (1934), adding alternating chapters of her own, and evoking 1920s Paris in a way that few books had done before. '[Harold] suggested that we meet on the terrace of the Café de la Paix that afternoon at four,' she wrote in *Being Geniuses Together*.

I looked up the café in the telephone directory, arrived a half hour early, and walked around the block until I saw Harold arrive in a taxi and make his way across the crowded terrace to one of the small, round-topped tables where a young man in a grey suit [McAlmon] had already begun his apéritif. Before I could bring myself to join them I had to walk twice around the block again, berating my own reflection in the shop windows, saying to it, *Oh overweening ego! Who cares that you are thin as a rail and smeared with make-up like a whore? Yes, the earrings are uproarious, and the hat is a scream, and the skirt may split up the sides at any minute, but these men and I have died the same deaths for the same poets, and they will hear me saying all the things I have not said yet and cannot say, and all the things I have not yet written they will know I will one day write. They move on the same sad, troubled waters with me.*

Kay Boyle went on to publish over forty books during her lifetime. She died in California in 1992, aged ninety.

See Also: Kay Boyle, Robert McAlmon, Adam Worth, Sylvia Beach.

Further Reading: R. McAlmon & K. Boyle, *Being Geniuses Together* (1920–1930) (Doubleday, 1968); R. Service, *The Best of Robert Service* (A&C Black, 2007).

Terrace of the Café de la Paix, 1935

ADAM WORTH

2 RUE SCRIBE

(Métro: Opéra)

LE GRAND HÔTEL

FORMER HEADQUARTERS OF

ADAM WORTH

INSPIRATION FOR

PROFESSOR MORIARTY

NEMESIS OF SHERLOCK HOLMES

Adam Worth

He is the Napoleon of Crime, Watson. He is the organiser of half that is evil and of nearly all that is undetected in this great city. He is a genius, a philosopher, an abstract thinker. He has a brain of the first order.

Sherlock Holmes describing Professor Moriarty in Sir Arthur Conan Doyle's 'The Final Problem' (1893)

Many of Conan Doyle's fictional characters were based upon, or were a composite of, real people. Holmes was based on Dr Joseph Bell, lecturer in clinical surgery at Doyle's Edinburgh medical school, and Watson, on forensic expert Dr Patrick Watson. But Conan Doyle's prime inspiration for Professor Moriarty – the arch-enemy of Sherlock Holmes – was a villain he had never met: Adam Worth, the greatest thief of modern times.

Worth was born in East Germany in 1844 to a Jewish family who emigrated to the United States when he was five years old. Short in stature, streetwise and quick-witted, he grew up thieving in his hometown of Cambridge, Massachusetts where he was known as 'Little Adam'. At the age of fourteen he ran away from home. He drifted to Boston and New York, and with the outbreak of the American Civil War he joined the Union Army when he was seventeen and became a 'bounty jumper': a soldier who deserted and re-enlisted in other regiments under an assumed name to collect the financial bounty offered to those who joined up. Worth even deserted the Union and joined the Confederate Army purely for the bounty.

When the war ended he returned to New York where he became a pickpocket, and in 1864 he was sentenced to three years' imprisonment in Sing Sing for stealing. At barely twenty years old, he ingeniously escaped prison after only a few weeks and made his way back to New York, where he returned to a life of crime. But unlike his criminal contemporaries, Worth did not drink alcohol, nor did he countenance violence, the vulgar attributes of the thug. Worth desperately wanted to elevate himself from the sleazy world of street crime to that of intelligent and calculating crooks where the objective was not picking a pocket, but robbing a bank. In November 1869, Worth and his accomplices successfully tunnelled into the vault of a major Boston bank, stealing one million dollars in money and securities. To evade capture, Worth and an associate sailed for Europe, ending up in Paris in the summer of 1871.

With their loot they purchased a large building at No. 2 rue Scribe, which is now part of the famous Grand Hôtel. They named their new premises the American Bar, and spent seventy-five thousand dollars refurbishing it. The second floor was a welcoming clubhouse for visiting Americans and the upper floors constituted an illegal gambling casino with roulette wheels and games of baccarat and poker. It was the first American-style nightclub in Paris, and it was a runaway success. The Paris authorities regularly raided the building, but local police were bribed to tip Worth off when a raid was expected, so no gambling was ever discovered on the premises.

By this time the famous Pinkerton Detective Agency was on to Worth, and were closely observing him. Reputedly, the detectives who had trailed Jesse James and Butch Cassidy never gave up, and they spent the next twenty-five years trying to put Worth behind bars. William Pinkerton actually paid a surprise visit to the bar. Worth immediately recognised him and, after shaking his hand, bought him a drink. Worth knew his time was running out in Paris. In 1875, aged thirty-one, Worth sold the American Bar and headed across the Channel where he began a new chapter in his life of crime. In London, he bought a mansion on the edge of Clapham Common and an apartment in Mayfair where he set about masterminding his criminal future. No longer would he get physically involved in a crime; he would subcontract the work to other criminals on a commission

basis, making himself virtually immune from the law. His success was unparalleled in the history of crime, making the Pinkerton detectives describe him as 'the most remarkable, most successful and most dangerous professional criminal known to modern times'.

Worth died in 1902, aged fifty-six, supposedly in reduced circumstances, and is buried under the alias Henry Judson Raymond in an unmarked common grave with no headstone in London's Highgate Cemetery. His death certificate describes him as a man of 'independent means'. To popular culture he was, according to the *New York Journal*, 'a singular modern romance'.

Further Information: The upper floors that were once Worth's gambling casino are now bedrooms of Le Grand Hôtel. Moriarty only makes an appearance in one Sherlock Holmes story, 'The Final Problem', where Moriarty and Holmes plunge over the Reichenbach Falls, but he is mentioned in many others. Moriarty's character was created by Doyle from a variety of sources, but his primary source was Adam Worth.

Le Grand Hôtel and Café de la Paix

HÔTEL SCRIBE

1 RUE SCRIBE

(Métro: Opéra)

**RESIDENCE FOR WAR CORRESPONDENTS
AFTER THE LIBERATION OF PARIS**

*We drove off, with a cluster of girls hanging
onto the jeep, and found the Hôtel Scribe,
where we had been told to report with our
film. Outside the hotel, inundating the army
vehicles there, were hundreds of Parisians,
singing, shaking hands, asking questions,
examining jeeps and guns, extending invitations, weeping, kissing the soldiers, kissing
the correspondents, kissing each other. ...
There was no hot water [in the hotel], but I
luxuriated in the bath nevertheless, listening
to the voice of the crowd down below ...
Just before I fell asleep I remembered what
I had heard a GI say that momentous afternoon: 'This is the day the war should end.'*
Irwin Shaw, writing about the liberation in
Paris! Paris! (1976)

When the Germans occupied Paris
in the summer of 1940 they
requisitioned Hôtel Scribe for their
propaganda staff. After the liberation
on 25 August 1944, the hotel became a
base for military public relations officers
and allied war correspondents including
John Dos Passos, Robert Capa, Janet
Flanner, William Saroyan, Irwin Shaw,
Ernest Hemingway and George Orwell.
On his return home from the Spanish
Civil War in 1945, Orwell stayed at the
hotel for a month. It was his first time
in Paris for eight years, and he lamented
how 'horribly depressing [Paris was]
compared with what it used to be'.
Noticing Ernest Hemingway's name in
the hotel register one day, he tracked
down the room and knocked on the

Top: US armoured vehicle on the Champs-
Élysées.   Centre: Ernest Hemingway and
Col. Buck Lanham in 1944.   Above: GIs
view the Eiffel Tower after liberation

door. Orwell introduced himself as Eric Blair, to which Hemingway, who was busy packing, retorted, 'Well what the fucking hell do you want?'

'I'm George Orwell.'

'Why the fucking hell didn't you say so!' Hemingway exclaimed, reaching for a bottle in his bag. 'Have a drink. Have a double. Straight or with water, there's no soda.' They only had a few minutes together as Hemingway was moving out, but neither of them ever forgot their brief encounter.

The Grand Café at the Hôtel Scribe was a favourite haunt of science fiction and adventure writer, Jules Verne. Perhaps he foresaw that history would one day be made here, because on 28 December 1895 in the Salon Indien of the Grand Café, the Lumière brothers demonstrated their cinematograph, and the motion picture industry was born.

See Also: George Orwell, Ernest Hemingway, Irwin Shaw, John Dos Passos, Janet Flanner, Eugène Scribe, Jules Verne, William Saroyan.

Further Information: Hôtel Scribe was built in 1861 and was part of the new Opéra district designed by Baron Haussmann. In 1864 the street and the hotel were named after French dramatist and librettist, Eugène Scribe (1791–1861). The hotel would become a focal point for the elite of Parisian society, including Duc de Morny, Marcel Proust, Serge Diaghilev, Josephine Baker, and the prestigious Jockey Club, who visited and took up residence here.

Further Reading: M. Cobb, *Eleven Days in August: The Liberation of Paris in 1944* (Simon & Schuster, 2013); A. Beevor, A. Cooper, *Paris After the Liberation: 1944–1949* (Penguin, 1995); I. Shaw, *The Young Lions* (1948).

Hôtel Scribe

PIERRE LOTI

3 RUE AUBER

(Métro: Opéra/Havre–Caumartin)

FORMER PUBLISHING HOUSE
OF CALMANN-LÉVY
PUBLISHER OF *AZIYADÉ*
BY PIERRE LOTI

At his best Pierre Loti was unquestionably the finest descriptive writer of the day. ... When all his limitations, however, have been rehearsed, Pierre Loti remains, in the mechanism of style and cadence, one of the most original and most perfect French writers of the second half of the 19th century.
Edmund Gosse

Pierre Loti in naval uniform

The above assessment is high praise from the distinguished British critic and writer, Edmund Gosse (1849–1928); today, however, few remember Loti or the writing Gosse applauds. But although the outmoded exoticism of Pierre Loti's work may have faded in the West, in Asia Minor his star still reigns supreme. In Turkey, a hill and a street are named after him, and in 1920 he was made an honorary citizen. On the day of his funeral, 10 June 1923, the flags of Constantinople flew at half mast.

Pierre Loti was the pseudonym of Louis Marie-Julien Viaud, who was born in Rochefort, south-west France, in 1850, and brought up by his widowed mother and aunts. In 1867 he joined the navy, and by 1906 he was captain of his own ship. He sailed all over the world as a naval officer, and his ports of call became the exotic locations for his novels and travel books, namely Polynesia, Africa, Palestine, India, Persia, Japan, China, and his beloved Turkey. He wrote over forty books, many of them autobio-graphical and inspired by his travels.

His first and most celebrated novel, *Aziyadé*, was a semi-autobiographical 'behind the veil' love story mainly set in Constantinople. Published anony-mously by Calmann-Lévy in 1879, it was based on Loti's love affair with an eighteen-year-old harem girl in Saloni-ka, which was then part of the Ottoman Empire. Loti had arrived in Salonika in May 1876 with the allied fleet, which had been sent to seek reprisals over the assassinations of the French and Ger-man Consuls by Turkish nationalists. It was a tense and hostile time, but Loti, with his usual inquisitiveness, was un-daunted, and explored the old Muslim quarter of the town regardless. Passing the barred windows of an old Turkish harem one day, he felt he was being watched. In *Aziyadé*, he recalls that:

Behind those heavy iron bars, two large green eyes were fixed on me. The eye-brows were drawn across, so that they met. The expression of those eyes was a mixture of energy and naïveté – one might have said it was that of a child, so fresh, so young it appeared ... A white veil was wound tightly round the head, leaving only the brow and those great eyes free. They were green – that sea-green which poets of the Orient once sang. This young woman was Aziyadé.

Loti travelled to Constantinople where he adopted the local dress, he studied the language, and he continued his affair with Aziyadé. Soon he was moving around the countryside unnoticed. Had he been caught he would have been arrested as a spy, but all Loti was doing was immersing himself in a world he had come to love. He returned to Constantinople time and again, and ended up writing seven books about Turkey, which were always in support of the Turkish people and defended them against harsh Western policies. His final visit was in 1913, when his reputation as a writer and orientalist was at its height. Crowds cheered him at the dockside and the Sultan gave him an audience.

His three novels of Breton fishing life: *Mon Frère Yves* (1883), *Pêcheur d'Islande* (1886), and *Matelot* (1893), are now considered amongst the best of his writing. Puccini's 1904 opera, *Madama Butterfly*, was partially based on Loti's Japanese-inspired *Madame Chrysanthème* (1887).

Throughout his life Loti was a passionate collector of artefacts and animals procured on his travels. Some were treasured gifts from potentates who hosted him and rewarded him with gifts, notably the Sultan of Oman, the Sultan of Morocco and the Khedive of Egypt. 'Soon the familiar things', he wrote, 'will seem very astonishing, when I'm back in the modern world and I reconstruct them from afar.' 'Reconstruct' them he did, in lavish style, back in his three-storey family home in Rochefort, and the extraordinary microcosm of the Islamic world he created there still exists today as a museum.

The love of his life, Aziyadé, who always believed he would return for her, died in 1880, and although Loti married a French woman in 1886, he returned to Constantinople a year later and found Aziyadé's grave. For the rest of his life he wore a gold ring with her name engraved on it.

Further Information: Michel Lévy and his brother Kalmus 'Calmann' Lévy founded the publishing house of Michel Lévy frères in 1836. After Michel's death in 1875 it was renamed Calmann-Lévy. Together the brothers created one of Europe's leading publishing houses, which published the cream of nineteenth-century French literature, notably that of Balzac, Dumas, Flaubert, Hugo, Stendhal, Sand, Baudelaire and Lamartine.

Further Reading: L. Blanch, *Pierre Loti:Travels with the Legendary Romantic* (Tauris Parke, 2004).

Pierre Loti (1850–1923) at home in his study

AMERICAN EXPRESS

11 RUE SCRIBE

(Métro: Opéra/Chaussée d'Antin–La Fayette)

ONCE THE WORLD'S MOST FAMOUS
TOURIST ADDRESS AND LIFELINE FOR
EXPATRIATE WRITERS AND ARTISTS

*During his 'bum' period, [Henry] Miller
turned up in Montparnasse almost every
evening, looking for that charitable soul
who might take him in. ... For many years
he had only one permanent address: 11 Rue
Scribe, the location of the American Express
office. To get there from Montparnasse, you
descended Boulevard Raspail, crossed the
Seine at Pont-Royal, traversed the Tuileries
to the Avenue de l'Opéra, then up to Rue
Scribe. By taxi, car, subway, bus, carriage,
and most often on foot, every American who
has ever lived in Paris, from Gertrude Stein
to Fitzgerald, Isadora Duncan to Hemingway and Steinbeck, has trod this path of hope
and dreams.*

Brassaï, *Henry Miller: The Paris Years*
(1975)

Opened in 1896, the American
Express office in Rue Scribe (now
closed) served as a meeting place,
mailing address and financial saviour
to expatriate writers and artists for over
eighty years. To many of them it was
their only permanent address. Here
one could scan the visitors' book to see
who was in town, buy a plane ticket or
locate a lost passport. In its heyday it
was equipped with reading and writing
rooms, a post office, telephones, a left
luggage office and an information bureau: services that were equivalent – and
probably superior – to those at most
foreign embassies. It has also been used
as a setting in literature, notably in the
novels *Dodsworth* (1929), by Sinclair
Lewis, and *Comedy: American Style*
(1933), by Jessie Redmon Fauset.

When, in 1901, the company's iron
safe was dynamited, it was said to be
the first time that this new explosive,
invented thirty-four years earlier in
Sweden by Alfred Nobel, had been used
for safe-blowing. The office's oriental
rugs were wrapped around the safe to
deaden the sound of the explosion.
Twisted gold napoleons and other coins
littered the floor. But the robbery turned
out to be a fiasco as little cash had been
left in the safe, which mostly contained
a considerable quantity of the newly
invented, and easily identified and numbered, traveller's cheque. The thieves
were later captured and sentenced to
penal servitude on Devil's Island.

See Also: Henry Miller, Ernest Hemingway, Gertrude Stein, Scott Fitzgerald.

GASTON GALLIMARD

79 RUE SAINT-LAZARE

(Métro: Trinité–d'Estienne d'Orves/St-Lazare)

BIRTHPLACE OF GASTON GALLIMARD

FRENCH PUBLISHING LEGEND

The rejection of this book will remain the most serious mistake ever made by the NRF and (since I bear the shame of being very much responsible for it) one of the most stinging and remorseful regrets of my life.
André Gide in 1913 lamenting to Marcel Proust his rejection of *Du Côté de chez Swann*, the first volume of Proust's master-piece, *À la recherche du temps perdu.*

Gaston Gallimard in his latter years

Gaston Gallimard (1881–1975) published most of France's twen-tieth-century literary legends, including André Gide, Marcel Proust, Albert Camus, Simone de Beauvoir, Jean Genet, Jean-Paul Sartre, Antoine de Saint-Exupéry, Georges Simenon, André Malraux and many others. During his lifetime Gallimard could boast eighteen Nobel Prize winners, and twenty-seven winners of Le Prix Goncourt, France's highest literary honour. He also pub-lished *La Pléiade*, the French series of literary classics, and *Série Noire*, a series of more than 2000 thrillers, detective novels and spy thrillers: a dazzling array of literature that made Gallimard the leading French publisher of the twenti-eth century.

It began in 1908, when a small group of writers created their own literary magazine called *La Nouvelle Revue Française*, known as the *NRF*. Among its co-founders were Jean Schlumberger and André Gide. By December 1910 the magazine's content had improved and circulation had grown, but its income was precarious. Undaunted, they pressed ahead with ambitious plans to launch their own publishing house; but they desperately needed to find a business manager: someone wealthy enough, and interested enough, to invest in their new enterprise.

They approached somebody they all vaguely knew. Thirty-year-old Gaston Gallimard was the son of Paul Galli-mard, a prosperous art collector whose house on Rue Saint-Lazare was lined with masterpieces. As a young man, Gaston inherited his father's tastes for the good life: the best tailor, beautiful women, the top restaurants, the theatre, and the skills for dealing in fine art. He had business instincts, a taste for liter-ature and – crucially – wealth. He was exactly the kind of person the *NRF* were looking for.

Gallimard eagerly accepted the offer, promptly borrowed 20,000 francs from an uncle, and became a partner in the fledgling publishing house Les Éditions de la NRF at 1 rue Saint-Benoît. Its first three books, released in 1911, were

Gide's *Isabelle*, Paul Claudel's *L'Otage* and Charles-Louis Philippe's *La Mere et l'enfant.* In 1912 the firm moved to 35 rue Madame. The following year they almost lost the publishing opportunity of a lifetime. A virtually unknown writer named Marcel Proust submitted a manuscript which was the first volume of what would become his masterpiece, À *la recherche du temps perdu (In Search of Lost Time)*, but the editorial board rejected it on the grounds that it was superficial, old fashioned, and too long. After further rejections Proust published the novel at his own expense, but as soon as the *NRF* editors saw the published book they realised their mistake. Proust later agreed that Les Éditions de la NRF could have it, but only if they agreed to publish it in its entirety. By the time of Proust's death in 1922, NRF had published the first four volumes of *À la recherche du temps perdu*. The last three were published posthumously, without Proust's final corrections and revisions.

In 1913, André Gide, who was worried that Les Éditions de la NRF was overextending itself, tried to have Gallimard replaced. In response Gallimard formed an editorial board, which in turn supported him and rejected the successor Gide was proposing. It also gave Gallimard a seat on the board and a voice in editorial decisions.

During World War I, in the spring of 1915, Gallimard had a physical and mental collapse and had to be hospitalised. But despite illness and the horrors of the war, Gallimard kept Les Éditions de la NRF afloat. Financially, things were bleak, but on the positive side they had signed Paul Valéry and acquired the French rights to the works of Joseph Conrad. The strained relations between Gide and Gallimard continued, but

André Gide seated and, from left to right, Jean Schlumberger, Jacques Rivière, and Roger Martin du Gard

slowly NRF emerged from the wilderness of war and survived. In July 1919 Les Éditions de la NRF was renamed Librairie Gallimard, and by the early 1930s it had become a publishing force to be reckoned with.

During the German occupation of France (1940–1944), the Nazis wanted control of the company, but Gallimard negotiated terms. He accepted the Nazi censorship lists, agreed to the appointment of a fascist editor for La Nouvelle Revue Française, and Jewish employees were removed from the staff. But Gallimard retained control of the publishing side. After the Liberation in 1944, there was a purge of collaborators and 50,000 French men and women were put on trial, with 1500 executed. *La Nouvelle Revue Française* was banned for a year, and Gaston Gallimard was threatened with being purged; however, his authors – notably Sartre and Camus – spoke up for him, and he was fully exonerated.

In later years Gaston Gallimard eventually relinquished the daily administration of the company to his son Claude and grandson Christian, but he was still actively involved until shortly before his death in 1975, aged ninety-four. Éditions Gallimard is the third largest publishing group in France, publishing approximately 750 new titles every year, with a backlist of over 17,000 titles.

See Also: Le Prix Goncourt, André Gide, Marcel Proust, Albert Camus, Jean-Paul Sartre, Antoine de Saint-Exupéry, Georges Simenon, André Malraux, Simone de Beauvoir, Jean Genet, Robert Brasillach.

Further Information: Michel Gallimard, Gaston's nephew, and Albert Camus were killed in a car crash in 1960. Gallimard's headquarters on Rue Sébastien-Bottin was renamed Rue Gaston-Gallimard in 2011, to mark the centenary of Éditions Gallimard.

Further Reading: P. Assouline, *Gaston Gallimard* (Éditions Balland, 1984).

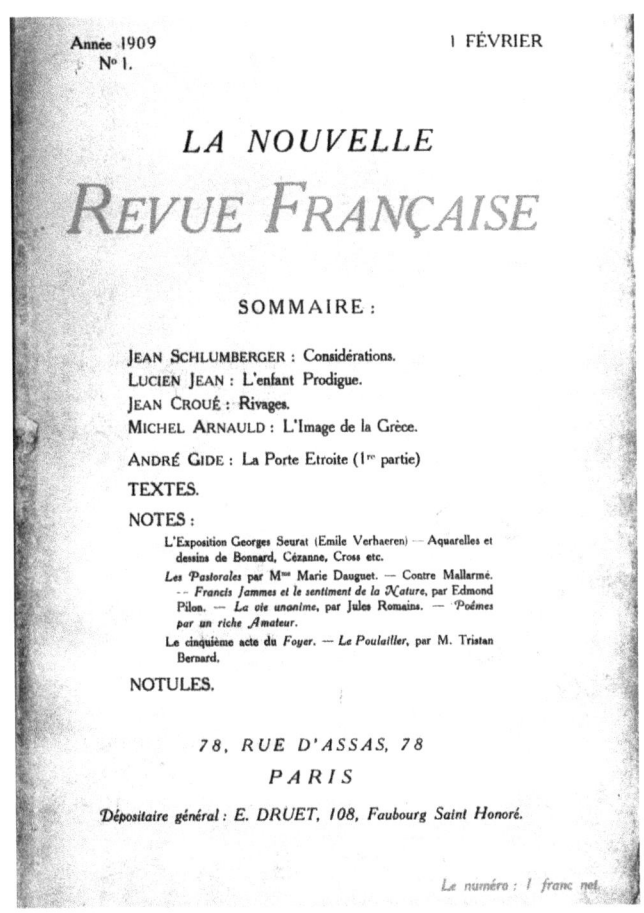

First edition of *La Nouvelle Revue Française*, February, 1909

305

WILLIAM SAROYAN

74 RUE TAITBOUT

(Métro: Trinité/Notre-Dame-de-Lorette)

**FORMER 6TH FLOOR APARTMENT
OF WILLIAM SAROYAN
ARMENIAN–AMERICAN DRAMATIST
AND SHORT-STORY WRITER**

*Good people are good because they've come
to wisdom through failure. We get very little
wisdom from success.*
William Saroyan

William Saroyan

Born in 1908 in Fresno, California, William Saroyan was the fourth child of Armenian refugees, and he spent most of his life writing about the Armenian–American experience. He was one of America's most talented and influential writers, achieving popularity during the 1930s with his first book, *The Daring Young Man on the Flying Trapeze*, which became an overnight success in 1934. Short stories, novels and plays followed, to great acclaim. In 1939 he was awarded the Pulitzer Prize for Drama for his play, *The Time of Your Life*. This he turned down, his rationale being that the arts should not be judged by commerce. He conquered Broadway and wrote for Hollywood, but after World War II his popularity waned and his outspoken, hard-boiled style of romanticism fell out of fashion; today he remains one of the twentieth century's most underrated and little read writers.
He first visited Paris in 1935 and was taken to a bordello near the Opera. '[The Madam] took me to a room', he wrote in *Places Where I've Done Time*, 'about the size of a circus ring ... a whole school of girls, stark naked except for jewelry and shoes, came into the room, smiling, and stood in a circle around me. All of a sudden I had everything, as well as truth.' He never found the bordello again, much to his dismay. In 1944 he was drafted into the Signal Corps, and was briefly posted to Paris, where his room-mate at the Hôtel Scribe was Irwin Shaw. By the early 1960s, determined to have a base in the city in order to find peace to write while at the same time distancing himself from his income tax debt of thousands of dollars, William Saroyan bought his dilapidated apartment on Rue Taitbout in the 9th arrondissement, home to the city's scattered Armenian community, where he divided his time between Paris and America for the next twenty years. Situated in a working-class neighbourhood, the apartment had neither elevator nor central heating, and the floorboards

had rot, but he had a soft spot for 'this old building which I have come to believe in and to love, although it is falling to pieces'.

A heavy drinker, an inveterate gambler and voice for the Armenian diaspora, William Saroyan wrote over sixty books, all of which reflect the fundamental goodness of people. In *Obituaries*, he wrote: 'My work is writing, but my real work is being.' He died of prostate cancer in 1981, aged seventy-two. 'Everybody has got to die,' he said, 'but I always believed an exception would be made in my case.'

See Also: Irwin Shaw, Hôtel Scribe.

Further Information: William Saroyan was twice married to actress Carol Marcus (1924–2003) with whom he had two children. Half of his ashes were buried in Fresno and the remainder in Armenia.

Select Bibliography: *The Daring Young Man on the Flying Trapeze* (1934); *My Heart's in the Highlands* (1939); *The Time of Your Life* (1939); *My Name is Aram* (1940); *The Human Comedy* (1943); *Tracy's Tiger* (1952); *I Used to Believe I Had Forever, Now I'm Not So Sure* (1968); *Letters from 74 rue Taitbout or Don't Go, But If You Must Say Hello To Everybody* (1969); *Obituaries* (1979).

Further Reading: L. Lee, B. Gifford, *Saroyan* (Harper & Row, 1984); J. Leggett, *A Daring Young Man: A Biography of William Saroyan* (Knopf, 2002); A. Saroyan, *Last Rites: The Death of William Saroyan* (Morrow, 1982); P. Hunter, *William Saroyan: Places in Time* (Craven St. Books, 2008); L. Hamalian, *William Saroyan: The Man and the Writer Remembered* (Fairleigh Dickinson Uni. Press, 1987); N. Balakian, *The World of William Saroyan* (Bucknell Uni. Press, 1998).

Rue Taitbout

PARIS *TRIBUNE*

5 RUE LAMARTINE

(Métro: Cadet)

FORMER OFFICES OF THE EUROPEAN
EDITION OF THE *CHICAGO TRIBUNE*

*In those days one could get a powerful lot
of refreshments for ten francs. At 7.45 he
staggered eastward towards the Panthéon
and I sashayed westward to the rue Lafayette
to the* Chicago Tribune *office, where another
drunken re-write man, more or less, made no
difference at all.*
Elliot Paul, *The Last Time I Saw Paris* (1942)

The origins of the *Chicago Tribune*'s
Paris edition hark back to the First
World War, when in 1917 its parent
paper in Chicago announced the issue
of an 'Army Edition' intended for the
American Expeditionary Forces who
were then entering the war in Europe.
When the war ended, it continued as the
European Edition, and became known
as the Paris *Tribune*, directed, in the
main, at Left Bank expatriates. A paper
'mostly written', wrote one of its journalists, 'and almost entirely read by the
bohemians of Montparnasse'.

Over the years its staff has included
many writers of outstanding literary
and journalistic talent, including Henry
Miller, James Thurber, Elliot Paul, Kay
Boyle, Waverley Root, Harold Stearns,
Eugene Jolas, Wambly Bald and William
L. Shirer. Many of them had their own
columns, notably Elliot Paul's 'From A
Litterateur's Notebook', Eugene Jolas's
'Rambles Through Literary Paris' and
Wambly Bald's 'La Vie de Bohème'.
Henry Miller had two brief jobs on the
Tribune, the first as a proofreader, an
experience he would recreate in *Tropic*
of Cancer, and later as an assistant
finance editor. 'The very atmosphere
of the place has gotten into my blood,'
wrote Miller. 'I miss it on my night off.
In the first place, it is a perfect maze of
machinery. The air is fetid. And then
there is the noise – a deafening noise,
and the blinding lights.'

In 1955 James Thurber reminisced about
the *Tribune* in *The Paris Review*:

> I remember Elliot Paul and I used to ar-
> gue about re-writing back in 1925 when
> we both worked for the Chicago Trib-
> une in Paris. It was his conviction you
> should leave the story as it came out of
> the typewriter, no changes. Naturally, he
> worked fast. Three novels he could turn
> out, each written in three weeks' time. I
> remember once he came into the office
> and said that a sixty-thousand-word
> manuscript had been stolen. No carbons
> existed, no notes. We were all horrified.
> But it didn't bother him at all. He'd just
> get back to the typewriter and bat away
> again.

The *Tribune*'s great rival was the Paris
edition of the *New York Herald*, a more
conservative and cautious paper, over
which the *Tribune* always tried to get
an exclusive. 'We invented our own
grotesque cable stories as fillers,' wrote
Eugene Jolas, 'and played gaily with
nerve-demoralizing headlines. But we
also tried especially to emphasize the
new intellectual and aesthetic develop-
ments in Paris, and whenever possible,
to scoop the *Herald* ... the disorder that
reigned in the editorial rooms was an
exact reflection of our state of mind.'

Journalists are renowned for inventing
the news, either through boredom,
necessity or just plain mischief. One
of the *Tribune*'s legendary concoctions
involved a reporter named Spencer Bull.

During the early 1920s the Prince of Wales arrived in Paris and one of his official engagements was to review a troop of British Boy Scouts. Bull wrote up his own account of events, which appeared in the *Tribune* the day after the Prince's review:

> Stopping before one manly youth the Prince inquired: 'What is your name, my lad?'
> 'None of your goddamned business, sir,' the youngster replied. At that, the Prince snatched a riding crop from his equerry and beat the boy's brains out.

The story, which slipped through the net of copy-editors and proofreaders, was published in the paper under the headline: 'Prince of Wales Bashes Boy's Brains Out with Bludgeon.' Fortunately for the *Tribune* the prince accepted an apology and did not sue. Spencer Bull was dismissed, and has since entered the annals of newspaper folklore.

During the early years of the Depression two Paris–American newspapers was a luxury that was no longer financially tenable. On 26 October 1934, the *Tribune* was sold to the Herald for $50,000, and became the *Herald Tribune*, evolving into the *International Herald Tribune* in 1967.

See Also: Elliot Paul, Eugene Jolas, Henry Miller, Kay Boyle, James Thurber, *Paris Herald.*

Further Information: Between the wars there were four English language newspapers published in Paris: the *Continental Daily Mail*, the *Times*, the *New York Herald* and the *Chicago Tribune*. The *Tribune* was located on the fourth floor at No. 5 rue Lamartine, where it used the print shop, distribution network, and floor space of the French paper, *Le Petit Journal*. The *Tribune* also maintained a public reading room and information office at No. 5 rue Scribe, where tourists could register their names and addresses in the paper's 'Arrivals' column to let their friends know they were in Paris.

Further Reading: R. Weber, *News of Paris* (Ivan R. Dee, 2006); H. Stearns, *The Street I Know* (Furman, 1935); H. Ford, *Published in Paris* (Garnstone, 1975); W. Shirer, *Twentieth Century Journey, Vol. 1* (Little Brown, 1984).

Jean-Paul Belmondo with Jean Seberg sporting a *Herald Tribune* top strolling down the Champs-Élysées in an iconic scene from Jean-Luc Godard's 1960 film, *À bout de souffle (Breathless)*

JEAN RHYS

44 RUE DE TRÉVISE

(Métro: Cadet)

HÔTEL DE HAVANE

FEATURED IN JEAN RHYS'S *QUARTET*

The hotel, which was called the Hôtel de Havane, was brand new. It smelt of paint and there were ladders and pails of whitewash on the staircase. Marya had often wandered about that part of Paris with Stephan when they lived in Montmartre, and she remembered the dingy streets, the vegetable shops kept by sleek haired women, the bars haunted by gaily dressed little prostitutes ...
Jean Rhys, *Quartet* (1928)

Jean Rhys

Today Jean Rhys is acknowledged as one of the outstanding writers of the twentieth century, but upon receipt of a major literary award in 1967, when she was in her mid-seventies, she observed ruefully, 'It has all come too late.' Most of her life's work was produced between 1928 and 1939, and during the next three decades she wrote very little until *The Wide Sargasso Sea*, a prequel to Charlotte Brontë's *Jane Eyre*, was published to great acclaim in 1966. Although its reception was a long overdue recognition of her genius, it was a curtain call 'too late' in a life of unhappiness and impoverishment.

Many of her early novels are set in Paris between the wars, where she lived in the early 1920s, but she was never part of the literary Left Bank and its expatriate cafe crowd. She was an outsider who unearthed her own Paris underworld of despair and degradation that inspired the doomed quality of many of her novels.

Born Ella Williams in 1890 on the Caribbean island of Dominica to a Welsh father and Creole mother of Scottish ancestry, she arrived in England to start boarding school in 1907, just prior to her seventeenth birthday. Compared to her Caribbean homeland, England was a bleak, cold and cheerless place: a country she would never have any deep affection for. After a brief spell at drama school and touring with a theatre company, she had her first affair in 1913, which resulted in an abortion, a story retold in her semi-autobiographical novel, *Voyage in the Dark*. In 1917 she met, and later married, Jean Lenglet, a Dutch-Frenchman with a questionable past.

In the summer of 1919 they both arrived in Paris and moved into a hotel on Rue Lamartine, near the Gare du Nord. Ella, who was by this time pregnant, soon got a job helping the children of a wealthy Parisian family to improve their English, but her husband's efforts to earn a living were often shrouded in secrecy. In December that year Ella gave birth to their son, who died three weeks later from pneumonia. An interval in Vienna and Eastern Europe followed, but Ella and Lenglet returned to Paris with their second child, a daughter, born in 1922. Meanwhile the police were running Lenglet to earth, and in 1923 he was arrested for fraud and imprisoned for eight months, and later expelled from France. During Lenglet's imprisonment Ella befriended English novelist and editor, Ford Madox Ford (1873–1939), who was at that time living in Paris with Australian artist, Stella Bowen (1893–1947). Ford was editor and publisher of the short-lived literary magazine, the *Transatlantic Review*, which had published many of the key modernists of the day, including Gertrude Stein, Ernest Hemingway, James Joyce and Djuna Barnes. After reading Ella's diaries Ford encouraged her to write, and in December 1924 her first published story, *Vienne*, appeared in the *Transatlantic Review* under the name Jean Rhys, a nom de plume suggested by Ford. She subsequently became Ford's lover in a suffocating *ménage à trois*, described in Rhys's novel *Quartet*:

What mattered was that, despising, almost disliking, love, he was forcing her to be nothing but the little woman who lived in the Hôtel du Bosphore for the express purpose of being made love to. A *petite femme*. It was, of course, part of his mania for classification. But he did it with such conviction that she, miserable weakling that she was, found herself trying to live up to his idea of her.

In 1927, Rhys's *The Left Bank and Other Stories*, with an introduction by Ford, was published by Jonathan Cape, and was the beginning of her most creative period, which lasted up until the outbreak of war in 1939.

Rhys divorced Lenglet in 1932 and went on to have two more disastrous marriages. Max Hamer, her last husband, was, like her first, jailed for fraud. She had always maintained that, had she had a happy life, she would never have wanted to write, but even her writing brought her little comfort in a life of straitened circumstances, alcohol and obscurity. Once, when contemplating suicide, she confided wryly in a letter to a friend:

Last night I was thinking 'If I could jump out of the window one bang and I'd be out of it.' For this is the sixth floor. Then I thought of Max's story of the old lady who went to church with her ear trumpet. And so the stern Scotch sexton or verger or something, eyed her a bit. Then he said 'Madam one toot and you're oot.' Perhaps that's what it would be like, One toot and you're oot.

See Also: Ford Madox Ford, *Transatlantic Review*, Gertrude Stein, Ernest Hemingway, James Joyce, Djuna Barnes.

Further Information: Jean Rhys died in Devon in 1979, aged eighty-eight, where she had lived for nineteen years in the village of Cheriton Fitzpaine: 'a dull spot which even drink can't enliven much'. Between 1967 and 1973 all her novels were reissued by André Deutsch and published in paperback by Penguin.

Select Bibliography: *The Left Bank and Other Stories* (1927); *Postures* (1928), (later known as *Quartet* (1929)); *After Leaving Mr. Mackenzie* (1931); *Voyage in the Dark* (1934); *Good Morning, Midnight* (1939); *Wide Sargasso Sea* (1966); *Sleep it Off Lady* (1976); *Smile Please* (1979).

Further Reading: F. Wyndham, D. Mell (eds.), *Jean Rhys Letters 1931–1966* (André Deutsch, 1984); S. Bowen, *Drawn From Life* (Virago, 1984).

ÉMILE GABORIAU

39 RUE NOTRE-DAME-DE-LORETTE

(Métro: Saint-Georges)

FORMER HOME OF ÉMILE GABORIAU, FATHER OF THE FRENCH DETECTIVE NOVEL, AND CREATOR OF MONSIEUR LECOQ

It is at the family fireside, often under the shelter of the law itself, that the real tragedies of life are acted; in these days traitors wear gloves, scoundrels cloak themselves in public esteem, and their victims die broken-hearted, but smiling to the last. What I have just related to you is almost an every-day occurrence; and yet you profess astonishment.
Émile Gaboriau, *File No. 113* (1867)

Émile Gaboriau

Émile Gaboriau is best remembered as the father of the *roman policier* (detective story) in France, a genre which today is a staple of the book world. But in Gaboriau's day, novels involving crime detection were virtually non-existent, and for good reason, as the Parisian police were generally despised. 'Even the ordinary street policeman', wrote Gaboriau, 'is the object of aversion; and the detective is loathed as intensely as if he were some monstrous horror.' Given this prejudice it seems fair to say that the reading public would be disinclined to bury themselves in stories about the forces of law and order. The public didn't bargain for Gaboriau's Monsieur Lecoq, however.

Lecoq was the antithesis of the conventional Parisian policeman. He could 'mould his features according to his will, as the sculptor moulds clay for modelling'. He was a master of disguise, who accused and criticised his fellow officers for incompetence and slipshod behaviour. The first fictional detective to mould a plaster cast of a footprint, he was egocentric, conceited and rather humourless, but above all, he was honest. Lecoq was partly inspired by Edgar Allan Poe's pioneering detective, Auguste Dupin, and by former criminal Eugène

François Vidocq, founder and first chief of the French crime detection unit, which evolved into the Sûreté Nationale. Émile Gaboriau was born in 1832 in the village of Saujon, Charente-Maritime, on the south-western coast of France. In 1855, after a spell in the military, he moved to Paris where he began writing for some small newspapers, soon becomimg secretary and ghostwriter for the novelist Paul Féval (1816–1887). Amongst other genres, Féval wrote crime fiction, and it was under his wing that Gaboriau learned the art of crime writing, and how to conduct investigative research, by touring the morgues, prisons and police courts. In 1866 he shot to fame when he published his first detective novel, *The Widow Lerouge*, and before long he had amassed a huge following. But he only lived for another seven years, dying of pulmonary apoplexy at 39 rue Notre-Dame-de-Lorette, aged forty, in 1873. During his short life he published over twenty novels, but his greatest creation was Monsieur Lecoq: 'We hold the clue; we follow it to the end. Onward, then.'

See Also: Eugène François Vidocq, Maurice Leblanc, Eugène Sue, Edgar Allan Poe.

Select Bibliography: *The Widow Lerouge* (1866); *File No. 113* (1867); *The Mystery of Orcival* (1867); *The Slaves of Paris* (1868); *Monsieur Lecoq* (1869); *Baron Trigault's Vengeance* (1870); *The Count's Millions* (1870); *Within an Inch of His Life* (1873); *Other People's Money* (1874).

Further Reading: E. Vidocq, *Memoirs of Vidocq, Vols. 1–4* (The first English edition of the series was started by Hunt & Clarke and taken over by Whittaker, Treacher & Arnot, 1828–1829); J. Symons, *Bloody Murder* (Pan, 1994).

BRICKTOP'S

1 RUE PIERRE FONTAINE

(Métro: Blanche/Pigalle)

SITE OF BRICKTOP'S
LEGENDARY NIGHTCLUB OF
ADA 'BRICKTOP' SMITH
QUEEN OF MONTMARTRE

T.S. Eliot expressed my life in those days better than I can. ... Somebody would usually ask me, 'Where were you born, Brick?' and I had this stock answer: 'On the fourteenth day of August 1894, in the little town of Alderson, West-by-God-Virginia, the doctor said, "Another little split-tail," and on that day Bricktop was born.'
T.S. Eliot ... added a line of his own:
... and on that day Bricktop was born,
And to her thorn, she gave a rose.
Ada Smith Ducongé (Bricktop) with James Haskins, *Bricktop* (1983)

The Jazz Age in Paris lasted roughly from 1914 to 1941, and one of its key players was Ada Smith (1894–1984), nicknamed Bricktop, because of her flaming red hair. The youngest child of an Irish father and a black mother, she served her apprenticeship singing and dancing in Chicago's saloons and cabarets. In 1924 she was invited to Paris to work for a small, ailing club called Le Grand Duc at 52 rue Pigalle (now Rue Jean-Baptiste Pigalle), one of the first nightclubs in Paris to perform jazz. Bricktop was shocked at the size of the place: '[It was] a tiny room that contained about twelve tables and a small bar that would feel crowded with six pairs of elbows leaning on it.' Waiting tables and dishwashing at the club, was a young black poet from Harlem named Langston Hughes, who described

Top: 1 rue Pierre-Fontaine
Bottom: Bricktop in her middle years

Bricktop on her arrival as 'short and freckled and slightly lighter than mustard. She was plainly dressed. She had reddish hair and was not very pretty. But she went around and met everybody in the place and shook hands with each one, and smiled. And you liked her right away.'

Business was often so bad at Le Grand Duc that on some nights Bricktop and the small band would play to a single customer. 'What made the difference', she wrote in her autobiography, 'was that the Montparnasse crowd of writers and artists discovered Le Grand Duc, led by F. Scott Fitzgerald.' Others followed in the wake of Fitzgerald (whom Bricktop described as 'a little boy in a man's body'), namely Ernest Hemingway, Louis Bromfield, Kay Boyle, T.S. Eliot, Robert McAlmon, Picasso and Cole Porter. 'My greatest claim to fame', wrote Scott Fitzgerald, 'is that I discovered Bricktop before Cole Porter.' Before long Bricktop was running the entire club, but she always yearned for 'a better-looking place', and in 1926 she moved to new premises across the street at 1 rue Fontaine. Undecided on a name for the new club, Cole Porter suggested she call it simply 'Bricktop's, [because] you're the reason why people come.' Bricktop's went from strength to strength, and its success in the early days was down to Cole Porter, who filled the club with his celebrated friends, from Noël Coward to the Aga Khan. Its performers over the years included Sidney Bechet, Louis Armstrong, Paul Robeson, Stéphane Grappelli and Django Reinhardt. Everyone who was anyone came to Brick's. The Jazz Age may not have been born here, but Bricktop's helped turn its status into art.

In Scott Fitzgerald's 1931 story, 'Baby-lon Revisited', his protagonist expresses a kind of passionate grief when returning to his debauched past:

After an hour he left and strolled towards Montmartre, up the Rue Pigalle into the Place Blanche. The rain had stopped and there were a few people in evening clothes disembarking from taxis in front of cabarets, and *cocottes* prowling singly or in pairs, and many Negroes. He passed a lighted door from which issued music, and stopped with the sense of familiarity; it was Bricktop's, where he had parted with so many hours and so much money.

See Also: F. Scott Fitzgerald, Ernest Hemingway, T.S. Eliot, Kay Boyle, Robert McAlmon, Langston Hughes.

Further Information: Rue Pierre-Fontaine was originally known as Rue Fontaine, but was renamed in 2004. In 1931 Bricktop moved to larger premises at No. 66 rue Pigalle and later went on to open nightclubs in Biarritz, Mexico City, Rome and New York. She was still performing in her eighties, and died in her Manhattan apartment in 1984, aged eighty-nine.

Further Reading: Bricktop with J. Haskins, *Bricktop* (McClelland & Stewart Ltd., 1983).

Ada Smith in 1917

GEORGE SAND

16 RUE CHAPTAL

(Métro: Blanche/Pigalle/St-Georges)

MUSÉE DE LA VIE ROMANTIQUE

DEVOTED TO GEORGE SAND

AND THE FRENCH ROMANTIC PERIOD

You ill-starred provincial, who have left your fields, your blue sky, your verdure, your house and your family, to come and shut yourself up in this dungeon of the mind and the heart – see Paris, lovely Paris, which in your dreams has seemed to you such a marvel of beauty! See it stretch away yonder, black with mud and rainy, as noisy and pestilent and rapid as a torrent of slime!

George Sand, *Indiana* (1832)

George Sand by Nadar, 1864

Remembered today for her uncon-ventional ways and her scandalous love affairs, George Sand was once France's bestselling writer, placed at the centre of French intellectual and artistic life. The risqué themes of sex, sexuality, incest, female independence and a woman's right to love, were recurring topics in her novels and plays and gained her wide critical acclaim. She wrote over sixty novels, twenty-five plays, an autobiography stretching to 1600 pages, and thousands of letters. George Eliot, Elizabeth Barrett Browning and the Brontë sisters were all influenced by her. Her circle of friends included Balzac, Flaubert, Delacroix, Liszt and Chopin. She wore men's clothes in public, smoked cigars and shocked society with her amoral behaviour, convincing many that she was a bisexual nymphomaniac. 'What a brave man she was', wrote Ivan Turgenev, 'and what a good woman'. The poet Charles Baudelaire, however, was not convinced. 'The fact that some men', he wrote, 'have been able to become infatuated with that latrine [George Sand] is proof of the degrada-tion of man this century.' But despite her horrified critics, which included the Church, none can deny she was a far-reaching rebel who, regardless of the restrictions thrust upon the women of her day, had a dazzling literary career and a remarkable life.

She was born Amantine Aurore Lucile Dupin in 1804, to Sophie Delaborde, a former prostitute, and Maurice Dupin, an aristocrat and soldier. Her father died when she was four, and she was raised by her paternal grandmother on her estate in Nohant, near Châteauroux in the heart of the Berry region, a location used in many of her novels. She was convent educated and in 1822 she mar-ried Casimir Dudevant (1798–1871), with whom she had a son and a daughter. The marriage failed and she moved to Paris to be with her lover, novelist Jules Sandeau (1811–1883), with whom she wrote some stories and the novel, *Rose et Blanche* (1831). Sandeau introduced her to the Parisian literary scene and it was from his surname that she took her pseudonym. In early 1832 she began writing her first independent novel, *Indiana*, which was published a few months later and became an instant bestseller. Other works soon followed, and her immense popularity as a writer enabled her to support herself and her family with her publications. Throughout her life she conducted affairs with many poets and artists, including dramatist Prosper Mérimée (1803–1870), novelist Alfred de Musset (1810–1857) and, most notably, the Polish composer, Frédéric Chopin (1810–1849), with whom she lived for over eight years. One of her most passionate love affairs was with a woman, the celebrated Parisian stage actress, Marie Dorval (1798–1849).

She remained a prolific writer up until the end of her life and became one of the most famous women of her time; but today, regrettably, it is only the myth of George Sand that is remembered. The real woman – subversive, modest, compassionate and honest in her writing – has been all but vanquished by the flamboyant legend. 'The world will know and understand me someday,' she wrote. 'But if that day does not arrive, it does not greatly matter. I shall have opened the way for other women.' She died on 8 June 1876, aged seventy-one. Shortly after her death her old friend and confidant, Gustave Flaubert (1821–1880) wrote to his friend Ivan Turgenev, 'At her funeral I cried like an ass.'

See Also: Jules Sandeau, Honoré de Balzac, Gustave Flaubert, Eugène Delacroix, Charles Baudelaire, Charles Dickens, Nadar.

Further Information: The Musée de la Vie Romantique was originally one of two workshops built alongside the Hôtel Scheffer-Renan, the townhouse of the Dutch painter Ary Scheffer (1795–1858). One workshop was his painting studio, and the other (now the Musée de la Vie Romantique) became a salon where Scheffer hosted his many guests, including Delacroix, Liszt, Rossini, Dickens, Chopin and George Sand. The museum houses documents and memorabilia relating to Sand, including furniture, paintings, *objets d'art*, jewellery and a plaster cast of Chopin's hand. The museum also contains paintings by Scheffer and his contemporaries.

Select Bibliography: *Indiana* (1832); *Valentine* (1832); *Jacques* (1833); *Lélia* (1833); *Mauprat* (1837); *Consuelo* (1842); *La Petite Fadette* (1849).

Further Reading: B. Jack, *George Sand, A Woman's Life Writ Large* (Vintage, 2001); G. Sand, *The Story of My Life* (State University of NY Press, 1991).

Musée de la Vie Romantique

ALFRED JARRY

55 RUE DE CLICHY

(Métro: Place de Clichy/Liège)

**LE THÉÂTRE DE L'OEUVRE
WHERE ALFRED JARRY'S
NIHILISTIC FARCE
UBU ROI PREMIERED IN 1896**

*Ah! What a marvellous evening the first
night of* Ubu Roi *has provided us with! Ever
since then, literature, art, and politics all
are impregnated with Ubu. One can smell
the perfume of Ubu everywhere. People fight
over Ubu and massacre each other over Ubu.*
La Revue Blanche

Often described as a precursor of
surrealism and the Theatre of the
Absurd, Alfred Jarry's work is characterised by his attacks on the conventions
of his day and by the grotesque. But he is
remembered today more for his eccentric
lifestyle – notably cycling around Paris
firing a pistol into the air, and living in
an apartment adorned with human skulls
– than for his literary works.

'Creatively he never grew up,' writes
Martin Seymour-Smith. 'His role is
rather one of a culture-hero than an important author in his own right. He was
rightly important to the surrealists; but
need not be as important to us. He is not
a hero of literature, but of the politics of
literature – and of nonconformity'.

Jarry was born in 1873 in Laval,
Mayenne, in north-west France, and
was educated in Rennes. His satirical
farce, *Ubu Roi* (King Ubu), was first
performed at the Théâtre de l'Oeuvre
in 1896, but its beginnings go back to
Jarry's schooldays in Rennes, when he
wrote a caricature of one of his pompous
masters and performed it as a puppet

Top: Alfred Jarry
Above: Artwork by Alfred Jarry *c.*1898

show when he was fifteen years old.
Ubu Roi, which outraged audiences,
ran for only two performances at the
Théâtre de l'Oeuvre. It did not make
Jarry's fortune, but it made his name,

318

which would be forever linked with notoriety and eccentricity. He went on to produce a cycle of *Ubu* productions and, eerily, he adopted the mannerisms of his character King Ubu: a squeaky voice, a puppet-like gait and extravagant dress. Gradually, he lost his own identity and disappeared into the character of his imagination. He also wrote novels, short stories and poems, and he invented a logic of the absurd which he called 'pataphysique', which he describes in full in his novel, *Gestes et opinions du docteur Faustroll* (1911). British poet Arthur Symons summed up his artistic objective perfectly when he wrote that Jarry was 'sweeping all art, along with all humanity, into the same inglorious slop-pail'. Jarry died of tuberculosis aggravated by alcoholism in 1907, aged thirty-four.

See Also: Surrealism, Dada, Arthur Symons, Oscar Wilde.

Further Information: Alfred Jarry is buried in the Cimetière de Bagneux (Division 23). Théâtre de l'Oeuvre was founded in 1893 by the French actor and theatrical producer, Aurélien Lugné-Poë (1869–1940). It made enormous contributions to the development of French theatre, staging the plays of Ibsen, Strindberg, Wilde, Claudel, and those of Dadaist and surrealist writers.

Select Bibliography: *Ubu Roi* (Exit Press, 2014); *Selected Works of Alfred Jarry* (Grove Press, 1965).

Further Reading: A. Brotchie, *Alfred Jarry: A Pataphysical Life* (MIT Press, 2015); R. Shattuck, *The Banquet Years: The Origins of the Avant Garde in France, 1885 to World War 1* (Random House, 1988).

Le Théâtre de l'Oeuvre

ARNOLD BENNETT

4 RUE DE CALAIS

(Métro: Place de Clichy/Blanche)

FORMER APARTMENT OF
ARNOLD BENNETT
ENGLISH NOVELIST AND PLAYWRIGHT
REMEMBERED FOR HIS STORIES SET IN
THE POTTERIES OF ENGLAND

The moment you're born you're done for.
Arnold Bennett

Arnold Bennett

Underrated although outdated today, Arnold Bennett (1867–1931) was once one of the most admired and successful novelists of his generation, whose books sold in huge numbers. He was born in the scarred and grimy landscape of the Potteries of Staffordshire, in England's industrial Midlands, where clean air in the nineteenth century was a rarity: an environment that not only hastened his escape south, but also inspired many of his works. The son of a solicitor, he became a solicitor's clerk in London and eventually moved into journalism. His first stories were published in *Tit-Bits* (1890) and the *Yellow Book* (1895), and his first novel, suitably entitled *The Man from the North*, was published in 1898.

To improve his writing skills and to study the arts, he moved to Paris in 1903, where he met and married his first wife, and where he lived for eight years. Initially he moved to the Hôtel du Quai Voltaire before finding permanent accommodation on Rue de Calais. 'Every afternoon and sometimes in the evening', he wrote, 'a distant violin used to play, very badly, six bars – no more – of an air of Verdi's over and over again;

never any other tune! The sound was too faint too annoy me, but it was the most melancholy thing that I have ever heard.' One of Bennett's Paris friends was Somerset Maugham, who recalled being offered a share in Bennett's mistress, which he refused, thinking it 'rather cold-blooded'. Maugham, who never liked Bennett much, described him as 'cocksure', 'bumptious', and 'rather common'. It took Bennett a few years to find real friends in Paris, and much of his early time there was a lonely, fish-out-of-water existence. Clive Bell sums up the impression Bennett made on the expatriates of the day in *Old Friends* (1956). 'He was the boy from Staffordshire who was making good and

320

in his bowler hat and reach-me-downs he looked the part. He was at once pleased with himself and ashamed – we rather liked him, but we thought nothing of his writing.' In Paris Bennett met Marguerite Soulié, his future wife: 'one of the most wonderful things that ever happened to me'. But the wonder did not last, and they separated in 1921. Bennett spent the rest of his life with actress Dorothy Cheston, with whom he had a daughter.

Bennett wrote over thirty novels, notably the *Clayhanger* series set in the Potteries; but he was also a successful playwright and an influential critic. Like many writers he needed to distance himself from his bleak roots in order to shape them into his own artistic reality, and like Joyce's Dublin or Stevenson's Scotland, they lived on in his imagination for the rest of his days, as did his sojourn in Paris. Bennett died aged sixty-three from typhoid fever two months after drinking a glass of tap water at a Paris restaurant in 1931. When Bennett lay dying in his London flat the police slowed down the traffic outside and swathed the street in straw to deaden the noise. It is believed to be one of the last occasions that this Victorian tradition was carried out. The menu at London's Savoy Hotel still lists an omelette named after him.

See Also: Somerset Maugham.

Select Bibliography: *Anna of the Five Towns* (1902); *The Old Wives' Tale* (1908); the *Clayhanger* trilogy – (*Clayhanger*, 1910, *Hilda Lessways*, 1911, *These Twain*, 1915); *The Card* (1911); *Riceyman Steps* (1923); *Lord Raingo* (1926).

Further Reading: M. Drabble, *Arnold Bennett* (Faber and Faber, 2009).

ANDRÉ BRETON

42 RUE PIERRE FONTAINE

(Métro: Blanche)

FORMER HOME OF ANDRÉ BRETON
WRITER, POET, CRITIC
AND FOUNDER MEMBER
OF THE SURREALIST MOVEMENT

The man who cannot visualise a horse galloping on a tomato is an idiot.
André Breton

Although André Breton (1896–1966) is usually referred to as co-founder of the surrealist movement along with Louis Aragon and Philippe Soupault, he was also its life force and backbone. Surrealism, a term created by Apollinaire, was his passion.

In its early years surrealism was a revolutionary artistic movement, created in part as a reaction to the carnage and pointlessness of World War I, demanding a reappraisal of everything that had gone before. It rejected a rational vision of life and adopted one that advocated the merit of the unconscious and dreams. It matured into an international movement attracting not only writers, but also film makers and artists such as Picasso, Miró, Man Ray, Magritte, and Dalí. Often out to shock, their individual interpretations of surrealism rarely had much in common, and each had their own definition of reality. Some were left wing revolutionaries and some, like Dalí, who was an admirer of Hitler and Franco, favoured the status quo and were politically right wing. Surrealism, therefore, was a great melting pot of the illogical in literature, painting, cinema and politics. Some even saw it as shaping the future destiny of the world. But it all ended with the death of its cornerstone, André Breton, in 1966.

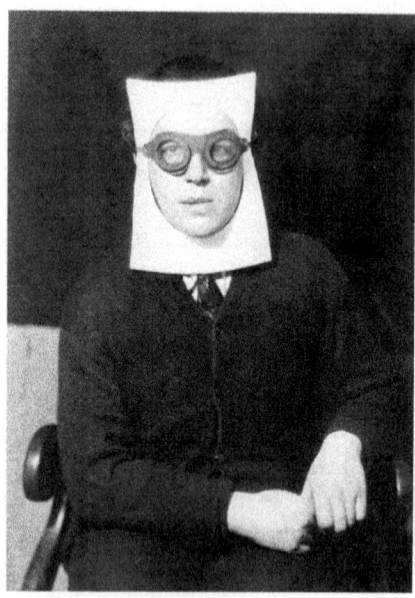

André Breton the Dadaist, 1930

Born in Normandy, Breton was the only child of a former seamstress and a ledger clerk. 'I believe I was very well brought up,' he wrote in his book *The Magnetic Fields*, adding, 'may it be said with rancor and hatred.' As a teenager he developed a fondness for reading and writing poetry, inspired by the works of Huysmans, Baudelaire, Mallarmé and Rimbaud. On leaving school he chose to study medicine, but in 1915 his studies ended when he was conscripted into the French military, and 'flung into a cesspool of blood, mud, and idiocy'. Basic training, combined with his minimal medical experience, made a nurse of him in the medical corps of the army. He worked in a number of psychiatric wards and, becoming interested in mental illness, he began to read the strongly influential Sigmund Freud, whom he would meet some time later, in 1921.

In 1916 Breton had become involved with the Dada movement, but after the war he settled in Paris where the now-waning Dadaist movement evolved into surrealism, the movement which was led by Breton, and to which he remained unswervingly loyal throughout his life. Breton was also one of the co-founders of the surrealistic journal *Littérature* in 1919, which featured automatic writing, the first written example of automatism, a method of creating art involuntarily and retrieving material from the subconscious mind. But the movement was officially launched with the publication of Breton's *Manifeste du Surréalisme (The Manifesto of Surrealism)* in 1924, encouraging writers and artists to reject social and moral conventions, and to embrace impromptu means of expression.

Amidst all this Breton was also writing poetry and fiction. The novel for which he is best remembered is his 1928 surrealist romance, *Nadja*. A committed Marxist, he joined the French Communist Party in 1927, later travelling to Mexico in 1938, where he met and collaborated with Leon Trotsky on *Manifesto for an Independent Revolutionary Art*. After the Nazi invasion of France, Breton fled to the USA in 1942 where he lived for several years in New York. He was married three times and lived in his Rue Pierre Fontaine apartment, on and off, from 1922 until his death in 1966. Breton was a great collector and his apartment was filled with thousands of items, including paintings, drawings, sculptures, photographs, books and manuscripts, most of which were auctioned off after his death. In 2008 Sotheby's in Paris sold a set of nine surrealist manuscripts by Breton, including *The Manifesto of Surrealism*, for 3.2 million euros.

See Also: Apollinaire, Louis Aragon, Robert Desnos, Stéphane Mallarmé, Tristan Tzara, Charles Baudelaire, Arthur Rimbaud, Dada.

Further Information: André Breton is buried in Paris's Batignolles Cemetery, Division 31. Place André Breton, at the intersection of Rue de Douai and Rue Pierre Fontaine, was inaugurated in 2005. In 1939 Breton expelled Salvador Dalí from the surrealist community over concern for Dalí's 'obsessions', namely his fondness for Hitler and apparent endorsement of fascism.

Select Bibliography: *Selected Poems* (Penguin, 1969); *What is Surrealism?: Selected Writings* (Pathfinder, 1978); *Mad Love* (Bison, 1988); *Nadja* (Penguin, 1999); *Manifestoes of Surrealism* (University of Michigan Press, 1972).

Further Reading: M. Polizzotto, *Revolution of the Mind: The Life of André Breton* (Black Widow Press, 2017).

LE CHAT NOIR
84 BOULEVARD DE ROCHECHOUART

(Métro: Anvers)

SITE OF THE ORIGINAL LE CHAT NOIR MONTMARTRE'S FIRST MODERN CABARET

Degrading.
Composer Erik Satie's comment on his time as Le Chat Noir's resident pianist from 1888 to 1891

The founding in 1881 of the artistic cabaret, Le Chat Noir, changed the face of Montmartre forever, and it was the beginning of a transformation that would eventually turn it into Paris's first modern entertainment quarter. The roots of this change lay in the construction in 1784 of a customs wall around the city, whose checkpoints imposed heavy taxes on products entering Paris. Montmartre, then with a population of around 400, took advantage of the situation and transformed itself into the archetypal frontier town, supplying cheap booze, dance halls and other pleasures of the night. Meanwhile, the population of Paris was exploding and the city was becoming cramped and expensive. Those who could no longer afford to live there flooded into the cheaper suburbs and engulfed Montmartre. The artists settled on La Butte, and lower Montmartre, especially around Pigalle, became an area of drinking dens, crime and prostitution. What changed everything and, in its way, diffused these social divisions, was the birth in the late nineteenth century of Montmartre's cabarets and music halls, which attracted a new audience: the

323

Théophile Steinlen's iconic Le Chat Noir poster

A drawing of Théophile Steinlen by Adolphe Willette (1857–1926)

well-heeled and cultured middle class. The first of these cabarets was Le Chat Noir.

The origins of Le Chat Noir grew out of a meeting between the artist, Rodolphe Salis (1851–1897), and writer, Émile Goudeau (1849–1906), who had founded the Club des Hydropathes, which was a platform for bohemian writers and artists with a thirst for culture washed down with alcohol to read and discuss their work. Unfortunately, the club's Left Bank venue had been forced to close due to rowdy behaviour, and Goudeau was on the lookout for a new one. Salis proposed they use his studio on Montmartre's Boulevard de Rochechouart; and so Le Chat Noir was born.

Thanks to the talents and entrepreneurship of Salis, the Hydropathes's artistic drinking forums were taken to another level, creating something unique for its time: the first modern cabaret. It was a mix of theatre, music, readings, political commentary, shadow plays and satire, with Salis as impresario. The formula proved a great success and attracted a diverse clientele, including artists, writers, journalists, students, prostitutes, grandes dames and the bourgeoisie. Writers who read on the floor in its early days included Guy de Maupassant, Paul Verlaine, Stéphane Mallarmé, Léon Bloy, Jean Lorraine, and dramatist Villiers de l'Isle-Adam. But amongst all this avant-garde entertainment and talent, the real cabaret stars were the *chansonniers*, a blend of comedian and monologuist, the most famous of which was Aristide Bruant. Dressed in his characteristic black cape, red scarf and wide-brimmed hat, he would later be immortalised on the posters of Le Chat Noir by Toulouse-Lautrec.

By 1885 Le Chat Noir had outgrown Salis's old studio on Boulevard de Rochechouart and moved to larger premises nearby, at No. 12 rue Laval (now Rue Victor Massé), where Salis converted the interior to resemble a 'fashionable country inn'. The third, and final, location of Le Chat Noir, was at No. 68 boulevard de Clichy. By the 1890s the popularity of the cabaret began to wane and was eventually supplanted by the music halls.

See Also: Céline, Guy de Maupassant, Paul Verlaine, Stéphane Mallarmé.

Further Information: In 1882 Salis launched the journal *Le Chat Noir*, and in the late 1880s published his *Contes du Chat Noir* (Stories from Le Chat Noir). A series of four volumes was proposed, but only two were ever published. The site of Le Chat Noir at No. 84 boulevard de Rochechouart is marked by a *Histoire de Paris* plaque. A few surviving relics from Le Chat Noir can be viewed at the Musée de Montmartre on Rue Cortot, including some zinc plates from its shadow theatre, and Adolphe Willette's 1884 painting *Parce Domine*, which he painted for Le Chat Noir. Its most famous surviving artefact is Théophile Steinlen's (1859–1923) iconic Le Chat Noir poster, which is now part of Parisian folklore and adorns everything from postcards to tacky souvenirs: a fitting tribute to a graphic design masterpiece.

Further Reading: R. Salis, *Contes du Chat Noir: L'Hiver* (Dentu, 1888); *Contes du Chat Noir: Le Printemps* (Dentu, 1891); P. Cate & M. Shaw (eds.), *The Spirit of Montmartre: Cabarets, Humor, and the Avant-Garde, 1875–1905* (Rutgers University Press, 1996); A. Fields, *Le Chat Noir: A Montmartre Cabaret and Its Artists in Turn-of-the-Century Paris* (Santa Barbara Museum of Art, 1993).

Aristide Bruant

Henri de Toulouse-Lautrec, 1892

10th

Arrondissement

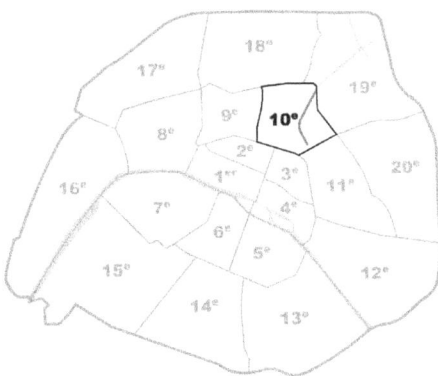

CYRANO DE BERGERAC

18 BOULEVARD SAINT-MARTIN
(Métro: Strasbourg–St-Denis)

THÉÂTRE DE LA PORTE SAINT-MARTIN
WHERE EDMOND ROSTAND'S PLAY
CYRANO DE BERGERAC **WAS FIRST**
PERFORMED IN 1897

In the early hours of 29th December, 1897, late strollers along the Boulevard Saint Martin, in Paris, witnessed extraordinary scenes. Knots of people were forming and reforming outside the Porte-Saint-Martin Theatre, which had only just shut its doors. They were laughing, crying, gesticulating, embracing – and none of them seemed to want to go home. Those who were present on that momentous occasion would always feel a special bond between them, as if they had been present at a miracle. The play whose première they had just been watching had finished late because

of constant interruptions for applause and encores. Even then the audience had refused to leave, demanding one curtain call after another. The young author was, however, too shy to appear. He had slipped out of the theatre and into a cab...
Sue Lloyd, *The Man Who Was Cyrano: A Life of Edmond Rostand, Creator of Cyrano de Bergerac* (2007)

So familiar are audiences today with the romantic legend of Cyrano de Bergerac, portrayed in novels, plays and film, that few realise this eccentric character was a real person. Descended from Sardinian immigrants, he was born Savinien de Cyrano in Paris in 1619 to Abel de Cyrano, a lawyer, and Espérance Bellanger. In later life, by taking the name 'de Bergerac' from a family estate outside Paris near where he was born, Savinien erased his relatively undistinguished roots and metamorphosed into

327

Gascon nobleman, Cyrano de Bergerac. The body of information available about the real Cyrano is slim, and with the fictional Cyrano always lurking in the shadows, historical researchers have often unwittingly entwined myth with fact. The real Cyrano, however, was certainly a celebrated swordsman who fought many duels, and he did have a prominent nose. He joined the military, but he was also a freethinker and writer of plays, poetry and science fiction novels, notably *Histoire comique contenant les états et empires de la lune* and *Histoire comique des états et empires du soleil* (published posthumously in 1655 and 1657 respectively). In these fantastic voyages the author journeys to the moon and the sun where he meets their inhabitants and experiences their customs, satirising the social issues of his day. His works inspired Molière, Voltaire, Jonathan Swift, Jules Verne and H.G. Wells. A talented writer, an academic, a legendary soldier, and very much a controversial figure in his day, Cyrano was much more than the chivalrous and lovesick two-dimensional knight errant popular history has framed him as.

The legend of the Cyrano we know today originates from the five-act tragicomedy in verse, *Cyrano de Bergerac* written by Edmond Rostand, which captivated the world stage in 1897 and has served as the model for all future creators of Cyrano's fictional life. The success of the play turned Rostand into a national hero, for which he was awarded the Légion d'honneur. After just a matter of weeks the printed edition of the play was in its sixth edition, and Cyrano-branded products appeared all over Paris, on everything from wine to chocolate bars. The triumph of *Cyrano de Bergerac* had restored French national pride and

Edmond Rostand

created a fiction that no facts, no matter how unshakeable, could ever topple.

Edmond Rostand was born on 1 April 1868 in Marseilles, the only son of a wealthy Provençal family. He studied law in Paris, but never practised, preferring to pursue a career as a poet and dramatist. His early efforts failed, but in 1894 the Comédie-Française staged his verse play *Les Romanesques*, based on *Romeo and Juliet*, to great success. His future plays had a mixed reception from critics and audiences, even when the great Sarah Bernhardt starred in them, but Bernhardt had confidence in Rostand and encouraged him to keep writing. Moderate success came in 1897 with *La Samaritaine*; by now he was slowly climbing the ladder of fame. But it was *Cyrano de Bergerac*, premiered at the Théâtre de la Porte Saint-Martin in 1897 that made him, along with Cyrano, immortal. And although Rostand kept writing accomplished plays, notably *L'Aiglon* (1900) and *Chantecler* (1910) – often under great pressure to repeat his amazing success – he would never again achieve the triumph of *Cyrano*. He died of pneumonia on 2 December 1918, aged fifty, leaving a wife and two sons. The real Cyrano died in 1655 unaware of his future immortality, and it's not known if he ever visited the town of Bergerac in Gascony. Nonetheless, the town exploits his fictitious Gascon pedigree to the full. Here you can tune into Cyrano FM, stay at the Cyrano Hotel, visit the Cyrano cinema, hire a cab from the Cyrano taxi company, or just watch the world go by on Cyrano Street. Two statues have also been erected to the town's hero, the older of the two frequently seen minus its celebrated proboscis, chipped off by trophy hunters and drunks. As the saying goes: when the legend becomes fact, print the legend.

See Also: Comédie-Française, D'Artagnan, Molière, Voltaire, Jules Verne.

Further Information: The original Théâtre de la Porte Saint-Martin was destroyed by fire during the Paris Commune of 1871. The new theatre where *Cyrano* was premiered was built in 1873 and was designed by architect Oscar de la Chardonnière. Cyrano de Bergerac died in Sannois, a commune in the north-western suburbs of Paris. His bronze bust, created by the sculptor Dan-Robert, can be found on Boulevard Charles de Gaulle. The Edmond Rostand Museum is located at Villa Arnaga in Cambo-les-Bains, Rostand's former home in the Basque province of Labourd, south-western France. Edmond Rostand is buried in the Cimetière Saint-Pierre, Marseille. Cyrano's final resting place remains unknown.

Select Bibliography: *Cyrano de Bergerac*, translated by A. Burgess (Nick Hern Books, 1991); *L'Aiglon*, translated by L. Parker, (Wildside Press, 2011); *Chantecler* (Genge Press, 2010).

Further Reading: I. Addyman, *Cyrano: The Life and Legend of Cyrano de Bergerac* (Simon & Schuster, 2009); S. Lloyd, *The Man Who Was Cyrano: A Life of Edmond Rostand, Creator of Cyrano de Bergerac* (Genge Press, 2007).

Top: An engaving of Cyrano de Bergerac by Zachary Heince, *c.*1654

Above: French actor Constant Coquelin (1841–1909), the original Cyrano, who first played him in 1897, subsequently performing the role over 400 times

11th

Arrondissement

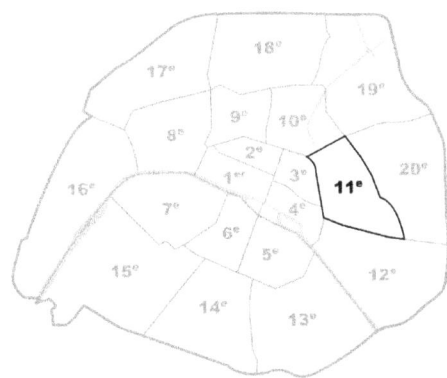

LA BASTILLE

PLACE DE LA BASTILLE

(Métro: Bastille)

SITE OF THE BASTILLE
PLACE OF IMPRISONMENT
AND INSPIRATION FOR WRITERS
THROUGHOUT HISTORY

Once in the Bastille, there is no afterwards.
Alexandre Dumas, *The Three Musketeers*
(1844)

The Bastille was built in the mid four-teenth century as an eight-towered fortress to protect the eastern part of the city from English attack during the Hundred Years War. It stood on the site of the Place de la Bastille, now one of the main squares of Paris. Although primarily a fortress, it also served periodically as a prison, and by the time of Louis XI's reign (1461–1483) it was used predominantly as a penal institution. Remembered today as a symbol of tyranny and torture, and a flashpoint of the French Revolution, most people's conception of this grim fortress is derived from literary portrayals, which were often inventive and far removed from the hard facts of history.

It was Dickens who gave audiences the definitive image of Bastille life in *A Tale of Two Cities* (1859), probably the most enduring and romanticised version of the French Revolution ever written. A tale of revenge and forgiveness, the Bastille is recalled in all its horror through the madness and pain of Doctor Manette who was locked up for years in a cell in the North Tower:

I, Alexandre Manette … write this melancholy paper in my doleful cell in the Bastille, during the last month of the year, 1767. I write it at stolen intervals, under every difficulty. I design to secrete it in the wall of the chimney, where I have slowly and laboriously made a place of concealment for it. Some pitying hand may find it there, when I and my sorrows are dust.

The most mysterious inmate the Bastille has ever held was the prisoner who became known as The Man in the Iron Mask, whose life was fancifully fictionalised by Alexandre Dumas in 1847. We know very little about this prisoner because of the secrecy that surrounded him, and to date nobody has solved the mystery of his identity, but hearsay, theories and counter-theories abound, ranging from his being the twin brother of Louis XIV to the Emperor of China. What we do know is that he wore a mask at all times, most likely of velvet, and that he arrived at the Bastille in 1698 having come from the fortress prison on Île Sainte-Marguerite. At the Bastille he was confined in a solitary cell where he died in 1703. He was buried, still wearing his mask, in the cemetery of Saint Paul. The register of deaths entered his name as unknown.

The Bastille, however, was not all doom and gloom. It even had a small library, and if you were wealthy enough you could still enjoy all your home comforts, from vintage wines to a four-poster bed. 'I only took with me two valets and a cook,' commented the Maréchal de Biron on his confinement in 1631. During his five-year stretch (1784–1789) in the Bastille the Marquis de Sade complained relentlessly in his letters about the unpalatable prison food 'to one accustomed to a dainty table', but Bastille archives reveal his menus often consisted of oysters, pâtés, truffled chickens, pigeons, brandy and wine. It was in the Bastille that Sade wrote *The 120 Days of Sodom*, a catalogue of sexual perversions that remained unpublished until the latter half of the twentieth century. Considered by many to be Sade's masterpiece, he wrote it in his cell on a twelve-metre long roll of paper.

Another famous inmate of the Bastille was writer and philosopher, François-Marie Arouet, known by his pen name Voltaire. Best known as a satirist, his cutting wit often landed him in trouble. In 1717 he was imprisoned for almost a year in the Bastille for accusing France's regent, the Duke of Orléans, of incest, and in 1726 he found himself back in the Bastille after a dispute with Parisian nobleman, the Chevalier de Rohan. His second stay, however, only lasted a few weeks until he was exiled to England.

The storming of the Bastille by crowds on the morning of 14 July 1789 was not concerned with the release of its inmates (there were only seven inside); it was about the gunpowder stored there. Thousands of muskets without powder and shot had been acquired that day by partisans, and the Bastille had a massive store of it. Hundreds were killed in the ensuing attack and the prison governor was beheaded. The King had been out hunting that day and, much to his regret, had killed nothing. When he was told what had happened at the Bastille, the King replied, 'Is this a revolt?' His advisor answered, 'No Majesty, this is a revolution.'

See Also: Victor Hugo, Charles Dickens, Alexandre Dumas, Marquis de Sade, Voltaire, Guillotine, *Les Misérables*.

Further Information: After the Bastille fell in July 1789, its ruins were cleared and many of its stones were used to build the Pont de la Concorde or sold off as souvenirs. In 1792 the site was turned into a square dedicated to liberty, and many suggestions were mooted for its centerpiece. In 1811 Napoleon decreed that a gigantic monument of an elephant be erected, 24 metres high and cast in bronze using metal from captured canon. A full-sized plaster model was duly erected on the spot and remained there for many years, rat-ridden and falling into ruin. Victor Hugo, in his novel *Les Misérables*, described it as 'unclean, despised, repulsive, and superb', making it the home of the novel's street urchin, Gavroche. The elephant was finally demolished to make way for the Colonne de Juillet (July Column), which was inaugurated in 1840 to commemorate the July Revolution of 1830. The outline of the Bastille is marked in the square's cobblestones.

A steel engraving of the full-scale plaster model that was intended as a bronze centre-piece to mark the site of the Bastille, but was never fulfilled

The storming of the Bastille by Jean-Pierre Houël (1735–1813)

12ᵗʰ
Arrondissement

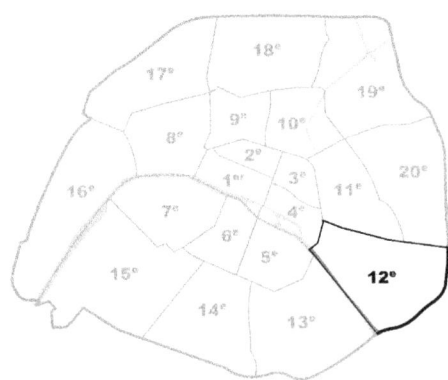

GARE DE LYON
20 BOULEVARD DIDEROT

(Métro: Gare de Lyon)

**WHERE THE PARIS–DIJON EXPRESS
ARRIVED IN 1922 WITH THE FIRST TWO
COPIES OF JAMES JOYCE'S *ULYSSES***

*Ulysses is the most important contribution
that has been made to fictional literature in
the twentieth century ... It is likely that there
is no one writing English today that could
parallel Mr. Joyce's feat, and it is also likely
that few would care to do it if they were
capable.*
Joseph Collins, *New York Times* (1922)

When Sylvia Beach, proprietor of
the bookshop Shakespeare and
Company, offered to publish James
Joyce's *Ulysses* she had no idea of the
magnitude of the task ahead of her. She
was a bookseller, not a book creator, but
her shop gave birth to one of the most important books in the history of literature.
Joyce was hoping to see the first copy
around the time of his fortieth birthday
on 2 February 1922. After countless difficulties, which included Joyce writing
a third more text on the page proofs,
Maurice Darantière, the book's Dijon
printer, completed two editions which he
dispatched on the Paris–Dijon express,
due to arrive in Paris at seven o'clock on
the morning of 2 February. 'I was on the
platform,' Beach wrote, 'my heart going
like the locomotive, as the train from
Dijon came slowly to a standstill and I
saw the conductor getting off, holding a
parcel and looking around for someone
– me.' She was handed a large parcel,
which she excitedly opened. Inside were
two copies of *Ulysses* in their distinct
cobalt blue covers. Copy number one
she handed into Joyce's pension at No.

9 rue de l'Université (now Hôtel Lenox), and copy number two, which was her personal copy, went on display in the window of Shakespeare and Company in Rue de l'Odéon. She later calculated that in the 732 pages of the first two copies there were one to half-a-dozen typographical errors per page. But who cared? The book, after a long and arduous journey, was at last in print. Janet Flanner summed up the occasion when she wrote that the book 'burst over the Left Bank like an explosion in print whose words and phrases fell on us like a gift of tongues, like a less than holy Pentecostal experience.'

See Also: Sylvia Beach, James Joyce, Janet Flanner, Ernest Hemingway, Ezra Pound.

Further Information: Gare de Lyon was also where Ernest Hemingway's first wife, Hadley, was robbed. On 2 December 1922, she arrived at the station to board an overnight train to Lausanne, Switzerland, to join her husband for a mountain holiday. She thought she would bring along his manuscripts as a surprise, for him to work on over the holiday. She packed everything she could find into a valise, including the pages of his first unfinished novel. When she boarded the train and found her compartment, she discovered the valise was missing. A search was made of the train, but to no avail: the valise had been stolen. When she met Hemingway at Lausanne station and tearfully broke the news, the loss of three years' work hit Hemingway like a ton of bricks. Ezra Pound's advice to his friend was that he should look on the loss as an 'act of Gawd'. The Gare de Lyon was built in 1900 for the World Exposition and is renowned for its architecture, notably that of Le Train Bleu restaurant in the main hall.

Gare de Lyon

Clockwise: James Joyce, Sylvia Beach, Hadley Hemingway, Maurice Darantière

336

13th

Arrondissement

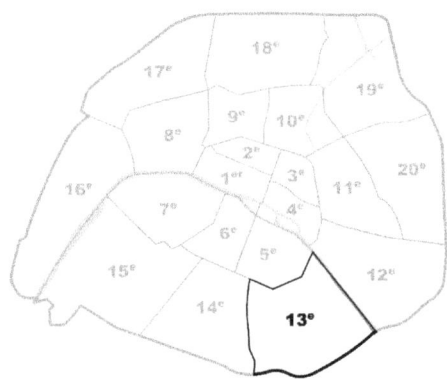

BIBLIOTHÈQUE NATIONALE DE FRANCE

QUAI FRANÇOIS-MAURIAC

(Métro: Bibliothèque François Mitterrand)

THE FRANÇOIS-MITTERRAND
LIBRARY

In October, while the Sorbonne was closed, I spent my days in the Bibliothèque Nationale ... From time to time I would look up at the other readers and lean back proudly in my armchair: among these specialists, scholars, researchers, and thinkers I felt at home. I no longer felt myself to be rejected by my environment; it was I who had rejected it in order to enter that society – of which I saw here a cross-section – in which all those minds that are interested in finding out the truth communicate with each other across the distances of space and time. I, too, was taking part in
the effort which humanity makes to know, to understand, to express itself: I was engaged in a great collective enterprise which would release me for ever from the bonds of loneliness. What a victory!
Simone de Beauvoir reminiscing about the BNF at Rue de Richelieu, in *Memoirs of a Dutiful Daughter* (1958)

The origins of the National Library of France go back to the fourteenth century, when, in 1368, Charles V founded his royal library, the Bibliothèque du Roi (King's Library), at the Louvre Palace. Charles was a book lover who had a great passion for the written word and for collecting the very best of it. The library was enriched, plundered and dispersed over the years by Charles's heirs, and in 1544 François I moved the library to Fontainebleau. From 1537 it received a copy of every

French publication, as it does to this day. It first opened to the public in 1692, and in 1721 the library was moved to the Mazarin Palace in the Rue de Richelieu. During the French Revolution it mercifully escaped destruction, but when the First Republic was founded in 1792 the Assembly declared that it was now no longer the property of the Crown, but of the French people and they named it the Bibliothèque Nationale. In 1896 the library became the largest repository of books in the world, and by 1920 the library's collection contained over four million volumes and eleven thousand manuscripts. During World War II more than two million books were lost in the conflict, and thousands

more were seized and confiscated by the Germans. From 1868, for almost 130 years, the major collections were held at the Rue de Richelieu, but in 1996 the new François-Mitterrand Library was inaugurated at Quai François-Mauriac where it is now one of the largest and most modern libraries in the world.

See Also: Bibliothèque Mazarine, Bibliothèque de l'Institut de France, Bibliothèque Sainte-Geneviève, The American Library in Paris, Simone de Beauvoir, Sylvia Beach.

Further Information: The Bibliothèque Nationale is spread across four sites in Paris: Richelieu-Louvois Library, 58 rue de Richelieu; François-Mitterrand Library, Quai François-Mauriac; Arsenal Library, 1 rue de Sully; Opéra Library, Place de l'Opéra.

In the print department of the Bibliothèque Nationale, 1897

WILKIE COLLINS

47–83 BOULEVARD DE L'HÔPITAL

(Métro: St-Marcel/Gare d'Austerlitz)

HÔPITAL DE LA SALPÊTRIÈRE
WHERE MADAME DE DOUHAULT,
INSPIRATION FOR WILKIE COLLINS'S
THE WOMAN IN WHITE,
WAS UNLAWFULLY CONFINED

This is the story of what a Woman's patience can endure, and what a Man's resolution can achieve.
If the machinery of the Law could be depended on to fathom every case of suspicion, and to conduct every process of inquiry, with moderate assistance only from the lubricating influences of oil of gold, the events which fill these pages might have claimed their share of the public attention in a Court of Justice.
Wilkie Collins, *The Woman in White* (1859)

English author Wilkie Collins (1824–1889) was an immensely popular writer in his day, but he was more a great storyteller than a great novelist. His plots were gripping and inventive, and were the bedrock of the Victorian genre known as 'sensation fiction', which is composed of mysterious, romantic, and suspenseful plots riddled with guilty secrets, aristocratic villains, heroines in danger, bigamy, poison and a gory death. Collins, with *The Woman in White*, is considered the innovator of the 'sensation novel'. As well as having an ingenious and engrossing plot it is also recognised as the first full-length detective story in English. It was immensely popular with its Victorian audience.

One of Collins's closest friends and collaborators was Charles Dickens, who serialised much of Collins's work

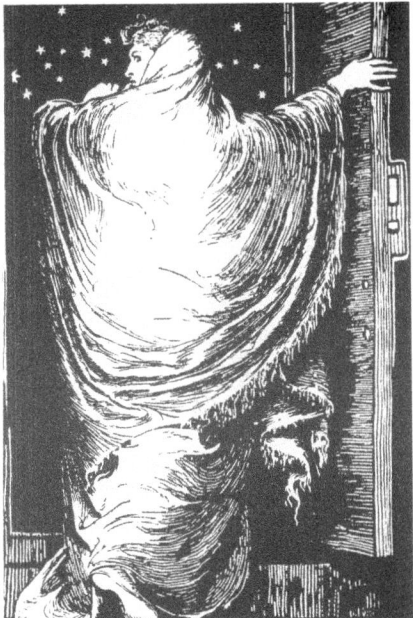

Top: Wilkie Collins Above: Poster advertising the stage version of *The Woman in White*

339

in his journal *All the Year Round*, the sales of which were boosted, thanks to *The Woman in White*, from around 40,000 to over 250,000. Dickens, who was enthralled by the novel, wrote him a letter of congratulation, signing himself Collins's 'obedient disciple'. The two of them often travelled together throughout Europe, and the disreputable corners of Paris were among their favourite haunts. In March 1856 while Collins was browsing the second-hand books of the bouquinistes – the riverside bookstalls along the Seine – he came across copies of Maurice Méjan's *Recueil des Causes Célèbres*, a collection of criminal archives published in 1808, or in his own words 'some dilapidated volumes of French crimes'. These volumes were to provide the crux of some of his best plots, including that of *The Woman in White*, which he based on the case of Madame de Douhault, who was unlawfully confined to the Salpêtrière asylum for the incurably insane in the late eighteenth century.

In 1764 Adélaïde de Champignelles (1741–1817) was married to the Marquis de Douhault. It was an unhappy and abusive marriage, during which time the marquis slowly descended into madness, no doubt relieving his wife of a great burden when he died in 1787. A few years previously, when Adélaïde's father had died, her recalcitrant and grasping brother had seized most of the father's estate, much of which rightfully belonged to Adélaïde and her mother and sister. In December 1787, Adélaïde left her home in Chazelet in central France on a proposed journey to Paris to resolve the matter, but before her departure she wrote a letter to a friend, Madame de Polignac, informing her of her intentions.

Accompanied by a coachman, a chambermaid and a servant, she stopped at Orléans to lodge with a nephew. The nephew, however, persuaded her to stay with Madame de la Roncière, another relative who lived a short distance away. On 15 January 1788, the day before she was due to continue her journey to Paris, Adélaïde went for a drive along the banks of the Loire with Madame de la Roncière. During the drive she was offered a pinch of snuff that gave her a violent headache and put her to sleep. When she awoke from her slumber, which she believed lasted for several days, she found herself in Paris's Salpêtrière insane asylum, registered under the name of Blainville. With Adélaïde now presumed dead, her brother and a few colluding heirs dissolved the estate. Any letters Adélaïde wrote from the asylum were seized by the authorities, but in June 1789, almost one and a half years later, she managed to smuggle out a letter to Madame de Polignac, and through the efforts of her friend she gained her release.

Collins's plot treads similar ground, where the evil Count Fosco plots to rob Laura of all her property by erasing her identity and confining her in an asylum. The novel also reveals how women in Victorian society were at the mercy of their husbands and often unprotected by the law. In the late 1850s the English novelist Edward Bulwer-Lytton had his perfectly sane wife, Rosina, committed to a lunatic asylum. Following a public enquiry, she was released a few weeks later. Wilkie Collins dedicated *The Woman in White* to the man who had helped secure Rosina's release. Predictably, perhaps, Bulwer-Lytton described *The Woman in White* as 'trash'.

See Also: Les Bouquinistes, Charles Dickens.

Further Information: The Salpêtrière was originally a gunpowder works, where a mine for saltpetre (potassium nitrate), a component of gunpowder, had existed. In the mid 1600s it was demolished and replaced with a hospital, which, a hundred years later, would become the world's largest hospital, capable of accommodating 10,000 patients. By the early nineteenth century it had gained a reputation as an innovative psychiatric hospital.

Today it is an acclaimed centre for teaching medicine, and is still one of Europe's largest hospitals.

Select Bibliography: *Basil* (1852); *The Woman in White* (1860); *No Name* (1862); *Armadale* (1866); *The Moonstone* (1868).

Further Reading: C. Peters, *The King of Inventors: A Life of Wilkie Collins* (Secker & Warburg, 1991).

Top: French neurologist, Jean-Martin Charcot, known as 'the founder of modern neurology' demonstrates hypnosis on a Salpêtrière patient (André Brouillet, 1897)
Above: Hôpital de la Salpêtrière

FORD MADOX FORD

65 BOULEVARD ARAGO

(Métro: Glacière)

Ford Madox Ford and Stella Bowen

LA CITÉ FLEURIE,
FORMER HOME OF FORD MADOX FORD
ENGLISH NOVELIST, CRITIC AND EDITOR
FOUNDER OF *THE TRANSATLANTIC
REVIEW*, AND A MAJOR INFLUENCE
ON EARLY TWENTIETH-CENTURY
LITERATURE

*We are all so afraid, we are all so alone, we
all so need from the outside the assurance of
our own worthiness to exist.
So, for a time, if such a passion come to frui-
tion, the man will get what he wants. He will
get the moral support, the encouragement,
the relief from the sense of loneliness, the
assurance of his own worth. But these things
pass away; inevitably they pass away as the
shadows pass across sun-dials. It is sad, but
it is so. The pages of the book will become
familiar; the beautiful corner of the road will
have been turned too many times. Well, this
is the saddest story.*

Ford Madox Ford, *The Good Soldier* (1915)

La Cité Fleurie

Ford Madox Ford had a varied and extremely productive career that lasted
over forty years, during which time he
published over eighty books. He also
had a talent for befriending, collaborating with, and discovering writers, many
of whom would go on to shape the future
of twentieth-century literature. Today
he is a sadly neglected writer, possibly
because of the vast variety of his work,
which ranges through novels, memoirs,
children's books, poetry, criticism, travelogues and literary history. He was also
a braggart and a liar who made an utter
mess of his life. Stella Bowen, his partner of many years, wrote: 'Ford's weakness of character, unfairness, disregard
of truth, and vanity must be accepted.
… On the other hand, his tenderness,
understanding, wisdom (about anything
that didn't apply to himself!) and the
tremendous attraction of his gorgeous
mind, must make him always regretted.'
He was born Ford Hermann Hueffer
in 1873 in Surrey, England, the eldest
child of German émigré, Francis Hueffer, and Catherine Madox Brown. He
would change his name to Ford Madox
Ford in 1919, ditching his German
surname, which had attracted too much
unpleasant attention during and after
the war. He had considered becoming

a composer, but eventually decided on a literary career, and his first book, *The Brown Owl*, a book of fairy stories, was published in 1891. In 1894 he eloped with, and married, his girlfriend Elsie Martindale, with whom he had two daughters. By the early 1900s his novels were gaining in popularity, and in 1908 he founded and edited the literary magazine, *The English Review*. The same year he began a relationship with feminist writer, Violet Hunt, which, like his marriage to Elsie, would eventually collapse amid a desperately complicated and ongoing emotional life.

In 1915 he joined the army and published *The Good Soldier*, the novel he regarded as his greatest achievement and for which he is best remembered.

Suffering from shell shock during the Battle of the Somme, he was invalided home, where he met Australian artist Stella Bowen. They set up home together in Sussex where Ford attempted pig farming, but shortly after their daughter was born, the harsh English winters and the failure of the farm drove them to France.

They arrived in Paris in September 1923, and settled into a cottage in the artist's colony at La Cité Fleurie (The Flowered City). Here, Bowen recalled that:

> in those warm early autumn days when we first began to feel the exhilaration of being in Paris, it was fun to lead people down [the] yellowing greenery of the little winding path behind the studios and give them tea in the tiny room with the shabby divan and the big French windows, and the sun pouring through the hanging sprays of creeper.

It was while living at La Cité Fleurie that Ford was inspired to create *The Transatlantic Review*, a monthly literary magazine. It only published twelve issues, during 1924, but it had a huge impact on early modernist literature, publishing the works of James Joyce; Gertrude Stein; Ernest Hemingway; Hilda Doolittle (HD); E.E. Cummings; Djuna Barnes; Ezra Pound, who helped Ford establish the *Review*; and Jean Rhys, who lived for a time at Ford's cottage and with whom he had a brief affair.

All the while Ford was still writing, and in the same year the *Review* was launched he published the first part of his major work of fiction now known as *Parade's End*, the success of which eventually took him to America and the lecture tour circuit in the late 1920s. Stella Bowen and Ford separated in 1928, and he spent the remainder of his turbulent life with American painter Janice Biala. He died in Deauville, on 26 June 1939, aged sixty-five, leaving behind his legacy as one of the great pioneers of modernism.

See Also: Jean Rhys, Ezra Pound, Amedeo Modigliani, James Joyce, Djuna Barnes, Ezra Pound, E.E. Cummings, Ernest Hemingway, Gertrude Stein, Three Mountains Press.

Further Information: La Cité Fleurie is a collection of around thirty artists' studios, located between Nos. 61 and 67 boulevard Arago and Rue Léon-Maurice-Nordmann, which were built between 1878 and 1888 using materials from one of the pavilions at the 1878 Exposition Universelle (World's Fair). Artists who have lived and worked here include Paul Gauguin and Amedeo Modigliani. A plaque at the entrance pays tribute to the Deutsche Freiheitsbibliothek (German Library of Freedom) founded by German émigré writers opposed to Hitler's practice of banning and burning books. More than 11,000 books banned by the Nazis were stored here from 1934 to 1939. In the 1980s, La Cité Fleurie came under threat from de-

developers, but the resulting public protest has, to date, successfully safeguarded its future.

Select Bibliography: *The Fifth Queen* trilogy (1906, 1907, 1908); *The Good Soldier* (1915); *Parade's End* tetralogy (sometimes known as 'Tietjens' tetralogy, published in four parts between 1924 and 1928); *Return to Yesterday* (1932).

Further Reading: A. Mizener, *The Saddest Story: A Biography of Ford Madox Ford* (Harper & Row, 1971); A. Judd, *Ford Madox Ford* (Flamingo, 1991); M. Saunders, *Ford Madox Ford: A Dual Life* (Oxford, vols. 1 & 2, 2012); R. Ludwig (ed.), *Letters of Ford Madox Ford* (Princeton University Press, 2015); S. Stang (ed.), *Correspondence of Ford Madox Ford and Stella Bowen* (Wiley, 1994).

14ᵗʰ
Arrondissement

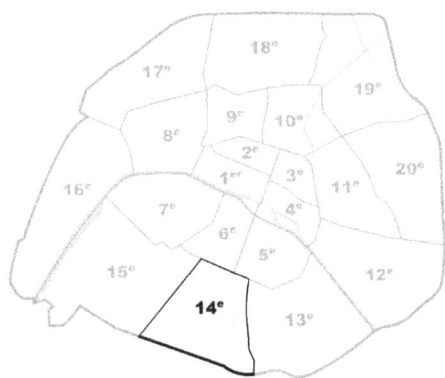

LE DÔME CAFÉ

108 BOULEVARD DU MONTPARNASSE

(Métro: Vavin)

When I have nothing better to do I take a taxi and go and sit in the old Café du Dôme. It is no longer what it was then, the meeting place exclusively of Bohemia, the small tradesmen of the neighbourhood have taken to visiting it, and strangers from the other side of the Seine come to it in the hope of seeing a world that has ceased to exist. Students come to it still, of course, painters and writers, but most of them are foreigners, and when you sit there you hear around you as much Russian, Spanish, German, and English as French. But I have a notion that they are saying very much the same sort of things as we said forty years ago, only they speak of Picasso instead of Manet and of André Breton instead of Guillaume Apollinaire. My heart goes out to them.

Somerset Maugham, *The Razor's Edge* (1944)

Founded in 1898, and located at the south-west corner of the Montparnasse–Raspail intersection, Le Dôme became known as 'the Anglo-American café', the favourite haunt of expatriate artists and writers. Through Hemingway's rose-coloured spectacles in *A Moveable Feast* (1964) he proclaims Le Dôme to be a more reputable hang-out than the other neighbourhood watering holes because its clientele is made up of 'serious and working artists rather than poseurs and layabouts', yet in a 1920s article he wrote for the *Toronto Star* he had described the Americans who went there as 'nearly all loafers expending the energy an artist puts into his creative work in talking about what they're going to do'. But whether 'serious' or 'poseur', Le Dôme's clientele, or Dômiers as they were known, was nothing, over the years, if not international, and included Kahlil Gibran, Max Ernst, Aleister Crowley, Robert Capa, Henry Miller, Ezra Pound, Anaïs Nin, Simone de Beauvoir and Somerset Maugham.

'From 1930 to 1939 I went regularly to the "Dôme" in Montparnasse', wrote Jean-Paul Sartre,

> As I was a teacher and hadn't much money I lived in a hotel; and like all people who live in hotels I spent most of the day in cafés. In 1940 the 'regulars' of the Dôme began to go elsewhere, for two reasons: the Métro station 'Vavin' was closed, and we had to make our way to the Dôme in the evenings, in complete darkness and on foot from the Gare Montparnasse. Besides, the Dôme was overrun with Germans, and these Germans were tactless enough to bring their own tea and coffee, and to have these prepared and served in front of us Frenchmen, who were already reduced to drinking some anonymous and ghastly substitute.

Le Dôme, like most expatriate enclaves, was not an ideal place for practising one's French, and as American writer Sinclair Lewis observed, 'all the waiters understand Americanese, so that it is possible for the patrons to be highly expatriate without benefit of Berlitz. It is, in fact, the perfectly standardized place to which standardized rebels flee from the crushing standardization of America.'

See Also: Henry Miller, Ernest Hemingway, Anaïs Nin, Simone de Beauvoir, Jean-Paul Sartre.

LA COUPOLE

102 BOULEVARD DU MONTPARNASSE

(Métro: Vavin)

'A piece of notepaper with the top cut off,'
observed Maigret. 'No doubt to get rid of a
printed heading.'
'Exactly. I thought so at once, and I thought
it would most likely have been written in a
cafe. I took it to Moers, who claims to know
the notepaper of most of the cafes in Paris.'
'Could he spot it?'
'It didn't take him ten minutes. This sheet
came from the Coupole, on Boulevard Mont-
parnasse. I've just been there. Unfortunately,
they have a thousand customers a day if they
have one, and at least fifty ask for writing
materials.'
Georges Simenon, *La Tête d'un homme*
(1931)

La Coupole opened its doors for business on 27 December 1927, advertising itself as a 'Bar Americain'. With its vast and airy interior, high ceilings, basement dancehall, and art deco pillars and walls, it soon became one of the favourite watering holes of the Montparnasse artistic community, including Ernest Hemingway, Colette, Jean Cocteau, Louis Aragon, André Malraux, Picasso, Simone de Beauvoir and the prolific Georges Simenon, creator of Maigret.

Occasionally Simenon would write his crime novels in the locality in which they were set. In March 1931 he booked himself into Montparnasse's Hôtel Aiglon on Boulevard Raspail and wrote *La Tête d'un homme (A Battle of Nerves)*. One of the novel's main locations was La Coupole, where Inspector Maigret first encounters its main protagonist.

American novelist Kay Boyle wrote about a visit to La Coupole in August 1929, during which time she conversed with Gascon, the barman and part-owner, observing that, 'without his handsome presence, his quiet generosity to artists, his beguiling smile, and his white-lipped fury for any kind of violence, the Coupole would have been a quite undistinguished place.'

See Also: Ernest Hemingway, Colette, Jean Cocteau, Louis Aragon, André Malraux, Picasso, Simone de Beauvoir, Georges Simenon, Kay Boyle.

BLACK MANIKIN PRESS

4 RUE DELAMBRE

(Métro: Vavin)

SITE OF EDWARD TITUS'S BOOKSHOP,
AT THE SIGN OF THE BLACK MANIKIN
HOME OF BLACK MANIKIN PRESS
AND LITERARY MAGAZINE
THIS QUARTER

How was I to know all those writers were worth a sou ... I never had a moment to read their books ... and I always had to pay for their meals! ... [Joyce] smelled bad ... couldn't see ... ate like a bird ... [Hemingway was] a loud-mouth and a show-off. Women liked him, but I didn't.

Helena Rubinstein, wife and benefactor of Edward Titus.

Polish-born American journalist Edward Titus had a distinct financial advantage over literary Paris in the 1920s: he was married to one of the world's richest women, cosmetics entrepreneur Helena Rubinstein (1862–1965). In Paris they lived at separate addresses – Rubinstein in a palatial house on the Île Saint-Louis, and Titus in a modest apartment at 4 rue Delambre. Described variously by Rubinstein's biographers as a waster, a dandy and a womaniser, Titus was also, thankfully for literary Paris, a book lover. In 1924, subsidised by his wife, he opened a shop dealing in rare books, named At the Sign of the Black Manikin. By 1926 Titus had begun transforming his enterprise into a publishing house that evolved into Black Manikin Press, which went on to publish such notable works as *Ladies Almanack*, by Djuna Barnes, D.H. Lawrence's *Lady Chatterley's Lover*, and the English version of *Kiki's Memoirs*, translated from the French by Samuel Putnam. In the late 1920s Titus began making plans to publish a quarterly literary magazine that would be 'devoted to encouraging the modern young American and English writers in Paris', and in the spring of 1929 he acquired and revived, albeit to his own agenda, the ailing magazine *This Quarter*. Founded by Ethel Moorhead and Ernest Walsh in 1925 'to publish the artist's work while it is still fresh', it was devoted to the rising stars of modernism, including Ernest Hemingway, Kay Boyle, James Joyce, Djuna Barnes, Ezra Pound, Eugene Jolas and many unknown novices. With Titus at its helm, the unpredictability and experimental edge was lost, but the magazine thrived nevertheless, and its future, though limited, was assured. In 1932 Titus published the final number of *This Quarter*, and with it, the last publication of Black Manikin Press, Anaïs Nin's *D.H. Lawrence, An Unprofessional Study*. Titus's place in the literary history of Paris was guaranteed; however, following his retirement to the countryside with his new wife, he never again returned to the literary scene of Montparnasse.

See Also: James Joyce, Ernest Hemingway, Anaïs Nin, Djuna Barnes, Ezra Pound, Eugene Jolas.

Further Information: Edward Titus and Helena Rubinstein married in 1908 and had two sons. After their divorce in 1938 Titus married a Swiss heiress and Rubinstein married Russian Prince Artchil Gourielli-Tchkonia, becoming Helena Princess Gourielli.

Further Reading: H. Ford, *Published in Paris* (Garnstone, 1975); J. Glassco, *Memoirs of Montparnasse* (NYRB Classics, 2007).

ERNEST HEMINGWAY
AND SCOTT FITZGERALD

10 RUE DELAMBRE

(Métro: Vavin)

AUBERGE DE VENISE

FORMERLY THE DINGO BAR

WHERE ERNEST HEMINGWAY FIRST MET

SCOTT FITZGERALD IN THE SPRING OF

1925

Walking ten feet or so ahead of me was Flossie, both of us on our way from the Dôme to the Dingo. As Flossie came abreast of the bar entrance, a handsome Rolls-Royce drove up to the curb and from it stepped two lavishly dressed ladies.
For a moment they hesitated. They looked at the Dingo questioningly. They peered in the windows between the curtains.
Flossie, seeing them, looked her contempt. As she passed into the bar she tossed a single phrase over her shoulder: 'You bitch!'
Whereupon the lady so addressed nudged her companion anxiously. 'Come on, Helen,' she said, 'This must be the place!'
Jimmie 'The Barman' Charters, *This Must Be The Place* (1934)

Hemingway wrote about his first meeting with Scott Fitzgerald in his memoir, *A Moveable Feast*, published posthumously in 1964, which recalls his life in Paris after World War I. In it he captures the Paris of the expatriates and his then idyllic marriage to his first wife, Hadley Richardson, with whom he appeared to live in romantic poverty with their baby son, Jack (Bumby). It is an excellent read; nonetheless, Hemingway's sentimental idealism conveys a somewhat suspect recollection of a period of his life more than thirty years previously. He summed up the work in its preface when he wrote: 'If the reader prefers, this book may be regarded as fiction.' And yet, the main criticism that has been aimed at the narrative over the years is not concern over its blurring of fact and fiction, but with Hemingway's scathing attacks on his contemporaries, most notably his savage portrayal of Scott and Zelda Fitzgerald. In fairness to Hemingway, *A Moveable Feast* was written in the late 1950s, at a time when he was drifting into the dementia that would lead, tragically, to his suicide in 1961.

According to Hemingway, Fitzgerald was drunk when he arrived at the Dingo Bar with a friend, baseball pitcher

Duncan (Dunc) Chaplin. Hemingway, who was sitting at the bar, described Fitzgerald as,

> a man then who looked like a boy with a face between handsome and pretty. He had very fair wavy hair, a high forehead, excited and friendly eyes and a delicate long-lipped Irish mouth that, on a girl, would have been the mouth of a beauty. … The mouth worried you until you knew him and then it worried you more.

Fitzgerald talked incessantly about the greatness of Hemingway's writings, much to the discomfiture of Hemingway, who believed that 'praise to the face was open disgrace'. Hemingway focused instead on Fitzgerald's well-fitting Brooks Brothers clothes, his white shirt and Guard's tie, noting his light build, his short legs and 'capable-looking hands', and his faintly puffy-faced appearance.

Getting drunker and drunker, Fitzgerald started interrogating Hemingway: 'Tell me, did you and your wife sleep together before you were married?' This was when, wrote Hemingway, 'the strange thing happened … [Fitzgerald's] eyes sank and began to look dead and the lips were drawn tight and the color left the face so that it was the color of used candle wax.' Thinking he was dying, Hemingway suggested taking Fitzgerald to a first aid station, but Dunc assured him that 'that's the way [champagne] takes him', and Fitzgerald was bundled into a taxi.

Fitzgerald was reading Hemingway long before their first meeting that day in the Dingo Bar. In October 1924 Fitzgerald had written to editor Max Perkins: 'This is to tell you about a man named Ernest Hemingway who lives in Paris, (an American) writes for the Transatlantic Review & has a brilliant future.' Fitzgerald died almost a quarter of a century before the publication of *A Moveable Feast*, unaware of his friend's character assassination of him and never able to set the record straight.

See Also: Ernest Hemingway, Scott Fitzgerald.

Further Information: Le Dingo, originally a simple workmen's bistro, became popular with English and American expatriates. It was also where Jimmie 'The Barman' Charters, one of the city's most famous bartenders of the period, worked in the early 1920s. 'I'm told', wrote Charters in his memoir, 'the unpaid bills over a nine-year period in the Dingo totalled half a million francs.' The Dingo Bar is, at the time of writing, an Italian restaurant, but the original mahogany bar can still be seen inside.

Further Reading: E. Hemingway, *A Moveable Feast* (Arrow, 2011); J. Charters, *This Must Be The Place* (Macmillan, 1989).

EDGAR ALLAN POE

RUE DE L'OUEST

(Métro: Pernety)

CRIME SCENE OF THE FIRST FRENCH
TRANSLATION OF EDGAR ALLAN POE'S
'THE MURDERS IN THE RUE MORGUE'
THE WORLD'S FIRST MODERN
DETECTIVE STORY

Poe's paternity of the detective story is not in dispute, but his fatherhood was unintended. He thought his mistress was Art, but really she was Sensation.
Julian Symons, *Bloody Murder* (1992)

Edgar Allan Poe in 1849

Edgar Allan Poe (1809–1849) chose to name his fictitious street in Paris after the house of the dead to generate terror in the reader and to lend atmosphere to his tale. French social reformer Victor Considerant, writing in 1845, just four years after the publication of 'The Murders in the Rue Morgue', described Paris as 'an immense workshop of putrefaction, where misery, pestilence and sickness work in concert, where sunlight and air rarely penetrate. [It is] a terrible place where plants shrivel and perish, and where, of seven small infants, four die during the course of the year.' Paris, therefore, was not yet a city of light; it was a city of darkness, disease and death: what better habitat for the birth of the world's first modern detective story? The short story 'The Murders in the Rue Morgue' was first published in 1841 by the Philadelphia periodical, *Graham's Magazine*, where Poe was the editor. Five years later it was published in France in serial form by the Parisian newspaper, *La Quotidienne* (The Daily), but the French translator failed to appreciate the allure of the fictional 'Rue Morgue', and changed the street name to Rue de l'Ouest, a real street in Montparnasse. It was a brutal transformation that appeared, nevertheless, to do no harm and woke the French up to the talents of Edgar Allan Poe, with better translations soon following in *La Quotidienne*'s clumsy wake.

The plot of 'The Murders in the Rue Morgue' revolves around an unnamed narrator who, in an 'obscure library in the Rue Montmartre' meets and befriends a man named C. Auguste Dupin who has a brilliant analytical mind. Shortly afterwards they both read about a horrible murder in the Rue Morgue where a mother and daughter are found dead. The daughter's strangled body has been thrust up the chimney of their locked apartment, and the mother's body found in the courtyard beaten to

351

death, with her throat so severely cut that her head falls off when the police try to move her. Money is found in their apartment, ruling out robbery as a motive. Also found is a blood-stained razor and locks of human hair, seemingly pulled out at the roots. Witnesses from the building agree they heard two voices: one, a Frenchman's deep voice; and the other a higher voice whose origin was unknown to them.

After examining the crime scene and finding a strand of hair that is not human, Dupin concludes that the witnesses were not hearing a high-pitched human voice at all but that of an 'Ourang-Outang' who entered the locked apartment through the window and killed both women. The deep Frenchman's voice was that of the ape's master, a sailor who had captured the animal in Borneo and returned with it to Paris, but who now had difficulty keeping it under control. Fleeing into the streets clutching his master's razor, the errant ape had been pursued by the sailor to the Rue Morgue whereupon it slashed the throat of the mother and strangled the daughter.

Today 'The Murders in the Rue Morgue' is credited with being the first modern detective story and the first locked-room mystery, but it also became a template for the fictional detectives of the future, whose exploits, like those of Dupin, would be faithfully written down by their admiring, yet dull-witted associates, notable among whom are Sherlock Holmes's Dr Watson, and Hercule Poirot's Captain Hastings. And so the golden age of the detective story was born.

See Also: Eugène François Vidocq, La Morgue, Charles Baudelaire, Stéphane Mallarmé, Paul Verlaine, Arthur Rimbaud.

Further Information: The character C. Auguste Dupin was based on Eugène François Vidocq (1775–1857), reformed criminal and founder of the French Sûreté. Poe described his stories as 'tales of ratiocination' (forming judgements by a process of logic). The word 'detective' did not come into existence until two years after the publication of 'The Murders in the Rue Morgue' when the then British Home Secretary, Sir James Graham, authorised the establishment of a Detective Department at Scotland Yard. One of Poe's biggest fans was Charles Baudelaire who translated many of his works into French. Others included Stéphane Mallarmé, Paul Verlaine and Arthur Rimbaud.

French criminologist, Edmond Locard (1877–1966), created France's first forensic science laboratory in Lyon in 1910. One of his strangest cases involved a series of jewel thefts in which the thief entered through upper-floor windows in daylight and stole just one item of jewellery, ignoring any other gems. Locard, who had obviously read Poe, summoned all the city's organ grinders to police headquarters and fingerprinted their performing monkeys. The monkey whose prints matched those at the crime scenes spent the rest of its days in the local zoo. The organ grinder was jailed.

Select Bibliography: 'The Fall of the House of Usher' (1839); 'The Murders in the Rue Morgue' (1841); 'The Masque of the Red Death' (1842); 'The Pit and the Pendulum' (1842); 'The Gold-Bug' (1843); 'The Tell-Tale Heart' (1843); 'The Purloined Letter' (1844).

Further Reading: J. Meyers, *Edgar Allan Poe: His Life and Legacy* (John Murray, 1992); N. Barnes, *A Dream Within A Dream: The Life of Edgar Allan Poe* (Peter Owen, 2009); D and T Hoobler, *The Crimes of Paris* (Little, Brown and Company, 2009); J. Symons, *Bloody Murder* (Pan, 1994); C. Emsley, *Police Detectives in History, 1750–1950* (Routledge, 2006).

JEAN GENET

42 RUE DE LA SANTÉ

(Métro: Saint-Jacques/Glacière)

LA SANTÉ PRISON
THE NOTORIOUS PENAL INSTITUTION
WHERE JEAN GENET BEGAN HIS FIRST
NOVEL *OUR LADY OF THE FLOWERS*

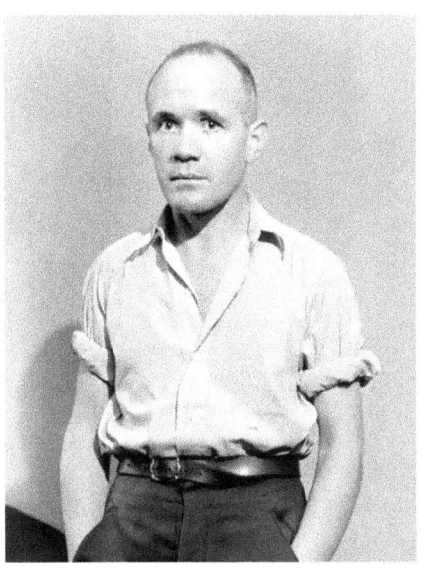

Jean Genet in 1947

Our Lady of the Flowers, *which is often considered to be Genet's masterpiece, was written entirely in the solitude of a prison cell ... French prison authorities, convinced that 'work is freedom', give the inmates paper from which they are required to make bags. It was on this brown paper that Genet wrote, in pencil,* Our Lady of the Flowers. *One day, while the prisoners were marching in the yard, a turnkey entered the cell, noticed the manuscript, took it away, and burned it. Genet began again. Why? For whom? ... Yet he wrote on, he persisted in writing. Nothing in the world mattered to him except those sheets of brown paper which a match could reduce to ashes.*
Jean-Paul Sartre

Thief, beggar, pimp, homosexual prostitute, convict, novelist and playwright, Jean Genet was an artistic outlaw who became a legend. His unique literary world evoked his experiences of life among the Paris underworld and years of imprisonment for petty thieving. He brought to life fantasies and nightmares employing unadulterated and powerful poetic prose drawn from his own anguish and loneliness as an outcast. 'On the planet Uranus', he writes in *Journal du voleur (The Thief's Journal)*,

it seems the atmosphere is so heavy ... that the animals drag themselves about crushed by the weight of the gases. It is

with these humiliated creatures always crawling on their bellies that I want to mingle. If in the transmigration of souls I am granted a new dwelling place, I shall choose that cursed planet to inhabit it with the convicts of my race.

Jean Genet was born at the Tarnier Childbirth Clinic, 89 rue d'Assas, Paris, on 19 December 1910. Six months later, his mother, Camille Genet, abandoned him to a children's home where he became a ward of the state. His father remains unknown. His childhood was spent with foster parents in the Massif Central, where his life of petty crime began at the age of ten when he was accused of thieving. Three years later, he began a short-lived apprenticeship as a typographer in Paris. Having fled the position after only ten days, he was found in Nice and subsequently taken to a children's home in Paris. Successive runaway attempts followed, as well as placements in other homes and psychiatric clinics. Having established

353

La Santé Prison (Eugène Atget, 1898)

himself as a petty thief, he was eventually sentenced to two-and-a-half years at Mettray Penal Colony, an open prison for boys.

'It was not at any particular period of my life that I decided to be a thief,' he writes, in *Journal du voleur*. 'My laziness and my daydreaming having led me to the *maison correctionelle* at Mettray, where I was to stay till I was twenty-one, I escaped, and to gain the signing-up bonus, joined up for five years.'

From 1929 until 1942 Genet led an erratic and itinerant life of stints in the army, which consisted of deserting, re-joining and internment in military jails, littered with repeated arrests for theft, and short prison sentences, in his civilian life. In December 1941, after being caught shoplifting, he was sentenced to three months at La Santé Prison. It was here that he began writing his first novel, *Our Lady of the Flowers*, a work depicting the Paris underworld of pimps, perverts, cut-throats and thugs: a piece of writing that Jean-Paul Sartre characterised as an 'epic of masturbation'. A month after his release from La Santé he was arrested again, for stealing books, and sentenced to eight months in Fresnes Prison where he composed the poem *The Man Condemned to Death*, which he later printed at his own expense. A few months after Genet's release in February 1943, he introduced himself to poet and novelist Jean Cocteau, who found a publisher for *Our Lady of the Flowers*, having read and been impressed with its content. Shortly afterwards, Genet was arrested once again for stealing a rare edition of Paul Verlaine's poetry. This time, because of his previous record, he faced a possible sentence of life imprisonment. However, with the help of Cocteau, who found him a distinguished defence lawyer, and a psychiatrist who declared to the court that Genet's 'will and moral sense' was weak, but that Genet was the 'greatest writer of the modern era' the judge relented, and sentenced Genet to three months in La Santé. Here, he would write his second novel, *Miracle de la Rose (The Miracle of the Rose)*. Three weeks after his release he was again arrested for stealing books, and jailed for four months. Freed on 15 March 1944, he was never incarcerated again.

By 1947 Genet's writing had become concentrated purely on drama, a genre in which he became the master of social protest, studying in depth the human condition and society's outcasts, notably in *Le Balcon (The Balcony)* and *Les Nègres (The Blacks)*. In later life he became a political activist, where he supported militancy in the American Civil Rights movement among the Black Panthers, and later he voiced support for the Baader–Meinhof terrorists. Today he is a counter-culture icon for many writers and artists, such as David Bowie, the title of whose 1972 song, *The Jean Genie*, was, in Bowie's words, 'a clumsy pun upon Jean Genet'.

Jean Genet died in April 1986, aged seventy-five, following a fall in his room at Jack's Hotel in the 13th arrondissement.

He was buried in his beloved Morocco in the Spanish Cemetery at Larache. 'The gravediggers did not know how to bury a Christian,' wrote his biographer Edmund White, 'so they orientated the grave toward Mecca. The tomb also looks out towards the old Spanish prison and bordello – two of the mainstays of Genet's imagination.'

See Also: Jean-Paul Sartre, Jean Cocteau, Guillaume Apollinaire, Hart Crane, *The Day of the Jackal*, Guillotine.

Further Information: La Santé Prison was built in 1867. Notable inmates over the years have included French poet Guillaume Apollinaire, American poet Hart Crane, Venezuelan terrorist Carlos the Jackal, and bank robber Michel Vaujour, whose wife piloted a helicopter on to the prison roof flying her husband to short-lived freedom in 1986. Public executions by guillotine were held on the pavement at the corner of Rue de la Santé and Boulevard Arago. The penultimate public execution in France took place on this spot in 1939. From that time, all executions were held in the prison courtyard. During the occupation the Nazis executed eighteen members of the Resistance at La Santé. A plaque is erected to their memory on the prison wall at the corner of Rue Jean-Dolent and Rue de la Santé.

Select Bibliography: *Notre Dame des Fleurs (Our Lady of the Flowers)* (1943); *Miracle de la Rose (The Miracle of the Rose)* (1951); *Pompes Funèbres (Funeral Rites)* (1953); *Querelle de Brest (Querelle of Brest)* (1953); *Journal du voleur (The Thief's Journal)* (1949). Plays: *Le Balcon (The Balcony)* (1956); *Les Nègres (The Blacks)* (1958).

Further Reading: E. White, *Genet* (Picador, 1994); Jean-Paul Sartre, *Saint Genet: Actor and Martyr* (University of Minnesota Press, 2012); M. Choukri, *Jean Genet in Tangier* (Ecco, 1974).

HENRY MILLER

18 VILLA SEURAT

101 RUE DE LA TOMBE-ISSOIRE

(Métro: Alésia)

FORMER HOME OF HENRY MILLER
AMERICAN WRITER BEST KNOWN FOR
HIS SEMI-AUTOBIOGRAPHICAL NOVEL
TROPIC OF CANCER

When Henry Miller's novel, Tropic of Cancer, *appeared in 1935, it was greeted with rather cautious praise, obviously conditioned in some cases by a fear of seeming to enjoy pornography. ...*
But read him for five pages, ten pages, and you feel the peculiar relief that comes not so much from understanding as from being understood. 'He knows all about me,' you feel; 'he wrote this specially for me'.
George Orwell, *Inside the Whale* (1940)

Henry Miller in 1932

During his time in Paris Henry Miller transformed himself from a down-and-out drifter into an imaginative writer who dazzled and shocked the literary world with his fearless and sexually explicit language. Whether his achievements are judged to be those of a perceptive writer or a pornographic misogynist, Henry Miller uniquely evoked the underbelly of Parisian life through the eyes of an expatriate in a way none had dared to do before. The whores and pimps, the greasy cafes and seedy hotels, the stink of the pissoirs and the fragrance of the Métro all embodied a Parisian cityscape that Miller described as an 'immense world of grey'.

Born to German immigrants in New York in 1891, he spent most of his childhood in Brooklyn. At the age of twenty-five he married his first wife, Beatrice Wickens, a pianist, with whom he had a daughter. In the early 1920s he worked as an employment manager at Western Union, and it was during this time that he wrote his first, never published, novel, *Clipped Wings*. In 1923, when he met Romanian-born dancer June Mansfield, their ensuing affair resulted in Miller's divorce from his wife at the end of that year, and his marriage to Mansfield some five months later. His second wife became a huge influence on his writings, featuring in many of his books, notably *The Rosy Crucifixion* trilogy: *Sexus, Plexus* and *Nexus*, and *Tropic of Cancer*. But their relationship was tempestuous, and would finally end in divorce in 1934.

Miller arrived in Paris in 1930, alone, penniless and with zero prospects. 'The man's entire fortune consisted of a toothbrush, a razor, a notebook, a pen, a raincoat, and a Mexican cane,' wrote his friend Brassaï. Miller was pushing forty, and with no roof over his head and no meal ticket, he was the archetypal vagrant. But rather than dishearten him, the freedom his situation offered seemed to be uplifting, and it was during these days 'on the bum' he began writing *Tropic of Cancer*, in which he recalls 'the splendor of those miserable days when I first arrived in Paris, a bewildered, poverty-stricken individual who haunted the streets like a ghost at a banquet'.

In the autumn of 1930 June joined him for a time in Paris, and the following year a friend introduced him to the essayist and writer of erotic literature, Anaïs Nin, who at that time was leading the life of a sheltered married woman of the French bourgeoisie. Miller represented to Nin a kind of sensual and poetic freedom, and what began as a literary friendship soon became sexual. 'I want to undress you,' wrote Miller to Nin, 'vulgarize you a bit.' There was also strong mutual attraction between Nin and June, and a love triangle with Miller unfolded. But beyond the 'literary fuck fests', as they called them, Miller and Nin developed a lifelong friendship.

In 1932 Miller sent the manuscript of *Tropic of Cancer* to Paris's Obelisk Press. Jack Kahane, Obelisk's founder, described it as 'a work of genius', and agreed to publish it. The process, however, took all of two years, giving Miller plenty of time for revision.

The day *Tropic of Cancer* was finally published, 1 September 1934, Miller moved into a rented top-floor apartment at 18 villa Seurat, paid for by Anaïs Nin. 'The whole street is given up to quiet, joyous work,' he wrote. 'Every house contains a writer, painter, musician, sculptor, dancer, or actor. It is such a quiet street and yet there is such activity going on, silently, becomingly, shall I not say reverently too?'

On publication, the United States Customs immediately banned *Tropic of Cancer*, and thirty years would pass

until the US Supreme Court lifted the obscenity ruling, in 1964. In spite of the hue and cry stirred up by the book's publication, which echoed in many countries around the world, it is now considered a modern classic, frequently appearing on lists of the best English-language novels of the twentieth century.

Fleeing the Nazis' inevitable invasion of France, Miller left Paris in May 1939 to join Lawrence Durrell in Greece. Once again, he was virtually penniless, but by now his writing had begun to fire the imagination of a generation. Henry Miller was their inspiration.

See Also: The Obelisk Press, Anaïs Nin, Brasserie Wepler, American Express, The American Hospital in Paris.

Further Information: Henry Miller married three more times and had two more children. He died of circulatory problems at his home in Los Angeles in 1980. June Mansfield Miller died in 1979, aged seventy-seven, and Anaïs Nin died in 1977, aged seventy-three. Miller had numerous residencies in Paris. On the day of his arrival in the city he shared a room at the Central Hotel on Rue du Maine, and during that first winter of 1930 he was offered a rent-free room on the seventh floor at No. 2 rue Auguste-Bartholdi. From 1932 to 1934, he lived with his friend Alfred Perlès in the suburbs of Clichy at No. 4 rue Anatole-France, where he finished *Tropic of Cancer*. Of all his lodgings, his claimed preference was for the house at Villa Seurat, which was built around 1925.

Select Bibliography: *Tropic of Cancer* (1934); *Black Spring* (1936); *Tropic of Capricorn* (1939); *The Colossus of Maroussi* (1941); *The Air-Conditioned Nightmare* (1945); *Sexus* (1949); *Plexus* (1953); *The Time of the Assassins* (1956); *Quiet Days in Clichy* (1956); *Big Sur and the Oranges of Hieronymus Bosch* (1957); *Nexus* (1959).

Further Reading: Brassaï, *Henry Miller: The Paris Years* (Arcade, 1975); N. Mailer, *Genius and Lust: A Journey Through the Major Writings of Henry Miller* (Grove Press, 1976); A. Nin, *Henry and June: From the Unexpurgated Diary of Anaïs Nin* (Harcourt Brace, 1986); R. Ferguson, *Henry Miller: A Life* (Norton, 1993); E. Jong, *The Devil at Large: Erica Jong on Henry Miller* (Random House, 1993).

18 villa Seurat

LAWRENCE DURRELL

21 RUE GAZAN

(Métro: Porte d'Orléans)

FORMER RESIDENCE OF

LAWRENCE DURRELL

POET, NOVELIST, TRAVEL WRITER

AND AUTHOR OF

THE ALEXANDRIA QUARTET

My dear Durrell,
... You've crossed the equator. Your commercial career is finished. From now on you're an outlaw, and I congratulate you with all the breath in my body. I seriously think that you truly are 'the first Englishman!' This is way beyond Lawrence and the whole tribe. You are out among the asteroids – for good and all, I hope. ...
Henry Miller praising Lawrence Durrell's manuscript of *The Black Book* in a letter dated 8 March 1937

Lawrence Durrell first gained recognition as a poet, but today his reputation as a writer rests mostly on four novels inspired by his wartime sojourn in Egypt: *Justine* (1957), *Balthazar* (1958), *Mountolive* (1958) and *Clea* (1960), known collectively as *The Alexandria Quartet*, a tetralogy that sets out to describe the same set of events from different perspectives. Its central theme, claimed Durrell, is 'an investigation of modern love'.

Durrell was born in Bengal in 1912, the eldest of four children of an English railway engineer. Following the death of his father in 1928, his family returned to England, eventually settling in Bournemouth. In 1932, while working for an estate agent, Durrell met, and later married, Nancy Myers, the first of his four wives – all of whom he

358

Lawrence Durrell

would treat abysmally and, sometimes, violently. In 1935 he persuaded his entire family, including his new bride, to leave England, or 'Pudding Island' as he always referred to it, and move to the Greek island of Corfu. Durrell and Nancy settled on Corfu's north-eastern coast at Kalamai in what has become known as the famous White House. He fictionalised this period of his life in his 1945 novel *Prospero's Cell*.

When Durrell read Henry Miller's novel *Tropic of Cancer*, which was, at the time, banned in the USA on the grounds of obscenity, it mesmerised him, and he and Miller began corresponding between the Mediterranean and Paris. 'I used to think', wrote Miller, 'when these heraldic messages arrived at the Villa Seurat on a cold summer's day in Paris, that he had taken a sniff of coke before oiling his pen.' But Durrell was writing to his god, convinced that Miller's *Tropic of Cancer* and *Black Spring* were 'the most religious books written since the authorized bible'. Following a two-year period during which time mutual fan mail passed between the two writers,

Durrell and Nancy travelled to Paris in August 1937 where they finally met Miller. It was the beginning of a lifelong friendship.

Miller and his lover, essayist and novelist Anaïs Nin, got on very well with the Durrells. It must have seemed like a friendship made in heaven for Durrell, whose enthusiasm for the erotic was a match for that of his friends. But while the three of them seemed to be on the same wavelength in this respect, Nancy was very much on the sidelines, which is where Durrell made sure she remained.

Durrell's stay in Paris included an interchange of literary ideas and a brief visit to London, and it was during this time that he was unfaithful to Nancy for the first time. Miller, the Durrells and the Austrian writer Alfred Perlès briefly took editorial control of an American country club magazine based in Paris called *The Booster*; however, the magazine's new content, brought together by this meeting of bohemian minds, was not well received by many of the more conservative original advertisers and subscribers, and after only four issues their connection with the magazine was severed.

In April 1938 the Durrells returned to Corfu, and the following year Henry Miller took the boat from Marseilles to Piraeus to pay them a visit and see Greece for the first time. For Miller it was the great adventure of his life and he recounted the experience in his travel book *The Colossus of Maroussi* (1941). 'The light of Greece opened my eyes,' he wrote, 'penetrated my pores, expanded my whole being.' In 1940 Nancy gave birth to a daughter, and after the fall of Greece in 1941, the Durrells fled to Alexandria where they separated some months later. After various

British diplomatic posts, Durrell, who suffered from emphysema, lived out the remaining years of his life in the south of France, where he died following a stroke in 1990.

In 1985 his second daughter, Sappho, from his second wife Eve Cohen, committed suicide by hanging. She was thirty-three years old and had suffered from a long-term psychiatric illness. In 1991 excerpts of her journals were published in which she claimed to have had an incestuous relationship with her father. Whether her writings were accurate, or the results of a deranged mind, it has never been possible to ascertain, but the allegation casts an enduring cloud over Durrell's memory.

In 1960 Lawrence Durrell was a candidate for the Nobel Prize in Literature, but the committee ruled him out because he 'gives a dubious aftertaste ... because of [his] monomaniacal preoccupation with erotic complications'.

See Also: Henry Miller, Anaïs Nin, Obelisk Press.

Further Information: Initially the Durrells lodged at 18 villa Seurat in an apartment below Henry Miller's top floor flat, owned by the American painter, Betty Ryan, who was on holiday. After her return they moved in with Alfred Perlès across the street, eventually renting a flat overlooking Parc Montsouris at 21 rue Gazan.

Select Bibliography: *The Black Book* (1938); *Prospero's Cell* (1945); *Reflections on a Marine Venus* (1953); *Bitter Lemons* (1957); *The Alexandria Quartet* (1962); *Collected Poems* (1960); *The Dark Labyrinth* (1961); *The Avignon Quintet* (1974–1985).

Further Reading: J. Hodgkin, *Amateurs in Eden* (Virago, 2012); I. MacNiven, *The Durrell–Miller Letters, 1935–1980* (New Directions, 1988); *Lawrence Durrell: A Biography* (Faber & Faber, 1998); G. Bowker, *Through the Dark Labyrinth: A Biography of Lawrence Durrell* (Endeavour, 2019); H. Miller, *The Colossus of Maroussi* (Minerva, 1991).

Top: 21 rue Gazan

Above: The White House, Kalamai

ALAIN ROBBE-GRILLET

30 RUE GASSENDI

(Métro: Denfert-Rochereau)

CHILDHOOD HOME OF

ALAIN ROBBE-GRILLET

AVANT-GARDE NOVELIST, FILM-MAKER

AND LEADING PRACTITIONER OF THE

NOUVEAU ROMAN

The room where I slept in the small Parisian apartment on Rue Gassendi was separated by a glass double door from the dining room, where my mother would stay up late into the night reading ... Her gaze, reaching me from time to time above the outspread newspaper, would disturb my solitary pleasures, which already had a strong sadistic tendency. As for the ghosts, they usually appeared opposite me, in a corner of the ceiling.
Alain Robbe-Grillet, *Le Miroir qui revient (Ghosts in the Mirror)* (1984)

Alain Robbe-Grillet was a major figure in French post-war literature, and also one of its most controversial. In the 1950s he launched and promoted the *nouveau roman* (new novel), which challenged the conventions and constraints of the traditional novel by reinventing its form. Early adherents of the *nouveau roman* included Nathalie Sarraute, Claude Simon and Michel Butor, all of who expounded their idea of a 'new realism' in their own distinct style. It was Robbe-Grillet, however, who was its champion, and who became known as the 'pope of the new novel'. 'Although all the articles written about us at the beginning were condemnations,' he observed, 'they paid us the compliment of talking about us constantly. We became famous without having any readers. Paradoxically, we began to have readers from the moment the tide of fashion turned – in the seventies. I even began to live on my earnings as a writer. Now everyone reads us.'

Robbe-Grillet was born into an engineering family in 1922 at Saint-Pierre-Quiberon, near Brest, in Brittany. He was educated in Brest, and Paris, where he started his studies in agricultural engineering shortly after the German occupation in 1940. At the end of spring 1943, along with other students, he was sent to work in a German labour camp in Nuremberg where he worked as a lathe operator in a heavy armaments factory. In 1955 he became a literary editor with Les Éditions de Minuit (The Midnight Press), an underground publishing house during the Nazi occupation, which is still in existence today.

The book that launched the *nouveau roman* in 1963 was *Pour un nouveau roman (Towards a New Novel)*, a collection of theoretcial writings which claimed that the traditional novel falsified the reality of experience through the illusion of order; but the work that brought him critical acclaim was *Le Voyeur* (1955). The novel, he commented, met with 'massive and violent rejection' from the press, a familiar and predictable reaction that he would encounter throughout his career for discarding the 'dead rules' of literary history. In the early 1960s he took up the mantle of screenwriter and film-maker and became part of French cinema's *nouvelle vague* (new wave). He died in 2008, aged eighty-five.

See Also: Les Éditions de Minuit, Claude Simon.

Select Bibliography: *Les Gommes (The Erasers)* (1953); *Le Voyeur (The Voyeur)* (1955); *La Jalousie (Jealousy)* (1957); *Dans le labyrinthe (In the Labyrinth)* (1959).

CIMETIÈRE DU MONTPARNASSE

3 BOULEVARD EDGAR QUINET

(Métro: Raspail/Edgar Quinet/Gaîté)

THE SECOND LARGEST NECROPOLIS IN PARIS

Personally I have no bone to pick with grave-yards, I take the air there willingly, perhaps more willingly than elsewhere, when take the air I must. The smell of corpses, distinctly perceptible under those of grass and humus mingled, I do not find unpleasant, a trifle on the sweet side perhaps, a trifle heady, but how infinitely preferable to what the living emit, their feet, teeth, armpits, arses, sticky foreskins and frustrated ovules.

Samuel Beckett, *First Love* (1946)

Montparnasse cemetery, originally known as Le Cimetière du Sud (The Southern Cemetery), was officially opened in 1824, on estates that once belonged to Hôtel-Dieu, Paris's oldest hospital, and the frères de la Charité (Brothers of Charity). In 1878 the cemetery was split in two by Rue Émile Richard, creating the *petit* cemetery to the southeast, and the *grand* cemetery to the northwest. To date over 300,000 remains have been buried beneath its 47 acres.

Further Information: Cimetière du Montparnasse is just a short distance from the Catacombes de Paris at 1 avenue du Colonel Henri Rol-Tanguy. The catacombs are a series of abandoned limestone and gypsum mines where the skeletal remains of over six million Parisians have been deposited over the centuries from Paris's overflowing graveyards and cemeteries. It is now a tourist attraction.

SERGE GAINSBOURG

(1928–1991)

DIVISION 1

POET, NOVELIST, LYRICIST AND SINGER

Gainsbourg is both the best and the worst, yin and yang, white and black. This Jewish little Prince from Russia whose dreams were probably fueled by Anderson, Perrault and Grimm, became, when confronted by the tragic reality of life, a moving or repugnant Quasimodo, depending on his and your state of mind. Hidden deep within this fragile, shy and aggressive man lies the soul of a poet craving tenderness, truth and integrity.
Brigitte Bardot

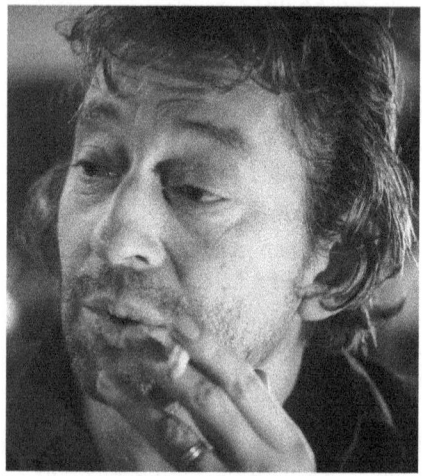

Serge Gainsbourg in 1981

'He was our Baudelaire, our Apollinaire', lamented President Mitterand, 'through his love for the language and his musical genius, he lifted the song to the realm of art.' Outside France, however, Serge Gainsbourg is more famous for his notoriety than for his art, and is remembered mainly for one song, his 1969 hit with English actress Jane Birkin, *Je T'aime ... Moi Non Plus*. It is an understandable neglect, as French

362

culture and language have often seemed impenetrable to the rest of the world, much of which thinks the French music scene peaked with Edith Piaf and the Singing Nun. But in his native France, Serge Gainsbourg was a poetic and musical icon.

He was born Lucien Ginsburg, with his twin sister, Liliane, at Paris's Hôtel Dieu hospital adjacent to Notre-Dame Cathedral on 2 April 1928. His parents were Jewish immigrants who had fled revolutionary Russia, and his father was a talented pianist who played around the clubs. During the Nazi occupation the family members were forced to wear the Yellow Star, to identify themselves as Jewish. 'It was like you were a bull', said Gainsbourg, 'branded with a red-hot iron.' When it became more and more difficult for his father to find work, the family moved to Limoges in the unoccupied zone, where they lived until Paris was liberated in 1944.

After initially pursuing painting as a career he switched to music in the early 1950s, changing his name from Lucien Ginsburg to Serge Gainsbourg – 'Serge' for its Russianness, and 'Gainsbourg' in homage to the English artist Thomas Gainsborough. In 1958 he was signed to the Philips label and recorded his first album, *Du chant à la une!*. His music became an eclectic mix of jazz ballads, the French *chanson*, and pop, mixed in later years with rock, reggae, funk, hip-hop and many other genres. By the late 1960s he had been twice married, and had an affair with Brigitte Bardot, for whom he wrote the erotic *Je T'aime ... Moi Non Plus*. Bardot was reluctant to proceed beyond the recording, however, and it was with singer and actor, Jane Birkin, who became Gainsbourg's next lover, that the song was released in 1969.

Some ten years later, Gainsbourg's life seemed to have entered a mode of self-destruction. At that time he was drinking heavily, chain-smoking, and engaging in more and more outrageous behaviour, which included performing a reggae version of the French national anthem, setting a 500-franc note alight on French television in protest against tax increases, and recording the 1984 song *Lemon Incest* with his and Birkin's thirteen-year-old daughter Charlotte, singing about 'the love we will never make together'. In the end his lifestyle caught up with him and he died of a heart attack in 1991 at his house at 5 *bis* rue de Verneuil in Saint-Germain-des-Prés. He was sixty-two years old. His death was comparable with that of President John F. Kennedy in that many Parisians claim to remember what they were doing when they heard the news that Serge Gainsbourg had died.

See Also: Charles Baudelaire, Guillaume Apollinaire, Charles Perrault.

Further Information: Gainsbourg moved to his Rue de Verneuil house in 1969, which, since his death, has become a graffiti-covered shrine. In 1969, *Je T'aime* was the first banned number one single in the UK. The title, *Je T'aime ... Moi Non Plus* (I Love You ... Me Neither), was inspired by Salvador Dalí's remark: 'Picasso is Spanish, me too. Picasso is a genius, me too. Picasso is a communist, me neither.' Gainsbourg first recorded *Je T'aime* with Brigitte Bardot in 1967, but fearing it might damage her career she did not sanction its release until 1986.

Further Reading: S. Simmons, *Serge Gainsbourg: A Fistful of Gitanes* (Da Capo, 2002).

JORIS-KARL HUYSMANS
(1848–1907)
DIVISION 2

FRENCH NOVELIST AND ESSAYIST

The only people who are worth knowing are either saints, scoundrels or madmen; at least their conversation is always interesting. Sensible people are dull by definition, because they are always harping on to the same boring tune about everyday life. They form part of the crowd, the more intelligent part perhaps, but the crowd for all that, and I'm sick of them.
Joris-Karl Huysmans

Huysmans was not a literary giant like his contemporaries, and he could never be described as fashionable, but he was a prominent and influential figure in the period's Decadent movement, of which his 1884 novel, *À rebours* (*Against Nature*), is a key example, establishing Huysmans as one of its major proponents. Oscar Wilde, whose own work was greatly influenced by the novel, referenced it, although not by name, in his *The Picture of Dorian Gray* (1891).

There has been little written on Huysmans over the years, other than Robert Baldick's celebrated biography in English written in 1955, followed by two French editions in 1958 and 1975. The reason, writes Baldick, was that in his will,

> Huysmans directed that his correspondence and private papers should remain unpublished. ... For nearly forty-three years [his executor] threatened erring authors, journalists, and *marchands d'autographes* with sanctions ranging from legal action and professional opprobrium to personal vilification; and it was only on his death, in September 1949, that the publication of Huysmans' correspondence and the writing of a full documented Life became practical possibilities.

Huysmans was born Charles Marie Georges Huysmans in Paris in 1848 to a French mother, and a Dutch father who was a lithographer and miniaturist. Educated in Paris, he worked for many years in the Ministry of the Interior as a civil servant, the boredom from which he relieved by penning his own works, from prose poems to novels. He lived through the siege of Paris (1870–71) and later became part of the literary circle surrounding Zola and his coterie.

One of his early works was *Marthe* (1876), on prostitution, but it was his 1884 novel, *À rebours*, exploring a decadent, aesthetic hero who rejects the real world and builds his own devious and evasive one that remains his best-known work. After *À rebours*, his most famous piece of writing, which describes a subject he had studied and personally experienced, is his once-controversial novel, *Là-bas* (*Down There*) published

Portrait of Huysmans by Adolphe Gumery, 1884

in 1891, dealing with medieval alchemy and Satanism in France during the late nineteenth century. After retiring from the French civil service in 1898, he pursued a monastic life, becoming a lay member of the Benedictine brotherhood. He died in 1907, aged fifty-nine, from cancer of the mouth, a malignancy for which he refused to accept painkilling drugs.

See Also: Émile Zola, Victor Hugo, Charles Baudelaire, Honoré de Balzac, Gustave Flaubert, Theophile Gautier, Stéphane Mallarmé, Arthur Rimbaud, Paul Verlaine, Oscar Wilde.

Further Information: The Decadent movement of the late nineteenth century, although fleeting, aimed to set literature and art free from the material world, rejecting the modernist vogue towards realism. Mostly asso-ciated with French literature, its foremost adherents included Charles Baudelaire, Joris-Karl Huysmans, Theophile Gautier, Stéphane Mallarmé, Arthur Rimbaud and Paul Verlaine. The works that are the movement's most groundbreaking are often at-tributed to Huysmans' novel *Against Nature*, and the poetry of Baudelaire. Originally the word 'decadent' was used as a term of abuse for certain writers by French critics, but was later adopted by those same writers as the *raison d'être* and masthead of their movement.

Select Bibliography: *Marthe* (1876); *À rebours (Against Nature)* (1884); *Là-bas (Down There)* (1891), *En route* (1895); *La Cathédrale (The Cathedral)* (1898); *L'Oblat (The Oblate)* (1903).

Further Reading: R. Baldick, *The Life of J-K Huysmans* (Clarendon Press, 1955).

CHARLES BAUDELAIRE
(1821–1867)
DIVISION 6

POET, CRITIC, ESSAYIST AND
TRANSLATOR WHO WAS A MAJOR
INFLUENCE ON MODERN POETRY

Souvenirs?
More than if I had lived a thousand years!

No chest of drawers crammed
with documents,
love-letters, wedding-invitations, wills,
a lock of someone's hair rolled up in a deed,
hides so many secrets as my brain.
This branching catacombs, this pyramid
contains more corpses than the potter's field:
I am a graveyard that the moon abhors,
where long worms like regrets come out
to feed
most ravenously on my dearest dead.
I am an old boudoir where a rack of gowns,
perfumed by withered roses, rots to dust;
where only faint pastels and pale Bouchers
inhale the scent of long-unstopped flasks.
Charles Baudelaire, *Spleen (II), Les Fleurs*
du Mal (1857)

Baudelaire by Étienne Carjat *c*.1862

Today Baudelaire still remains a controversial writer, but his place as an influential poet is firmly established. His *Les Fleurs du Mal (The Flowers of Evil)* was so powerful when it was first published in 1857 it set in motion the Symbolist movement of late nineteenth-century France, and became an enormous influence on modern poetry. The poems are a sweeping collection of sexual passions engulfed in horror and decay, themes that were considered shocking by many readers. Baudelaire's inspiration was the ugliness of a modern urban existence from which he extracts a kind of graceful allure from its hideous reality and oppressiveness. Shortly after the publication of *Les Fleurs du Mal*, Baudelaire, his printer and his publisher were prosecuted and fined for offences to public morals, and all copies of the book ordered to be confiscated. Six of the poems in the book were officially banned, a proscription that remained in place in France until 1949.

The only child of Caroline Dufaÿs and François Baudelaire, Charles Pierre Baudelaire was born on 9 April 1821 at No. 13 rue Hautefeuille (now demolished) in the Latin Quarter. His mother's origins are obscure, but François, who was considerably older than his wife, is listed as 'painter' on his son's birth certificate. Baudelaire once remarked that his 'execrable temperament' was due to being the child of ill-matched parents.

Top: The family tomb with Baudelaire's name smeared with lipstick
Above: Baudelaire's controversial cenotaph

'My frayed nerves are due to their disparity. That's what comes of being the unbalanced child of a mother of twenty-seven and a father aged sixty-two.' In 1784 François Baudelaire had been ordained a priest, but the following year he left the ministry to become a private tutor, wisely resigning the priesthood during the Reign of Terror in 1793. It was this background that gave rise to his son's frequent referral to himself as 'the son of a priest'.

In 1828, the year after his father's death from cancer, and Charles's sixth year, Caroline Baudelaire, to whom her son was devoted, married Jacques Aupick, a career soldier. Baudelaire grew to loathe his stepfather, chiefly because he had been robbed of his mother's love, but also because in later life Aupick tried to veto his chance of a literary career. Aupick even went to the extent, in 1841, of sending his stepson on a journey to India in the hope that a long sea voyage to the mysterious east would make him forget his unconventional ways.

Baudelaire, however, jumped ship in Mauritius and made his way back to Paris and bohemian life, despite his family's disapproval. After his return in 1842 he was bequeathed a paternal legacy of around a hundred thousand francs and some land: sufficient income for a young bachelor's needs, if he was careful, but Baudelaire was never one to live within his means. He spent his new wealth on an apartment and transformed himself into a dandy with voguish and expensive clothes. He collected antiques and artworks, wrote promissory notes to his creditors that he couldn't fulfil, and footed the bills for his mistress and muse, Jeanne Duval, his 'Vénus Noire' ('Black Venus'), with whom he had a stormy relationship for twenty years. With his small fortune evaporating rapidly, his family, fearing his ruin, obtained a court-appointed guardian to control his finances, which Baudelaire resented bitterly.

Amid the volatility of his life he still managed to write poetry, and regular literary and art criticisms. In 1847 he published an autobiographical novel, *La Fanfarlo*. Later works include *Les Paradis artificiels (Artificial Paradises)* (1860) and *Petits Poèmes en prose*, also known as *Le Spleen de Paris (Little Poems in Prose)* (1869). He also translated the works of Thomas De Quincey and Edgar Allan Poe, but it is for *Les Fleurs du Mal* that he is chiefly celebrated.

By the early 1860s Baudelaire's health was in decline. After years of alcohol and laudanum abuse, venereal disease, poverty and stress, he was stricken with paralysis and aphasia and died in his mother's arms at a Paris nursing home on 31 August, 1867, aged only forty-six. His funeral took place two days later and around sixty mourners gathered at the graveside, including Paul Verlaine, Édouard Manet, and the photographer, Nadar, who fancifully summed up Baudelaire's tortured life when he wrote: 'That man who lived in perpetual torment, feverish, unappeased and undefeated, that hysteric, that maniac, that werewolf, never harmed a soul. He did not even stoop to hate.'

See Also: Palais de Justice. Nadar, Paul Verlaine.

Further Information: Baudelaire died from paralysis and aphasia, a language and communication disorder usually caused by injury to the brain, such as occurs following a stroke. Ironically, he was buried alongside his stepfather, Jacques Aupick. His mother joined them on her death four years later.

Baudelaire's cenotaph is located between Divisions 26 and 27 at the eastern end of the crossroads, and is attached to the wall separating the western part of the cemetery and Rue Émile Richard. Sculpted by José de Charmoy (1879–1914) and erected in 1902, the sculpture was extremely controversial in its day. Initially Auguste Rodin (1840–1917) was commissioned to create the cenotaph, but after years of quarrelling among the organisers he abandoned the project.

Select Bibliography: *Flowers of Evil* (Oxford, 1993); *Twenty Prose Poems* (City Lights, 2001); *Selected Poems* (Penguin, 1995).

Further Reading: C. Pichois and J. Ziegler, *Baudelaire* (trans. G. Robb, Vintage, 1991).

Rue Hautefeuille, Baudelaire's birthplace *c.* 1866

EUGÈNE IONESCO
(1909–1994)

DIVISION 6

ROMANIAN FRENCH PLAYWRIGHT
ONE OF THE LEADING EXPONENTS
OF THE THEATRE OF THE ABSURD

Macbeth, for example, says that the world is a tale told by an idiot, full of sound and fury, signifying nothing. That is the pure definition of the Theatre of the Absurd – and perhaps of the world. Shakespeare was the great one before us. His place was between God and despair.
Eugène Ionesco

Eugène Ionesco

Ionesco wrote: 'I started to write for the theatre because I hated it.' It was a loathing that pushed him towards the antithesis of conventional drama, which became known as the Theatre of the Absurd: a movement that jettisons methodical plot development, meaningful dialogue and comprehensible characters, and substitutes them with a pessimistic and, usually, humorous vision of humanity, conveying the meaninglessness of man's existence in a world ruled by chance, but often with an element of hope. 'To tear ourselves away from the everyday,' he wrote, 'from habit, from mental laziness which hides from us the strangeness of reality, we must receive something like a real bludgeon blow.' Ionesco's 'bludgeon blow' – of which there were many, in his scathing satires – inspired a radical change in modern dramatic approach and helped lay the foundations for what would become the Theatre of the Absurd.

Eugène Ionesco, who was born in Romania of a Romanian father and French mother, spent the majority of his childhood in France. He returned to Romania in 1925, and later studied for a degree in French at the University of Bucharest. In 1936 he married Rodica Burileanu with whom he had a daughter. Two years later the family moved to Paris where Ionesco finished his doctoral thesis, and where he eventually made his home. He began his writing career in Romania, writing poetry and criticism and, notably, a scathing satirical biography of Victor Hugo: *Hugoliade, or The Grotesque and Tragic life of Victor Hugo.* His first play, or 'antiplay', as he called it, entitled *La Cantatrice chauve (The Bald Soprano)*, was not written until 1948. In one of the scenes two strangers exchange platitudes about the weather, about where they live, and about how many children they have, and soon they are amazed to discover they are actually husband and wife. It was an early example of what would become Ionesco's recurring topics of

isolation, communication breakdown and bourgeois conformity. Following the first performance of *The Bald Soprano* in his late thirties, he went on to write many more plays and, in so doing, exasperated traditionalists on both the right and the left of the political spectrum. He died aged eighty-four on 28 March 1994, and is now regarded as one of the great dramatists of the twentieth century.

See Also: Samuel Beckett, Jean Genet, Victor Hugo, Académie francaise.

Further Information: Hungarian-born Martin Esslin conceived the term 'Theatre of the Absurd' in his book of the same name, published in 1961. He observes that he 'was motivated to write it at the end of the 1950s by impatience, even rage, with theatre critics who seemed to me to have missed the importance and beauty of plays that had deeply moved me when I ran across them, almost by chance, in little theatres on the Paris Left Bank.' Ionesco may have been a proponent of the antiplay, but he was not anti-establishment; in 1970 he became a member of one the most traditional institutions in France, the Académie francaise.

Select Bibliography: *The Bald Soprano* (1950); *Salutations* (1950); *The Lesson* (1951); *The Chairs* (1952); *Victims of Duty* (1953); *Amédée, or How to Get Rid of It* (1954); *Jack, or The Submission* (1955); *The New Tenant* (1955); *The Picture* (1955); *The Killer* (1958); *Rhinoceros* (1959); *Exit the King* (1962); *Hunger and Thirst* (1964);

Fragments of a Journal (1967); *Present Past: Past Present: A Personal Memoir* (1968); *Macbett* (1972).

Further Reading: H. Bloom, *Eugène Ionesco* (Chelsea, 2002); D. Gaensbauer, *Eugène Ionesco Revisited* (Twayne, 1996); L. Pronko, *Eugène Ionesco* (Columbia University Press, 1965); M. Esslin, *The Theatre of the Absurd* (Methuen, 2001).

MAURICE LEBLANC
(1864–1941)
DIVISION 10

CREATOR OF ARSÈNE LUPIN
'THE PRINCE OF THIEVES'

The greatest thief in the whole world
Ellery Queen describing Arsène Lupin

Maurice Leblanc was a French author and journalist, best known today as the creator of the gentleman thief and detective, Arsène Lupin. Born in 1864 in Rouen, Normandy, to an Italian father and a French mother, Leblanc studied law and worked in the family shipping business. He also wrote competent novels and short stories, but with little financial success. His journalistic work, however, attracted the attention of the editor of the magazine *Je Sais Tout,* who commissioned him to write a story in the spirit of Sherlock Holmes, who had become a journalistic sensation a decade or so earlier in London's *Strand Magazine*. The end result, which first appeared in 1905, was *L'Arrestation d'Arsène Lupin (The Arrest of Arsène Lupin)*, a story about a gentleman rogue who pursues a career of burglary and confidence trickery while outwitting the police at every turn. The novel was a surprise success. Lupin was the antithesis of Sherlock Holmes, with a sense of humour to boot. Arsène Lupin went on to be featured in over sixty of Leblanc's novels and stories, and has never been out of print in France for well over a hundred years.

In winter Leblanc lived in Paris, and in summer he returned to his beloved Normandy, where he set many of his stories. Each of his homes had a garden shed where he would write, regardless of the weather, in undisturbed tranquility. In response to a query about how he knew so much about criminology, Leblanc replied,

> But I am blankly ignorant! I never met or talked with thieves and rogues. They do not interest me. I never had the faintest wish to know them. My stories are pure romance – the fictions of my brain – the merest fancies. …
>
> All the romance of crime was suggested in Poe's works. I don't remember anything besides Poe and Balzac that could have helped me work out my plots.

The romance may have been Poe and Balzac, but the humour was pure Leblanc, especially when he introduces Sherlock Holmes (for copyright reasons known as Herlock Sholmes), whom Lupin outwits and on one occasion steals Sholmes's watch. Lupin was also an inspiration to many. Agatha Christie, while doing the groundwork for her first detective story, contemplated using him as the model for her sleuth. Jean-Paul Sartre called Lupin 'the Cyrano of the underworld', while T.S. Eliot once commented, 'I used to read him, but I have now graduated to Inspector Maigret.'

No doubt Leblanc dreamt that posterity would lay his literary creations alongside those of Flaubert, but it was Arsène

Maurice Leblanc

Lupin, the character who brought him fame and fortune, that was to secure his destiny.

Revered as one of the great writers of the detective genre, he died at the age of seventy-five in Perpignan, 6 November 1941.

See Also: Émile Gaboriau, Eugène Vidocq, Georges Simenon, Honoré de Balzac.

Further Information: Le Clos Arsène Lupin, a museum dedicated to Leblanc and Lupin, is located in Leblanc's former home at 15 rue Guy de Maupassant, Étretat, Normandy.

Select Bibliography: *Arsène Lupin, Gentleman Burglar* (1906); *Arsène Lupin, versus Herlock Sholmes* (1908); *The Hollow Needle* (1909); *The Confessions of Arsène Lupin* (1913).

SAMUEL BECKETT

(1906–1989)

DIVISION 12

IRISH NOVELIST AND PLAYWRIGHT
AWARDED THE NOBEL PRIZE
IN LITERATURE IN 1969

Have you not done tormenting me with your accursed time! It's abominable! When! When! One day, is that not enough for you, one day he went dumb, one day I went blind, one day we'll go deaf, one day we were born, one day we shall die, the same day, the same second, is that not enough for you? They give birth astride of a grave, the light gleams an instant, then it's night once more.
Samuel Beckett, *Waiting for Godot* (1953)

Samuel Beckett in 1973

In 1953 Samuel Beckett became famous overnight after the Paris debut of his play *En attendant Godot (Waiting for Godot)* was performed at the Théâtre de Babylone on Paris's Boulevard Raspail. Many, however, consider his fiction, some of which was written long before *Godot*'s triumph, to be the crowning point of his literary achievement. But whether fiction or drama, the same ethical and philosophical principles are to be found, all written with the same motive: to make the audience face up to the truth of human existence and the pointlessness of life. Beckett naturally became associated with the Theatre of the Absurd, a movement that essentially presents the absurdity of the human condition in a world ruled by happenstance. 'On a day like this', someone once remarked to him, 'it's good to be alive', whereupon Beckett replied: 'Well, I wouldn't go as far as that!'

Born in Dublin to a Protestant family, Beckett went to Paris as an exchange lecturer in English at the École Normale Supérieure in 1928. He soon became a member of the literary circle surrounding James Joyce, the subject of Beckett's first published work, 'Dante... Bruno. Vico.. Joyce:', an essay published in 1929. Joyce and Beckett, who shared the same fascination with language, became quite close. Occasionally Beckett acted as amanuensis to Joyce during the writing of *Finnegans Wake*. 'In the middle of one such session', writes Joyce's biographer Richard Ellmann, 'there was a knock at the door which Beckett didn't hear. Joyce said, "Come in," and Beckett wrote it down. Afterwards he read back what he had written and Joyce said, "What's that 'Come in'?" "Yes, you said that," said Beckett. Joyce thought for a moment, then said, "Let it stand."' They were obviously cut from the same cloth. Beckett settled permanently in Paris in 1937. That same year, on Avenue d'Orléans, he was stabbed in the chest and nearly killed in a random attack.

Lucien Raimbourg as Vladimir, Pierre Latour as Estragon, Roger Blin as Pozzo, in the 1953 world premiere of *En attendant Godot* at the Théâtre de Babylone in Paris

In hospital he received visits from his friend, Suzanne Dechevaux-Dumesnil, whom he would marry in 1961, and who would remain his lifelong companion despite Beckett having numerous affairs. The following year he published his first novel, *Murphy*, a bleak, absurdist masterpiece, strongly influenced by Joyce. Written in English, Beckett almost immediately translated it into French, a practice he would employ for most of his works, his reasoning being that he wanted to escape his mother tongue. Writing in English, he could too easily lapse into rhetoric, but being creative in a language other than his own demanded greater self-discipline.

Following the occupation of Paris by the Germans in 1940, Beckett joined a Resistance cell called 'Gloria SMH', founded by Jeanine Picabia, daughter of the painter Francis Picabia. Beckett's role involved typing and translating information reports that were subsequently transmitted back to England.

In 1941 he started to write his second novel, *Watt*, which provided him with 'a means of staying sane'. In August 1942 his Resistance cell was betrayed and he narrowly escaped being caught by the Gestapo. Fearing for their lives, Beckett and Suzanne fled south to the village of Roussillon, Vaucluse, in the mountains of Provence-Alpes-Côte-d'Azur. Here they found refuge and continued to work for the Resistance. A few months after Paris had been liberated by French and American troops in early 1945, they returned to their flat in Rue des Favorites which, miraculously, had not been ransacked. Here they began to pick up their life again. After the war Beckett was awarded the Croix de guerre and the Médaille de la Resistance by the French government for his Resistance exploits which he famously referred to as 'boy scout stuff'.

Watt was completed late in 1945, but it was rejected by 'a good score of London publishers', noted Beckett, and it was only after the success of *Waiting for Godot* that Olympia Press published it in 1953. His best-known novels, *Molloy, Malone meurt (Malone Dies),* and *L'innommable (The Unnamable)*, were written in the 1950s. In the following decade he frequently wrote for television and radio.

On reflection, Beckett's works, although ambiguous and desolate, are also filled with abounding wit, pathos and eloquence, achievements that resulted in his becoming one of the most significant writers of the twentieth century. 'I couldn't have done it otherwise,' he said. 'Gone on, I mean. I could not have gone through the awful wretched mess of life without having left a stain upon the silence.'

See Also: Les Éditions de Minuit, French Resistance, Jean Anouilh, Eugène Ionesco, James Joyce, Olympia Press, The Tartan Pimpernel.

Further Information: Théatre de Babylone closed in September 1954 due to financial difficulties. Beckett and Suzanne moved in 1959 from their small, top-floor flat at 6 rue des Favorites to a larger, seventh-floor apartment at 38 boulevard Saint-Jacques. Suzanne died in July 1989, aged eighty-eight. Beckett was admitted to the Tiers Temps nursing home in Rue Rémy-Dumoncel in 1988, where he died from emphysema in December the following year, aged eighty-three. The couple are interred beside each other in the Cimitière du Montparnasse.

Select Bibliography: Prose: *Watt* (1953); *Molloy* (1951) (Eng. Trans., (1955)); *Malone meurt* (1951) *(Malone Dies* (1956)); *L'Innommable* (1953) *(The Unnamable* (1958)).
Plays: *En attendant Godot* (1952) *(Waiting for Godot* (1954)); *Fin de Partie (Endgame* (1957)); *Krapp's Last Tape* (1958); *Happy Days* (1960).

Further Reading: D. Bair, *Samuel Beckett* (Jonathan Cape, 1978); J. Knowlson, *Damned To Fame: The Life of Samuel Beckett* (Bloomsbury, 1996); E. Brater, *The Essential Samuel Beckett: An Illustrated Biography* (Thames & Hudson, 2003); J. Calder, *The Philosophy of Samuel Beckett* (Alma, 2018).

Top: 38 boulevard Raspail, site of the Théatre de Babylone where *En attendant Godot* premiered in 1953. Above: Beckett's grave

PIERRE LAROUSSE

(1817–1875)

DIVISION 14

GRAMMARIAN, LEXICOGRAPHER,
ENCYCLOPÉDISTE AND PUBLISHER OF
THE *GRAND DICTIONNAIRE UNIVERSEL
DU XIX SIÈCLE*

I sow to all winds.
Motto of Pierre Larousse

Pierre Athanase Larousse, the son of a blacksmith, was born on 23 October 1817 in Toucy, in the Burgundy region. At the age of sixteen he won a scholarship to a teacher training school in Versailles, afterwards returning to Toucy as a teacher. However, education methods in rural Burgundy, being crude and set in their ways, prompted him to move to Paris in 1840 to broaden his horizons. In Paris he taught at a private boarding school where he met his future wife, Suzanne Caubel, with whom he published a French language course for children. In 1852, with publisher and former teacher Pierre Boyer, he opened the Larousse and Boyer Book-shop in Paris. Together they published innovative textbooks for children and reference guides for teachers. In 1856 Larousse and Boyer published the *New Dictionary of the French Language*, the predecessor of *Le Petit Larousse*, the famous dictionary and encyclopedia of proper nouns that is still in print today. But Larousse's major work, for which he is chiefly remembered, was his *Grand dictionnaire universel du XIXe siècle* (Great Universal 19th Century Dictionary), in 15 volumes, which was issued in fortnightly parts between 1866

and 1876. Larousse devoted the rest of his life to the dictionary, but died of a stroke on 3 January 1875, shortly before its completion.

ROBERT DESNOS
(1900–1945)
DIVISION 15

FRENCH POET, NOVELIST AND JOUR-
NALIST, AND LEADING EXPONENT OF
FRENCH SURREALISM

I'll be forgotten. Someday no one will know
my name but will know hers. One evening,
naked in glory and rich, I will come back, I
will knock on her door, completely nude,
but no one will answer, even when, having
opened the door, I'll appear in her sight.
I have grasped, at least, the meaning of per-
petuity. Not the ridiculous one of cemetery
plots.

Robert Desnos, from 'Tour of the Tomb'

Robert Desnos did not live long
enough to take his place amongst
France's celebrated post-war poets, a
destiny he assuredly deserved. He was
arrested by the Gestapo for his Resistance activities on 22 February 1944 and
died following his imprisonment in June
the following year.
Born in Paris, he became a literary
columnist for the newspaper *Paris-Soir*.
His first poems were published in 1917,
and in 1922 he published his first book,
Rrose Sélavy, a collection of surrealistic
aphorisms. In the early 1920s he met
the key figures of French surrealism:
André Breton, Louis Aragon and Paul
Éluard. Desnos soon became an active
member of the group, which performed
the technique of automatic writing that
entailed falling into a hypnotic trance (of
which Desnos proved to be adept) while
writing, drawing and reciting dreams.

'Surrealism is the order of the day',
wrote Breton, 'and Desnos is its
prophet.' He parted company with the
surrealists in 1929, but the decade had
been a very creative period of his life,
during which time he had published a
prodigious amount of poetry.
In 1931 he married Youki Foujita (Lucie Badoul), former wife of the Japanese
artist Tsuguharu Foujita. During the
1930s he began to immerse himself in a
greater number of commercial projects:
journalism, radio, and film, as well as
developing his talent as a natural lyric
poet. On 22 February 1944, the Gestapo
arrived at the Desnos's flat at 19 rue
Mazarine looking for the names of
members of the Resistance. Although
Desnos had been tipped off, and was
aware the raid was coming, he refused
to flee as his wife was not at home.
Had she been found, she would have
been tortured in his stead. When the
Gestapo's search of the flat revealed a
list of names concealed in the binding
of a book, Desnos was arrested. A
month before his forty-fifth birthday
he died from typhus as a consequence
of the ill treatment he had received in
a Czech concentration camp at Terezin.

See Also: André Breton, Louis Aragon, Paul
Éluard.

Select Bibliography: *The Voice: Selected*
Poems of Robert Desnos (2005); *Essential*
Poems and Writings of Robert Desnos
(2008).

Further Reading: K. Conley, *Robert*
Desnos, Surrealism, and the Marvelous in
Everyday Life (Univ. of Nebraska, 2004).

LOUIS HACHETTE
(1800–1864)

DIVISION 15

FRENCH BOOKSELLER AND PUBLISHER
WHO TRANSFORMED THE WORLD OF
BOOKS

*In this happy situation, there is a place
for everyone under the sun. One can live
peacefully and happily in a country where
the earth can nourish generously all of its
inhabitants.*
Louis Hachette on the unlimited market for
literature.

Born in 1800 at Rethel in the
Ardennes, Louis Hachette was the
eldest son of a pharmacist and a textile
merchant's daughter. He was educated
in Paris where his mother worked as
a laundress following her separation
from his father. He was enrolled at
the elite École Normale Supérieure
in 1819 where he was on course for a
career in teaching or law; however,
on entering the book trade he bought
a small bookshop in 1826 near the
Sorbonne called Librairie Brédif, which
he renamed Hachette. From here he
published educational books and, later,
dictionaries and encyclopedias. Seven
years later, in 1833, the French government passed the Guizot Schools Law,
one of the foundations of the French
education system, making it obligatory
for every municipality to open a school.
Books were now desperately needed
for schoolchildren all over France, and
Hachette, who had been working on an
alphabet primer since 1829, was the
only supplier capable of responding to a
government order for one million textbooks. In 1836 he further strengthened
his grip on the educational market when
he became the official publisher of the
University of France. In 1852 Hachette
signed a contract with France's railway
companies to create station bookstalls
that would sell novels and travel guides,
including Hachette's own *Guides
Joanne*, eventually renamed *Guides
bleu*. By the mid 1890s Hachette had a
network of more than a thousand station
bookstalls throughout France. Today
Hachette Livre is the largest publisher
in France, and the third largest trade
and educational publisher in the world.
When Hachette died in 1864, aged six-
ty-four, he was not only one of the most
successful publishers in the book trade,
but he could also lay claim to having
revolutionised it.

See Also: Gaston Gallimard, Pierre-Jules
Hetzel, Émile Zola.

Further Information: In the early 1860s
one of the clerks in Hachette's dispatch department was the young, as yet unpublished,
Émile Zola. The present-day location of Hachette's headquarters is 43 quai de Grenelle,
in the 15th arrondissement.

Louis Hachette

CHARLES AUGUSTIN
SAINTE-BEUVE
(1804–1869)
DIVISION 17

POET, NOVELIST AND MASTER OF
MODERN FRENCH CRITICISM

Nothing is more painful to me than the disdain with which people treat second-rate authors, as if there were room only for the first-raters.
Charles Augustin Sainte-Beuve

The Goncourt brothers wrote: 'He is a short, tubby little man, stockily built with a peasant's neck and shoulders, dressed in a simple country manner … one might take him for an intelligent provincial coming out of a library, a cloister of books, under which there was a cellar of rich burgundy.' Sainte-Beuve was obviously no dandy, but all he really needed was his pen, which made him one of the most influential, enduring and passionate literary critics of nineteenth-century France. Born at Boulogne-sur-Mer in 1804, Charles Augustin Sainte-Beuve was the only child of a tax collector. He studied medicine for three years, 'where I lived in such isolation, that nobody came to see me for seven months, except my mother, and she came only once'. However, being drawn to journalism, he began writing literary articles, cutting short his medical career in 1824 when he began contributing to the French newspaper, *Le Globe*. It was for this publication that, in 1827, he wrote a review of Victor Hugo's *Odes et Ballades*. The piece won him great favour with both Hugo, and his wife, Adèle, with whom he later had an affair, and who provided the inspiration for his 1834 novel, *Volupté*. He lectured on criticism in Lausanne, Liège, and the École Normale Supérieure, all discourses that were later collected and published; but his reputation as one of the great literary critics of France rests on his weekly columns published in *Le Constitutionnel* newspaper from 1849 to 1869. These critical essays, six hundred and forty in total, each 3000 words in length, covered all genres of literature, predominantly French, but also classical and foreign. The weekly columns were collected in the 16-volume *Causeries du lundi* (Monday chats) (1851–1881) and their continuation, the 13-volume *Nouveaux lundis* (1863–1870).

Sainte-Beuve's reputation as the father of modern French criticism was not without its limitations, however. He championed many writers who are now forgotten, while dismissing writers such as Balzac and Baudelaire as licentious, and Hugo as too political. He was known to praise some writers while they were alive, and then denigrate their work after their death.

'How ghastly to be survived by Sainte-Beuve,' wrote the Goncourt brothers. Nevertheless, the critic's responsibility is to be critical. Sainte-Beuve's work is 'almost unique', wrote American literary critic Irving Babbitt, 'in the way it combines extent with richness and variety. Perhaps no other writer has written more than fifty volumes and repeated himself so little, or fallen so rarely, even towards the end, below his own best standard.'

See Also: Victor Hugo, Honoré de Balzac, Charles Baudelaire, Goncourt brothers, Irving Babbitt, Luxembourg Gardens.

378

Further Information: Sainte-Beuve died in 1869 after surgery for the removal of a bladder stone. A statue of him can be seen in the Luxembourg Gardens.

Select Bibliography: *Essays on Men and Women* (1890); *Select Essays of Sainte-Beuve* (1895); *Causeries du lundi, 8 vols.* (1909–1911).

Further Reading: H. Nicolson, *Sainte-Beuve* (Greenwood, 1978); R. Chadbourne, *Charles Augustin Sainte-Beuve* (Twayne, 1978); G. Harper, *Charles Augustin Sainte-Beuve* (University of Michigan Library, 2009); R. Baldick (ed. & trans.), *Pages From The Goncourt Journals* (NYRB Classics, 2007); *Dinner at Magny's* (Penguin, 1973); I. Babbitt, *Masters of Modern French Criticism, 1912* (Kessinger, 2010); M. Proust, *By Way of Sainte-Beuve* (Hogarth, 1984).

The grave of Sainte-Beuve

JEAN-PAUL SARTRE
(1905–1980)
SIMONE DE BEAUVOIR
(1908–1986)
DIVISION 20

LEGENDS OF TWENTIETH-CENTURY
COUNTERCULTURE

Simone pledged herself to Jean-Paul, the only man she'd met who was her intellectual equal. The lifetime commitment that followed would prove more enduring than many a marriage. Bound together by their difficult childhoods, by the intellectual fireworks they created, and by a deep, visceral need, together they would light up their century.
Carole Seymour-Jones, *A Dangerous Liaison* (2008)

Jean-Paul Sartre and Simone de Beauvoir's relationship – from Sorbonne lecture halls to the cafes of the Left Bank – endured for fifty-one years. While Sartre wrote about a godless world, Beauvoir produced the seminal text on feminism. They never married, they practised free love; they refused order, family, children and the moral standards of their parents; they challenged political issues during turbulent times and had a wilful disregard for convention. They became France's most famous twentieth-century intellectuals, and they inspired a generation.

Sartre lived out his final years, from 1973 until his death in 1980, in a two-bedroomed flat on the tenth floor of 29 boulevard Edgar-Quinet, overlooking Montparnasse Cemetery. Sartre lost the use of his right eye when he was a child, but in 1973, aged sixty-seven, a haemorrhage in his other eye virtually blinded him. It was therefore no longer safe for him to live on his own, and the flat's

379

spare room could conveniently accommodate alternating mistresses, including Beauvoir, to care for him nightly.

On the morning of 20 March 1980, Beauvoir discovered Sartre sitting on his bed fighting for breath. Phoning for an ambulance proved futile as the phone was disconnected (Sartre's secretary had failed to pay the bill). Finally the concierge got through to emergency services and Sartre was taken into intensive care at Broussais hospital on Rue Didot in the 14th arrondissement. He was diagnosed with pulmonary oedema. On 15 April he slipped into a coma and died two days later, just a few weeks short of his seventy-fifth birthday.

It was estimated that over 50,000 people lined the streets on Saturday, 19 April to view his funeral cortège. Millions watched on television. Beauvoir struggled through the swelling crowds and paparazzi on whisky and valium, finally throwing a white rose into Sartre's open grave at Montparnasse. 'You are in your little box; you will not come out of it and I shall not join you there,' she wrote in *Adieux: A Farewell to Sartre*. 'Even if I am buried next to you there will be no communication between your ashes and mine.'

A few days later Sartre's body was exhumed and taken to Père Lachaise cemetery for cremation. His ashes were later returned to the Montparnasse tomb. Beauvoir was too ill to attend the cremation ceremony. 'I took too many tranquillizers', she later commented, 'and drank too much alcohol, while he was ill, to try to hold on, not to break down. I was in a very bad shape when he died. My lungs were congested, I could no longer walk.' Shortly after the funeral she was diagnosed with pneumonia and depression, and hospitalised for a month.

Beauvoir was a heavy drinker and suffered from cirrhosis of the liver. In March 1986 she was admitted to hospital for surgery, and after several weeks of struggling with the congestion on her lungs, she drifted into a coma and died on 14 April. She was buried beside Sartre in Montparnasse Cemetery. Thousands lined the streets for a glimpse of the hearse, and many more blocked the cemetery entrance and climbed its walls. 'My life was hurrying, racing tragically toward its end,' she wrote in *The Woman Destroyed*, 'And yet at the same time it was dripping so slowly, so very slowly now, hour by hour, minute by minute. One always has to wait until the sugar melts, the memory dies, the wound scars over, the sun sets, the unhappiness lifts and fades away.'

See Also: Jean-Paul Sartre, Simone de Beauvoir, Café de Flore, Sorbonne.

Further Reading: S. de Beauvoir, *Adieux: A Farewell to Sartre* (Pantheon, 1984); C. Seymour-Jones, *A Dangerous Liaison* (Century, 2008); S. Bakewell, *At The Existentialist Café* (Chatto & Windus, 2016).

GUY DE MAUPASSANT

(1850–1893)

DIVISION 26

FATHER OF THE MODERN SHORT STORY

Great minds that are healthy are never considered geniuses, while this sublime qualification is lavished on brains that are often inferior but are slightly touched by madness. Guy de Maupassant, 'The Englishman of Étretat' (L'Anglais d'Étretat) (1882)

Guy de Maupassant was privileged to have been a pupil and protégé of Gustave Flaubert, one of the great masters of the contemporary novel. 'I don't know whether you will have any talent,' Flaubert once told him, after perusing some of his early attempts at writing. 'What you have brought to me proves you have some intelligence, but don't forget this, young man, that talent, as Buffon said, is simply long patience. Work.' With Flaubert's guidance and training Maupassant ultimately perfected the writer's craft in virtually all genres, from the novel to verse. But his name will always remain synonymous with the short story, a medium for which he became the standard-bearer, and which made his fortune. However, his dazzling success and subsequent fame was to be his downfall, where a combination of extravagant living, overwork and failing health led to his ruin and attempted suicide.

Maupassant was born in Normandy, near Dieppe, in 1850. When he was nineteen he began studying law in Paris, but his studies were interrupted by the Franco-Prussian war of 1870, at which time he joined the army. The following year, after the war, he became a civil servant at the Naval Ministry in Paris: a tedious, bureaucratic routine he explored in some of his early short stories. Although he had strong literary ambitions, he published little until 1880, when one short story, 'Boule de suif' ('Ball of Fat'), launched him from obscurity to national fame.

Set during the Franco-Prussian war, ten stagecoach passengers are fleeing the Prussians and heading for the coast at Le Havre. One of the passengers is a prostitute named Elisabeth Rousset, and her travelling companions are a mixture of people from all social levels. Essentially, the carriage and passengers are a microcosmic representation of French society in the late nineteenth century. Predictably, the passengers initially spurn the prostitute, but warm to her when she offers to share her food with them. When the coach is halted by the Prussians at a coaching inn, it soon becomes apparent that the travellers will not be allowed to proceed until Elisabeth sleeps with their officer. Elisabeth persistently refuses, and the other passengers, who are supportive of her stance at first, grow impatient, and after many spurious, seemingly moral, arguments, they convince Elisabeth it

381

is the right thing to do. Elisabeth gives in and sleeps with the officer, and the next morning their journey continues. Back in the coach the passengers again ignore Elisabeth, who weeps for her lost dignity.

Flaubert described the story as 'nothing more or less than the work of a master'. 'Boule de suif' first appeared in the short story collection, *Les Soirées de Médan* (Evenings at Médan), which went through eight reprints in two weeks. Its six contributors included Émile Zola, Joris-Karl Huysmans and Paul Alexis. The anthology's title, *Les Soirées de Médan*, refers to Zola's house at Médan, near Paris, where writers including Maupassant would meet for dinner and promote their ideals of Naturalism, a French literary movement in prose fiction that sought its inspiration from everyday life. After the publication of 'Boule de suif' in 1880, when Maupassant's career was well and truly established, he was at last able to live by his pen. During the next ten years he achieved great success with his short stories and novels. The trappings of success brought wealth, mistresses, houses, yachts, influential friends and the means to travel widely. But there was another side to Maupassant; his health was weakened by the syphilis he had been infected with in his twenties, and he was fretful, and prone to depression and suicidal thoughts. He also had the worry of inherited psychiatric disorders: his mother was depressive and his sister and brother died insane. By 1890 his health had gone into a rapid decline, with fits of depression and paralysis. During Christmas 1891, at Cannes, he wrote to his doctor:

I am utterly without hope. I am in my death agony. I have a softening of the brain brought on by my bathing my nostrils with salt-water. The salt has fermented in my brain and every night my brains are dripping through my nose and mouth in a sticky paste … It means Death is near and I am going mad.

During the night in early January 1892 Maupassant attempted to shoot himself, but his valet had already removed the bullets from his gun. In his frustration he grabbed a paperknife from his desk and stabbed himself in the throat. This, too, was a failed suicide attempt. A few days later he was conveyed by train to Paris and taken in a straitjacket to a clinic in Passy, where he died, insane, on 6 July 1893, a few weeks before his forty-third birthday.

See Also: Gustave Flaubert, Émile Zola, Joris-Karl Huysmans.

Select Bibliography: Short story collections: *Les Soirées de Médan* (1880); *La Maison Tellier* (1881); *Mademoiselle Fifi* (1883); *Miss Harriet* (1884); *Toine* (1886). Novels: *Une Vie* (1883); *Bel-Ami* (1885); *Pierre et Jean* (1888).

Further Reading: M. Lerner, *Maupassant* (George Allen & Unwin Ltd., 1975).

JOSEPH KESSEL
(1898–1979)
DIVISION 28

NOVELIST AND JOURNALIST
BEST KNOWN FOR HIS EROTIC NOVEL
BELLE DE JOUR

To reach her mother's room from her own, Séverine who was eight had to go down a long hallway. She disliked the trip, and invariably ran all the way. But one morning Séverine was brought up short halfway down the corridor. A door leading to the bathroom had just opened. A plumber appeared: short, squat. From under sparse reddish lashes his eyes contemplated the girl. Bold as she was, Séverine was scared, took a step back. Her movement decided him. He glanced around sharply and grabbed Séverine with both hands. An odor of gas, of animal strength closed against her. Two ill-shaven lips burned her neck. She fought back. The workman laughed silently, sensually. Under her frock his hands slipped over the soft flesh. Suddenly Séverine stopped struggling. She was stiff, white. The man put her on the floor and left noiselessly.

Joseph Kessel, *Belle de Jour* (1928)

Joseph Kessel would be little remembered today outside France had it not been for the publication of his controversial novel, *Belle de Jour*, in 1928, and the subsequent film of the book, directed by Luis Buñuel, in 1967. Partly serialised in the French newspaper *Gringoire* in 1927, it was deemed a scandalous book at that time, telling the story of a society woman who spends her days working in a brothel as a prostitute while her husband is at work. Although there are neither graphic sex scenes nor racy language in the story, the book was misunderstood by many and accused of being pornographic and gratuitously licentious.

'From the moment I chose to write on this subject', wrote Kessel, 'I knew the risks I ran ... What I tried to do in *Belle de Jour* was show the desperate divorce that can exist between body and soul; between a true, tender, immense love and the implacable demands of the senses. ... I chose my subject as one examines a sick heart: in order better to know how a healthy one functions.'

Kessel, a Russian Jew, was born in Argentina due to the peripatetic lifestyle of his father, a Lithuanian doctor, but his early life was spent in Orenburg, Russia, close to the Kazakhstan border. When he was ten years old the family moved to France. An adventurer at heart, he was a bombardier in World War I, later becoming a travel writer and a journalist, and, in World War II, a Resistance fighter. He wrote over sixty novels and short stories, many of them autobiographical. The author Irwin Shaw recalls that Kessel was 'a giant of a man physically and morally, who could at the age of seventy still crush you in his arms when he embraced you after returning from one of his voyages to the far corners of the earth ... Kessel was a drinker, not a drunk. No drunk could have produced what he did in his lifetime.' Joseph Kessel died in 1979 at his home near Paris, aged eighty-one.

Further Information: The title *Belle de Jour* is a French pun. 'Belle de nuit' translates in English as 'lady of the night': a prostitute. But as Séverine, the prostitute in the novel works during the day, she is 'Belle de jour'. In 1943 Kessel co-authored with his nephew, Maurice Druon, the unofficial anthem of the Free French Forces, 'Chant des Partisans'. Kessel became a member of the Académie française. Prix Joseph Kessel is now a prestigious prize in French language literature.

383

HUBERT BEUVE-MÉRY

(1902–1989)

DIVISION 11

JOURNALIST, EDITOR

AND FOUNDER OF *LE MONDE*

What good will it do? You know my ideas and I know yours.
President de Gaulle's reply to Beuve-Méry's request for an interview.

When Hubert Beuve-Méry died at the age of eighty-seven on 6 August 1989, he was widely regarded as the conscience of the French press and the voice of the free press. From the ruins of the once liberal daily, and later pro-Vichy, *Le Temps*, Beuve-Méry founded *Le Monde* at President de Gaulle's request, following the expulsion of the German army from Paris. Taking over the old offices of *Le Temps*, he dismissed all its collaborationist staff members and rolled out the first issue of *Le Monde* on 19 December 1944.

Initially, financial support came from de Gaulle's government, but Beuve-Méry was insistent on the newspaper having editorial independence. De Gaulle conceded, but it was a decision he would later regret. Over the years Beuve-Méry, whose pen name was 'Sirius', stood up to de Gaulle on countless issues, notably France's involvement in Indochina and Algeria. His principle of total freedom for the press, with no political compromise, eventually established *Le Monde* as one of the most important and respected newspapers in the world.

See Also: Paris *Tribune*, Paris *Herald*, President de Gaulle, Pierre Beaumarchais.

Further Information: *Le Temps* was founded in 1861 by Edmund Chojecki and Auguste Nefftzer, and became one of the French Republic's most important newspapers until its closure by President de Gaulle's government in 1944. After *Le Monde*, France's second-largest newspaper is *Le Figaro*. Founded as a satirical gossip sheet in 1826, it was named after the eponymous hero in Beaumarchais's play, *Le Mariage de Figaro*, who declares 'Sans la liberté de blâmer, il n'est point d'éloge flatteur' ('Without the freedom to criticise, there is no true praise'). *Le Figaro* became a daily in 1866, and up until the start of World War II, it was France's leading newspaper. Rather than suffer censorship under the Vichy government it suspended production, but today it remains the conservative voice of France.

First edition of *Le Monde* on 19 December 1944

15th Arrondissement

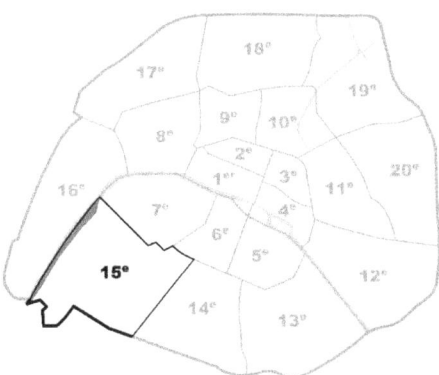

WALTER BENJAMIN

10 RUE DOMBASLE

(Métro: Convention)

FORMER HOME OF WALTER BENJAMIN GERMAN JEWISH PHILOSOPHER AND ESSAYIST, REGARDED AS GERMANY'S MOST SIGNIFICANT LITERARY CRITIC DURING THE FIRST HALF OF THE TWENTIETH CENTURY

A Klee painting named Angelus Novus shows an angel looking as though he is about to move away from something he is fixedly contemplating. His eyes are staring, his mouth is open, his wings are spread. This is how one pictures the angel of history. His face is turned toward the past. Where we perceive a chain of events, he sees one single catastrophe which keeps piling wreckage upon wreckage and hurls it in front of his feet. The angel would like to stay, awaken the dead, and make whole what has been smashed. But a storm is blowing from Paradise; it has got caught in his wings with such violence that the angel can no longer close them. The storm irresistibly propels him into the future to which his back is turned, while the pile of debris before him grows skyward. This storm is what we call progress.

Walter Benjamin, *Theses on the Philosophy of History* (1942)

Born in Berlin in 1892, Walter Benjamin's life was a succession of problems, failures, and dreams destroyed, ending in his death in 1940 while fleeing the Gestapo. After studying literature and philosophy in Germany, Benjamin worked as a freelance critic and translator, notably of Baudelaire and Proust. In 1933 he fled Germany to escape the rise of Nazism and eventually settled in Paris. Throughout his relatively short life Benjamin struggled to make a living at writing, and with Hitler in power hopes of a Jewish author publishing in Germany were unthinkable. He experimented with most literary forms, including short stories, novellas, essays, fables and parables, and the critical writings that made his name. He even penned an outline for a crime novel, and his autobiographical vignettes, entitled *Berlin Childhood Around 1900*, were published posthumously in 1950. His old friend Bertolt Brecht, living in exile in Denmark, eventually turned him towards Marxian materialism, and it was his study in this field that resulted in his well-known essays, *The Work of Art in an Age of Mechanical Reproduction* (1936), and his last complete work, *Theses on the Philosophy of History*, completed before his death in 1940 but published posthumously two years later. In the late 1920s he had begun work on his magnum opus, which would become known in English as *The Arcades Project*. It consists of a mammoth collection of writings on nineteenth-century Paris focusing on its iron and glass covered arcades, known in French as the *passages couverts de Paris*. These were early centres of consumer culture, and the forerunners of the modern day shopping mall. Originally Benjamin saw the project as a short article on the rise and fall of the arcades, but it kept on growing until it became a vast framework for a far-reaching cultural theory of modernity.

With the outbreak of war in 1939, Benjamin, as a German national, was temporarily interned in a French prison camp. After his release a few months later he returned to Paris and continued his work on *The Arcades Project* at his home from home in the Bibliothèque Nationale on Rue Richelieu.

Walter Benjamin in the late 1930s

His real home, from 1938 to 1940, was a seventh-floor apartment at No. 10 rue Dombasle (now marked by a plaque), where his friend and neighbour, Arthur Koestler, also lived. When the Germans advanced on Paris in the summer of 1940, Benjamin left the unfinished manuscript of *The Arcades Project* with a friend to hide before fleeing south to the uncertain safety of Vichy France, where he intended to make arrangements to cross the Spanish frontier and hopefully sail to America. In Marseille he ran into Koestler who was also searching for an escape route. 'He asked me,' wrote Koestler in his memoir, *Scum of the Earth*,

'If anything goes wrong, have you got anything to take?' For in those days we all carried some stuff in our pockets like conspirators in a penny dreadful, only reality was more dreadful. I had none, and he shared what he had with me, 62 tablets of a [morphine] sedative … He did it reluctantly, for he did not know whether the 31 tablets left him would be enough. It was enough.

A few days later, and lacking an exit visa from France, Benjamin joined a guided party that attempted to cross the Pyrenees. The Spanish authorities refused the group entry and, fearing his fate at the hands of the Gestapo, Benjamin took his own life in a hotel room in Portbou, in the foothills of the Pyrenees on 26 September 1940. He is buried in the local Cementiri de Portbou where the exact location of his grave is unknown, but a plaque commemorates him with his own words: 'There is no document of civilisation that is not at the same time a document of barbarism.'

See Also: Marcel Proust, Charles Baudelaire, Bibliothèque Nationale.

Further Information: The cause of death on Benjamin's death certificate read 'cerebral haemorrhage'. Koestler, however, later took the same quantity of morphine tablets in Lisbon and survived. A theory persists that Benjamin didn't commit suicide, but was murdered by Stalin's agents.

Select Bibliography: *The Arcades Project* (Harvard University Press, 2002); *Walter Benjamin: Selected Writings,* (4 vols. covering work from 1913 to 1940, Harvard University Press, 2004).

Further Reading: H. Eiland, M. Jennings, *Walter Benjamin: A Critical Life* (Harvard University Press, 2014); R. Wolin, *Walter Benjamin: An Aesthetic of Redemption* (University of California Press, 1994).

Top: Passage des Princes, 5 boulevard des Italiens. Above: Rue Dombasle

387

BLAISE CENDRARS

PASSAGE DE DANTZIG

(Métro: Convention)

LA RUCHE

FORMER ATELIER OF

BLAISE CENDRARS

NOVELIST, POET AND TRAVELLER

Blaise Cendrars

Personally, since I have no faith, I will not be there to see the Second Coming. But nor will I be on the side of the sensitive souls. I chose my corner a long time ago, not in the graveyard of the Church, but in an ideal spot on a steamer's course, where a suicide can easily dive overboard and plunge in among the sargasso weed that floats there in the great indigo vat. This is situated at: latitude zero, 1, 2, or 3-tenths South, by 1, 2, or 3-dozen degrees West, due West, let us say from 13 to 33 ...

I hope they will let me choose this spot in peace.

I will not ask for any fanfares.

At the most, a big sperm whale to swallow me.

Blaise Cendrars, *Sky: Memoirs* (1949)

In a way, Swiss-born Blaise Cendrars invented himself, along with his name, creating legend out of his life and writings. Eccentric and temperamental, he led a life of travel and adventure, and his itinerant wanderings were at the roots of his verse and prose. The New York news and culture paper, *The Village Voice*, described him as 'The Indiana Jones of French literature', a moniker he would no doubt have approved of; and his friend Henry Miller wrote that his life read 'like the Arabian Nights Entertainment'. But Cendrars's accounts of his early life should be read as an intriguing blend of fact and fiction,

or a '*divertissement*' as he liked to call it. They were also an essential part of what made this great raconteur one of the grand figures of modernism. 'The most famous imaginary hero created by the Swiss writer', wrote one critic, 'could well be Blaise Cendrars.'

In 1887, Frédéric-Louis Sauser, who would become known as Blaise Cendrars, was born to a French father and a Scottish mother in the watchmaking town of La Chaux-de-Fonds in Switzerland. His nomadic life began as a teenager when he was apprenticed to Swiss watchmakers in Russia. In the winter of 1911 he visited New York, which inspired his poem *Les Pâques à New York (Easter in New York)* (1912), and in 1913 he wrote *La Prose du Transsibérien*, an epic poem recounting an imaginary transcontinental train journey. These poems not only ensured his place among the avant-garde poets of Paris, they also altered the face of modern verse.

In 1914 he joined the Foreign Legion and lost his right arm in battle, an experience he later wrote about in *La Main Coupée (The Bloody Hand)*

(1946). After the war he became part of the artistic community in Montparnasse, where he concentrated on writing novels and short stories. It was here that Ernest Hemingway, in *A Moveable Feast*, describes an encounter with him:

> The only poet I saw [at La Closerie des Lilas] was Blaise Cendrars, with his broken boxer's face and his pinned-up empty sleeve, rolling a cigarette with his one good hand. He was a good companion until he drank too much, and at that time, when he was lying, he was more interesting than many men telling a story truly.

Cendrars became immersed in the film industry for a while and was a war correspondent during World War II. He travelled all over the world, but for a period prior to the outbreak of the First World War, he lived and worked in what became one of the largest artistic communes in Paris, known as La Ruche (the beehive) in the Passage de Dantzig. Among its inhabitants were Amedeo Modigliani, Marc Chagall, Max Jacob, Chaim Soutine, Guillaume Apollinaire and Fernand Léger. 'These ateliers were occupied by artistic Bohemians from all over the world', wrote Chagall. 'While an offended model sobbed in the Russian ateliers, the Italian studios rang with songs and the sound of guitars, the Jewish ones with discussions.' La Ruche was the creation of philanthropic French sculptor, Alfred Boucher (1850–1934), who purchased land in 1902 near the slaughterhouses on Rue de Vaugirard, where he erected leftover buildings and materials from the 1900 Paris World's Fair. The major part of the building came from the Médoc wine pavilion, the rotunda of which had an octagonal exterior on three levels, which housed many studios. Its wrought-iron gates came from the Palace of the Woman, and the classical statues guarding its threshold, from the British India pavilion. Threatened with demolition in 1968, it has since been preserved and renovated and is now home to a new generation of artists.

Contrary to his expectations, Blaise Cendrars did not die by diving overboard from a steamer and plunging into the Sargasso Sea, as he had predicted in his *Sky: Memoirs*, but died in Paris following a stroke in 1961.

See Also: Henry Miller, Guillaume Apollinaire, Foreign Legion, Ernest Hemingway, La Closerie des Lilas, Eiffel Tower.

Select Bibliography: *Blaise Cendrars Complete Poems* (1993); *Moravagine* (1926); *Blaise Cendrars Selected Writings* (2010); *La Main Coupée (The Bloody Hand)* (1946).

Entrance to La Ruche, Passage de Dantzig

ANNA AKHMATOVA

CITÉ FALGUIÈRE

(Métro: Pasteur)

STUDIO OF ITALIAN PAINTER AND
SCULPTOR AMEDEO MODIGLIANI
LOVER OF RUSSIAN POET
ANNA AKHMATOVA

Bitter languor has been weathered
With the winter snows.
Why, o why, must you be better
Than the one I chose?
Anna Akhmatova, from 'Nothing chains a
heart to heart'

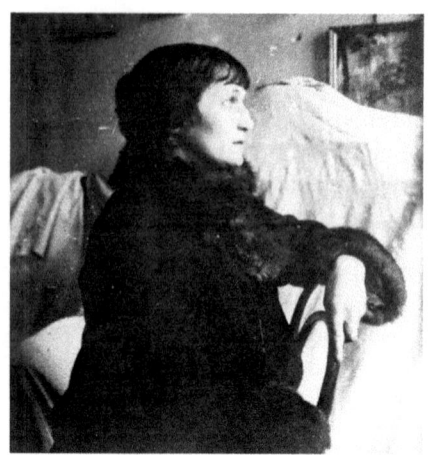

Anna Akhmatova (1889–1966) was the outspoken poet of Russian wretchedness and persecution under Stalin. Officially silenced from 1922 until 1940, and her poetry banned in 1946, she would not flee from Stalin's terror. 'I am not one of those who left their land to the mercy of the enemy,' she later wrote. But in 1910 the door to an alternative future briefly opened, and it led to the West. That year she married the poet Nikolay Gumilyov (1886–1921), and the newly-weds spent their honeymoon in Paris. It was an unhappy union, which would end in divorce in 1918, but for the present the cultural capital of the world lay before them. Akhmatova was twenty-one and it was her first experience of western Europe. Being poets, they mixed with the artistic avant-garde, and it was here that Akhmatova met and later had an affair with the then unknown Amedeo Modigliani. 'In 1910 I saw him very rarely, just a few times,' wrote Akhmatova in 'Memories of Modigliani' in *The London Magazine* (1964):

But he wrote to me during the whole winter. I remember some sentences from

Top: Anna Akhmatova
Above: Amedeo Modigliani *c.*1912

his letter. One was: *Vous êtes en moi comme une hantise* (you are obsessively a part of me). …
We both probably failed to realise a crucial point: everything that was happening was for both of us but the prehistory of our lives – of his very short life, of my long life. …
He lived in dire poverty, and I don't know how he lived. He enjoyed no recognition whatsoever as a painter. At that time (1911) he lived in the Impasse Falguière. He was so poor that in the Jardin du Luxembourg we sat on a bench and not, as was usual, on chairs since

you had to pay for them. He complained neither about his poverty nor about the lack of recognition, both of which were clearly apparent. ...

He did not draw me from life but alone at home. He gave me these drawings as a gift; there were sixteen of them. He asked me to frame them and to hang them in my room. They were lost in Tsarskoye Selo during the first revolution.

Akhmatova visited Paris again in 1911, but unlike many other Russian artists she did not permanently embrace the artistic freedom of the West, and returned to live through the 1917 revolution and Stalin's purges. When she died in 1966 she was the most celebrated woman poet in Russian literature.

Modigliani never achieved fame or fortune during his short life, dying of tubercular meningitis in 1920 at the Hôpital de la Charité in Paris. At a New York auction house in 2015, a Modigliani 1917–1918 canvas, *Nu Couché*, sold for $170.4 million.

'Once when I went to call on Modigliani, he was out,' wrote Akhmatova:

We had apparently misunderstood each other so I decided to wait several minutes. I was clutching an armful of red roses. A window above the locked gates of the studio was open. Having nothing better to do, I began to toss the flowers in through the window. Then without waiting any longer, I left. When we met again, he was perplexed at how I had entered the locked room because he had the key. I explained what had happened, 'but that's impossible – they were lying there so beautifully'.

Further Information: Modigliani is buried in Père Lachaise Cemetery, Division 96, beside his partner Jeanne Hébuterne

(1898–1920), who jumped from a fifth-floor window the day after Modigliani's death, killing herself and their unborn baby. Their daughter, Jeanne Modigliani (1918–1984) survived them. The cul-de-sac Cité Falguière was built in the late nineteenth century as an area of low-cost studios that served as work and living space for several modern artists, including Amedeo Modigliani, Paul Gauguin, Chaim Soutine, Tsuguharu Foujita and Constantin Bracusi. Modigliani's studio was number 14, but now only numbers 9 and 11 survive, which, at the time of writing, are still used as artists' studios.

Select Bibliography: *Vecher (Evening)* (1912); *Chokti (The Rosary)* (1913); *Belaya Staya (White Flock)* (1917); *Anno Domini MCMXXI* (1922); *Poema bez geroya (Poem without a Hero)* (1940–1962); *Rekviem (Requiem)* (1963).

Further Reading: A. Haight, *Anna Akhmatova: A Poetic Pilgrimage* (Oxford University Press, 1976); E. Feinstein, *Anna of all the Russias* (W&N, 2006); J. Modigliani, *Modigliani: Man and Myth* (Andreì Deutsch, 1959).

Cité Falguière

16th

Arrondissement

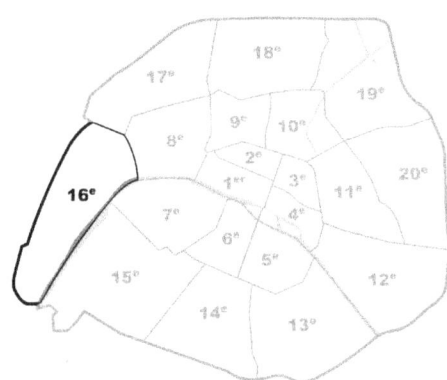

HONORÉ DE BALZAC

47 RUE RAYNOUARD

(Métro: Passy/La Muette)

MAISON DE BALZAC

FORMER HOME OF HONORÉ DE BALZAC

FOUNDER OF THE MODERN NOVEL

Balzac's style is bad; in spite of the electric vigour that runs through his writing, it is formless, clumsy, and quite without distinction; it is the writing of a man who was highly perspicacious, formidably powerful, and vulgar. But, on the other hand, he possessed one great quality which Hugo altogether lacked – the sense of the real. Hugo was most himself when he was soaring on the wings of fancy through the empyrean; Balzac was most himself when he was rattling in a hired cab through the streets of Paris. He was of the earth earthy.

Lytton Strachey, *Landmarks in French Literature* (1912)

Honoré de Balzac's fictional world represents the kaleidoscope of nineteenth-century Parisian society, which was filled with wretchedness and poverty, greed and jealousy, and was littered with characters on the road to destruction: disreputable dealers, abandoned lovers, erotomaniacs, crooks, misers and the ruthlessly ambitious. His greatest creation was the monumental *La Comédie humaine*, a study of the whole of contemporary society from the French Revolution to the fall of Louis-Philippe in 1848. Published in 17 volumes between 1842 and 1847, it was an astonishing achievement.

A labour of love, but also a financial necessity, Balzac produced 85 novels in 20 years. Working mostly through the night and wearing his customary monk's robe, he could write for ten to fourteen hours a day. His range of characters (*La Comédie humaine* has over 2,000) and the sheer scale of his work made him one of the giants of realism and the founder of the modern novel.

Balzac's father, Bernard-François Balssa, was an ambitious young man who elevated himself from peasant stock to become Secretary to the King's Council by the time he was thirty. During this rapid rise he changed his name from Balssa to Balzac. In 1795 he was posted to Tours, where he supervised food provisions for the army. Two years later, at the age of fifty, he married eighteen-year-old Anne-Charlotte-Laure Sallambier. Their son Honoré was born on 20 May 1799, in Tours, where the family remained for fifteen years before moving to Paris.

Honoré de Balzac

Honoré became a clerk in various law offices, but soon wearying of the predictability of the work, he turned to literature. His parents gave the change their grudging consent and furnished him with a meagre allowance, the caveat being that if he hadn't succeeded within two years he would have to get himself a proper job. Predictably, at first he earned neither fame nor money, publishing mostly unmemorable, sometimes scandalous, novels, under pseudonyms. He also got involved in reckless business schemes, and by the age of twenty-nine he was over 100,000 francs in debt.

Lesser men would have buckled under the strain, but for Balzac the pressure seemed to nurture him. Undaunted, he published *Les Chouans* in 1829, his first novel under his own name. His first success, Balzac was now beginning to understand the novel and map out his literary future. Boosted, no doubt, by his growing expertise, it was around this time that he added the aristocratic-sounding 'de' to his name, observing, in 1830, that 'the aristocracy and authority of talent are more substantial than the aristocracy of names and material power.'

His first great public triumph was *La Peau de chagrin (The Wild Ass's Skin)*, written in 1831. Shortly after its publication he received an anonymous letter of literary criticism from a woman, signed mysteriously, 'l'Étrangère'. This began a long correspondence with Polish noblewoman, Ewelina Hańska, the woman he would eventually marry shortly before his death.

In 1834 Balzac came up with the idea of grouping his novels together under a common title. The result was a gargantuan study of a living city, from its summit to its lowest depths, which he called *La Comédie humaine*.

Throughout his life creditors relentlessly pursued Balzac. He even wrote a play, 'about a man and the battles he has with his creditors, the tricks he uses to escape their clutches', called *Mercadet*. From October 1840 until April 1847 he rented a house at 19 rue Basse (now 47 rue Raynouard) in Passy. The lease was not signed by Balzac, but by his housekeeper, and thus he hid himself behind the name Madame de Breugnol.

The house was concealed between two roads: a higher and a lower and, crucially, it had two entrances. Should creditors call at one of them, the other could become a hasty exit route.

Balzac lived out his final years, from 1847 until his death in 1850, at his house on Rue Fortunée (now Rue Balzac). Here the great realist died, aged fifty-one, from a gangrene associated with congestive heart failure, only five months after his marriage to the Countess Ewelina Hańska. 'But Balzac is no more a realist than Holbein was,' wrote Oscar Wilde. 'He created life, he did not copy it.'

See Also: Tomb of Balzac, Oscar Wilde.

Select Bibliography: *Les Chouans* (1829); *La Peau de Chagrin* (1831); *Eugénie Grandet* (1833); *Séraphîta* (1834); *Le Père Goriot* (1835); *La Cousine Bette* (1846).

Further Reading: G. Robb, *Balzac* (Picador, 1994); M. Sandars, *Honoré de Balzac* (Kennikat, 1970); A. Maurois, *Prometheus: The Life of Balzac* (Carroll & Graf, 1993).

Above: Maison de Balzac Top: side entrance of house

395

HENRI BERGSON

47 BOULEVARD DE BEAUSÉJOUR

(Métro: La Muette)

FORMER HOME OF HENRI BERGSON

FRENCH PHILOSOPHER

AND NOBEL PRIZE WINNER

Henri Bergson in 1900

I had remained up to that time wholly imbued with mechanistic theories to which I had been led at an early date by the reading of [English sociologist and philosopher] Herbert Spencer. It was the analysis of the notion of time, as it enters into mechanics and physics, which overturned all my ideas. I saw to my great surprise, that scientific time does not endure, that positive science consists essentially in the elimination of duration. This was the point of departure of a series of reflections which brought me by gradual steps to reject almost all of what I had hitherto accepted, and to change my point of view completely.

Henri Bergson explaining his awakening in a letter to American philosopher and psychologist, William James, in 1908.

Henri Bergson's theories on modern thought and literature had a far-reaching influence on writers of the modernist generation at the turn of the twentieth century. The way he set about portraying consciousness and time profoundly affected Marcel Proust, Virginia Woolf, T.S. Eliot and others who, in their writing, employed the style coined by William James as stream of consciousness.

The rudiments of Bergson's philosophy see the world divided into consciousness and matter, with the inherent creativity possessed by consciousness seeking to impose itself on matter to create new forms of life.

Bergson was very much in vogue in the early twentieth century and he became something of a fashionable cult figure. Between 1896 and 1907 he published the three major works that cemented his reputation and gained him worldwide renown: *Time and Free Will, Matter and Memory* and *Creative Evolution*.

He was born at 18 rue Lamartine in 1859, the second of seven children of Jewish parents. His father, a musician, was from a wealthy Polish family, whose name Bergson derives from 'Bereksohn' or 'the sons of Berek'. His mother's background was English and Irish Jewish. The family lived in London for several years after his birth, returning to Paris before his ninth birthday. In Paris, Bergson studied philosophy, and after a career as a schoolteacher, he was appointed to the École Normale Supérieure in 1898. Four years later, until his retirement in 1921, he held the Chair of Modern Philosophy at the Collège de France. In 1915 he became one of the '40 immortals' of the Académie française, and in 1927 he was awarded the Nobel Prize in Literature.

'It is in a sense appropriate', wrote British literary critic, Martin Seymour-Smith,

> that Bergson, although not an imaginative writer, should have received the Nobel Prize for Literature: his influence on literature has been wide and deep. He demanded a return to the 'immediate data of consciousness', and he believed that this could be grasped by means of what he called 'intuition'. Like a number of modern novelists he saw character not as 'personality' but as a process of ceaseless becoming.

Bergson was too ill to attend the Nobel ceremony in Stockholm as he was suffering from a degenerative form of rheumatism that paralysed much of his body. His time of prominence waned somewhat during the late 1920s, and he lived out the rest of his days with his wife and daughter in Paris. From 1940 until his death in 1941, he suffered the horror and humiliation of the Nazi occupation when all Jews were made to register with the German authorities. Bergson wrote on his registration form, 'Academic. Philosopher. Nobel Prize winner. Jew.' He died shortly afterwards from bronchitis, aged eighty-one, and is buried in the Cimetière de Garches, in the western suburbs of Paris.

See Also: Marcel Proust, T.S. Eliot, Henry James, Maurice Merleau-Ponty.

Further Information: Born a Jew, Bergson was inclined in later life towards Catholicism. However, unwilling to seem to be deserting the Jewish people during their time of persecution under the Nazis, he did not undergo conversion. The term 'stream of consciousness' was introduced by American philosopher and psychologist, William James, in his *Principles of Psychology* (1890).

Select Bibliography: *Time and Free Will* (1889); *Matter and Memory* (1896); *Creative Evolution* (1907).

Further Reading: K. Ansell-Pearson, *Philosophy and the Adventure of the Virtual: Bergson and the Time of Life* (Routledge, 2002); S. Guerlac, *Thinking in Time: An Introduction to Henri Bergson* (Cornell University Press, 2006).

Top: 47 boulevard de Beauséjour
Above: Plaque to the right of the entrance

RENÉE VIVIEN

2 RUE DU COMMANDANT SCHLOESING

(Métro: Trocadéro)

ENGLISH–BORN SAPPHIC POET

CIMETIÈRE DE PASSY (DIVISION 13)

There is not a single feature of her youthful face that I do not vividly recall. Everything in it bespoke childishness, roguishness, and the propensity to laughter. Impossible to find anywhere in that face, from the fair hair to the sweet dimple of the weak little chin, any line that was not a line of laughter, any sign of the hidden tragic melancholy that throbs in the poetry of Renée Vivien. I never saw Renée sad. She would exclaim, in her lisping English accent, 'Oh, my dear little Colette, how disgusting this life is!' Then she would burst into laughter. In all too many of her notes, I find that same exclamation repeated, often spelled out frankly in the coarsest words: 'Isn't this life sheer muck? Well, I hope it will soon be over!'

Colette, *The Pure and the Impure* (1932)

Renée Vivien was born Pauline Mary Tarn to a British father and an American mother in London, in 1877. On inheriting her father's fortune at the age of twenty-one, she settled permanently in Paris where, living openly as a lesbian, she became one of the first modern women poets to write about love between women. She was a disciple of the Greek poet, Sappho, whose lyric poetry she translated. Her literary output was impressive. Within ten years she had written over twenty volumes of poetry, short stories, prose poems and one novel. Most of her poetry, including her translations of Sappho, was written in French, and very little of her work exists in English translation, which is a legacy that has denied her the recognition she deserves in the English-speaking world.

Renée Vivien had a genuine gift for poetry, but her short, self-destructive life, fuelled by alcohol and drugs, contributed to her early death at the age of only thirty-two.

One of the most famous portraits by a contemporary of Vivien's eccentric world was a character sketch by her near neighbour and friend, Colette, in *The Pure and the Impure*. The sketch doesn't reveal anything about Vivien's poetry as their friendship, according to Colette, was 'not literary'. Instead, Colette focuses on Vivien's unorthodox lifestyle in a dark and exotic apartment filled with incense and gigantic Buddhas, concealing her poems in baskets of fruit to be given as gifts, or hiding them under cushions from inquisitive eyes. Colette was, however, intrigued to know her working methods, but the 'secretive' Vivien never revealed them.

Vivien had various relationships throughout her short life, notably with writer and salonnière, Natalie Barney, and Baroness Hélène van Zuylen, one of the Paris Rothschilds. Vivien died in 1909 from pneumonia, following complications from drug abuse, alcoholism, and anorexia nervosa. Shortly before her death she converted to Roman Catholicism, having thought she'd seen, as Colette observes in *The Pure and the Impure,*

in her spells of giddiness, in the aurora borealis of starvation … the flames of the Catholic hell. … I was by chance spared the sight of Renée dying, then dead. She carried off with her more than one secret, and beneath her purple veil, Renée Vivien, the poet, led away – her throat encircled with moonstones, beryls, aquamarines, and other anaemic gems – the immodest child, the excited little girl who taught me, with unembarrassed competence: 'There are fewer ways of making love than they say, and more than one believes … '

See Also: Colette, Natalie Barney.

Further Information: Cimetière de Passy officially opened in 1820 and has an area of roughly four acres, lined with hundreds of horse chestnut trees. Located in one of the wealthiest residential areas of the city, it is amply stocked with the well-to-do. Notable residents include Claude Debussy, Édouard Manet and Gabriel Fauré. The grave of Vivien's lover, Natalie Barney, can be found in Division 9. Renée Vivien's Paris home was a ground floor apartment at 23 avenue du Bois de Boulogne (now 23 avenue Foch).

Select Bibliography: J-P Goujon (ed.), *Oeuvre poétique complète de Renée Vivien: 1877–1909* (1986).

Further Reading: Colette, *The Pure and the Impure* (Penguin, 1980); K. Jay, *The Amazon and the Page: Natalie Barney and Renée Vivien* (Indiana University Press, 1988).

Renée Vivien *c.*1905

ANATOLE FRANCE

5 VILLA SAÏD

(Métro: Port Dauphine)

FORMER HOME OF ANATOLE FRANCE
FRENCH POET AND NOVELIST
WINNER OF THE NOBEL PRIZE
IN LITERATURE

The good critic is he who relates the adventures of his soul in the midst of masterpieces.
Anatole France, *La Vie Littéraire* (1888)

Anatole France (1844–1924) is a neglected writer today, but he once had a huge international reputation, bodily endorsed by the 200,000 mourners who lined the streets of Paris for his funeral cortège. He is also a writer who cannot be pigeonholed in a particular genre because he cast his talents wide, scattering them across novels, essays, plays, short stories, poetry, criticism and journalism. He was witty, satirical, passionate and scholarly, winning the Nobel Prize in Literature in 1921, shortly before his death. His critics, though, have accused him of lacking in creative imagination and producing sparse plots. Today Anatole France is largely unacknowledged and, sadly, mostly unread.

The only son of a bookseller, Anatole-François Thibault, who would become known as Anatole France, was born at 19 quai Malaquais in Saint-Germain-des-Prés on 16 April 1844. Edmond de Goncourt, one of his father's customers, remembered him as a 'young wretch who seemed to have a perpetual cold in the head'. His father had hopes he would carry on the family trade, but France's ambition was to write, rather than sell, literature. It was around the

Anatole France in 1893

a candle in her hand. It became a sort of rite.' In 1877, following a six-month romance, escape arrived on his marriage to twenty-year-old Valérie Guérin de Sauville, with whom he had a daughter four years later. However, as a consequence of France's numerous affairs, the marriage ended in divorce in 1893. One of his most notable love affairs was with the wealthy *salonièrre* Madame Arman, the inspiration for Madame Verdurin in Proust's *In Search of Lost Time*.

During the Dreyfus Affair that split the French nation in the late-nineteenth and early-twentieth centuries, when Alfred Dreyfus, a Jewish army captain was falsely convicted of espionage, France, along with Émile Zola, supported the innocent Dreyfus. When Zola was stripped of his Légion d'honneur and tried for treason for writing *J'Accuse...!*, France publicly resigned his own membership.

By the 1890s France's fame and fortune were well and truly accomplished, and in 1894 he bought a house in keeping with his growing reputation. No. 5 villa Saïd, with its tall and narrow Second Empire facade, was purchased in 1894 for seventy thousand francs. France later installed, as housekeeper, Madame Arman's former maid, Emma Laprevotte, whom he subsequently married. France lived at 5 villa Saïd for the next twenty years; but it was an awkward and, in some ways, impractical house, being tall and narrow, lit by candles and oil lamps, having poor ventilation with smoking fires, and where both bathroom and kitchen were inconveniently situated in the basement. In 1914 he decided to demolish, then rebuild it, and by 1920, considerably delayed by the war, the new improved house was ready. In the meantime, France and Emma had been living in a small manor house near Tours

time he was working at his first job, as a part-time editorial assistant in 1865, that he started to fully concentrate on his writing. The following year a publisher gave him editorial control of a short-lived periodical, in which he included some of his own articles and poems. From 1876 to 1890 he was assistant librarian at the Senate, the upper house of the French parliament, though he was still writing and contributing to journals. His first novel, *Jocasta and the Famished Cat*, was published in 1879, but it was with the publication of *The Crime of Sylvestre Bonnard*, two years later, that his artistic reputation was established.

Meanwhile he was still living in the claustrophobic atmosphere of his parents' home. 'Until I was thirty-five,' he wrote, 'my mother never went to bed before she had seen me come in. At midnight, or at four in the morning, I would find her, silent and implacable, and discovered how much country life suited them. Consequently, France never felt comfortable in the new house and for the rest of his life he only lived there during the winter months, escaping the cold of the country. Suffering very poor health, he took to bed in August 1924, where he lingered on the point of death for two months. During one of his brief periods of lucidity, he was heard to sigh, 'So this is what it's like to die; it takes a long time.' Anatole France is buried in the Cimetière de Neuilly-sur-Seine, Division 106.

See Also: Les Bouquinistes, Émile Zola, Marcel Proust, Edmond de Goncourt.

Select Bibliography: *The Crime of Sylvestre Bonnard* (1881); *The Red Lily* (1894); *The Elm Tree on the Mall* (1897); *The Wicker-Work Woman* (1897); *The Amethyst Ring* (1899); *Monsieur Bergeret in Paris* (1901); *Penguin Island* (1908); *The Gods are Athirst* (1912); *Little Pierre* (1918); *The Bloom of Life* (1922).

Further Reading: D. Tylden-Wright, *Anatole France* (Collins, 1967).

Villa Saïd in 2019

PIERRE BOULLE

18 RUE DURET

(Métro: Argentine)

FORMER HOME PIERRE BOULLE

AUTHOR OF *THE BRIDGE OVER THE RIVER KWAI* AND *PLANET OF THE APES*

That perfected machines may one day succeed us is, I remember, an extremely commonplace notion on Earth. It prevails not only among poets and romantics but in all classes of society. Perhaps it is because it is so widespread, born spontaneously in popular imagination, that it irritates scientific minds. Perhaps it is also for this very reason that it contains a germ of truth. Only a germ: Machines will always be machines; the most perfected robot, always a robot. But what of living creatures possessing a certain degree of intelligence, like apes? And apes, precisely, are endowed with a keen sense of imitation.
Pierre Boulle, *Planet of the Apes* (1963)

Pierre Boulle wrote mainly in two genres: war and science fiction. It was a writing career that lasted over forty years, during which time he created more than thirty novels and numerous short stories; however, he would possibly be forgotten today had it not been for the film versions of his two novels *Le pont de la rivière Kwaï (The Bridge Over the River Kwai)* and *La planète des singes (Monkey Planet*, later issued as *Planet of the Apes)*. And although both films became classics of their genres, the talents of their creator remain virtually unsung, if not unknown.
Pierre Boulle was born in Avignon in 1912, and trained as an engineer in Paris. In the late 1930s he worked as a rubber planter in Malaya, but at the outbreak of war in 1939 he was mobilised as a second

Pierre Boulle

in *My Own River Kwai.* 'This was the course I had to take, and at once, without waiting another second.'

Selling everything he owned, he moved back to Paris in 1948 and rented a room in a small hotel (now demolished) in Montparnasse where he started writing on an old second-hand typewriter. His first published novel was *William Conrad*, a spy story published in 1950, but in 1952 he wrote the book for which he would be best remembered: *The Bridge Over the River Kwai*, a fictional story set around the construction of a bridge on the Burma Railway, known as the Death Railway because so many died building it during World War II. The novel won France's prestigious Prix Sainte-Beuve in 1952.

Boulle never married, and in 1955 he moved into his widowed sister's apartment on Rue Duret, where he helped care for her young daughter, and where he would write *Planet of the Apes* in 1963. It was here he died on 30 January 1994, aged eighty-one.

lieutenant and posted to Indochina. With the Fall of France in June 1940 he joined the Free French in Singapore, where he received commando training on how to blow up bridges, derail trains, and kill the enemy silently. After Japan entered the war in December 1941, the Free French moved their base to Kunming in China. When attempting to infiltrate Indochina by raft from China, Boulle was captured and handed over to the Vichy authorities, who court-martialled him for treason. Condemned to hard labour for life, he spent two years in prison from 1942 to 1944, eventually escaping and being repatriated to France in 1945. After the war he returned to his life on the rubber plantations of Malaya, but after experiencing something of a literary epiphany he decided to change the course of his life and become a writer. 'It was an instant revelation,' he wrote

Further Information: Pierre Boulle is buried in the Cimetière Saint-Véran (Plot Division 1), Saint-Véran, Hautes-Alpes department in south-eastern France.

Select Bibliography: *William Conrad* (1950); *The Bridge Over the River Kwai* (1954); *A Noble Profession* (1960); *Monkey Planet* (1963) (later issued as *Planet of the Apes*); *Garden on the Moon* (1965); *Time Out of Mind: And Other Stories* (1966); *The Source of the River Kwai* (1967); *An Impartial Eye* (1968).

Further Reading: L. Becker, *Pierre Boulle* (Twayne, 1996); J. Summers, *The Colonel of Tamarkan: Philip Toosey and the Bridge on the River Kwai* (Simon & Schuster, 2006).

ERICH MARIA REMARQUE

8 RUE DE SAIGON

(Métro: Argentine)

FORMERLY HÔTEL ANSONIA
PERIODIC RESIDENCE OF
ERICH MARIA REMARQUE
AND SETTING FOR HIS NOVEL
ARCH OF TRIUMPH

The dining room of the Hôtel International was in the basement. The lodgers called it the Catacombs. During the day a dim light came through several large, thick, opalescent-glass panes which faced on the courtyard. In the winter it had to be lighted all day long. The room was at once a writing room, a smoking room, an auditorium, an assembly room, and a refuge for those emigrants who had no papers – when there was a police inspection they could escape through the yard into a garage and from there to the next street.
Erich Maria Remarque, *Arch of Triumph* (1945)

DANS CET IMMEUBLE
A VECU L'ECRIVAIN
PIERRE BOULLE
DE 1956 A 1994

Top: 18 rue Duret
Above: Plaque to the left of the entrance

The Hôtel Ansonia was a safe house in the 1930s for refugees fleeing Nazi Germany: a place where stateless people without papers were admitted and no questions were asked. If they were lucky, it was only a brief staging post to flee a Europe on the brink of another world war. If they were not so lucky, it was a place to fester and remember a past that had vanished while waiting for an uncertain future. The German composer, Friedrich Hollaender, described it in his memoirs as 'this nest for the expelled, refuge of the expropriated, holding tank, transition camp, hotbed for all finds of premature births – of ideas for the future to suicide plans. The rooms are small but dirty – dirty but cheap'.

German novelist Erich Maria Remarque

preferred to stay at the Ansonia when he was in Paris, and used it as a setting in his novels *Flotsam* and *Arch of Triumph*, where he named it, ironically, Hôtel International. Remarque was an acclaimed author, accustomed to the luxury hotels of Europe, but when in Paris he favoured the Ansonia for its refugee grapevine and as a meeting place for friends from Berlin.

He was born Erich Paul Remark in Osnabrück, Lower Saxony, in 1898. His forebears were French, and his grandfather had Germanised their surname from Remarque to Remark. When he was fourteen he attended a preparatory school for student teachers, but when the war interrupted his studies he was conscripted into the army in 1917, aged eighteen, and sent to the Western Front. By this stage of the war the initial patriotic enthusiasm of recruits was ebbing away as the horrors of the Front filtered back to the German people, and Remarque was a reluctant recruit. His experience at the Front was brief, but long enough to be exposed to its barbarity. In mid July 1917, the Front was preparing for the Battle of Passchendaele. During the initial barrage, and while carrying a wounded comrade to safety, shrapnel from a shell hit Remarque in five places, hospitalising him for the next fifteen months, and ending his war service.

He had various jobs after the war, including those of teacher, librarian, journalist and editor, and he also published two novels, neither of them to any great acclaim. In 1927 he started writing the book which would make his name and whose title, *All Quiet on the Western Front*, would become a universal catchphrase. After the armistice, however, bookshops had been flooded with novels and autobiographies, and memoirs of the war. For this reason, Remarque was reluctant to publish the manuscript and it lay in his desk drawer for six months. When it was eventually published on 31 January 1929 the initial print run sold out on the first day. Sales in the following weeks were around 20,000 a day, with almost a million copies sold in Germany by the end of the year. Other countries followed the same pattern, and made the unsuspecting Remarque a rich, famous and controversial writer. It was at this time that, possibly in order to disassociate himself from his earlier work, he reverted to the former spelling of his family name, from Remark to Remarque.

His anti-war narrative, however, led to Remarque's citizenship being revoked by the Nazis and his books being banned and publicly burned in the streets. It was a criminal offence to own his books in Germany and all copies were handed over to the Gestapo. In 1933 Remarque wisely fled Nazi Germany for the safety of neutral Switzerland, and in doing so became a refugee.

His second worldwide bestseller after *All Quiet on the Western Front* was *Arch of Triumph*. Written during WWII it highlights the plight of Ravic, a German refugee surgeon in 1930s Paris. Stateless, and in constant fear of being deported, Ravic performs surgery in secret for a French hospital, while living a seedy existence at the Hôtel International, alias Hôtel Ansonia.

With Remarque's success came wealth and celebrity, and the injudicious trappings of heavy drinking, fast cars and broken marriages. But he never forgot his past and how the Nazis condemned and hounded him. After WWII, and for the remainder of his life, he always kept a packed suitcase nearby. 'It's a case that's always kept ready', he said, 'if sometimes I should suddenly have to take off.'

Further Information: Embittered that Remarque was beyond their grasp the Nazis went after his sister, Elfriede, instead. In 1943 the Gestapo guillotined her because of anti-state remarks, afterwards sending the bill for the execution to her sister Erna. Remarque is buried in Ronco village cemetery, near Locarno in Switzerland. His papers and manuscript collections are housed at New York University's Fales Library. In 1922 Remarque removed his middle name Paul and substituted it with Maria. The reason remains a mystery. It may have been a tribute to his mother, as Maria was her middle name, or simply a salute to his literary hero Rainer Maria Rilke.

Select Bibliography: *All Quiet on the Western Front* (1929); *The Road Back* (1931); *Three Comrades* (1937); *Flotsam* (1941); *Arch of Triumph* (1945).

Further Reading: H. Tims, *Erich Maria Remarque: The Last Romantic* (Constable, 2003).

8 rue de Saigon

ERNST JÜNGER

17 AVENUE KLÉBER

(Métro: Kléber)

HÔTEL RAPHAEL

FORMER QUARTERS OF ERNST JÜNGER

NAZI OFFICER IN OCCUPIED PARIS

AND AUTHOR OF *STORM OF STEEL*

A sweetish smell and a bundle hanging in the wire caught my attention. In the rising mist, I leaped out of the trench and found a shrunken French corpse. Flesh like mouldering fish gleamed greenishly through splits in the shredded uniform. Turning round, I took a step back in horror: next to me a figure was crouched against a tree. It still had gleaming French leather harness, and on its back was a fully packed haversack, topped by a round mess-tin. Empty eye-sockets and a few strands of hair on the bluish-black skull indicated that the man was not among the living ... All around were dozens more, rotted, dried, stiffened to mummies, frozen in an eerie dance of death.
Ernst Jünger, *In Stahlgewittern (Storm of Steel)* (1920)

Ernst Jünger's powerful and graphic memoir, *Storm of Steel*, was one of the first books to depict the savagery of trench warfare, and it stands alongside Remarque's *All Quiet on the Western Front* and Barbusse's *Under Fire* as one of the iconic testimonies of the unprecedented slaughter and carnage of the First World War. Jünger, who served as an officer in the German military in both world wars, was wounded several times, and was awarded the Iron Cross 1st Class, and the *Pour le Mérite*, one of Germany's highest awards for gallantry. He was a passionate militarist and a complex writer whose intention was not to write a testament to pacifism, but to

405

recount the horror of war straightfor-
wardly, and without any adornment,
in his own sober and impassive prose.
'We were enraptured by war,' he wrote,
through the eyes of a raw recruit, in
Storm of Steel. 'We had set out in a rain
of flowers, in a drunken atmosphere of
blood and roses. Surely the war had to
supply us with what we wanted; the
great, the overwhelming, the hallowed
experience.' Some critics accused him
of glorifying war, while others revered
him, and throughout his writing career,
which ranged over eighty years, he
remained a controversial and contradic-
tory figure.

He was born in Heidelberg in 1895, the
eldest of six children of Ernst Georg
Jünger, a pharmacist, and Karoline
Lampl. At the age of eighteen, by which
time he was developing a reputation as a
promising poet, he ran away from school
and joined the French Foreign Legion,
from which he was later dismissed on
the grounds of being a minor.

On the outbreak of World War I, he
volunteered with the 73rd Infantry
Regiment of the German army. He
wrote about his war experiences in
several books, but it was *Storm of Steel*
that made his fame. It was not an immediate bestseller, but it sold steadily until
the 1930s when sales rocketed into six
figures. By this time an acclaimed war
writer amid the rise of fascism, he was
courted by the Nazis, and offered a seat
in the Reichstag, which he refused. He
'hated democracy like the plague', he
once said, but, ironically, he never joined
the Nazi party, and although admired by
the Nazis, he continued to be critical of
their 'blood and soil' doctrine.

With the outbreak of the Second World
War and his promotion to Captain, much
of his time was spent in Paris where he

Ernst Jünger in First World War uniform

was posted as a staff officer in the spring
of 1941. He was based at the Hôtel Majestic, on Avenue Kléber, which had been
requisitioned as the headquarters of the
German military commander in France,
General Carl-Heinrich von Stülpnagel,
who was responsible for deporting thousands of Parisian Jews to concentration
camps. Jünger was quartered, along with
other Nazi officials, next door in the
luxurious Hôtel Raphael. Aside from his
administrative duties, he enjoyed Paris
to the full. He mingled with its writers
and intellectuals, including Cocteau and
Céline. He visited Picasso and Braque at
their studios, and he wined and dined in
the best restaurants. Jünger was eventually dismissed from the army in 1944 for
his association with the officers involved
in the failed bomb plot to assassinate
Hitler on 20 July 1944. The Gestapo
subsequently arrested 7000 people, of
whom 4980 were executed. Jünger was
lucky, as he had not actively participated
in the plot, but he received a dishonoura-
ble discharge for anti-Nazi activities.

After the war Jünger was not allowed to
publish in Germany for a few years, but
by the time of his death in 1998, aged
one hundred and two, Europe had show-

ered him with innumerable literary and civic awards. Admired by the politically far Right and disapproved of by the Left, he is still a contentious figure today. The dispassionateness and detachment of *Storm of Steel* once enraged a Berlin theatre group so much they turned it into a musical: not out of lack of respect for the fallen, but as an act of revenge.

See Also: Erich Maria Remarque, Henri Barbusse, Louis-Ferdinand Céline, Jean Cocteau.

Select Bibliography: *Storm of Steel* (1920); *Sturm* (1923); *On the Marble Cliffs* (1939); *Heliopolis* (1949); *The Glass Bees* (1957).

Further Reading: J. Hervier, *The Details of Time: Conversations with Ernst Jünger* (Marsilio, 1995); E. Neaman, *A Dubious Past: Ernst Jünger and the Politics of Literature after Nazism* (University of California Press, 1999); T. Nevin, *Ernst Jünger and Germany: Into the Abyss, 1914–1945* (Constable, 1997).

Hôtel Raphael, Avenue Kléber

PAUL VALÉRY

40 RUE PAUL VALÉRY

(Métro: Victor Hugo)

FORMER HOME OF PAUL VALÉRY
POET, ESSAYIST AND CRITIC
UNIVERSALLY CONSIDERED
FRANCE'S GREATEST POET
OF THE TWENTIETH CENTURY

Were purpose clear, all would seem vain to you.
Your ennui would haunt a shadowless world
Of neutral life and untransforming souls.
Something of disquiet is a holy gift:
Hope, which in your eyes lights up dark alleyways,
Does not arise from a more settled earth;
All your splendours spring from mysteries.
The most profound, not self-understood,
From certain night derive their riches
And the pure objects of their noble loves.
The treasure that irradiates your life
Is dark; from misty silence poems arise.
Paul Valéry, from *La Jeune Parque* (1917)

Paul Valéry, one of the last great archetypes of the Symbolist movement, was a 'revelation' to T.S. Eliot. Valéry 'will remain for posterity the representative poet,' wrote Eliot, 'the symbol of the poet, of the first half of the twentieth century – not Yeats, not Rilke, not anyone else.' But above all the praise, Valéry yearned primarily to be neither poet nor writer, but thinker. Poems and writings, to him, were just a side effect of his analytical mind.

Paul Valéry was born on 30 October 1871 in the small Mediterranean seaport of Sète, on the eastern side of the Pyrenees, to a mother of Italian descent and a Corsican father who was a customs officer. All his life Valéry would retain

407

Portrait of Paul Valéry in 1923 by Jacques-Émile Blanche (1861–1942)

strong memories of his Mediterranean childhood. In his essay 'Inspirations méditerranéennes' he describes how the three 'deities' of Sea, Sky, and Sun shaped his thought. In 1884, the year he and his family moved to Montpellier, Valéry began writing poems; by the time he was nineteen, he had penned nearly three hundred of them. Following his law studies at university, he moved to Paris in the early 1890s, where he worked briefly for the War Office before being employed by a news agency for over twenty years. Through a meeting with the Symbolist poet, Pierre Louÿs, he was introduced to the literary figures of Paris, notably André Gide, and his poet hero, Stéphane Mallarmé, who became a deep and lasting influence throughout his life. Valéry's earliest published poem appeared in 1891, but in 1892 he suddenly rejected poetry

and all creative writing. Two years later, having moved into a small room on Rue Gay-Lussac, he began writing his monumental *Cahiers* (notebooks), ultimately comprising 30,000 pages of analytical observations, mainly on the functioning of the human mind, which became a crucial part of his prose work. Rising at dawn most days, he continued writing his *Cahiers* until his death over fifty years later. Valéry returned to writing poetry in 1912, after what became known as 'the great silence'. He was persuaded to collect some of his early poems for publication, a process that aroused his enthusiasm for working with poetry again, giving rise to *La Jeune Parque* (The Young Fate) in 1917, which he expanded into a major work, and *Charmes* (Incantations) (1922), a further volume of poems written between 1913 and 1922.

In 1945 he died aged seventy-three from cancer, on the fourth floor at 40 rue Paul Valéry (formerly Rue Pauquet). He was given a state funeral and his coffin was carried from the Place Victor Hugo to the Trocadéro and placed on a catafalque draped with the French colours. Students held a vigil and the public filed past throughout the night. All public buildings, except the Panthéon, remained in darkness. Valéry was later buried in the cemetery at Sète.

See Also: Stéphane Mallarmé, André Gide, T.S. Eliot, Charles Baudelaire, Académie française.

Further Information: In 1900 Valéry married Jeannine Gobillard, niece of the painter Berthe Morisot. Valéry was admitted to the Académie française in 1925. A bronze bust of Valéry, sculpted by Renée Vautier (1898–1991), was erected in the Jardins du Trocadéro in 1975.

Select Bibliography: *Paul Valéry: An Anthology* (1977); *Selected Writings of Paul Valéry* (1964); *The Idea of Perfection: The Poetry and Prose of Paul Valéry* (Farrar, Straus and Giroux, bilingual edition, 2020); *Collected Works of Paul Valéry, Volume 1: Poems* (2015); *Cahiers / Notebooks, Volume 1* (2000).

Further Reading: F. Scarfe, *The Art of Paul Valéry* (Heinemann, 1954); W. Ince, *Poetic Theory of Paul Valéry: Inspiration and Technique* (Leicester University Press, 1970); C. Crow, *Paul Valéry: Consciousness and Nature* (Cambridge University Press, 1972); C. Whiting, *Paul Valéry* (Athlone Press, 1978); J. Lawler, *Poet as Analyst: Essays on Paul Valéry* (University of California Press, 1992).

40 rue Paul Valéry

JAMES THURBER

5 RUE DE CHAILLOT

(Métro: Iéna)

SITE OF THE US EMBASSY WHERE HUMOURIST, AUTHOR AND CARTOONIST JAMES THURBER WORKED AS A CODE CLERK

'You are all a lost generation,'Gertrude Stein said to Hemingway. We weren't lost. We knew where we were, all right, but we wouldn't go home. Ours was the generation that stayed up all night.
James Thurber, *Selected Letters* (1981)

James Thurber, one of the great American humourists, took the average twentieth-century person, bewildered and plagued by a world they could never quite comprehend, and allowed them to escape into a world of fantasy. This bewilderment was a disorder Thurber summed up when he wrote: 'I used to wake up at 4 a.m. and start sneezing, sometimes for five hours. I tried to find out what sort of allergy I had but finally came to the conclusion that it must be an allergy to consciousness.'

His most famous short story was 'The Secret Life of Walter Mitty' (1939), but he became best known for his cartoons and stories published in *The New Yorker* magazine.

Born in 1894 in Columbus, Ohio, on a 'night of wild portent', he was the second of three sons of Mary, and Charles Thurber, a father who inspired many of the self-effacing characters in his stories. Tragically, when he was six years old, James was blinded in his left eye by an arrow fired from his brother's toy bow. As a consequence of the accident, the

James Thurber

sight in his other eye failed gradually throughout his life, resulting in near blindness.

Because of his poor eyesight, Thurber left university without graduating, and went to work as a code clerk for the State Department in 1918. His first job was in Washington DC, but shortly afterwards he was posted to the American Embassy in Paris where the entire city was celebrating the armistice. 'Paris' heart was warm and gay, all right,' he wrote,

> but there was hysteria in its beat. ... Girls snatched overseas caps and tunic buttons from American soldiers, paying for them in hugs and kisses, and even warmer coin. ... The Folies-Bergère and the Casino de Paris, we found a few nights later, were headquarters of the New Elation, filled with generous ladies of joy, some offering their charms free to drinking, laughing and brawling Americans in what was left of their uniforms. ... The Americans have never been so loved in France, or anywhere else abroad, as they were in those weeks of merriment and abandon.

Two months after his arrival, the Paris Peace Conference convened in January 1919 at Versailles. Thurber presumed he would be assigned to the conference's American mission as a code clerk, but it turned out that the mission had not requested code 'clerks' from Washington, but code 'books', and Thurber was re-assigned to the American Embassy.

Thurber was in his mid-twenties during his time in Paris, and still a virgin. His literary hero was not, as one might have expected, Mark Twain, to whom he is often compared, but that great literary realist, Henry James. But unlike James, who maintained his sexual purity, Thurber succumbed in Paris. What actually happened remains a mystery, but the ordeal was an extremely distressing experience for him. Was the girl pregnant? Did he contract a venereal disease? Or was it just despair at having betrayed the Jamesian code of ethics? Whatever the trauma was it affected him deeply. On his return to America he wrote to a friend: 'You see I am not in très excellent condition, having had a very bad time of it with nerves in Paris – which is a hint of the silence story – untold yet by the way.'

In later life he partially related the experience in 'The Other Room', one of the last stories he ever wrote which was published in *Harper's Magazine* in 1962, the year after he died:

> The other day I took a taxi up to the street where [she] used to have an apartment. I remembered the street, and even the number. ... They call it Rue Marcadet, and it's ... in Montmartre. I didn't get out of the cab ... I just looked at the building, the windows on the second floor. ... She would be sixty now ... twenty then. ...There were pictures of guys [in uniform] all over her living room [including] a young Canadian soldier ... He gets into my dreams too,

Rue Marcadet

See Also: Paris *Tribune*, Henry James, Mark Twain.

Further Information: In 1925 James Thurber returned with his first wife to Paris, where he was hired as a rewrite man for the Paris *Tribune*. He was later transferred to the Riviera edition in Nice, returning to America in 1926.

Select Bibliography: *The Owl in the Attic and Other Perplexities* (1931); *My Life and Hard Times* (1933); *The Last Flower* (1939); *Fables for Our Time and Famous Poems Illustrated* (1940); *The Thurber Carnival* (1945).

Further Reading: H. Kinney, *James Thurber: His Life and Times* (Henry Holt, 1995).

ELIHU WASHBURNE

95 RUE DE CHAILLOT

(Métro: Iéna)

**SITE OF THE AMERICAN LEGATION
AND OFFICE OF ELIHU WASHBURNE
AMERICA'S MINISTER TO FRANCE
DURING THE PRUSSIAN SIEGE AND
THE AFTERMATH OF THE COMMUNE**

kinda banged up, with his uniform all bloody. ... He had been killed in action. ... This good-looking boy on the piano kept staring at me, and looking sad, and awful young.

Thurber sailed home to America in February 1920, after fifteen months in Europe. Blindness curtailed his career as a cartoonist in middle age, but he continued to dictate his stories. He died in 1961 when pneumonia set in after the removal from his brain of a tumour. According to his second wife, Helen, his last words were 'God bless, goddam'.

77th day of the siege. ... There has been no fighting at all anywhere today. There was a very light snow last night and this evening it rains a little. The suffering of the troops on both sides must have been fearful these last days. The French are without blankets and with but little to eat, half-frozen, half-starved, and raw troops at that. ... I have just come from the American Ambulance where I saw a poor captain of the regular army breathing his last and his last moments were being soothed by some of our American ladies who are devoting themselves to the sick and dying.

Elihu Washburne, diary entry, 3 Dec. 1870

411

During his eight years of service as American minister to France, Elihu Washburne (1816–1887) lived through the Franco-Prussian War of 1870–71, which ended with the siege of Paris and led to the rise and fall of the Paris Commune. Rather than return home during this dangerous and turbulent period of history, Washburne decided to stay and offer whatever help he could to his countrymen and other foreign nationals. This was a decision that not only saved many lives, but also resulted in his celebrated Paris diary, which, written with genuine insight and understanding, recorded the extraordinary events of the time.

Washburne was born in Livermore, Maine, in the USA, on 23 September 1816. Having started his working life as a printer's apprentice, he went on to practice law. Elected to Congress in 1853, then, in 1868, appointed as Secretary of State to President Ulysses S. Grant, he resigned after a very short time in order to accept the diplomatic mission to France. When war broke out with the Prussians Washburne sent his family to Brussels for their safety, but he felt duty-bound to stay in Paris. All the other ambassadors, he recorded in his diary, 'ran away'.

'There are no carriages passing on the grand avenue,' wrote Washburne during the Siege, 'that great artery through which has passed for so many years all the royalty, the wealth, the fashion, the frivolity, the vice of Paris ... and there is the silence of death.' The Prussian Siege, which lasted from 19 September 1870 until 28 January 1871, and during which time Paris was starved into surrender and forced to eat cats, dogs, rats and zoo animals, culminated in a death toll of more than 65,000 citizens. The Prussians did not occupy Paris for

Elihu Washburne

long, but the humiliation of the French was complete. Mass insurrection followed, which became known as the Paris Commune, in which the so-called Communards fought a losing battle against government troops. Hundreds of Communards were killed, executed or imprisoned. 'There has been nothing but general butchery,' wrote Washburne in his diary. 'The rage of the soldiers and the people knows no bounds. No punishment is too great, or too speedy, for the guilty, but there is no discrimination. Let a person utter a word of sympathy, or even let a man be pointed out to a crowd as a sympathizer and his life is gone.'

Elihu Washburne retired in 1877 and returned to America where he wrote his *Recollections of a Minister to France* in 1887. His greatest gift to posterity was his diary, recording, like no other, the colossal struggle of the French people and one man's heroic stand.

Further Information: The diary and correspondence of Elihu Washburne are housed in the Library of Congress, Washington DC. Other papers and journals can be viewed at the Washburn-Norlands Living History Center, Livermore, Maine. At the outbreak of the Franco-Prussian War in 1870, members of the American Colony in Paris set up a makeshift tented hospital to care for wounded soldiers which they called an 'ambulance', from *hôpital ambulant* (mobile field hospital).

Further Reading: D. McCullough, *The Greater Journey: Americans in Paris* (Simon & Schuster, 2011); D. McCullough, M. Hill, *Elihu Washburne: The Diary and Letters of America's Minister to France During the Siege and Commune of Paris* (Simon & Schuster, 2013).

Barricade at Passage Raoul (now Rue Bréguet) during the Paris Commune in 1871

17th

Arrondissement

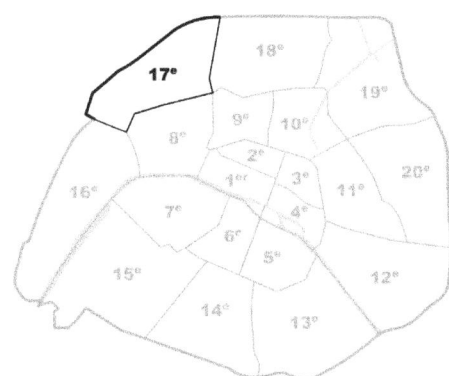

LANGSTON HUGHES

15 RUE NOLLET

(Métro: Place de Clichy/La Fourche)

FORMER ATTIC ROOM OF

LANGSTON HUGHES

POET, PLAYWRIGHT, NOVELIST AND

KEY FIGURE OF THE 1920S HARLEM

RENAISSANCE

We younger Negro artists who create now in-tend to express our individual dark-skinned selves without fear or shame. If white people are pleased, we are glad. If they are not, it doesn't matter. We know we are beautiful. And ugly too. The tom-tom cries and the tom-tom laughs. If colored people are pleased we are. If they are not, their displeasure doesn't matter either. We build our temples for tomorrow ...

Langston Hughes 'The Negro Artist and the Racial Mountain' (1926)

Langston Hughes (1902–1967) was a young poet who achieved fame during a period that became known as the Harlem Renaissance, a movement of artistic, social and cultural outpourings of African American culture in the Harlem neighbourhood of New York from around 1918 to the mid 1930s. What made Hughes different from other poets of his day was the way his poetry was mostly aimed at people – almost exclusively black people – using a simple and direct language familiar to all. He was one of the pioneers of Jazz Poetry, which has been described as demonstrating a 'jazz-like rhythm or the feel of improvisation'. Hughes was also a prolific writer of novels, short stories and plays, and in doing so told the story of his people to the world. 'Hang yourself, poet, in your own words,' he wrote, impelling fellow poets to express the truth. 'Otherwise, you are dead.'

Publicity photo of Langston Hughes dressed as a bellhop for his first collection of poetry, *The Weary Blues*

his pocket. A few weeks later he found a job as a dishwasher at Le Grand Duc, a nightclub at 52 rue Pigalle (now Rue Jean-Baptiste Pigalle), with a salary of fifteen francs a night including breakfast. Here he met the legendary performer, Ada Smith, known as Bricktop, as well as a 'great many celebrities and millionaires', and by April he had moved to an attic room at 15 rue Nollet near Place Clichy,

> in a room with slanting roofs up under the eaves, overlooking the chimney pots of Paris. ... That room was right out of a book, and I began to say to myself that I guess dreams do come true, and sometimes life makes its own books, because here I am living in a Paris garret, writing poems and having champagne for breakfast (because champagne is what we had with our breakfast at the Grand Duc from the half-empty bottles left by unsuspecting guests, in their ice buckets ...).

He was born in 1902 in Joplin, Missouri. His parents divorced when he was very young, after which time he was raised mainly by his maternal grandmother. He led a peripatetic life from an early age, travelling to Mexico, Europe, Africa, Russia, China and Japan, and to Madrid during the Spanish Civil War. In the winter of 1924, while working as a deckhand on a cargo ship, he drew his wages upon docking in Rotterdam, and, having packed his bags, he caught the night train to Paris.

After paying for his ticket and visa expenses he arrived at the Gare du Nord on 23 February with only seven dollars in

After his sojourn in Paris, he briefly visited Italy, where he was robbed and compelled to live in dosshouses. In Genoa, he was sometimes so hungry, he wrote, 'I would stand in front of a bakery window ... and wonder how I could steal something to eat and not get caught and locked up. But I never had the nerve, nor the ultimate necessity of stealing, for something always seemed to turn up just when I was the hungriest.' He eventually signed on as a deckhand with no pay on a cargo boat sailing from Genoa to New York. 'Ten months before, I had got to Paris with seven dollars ... I came home with a quarter, so my first European trip cost me exactly six dollars and seventy-five cents!'

See Also: Bricktop's.

Further Information: Langston Hughes died in New York of complications from prostate cancer on 22 May 1967. His Harlem residence at 20 East 127th Street has since been renamed Langston Hughes Place.

Select Bibliography: Poetry: *The Weary Blues* (1926); *Fine Clothes to the Jew* (1927); *A New Song* (1938); *Montage of a Dream Deferred* (1951); *Collected Poems of Langston Hughes* (Vintage, 1995). Fiction : *Not Without Laughter* (1930); *The Ways of White Folks* (1934). Plays: *Mule Bone* (with Zora Hurston, 1931); *Tambourines to Glory* (1956); *Black Nativity* (1961); *Jerico-Jim Crow* (1964). Autobiography: *The Big Sea* (1940).

Further Reading: A. Rampersad, *The Life of Langston Hughes, Vol. 1: 1902–1941: I, Too, Sing America* (Oxford University Press, 2002); *The Life of Langston Hughes, Vol. 2: 1941–1967: I Dream a World* (Oxford University Press, 2002); A. Rampersad (Ed.), *Selected Letters of Langston Hughes* (Knopf, 2015).

15 rue Nollet

STÉPHANE MALLARMÉ

89 RUE DE ROME
(Métro: Rome)

FORMER APARTMENT OF
STÉPHANE MALLARMÉ
FRENCH SYMBOLIST POET, CRITIC AND
ONE OF THE FOUNDING FATHERS
OF MODERNISM

Mallarmé came from his small flat in the rue de Rome, where he had perhaps left the young Claudel or the young Valéry, and then crossed the place and the pont de l'Europe. Each day, he told George Moore, he was gripped by the temptation to throw himself from the top of the bridge onto the tracks, in order finally to escape the mediocrity in which he was imprisoned. ...
He sat there in the teacher's chair; and we, in front of him, sat there on our benches, and we had the impression that, just as we did, he came to class with no great taste for it and no great repugnance, driven by the force of circumstance.
Daniel Halévy, remembering his English teacher, Stéphane Mallarmé, at the lycée Condorcet in *Pays parisiens* (1932)

Stéphane Mallarmé (1842–1898) worked for much of his life as a schoolmaster, balancing a somewhat humdrum teaching livelihood with his parallel career as a poet. Outside the classroom he was the guiding light and leader of Symbolism, the literary and artistic movement that had liberated itself of all traditional conventions. After a lifetime devoted to literature, his poetry, much of which is obscure and impenetrable to many, totals fewer than a hundred poems and can be contained in one slim volume. '[He] was one of those who love literature too much to write it except by fragments; in whom the desire of perfection brings its own defeat,' wrote Arthur Symonds.

> It was a matter of sincere indifference to him whether he left one or two little, limited masterpieces of formal verse and prose, the more or the less. It was 'the work' that he dreamed of, the new art, more than a new religion, whose precise form in the world he was never quite able to settle.

On Tuesday evenings he hosted a literary salon where writers would rendezvous at Mallarmé's flat on Rue de Rome. Those who climbed the four flights to his small, but celebrated salon, sought advice and encouragement, and included Paul Valéry, Paul Verlaine, Guy de Maupassant and André Gide. 'Here was a house', wrote Symonds, 'in which art, literature, was the very atmosphere, a religious atmosphere; and the master of the house, in his just a little solemn simplicity, a priest.'

Mallarmé was born in 1842 in Paris, where his father was a civil servant. Following his mother's death when he was five years old, he was raised by his maternal grandparents, later attending boarding school. By the age of twenty he was teaching French in London, and studying English. In England he married a young German governess before returning to France, where he took up a series of posts as an English master in provincial schools, finally obtaining a teaching job in Paris in 1871. Unlike many writers he did not live a life full of incident. The uneventful treadmill of the classroom was his lot. But the grief and sense of loss he suffered following the untimely deaths of his mother, his sister and his second child played a major part in his writing, inspiring his *tombeau*

Stéphane Mallarmé

(tomb) poems: *Pour un tombeau d'Anatole* for his son, a *tombeau* poem after the death of Edgar Allan Poe, and later *tombeaux* for his literary heroes Charles Baudelaire and Paul Verlaine. 'L'Après-midi d'un faune' ('A Faun's Afternoon'), which inspired the Prelude by Debussy, is one of his best-known poems; and his last major poem, 'Un coup de dés jamais n'abolira le hazard' ('A roll of the dice will never abolish chance'), written in 1897, is like a work out of time, anticipating the typographic free spirit of the twentieth century. The multi-layered, free-form nature of Mallarmé's poetry has often made his poems difficult to unravel, especially in translation, yet his influence has been immense.

He published little, but what he did produce ranks among the masterpieces of French poetry, ensuring his place among the great poets of the nineteenth century.

See Also: Paul Valéry, Paul Verlaine, Guy de Maupassant, André Gide, T.S. Eliot.

Further Information: No. 89 rue de Rome is marked by a plaque. In 1893 Stéphane Mallarmé settled with his wife and daughter at their country house in Valvins on the Seine, near Fontainebleau (now Musée Stéphane Mallarmé). On 9 September 1898, aged fifty-six, Mallarmé died at Valvins from laryngospasm, an involuntary contraction of the vocal cords, and is buried in the nearby Cimetière de Samoreau.

Select Bibliography: *Collected Poems and Other Verse* (Oxford World Classics, 2008).

Further Reading: A. Symons, *The Symbolist Movement in Literature* (Fyfield, 2014); G. Millan, *A Throw of the Dice: The Life of Stéphane Mallarmé* (Secker & Warburg, 1994); R. Pearson, *Stéphane Mallarmé* (Reaktion, 2010).

89 rue de Rome

D'ARTAGNAN

PLACE DU GÉNÉRAL CATROUX

(Métro: Malesherbes)

SCULPTURE OF D'ARTAGNAN
CAPTAIN OF THE MUSKETEERS
ONE OF THE IMMORTAL HEROES
OF WORLD LITERATURE

My son, be worthy of your noble name, worthily borne by your ancestors for over five hundred years. Remember it's by courage, and courage alone, that a nobleman makes his way nowadays. Don't be afraid of opportunities, and seek out adventures. My son, all I have to give you is fifteen ecus, my horse, and the advice you've just heard. Make the most of these gifts, and have a long, happy life.
Alexandre Dumas, *Les Trois Mousquetaires (The Three Musketeers)* (1844)

Mystery, intrigue and espionage: Alexandre Dumas's *Les Trois Mousquetaires* has it all. Now one of the great classics of world literature and popular with both adults and children, it was first published in serial form in 1844. It is set in the time of Richelieu, where the three musketeers Athos, Porthos and Aramis, and the hotheaded, yet indestructible D'Artagnan, are the King's bodyguard, who repeatedly come head-to-head with Richelieu's guard and his beautiful spy 'Milady'.

All three musketeers and D'Artagnan were based on real people: Armand d'Athos (*c.*1615–1643), of whom little is known; Isaac de Porthau (1617–1712), who became Secretary of the Parliament of Béarn; Henri d'Aramitz (*c.*1620-1674), who was a Catholic clergyman; and Charles de Batz-Castelmore d'Artagnan (*c.*1611–1673), a Gascon nobleman of questionable lineage. They all originated from Gascony in the south-west of France, and they were all men-at-arms during the 1640s in the Black Musketeers, the elite royal guard of Louis IV.

The historical d'Artagnan was born Charles de Batz-Castelmore on or around 1611 in the village of Lupiac in Gascony, although his family's claim to nobility is suspect: in 1565 Arnaud de Batz, a local tradesman, bought the small chateau of Castelmore near Lupiac, and by the end of the sixteenth century a descendant of his was using a title of nobility. In 1608 Bertrand de Batz-Castelmore married Françoise de Montesquiou d'Artagnan, daughter of Jean de Montesquiou, lord of Artagnan, an estate near Lupiac. The Montesquiou family were ancient nobility and Jean de Montesquiou had served in the French Guards and was well known to the Royal Household. For Bertrand, the marriage was a profitable and tactical alliance. Bertrand and Françoise had six children. Three of their sons joined the military, and by March 1633, their son, Charles de Batz-Castelmore, had become Charles d'Artagnan, musketeer. As a loyal musketeer his career thrived on battles, swashbuckling, espionage and military honours, culminating in a noble death fighting for his King at the Siege of Maastricht in 1673, where he was shot through the throat with a musket ball. His burial place is unknown.

Dumas based much of his portrayal of D'Artagnan on Courlitz de Sandras's *Mémoires de M. d'Artagnan* (1700), a semi-fictional account of d'Artagnan's life written twenty-seven years after his death. Pseudo-memoirs were a speciality of Courlitz de Sandras, and Dumas was never one to let fact get in the way of

Former travelling salesman Albert Kanter (1897–1973) created *Classic Comics* in October 1941, becoming *Classics Illustrated* in 1947. Its first issue was *The Three Musketeers.* Some comics were reprinted up to 25 times

fiction. In *Mes Mémoires* (1852–1855) Dumas writes:

I start by devising a story. I try to make it romantic, moving, dramatic, and when scope has been found for the emotions and the imagination, I search through the annals of the past to find a frame in which to set it; and it has never happened that history has failed to provide this frame, so exactly adjusted to the subject that it seemed it was not a case of the frame being made for the picture, but that the picture had been made to fit the frame.

One of the reasons Dumas's fiction endures is because it doesn't get bogged down with historical accuracy, but gives us the characters, the setting, and the romance from his wonderfully naïve and optimistic viewpoint. The reader knows they are in the seventeenth century, because they meet Cardinal Richelieu and the Duke of Buckingham, but Dumas has simply purified it of some of its real horrors, such as starvation, epidemics, massacres and lawlessness.

Two sequels followed the success of *Les Trois Mousquetaires*: *Vingt ans après (Twenty Years After)* (1845) and *Le Vicomte de Bragelonne (Ten Years Later)* (1847).

See Also: Alexandre Dumas, Alexandre Dumas *fils*, Gustave Doré, Cardinal Richelieu, Auguste Maquet, Palais de Justice.

Further Information: D'Artagnan's bronze sculpture is situated on a ledge below, and to the rear of, the pedestal of Alexandre Dumas's statue. Seated beneath the front of the pedestal is a bronze group symbolising readers perusing his books. All sculptures are the work of the French artist, Gustave Doré (1832–1883). Because not enough money could be raised to fund the project, Doré, who started sculpting late in life, created the sculptures for the Dumas monument for no fee. Sadly, he died before he could see the monument's completion, which was inaugurated by Alexandre Dumas *fils* on 4 November 1883. Place du Général Catroux was formerly known as Place Malesherbes, and the monument was erected here because Alexandre Dumas had lived nearby at 94 avenue de Villiers.

The origin of the musketeers goes back to 1600, during the reign of Henri IV who formed a lightweight cavalry unit of skilled marksmen known as the *Carabins*. In 1622 Henri's son, Louis XIII, renamed them the King's Musketeers, who, in peacetime, acted as the King's escort while the King was travelling. The Black Musketeers were so called because of the colour of their horses. The musketeers disbanded in 1776. A museum dedicated to d'Artagnan is located in the historic Chapelle Saint-Jacques in Lupiac.

Further Reading: K. Maund & P. Nanson, *The Four Musketeers, The True Story of D'Artagnan, Porthos, Aramis & Athos* (Tempus, 2005); R. Chartrand, *French Musketeer 1622–1775* (Osprey, 2013); J. Lynn, *The French Wars 1667–1714* (Osprey, 2014); *Giant of the Grand Siècle: The French Army, 1610–1715* (Cambridge, 2006); J. Blanchard, *Eminence: Cardinal Richelieu and the Rise of France* (Walker, 2011).

Gustave Doré's D'Artagnan, ready for action sitting in the shadow of Dumas in Place du Général Catroux

421

FRANÇOISE SAGAN

158 BOULEVARD MALESHERBES

(Métro: Wagram)

FORMER HOME OF FRANÇOISE SAGAN WHERE SHE WROTE MUCH OF HER ACCLAIMED DEBUT NOVEL, *BONJOUR TRISTESSE*

It would be bad form for me to describe people I don't know and don't understand. Think about it. Whisky, Ferraris and gambling; aren't they rather more amusing than knitting, housekeeping and one's savings ... All my life, I will continue obstinately to write about love, solitude and passion among the kind of people I know. The rest don't interest me.

Françoise Sagan

Françoise Sagan with her son, Denis

Written when she was a teenager, Françoise Sagan's 1954 debut novel *Bonjour Tristesse* (Hello Sadness), earned her international acclaim and scandal. The book, disregarding accepted standards of the times, paints a cynically amoral and pessimistic portrait of love, in which a teenage girl rebuffs the conventional concepts of love and marriage and seeks her own sexual freedom. Today, few people in Western cultures are fazed by the concept of teenage free love and self-indulgence, but in the 1950s such behaviour was considered morally and legally unacceptable. As a teenager Françoise Sagan ignored, or perhaps was just oblivious to, these stifling conventions, and *Bonjour Tristesse* became a worldwide bestseller, turning its creator into French literature's *enfant terrible.* 'I could not understand what all the fuss was about at first,' she wrote,

and today I can think of only two ridiculous reasons for it. It was inconceivable that a young girl of seventeen or eighteen should make love, without being in love, with a boy of her own age, and not be punished for it. People couldn't tolerate the idea that the girl should not fall madly in love with the boy, and not be pregnant by the end of the summer. It was unacceptable too in those days that a young girl should have the right to use her body as she will, and derive pleasure from it without incurring a penalty, one which had always been thought inevitable. And furthermore, people couldn't accept that this same young girl should know about her father's love affairs, discuss them with him, and thereby reach a kind of complicity with him on subjects that had until then been taboo between parents and children.

Françoise Quoirez was born in 1935 in the town of Cajarc in south-west France, the third and youngest child of Pierre Quoirez, a wealthy industrialist, and Marie Laubard. Much of her childhood was spent in Lyon, but after the liberation of France in 1944, the family settled in Paris. Educated at convent schools, and the Sorbonne, where she studied literature

422

PENGUIN BOOKS

BONJOUR TRISTESSE

Françoise Sagan

COMPLETE 2/6 UNABRIDGED

than by her talent. But despite her hedonistic, devil-may-care attitude, whatever demons Sagan was out to exorcise made her the writer she was and would become in the future.

'Writing requires a precise, precious and rare talent', she wrote in *Avec Mon Meilleur Souvenir*,

the truth of this is unseemly and almost incongruous these days. In any event, literature, with its gentle disdain for its false priests and pretenders, takes its own revenge, turning those who dare meddle with it, even at arm's length, into impotent and bitter cripples – and gives them nothing, except sometimes, with cruel intent, a transient success that will torment them for life.

See Also: Marcel Proust, Paul Éluard.

but due to indifference failed to graduate, she began to write *Bonjour Tristesse* in the bistros around the Sorbonne and at home on Boulevard Malesherbes. The title of the book came from the poem 'À peine défigurée' ('Barely Disfigured') by Paul Éluard, and, as her father had forbidden her to put her family name to the book, she took her nom de plume from the Princesse de Sagan in Marcel Proust's *À la recherche du temps perdu (In Search of Lost Time)*.

Bonjour Tristesse was first published in 1954 by René Julliard, in Rue de l'Université. When its staggering success landed celebrity and wealth into Sagan's teenage lap, the world's media became more tantalised – as they would continue to do until her death – by her lifestyle

Further Information: Françoise Sagan was twice married and had one son. She died of heart and lung ailments on 24 September 2004, aged sixty-nine, and was buried in Seuzac village cemetery, Cajarc, Département du Lot, Midi-Pyrénées.

Select Bibliography: *Bonjour Tristesse* (1954); *Un certain sourire (A Certain Smile)* (1955); *Dans un mois, dans un an (Those Without Shadows)* (1957); *Aimez-vous Brahms?* (1959); *Les merveilleux nuages (Wonderful Clouds)* (1961); *Le garde du coeur (The Heart-Keeper)* (1968); *Des bleus à l'âme (Scars on the Soul)* (1972); *Avec mon meilleur souvenir (With Fondest Regards)* (1984); *Réponses, The Autobiography of Françoise Sagan* (1979).

Further Reading: J. Miller, *Françoise Sagan* (Twayne, 1988).

CIMETIÈRE
DES BATIGNOLLES

8 RUE SAINT-JUST

(Métro: Porte de Clichy)

Established in 1833, the Cimetière des Batignolles has today around fifteen thousand graves occupying its 27 acres, and is located next to the Boulevard Périphérique, Paris's ring road around the city, completed in 1973. As it is the busiest road in France at the time of writing, the traditional phrase bestowed on the deceased, *Repose en Paix* (Rest in Peace) now has a rather hollow ring to it for those in this once garden of peace.

PAUL VERLAINE

(1844–1896)

DIVISION 11

ONE OF THE FOUNDING FATHERS OF MODERN POETRY

I believe, and I sin in thought as in action; I believe, and I repent in thought, if no more. Or again, I believe, and I am a good Christian at this moment; I believe, and I am a bad Christian the instant after. The remembrance, the hope, the invocation of a sin delights me, with or without remorse, sometimes under the very form of sin, and hedged with all its natural consequences; more often – so strong, so natural and animal, are flesh and blood – just in the same manner as the remembrances, hopes, invocations of any carnal freethinker. This delight, I, you, some one else, writers, it pleases us to put to paper and publish more or less well expressed: we consign it, in short, into literary form, forgetting all religious ideas, or not letting one of them escape us. Can any one in good faith condemn us as poet? A hundred times no.
Paul Verlaine

The tormented life of poet Paul Verlaine ended in poverty at 39 rue Descartes, on 8 January 1896. He died, aged fifty-one, from a combination of heart disease, diabetes, syphilis, and his long association with drugs and alcohol. Over five thousand mourners attended his funeral, including Rachilde, Stéphane Mallarmé, and Gabriel Fauré, who played the organ at the funeral service.

During a life that was absinthe-soaked and full of scandal, Verlaine was jailed, ostracised, pilloried and praised. 'Life is a farce which everyone has to perform,' wrote his former lover Arthur Rimbaud. Verlaine performed his 'farce' to the bitter end.

See Also: Paul Verlaine (Rue Nicolet), Arthur Rimbaud, Stéphane Mallarmé, Rachilde, Ernest Hemingway (Rue du Cardinal Lemoine).

Further Information: Verlaine was initially buried in the 20th Division, but after a road bridge was built over the site funds

424

were raised in 1989 to clean and relocate his tomb to its present location. A commemorative plaque to Verlaine can be seen at 39 rue Descartes, the same building in which Ernest Hemingway briefly rented an attic room for his writing studio when he was living at nearby 74 rue du Cardinal Lemoine in the early 1920s.

Select Bibliography: M. Sorrell (ed.), *Paul Verlaine: Selected Poems* (Oxford World's Classics, 2009, includes parallel French text).

Further Reading: J. Richardson, *Verlaine* (Weidenfeld & Nicolson, 1971); S. Zweig, *Paul Verlaine* (Leopold Classic Library, 2015); A. Symons, *The Symbolist Movement in Literature* (Dutton, 1919).

ÉRIC LOSFELD
(1922–1979)

DIVISION 9

PUBLISHER OF EROTIC

AND FANTASY LITERATURE

NOTABLY THE CLASSICS

EMMANUELLE AND *BARBARELLA*

What misadventures, what disappointments in love have led this girl to wander alone through a solar system far removed from ours?
Jean-Claude Forest, *Barbarella* (1962)

Born in Mouscron in Belgium, near the French frontier, Éric Losfeld was a pioneering avant-garde publisher of risqué books. Many of his publications were ruled obscene, and in the 1950s and early 1960s he often worked clandestinely. During his life he published the books of hundreds of surrealist and erotic writers, from the Marquis de Sade to Emmanuelle Arsan, under various imprints. Little is known of Losfeld's early

Emmanuelle Arsan, pen name of Marayat Bibidh

life; even his own memoirs circumvent most of his formative years. In 1951 he founded Éditions Arcanes and launched his independent publishing career. He was also a bookseller and a writer who wrote under the pseudonym Delfos. He published comic books and periodicals, notably *Postif*, which Martin Scorsese described as 'the best movie magazine in the world', and *Midi Minuit Fantastique*, dedicated to fantasy, horror and sci-fi films. His longest running imprint was Éditions Le Terrain Vague, founded in 1955, which published the international bestseller *Emmanuelle* and the comic book *Barbarella*.

Emmanuelle is a series of explicit erotic encounters written under the pen name Emmanuelle Arsan by Thai-born Marayat Bibidh (1932–2005). Losfeld first published it anonymously in 1967, crediting later editions to the author. The book has since taken its place among the world's erotic classics.

The *Barbarella* comic strip, created by

JEAN-CLAUDE FOREST / ERIC LOSFELD 1966

Front cover of one of Losfeld's hardback editions of *Barbarella* from the 1960s that sold over 200,000 copies worldwide

writer and illustrator Jean-Claude Forest (1930–1998), was first serialised in the French *V Magazine* edited by Georges Gallet in 1962. 'One day he asked me if I wanted to do a strip for him – no holds barred!' recalled Forest.

> Gallet had asked me to do a kind of female Tarzan, Tarzella, but that idea didn't particularly interest me. It led me

to come up with Barbarella. For the next two years, at the rate of eight pages every three months, I told her adventures, going with the flow of inspiration, without any pre-planning.

In 1964 Losfeld's imprint, Éditions Le Terrain Vague, published a hardback edition of *V Magazine*'s *Barbarella* stories that went on to sell over 200,000 copies. The book's eroticism, however, succeeded in getting the book banned from public display in France, which in 1949 had imposed strict censorship laws controlling publications intended for minors. 'Of the 600 books I've published in twenty years', wrote Losfeld, 'six got me into trouble with the Surveillance Commission, and the first of these was *Barbarella*.'

Today its troubled history is all but forgotten, and the girl in the skintight spacesuit is part of the sixties sexual revolution and a science fiction classic. Its success is due in part to the vision of Éric Losfeld, whose tombstone inscription reads: 'Tout ce qu'il éditait avait le souffle de la liberté' ('Everything he edited had the breath of freedom').

See Also: Olympia Press, Obelisk Press.

Further Reading: E. Arsan, *Emmanuelle* (Harper Perennial, 2009); J-C. Forest, *Barbarella* (Humanoids Inc., 2014).

18th
Arrondissement

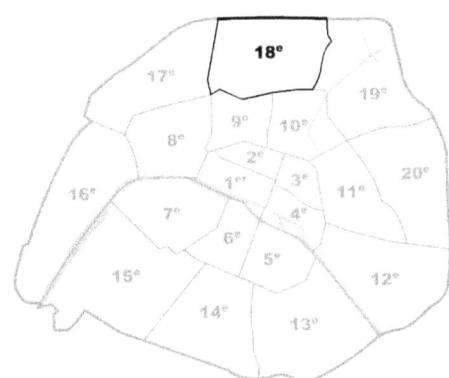

GEORGE BERNARD SHAW

RUE DE LA CHAPELLE

(Métro: Marx Dormoy)

SAINT-DENYS DE LA CHAPELLE BASILICA OF SAINTE-JEANNE-D'ARC DEDICATED TO THE FRENCH HEROINE WHO HAS INSPIRED LITERATURE FOR MORE THAN 500 YEARS

Joan of Arc, a village girl from the Vosges, was born about 1412; burnt for heresy, witchcraft, and sorcery in 1431; rehabilitated after a fashion in 1456; designated Venerable in 1904; declared Blessed in 1908; and finally canonized in 1920. She is the most notable Warrior Saint in the Christian calendar, and the queerest fish among the eccentric worthies of the Middle Ages. ...
She claimed to be the ambassador and plenipotentiary of God, and to be, in effect, a member of the Church Triumphant whilst still in the flesh on earth. She patronized her own king, and summoned the English king to repentance and obedience to her commands. She lectured, talked down, and overruled statesmen and prelates. She pooh-poohed the plans of generals, leading their troops to victory on plans of her own. ... As her actual condition was pure upstart, there were only two opinions about her. One was that she was miraculous: the other that she was unbearable.

George Bernard Shaw, Preface to *Saint Joan* (1924)

Throughout history, the curious, the infatuated and the sceptical have written their version of the legend of Joan of Arc: Christine de Pizan ('Chanson en l'honneur de Jeanne d'Arc', 1429), William Shakespeare (*Henry VI, Part 1,* 1590), Robert Southey (*Joan of Arc,* 1796), Friedrich Schiller (*The Maid of Orleans,* 1801), Samuel Taylor

Coleridge (*The Destiny of Nations*, 1821), Mark Twain (*Personal Recollections of Joan of Arc*, 1896), Bertolt Brecht (*Saint Joan of the Stockyards*, 1930) and Jean Anouilh (*L'Alouette*, 1953); but probably the most celebrated, and certainly the most enduring, is George Bernard Shaw's 1923 drama, *Saint Joan*. 'The most inevitable dramatic conception, then, of the nineteenth century', wrote George Bernard Shaw', 'is that of a perfectly naïve hero upsetting religion, law and order in all directions, and establishing in their place the unfettered action of Humanity … This conception, already incipient in Adam Smith's *Wealth of Nations*, was certain at last to reach some great artist, and be embodied by him in a masterpiece.' Shaw, of course, was not thinking of himself when he wrote this. In his notes to *Caesar and Cleopatra* (1898) he categorised Joan of Arc along with Lord Nelson and Charles XII, whom he described as 'half-witted geniuses, enjoying the worship accorded by all races to certain forms of insanity'. Ten years later, however, in the Preface to his 1908 play, *Getting Married*, Joan was bestowed with 'exceptional sanity', and no longer grouped with 'half-witted geniuses'. Seventeen of Shaw's plays were produced in Paris during his lifetime, but, apart from *Saint Joan*, all of them were failures. 'I have educated London,' he wrote in 1924:

> I have educated New York, Berlin and Vienna: Moscow and Stockholm are at my feet, but I am too old to educate Paris; it is too far behind and I am too far ahead. Besides this, my method of education is to teach people how to laugh at themselves, and the pride of Paris is so prodigious that it has beaten all its professors from Molière to Anatole France and might even beat me.

George Bernard Shaw (1856–1950)

Shaw's basic problem was that the French thought his plays too parochial, and he thought the Parisian stage fundamentally provincial and unprogressive, all of which was compounded by Shaw's insistence on using Augustin Hamon as his authorised translator. Hamon was a French social psychologist with little knowledge of drama, and, being linguistically unsuited to the task, his inaccurate translations estranged French audiences in their droves. Shaw still insisted on using him, but with *Saint Joan* he made an exception.

The task of deciphering *Saint Joan* for the Paris stage in 1925 fell to the Russian couple Georges Pitoëff, the play's producer, and his actor wife, Ludmilla, who played the role of Joan. The Pitoëffs' blood had run cold after a reading of Hamon's translation, but in collaboration with French playwright Henri-René Lenormand they completely revised it, and for the first time French audiences and critics praised the work of George Bernard Shaw. 'Woe

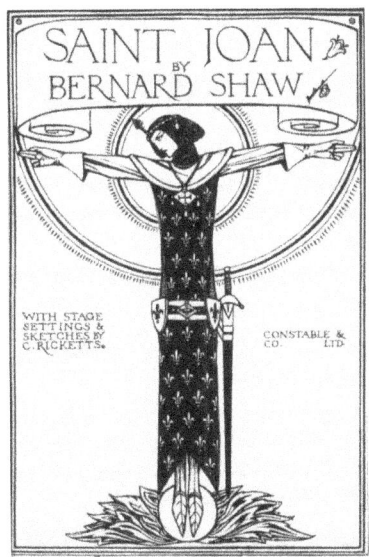

Constable & Co. Ltd cover, 1924

when Joan of Arc was burnt at the stake by the English in 1431. In 1920, nearly 500 years after her death, she was canonised as a Roman Catholic saint.

Select Bibliography: George Bernard Shaw wrote more than sixty plays, but his major dramatic works include *The Devil's Disciple* (1897); *Caesar and Cleopatra* (1898); *Man and Superman* (1903); *The Doctor's Dilemm*a (1906); *Major Barbara* (1907); *Pygmalion* (1913) and *Saint Joan* (1923).

Further Reading: M. Holroyd, *Bernard Shaw* (Chatto & Windus, 1997); B. Tyson, *The Story of Shaw's Saint Joan* (McGill-Queen's University Press, 1982); M. Pharand, *Bernard Shaw and the French* (University Press of Florida, 2001).

unto me when all men praise me!' says Saint Joan, anguish Shaw himself would soon experience: shortly after the success of *Saint Joan* Shaw was awarded the Nobel Prize in Literature, in 1925. As a man who had always discouraged the bestowal of prizes, he told Augustin Hamon, 'The Nobel Prize has been a hideous calamity for me. It was really almost as bad as my seventieth birthday.'

See Also: Christine de Pizan, Mark Twain, Anatole France, Molière.

Further Information: Legend has it that Joan of Arc spent a night of prayer in Saint-Denys de la Chapelle in 1429. To commemorate both this occasion and the 1914 Anglo-French forces' victory at the first Battle of the Marne, the Basilica of Sainte-Jeanne-d'Arc was built next door to Saint-Denys de la Chapelle in 1930. Many Catholics attributed the Anglo-French Marne victory to the divine intervention of Joan of Arc, and afterwards effigies of her began to appear on many French war memorials. Divine intervention, however, was absent

Statue of Joan of Arc outside the Basilica of Sainte-Jeanne-d'Arc

ANDRÉ MALRAUX

53 RUE DAMRÉMONT

(Métro: Lamarck-Caulaincourt/Guy Môquet)

BIRTHPLACE OF ANDRÉ MALRAUX

NOVELIST, ADVENTURER

AND POLITICIAN

His first overseas adventure was the one that made him notorious: an expedition in 1923 to French-ruled Cambodia, during which he amputated priceless bits of sculpture and statuary from some ancient temples. Arrested and charged for this, he managed to induce quite a number of Parisian intellectuals and aesthetes, including André Gide and André Maurois, to take up his case as if it were an injustice being committed by the colonial authorities. ... the Surrealist André Breton added, with magnificent condescension to the Cambodians, 'Who in their homeland really cares about the preservation of these works of art?'
Christopher Hitchens, *The New York Times* (2005)

André Malraux in 1976

André Malraux as a young man is reminiscent of the action hero, Indiana Jones: a daredevil who travelled the globe dressed in his iconic fedora and leather jacket, bullwhip in hand, having extraordinary adventures unlikely except in a movie script. Malraux may not have carried a bullwhip, but he was nothing if not a man of diversity who recast himself in many different roles throughout his life: critic, rare book dealer, publisher, archaeologist, novelist, Resistance fighter and statesman, to name a few. At the age of twenty-three he organised a raid to loot a ruined temple of its Khmer sculptures in French Cambodia, for which he was arrested and sentenced to three years in prison. He witnessed the birth of the Chinese Revolution, and was a prominent anti-fascist. In 1934 he claimed to have found the lost capital of the Queen of Sheba while exploring Arabia. During the Spanish Civil War he organised a volunteer bomber squadron for the Republicans, yet he had never piloted an aeroplane. In World War II he joined a tank regiment and was captured and imprisoned by the Nazis. He later escaped and joined the Resistance. His final roles were as Minister of Information (1945–1946), and later as the first Minister for Cultural Affairs (1959–1969) in General de Gaulle's governments.

His first role, as a baby, was played out at No. 53 rue Damrémont in Montmartre, where he was born on 3 November 1901 to Berthe Lamy and Fernand-Georges Malraux, a small-time stockbroker. A year later Berthe gave birth to another son who lived for only three months. The Malrauxs' marriage collapsed shortly afterwards, whereupon Berthe and André went to live with

Berthe's mother and sister in Bondy, a small town north-east of Paris. When he was seventeen he was turned down for Paris's prestigious Lycée Condorcet, an event that for him was a deciding factor; he would end his schooling for good and pursue the love of his life: the world of books. Whether it was dealing in rare books, writing literary criticism, editing or publishing, Malraux experienced it all; but rare books were his passion. 'What is the difference', he once wrote, 'between a good fake and a bad original? Hoax is eminently creative.'

He began his own writing career in the 1920s, writing essays and short stories, many of them influenced by the cubism and surrealism vogue of the day, but it was *La Condition humaine (Man's Estate)* (1933) that established him as an important writer. Set during Chiang Kai-Shek's 1927 coup against the communists, it was one of the first books to expose the reality of twentieth-century politics and the suffering and mayhem of a coup. The book won the Prix Goncourt in 1933. Malraux's 1937 novel, *L'Espoir (Man's Hope)*, which is considered one of his best, was based on his experiences during the Spanish Civil War. From the late 1940s his faith in the power and importance of art strongly influenced his writing, and this was the time of his life when he produced numerous books and essays on painting and sculpture.

Malraux died from cancer, aged seventy-five, in 1976, and was buried in Verrières-le-Buisson, a southern suburb of Paris, where he had lived out his final years. On the twentieth anniversary of his death, his body was exhumed and enshrined in the Panthéon, France's mausoleum for national heroes. President Chirac's speech on the day spoke of Malraux's great achievements but,

53 rue Damrémont

unsurprisingly, played down his temple-robbing exploits. French philosopher, Raymond Aron, later gave a more honest account, describing Malraux as 'One third genius, one third false, one third incomprehensible.'

See Also: Prix Goncourt , Panthéon, André Breton, André Gide.

Further Information: Malraux's attempt to rob the temple at Banteay Srei in Cambodia of Khmer statuary to sell to the museum market was nothing new. Countless sites have been robbed over the centuries and their contents can still be seen in respectable museums today. Although Malraux was caught in the act, arrested, and sent to trial, he was eventually given a suspended prison sentence of one year.

Select Bibliography: *Les Conquérants (The Conquerors)* (1928); *La Condition humaine (Man's Fate)* (1933); *L'Espoir (Man's Hope)* (1937); *La Psychologie de l'art (The Psychology of Art)* (1947–1949).

Further Reading: C. Cate, *André Malraux: A Biography* (Hutchinson, 1995); O. Todd, *Malraux: A Life* (Knopf, 2005).

PAUL VERLAINE
AND ARTHUR RIMBAUD

14 RUE NICOLET

(Métro: Château Rouge)

SCENE OF VERLAINE AND RIMBAUD'S
FIRST MEETING IN 1871. AN INTENSE
RELATIONSHIP THAT WOULD END
WITH VERLAINE'S IMPRISONMENT

Art wants no tears and takes no prisoners ...
Paul Verlaine, from 'Golden Lines'

One of history's most shocking and impassioned literary friendships was that of poets Paul Verlaine (1844–1896) and Arthur Rimbaud (1854–1891), whose frenzied love affair involving drugs, drinking bouts, violence and sex finally ended with Verlaine being sent to prison for wounding Rimbaud with a gun. They both led infamous lives, and there is a tendency for them to be remembered more for their notoriety than for their art. But despite their scandalous reputations, they were groundbreaking pioneers of Symbolism and free verse, and today are ranked among the founding fathers of modern poetry.

Verlaine was born in Metz in northeast France, the only child of Nicolas Verlaine, a retired army captain, and Stéphanie Dehée, a farmer's daughter. In contrast to Nicolas's natural steely imperiousness, Stéphanie was a frivolous and indulgent mother, perhaps the more so because her son had been a late child, born thirteen years into the marriage after a succession of miscarriages. In 1851 the family moved to Paris where Verlaine studied law, but his total lack of interest prompted his father to terminate his studies. Various clerical posts

Above: Arthur Rimbaud aged seventeen in December 1871. Photo by Étienne Carjat. Top: Paule Verlaine in 1893. Photo by Otto Wegener

followed, but it was in the cafe life of literature, the avant-garde and absinthe that Verlaine flourished and where, mixing with the leading Parnassian poets of the day, his ability as a poet turned him into a rising star. His first volume of poems, *Poèmes saturniens*, was critically received in 1866, and his second work, *Fêtes galantes*, published three years later, is often considered his masterpiece. But his talent had a dark side. He was an unstable and capricious character, full of contradictions and prone to violence. In later life one of his former teachers observed, 'I never doubted that there was something in that hideous head which resembled a half-witted criminal.' Plagued by homosexual cravings and yearning to be rid of his 'vice', Verlaine met and married Mathilde Mauté in 1870, but heavy drinking, domestic cruelty (he once set fire to his wife's hair and threw his baby son against a wall), and his relationship with Rimbaud ultimately put an end to the marriage.

Rimbaud was born and raised by his austere, peasant mother in Charleville in the Ardenne, where he grew up into an obstinate and rowdy adolescent with a love of literature. By the time he was sixteen he was an aggressive, anarchistic figure, rebelling against the conventions of the day and pushing out the boundaries of poetry. Strongly influenced by Baudelaire and occult philosophies, he explored the subconscious and experimented with verse as no poet had done before. 'I turned silences and nights into words', he wrote in a *A Season in Hell*. 'What was unutterable, I wrote down. I made the whirling world stand still.' In the summer of 1871 he sent some verses to Verlaine, who immediately wrote inviting him to Paris. Verlaine was

14 rue Nicolet

twenty-seven, and Rimbaud was a few weeks short of seventeen.

At that time Verlaine was living at his in-laws' house in Rue Nicolet. Setting off from here to meet this young poetic genius, he accidentally went to the wrong station. Having nobody to greet him, Rimbaud was compelled to make his own way to Rue Nicolet. When Mathilde opened the door she was confronted with a long-haired, scruffy, ill-mannered young peasant lad who looked barely out of school. 'His eyes were blue and rather beautiful,' she wrote in her memoirs, 'but they had a sly expression which, in our indulgence, we mistook for shyness.' His drawn up trousers 'revealed his blue cotton socks knitted with his mother's care'. Rimbaud had no luggage, just a change of clothing, and the manuscript of 'Le Bateau Ivre' (The Drunken Boat), his 100-line verse-poem, which would influence a generation of writers.

Verlaine and Rimbaud's relationship soon became an intense love affair, during which time Rimbaud's insolent, arrogant and obscene behaviour alienated most of the literati in Paris. Verlaine soon abandoned his wife and child for his newfound lover and in the summer of 1872 they left Paris together to travel in Europe. Rimbaud eventually tired of their itinerant existence and, when he threatened to end their relationship the following year in Brussels, Verlaine shot and wounded Rimbaud in the wrist after a drunken quarrel. Verlaine was arrested and served eighteen months in prison with hard labour.

In prison he converted to Catholicism and wrote his *Romances sans paroles* in 1874. On his release he tried unsuccessfully to enter a monastery, and later taught languages in England and France. His final years were lived in dire poverty, but he was still writing. In 1884 he published *Les Poètes maudits*, short studies of various 'cursed poets' including Rimbaud. Ten years later, in 1894, he was voted 'Prince of Poets' by the artistic review, *La Plume*. He died in Rue Descartes, aged fifty-one, a victim of alcoholism and drug dependency, and is buried in Paris's Batignolles Cemetery.

Rimbaud wrote no more poetry after the age of nineteen. He wandered through Europe and the Far East where he joined and later deserted the Dutch army in the East Indies. A job with a coffee trader led him to the Horn of Africa where he became a trader, an explorer and a gunrunner, venturing into the interior of Ethiopia. A cancerous tumour on his knee sent him back to France in 1891, where his leg was amputated in Marseille, and where, in great pain, he died soon afterwards, at the age of thirty-seven. His body was shipped back to Charleville, where he was buried in the local cemetery, his mother and sister the only mourners. Today Rimbaud is a counterculture legend: 'The first poet', wrote René Char, 'of a civilization not yet born.'

See Also: Batignolles Cemetery, Charles Baudelaire.

Select Bibliography: M. Sorrell (ed.), *Paul Verlaine: Selected Poems* (Oxford World's Classics 2009); *Arthur Rimbaud: Collected Poems* (Oxford World's Classics, 2009).

Further Reading: S. Zweig, *Paul Verlaine* (Leopold, 2015); G. Robb, *Rimbaud: A Biography* (Norton, 2001); C. Nicholl, *Somebody Else: Arthur Rimbaud in Africa, 1880–91* (Vintage, 1998).

Paul Verlaine drinking absinthe in the Café François in 1892

LE LAPIN AGILE

22 RUE DES SAULES

(Métro: Lamarck–Caulaincourt)

OLDEST CABARET IN MONTMARTRE
HAUNT OF ARTISTS, WRITERS
AND LOLO THE DONKEY

All of them liked the casual life we led at the Lapin. And under the lights veiled with red foulards and the low painted ceiling of the main room, where Frédérique sang, who would not have succumbed, as though to a powerful drug? Neither dream nor pleasure approached the sensation. It was something else. A special kind of intoxication, a mingling of reverie and despair, indefinable, without echo. Like autumn rain that falls and stops and falls again, it caught hold of us, fondled us, enervated us. And it really did rain those nights – or else it snowed, while the drunkest of us slept stretched out on a bench, and inoffensive white mice, sly and unafraid, pattered across the chimney-piece. How to describe the atmosphere of our long vigils? It drew its essence from the haphazard setting, in which obscene clay models, a huge Christ figure in plaster, and canvases by Picasso, Utrillo and Girieud all had a place. The dense pipe-smoke added to it. And Frédérique, armed with his guitar, Mac Orlan dressed in cowboy style, the dampness of the walls, the barking dogs, the secret despair of each of us, our poverty, our youth, the time that had gone by – all these completed it.

Francis Carco, *De Montmartre au quartier latin* (1927)

Frédéric Gérard in 1927

B uilt in 1795, the Lapin Agile began life as an inn, and by 1869 it was known as the Cabaret des Assassins, after Douay's painting of the mass murderer Jean-Baptiste Troppman that hung on its walls: a fitting tribute to its disreputable clientele of rogues and thieves. In 1875, the caricaturist André Gill painted a sign depicting the cabaret's culinary *pièce de résistance*, a rabbit, dressed in a hat and sash jumping in lively fashion out of a saucepan while balancing a bottle of wine on his paw. So admired was the painting that the cabaret soon became known by locals as the 'Lapin à Gill' (Gill's Rabbit). Over time, however, the name gradually evolved into the punning 'Lapin Agile' (Agile Rabbit), the name by which it is known today. Following repeated brawls and shootings, and under constant threat of closure, the management of the Lapin Agile was handed over to Frédéric Gérard by its owner, Aristide Bruant, in 1902. Frédé, as he was known, got rid of the villains and opened his doors to the bohemians and artistes of Montmartre, with whom he would play his guitar during

435

evenings of poetry and song. All types began to cross the threshold of Lapin, from Montmartre locals to the wealthy bourgeoisie, and it became the favourite haunt of struggling artists, including Picasso, Modigliani and Utrillo, many of whom would sketch in exchange for a few drinks. A salon of writers emerged as well, notably Max Jacob, Apollinaire, Francis Carco, Pierre Mac Orlan, and Roland Dorgelès. The Lapin Agile had successfully metamorphosed from a den of thieves to a hub of modernism.

The writer Roland Dorgelès, however, was never fully convinced about modernism, and considered many of the cubists' artwork grandiose and pretentious. Dorgelès decided to play a practical joke. He invented an artist called Joachim-Raphaël Boronali from Genoa, the declared leader of the new artistic school of 'excessivism'. Then Dorgelès and a few friends attached a paint-covered brush to the tail of Frédéric Gérard's pet donkey, Lolo, who they encouraged to wag his tail against a strategically positioned canvas. The end result was submitted to the 1910 Salon des Indépendants in Paris as Boronali's *And the sun went down on the Adriatic.* Many of the critics took it seriously and mentioned it in their reviews alongside those of Matisse and Rouault who were exhibiting in the same salon. Dorgelès's hoax had proved his point and embarrassed the art world, making Lolo probably the most famous ass in France. Artistic cabarets are still performed at Lapin Agile today.

See Also: Max Jacob, Guillaume Apollinaire.

Further Information: André Gill, who suffered from mental illness, died at Charenton Asylum in 1885, aged forty-four. Montmartre's Rue André Gill is named after him, and his bust can be seen at the end of the street.

Lapin Agile in 1913

TRISTAN TZARA

15 AVENUE JUNOT

(Métro: Lamarck–Caulaincourt)

FORMER HOME OF TRISTAN TZARA
POET AND CO-FOUNDER OF DADA,
PRECURSOR OF SURREALISM IN PARIS

No one has written more foolishly at times, but many have written almost as foolishly and never once so well. He and his wife, on what the French law now probably calls his money, are building a huge modernist house in Montmartre. Tzara is a great man of small stature and wears a monocle.
Janet Flanner, *Paris Was Yesterday 1925–1939* (1972)

Tristan Tzara *c.*1928

Tristan Tzara was the pseudonym of Samuel Rosenstock, born in Romania in 1896 to Jewish parents, roots he intentionally kept obscure throughout his life. He left Romania in the bitter winter of 1915 aged twenty, with his manuscripts and poems, and settled in Zurich, where he became a struggling poet trying to find his own voice, something he could never have achieved in Romania. 'Boredom,' he wrote, during his early months, 'with its painful varieties of melancholy, invaded me. Sensations of happiness became rare.'

But Tzara's destiny was to change irrevocably in February 1916 when he responded to an advertisement that had appeared in the Swiss newspaper *Neue Zürcher Zeitung* (New Journal of Zurich), which stated that in a back room of a bar-cum-restaurant in Zurich's Neiderdorf district, a group of young artists were creating an entertainment to be called Cabaret Voltaire (named after the eighteenth century philosopher and satirist), where visiting artists could bring along ideas and contributions. 'The place was jammed,' wrote the Cabaret's founder Hugo Ball; 'many people could not find a seat. ... on that same evening Tzara read some traditional-style poems, which he fished out of his various coat pockets in a rather charming way.' The following week Cabaret Voltaire once again staged experimental 'happenings' of the spoken word, dance, music and art, with Tzara reading poems by Verlaine, Mallarmé, and Appollinaire. Cabaret Voltaire survived for only a few months, until the summer of 1916, but as a consequence of its desire to provoke outrage and its attacks on the values of the Establishment, Dada groups, as they became known, burst forth virtually simultaneously in cities around the world including Berlin, New York and Barcelona.

Hugo Ball and Tristan Tzara became the movement's figureheads, and in January 1920 Tzara arrived in Paris where the movement had established its headquarters, and where the journal, *Littérature*, was fast becoming its official mouthpiece. Tzara joined up with the city's resident Dadaists, notably Max Ernst, André Breton, Louis Aragon, Marcel Duchamp, Man Ray and Francis Picabia. A few Dadaist festivals and 'happenings' were held, at which members of the audience would hurl rotten vegetables at the stage, ending the events in brawls and scuffles. By the summer of 1922 Dada was predictably going through its death throes; but its life had paved the way for surrealism, which established its predominance in 1924 with the publication of André Breton's *Manifeste du surréalism*. But although Dada was a short-lived movement of anti-art that was against permanence, it did – ironically – bequeath a permanent legacy of Dadaist prose, poetry and paintings that has endured over the years through the art of Max Ernst and Francis Picabia, and the poems of Tristan Tzara and others.

See Also: André Breton, Paul Éluard, Louis Aragon, Paul Verlaine, Stéphane Mallarmé, Guillaume Apollinaire, Voltaire, Janet Flanner.

Further Information: Tristan Tzara made France his permanent home, and in 1925 he married Swedish artist, Greta Knutson. Together they commissioned modernist architect, Adolph Loos, to design them a house on Avenue Junot in Montmartre. They divorced in 1942. Tzara died in 1963, aged sixty-seven, and is buried in the Cimetière du Montparnasse, Division 8. The name Dada was reputedly chosen at random from a French–German dictionary, but it could have meant anything, or nothing, and for many Dadaists it was simply 'nothing at all'.

Select Bibliography: *Vingt-cinq Poèmes* (Twenty-five Poems) (1918); *Sept Manifestes Dada* (Seven Dadaist Manifestos) (1924).

Further Reading: M. Hentea, *TaTa Dada: The Real Life and Celestial Adventures of Tristan Tzara* (MIT Press, 2014); D. Hopkins, *Dada and Surrealism: A Very Short Introduction* (Oxford University Press, 2004).

15 avenue Junot

MARCEL AYMÉ

PLACE MARCEL AYMÉ

(Métro: Lamarck–Caulaincourt)

SCULPTURE OF LE PASSE-MURAILLE

A TRIBUTE TO WRITER MARCEL AYMÉ

In Montmartre, on the third floor of 75b rue d'Orchampt, there lived an excellent gentleman called Dutilleul, who possessed the singular gift of passing through walls without any trouble at all. He wore pince-nez and a small black goatee, and was a lowly clerk in the Ministry of Records. In winter he would take the bus to work, and in fine weather he would make the journey on foot, in his bowler hat.

Marcel Aymé, 'Le passe-muraille' (1941)

Marcel Aymé in 1929

An underrated and often overlooked writer of the French contemporary short story, Marcel Aymé's humorous and satirical fantasies range from the fairytale to science fiction. His most famous short story, published in 1941, is 'Le passe-muraille' ('The Man Who Walked Through Walls') in which a man discovers he has the ability to pass through walls with ease, but who eventually ends up trapped in one for eternity. In 'Le temps mort' ('Dead Time') the protagonist only exists on alternate days, and in 'La carte' (The Map), set in Nazi-occupied France, ration cards are only issued for a certain number of days per month depending how useful a citizen is to society, and where writers, coming under the 'Useless' category, receive only half the monthly allowance of food, fuel and clothing.

Aymé was born in Joigny in Burgundy in 1902 and brought up in the Jura countryside. He arrived in Paris in 1925 where he worked as a journalist. After the success of his novel *La Jument verte (The Green Mare)* in 1933, he became a full-time writer of children's stories, short stories, novels, plays and film scripts, many of which are set in Montmartre where he spent a great part of his life.

Politically, Aymé was a nonconformist who was against fascism and socialism. But many of his friends, prior to and during the Second World War, were fiercely anti-Semitic and supported the Nazi occupation of France. Notable among these was Céline, who once commented that Aymé had been 'absolutely ruined by prosperity', and that his 'careful, artistic writing is not at all my kind of thing'. Céline was eventually imprisoned as a collaborator, and although Aymé defended his friend, and also the French writer, Robert Brasillach, who was executed for advocating collaborationism, Aymé himself was never a collaborator and was most likely reacting to the political and bourgeois hypocrisy of the time.

See Also: Céline, Robert Brasillach, Jean Cocteau.

Further Information: Place Marcel Aymé is located at the junction of Rue Norvins and Rue Girardon. Aymé lived at No. 26 rue Norvins (now No. 2 place Marcel Aymé) for over thirty years, from 1934 until his death in 1967. The sculpture of Le Passe-Muraille was created in 1989 by French actor, director and sculptor, Jean Marais (1913–1998), muse and lover of Jean Cocteau. Place Jean-Marais is located near Place du Tertre, in front of the church of Saint-Pierre de Montmartre.

Select Bibliography: *La Table aux crevés (The Hollow Field)* (1929); *La Jument verte (The Green Mare)* (1933); *Le Moulin de la Sourdine (The Secret Stream)* (1936); *Travelingue (The Miraculous Barber)* (1941); 'Le passe-muraille' ('The Man Who Walked through Walls') (1943); *Les Contes du chat perché (The Wonderful Farm)* (1934).

Further Reading: C. Duneton, *L'art d'Aymé* (Le Cherche Midi, 2004); J-L. Dumont, *Marcel Aymé et le Merveilleux* (Nouvelles Éditions Debresse, 1970); J. Marais, *Histoires de ma vie* (Albin Michel, 1975).

LOUIS-FERDINAND CÉLINE

98 RUE LEPIC

(Métro: Abbesses/Lamarck–Caulaincourt)

FORMER HOME OF CÉLINE

WRITER, PHYSICIAN, AND AUTHOR OF

JOURNEY TO THE END OF THE NIGHT

Céline in 1932

You can lose your way groping among the shadows of the past. It's frightening how many people and things there are in a man's past that have stopped moving. The living people we've lost in the crypts of time sleep so soundly side by side with the dead that the same darkness envelops them all. As we grow older, we no longer know whom to awaken, the living or the dead.
Louis-Ferdinand Céline, *Journey to the End of the Night* (1932)

Best remembered today for his first novel, *Voyage au bout de la nuit (Journey to the End of the Night)* (1932), Céline, which was the pen name of Louis-Ferdinand Destouches, was a man of many identities and one of the most controversial novelists of the twentieth century. Yet his life and work has remained obscure due to his extreme political views. He wrote anti-Semitic leaflets, applauded Hitler, fled to Germany after the liberation, and went into exile in Denmark where he was imprisoned as a collaborator. In 1951, when he was eventually pardoned, he returned to France, a country whose critics had all but eliminated him from French literary history. Following his death in 1961 French newspapers devoted much of their coverage to Ernest Hemingway, who died on the same day, with Céline – a writer many still preferred to forget – consigned to the periphery.
Information about his early life is hazy,

and those members of the press who probed for details were told by Céline to 'invent them'. Some life events that we can be fairly sure of, however, are that he was born into a family of lower-middle-class shopkeepers in Courbevoie, a commune close to city centre Paris, in 1894. Shortly after his birth the family moved to Passage Choiseul, one of the covered passages of Paris near Avenue de l'Opéra, where his mother had a lace shop and which would later become the setting for his novel *Mort à crédit (Death on Credit)*. In 1924, after a spell in the army and a variety of jobs, he qualified as a doctor, establishing his own practice in the working-class suburb of Clichy in 1928, an area he described as 'a doormat thrown before the town where everyone wipes his feet'. He lived and practised at 36 rue d'Alsace, where a sign on the door read: 'Doctor Louis Destouches – General Practice – Paediatrics – First Floor, left'. In 1931, disillusioned with private practice, he moved to a three-roomed flat on the top floor at 98 rue Lepic in Montmartre, and took employment at a municipal clinic on the rue Fanny in Clichy. Here he worked long hours and met the people of the streets: beggars, pimps, prostitutes, drunkards and the destitute, whose wit, slang and perception of life seeped into his muscular prose.

His first novel, *Voyage au bout de la nuit*, was published in November 1932 and portrays a harsh, graphic picture of the First World War and its aftermath. The book, which made Céline famous, provoked controversy and debate, but its impact on the reading public was huge and it narrowly missed winning the Prix Goncourt, France's most prestigious literary prize. In 1936 he published *Mort à credit,* which was condemned by the same critics who had once praised him, and was a commercial disaster. But it was his three lengthy anti-Semitic pamphlets – *Bagatelles pour un Massacre* (Trifles for a Massacre), *L'École des Cadavres* (The School of Corpses) and *Les Beaux Draps* (A Fine Mess) – published before and during the Second World War, which led to his eventual conviction *in absentia* for collaboration with the Nazis, for which he was sentenced to one year's imprisonment.

When Céline returned in June 1951 to France from Denmark after being granted a pardon, he and his wife settled in the Paris suburb of Meudon, which was where he died in 1961 from a cerebral haemorrhage. As the parish priest refused to allow Céline to be buried in consecrated ground, he was buried in the Cimetière Meudon. Of the few mourners who attended his funeral, one was the French actress Arletty, who later wrote:

> I remember his wife, a doctor and a cat that circled his grave. He wanted a holly-tree, a holly-tree was in flower; a young child with a chequered apron straight out of a 1912 catalogue was watering the flowers on the next grave. The child, the animal, the flower he liked, this was how he finished his journey.

See Also: Ernest Hemingway, Le Prix Goncourt.

Further Information: Céline was married twice, fathered a child and had numerous affairs, notably with dancers, with whom he had a fascination. His pen name Céline was the first name of his maternal grandmother. Robert Denoël, publisher of the first edition of *Voyage au bout de la nuit* and Céline's anti-Semitic pamphlets, was murdered in 1945. Arletty (1898–1992) was briefly imprisoned for her wartime liaison with a German officer. 'My heart is French', she allegedly commented, 'but my ass is international'.

Select Bibliography: *Voyage au bout de la nuit (Journey to the End of the Night)* (1932); *L'Église (The Church)* (1933); *Mort à credit (Death on Credit)* (1936); *Mea Culpa* (1936); *Guignol's Band* (1944); *D'un château l'autre (Castle to Castle)* (1957); *Nord (North)* (1960); *Rigodon (Rigadoon)* (pub. posth. 1969).

Further Reading: P. McCarthy, *Céline* (Penguin, 1977).

98 rue Lepic

BATEAU LAVOIR

13 RUE RAVIGNAN

AT PLACE ÉMILE GOUDEAU

(Métro: Abbesses)

ARTISTS' RESIDENCE AND WORKPLACE
FROM THE 1890S UNTIL THE OUTBREAK
OF THE FIRST WORLD WAR

*The place was so jerry-built that the walls
oozed moisture – 'glacial in winter, and a
Turkish bath in summer' – hence a prevail-
ing smell of mildew, as well as cat piss and
drains. ... On a basement landing was the
one and only toilet, a dark and filthy hole
with an unlockable door that banged in the
wind, and, next to it, the one and only tap ...
There was no gas or electricity.*
John Richardson, *A Life of Picasso: 1881–
1906* (1991)

Pablo Picasso outside Bateau Lavoir *c.*1904

The Bateau Lavoir (Wash house Boat) was a legendary complex of ramshackle wooden shacks, which provided accommodation and workspace for artists in turn-of-the-century Paris. Originally a piano factory, it was bought in 1867 by a locksmith named François-Sébastien Maillard. Some twenty years later, a Monsieur Thibouville instigated the division of this damp and dilapidated building into twenty workshops by the architect Paul Vasseur. From the front, the building looked a deceptively small, single storey structure; but on entering, one would find oneself amid a maze of corridors and creaking stairs on a third floor, precariously overlooking Rue Garreau. But 'cat piss and drains' aside, the Bateau Lavoir was cheap, and it was in Montmartre: the avant-garde heart of artistic activity.

Its most famous resident was Pablo Picasso, who moved there sometime around 1903. Painter André Derain remembered his first encounter with him:

He was living in that strange wooden house in the Rue Ravignan which was inhabited by so many artists famous today or in the way of becoming so. I met him there in 1905. His reputation had not yet spread beyond the boundaries of the Butte. His blue workman's blouse, his occasionally cruel quips, the strangeness of his art, were the talk of Montmartre. His studio, cluttered with canvases representing mystical harlequins and drawings on which people walked and which everyone was allowed to carry off with him, was the meeting place of all the young artists, all the young poets.

Picasso's arrival was rapidly followed by that of Amedeo Modigliani, Juan Gris, Max Jacob and others, and the Bateau Lavoir also became a regular meeting place for a wide variety of artists and writers including Gertrude Stein, Guillaume Apollinaire, Jean Cocteau, Henri Matisse, André Salmon, Georges Braque, Maurice Utrillo and Raymond Radiguet. One of its early occupants was the French novelist, Pierre Mac Orlan (1882–1970), who observed:

> It was the worst time of my life! I've always hated that 'legendary' place. In truth, it was a nightmare for anyone who ventured inside! My experience of the place was one of hunger, cold, and humiliation; and I can tell you I'll never forget it. I was living in the most squalid and poorly lit basement studio and I used to sleep on a pile of old papers.

It is likely that many, if not all, residents would have shared Mac Orlan's experience; but living conditions aside, the Bateau Lavoir generated some legendary work, notably Picasso's *Les Demoiselles d'Avignon*, the painting which is generally regarded as being the forerunner of cubist art. Picasso left the Bateau Lavoir for good in 1912. On hearing in 1969 that the Bateau Lavoir was to be officially declared a historical monument, Picasso remarked to the Minister of Cultural Affairs, 'If only we'd been told that when we were living in it!' Five months later, on 12 May 1970, the building was destroyed by fire.

See Also: Gertrude Stein, Guillaume Appollinaire, Jean Cocteau, Max Jacob, Raymond Radiguet.

Further Information: It was Max Jacob who first named the building the Bateau Lavoir. After seeing washing drying and hearing the walls creaking in the wind, he said it reminded him of the wash house boats that plied their trade up and down the Seine.

Top: Bateau Lavoir in 1967
Above: Following the 1970 fire the Bateau Lavoir was completely rebuilt in 1978, but the original 'historical monument' was, alas, lost forever

ROBERT LOUIS STEVENSON

5 RUE RAVIGNAN

(Métro: Abbesses)

LODGINGS OF ROBERT LOUIS STEVENSON AND HIS LOVER FANNY OSBOURNE IN 1877

Every man has his own romance; mine clustered exclusively about the practice of the arts, the life of the Latin Quarter students, and the world of Paris as depicted by that grimy wizard, the author of the Comédie Humaine. I was not disappointed – I could not have been; for I did not see the facts, I brought them with me ready made.
Robert Louis Stevenson, *The Wrecker* (1892)

Top: RLS in his iconic velvet jacket
Above: Fanny Stevenson in 1885

Robert Louis Stevenson (1850–1894) had a lifelong love affair with France, but his 'first independent acquaintance with Paris' was in April 1874 when he visited his cousin, Bob Stevenson, who was studying painting at a studio close to his lodgings at 81 boulevard Montparnasse.

Sixty kilometres south of the city at Grez-sur-Loing, in the summer of 1876, he met the woman who would eventually become his wife. American-born Fanny Osbourne (1840–1914), along with her three children, arrived in Europe in October 1875. Escaping a failed marriage, she had come to Europe to continue her art studies along with her seventeen-year-old daughter, Belle. Her son Lloyd was seven, and Hervey, the youngest, was five. The family lived in Antwerp for three months, eventually moving to an apartment in Rue de Naples in Paris. In the spring of 1876 Hervey died, probably from consumption, and to help Fanny come to terms with her grief, the peace of Grez-sur-Loing, famous as a retreat for artists and writers, came highly recommended. Fanny soon encountered one such writer: 'a tall, gaunt Scotchman with a face like Raphael', she wrote, 'and between over-education and dissipation has ruined his health, and is dying of consumption … Louis is heir to an immense fortune which he will never live to inherit.' She also found him very emotional, prone to bursting into tears, and with a furious temper, but despite her misgivings they soon became lovers. Fanny moved back to Paris lodgings in Rue de Douai, and in the summer of 1877 she moved herself and her family to Rue Ravignan in Montmartre, where Louis also stayed for a short time before returning to his native Scotland. During the following year Louis and Fanny saw each other sporadically, but on the morning of 12 August 1878, Fanny and her family began their journey by train to London where they would board the train for Liverpool and the long voyage back to California. 'It was terribly short and sudden and final,' wrote her son Lloyd, 'and before I could realise it RLS was walking away down the long length of the platform, a diminishing figure in a brown ulster. My eyes followed him, hoping that he would look back. But he never turned, and finally disappeared in the crowd.'

Louis may have been rejected and bewildered, but he was determined not to allow the woman he loved to disappear from his life, and in the summer of 1879 he bought a one-way ticket on a steamer to New York. From there he journeyed overland to California. It was a journey that nearly killed him, but on Wednesday, 19 May 1880, Louis and Fanny were eventually married in San Francisco.

They returned briefly to Paris in the summer of 1881, visiting Saint-Germain-en-Laye in the western suburbs of the city, where Fanny's son Hervey was buried. They stayed at the plush Hôtel du Pavillon Henri IV, where it appears they were asked to leave because of Louis's flamboyant wardrobe: 'Louis was rather knocked to bits by the insults that were heaped upon him at the hotel,' wrote Fanny in a letter to Louis's parents.

I am glad to say that we marched away leaving them in utmost confusion and dismay. I think that they will now always believe that they turned from their doors the eccentric son of a wealthy English nobleman. I know that it all came from the fact that Louis had on a coloured flannel shirt, and the general suspicious appearance of his wardrobe. I could not blame for that, but they should not have piled insults upon him.

The Stevensons' last visit to Paris was in August 1886, shortly after which time they departed for the South Seas where the 'suspicious appearance of his wardrobe' would become part of the Stevenson legend. Following Louis's death in Samoa of a cerebral haemorrhage in 1894, Fanny returned to California where she lived until her death in 1914. The following year, Belle transported her mother's ashes to Samoa, for burial on the top of Mount Vaea, next to the grave of Louis. Fanny's marker reads, in Louis's words: Teacher, tender, comrade, wife, A fellow-farer true through life …

See Also: Honoré de Balzac, Jardin du Luxembourg.

Further Information: Stevenson wrote two travel books set in France: *An Inland Voyage* (1878), a travelogue about his canoeing trip through France and Belgium in 1876, and *Travels with a Donkey in the Cévennes* (1879) which recounts his 120-mile hike through the hills of the Cévennes with his stubborn donkey, Modestine, in 1878. He also recreated some of his early experiences of bohemian life in the Paris chapters of *The Wrecker* (1892), which he wrote in collaboration with his stepson Lloyd Osbourne.

Select Bibliography: *The Silverado Squatters* (1883); *Treasure Island* (1883); *A Child's Garden of Verses* (1885); *Kidnapped* (1886); *The Strange Case of Dr Jekyll and Mr Hyde* (1886); *Fables* (1896); *Weir of Hermiston* (1896).

Further Reading: L. Stott, *Robert Louis Stevenson and France* (Creag Darach Publications, 1994); M. Wiederanders, *Stevenson's Treasure* (Fireship Press, 2014); N. Rankin, *Dead Man's Chest: Travels after Robert Louis Stevenson* (Faber & Faber, 1987); W. Low, *A Chronicle of Friendships* (Hodder & Stoughton, 1908).

JEAN ANOUILH

1 PLACE CHARLES DULLIN

(Métro: Anvers)

THÉÂTRE DE L'ATELIER
WHERE JEAN ANOUILH'S PLAY
ANTIGONE WAS FIRST PERFORMED
DURING THE NAZI OCCUPATION IN 1944

In a tragedy, nothing is in doubt and everyone's destiny is known. That makes for tranquillity. There is a sort of fellow-feeling among characters in a tragedy: he who kills is as innocent as he who gets killed: it's all a matter of what part you are playing. Tragedy is restful; and the reason is that hope, that foul, deceitful thing, has no part in it. There isn't any hope. You're trapped. The whole sky has fallen on you, and all you can do about it is to shout.
Jean Anouilh, *Antigone* (1944)

Jean Anouilh

Playwright Jean Anouilh (1910–1987) became a leading figure in French theatre during the Second World War when his play, *Antigone*, was premiered at the Théâtre de l'Atelier on 6 February 1944 during the Nazi occupation of Paris. The play, a version of Sophocles's ancient Greek tragedy *Antigone*, is Anouilh's best remembered and most frequently performed work, and while the play was deemed by many to be an allegory of the Resistance movement under the occupation, others inter-preted it as a vindication of the Nazis. The opening night audience in 1944 consisted, therefore, of an ironic mix of collaborators and members of the Resistance, all of whom applauded the play's ambiguous lines. No doubt the Nazi censors were just as confused, and it seems likely that the play only escaped censorship because of its histor-ical context. Jean-Paul Sartre presented *Antigone* as the original existential pro-tagonist when he wrote, 'Anouilh stirred up a storm of discussion with *Antigone* being charged on the one hand with being a Nazi, on the other with being an anarchist.' But Anouilh always took an apolitical stance and did not openly take sides. 'My conscience is clear,' he wrote in his memoirs. 'I knew nothing of the resistance movement during the war.'

Jean Anouilh, the son of François Anouilh, a tailor, and Marie-Magdeleine, a violinist, was born in 1910 in Cérisole, near Bordeaux. When he was eight years old the family moved to Paris where, following his secondary education, he was accepted to the Sorbonne to study law; however, when his studies had to be cut short for financial reasons, Anouilh worked as a copywriter for an advertising agency. In 1935, at the age of twenty-five, he began to concentrate solely on his writing, and after two years of working on indifferent projects he had his first major success with *Le Vo-yageur sans bagage (Traveller without Luggage)*, when he began to establish himself as a major playwright.

In later years his works were eclipsed by the emergence of the Theatre of the Absurd playwrights, notably Eugène Ionesco, Samuel Beckett and Jean Genet. But Anouilh, although a victim of changing tastes, will always be regarded, along with his racy dialogue and comic genius, as one of the supreme entertainers of modern French drama. He died of a heart attack in Lausanne, Switzerland, in 1987, aged seventy-seven.

See Also: Joan of Arc, Eugène Ionesco, Samuel Beckett, Jean Genet, Nazi occupation of Paris.

Further Information: Classified as a historical monument in 1965, Théâtre de l'Atelier first opened its doors in 1822 under the name Théâtre Montmartre. From 1914 until the early 1920s it was a cinema, but in 1922 it returned to its theatrical roots when French actor Charles Dullin (1885–1949) took over its artistic direction. Dullin had recently founded a theatrical company called l'Atelier (the workshop) and thereafter the old Théâtre Montmartre became known as Théâtre de l'Atelier. In 1938 Ukrainian-born director André Barsacq (1909–1973) succeeded Dullin as artistic director, and it was Barsacq who would go on to produce most of Jean Anouilh's plays, including *Antigone* in 1944. At the time of writing Théâtre de l'Atelier is still a working theatre.

Select Bibliography: *Le Voyageur sans bagage (Traveller without Luggage)* (1937); *Antigone* (1942); *L'Invitation au château (Ring Round the Moon)* (1947); *La Valse des toréadors (The Waltz of the Toreadors)* (1952); *L'Alouette (The Lark)* (1952); *Becket ou l'Honneur de Dieu (Becket or the Honour of God)* (1959).

Further Reading: M. Archer, *Jean Anouilh* (Columbia University Press, 1971); L. Falb, *Jean Anouilh* (Ungar, 1977); A. Riding, *And The Show Went On* (Duckworth, 2011).

Théâtre de l'Atelier

MOULIN ROUGE

82 BOULEVARD DE CLICHY

(Métro: Blanche)

WHERE COLETTE AND HER LOVER
MISSY PROVOKED A RIOT
IN *RÊVE D'ÉGYPTE* IN 1907

I'm a bit disgusted by the cowardice of all these people who, last night and tonight, showered me with insults, and ... if I didn't get a footstool thrown smack in my face, it's only because I dodged it in time. Very attractive, don't you think?
From an interview with Colette in *La Semaine parisienne*, January, 1907

Moulin Rouge *c.*1900

French audiences seemingly have a penchant for a rampage on an opening night. Think back to the near-riots at the Paris premieres of Victor Hugo's *Hernani* (1830) and Stravinsky's *The Rite of Spring* (1913). Or the birth pangs of modernism at the opening night of Alfred Jarry's comic play, *Ubu Roi*, which closed after its first performance following riots in 1896. But at the Moulin Rouge on the evening of 3 January 1907 it was not the art of the avant-garde that caused uproar; it was a lesbian kiss and a slur on the aristocracy.

There were no empty seats on the opening night of *Rêve d'Égypte* (Egyptian Dream), a one-act pantomime for two actors, starring Colette, and 'Yssim', the anagrammatic artistic alias of Missy, Colette's lover Mathilde de Morny, the Marquise de Belbeuf. Colette played an Egyptian mummy, and Yssim portrayed the archaeologist who unearths her. Returning to life, the mummy rises from her sarcophagus; and as she begins to dance, the embalmer's bandages slowly unwind to reveal Colette wearing a jewelled bra.

At this point the archaeologist clasps the mummy in a passionate embrace. 'During the quarter of an hour that the pantomime lasted,' wrote a reporter for *Le Figaro*, 'the tumult didn't cease for a minute, and the actors confronting the storm continued the performance with a perseverance worthy of a better cause', and when Colette began 'to mime a love scene with her partner' the audience erupted and projectiles of cushions, coins and orange peel were thrown onto the stage. The orchestra was inaudible above the jeers and shouts of 'down with the dykes'. When Colette's estranged husband, Willy, who co-wrote the piece, was spotted in the audience, he had to fend off the angry crowds with his cane. The mob had, of course, arrived prepared, with the sole intention of undermining the show. In the audience, as well as Missy's family and friends, were around a hundred and fifty hired thugs, whose objections were not solely aimed at a lesbian kiss, but at Missy herself, who, in their eyes, was bringing disgrace to her family and dishonouring the nobility – of which Missy was a member. The proprietors of the Moulin Rouge had fanned the flames of the scandal by emphasising Missy's heritage to the full by using her family's coat of arms in their publicity, without her permission. If ever a show was doomed before the curtain even rose, *Rêve d'Égypte* was it. The Moulin Rouge refused to close the show, and the following evening the riotous behaviour of the audience was repeated, even though Missy had been replaced by a male actor. The next day the police issued a total ban of *Rêve d'Égypte*. The mob had achieved its objective.

Colette went on to have a successful writing career and became a formidable voice in women's writing. Her relationship with Missy ended in 1911. Missy's acting career was short-lived, and in 1944 she committed suicide.

See Also: Colette, Victor Hugo, Alfred Jarry.

Further Information: The Moulin Rouge (Red Mill) was opened in the Jardin de Paris, at the bottom of Montmartre hill, on 6 October 1889 by Joseph Oller (1839–1922) a Spanish entrepreneur, and his manager, Charles Zidler (1831–1897). The windmill erected on its roof was merely symbolic of the dozens of windmills that were once scattered across rural Montmartre grinding grain into flour or mash. 'All [the Moulin Rouge] ever ground was the customers' money', observed Jane Avril, one of its cabaret stars. It had a dance hall in the basement, a cabaret at street level, and an open-air theatre at the rear overlooked by a giant plaster elephant, purchased at the Paris Universal Exhibition of 1889. Best remembered for popularising the cancan, it went on to achieve immortality through the posters of Henri de Toulouse-Lautrec. The original building was destroyed by fire in 1915, but it was rebuilt and reopened in 1921. The Moulin Rouge is now a shadow of its former, belle époque self; nonetheless, it remains a popular tourist attraction.

Further Reading: J. Thurman, *A Life of Colette* (Bloomsbury, 1999); P. La Mure, *Moulin Rouge* (Fontana, 1967); J. Pessis, J. Crépineau, *The Moulin Rouge* (Sutton, 1990).

Colette and Mathilde "Missy" de Morny

CIMETIÈRE DE MONTMARTRE

20 AVENUE RACHEL

(Métro: Blanche)

THE THIRD LARGEST NECROPOLIS IN PARIS

The Caulaincourt bridge, which shakes when the trucks and buses cross over it, does nothing for the funereal grandeur of the place. This is just an odd sort of garden, a toy-town consisting of midget houses, chapels like huts, and mausoleums like shacks, all built out of massive stone, iron, or marble, all fashioned and carved in cheerful bad taste and with a childish self-importance which, instead of winning you over, makes you shrug and give a cynical laugh, turning the ritual visit into an indecent sort of outing.

Colette, 'Le Cimetière Montmartre', *Le Matin* (1913)

Montmartre Cemetery was built over the site of an abandoned gypsum quarry (the indigenous plaster of Paris) that had been used for mass graves during the Reign of Terror. After the Revolution it went by various names: Le Cimetière des Grandes Carrières (The Cemetery of the Large Quarries), Le Cimetière de la Barrière Blanche (The Cemetery of the White Barrier), and Le Cimetière du Nord, eventually evolving into Le Cimetière de Montmartre in 1825. The Caulaincourt Bridge was first proposed by Baron Haussmann in the 1860s, but the scheme was abandoned after a spirited press campaign opposed it. It was finally built in 1887–1888, much to the dismay of outraged Parisians. The cemetery's only entrance is on Avenue Rachel, named after the tragedienne, Mademoiselle Rachel who, ironically, is buried in Père Lachaise.

THÉOPHILE GAUTIER
(1811–1872)
DIVISION 3

POET, NOVELIST, DRAMATIST, CRITIC, JOURNALIST, AND CO-WRITER OF THE LIBRETTO FOR THE BALLET *GISELLE*

No one is truly dead until they are no longer loved.
Théophile Gautier, 'The Tourist' (1852)

Théophile Gautier by Nadar

Baudelaire called him *'Gautier inconnu'* (unknown Gautier). Critic Auguste Faguet wrote that 'His intellectual foundations were null and void. He had not a single idea in his head.' Renowned photographer Félix Nadar once compared his large wrinkled face to an unmade double bed on a Sunday morning. Not the most encouraging of descriptions for one of the most important Romantics of the mid nineteenth century, but Théophile Gautier, alas, has remained forgotten, ignored, and misjudged for more than 150 years, and very few of Gautier's works have been translated into English.

He was born in Tarbes, near Toulouse, in 1811, the son of a tax official. In 1814 his family moved to Paris where his father was appointed receiver of taxes. At school he met the poet Gérard de Nerval, who would become a lifelong friend. He studied art, but later, inspired by Victor Hugo, transferred to the discipline of literature, becoming a passionate Romantic. In 1830 he published his first book, *Poésies*, a collection of 42 poems. *Albertus*, a long, narrative poem about a young painter who falls into the clutches of a sorcerer, was published in 1832. Other poems and short stories followed, but it is for his long and sensuous 1835 novel, *Mademoiselle de Maupin*, that he will be remembered, with its celebrated passage on 'art for art's sake' that scandalised the reading public of his day. Through financial necessity much of his life was spent as critic and journalist, a career that allowed him to travel widely, inspiring a series of travel books, including *Voyage en Espagne* (1843) and *Voyage en Russie* (1867), which rank among the best of nineteenth-century travel literature. In 1852, with his collection of poems, *Émaux et camées* (Enamels and Cameos), Gautier turned his back on Romanticism and embraced the perfect form of the Parnassian school of poetry. It was a trend that would eventually evaporate with the arrival of the Symbolists, but Gautier was a successful pioneer of many styles and he influenced them all. His talent was immortalised by Baudelaire when he dedicated *Les Fleurs du mal* to him, inscribing it to 'a perfect magician of French letters'.

Gautier was always fascinated by dance and he became an acclaimed ballet critic. Following a visit to Spain in 1841, where he observed Andalusian women dancing the flamenco, he visited the Paris Opéra and was captivated by the ballerina Carlotta Grisi, with whom he fell in love and co-wrote the libretto for *Giselle*. Carlotta, however, did not return his love, and though he would retain his passion for her for the remainder of his life, he had a long-term, though unmarried, relationship with Carlotta's sister, Ernestina, with whom he had two daughters. In later life, to ease his financial situation, Gautier was given a sinecure as librarian to his friend Princess Mathilde, daughter of Napoleon Bonaparte's brother, Jérôme.

Gautier died in 1872 from chronic heart disease, aged sixty-one. But perhaps his death was not final: 'Nothing, in fact, actually dies,' he wrote in 'The Tourist': 'everything goes on existing, always. No power on earth can obliterate that which has once had being. Every act, every word, every form, every thought, falls into the universal ocean of things, and produces a circle on its surface that goes on enlarging beyond the furthest bounds of eternity.'

See Also: Victor Hugo, Nadar, Charles Baudelaire, Gérard de Nerval.

Further Information: The French literary style of Parnassianism, which was greatly influenced by Théophile Gautier, became a trend in the late nineteenth century and was led by a group of young poets known as Les Parnassiens, which had as its leader the poet Leconte de Lisle. The group's aim was to free poetry from the old-fashioned romantic concepts of emotionalism and vagueness, and replace it with content and form that was more controlled, precise and technically perfect.

Select Bibliography: *My Fantoms* (NYRB Classics, translated by Richard Holmes, 2008); *Mademoiselle de Maupin* (Penguin Classics, translated by Helen Constantine, 2005).

Further Reading: J. Richardson, *Théophile Gautier: His Life and Times* (Reinhardt, 1958); R. Grant, *Théophile Gautier* (Twayne, 1975).

HENRI MURGER
(1822–1861)
DIVISION 5

NOVELIST AND POET

AUTHOR OF *SCÈNES DE LA VIE DE BOHÈME,* INSPIRATION FOR PUCCINI'S OPERA *LA BOHÈME*

Henri Murger by Nadar

Today, as of old, every man who enters on an artistic career, without any other means of livelihood than his art itself, will be forced to walk in the paths of Bohemia. The greater number of our contemporaries who display the noblest blazonry of art have been Bohemians, and amidst their calm and prosperous glory they often recall, perhaps with regret, the time when, climbing the verdant slope of youth, they had no other fortune in the sunshine of their twenty years than courage, which is the virtue of the young, and hope, which is the wealth of the poor.
Henri Murger, *Scènes de la vie de bohème* (1851)

Although a talented writer, Henri Murger would probably be lost to literary history if the Italian composer Giacomo Puccini (1858–1924) had not based his 1896 opera *La bohème* on his book, *Scènes de la vie de bohème* (Scenes of Bohemian Life). Today *La bohème* is one of the world's most popular operas, but the book and the writer that inspired it have been all but forgotten.

Louis-Henri Murger was born in Paris in 1822, the son of a Savoyard immigrant who was a concierge in Rue Saint-Georges. Leaving school at fifteen he drifted into various unskilled jobs before starting to work with words in whatever way he could that would earn him a living – essays, poems, novels, lyrics, editing – much of the material

being taken from his own experiences and demonstrating the characteristic pathos and humour of the bohemian life he was living. His first real success was *Scènes de la vie de bohème*, which was first published serially in the Parisian newspaper *Le Corsaire* in 1848. Other writings followed, but none achieved the success of *Vie de bohème.*

He died in impoverished circumstances in 1861 aged thirty-eight. 'Saint-Victor, who came to see us today,' wrote the Goncourt brothers,

brought us the news that Murger is dying of an illness in which one rots alive ... When they tried to trim his moustache the other day, the lip came away with the hairs... It strikes me as the death of Bohemia, this death by decomposition, in which everything in Murger's life and the world which he depicted is combined ... a life opposed to all the principles of physical and spiritual hygiene, which results in a man dying in shreds ... without enough strength left in him to suffer, and complaining of only one thing, the smell of rotten meat in his bedroom – the smell of his own body.

See Also: Jardin du Luxembourg, Goncourt brothers, Nadar.

Further Information: After Murger's death a fund was started to raise money for a monument to his memory, which now stands in the Jardin du Luxembourg. Mimi, the dying heroine of *La bohème*, was suffering from consumption, the archaic name for pulmonary tuberculosis, which was particularly prevalent among the poor due to cramped living conditions, absence of sanitation, and poor nutrition. By 1918, one in six deaths in France were still caused by TB. The medieval bohemian life that Murger was writing about disappeared in the mid nineteenth century under the demolition hammer of town planner, Baron Haussman, who created the wide boulevards of Paris we know today.

Further Reading: R. Baldick, *Pages From The Goncourt Journals* (NYRB Classics, 2007).

THE GONCOURT BROTHERS

EDMOND DE GONCOURT **(1822–1896)**

JULES DE GONCOURT **(1830–1870)**

DIVISION 13

NOVELISTS AND MEN OF LETTERS
REMEMBERED FOR THEIR
JOURNALS OF PARISIAN LIFE

Edmond de Goncourt and his brother Jules were so inseparable that in twenty-two years after the death of their mother they were only twice apart for as much as twenty-four hours; so inseparable that they wrote their joint diary in the first person. They moved to Auteuil in 1868; Jules died from tertiary syphilis in 1870. During his final decline, Edmond asked him, 'Where are you, my dear chap?' and after a few moments Jules replied, 'Away in space, in empty space.'
Alphonse Daudet, *La Doulou* (1930, translated into English as *In the Land of Pain*, 2002 by Julian Barnes.)

The Goncourt brothers were prolific writers who published novels, plays, and books of criticism, all of them largely forgotten today. What saved the brothers' writings from the dust of anonymity were their journals: outspoken diaries of nineteenth-century literary and social comment, full of gossip, scandal and indiscretion, which has ensured their immortality. Success in their lifetime, however, escaped them, and bad luck was never far away. Their first journal entry was written on 2 December 1851, the day their first novel was published, but, as misfortune would have it, it was also the day Napoleon III overthrew the Republic, causing their novel to be ignored amid the general hubbub.
The Goncourt brothers were seldom apart from each other for long and did

everything collaboratively, including their writing. They wrote six novels together, of which their best known was *Germinie Lacerteux* (1865), based on the bizarre double-life of one of the Goncourts' domestic servants.

They never married, but had lovers, occasionally sharing the same one. Wealthy, and extremely artistic, their joint interests were literature, collecting *objets d'art* and dining with their literary friends, notably at the Restaurant Magny on Rue Mazet with writers such as Théophile Gautier, Gustave Flaubert, George Sand, Ivan Turgenev and Sainte-Beuve. Only when Jules died in 1870 were the brothers separated. Once described as an 'indiscreet individual', Edmond de Goncourt replied, 'I accept the reproach and I am not ashamed of it … For ever since the world began, the only memoirs of any interest have been written by 'indiscreet individuals'.'

'My constant preoccupation,' wrote Edmond, 'is to save the name of Goncourt from oblivion in the future by every sort of survival: survival through works of literature, survival through foundations, survival through the application of my monogram to all the *objets d'art* which have belonged to my brother and myself.'

In the end none of these ideas would 'save the name of Goncourt from oblivion'; it was their daily journal, memoirs of literary Paris, that will be read in perpetuity. It was, wrote the brothers, 'The confession of two lives never separated in pleasure, in work or in pain, the confession of two twin spirits, two minds receiving from the contact of men and things impressions so alike, so identical, so homogeneous, that this confession may be considered as the effusion of a single ego, of a single I.'

See Also: Le prix Goncourt, Alphonse Daudet, Restaurant Magny, Théophile Gautier, Gustave Flaubert, George Sand, Ivan Turgenev, Charles Sainte-Beuve.

Further Information: Edmond de Goncourt bequeathed much of his estate to create the académie Goncourt, a foundation to promote French literature and to honour the memory of his brother Jules. Since 1903 the académie has awarded Le prix Goncourt, France's most celebrated literary prize.

Select Bibliography: *Germinie Lacerteux* (1865); *Manette Salomon* (1867); *Madame Gervaisais* (1869); *Chérie* (1884).

Further Reading: R. Baldick, *Pages From The Goncourt Journals* (NYRB Classics, 2007); *Dinner at Magny's* (Penguin, 1973).

Edmond and Jules de Goncourt
in 1853 by Paul Gavarni

ALPHONSINE PLESSIS
(1824–1847)
DIVISION 15

LOVER AND MUSE OF ALEXANDRE DUMAS *FILS* AND INSPIRATION FOR HIS NOVEL *LA DAME AUX CAMÉLIAS*

For twenty-five days of the month the camellias were white, and for five they were red; no one ever knew the reason of this change of colour, which I mention though I can not explain it; it was noticed both by her friends and by the habitué's of the theatres to which she most often went. She was never seen with any flowers but camellias. At the florist's, Madame Barjon's, she had come to be called 'the Lady of the Camellias', and the name stuck to her.
Alexandre Dumas *fils*, *La Dame aux Camélias* (1848)

Alphonsine Plessis was a high-class prostitute and mistress of wealthy men. When she died from tuberculosis aged only twenty-three in 1847, crowds lined the streets for a glimpse of her funeral cortège. Charles Dickens, who was among the crowds, commented, 'One could have believed that she was Jeanne d'Arc or some other national heroine, so deep was the general sadness.' Giuseppe Verdi turned her life into opera in *La Traviata* (the fallen woman), and the stage and cinema knew her as *Camille*, but she was immortalised first in literature as the celebrated courtesan, Marguerite Gautier, in Alexandre Dumas *fils*'s 1848 novel, *La Dame aux Camélias*.

Alphonsine Plessis was born in Nonant-le-Pin, Normandy, in 1824 to Marin Plessis, a pedlar, and Marie Deshayes. Her mother died when she was six, and when she was fifteen she moved

American actress, Clara Morris (1849–1925), became a great success at playing the suffering heroine, *Camille*, on the New York stage in 1874

to Paris, where she had a succession of lovers. By the time she was sixteen she had blossomed into one of the most celebrated courtesans in Paris, and it was around this time that she adopted the moniker Marie Duplessis. Admirers bestowed property, clothes, and money on her, which she spent recklessly. Literary critic Jules Janin remembered 'her young and supple waist', and 'the beautiful oval of her face'. Men, especially those of means, found her intoxicating.

She was Dumas *fils*'s mistress for just under a year, but it is doubtful it was a love match, at least on her part, and Dumas would certainly not have had the income to keep her in the lavish circumstances she had become accustomed to.

457

Nonetheless, it is unlikely, given their relationship, that Dumas would have been unaware of the significance of the changing colours of the camellias as a signal of her availability for twenty-five days of the month, while menstruating for the remaining five; and it is possible, as Renée-Michèle Sasson observes, that, 'Dumas *fils*'s *faux naïf* remark about not understanding why Marguerite wore red camellias for five days out of every month is meant to create sexual innuendo in the novel.'

In 1845, the year of their break-up, she met the love of her life, Hungarian composer Franz Liszt; however, the relationship came to nothing. The following year she married a French nobleman, but by that time her health was deteriorating (and her money diminishing) rapidly, and she died of tuberculosis on 3 February 1847. Her effects were later auctioned off to pay her debts.

Dumas wrote *La Dame aux Camélias* very quickly during the month of June 1847, and it was published the following summer. It was a kiss-and-tell book of doomed passion that revealed the mysterious and controversial life of a courtesan. It sold well. In 1852, Dumas's dramatised version, which he wrote in a week, was even more successful than his novel, which led Dumas to devote his talents exclusively to the theatre, where he won rapid fame, becoming one of the leading playwrights of the Second Empire.

See Also: Alexandre Dumas *père*.

Further Information: Born in 1824, Alexandre Dumas *fils* was the illegitimate son of Alexandre Dumas and Marie Labay, a seamstress. His father legally recognised him in 1831, but the circumstances of his birth created in him a deep-rooted concern with the problems of adultery, illegitimacy and prostitution. 'I find the subject of my books in my dreams', said Dumas *père*, 'and my son finds his in reality.' He is buried in Montmartre Cemetery, Division 21. An inscription on his tomb reads: 'I am keenly interested in my life, which pertains to time, but I am more interested in death, which pertains to eternity.' The first performance of *La Traviata*, in Venice in 1853, closed after ten performances. '*La Traviata* last night was a failure,' wrote Verdi to a friend. 'Was the fault mine or the singers? Time will tell.'

Further Reading: J. Kavanagh, *The Girl Who Loved Camellias: The Life and Legend of Marie Duplessis* (Knopf, 2013); E. Saunders, *The Prodigal Father* (Longmans, 1951); A. Maurois, *The Titans: A three-generation biography of the Dumas* (Harper, 1957).

PAULINE VIARDOT

(1821–1910)

DIVISION 20

OPERA SINGER AND MUSE

OF IVAN TURGENEV

When he lay dying, in fierce agonies from the cancerous abscess that was attacking his upper vertebrae, Turgenev threw an inkwell at his lover Pauline Viardot. It may well just have been a sick man lashing out, but Turgenev never forgot anything that he had seen or read, and the gesture immediately recalls the moment when Marx's second most important intellectual forebear Martin Luther flung his inkwell at the Devil. For Turgenev, not woman, but the love she commanded was the very devil. Throwing ink at the problem never quite made it go away, but it resulted in some of the finest writing of the age.
Brian Morton, 'Turgenev at 200' *Scottish Review of Books* Vol 13, Number 2 (2018)

Berlioz described her as 'one of the greatest artists who comes to mind in the past and present history of music'. Saint-Saëns dedicated his opera *Samson and Delilah* to her. She premiered Brahms's *Alto Rhapsody*, and she was also a pianist and a composer, but the musical star of Pauline Viardot has all but faded away and she is better remembered today for the society she moved among than for her mezzo-soprano celebrity.

She entertained many of the literary giants of her time, including Charles Dickens and Henry James, and she was the inspiration for the heroine in George Sand's 1843 novel *Consuelo*. Her most celebrated literary relationship, however, was with the Russian novelist and dramatist, Ivan Turgenev, whom she first met in St Petersburg in 1843. Turgenev became besotted with her, showering her with flowers and gifts despite her being married by this time to Louis Viardot. Her dressing room floor was covered with a white bearskin and the right to sit on one of its four paws was a cherished privilege. Turgenev occupied paw number three, which was the beginning of his gradual access to Viardot's life as well as, from 1845 until Turgenev's death in 1883, her marital home and her children. It remains unclear whether it was a *ménage à trois* situation or whether Viardot and Turgenev's relationship was purely platonic. She retired from the stage in 1863, at the age of forty-two, and devoted herself to composition. History, however, remembers her celebrity more than her artistry.

See Also: Ivan Turgenev, George Sand.

Further Reading: G. Sand, *Consuelo* (Nabu Press, 2010); M. Steen, *Enchantress of Nations* (Icon, 2007); A. Fitzlyon, *The Price of Genius – A Life of Pauline Viardot* (Overture, 2011).

ERNEST RENAN

(1823–1892)

DIVISION 22

FRENCH PHILOLOGIST AND HISTORIAN BEST REMEMBERED FOR HIS *THE LIFE OF JESUS*

The man who has time to keep a private diary has never understood the immensity of the universe.
Ernest Renan

Ernest Renan was born at Tréguier, Brittany, the son of a fisherman who died by drowning when Ernest was five years old. It was a mysterious death, and suicide was suspected due to his extensive debts. Towards the end of his life, Renan spoke of the superstitions of his native Brittany in *Souvenirs d'enfance et de jeunesse (Memories of Childhood and Youth)* in which he relates an incident concerning one of his mother's neighbours, who was a sorceress. Wanting to learn about Ernest's life expectancy, she threw one of the boy's shirts into a sacred lake. 'No sooner had I thrown the little shirt onto the surface than it lifted itself up. Ah, if you had seen how the two arms stretched themselves out! He means to live!' she exclaimed. And live, he did, until the age of sixty-nine, in 1892.

As a young man he was educated for the priesthood, but when religious doubts and a growing interest in literature prevented him from taking his vows, he became a teacher in a private school. In 1850 he started work at the Bibliothèque nationale, and in 1861 he was appointed to the chair of Hebrew at the Collège de France, almost immediately being suspended following his inaugural lecture for casting doubt on the divinity of Christ. He went on to write many histories and philological works, and was considered by many to be one of the leading thinkers of the nineteenth century, but it was his controversial *Vie de Jésus (The Life of Jesus)* (1863), the first of a series on the history of the origins of Christianity, for which he is chiefly remembered. Although the book was denounced by the Church, and infuriated many, its controversial claims made it immensely popular with the reading public.

Renan was also an eminent Semitic scholar who held strong anti-Semitic views. 'It is not fair [of a Jew] to claim family rights in a house which one has not built,' he wrote, 'like those birds which come and take up their quarters in a nest which does not belong to them, or like the crustaceans which steal the shell of another species.'

Further Reading: R. Chadbourne, *Ernest Renan* (Twayne, 1968).

CLAUDE SIMON
(1913–2005)

DIVISION 25

NOVELIST AND WINE PRODUCER
WINNER OF THE NOBEL PRIZE IN
LITERATURE IN 1985

Claude Simon in 1932

... there was a second when I could see him that way his arm raised brandishing that useless ridiculous weapon in the hereditary gesture of an equestrian statue which had probably been handed down to him by generations of swordsmen ... the sun glinting for a second on the naked blade then everything – man horse and sabre – collapsing together sideways like a lead soldier beginning to melt from the feet up.
Claude Simon, *The Flanders Road* (1960)

Over the years Claude Simon has acquired a reputation as a difficult and controversial writer. His stream-of-consciousness pages of lengthy thousand-word sentences with no punctuation and lack of plot made critics mistakenly classify him alongside the French *nouveau roman* writers of the 1950s, a pigeonholing Simon always objected to. As with many writers, it was the events of his early life that formed his understanding of it, and which became the substance of his novels. Despite the fact that his storylines could be distorted and seemingly chaotic to some, he always maintained he was hopeless at inventing plots, and that his novels were taken from real life, distinct from a fictional or idealised world. It was a method that turned him into one of France's major post-war novelists.

Simon was born in Madagascar in 1913, but grew up in Roussillon, at the foot the Pyrenees. His father, a major in the cavalry, was killed in the First World War, and his mother died when he was

eleven. During the Spanish Civil War he helped run guns to the Republicans in Catalonia, an experience that inspired *Le Palace* in 1962 and *Les Géorgiques* in 1981. While attempting to write his first novel, *Le Tricheur (The Cheat)*, in the late 1930s, he was enlisted into a cavalry regiment in 1939, most of whom were massacred after they were ordered to attack German tanks on horseback with swords and rifles. Miraculously, Simon survived, but he was later imprisoned in a POW camp. After several months' imprisonment he managed to escape and return home, where he finished *Le Tricheur* in 1941. As well as influencing his personal life, the war and its aftermath influenced Simon's fiction, notable in *La Route des Flandres (The Flanders Road)*, published in 1960. It was an innovative work, in which Simon conceived a prose technique imitating the mind's fluid thought process.

'To my great shame,' he observed late in life, 'through all these ups and downs, I have, at the age of seventy, still not made any sense of all this, unless it is that, as I think Barthes has said, "if the world has any meaning, it is that it means nothing" – except that it exists.'

See Also: Alain Robbe-Grillet, Les Éditions de Minuit.

461

HEINRICH HEINE
(1797–1856)

DIVISION 27

GERMAN ROMANTIC POET
WHOSE LYRICS WERE POPULARISED
IN THE MUSIC OF SCHUBERT,
SCHUMANN AND BRAHMS

On the day I saw the grave it was almost covered with bunches of blue forget-me-nots. Heine died in 1856, but the youth of the world, seemingly, remembers him still. The flowers were probably from some young German sojourning in Paris; certainly they were a tribute from youth, for the melody of Heine's verse never rings quite so true as in the years that lie the other side of twenty. Probably the youth of countless generations to come will exultantly discover him, feverishly read him, and passionately proclaim him.
Willa Cather, 1902

Heinrich Heine is remembered today as the Romantic poet whose lyrics were popularised in the music of Schubert, Schumann and Brahms. But he was also deeply immersed in social and political issues, where his critical and satirical works frequently came up against German censorship laws, leading, in 1835, to an attempt by the Federal parliament to enforce a nationwide ban on his works. The Nazis, however, were more successful, and burned his 'degenerate' books along with thousands of others on Berlin's Opernplatz in 1933, ignoring Heine's warning in his play *Almansor* (1823) when he wrote, 'Wherever they burn books they will also, in the end, burn human beings.'

Heine was born in Düsseldorf, the eldest of six children of a Jewish textile merchant. His degree was in law, a career he never pursued, being more inclined to Romantic poetry. During the 1820s his fame as a poet was on the rise and much of his work became more concerned with contemporary social and political issues. He travelled through England and Italy, moving to Paris in 1831 when he became unable to find work and was discontented with German politics.

In Paris he became one of its leading literary personalities, and in 1834 he met, and later married, a nineteen-year-old illiterate shop girl whom he lived with for the rest of his life. His Paris days were undoubtedly his happiest and most creative, but this contentment came to an end in the late 1840s when syphilis attacked his nervous system. From 1848 his 'poor, unburied corpse' was confined to his 'mattress grave' surrounded by painkillers and work in progress. After eight years of suffering he died, aged fifty-eight, at 3 avenue Matignon, overlooking the Champs-Élysées, in 1856.

Select Bibliography: *The Complete Poems of Heinrich Heine: a Modern English Version* (Oxford University Press 1984); *The Harz Journey and Selected Prose* (Penguin Classics, 2007).

Further Reading: J.L. Sammons, *Heinrich Heine: A Modern Biography* (Princeton University Press, 2014).

STENDHAL
(1783–1842)

DIVISION 30

NOVELIST AND CRITIC

A novel is a mirror which passes over a highway. Sometimes it reflects to your eyes the blue of the skies, at others the churned-up mud of the road.
Stendhal, *Le Rouge et le noir* (1830)

Stendhal was the pen name of Marie Henri Beyle, now considered one of the great French novelists; however, it was not until after his death in the latter years of the nineteenth century, when the novel changed direction towards psychological observation, that his true status in French literature was finally recognised. But Stendhal was much more than a novelist. He was also a critic, art historian, musicologist, journalist and biographer. Today he is mainly remembered for two novels: *Le Rouge et le noir (The Red and the Black)* (1830), and *La Chartreuse de Parme (The Charterhouse of Parma)* (1839).

He was born in Grenoble in 1783, a town he described as 'the capital of pettiness'. When his mother, Henriette Gagnon, died in childbirth in 1790, the grieving seven-year-old soon found that life with his lawyer father, who constantly spouted piety and morals, inflamed a sense of bitterness in his bones. 'My father', he wrote in later life, 'loved me only as the bearer of his name, but never as a son.' Henri left his provincial childhood behind at the age of seventeen, setting out for Paris in the autumn of 1799.

In Paris he worked at first as a clerk at the Ministry of War, but the following year, having secured an army commission in Napoleon's army, he crossed the Alps into Italy, a country he became captivated by. In the early 1800s, surviving on a pension from his father, he lived in France, mainly in Paris, honing his skills as a writer and striving – though ultimately failing – to become a comic playwright and the next Molière. From 1806 to 1814 he was again involved with the military; however, Napoleon's disastrous retreat from Moscow in 1812, during which Henri was one of the few survivors, reinforced his serious doubts about his Emperor's strategies.

With the fall of Napoleon Henri retired to Milan where he adopted the nom de plume Stendhal and began writing books on Italian painting, and music, notably biographies of Haydn and Mozart. His income, however, came primarily from his journalism. In 1821, having been expelled from Milan as a suspected spy, he moved back to Paris where he would eventually write his two masterpieces, *Le Rouge et le noir* and *La Chartreuse de Parme*. Both books were admired by Honoré de Balzac, but otherwise received scant praise and understanding during his lifetime.

After the July Revolution in 1830 and the overthrow of the Bourbon monarchy, he became French consul at the port of Civitavecchia in the Papal States, a post he held until shortly before his death. In 1841, after suffering a series of strokes, he returned to Paris, where he died in spring of the following year after collapsing in Rue Neuve-des-Capucines. He was fifty-nine years old. 'I find that there's nothing ridiculous,' he had written to a friend shortly after his first stroke, 'about dropping dead in the streets, as long as one doesn't do it deliberately.'

Shortly after his death, critic Paul-Émile Forgues wrote of Stendhal: '[He was] a studious observer of human passions … the only man to whom Diderot, were he alive today, would stretch out his hand … the ingenious analyst to whom we owe the truest definition ever given of love … author of two novels which connoisseurs have already singled out from all the rubbish produced in the genre by our dismal age of magazine serials.'

See Also: Honoré de Balzac, Denis Diderot.

Select Bibliography: *The Red and the Black* (Penguin Classics, 2002); *The Charterhouse of Parma* (Penguin Classics, 2006); *Love* (Penguin Classics, 1975); *The Life of Henry Brulard* (New York Review of Books Classics, 2007); *Memoirs of an Egotist* (Turnstile, 1949); *Lucien Leuwen* (Penguin Classics, 1991); *Life of Rossini* (Calder Publications, 1970).

Further Reading: J. Keates, *Stendhal* (Sinclair-Stevenson, 1994); R. Pearson, *Stendhal's Violin* (OUP, 1992).

20th

Arrondissement

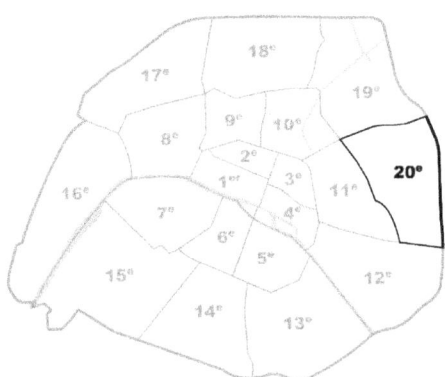

ROBERT BRASILLACH

119 RUE DE BAGNOLET

(Métro: Alexandre Dumas/Gambetta)

CIMETIÈRE DE CHARONNE

GRAVE OF AUTHOR AND EDITOR

ROBERT BRASILLACH

EXECUTED FOR TREASON IN 1945

One can hate or pity Brasillach. But if we condemn him, we should also challenge the motives of a vengeful France. A writer who loses his soul is not as dangerous as a nation that loses its mind.
Richard Corliss, 'Killed for His Words' *Time* (2000)

Robert Brasillach (1909–1945) was the novelist and journalist chiefly remembered as the editor of *Je suis partout*, one of the leading fascist and anti-Semitic newspapers in Paris during the Nazi occupation. After the liberation of France, when there was a purge of collaborators, 50,000 French men and women were put on trial and 1500 were executed, of whom Robert Brasillach was one. Convicted of 'intelligence with the enemy', he died before a firing squad aged thirty-five at Fort de Montrouge in the southern suburbs of Paris. But what made Brasillach's punishment unique was the fact that he was condemned to death for his words.

Brasillach's trial and verdict was what we might today call a done deal: Vichy versus the Resistance. The jurors were Resistance veterans and the judge, who had carried on with his duties under Vichy, perhaps viewed Brasillach's execution as his own absolution. A guilty verdict, therefore, was preordained and the outcome decided, no matter how

465

brilliant and calculated the defence. The trial lasted only six hours, during which time Brasillach's mitigations were annihilated by the prosecution. After the jury's deliberation of only twenty-five minutes, the judge read the death sentence, to which Brasillach's supporters in the courtroom erupted in rage. Brasillach himself shouted, 'It's an honour!'

A petition for clemency was sent to President de Gaulle signed by many artists and writers, including Albert Camus, who, although he detested Brasillach, was against the death penalty. Jean-Paul Sartre and Simone de Beauvoir refused to sign. It is beyond doubt that Brasillach was guilty of collaborating with the Nazis, but the moral dilemma remains: can words be translated into crimes? And why was he executed when a Paris police chief, responsible for signing the documents that sent thousands of French Jews to the death camps, was given only a two-year suspended sentence?

See Also: Albert Camus, Jean-Paul Sartre, Simone de Beauvoir, Charles de Gaulle.

Further Information: Brasillach's grave is in the first section on the right off the Avenue Principale. Fort de Montrouge was originally built in 1845 as part of the defensive fortifications encircling Paris in the mid nineteenth century. After the liberation of France the fort was used for the executions of members of the Carlingue, the French Gestapo. The former Chief of State of Vichy France, Philippe Pétain, was imprisoned at the fort for three months before his trial for treason in July 1945. Today the fort houses the national gendarmerie.

Select Bibliography: *Le Voleur d'étincelles (The Spark Thief)* (1932); *L'Enfant de la nuit (Child of the Night)* (1934); *Histoire du cinéma* (1935); *Le Marchand d'oiseaux (The Bird Merchant)* (1936); *Comme le temps passe (How The Time Passes By)* (1937); *Les Sept Couleurs (The Seven Colours)* (1939); *Poèmes* (1944).

Further Reading: A. Kaplan, *The Collaborator: The Trial and Execution of Robert Brasillach* (University of Chicago Press, 2001); H. Lottman, *The People's Anger: Justice and Revenge After the Liberation of France* (Hutchinson, 1986).

Left: Robert Brasillach seated to the left of reactionary French philosopher Charles Maurras
Top right: Grave of Robert Brasillach. Bottom right: Entrance to Fort de Montrouge

CIMETIÈRE DU PÈRE LACHAISE

8 BOULEVARD DE MÉNILMONTANT

(Métro: Philippe Auguste)

THE MOST VISITED NECROPOLIS
IN THE WORLD

In the cemetery of Père-Lachaise, in the vicinity of the common grave, far from the elegant quarter of that city of sepulchres, far from all the tombs of fancy which display in the presence of eternity all the hideous fashions of death, in a deserted corner, beside an old wall, beneath a great yew tree over which climbs the wild convolvulus, amid dandelions and mosses, there lies a stone. That stone is no more exempt than others from the leprosy of time, of dampness, of the lichens and from the defilement of the birds. The water turns it green, the air blackens it. It is not near any path, and people are not fond of walking in that direction, because the grass is high and their feet are immediately wet. When there is a little sunshine, the lizards come thither. All around there is a quivering of weeds. In the spring, linnets warble in the trees. ... This stone is perfectly plain. ... No name is to be read there.

Victor Hugo describing the unmarked grave in Père Lachaise of Jean Valjean in *Les Misérables* (1862)

Above: Views of the main entrance on Boulevard de Ménilmontant

467

By the late eighteenth century burial space within the city of Paris was in short supply. Its largest burial ground, the Cimetière des Saints-Innocents (Holy Innocents' Cemetery) on Rue Saint-Denis, was closed in 1780 because of overuse. Many of its corpses were later exhumed and transferred to the abandoned mines and quarries near Montparnasse known today as the Catacombs. But most of the cemeteries and graveyards of Paris had the same problem: they were full to capacity and something had to be done by the authorities to solve the dilemma. The obvious solution was to generate large burial grounds outside the city precincts, and the three largest municipal cemeteries created to meet this need were Cimetière du Père Lachaise, Cimetière du Montparnasse and Cimetière de Montmartre, established in 1804, 1824 and 1825 respectively.

Cimetière du Père Lachaise, Paris's first municipal cemetery, was named after the Jesuit priest, Père François de la Chaise (1624–1709), whose house had once occupied part of the site. Père Lachaise also became the world's first garden cemetery; it was to be a landscaped horticultural experience as well as a final resting place. At first, however, it attracted relatively few burials, mainly because Père Lachaise was too far out of the city, too expensive and not consecrated by the Church. During the first year only thirteen bodies had been buried there. The authorities helped solve the unpopularity problem to a certain extent by transferring the remains of Molière and Jean de La Fontaine to Père Lachaise in the hope of increasing burials by strengthening its prestige. By the time the remains of the lovers Abélard and Héloïse were transferred there in 1817, Père Lachaise's reputation as the fashionable place to be buried was rapidly gaining momentum, and by 1832 over 30,000 Parisians lay beneath its soil, buried either in common graves or spectacular mausoleums, the latter being

Engraving of the Cimetière des Saints-Innocents *c.*1550 by Theodor Hoffbauer (1839–1922)

described by Victor Hugo as: 'hideous, frilly little buildings with their boxes and compartments where good Parisians tidy their fathers away into drawers.' Today Père Lachaise is the most visited cemetery in the world with more than 3.5 million visitors annually.

A public collection box in Père Lachaise for *Les Pauvres De Paris* (The Poor of Paris)

COLETTE
(1873–1954)
DIVISION 4

NOVELIST, ACTRESS, DANCER, JOURNALIST AND CREATOR OF *GIGI*

Sidonie-Gabrielle Colette received the first state funeral that the Republic ever gave to a woman. At seven o'clock on the morning of August 7, 1954, her body was moved to the cour d'honneur of the Palais-Royal. The coffin was placed on a raised catafalque draped with the tricolor and flanked by a military guard in dress uniform. It was surrounded by a great embankment of flowers, most of them blue. ... After the orations, her immediate family and a few close friends buried Colette in Père-Lachaise. As the dirt was shoveled into the grave, the rain began, the winds rose, and a storm broke – one of the most violent in a century. She would have enjoyed it.
Judith Thurman, *Secrets of the Flesh: A Life of Colette* (1999)

When Colette died aged eighty-one, on the evening of Tuesday, 3 August 1954, she was regarded by many as one of the most outstanding literary figures of the first half of the twentieth century. Although a Burgundian, the origins of her novels lie in the bohemian Paris of her early life, steeped in nostalgia, remorse, eroticism, scandal and a healthy disdain for the moral standards of her day. In 1935, a readers' poll nominated her the greatest living master of French prose.

She was born in 1873 in Burgundy. Her mother was Parisian, her father a retired French army officer. Her early novels, the *Claudine* series, were published under the name of her first husband, a rascal named Henry Gauthier-Villars, who wrote under the pen name Willy. The collaboration ended in 1904, as did the marriage two years later, when they separated. Up until 1916, she wrote under the name Colette Willy. After her divorce in 1910 she performed as a vivacious dancer in music halls and became a star of the lesbian demimonde, baring her breasts and leaving a trail of scandal that repeatedly shocked her public. Later she became a journalist and she was the first woman to report from the Western Front during World War I. When she was forty she gave birth to her only child, and at forty-seven she seduced her stepson. Her novels, written in a musical and sensuous prose, include *Chéri* (1920), *La Fin de Chéri* (1926) and *Gigi* (1944). 'What a wonderful life I've had!' she wrote, 'I only wish I'd realised it sooner.'

See Also: Colette (Rue de Beaujolais).

Further Reading: J. Thurman, *Secrets of the Flesh: A Life of Colette* (Bloomsbury, 1999).

Left: Colette's final resting place. Right: Colette, Willy and Toby the dog *c.*1900

ALFRED DE MUSSET

(1810–1857)

DIVISION 4

POET, NOVELIST, DRAMATIST

LOVER OF GEORGE SAND

There are almost always fresh flowers lying before the bust of the poet, and below the bust runs an inscription in verse to this effect:

Friends of mine, when I shall die,
Plant a willow over me.
In its sad shade would I lie,

Its pallid leaf is dear to me.
Light its tender shade will weep
O'er the earth where I shall sleep.

This willow requested by the poet has become a subject of mirth even among Parisians, whose sense of the ridiculous is almost entirely lacking. Ever since 1857 gardener after gardener has tried to make a willow tree grow over the tearful singer's grave, but the soil of Père-Lachaise is high and sandy, and the result of fifty years of effort is a spindling yellow seedling, five feet high, so nearly dead that its shade is as light as even so sensitive a gentleman could have wished it. De Musset certainly never *got anything he wanted in life, and it seems a sort of fine-drawn irony that he should not have the one poor willow he wanted for his grave. On the other hand, no one ever quite so thoroughly enjoyed the idea of missing all he wanted, and the condition of this willow would certainly delight his artistic sense as a most effective instance of the relentlessness of a destiny of which he was never tired of complaining.*

Willa Cather, 'The Cemeteries of Paris' (1902)

Born in Paris in 1810, Alfred de Musset was the son of a well-to-do government official. After various dead-end careers in banking, law and medicine, Musset found a vocation in literature. His first published work was a translation of Thomas De Quincey's *Confessions of an English Opium Eater* in 1828. His first collection of poems, which were strongly influenced by the Romantic movement, were published a few years later to much acclaim by France's greatest Romantic, Victor Hugo. One of his poems, 'Ballade à la lune', offended many because he compared the moon to a dot over an 'i'. Perhaps people's sensibilities were more finely tuned in the early nineteenth century, which may have contributed to the failure of his play *La Nuit vénitienne* (The Venetian Night) in 1830; from that point, until 1847, his plays were for armchair consumption only, being published but not performed.

In 1833 he became one of the many lovers of George Sand, who was six years his senior. They visited Italy together, and when Musset fell seriously ill in Venice, Sand seduced the young Italian doctor who attended him. It was an episode in his life he would recall in his 1836 autobiographical novel, *La Confession d'un enfant du siècle (The*

Confession of a Child of the Century). His stormy relationship with Sand came to an end in 1835.

At that time, his lifestyle had degenerated into a fevered existence fuelled by sex and alcohol, but he was still managing to produce some of his finest work, immersed in his usual obsessive themes: loss of childhood innocence, masochistic pleasure in suffering, sexual desire, and death, which came to him in 1857 at the relatively young age of forty-seven. Its cause was a combination of alcoholism and heart disease. Today Musset is considered one of the major figures of the Romantic movement.

See Also: Victor Hugo, George Sand.

Select Bibliography: *The Confession of a Child of the Century* (Penguin, 2013); *A Comedy & Two Proverbs* (Oxford University Press, 1957); *Poems of Alfred De Musset* (Forgotten Books, 2018).

Further Reading: M. Rees, *Alfred De Musset* (Twayne, 1971); W. Cather, *Willa Cather in Europe* (University of Nebraska Press, 1988).

ABÉLARD AND HÉLOÏSE

DIVISION 7

LEGENDARY LITERARY LOVERS

How happy is the blameless vestal's lot!
The world forgetting, by the world forgot.
Eternal sunshine of the spotless mind!
Each pray'r accepted, and each wish
resign'd
Alexander Pope, from *Eloisa to Abelard*
(1717)

Abélard and Héloïse were a High-Middle-Ages teacher and his pupil whose all-consuming love affair had tragic consequences for both. Pierre Abélard (1079–1142) was a renowned cleric and teacher throughout Europe, but his fame today rests chiefly on his famous love affair. He was also Dean of Philosophy of Notre-Dame de Paris, and it was here that he became smitten with the niece of Fulbert, a fellow canon, who was persuaded by Abélard to give him lodgings in exchange for tutoring the girl, whose name was Héloïse. The exact ages of the pair at that time are unknown, but Abélard is considered to have been in his mid-thirties and Héloïse some twenty years his junior. Abélard described the beginning of their affair in his autobiographical *Historia Calamitatum (History of my Misfortunes)*:

> Her studies allowed us to withdraw in private, as love desired, and then with our books open before us, more words of love than of reading passed between us, and more kissing than teaching. My hands strayed oftener to her bosom than to the pages; love drew our eyes to look on each other more than reading kept them on our texts.

When Fulbert learned about the affair he forced the couple to separate. Nevertheless, they resolutely continued seeing each other and in due course Héloïse became pregnant, later giving birth to a son. Abélard wanted to marry, but although this was possible for a twelfth-century cleric, a firmer stance was taken at that time on chastity, and Héloïse did not want to compromise his career with a scandal. They were eventually married in secret, hoping to protect the family honour and assuage Fulbert's wrath. However, when Fulbert publicly disclosed their marriage, Héloïse repudiated it, whereupon 'her uncle, aroused to fury thereby, visited her repeatedly with punishments,' Abélard records.

In order to safeguard her against her uncle, Abélard sent Héloïse to stay at the convent at Argenteuil, near Paris, where she had grown up.

'When her uncle and his kinsmen heard of this', wrote Abélard in *Historia Calamitatum*,

> they were convinced that now I had completely played them false and had rid myself forever of Heloise by forcing her to become a nun. Violently incensed, they laid a plot against me, and one night while I all unsuspecting was asleep in a secret room in my lodgings, they broke in with the help of one of my servants whom they had bribed. There they had vengeance on me with a most cruel and most shameful punishment, such as astounded the whole world; for they cut off those parts of my body with which I had done that which was the cause of their sorrow. This done, straightway they fled, but two of them were captured and suffered the loss of their eyes and their genital organs. One of these two was the aforesaid servant, who even while he was still in my service, had been led by his avarice to betray me.

In the aftermath of his misery and disgrace Abélard retreated into a monastery and became a monk, and bid that Héloïse take the veil within the convent. Abélard's monastic life, however, was far from peaceful: when the Church declared him a heretic he was forced to leave Paris, and throughout the remainder of his life he lived in various monasteries, at one point living the life of a hermit south-east of Paris near Nogent-sur-Seine. When students from Paris discovered him in his retreat, he began teaching again there, eventually founding the Benedictine monastery, the Oratory of the Paraclete. Many years later, after Abélard had left the Oratory in search of another refuge, Héloïse became abbess here. After reading *Historia Calamitatum* she began corresponding with Abélard again, resulting in an exchange of letters after many years of silence. 'Even during the celebration of the Mass', wrote Héloïse, 'when our prayers should be purer, lewd visions of these pleasures take such a hold upon my unhappy soul that my thoughts are on their wantonness instead of on prayers. I should be groaning over the sins I have committed, but I can only sigh for what we have lost.'

Abélard died in 1142, and Héloïse in 1164, but their place of burial is disputed. The Oratory of the Paraclete claims they are both buried there; however, their bones have been moved several times throughout history, and Père Lachaise Cemetery is now regarded as being their most likely resting place.

Further Information: The tomb of Abélard and Héloïse was designed by Alexandre Lenoir. It is a Gothic blend of a *castrum doloris* (castle of grief) and a miniature chapel, incorporating stone from the ruined Oratory of the Paraclete.

Further Reading: P. Abélard, *Historia Calamitatum* (BiblioLife, 2007); P. Abélard and Héloïse, *The Letters of Abélard and Héloïse* (Penguin, 2003); M. Bragg, *Love Without End: A Story of Héloïse and Abélard* (Sceptre, 2019).

Tomb of Abélard and Héloïse

PIERRE LAZAREFF
(1907–1972)
HÉLÈNE LAZAREFF
(1909–1988)

DIVISION 7

FOUNDERS OF *FRANCE-SOIR*

AND *ELLE* MAGAZINE

The liberty of Elle's *tone was, at the time, revolutionary. Just think that before the war,* Marie-Claire *didn't venture to print the word 'lover'. Women only had friends, or fiancés.*
Susan Weiner, *Enfants Terribles* (2001)

1960s French *Elle* magazine, featuring Jean Shrimpton photographed by Brian Duffy

Husband and wife team Pierre and Hélène Lazareff, both of Russian Jewish origin, were a dynamic duo in the publishing world of post-war France. They met while working on the French daily newspaper *Paris-Soir* in the 1930s. Hélène (née Gordon) wrote the children's page under the pen name Tante Juliette (Aunt Juliette), and Pierre was the managing editor. They married in 1938, and with the outbreak of the Second World War moved to New York. *Paris-Soir* continued to publish during the German occupation but in collaboration with the Nazis, which resulted in the French government confiscating their printing plant after the liberation.

The Lazareffs returned to Paris in 1944 where Pierre joined the underground newspaper, *Défense de la France* (Defence of France) which had come out of hiding and taken over the printing plant of the disgraced *Paris-Soir*. After the war *Défense de la France* metamorphosed into *France-Soir*, and with Pierre Lazareff as its chief editor it achieved circulation figures of 1.5 million during the 1950s, one of the largest circulations in Europe.

While in New York, Hélène Lazareff had worked on several American magazines, including *Harper's Bazaar* and the *New York Times Magazine*, an experience that inspired her to create her own. The first issue of *Elle* magazine was published in October 1945.

Ten years later, one in six French women were reading it. In the early 21st century *Elle* had the largest readership of any fashion magazine in the world, with editions on six continents. Hence the famous catchphrase, 'Si elle lit, elle lit *Elle*'(If she reads, she reads *Elle*).

See Also: *Le Monde*, Paris *Tribune*, *Paris Herald*.

Further Information: *France-Soir* ceased publication as a hard copy newspaper in 2011. The clandestine newspaper of the French Resistance group, *Défense de la France*, had the largest circulation of any underground newspaper during the Second World War, with a circulation in January 1944 of 450,000.

REMY DE GOURMONT
(1858–1915)
DIVISION 10

CRITIC, POET AND NOVELIST
AND 'CRITICAL CONSCIENCE
OF HIS GENERATION'

[Arthur Rimbaud] ... from the most tender age showed traits of the most insupportable blackguardism. ... He is often obscure, bizarre and absurd. Of sincerity nothing, with a woman's character, a girl's, inherently wicked and even savage, Rimbaud has that kind of talent which interests without pleasing. In his works are pages which give the impression of beauty one feels before a pustulous toad, a good-looking syphillitic woman, or the Chateau-Rouge at eleven o'clock in the evening.
Remy de Gourmont, *Le Livre des Masques (The Book of Masks)* (1896)

Mostly forgotten today, Remy de Gourmont wrote in many forms: novel, play, poetry and criticism. T.S. Eliot described him as 'the critical conscience of his generation', and John Cowper Powys wrote that 'the death of Remy de Gourmont is one of the greatest losses that European literature has suffered since the death of Oscar Wilde.' Gourmont published over fifty works, but he is remembered primarily for his interpretations of the Symbolist movement in French poetry, notably in his 1896 classic *Le Livre des Masques.* He was born in Normandy to an aristocratic family of artists and writers who claimed descent from the poet François de Malherbe. After studying law at Caen, he obtained a post with the Bibliothèque nationale, but was dismissed a few years later for publishing an unpatriotic article. In 1889 he became one of the founders of the Symbolist review, *Mercure de France*, which published many of his articles, and eventually his books. His poetry and novels are little read today, but what does endure, and has had lasting effect and influence, is his critical writing. He was, as T.S. Eliot noted, 'a real master of fact – sometimes, I am afraid, when he moved outside of literature, a master illusionist of fact.'

From his early twenties, Gourmont suffered from a painfully disfiguring skin disease, which turned him into a semi-recluse, writing mostly from his home. In 1886 he met artists' model Berthe de Courrière, former mistress of the sculptor Auguste Clésinger, who had bequeathed his fortune to her on his death. She later became Gourmont's mistress, and they lived together until Gourmont's death from a stroke in 1915. Berthe died the following year, and they were both laid to rest in an eternal *ménage à trois* in Clésinger's vault at Père Lachaise. 'Gourmont is dead', wrote Ezra Pound, 'and the world's light is darkened.'

See Also: T.S. Eliot, Arthur Rimbaud, François de Malherbe, Bibliothèque nationale, Oscar Wilde, Ezra Pound.

Remy de Gourmont

MOLIÈRE
(1622–1673)
DIVISION 25

Molière in 1668

FRANCE'S GREATEST COMIC DRAMATIST

His wife had a stone slab laid on his grave [in Saint-Joseph cemetery] and ordered a hundred bundles of firewood delivered to the cemetery so that the homeless beggars could warm themselves. The next winter, which was especially severe, a huge fire was lit on the stone. The slab cracked from the heat and fell apart. Time scattered the pieces. And when, during the Great Revolution, 119 years later, the people's commissaires came to disinter the body of Jean-Baptiste Molière and transfer it to a mausoleum, no one could point precisely to the place of his burial. And although someone's remains were disinterred and placed in a mausoleum, no one can say with assurance that those were Molière's. It may well be that the honours were conferred on the ashes of an unknown man.

Mikhail Bulgakov describing the fate of Molière's remains prior to interment at Père Lachaise in *The Life of Monsieur de Molière* (1962)

Molière may have been France's greatest comic dramatist, praised by king and commoner alike, but that didn't entitle him to a decent Christian burial. To the Roman Catholic Church in the seventeenth century, actors were instruments of the Devil, and the French clergy were more neurotic about them than were their counterparts elsewhere. Threatened by anti-Catholic England and the spread of the Protestant Reformation throughout Europe, the Catholic Church in France waged a savage war on the theatre, and unless actors renounced their profession before dying they were refused burial in consecrated ground.

In romantic myth Molière died on the stage while performing in *Le Malade imaginaire*. He was certainly taken seriously ill during the performance and could well have died on stage, but he was immediately taken home where he began to haemorrhage. 'This same day,' wrote actor Charles Varlet,

> after the play, about 10 o'clock in the evening, Monsieur de Molière died in his house, rue de Richelieu, having played the role of the Imaginary Invalid, very ill of a cold and fluxion of the chest that caused him to cough heavily, so that with the great effort he made to spit he broke a vein in his body and lived no more than a half hour or three quarters after the vein broke'.

Molière, who was probably suffering from tuberculosis, died from a massive haemorrhage, aged fifty-one. But Molière had died without renouncing his profession. Two priests had been

476

contacted during his last hours of life, but both had refused to come and hear his renunciation, and when at last a priest did arrive Molière was already dead. His wife appealed to King Louis XIV, who could do nothing of consequence against the power of the Church, other than decree his body should be buried under cover of darkness and without fuss, but not in holy ground.

Despite misgivings by the Church, Molière was eventually buried in the cemetery of Saint-Joseph that belonged to the parish of Saint-Eustache, which has long vanished under the heel of modern Paris. The site of his burial in the cemetery was uncertain, but during the French Revolution in 1792 his supposed remains were exhumed, stored in the church for seven years, and eventually deposited in the newly inaugurated Musée des monuments français (a former convent of the Petits-Augustins, now part of the École des Beaux-Arts on Rue Bonaparte). After the Bourbon Restoration in 1814, the museum was closed, and Molière's alleged remains were later transferred to Père Lachaise in 1817 where they still lie. But whether they are in fact his remains, or, as Mikhail Bulgakov observed, 'the ashes of an unknown man', we shall probably never know.

See Also: The Fontaine Molière, Jean Racine, Pierre Corneille, Basilica of Sainte-Jeanne-d'Arc, École des Beaux-Arts.

Further Information: In 1680, seven years after Molière's death, the state theatre La Comédie-Francaise was created by royal decree. It is known affectionately as *La Maison de Molière* after its spiritual and artistic patron.

Further Reading: V. Scott, *Molière: A Theatrical Life* (Cambridge University Press, 2002); M. Bulgakov, *The Life of Monsieur de Molière* (Alma Books, 2009); J. Gaines (ed.), *The Molière Encyclopedia* (Greenwood, 2002).

JEAN DE LA FONTAINE

(1621–1695)

DIVISION 25

POET AND FABULIST

Jean de La Fontaine

Perched in a treetop, old Mister Crow
Was holding a cheese in his beak.
Drawn by the smell, Mister Fox, down below,
Peered up, then proceeded to speak.
'Why, hello, fair Sir Crow! Lovely day!
How you dazzle my eyes! How rare your
display!
Not to lie, if your voice when you sing
Is as fine as the cut of your wing
I'll know you're the Phoenix reborn in these
woods!'
At these words the old crow became giddy
with pleasure
And, thinking to prove his voice a treasure,
He opened his big beak – and promptly
dropped the goods.
Fox pounced upon his prize, then said, 'My
dear, dear sir,
Learn now that every flatterer
Lives at the cost of those who give him credit.
That lesson's worth a cheese no doubt, so
don't forget it!'
The crow, in shame and deep chagrin,
Swore, a bit late, never again to be taken in.
Jean de La Fontaine, 'The Crow and the Fox'
The Complete Fables of La Fontaine,
(Translated by Craig Hill, 2008)

Jean de La Fontaine's fables are often mistaken as poems created solely for children, but, as his translator Craig Hill points out, his fables are 'no more a work for children than are George Orwell's *Animal Farm* or William Blake's *Songs of Innocence*.' Using an assortment of animal characters La Fontaine depicted and tenderly mocked the society of his day with his humorous, subtle and moral observations. With sources from Aesop to Machiavelli, his *Fables* were published in twelve volumes from 1668 to 1694, and it is on these deceptively simple works that his fame rests today. He was born in Château-Thierry, Champagne, in 1621, the son of a government official. As with many poets throughout history, regular education and employment did not suit him, and after a few career dead ends he eventually drifted to Paris where he half-heartedly studied law and became a novice in a seminary. But it was a vocation he had no real interest in; what he really wanted was to become a writer, but his prospects then were non-existent. In 1647, aged twenty-five, he returned home where he was employed by his father for the next thirteen years. During this time he married a local girl with whom he had a son, and became more and more committed to the craft of writing.

Earning a living from writing, however, was practically impossible in France until the late eighteenth century. Publishers, and also the theatre, paid next to nothing. Unless one was fortunate enough to have another profession, or a private income, one's only hope was

to seek patronage from the rich and powerful, which in La Fontaine's day was an essential part of literary life. In 1657 he submitted one of his first major poems to the enormously wealthy Nicolas Fouquet, France's Superintendent of Finances, who subsequently invited La Fontaine to join his literary coterie and write verses for his pleasure in exchange for a regular salary. But the world of court patronage was often precarious, and when King Louis XIV sentenced Fouquet to life imprisonment for embezzlement in 1661, La Fontaine had to find other patrons to sustain and protect him, taking great care to avoid the displeasure of the King.

La Fontaine shrewdly dedicated his first volume of fables to the King's son, Louis, maintaining that his verse translations reached back to Aesop, whose wisdom the young dauphin might need some day to rule a nation. The fact that La Fontaine's versions of Aesop satirised the monarchy and its court may not have escaped their notice, but blame, along with its piercing wit, could always be laid at the door of Aesop, not La Fontaine. But for the tyrannical regime of Louis XIV and his court, literature was not about wisdom; it was about propaganda, praising the King, and the odd heroic ode. Anything else would

have required an uphill struggle to gain courtly recognition.

During his lifetime La Fontaine became famous for his fables, but he also wrote several other popular works, including his *Contes et nouvelles en vers*, a collection of bawdy erotic tales. His lasting legacy, however, was his fables, and his unique bestowal of verbal, witty humour on animals and vegetables, to which all children's literature, from *Alice in Wonderland* to *The Gruffalo*, is forever indebted.

See Also: Charles Perrault.

Further Information: La Fontaine died in April 1695 at Neuilly-sur-Seine. Nicolas Fouquet was imprisoned by order of the King on false charges of embezzlement and treason. La Fontaine, who remained loyal to Fouquet, campaigned fruitlessly for his release. Fouquet died in prison in 1680, after nearly sixteen years' imprisonment.

Select Bibliography: C. Hill, *The Complete Fables of La Fontaine* (Arcade, 2008).

Further Reading: M. Fumaroli, *The Poet and the King: Jean de La Fontaine and His Century* (Trans. J. Todd, University of Notre Dame Press, 2002).

Illustration from the first collection of La Fontaine's *Fables* (1668–1694) by François Chauveau (1613–1676)

ALPHONSE DAUDET

(1840–1897)

DIVISION 26

NOVELIST, DRAMATIST AND SHORT-STORY WRITER REMEMBERED FOR HIS HUMOROUS SKETCHES OF PROVENÇAL LIFE

Alphonse Daudet in 1891

From where I was, I used to see a kindly-looking old man trotting sedately along the paths. All day long he pruned the trees, dug, watered, removed the wilted flowers with minute care; then, at the setting of the sun, he would enter the little chapel where his family's dead were sleeping; he would replace the spade, the rake, the large watering cans; all was done tranquilly, with the serenity of a graveyard gardener. Yet, without his at all being aware of it, this good man worked with a kind of reverence, softening all noises and gently closing the door of the vault each time, as if he feared to waken someone. In the great, radiant silence, his care for that little garden disturbed not one bird, and it had nothing of sadness about it. It only made the sea seem more immense, the sky more high; and this siesta without end, amid the ever-restless, ever-triumphant life-forces of nature, diffused all around it the feeling of eternal rest.

Alphonse Daudet, *Lettres de mon Moulin* (1869)

Alphonse Daudet was a leading literary figure in French literature. Witty and exuberant, his prose was popular internationally in the late nineteenth century, but today, lamentably, it is little read outside the country of his birth. He won rapid fame with his novels, but it is his sentimental and humorous vignettes of the Midi, namely in *Lettres de mon Moulin (Letters from my Windmill)*, and his *Tartarin* parodies, for which he is remembered. Although happily married with three children, Daudet had casual sexual affairs with women throughout his life, which resulted in his contracting syphilis. In the early stages it was treated with mercury and lay dormant, but in the mid-1880s he was diagnosed with tabes dorsalis, a form of neurosyphilis, the symptons of which include a degeneration of the back and the inability to control body movements, resulting in paralysis. In 1897, after twelve years of excruciating pain alleviated by chloral, bromide and morphine, he died at the dinner table at 41 rue de l'Université, his family home. Daudet chronicled his physical decline in notes intended for a projected book with the proposed title *La Doulou*, a Provençal word meaning 'pain'. Prophetically, he wrote,

You have to die so many times before you die. … Pain has a life of its own. The ingenious efforts a disease makes in order to survive. People say, 'Let nature take its course.' But death is as much a part of nature as life. The forces of survival and destruction are at war within us and are equally matched.

La Doulou was published posthumously in 1930. The English translation, *In the Land of Pain* (translated by Julian Barnes), was published in 2002.

JEAN ANTHELME BRILLAT-SAVARIN
(1755–1826)
DIVISION 28

INFLUENTIAL WRITER ON THE ART OF GASTRONOMY AND AUTHOR OF *PHYSIOLOGIE DU GOÛT* (*THE PHYSIOLOGY OF TASTE*)

Those who have been too long at their labour, who have drunk too long at the cup of voluptuousness, who feel they have become temporarily inhumane, who are tormented by their families, who find life sad and love ephemeral ... they should all eat chocolate and they will be comforted.
Jean Anthelme Brillat-Savarin

The *Physiology of Taste; or, Meditations on Transcendental Gastronomy* is not a title that easily rolls off the tongue, nor is it even a cookbook or a guidebook to the culinary arts, but it helped launch a whole new genre of books on the practice and art of choosing, cooking and eating food. Published in 1825, Brillat-Savarin's idiosyncratic book, which has had many different English titles over the years, is more a collection of witty anecdotes, aphorisms ('Tell me what you eat, and I will tell you what you are'), guidelines and observations to improve the dining experience. Publishers rejected the original manuscript of *Physiology*, but Brillat-Savarin, under the pseudonym the 'Professor', printed 500 copies privately, which gave him – albeit briefly – the taste of success. Two months later, in February 1826, he contracted pneumonia and died.

Following the aftermath of the French Revolution everything was beginning to change in France, and not just polit-ically. A culinary revolution was also happening and public dining was altering dramatically. Antoine Beauvilliers opened the first grand restaurant, the Taverne anglaise, at the Palais-Royale in 1786, and later wrote *L'art du Cuisinier*, which became a classic of French gastronomic literature. Enterprising restaurants soon started cropping up everywhere, and France's first public critic and restaurant reviewer, Grimod de La Reynière, began to turn gastronomy and its literature into an art. By the time Brillat-Savarin published his *Physiology* in 1825 there was already an audience of aspiring gastronomes eager for his anecdotes and tongue-in-cheek witticisms. 'The discovery of a new dish', wrote Brillat-Savarin, 'does more for the happiness of the human race than the discovery of a star.'

Further Reading: G. MacDonogh, *Brillat-Savarin: The Judge and His Stomach* (John Murray, 1992); *The Physiology of Taste* (Vintage Classics, 2011).

An early nineteenth-century poster advertising *Physiologie du Goût*

HONORÉ DE BALZAC
(1799–1850)

DIVISION 48

FOUNDER OF THE MODERN NOVEL

Death is as unexpected in his caprice as a courtesan in her disdain; but death is truer – Death has never forsaken any man.
Honoré de Balzac, *L'Élixir de longue vie (The Elixir of Life)* (1830)

Honoré de Balzac was one of the great realists of French literature. A workaholic who regularly wrote for eighteen hours a day, he produced a colossal amount of work during his relatively short life. His greatest achievement was *La Comédie humaine*, a series of loosely connected novels spanning French society from the Revolution to the end of the July Monarchy in 1848. Included in the series are his masterpieces *Le Père Goriot* (1835) and *Cousine Bette* (1846).

On 18 August 1850, just five months after Balzac's marriage to the Countess Ewelina Hańska, he died from a gangrene associated with congestive heart failure at his home on Rue Fortunée (now Rue Balzac). Three days later, his funeral procession started from the Église Saint-Philippe-du-Roule on Rue de Courcelles, where a two-horse hearse followed by a long train of mourners led the way to Père Lachaise. Victor Hugo, who was eulogist as well as one of the four pall-bearers, recalled Balzac's death and funeral in *Actes et Paroles (Deeds and Words)* (1889):

> I perceived an open door. I heard a loud and sinister rattling noise. I was in the death-chamber of Balzac.

Above: Église Saint-Philippe-du-Roule
Top: Honoré de Balzac in 1842

A bed stood in the middle of the room, a mahogany bedstead having a suspensory arrangement at the head and foot for the convenience of moving the invalid. M. de Balzac was in this bed, his head supported on a pile of pillows, to which had been added the red damask cushions from the sofa. His face was purple, almost black, and drawn to the right side; his beard untrimmed, his grey hair cut short, his eyes fixed and open. I saw him in profile, and thus he resembled

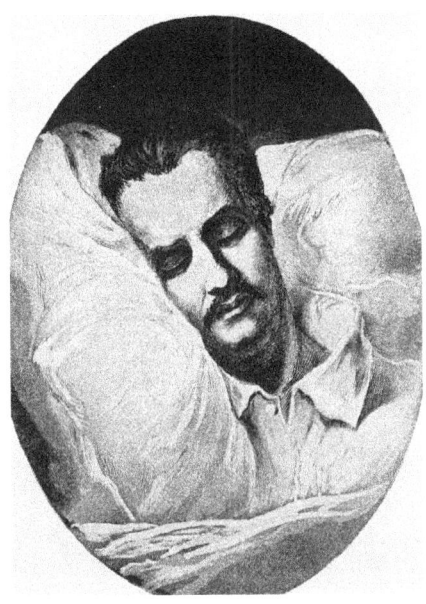

Portrait of Balzac, taken one hour after his death

the Emperor ...

An unsupportable smell issued from the bed. I lifted the counterpane and took the hand of Balzac. It was clammy. I pressed it. He did not respond to the pressure.

This was the same room in which I had come to see him a month previously. He was then cheerful, full of hope, having no doubt of his recovery, showing his swelled limb, and laughing ...

He died in the night. He was fifty-one years old ...

The [funeral] procession traversed Paris and went by way of the boulevards to Père la Chaise. A few drops of rain fell when we were leaving the church and when we reached the cemetery. It was one of those days on which it seems that the heavens must shed tears.

We walked all the way. I proceeded in front of the coffin, holding one of the silver tassels of the pall; Alexandre Dumas was on the other side.

When we came to the grave, which was some distance up the hill, we found an immense crowd. The road was rough and narrow; the horses had some difficulty in pulling the hearse, which rolled back again. I found myself imprisoned between a wheel and a tomb, and was very nearly crushed. The spectators who were standing on the tomb helped me up.

The coffin was lowered into the grave, which is close to those of Charles Nodier and of Casimir Delavigne. The priest said the last prayer, and I spoke a few words. As I was speaking the sun set. All Paris appeared in the distance enveloped in the splendid haze of the setting orb. The earth began to fall into the grave almost at my feet, and I was interrupted by the dull sound of this earth dropping on the coffin.

See Also: Honoré de Balzac (Maison de Balzac), Victor Hugo, Alexandre Dumas.

Further Information: Balzac had many lovers throughout his life, but the 'object of [his] sweetest dreams', the woman he eventually married in 1850, was Polish noblewoman, Ewelina Hańska. She died aged seventy-six in 1882 and is buried beside Balzac.

Close-up of the bust that crowns Balzac's tomb

483

GÉRARD DE NERVAL

(1808–1855)

DIVISION 49

ROMANTIC POET, WRITER AND TRAVELLER OFTEN REGARDED AS A PRECURSOR OF BOTH THE SYMBOLIST AND SURREALIST MOVEMENTS

Why should a lobster be any more ridiculous than a dog? ... or any other animal that one chooses to take for a walk? I have a liking for lobsters. They are peaceful, serious creatures. They know the secrets of the sea, they don't bark, and they don't gobble up your monadic privacy like dogs do. And Goethe had an aversion to dogs, and he wasn't mad! Gérard de Nerval justifying walking a lobster on a leash in the gardens of the Palais Royal in Théophile Gautier's *Portraits et Souvenirs Littéraires* (1875)

Gérard de Nerval by Nadar

On 27 January 1855, Gérard de Nerval left a curt note to his aunt: 'Do not wait up for me this evening, for the night will be black and white.' At dawn the following day his body was discovered hanging by a rope from the grill of a ventilation window in Rue de la Vieille-Lanterne, a dark, narrow alley (since demolished as part of the redevelopment of Paris) on the Right Bank of the Seine. There was no suicide note, and despite sub-zero temperatures and falling snow he wore no coat. He had 'delivered his soul', wrote Baudelaire, 'in the darkest street that he could find.' Nerval's friends were in agreement that he had died by his own hand, an act that would refuse him burial in consecrated ground; however, in a letter to the Archbishop of Paris, Nerval's doctor wrote that 'it was certainly in an extreme attack of madness that M. Gérard de Nerval put an end to his days.' The Church accepted the diagnosis and he was subsequently buried in Père Lachaise. Whatever were the reasons which brought about his death, in life Gérard de Nerval was a masterly and revolutionary writer, named by Proust as one of the three or four most important French writers of the nineteenth century.

He was born Gérard Labrunie on 22 May 1808 near the Place du Châtelet – only a few hundred metres from where he would die – the only child of Étienne Labrunie, an army doctor, and Marguerite Laurent, who died from fever in 1810, just two years after her son's birth. When Gérard was of age, his father sent him to the Lycée Charlemagne, and it was here that he met the writer Théophile Gautier, who would become a lifelong friend. At the Lycée, Nerval was a model pupil, especially in

were not reciprocated. The first signs of his schizophrenic personality appeared in 1841, and from then until his death he was periodically hospitalised at various clinics and asylums. Throughout his later life he seems to have been preoccupied with death. In an 1837 manuscript he wrote:

> It was then that I was tempted to go to God, that I might demand the account on my incomplete existence. There was only a single step to take. At the place where I stood, the hillside was cut away like a cliff, with the sea groaning at its foot, blue and pure. There was no more than a moment to suffer. Oh how terrible was the dizziness of that thought! Two times I threw myself forward, and I do not know what power flung me back, still alive, onto the grass which I kissed. No, my God, you have not created me for eternal suffering. I do not wish to outrage you with my own death. But give me the strength, give me the energy, give me above all the resolution, which helps some to power, some to fame, and some – to love.

languages, and here he published two pamphlets of poetry, later establishing his reputation as a writer of genius when he published a translation of Goethe's *Faust* during the winter of 1827. Praised by Goethe, and used by Berlioz for the libretto of his *Faust* opera, Nerval's translation was a triumph that spread literary Paris at his feet, securing Victor Hugo and Alexandre Dumas among his admirers.

Throughout his relatively short life Nerval produced a considerable outpouring of poetry, prose, essays, short stories, and literary and dramatic criticism. In 1834 he came into a sizeable inheritance of thirty thousand francs. Most of this he lost in a failed publishing venture, but it did allow him to travel and to write travelogues, notably *Voyage en Orient* (1851). He and Alexandre Dumas worked together writing for the stage; however, when in 1837 *Piquillo* was shown at the Opéra-Comique, only Dumas's name appeared on the libretto. Perhaps adding insult to injury, Nerval fell in love with Jenny Colon, who played the main role, but his feelings

When Gérard de Nerval did eventually take his own life he left for posterity a canon of works, some of which are miniature masterpieces, notably *Sylvie*. He wrote during periods of sanity and insanity, through a fog of hallucinations, dreams and depressions. Had he been born a few decades later psychoanalysis could possibly have saved his life. Today he is little remembered outside France, but his body of work confirms that he was an especially gifted writer with a fascination for the strange and the exotic – lobsters included.

See Also: Théophile Gautier, Marcel Proust, Charles Baudelaire, Victor Hugo, Alexandre Dumas, Nadar.

Further Information: Rue de la Vieille-Lanterne fell victim to Baron Haussmann's renovation of Paris in the mid 1800s and a theatre (now known as Théâtre de la Ville) was built over the site. In the garden of the adjacent Tour Saint-Jacques is a plaque commemorating Nerval, and next to it a stone inscribed with his poem *El Desdichado* (The Disinherited One).

Select Bibliography: *Voyage en Orient* (1851); *Lorely, souvenirs d'Allemagne* (1852); *Les Illuminés* (1852); *Sylvie* (1853); *Les Filles du feu* (1854); *Pandora* (1854); *Aurélia, ou le rêve et la vie* (1855).

Further Reading: R. Holmes, *Footsteps: Adventures of a Romantic Biographer* (Hodder & Stoughton, 1985); B. Sowerby, *The Disinherited: The Life of Gérard de Nerval* (Peter Owen, 1973); S. Rhodes, *Gérard de Nerval 1808–1855: Poet, Traveler, Dreamer* (Philosophical Lib., 1951).

Plaque commemorating Gérard de Nerval in the garden of the Tour Saint-Jacques

MAURICE MERLEAU-PONTY
(1908–1961)
DIVISION 52

FRENCH PHILOSOPHER AND ESSAYIST
LEADING PROPONENT OF EXISTENTIAL-
ISM AND PHENOMENOLOGY
AND CO-FOUNDER OF THE JOURNAL *LES
TEMPS MODERNES*

The full meaning of a language is never translatable into another. We may speak several languages but one of them always remains the one in which we live. In order completely to assimilate a language it would be necessary to make the world which it expresses one's own and one never does belong to two worlds at once.
Maurice Merleau-Ponty, from *Phenomenology of Perception* (1945)

Maurice Merleau-Ponty is remembered for his 1945 work *Phenomenology of Perception*, which established his reputation as one of the world's eminent phenomenologists. In the book he expounds his own unique evaluation of phenomenology's method, investigating the nature of consciousness and establishing his theory in bodily behaviour and in perception. Strongly influenced by Karl Marx, Edmund Husserl and Martin Heidegger, his early life was spent with the existentialist movement where he was a friend of Jean-Paul Sartre and Simone de Beauvoir. In 1945 he was one of the co-founders, along with Sartre and Beauvoir, of *Les Temps Modernes* (Modern Times), a journal which aimed to publish *littérature engagée* (engaged literature): literature of commitment with a philosophy propounding existentialism consisting of a practical element

486

as well as a cultural one. It was an attitude that many writers took exception to. Sartre's response to them was, 'the world can easily get along without literature. But it can get along even more easily without man'. Merleau-Ponty became the political editor for *Les Temps Modernes* and wrote regularly on politics and contemporary events, always probing their philosophical themes. In 1953 he left the journal and distanced himself from the neo-Marxism of Sartre and revolutionary politics, preferring a 'new liberalism'. Although Merleau-Ponty wrote leftist political essays and books until his death, notably *Humanism and Terror* (1947), it is for his philosophical works that he is celebrated.

Born in Rochefort-sur-Mer on the south-western coast of France, he studied in Paris and worked as a schoolteacher up until the outbreak of the Second World War, after which time he held various professorships. One of the leading French phenomenologists of his generation, he died suddenly from a stroke in 1961, at the age of fifty-three.

See Also: Jean-Paul Sartre, Simone de Beauvoir, Jean Genet, Samuel Beckett, Nathalie Sarraute, Boris Vian, Richard Wright.

Further Information: *Les Temps Modernes* ceased publication in 2019. Past contributors included Jean Genet, Samuel Beckett, Nathalie Sarraute, Boris Vian and Richard Wright.

Select Bibliography: *La Structure du comportement (The Structure of Behavior)* (1942); *Phénoménologie de la perception (Phenomenology of Perception)* (1945); *Les aventures de la dialectique (Adventures of the Dialectic)* (1955).

Further Reading: K. Morris, *Starting with Merleau-Ponty* (Continuum, 2012).

AUGUSTE MAQUET
(1813–1888)
DIVISION 54

**NOVELIST AND COLLABORATOR
WITH ALEXANDRE DUMAS**

If Maquet's role was that of mason, Dumas's was that of architect.
André Maurois

Auguste Maquet was the principal writing collaborator with the phenomenally successful novelist Alexandre Dumas (1802–1870). Maquet would usually supply the plot and the historical framework, and sketch out the bare bones of the story. Dumas would then embellish Maquet's rough draft, adding detail and colour. It was a very successful partnership that gave birth to *Les Trois Mousquetaires (The Three Musketeers)* and many other classics, but it all ended in acrimony.

Dumas and Maquet began working together in the 1840s after Dumas successfully rewrote an early play written by Maquet, for which Maquet was credited. But their collaborative writings usually bore the name of Dumas, who, it is said, would have willingly shared the credit with Maquet had it not been

MARIE D'AGOULT
(1805–1876)
DIVISION 54

NOVELIST AND HISTORIAN, AND LOVER
OF FRANZ LISZT, WHO WROTE UNDER
THE PSEUDONYM DANIEL STERN

*The truth is too simple: one must always get
there by a complicated route.*
Marie d'Agoult, *Letter to Armand Barbès*,
(1867)

Regrettably, many women writers in history are acknowledged more for their lovers, or for the scandals they provoked, than for their writing. Marie d'Agoult was no exception, as she is remembered primarily for her ten-year love affair with the composer, Franz Liszt (1811–1886), which produced three children, the second of whom became the wife and muse of Richard Wagner. But Marie de Flavigny, Comtess d'Agoult, established herself as an independent, freethinking woman long before the feminist movement had arrived, and went on to set up some of the nineteenth century's celebrated literary salons. The daughter of a German mother and a French aristocrat who had escaped the Revolution, Marie d'Agoult published under the pen name Daniel Stern. Her writings include the autobiographical novel, *Nélida* (an anagram of her pen name), and *Histoire de la Révolution de 1848* (1850–53). Although she never attained the great fame or status as a writer that she yearned for, she did achieve a substantial readership in her day, and never flinched from writing on sensitive subjects such as self-determination, social revolution, and liberty.

for his publisher's objections. Dumas's name was well known, and the publisher feared the inclusion of the unknown Maquet: 'A serial bearing the name of Dumas is worth three francs a line,' commented Dumas's publisher Emile de Girardin. 'Bearing the names of Dumas and Maquet, it is worth thirty sous.'
Despite earning more money than he could ever have earned from his own writing, frustration and lack of recognition forced Maquet to take Dumas to court in 1858 to gain the joint rights to their works. The court awarded Maquet financial compensation, but rejected his demands to be recognised as co-author.
Macquet continued writing novels, plays and serialised fiction under his own name, but it is as Dumas's co-author that he tends to be remembered. As French historian Alain Decaux observed regarding Dumas's authorship: 'Just like the Renaissance painters, someone had to prepare your frescoes – and it is right that Auguste Maquet be named – but in the end, the quill is yours.'

See Also: Alexandre Dumas.

Top: Marie d'Agoult in 1843 by Henri Lehmann. Above: Franz Liszt in 1858 by Franz Hanfstaengl

RAYMOND RADIGUET

(1903–1923)

DIVISION 56

NOVELIST, POET AND PRECOCIOUS GENIUS

Listen to a terrible thing. In three days I shall be shot by the soldiers of God.
Raymond Radiguet to Jean Cocteau, 9 December 1923, three days before his death

Raymond Radiguet is remembered for two things: writing *Le Diable au corps (The Devil in the Flesh)*, one of the most remarkable novels of the early twentieth century, and dying young from typhoid fever aged only twenty years. His debut novel, *Le Diable au corps*, caused a furore on publication in 1923, partly because it told the story of a wife having an affair with an adolescent while her husband was fighting at the front and partly because it was semi-autobiographical. Like many young writers who died before realising their full potential, Radiguet left us just a scant sample of his genius. 'Radiguet', wrote Martin Seymour-Smith, 'did not have time to grow a heart.'

He was born in Saint-Maur in the south-eastern suburbs of Paris in 1903, to Jeanne Tournier, and Jules-Maurice Radiguet, an artist and caricaturist for newspapers and magazines. When Raymond was fifteen his father enlisted him as his messenger, someone to take his artwork to various editors' offices in Paris. But Raymond was also artistic. He wrote poems and short stories as well as creating his own drawings, and he used this opportunity to promote his own work alongside his father's. One of the editors he visited was the writer André

489

Raymond Radiguet in 1920 by Picasso

Salmon, who remembered Radiguet's first appearance in his office, still in short trousers and wearing a stiff collar: '[He was a] nice little boy with the sharp gaze of an adult who was still naïve but very likely to become cruel; yes, a strange gaze darkened by a rebellious lock of hair hanging in heavy folds, like the hard visor of a helmet.' Some of his work did appear in print sporadically, but Radiguet wanted a career in writing, and he found its beginning in journalism. By 1919 he was mingling with the avant-garde community, meeting such writers as Max Jacob, Blaise Cendrars, André Breton, Louis Aragon, Tristan Tzara, and the modernist he is most associated with, Jean Cocteau. When Radiguet first met Cocteau he was seventeen and Cocteau was thirty. They soon became devoted companions and lovers. It was a stormy relationship, sporadically interrupted by Radiguet's female fascinations, notably artist's model Bronia Perlmutter, whom he planned to marry. But Cocteau became his tireless promoter right up to, and after, Radiguet's death. Cocteau realised Radiguet's star quality immediately: 'He skipped as he walked. For him pavements seemed to have been made of rubber. He would pull little sheets of copy-book paper out of his pockets, rolled up into balls. He would flatten them out with his hand ... and try to read a very short poem.'

Radiguet started writing *Le Diable au corps* in 1919, and when it was eventually published in 1923, it became a bestseller and made him rich. But 'the soldiers of God' were getting closer. In September 1923 he was diagnosed with typhoid fever, probably contracted through eating rancid oysters, and was admitted to a private nursing home on Rue Piccini. He died in the early hours of 12 December and his funeral Mass took place at Saint-Honoré-d'Eylau. Mourners included Pablo Picasso, Constantin Brâncusi and Coco Chanel. Jean Cocteau was too ill to attend.

'It was the most tragic sight that I have ever seen,' wrote Welsh artist and writer, Nina Hamnett,

Radiguet's sisters, the youngest being about six, stood in a row, their faces contorted with weeping. Marie and I burst into tears and went out into the street to see the procession start off. The hearse was covered in white and was drawn by two large white horses, like those in the war picture by Uccello in the National Gallery. They stood patiently and waited. The coffin was carried out with its white pall, and on it was one bunch of red roses. Many wreaths were carried out, and by the time the procession started the white hearse and a carriage following it were covered with white flowers. We walked down the boulevard, following the procession, and waited and watched the hearse and the long train of mourners disappear into the distance on their way to Père Lachaise. It was not yet ten o'clock and still pouring with rain.

See Also: Jean Cocteau, Max Jacob, Blaise Cendrars, André Breton, Louis Aragon, Tristan Tzara.

Further Information: Radiguet's second novel, *Le Bal du comte d'Orgel*, was published posthumously, in 1924.

Select Bibliography: *Le Diable au corps (The Devil in the Flesh)* (1923); *Le Bal du comte d'Orgel (The Count's Ball)* (1924); *Cheeks on Fire*, Collected Poems (1976); *The Flower-Girl* (1950).

Further Reading: M. Crosland, *Raymond Radiguet: A Biographical Study* (Peter Owen, 1976).

Église Saint-Honoré-d'Eylau, Avenue Raymond-Poincaré. Site of Raymond Radiguet's funeral Mass in 1923

ANNETTE VALLON
(1766–1841)
CAROLINE BAUDOUIN
(1792–1862)
DIVISION 57

LOVER, AND DAUGHTER,
OF ENGLISH ROMANTIC POET,
WILLIAM WORDSWORTH

A point made early in Legouis's book [William Wordsworth and Annette Vallon] is that Wordsworth was not a Victorian – he was 67 when the Queen ascended to the throne, and 'might have died before her accession without any loss to his poetry and to his glory'. 'No greater mistake can be made in literary history,' says Legouis, who co-authored what was for a long time the standard history of English literature, 'than the confusion of the two epochs, the one in which Wordsworth lived and the one in which he outlived himself and died.' Wordsworth was a Georgian, and should be judged according to the morals of his day.
James Fenton, *The Guardian* (2006)

When William Wordsworth (1770–1850) arrived in Paris in December 1791, he was twenty-one years old, a gentleman of slender means, and a budding poet who was eager to witness the Revolution at first hand. He trundled all over the city soaking up its Republican passion; he picked up souvenirs from the ruins of the Bastille, and immersed himself in the partisan spirit that was engulfing its people. It was a youthful, political idealism he would eventually discard in later life.

In the spring of 1792 he travelled to Orléans on the pretext of improving his knowledge of French and with a view to becoming a tutor. Shortly after his arrival he met and fell in love with twenty-six-year-old Marie Anne (Annette) Vallon, who gave birth to their child at the end of that year. The child was baptised 'Anne Caroline Wordsworth, and, although Wordsworth legally acknowledged his daughter, there was no marriage, the most likely reason being his inability to financially support a family. Wordsworth departed for England before his daughter was born with the intention of returning, but the outbreak of war with France prevented it. Letters were exchanged between Wordsworth and Annette over the years, but they did not meet again until 1802, when Wordsworth and his sister Dorothy met Annette and, for the first time, Caroline, in Calais. It was on this visit that Wordsworth told Annette about his forthcoming marriage to Mary Hutchinson. At Mary's insistence, Wordsworth made arrangements for Caroline's support, settling £30 a year on her on her marriage in 1816. Eighteen years later they met again when Wordsworth and his wife and sister were in Paris at the end of a continental tour. Annette was still single and Caroline was married with a daughter. The group visited the Louvre together, and afterwards Wordsworth took his French granddaughter for a stroll in the Jardin des Plantes.

After Wordsworth's death in 1850 all references to his French daughter (William and Mary had five children together) were expunged from official records by his widow. Wordsworth's first biographer, his nephew Christopher Wordsworth, also failed to mention the Gallic skeletons in the great Poet Laureate's cupboard.

Further Information: Annette Vallon died in Paris on 10 January 1841, at Boulevard des Filles du Calvaire, aged seventy-five. Her daughter, Caroline, died in 1862 on the Left Bank at 3 rue Jacob and was buried in the same grave as her mother. Part of the inscription on the gravestone reads: 'To the memory of our mother Anne Caroline William Wordsworth, the widow of Jean Baptiste Baudouin ... ' William Wordsworth died from pleurisy, aged eighty, and is buried in St Oswald's Church in Grasmere, England.

Further Reading: E. Legouis, *William Wordsworth and Annette Vallon* (J.M. Dent, 1922); J. Tipton, *Annette Vallon* (Harper, 2007); R. Holmes, *Footsteps: Adventures of a Romantic Biographer* (Hodder & Stoughton, 1985).

William Wordsworth aged 28 years, by William Shuter (1771–1799)

JEAN-GASPARD DEBURAU
(1796–1846)

DIVISION 59

LEGEND OF THE FRENCH ROMANTIC
THEATRE, WHO WAS FAMOUS FOR HIS
PORTRAYAL OF PIERROT

The pantomime is the real comédie humaine*;
and even though it does not employ two thousand characters like Balzac's, it is none the
less complete for that. It embraces everything
in four or five type-parts. Cassandra represents the family; Columbine the ideal woman
or the dream pursued, the flower of youth
and beauty; Arlequin with his monkey's snout
and snake-like body, his patchwork and his
shower of spangles, represents Love, Wit,
Impulse, Audacity, and all that glitters in vice
or virtue; while Pierrot, poor haggard, pallid
Pierrot in his glimmering draperies, always
hungry and always beaten, is the antique
slave and the modern proletarian, the pari-
ah, the helpless and disinherited being, who
witnesses the orgies and follies of his masters
with mournful and yet cunning eyes.*
Théophile Gautier

In 1945 Deburau was immortalised on the
screen by actor and mime artist, Jean-Louis
Barrault, in Marcel Carné's masterpiece, *Les
Enfants du Paradis*

Jean-Gaspard Deburau was a Bo-
hemian-born French pantomime
actor remembered for transforming the
simpleton figure of the sad, white-faced
clown known as Pierrot into a character
that became a muse for all the arts. As a
literary metaphor he fascinated and inspired writers, notably Gustave Flaubert,
Paul Verlaine, Charles Baudelaire, Jules
Laforgue, T.S. Eliot, Wallace Stevens
and George Sand. He appeared on the
canvases of Seurat (*Pierrot with a White
Pipe*, 1883), Cézanne (*Pierrot and Har-
lequin*, 1888) and Picasso (*Pierrot and
Columbine*, 1900). His beginnings reach
back to the *Commedia dell'arte*, an Italian theatrical form that flourished from
the sixteenth to the eighteenth century.
Pierrot had therefore survived three centuries of social and cultural change by
the time Deburau's talents changed him
into an artistic cult in nineteenth-century
Paris.

Deburau was born in Kolín, Bohemia
(now Czech Republic), in 1796, into a
family of touring acrobats. As a young
man he joined Paris's Théâtre des
Funambules (Theatre of the Tightrope
Walkers) on Boulevard du Temple,
founded in 1816 and originally conceived as a venue for circus performers.
Here Deburau perfected his creation of
Pierrot as a lovelorn, pitiful figure who
could be teasing and spiteful, but also
full of everlasting hope: an achievement
that turned Deburau into Europe's most
famous mime artist and had audiences
flocking to the Théâtre des Funambules
in droves. A chronic asthmatic, Deburau
died a theatrical legend in 1846 after

493

years of ill health. Baudelaire summed him up in a sentence: '[He was] pale as the moon, mysterious as silence, supple and mute as the serpent, thin and long as the gibbet.'

See Also: Gustave Flaubert, Paul Verlaine, Charles Baudelaire, George Sand, Théophile Gautier, Molière, Alphonsine Plessis, T.S. Eliot.

Further Information: In 1836 Deburau was arrested for murder after he struck down a street-boy with a blow from his cane, fracturing the boy's skull. The drunken youth, who had been relentlessly taunting Deburau in the street, died the following day. Deburau was detained in prison, but the court acquitted him. Deburau married twice and had several children. He also had an offstage relationship with Alphonsine Plessis (Marie Duplessis), the muse for Alexandre Dumas *fils*'s *The Lady of the Camellias* (1848). Théâtre des Funambules was demolished in 1862.

Further Reading: R. Storey, *Pierrot: A Critical History of a Mask* (Princeton University Press, 1978).

Théâtre des Funambules in 1862

JEAN DE BRUNHOFF
(1899–1937)
CÉCILE DE BRUNHOFF
(1903–2003)
DIVISION 65

CREATORS OF BABAR THE ELEPHANT

If you love elephants, you will love Babar and Celeste. And if you have never loved elephants, you will love them now.
A.A. Milne, from his preface to *The Story of Babar* (1948 edition)

In the summer of 1930 Laurent and Mathieu de Brunhoff were visiting their grandfather's house on the east side of Paris. To distract the children their mother, Cécile de Brunhoff, began to tell them the story of a young elephant whose mother is killed by a hunter and who flees the jungle for adventures in the city. The narrative so enthralled the children that the following day they rushed into the study of their artist father, Jean, to tell him all about it, and to ask him to illustrate the tale. Thus Babar the orphaned elephant was born. Cécile had originally named the elephant Bébé (Baby), but Jean changed his name to Babar. When the first book, *Histoire de Babar*, was published in 1931, Cécile insisted her name be omitted as she thought her role in Babar's creation was of little consequence. Jean wrote and illustrated seven Babar books before his death in 1937.

After the Second World War, in 1946, the Brunhoffs' artist son Laurent, then aged twenty-one, took up his father's mantle and wrote and illustrated his own Babar book, *Babar et ce coquin d'Arthur (Babar's Cousin: That Rascal Arthur)* in his father's distinctive style. Laurent proceeded to publish over forty

Babar books, which began, he claimed, as,

> a way of getting my father alive again. I wanted to be faithful. I didn't want to touch the heart of the Babar books – which is a human story. There may be some differences because we are not the same man. He was more well-balanced, symmetrical, and there is maybe more movement in my composition. After a while it was like Babar was my own and I didn't think of my father any more.

Today Babar is one of the world's most popular children's characters, and despite accusations over the years of its being an allegory of French colonialism (naked natives, walking upright Europeanised elephants, etc.), it remains a fable that has endured and survived in all its forms for generations.

Further Information: Jean de Brunhoff died in 1937 from tuberculosis aged thirty-seven. Cécile de Brunhoff, a graduate of the École Normale de Musique in Paris, was a classically trained pianist. She had three sons with Jean and never remarried after his death. She died in 2003 of a stroke in Paris at the age of ninety-nine.

Select Bibliography: *The Travels of Babar* (1934); *Babar the King* (1935); *A.B.C. of Babar* (1936); *Zephir's Holidays* (1937); *Babar and His Children* (1938); *Babar and Father Christmas* (1940); *Babar's Anniversary Album: 6 Favorite Stories* (Random House, 1993).

Further Reading: A. Hildebrand, *Jean and Laurent de Brunhoff: The Legacy of Babar* (Twayne, 1992); D. Charles, *Les Histoires de Babar* (BnF, 2012); C. Nelson, *Drawing Babar: Early Drafts and Watercolors* (Pierpont Morgan Library, 2008); N. Weber, *The Art of Babar* (Abrams, 1989).

Top: The Brunhoffs *c.*1930 Centre: Illustration from the first edition of *Histoire de Babar* (1931). Above: The Brunhoffs' tomb

MARCEL PROUST
(1871–1922)

DIVISION 85

AUTHOR OF *IN SEARCH OF LOST TIME*

ONE OF THE MAJOR WORKS OF

TWENTIETH-CENTURY FICTION

It is better to dream your life than to live it, and even though you live it, you will still dream it.

Marcel Proust, *Les plaisirs et les jours* (1896)

Portrait de Marcel Proust by Jacques-Emile Blanche, 1892

Graham Greene proclaimed that 'Proust was the greatest novelist of the twentieth century, just as Tolstoy was in the nineteenth.' Virginia Woolf was overwhelmed by his genius, and he inspired Jean Genet to write his first novel, *Our Lady of the Flowers*. 'Just as the voice of a ventriloquist comes out of his chest,' wrote Jean Cocteau, 'so Proust's emerged from his soul.'

Marcel Proust was born in Auteuil, Paris, on 10 July 1871 to affluent middle-class parents Adrien Proust, an eminent doctor, and Jeanne Weil, a widely-read woman from a wealthy Jewish family, who was the focus of her son's existence until her death in 1905, when Proust was thirty-four years old. Proust suffered from chronic asthma from the age of nine, and from that time he became a semi-invalid for most of his life. 'A child who from birth has always breathed without paying any attention', he later wrote, 'has no idea how much the air, which swells so sweetly in his chest that he doesn't even notice it, is essential to his life.' He was also neurotic, no doubt exacerbated by asthma, but caused largely by his concealed homosexuality. By the turn of the century he had become a well-known society figure until his withdrawal into his celebrated cork-lined apartment on Boulevard Haussmann, where he screened himself from noise and pollutants that could irritate his asthma. Here he devoted himself solely to writing, and it was in this apartment that he wrote most of *In Search of Lost Time*, a gargantuan series of novels in which the narrator recalls his past life, discovering that certain sensory perceptions can trigger the powers of memory, notably the famous dipping of a madeleine into a cup of herbal tea.

Towards the end of 1922 Proust's health worsened. He developed pneumonia, bronchitis and, ultimately, an abscess on the lungs. He died in the early evening of 18 November 1922 and his funeral service was held at the Église Saint-Pierre-de-Chaillot on Rue de Chaillot.

George Painter, Proust's biographer, describes the atmosphere that day:

> In that enormous concourse ... he was surrounded by all the friends of all his life, as though a throng of ghosts had risen to do honour to a living man. Ravel's *Pavane for a Dead Infanta* was played, the Abbé Delepouve pronounced absolution, the bells tolled, and the mourners waited for their carriages. Barrès, bowler-hatted, his umbrella dangling from his elbow, said to Mauriac: 'Ah, well, he was our young man.' ... Fernand Gregh's little dog Flipot had escaped and taken refuge, amid the vulgar laughter of sightseers, under Proust's hearse; and suddenly the desperate animal darted away through the torrent of motor-cars, never to be seen again. They buried Proust with his father and mother ... at the summit of Père Lachaise. For a few years, until no one came, the Abbé Mugnier held an anniversary mass in his memory at Saint-Pierre-de-Chaillot.

See Also: Marcel Proust (Boulevard Haussmann), Jean Genet, Jean Cocteau, Guy de Maupassant.

Further Information: The old Église Saint-Pierre-de-Chaillot (now demolished) also hosted the funeral service of Guy de Maupassant in 1893. The present church dates from 1938. The original Proust family tomb at Père Lachaise featured a large plaque of the bearded Doctor Proust, Marcel's father, by Marie Nordlinger. It has since been removed to the Proust Museum at Illiers and the tomb has been completely reconstructed in black marble.

Select Bibliography: *By Way of Sainte-Beuve* (trans. S. Townsend, Chatto & Windus, 1958); *In Search of Lost Time* (trans. C.K. Scott-Moncrieff, T. Kilmartin, A. Mayor, revised by D.J. Enright, Chatto & Windus, 1992); *Jean Santeuil* (trans. G. Hopkins, Weidenfeld & Nicolson, 1955); *Marcel Proust: Letters to his Mother* (trans. and ed. G. Painter, Rider & Co., 1956); *On Reading* (trans. and ed. J. Autret and W. Burford, Souvenir Press, 1972).

Further Reading: G.D. Painter, *Marcel Proust: A Biography* (Chatto & Windus, 1989); J-Y. Tadié, *Marcel Proust: A Life* (Penguin, 2001); J.E. Rivers, *Proust and the Art of Love* (Columbia, 1980); E. White, *Proust* (Weidenfeld & Nicolson, 1999); C. Albaret, *Monsieur Proust* (New York Review of Books, 2003); S, Beckett, *Proust*, (Chatto & Windus, 1931).

GUILLAUME APOLLINAIRE
(1880–1918)

DIVISION 86

**FRENCH POET, PLAYWRIGHT, ART
CRITIC AND CHAMPION OF MODERNISM**

*[In 1906 [French artist André] Derain]
formed a friendship with Picasso, and the
almost immediate effect of this friendship
was the birth of Cubism, which was the art
of creating new objects consisting not of
visual but of conceptual elements. Everyone
is capable of directly perceiving this inner
reality. One does not have to be cultivated to
grasp the fact, for instance, that a chair, no
matter how you view it, will always have four
legs, a seat, and a back. The Cubist paintings
by Picasso, Braque, Metzinger, Gleizes,
Léger, Jean [sic] Gris, etc. inspired Henri
Matisse to coin the grotesque term 'Cubism',
which was destined to go so far so quickly:
he had been greatly struck by the geometric
appearance of these paintings in which the
artists aimed at rendering essential reality
with great purity.*
Guillaume Apollinaire, from *Le Temps*, 1912

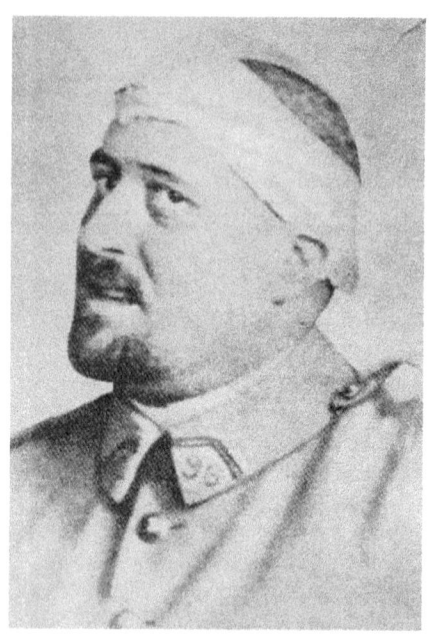

Apollinaire in spring 1916 after sustaining a
shrapnel wound to his temple

G uillaume Apollinaire could be
described as the literary counterpart
of cubism. As a leading modernist poet
during the belle époque, he rejected the
poetic traditions of rhythm and language
and championed everything new and
experimental in the thought, expression
and technique of art from the cubist
painters, bringing their ideals to his own
typographical experiments with poetry.
He also coined the term surrealism for
the first time in his programme notes
for the Satie–Cocteau–Picasso–Massine
ballet *Parade* in 1917, and also used
it to explain his own 1918 play *Les
Mamelles de Tirésias (The Breasts of
Tiresias)*. Most of Apollinaire's poetry
can be found in *Alcools* (1913) and

Calligrammes (1918), his interpretations of concrete poetry, the visual rather
than the linguistic components of poetry,
published shortly after his death in 1918.
He was born Guglielmo de Kostrowitzky in Rome in 1880 to Angelica de
Kostrowitzky, daughter of a Russian
army officer of Polish descent. His
paternity remains a mystery. His mother
had numerous lovers and his father could
have been anyone from an army officer
to the Pope, as Apollinaire often hinted.
Two years later, in 1882, Angelica bore
another son named Albert. Again the
father is unknown. When Albert was
five years old Angelica left Rome with
her two sons to settle in Monte Carlo,
where she was employed at a casino
as an *entraîneuse*, a woman who leads
men on to spend money at the gaming
tables. After a childhood that involved
relocating from one casino town to
another, the family moved – along with

Angelica's latest lover – to Stavelot, a small town in eastern Belgium, in 1899. The same year, the brothers, now in their late teens, decamped to Paris, where Guglielmo adopted the name Guillaume Apollinaire.

In Paris Apollinaire took various breadline jobs: addressing envelopes, teaching French, writing an erotic novel and, finally, working as a bank clerk, a job he held for six years. During these early years in Paris he managed to get some poems, stories and articles published. In 1909 his first collection of poetry, *L'enchanteur pourrissant (The Rotting Magician)*, was published, but it was *Alcools (Alcohols)* that established him as an important poet. By now he had become an accepted member of the Parisian artistic community where he befriended, and collaborated with, Pablo Picasso, Jean Cocteau, Georges Braque, Robert Delaunay, Jean Metzinger, Juan Gris and Francis Picabia who, along with others, became part of the new movement known as cubism. French poet and critic, Max Jacob, reminisced about his first meeting with Apollinaire in a crowded bar in October, 1904:

He was wearing a stained light-coloured suit, and a tiny straw hat was perched atop his famous pear-shaped head. He had hazel eyes, terrible and gleaming, a bit of curly blond hair fell over his forehead, his mouth looked like a little pimento, he had strong limbs, a broad chest looped across by a platinum watch-chain, and a ruby on his finger. The poor boy was always being taken for a rich man because his mother – an adventuress, to put it politely – clothed him from head to toe. She never gave him anything else. He was a clerk in a bank in the Rue Lepeletier.

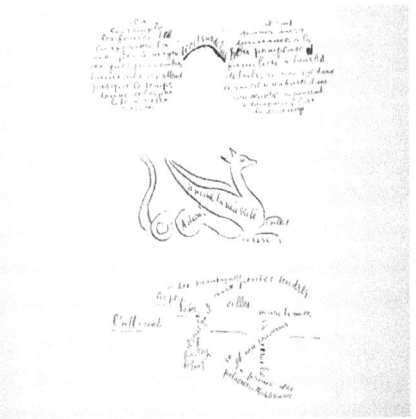

Top: A calligram from *Calligrammes* (1918)
Above: Apollinaire with former lover, Madeleine Pagès in Oran in 1916

In 1914 Apollinaire enlisted in an artillery regiment of the French army. 'I so love art', he wrote, 'that I have joined the artillery.' Soon afterwards, he transferred to the infantry, where he sustained a shell wound above the right temple. His helmet saved his head from being blown off, and a military surgeon operated in the back of an ambulance to

499

remove shell fragments. Further surgery followed, but he never fully recovered. Weakened by his wounds he died during the 1918 influenza pandemic. On his deathbed he pleaded with the doctor to cure him: 'Save me, doctor! I want to live! I still have so many things to say!'

See Also: Jean Cocteau, Pablo Picasso, Max Jacob, Louvre.

Further Information: Apollinaire eventually escaped his life as a bank clerk by offering his services as editor, translator, journalist and pornographer. Invalided out of the army after his head injury, he married Jacqueline Kolb in 1918, shortly before his death. Jacqueline, who was the inspiration for his poem 'La jolie rousse' ('The Pretty Redhead'), never remarried, and carried on living at their apartment at 202 boulevard Saint-Germain until her death in 1967.

Select Bibliography: *Selected Poems* (2015); *Selected Writings* (1982).

Further Reading: F. Steegmuller, *Apollinaire* (Penguin, 1973).

BERNARD GRASSET
(1881–1955)
DIVISION 88

FRENCH COLLABORATIONIST PUBLISHER DURING THE GERMAN OCCUPATION OF FRANCE

The occupiers are essentially racist. I have a clear tendency to be one.
Bernard Grasset writing to a friend in 1940

Bernard Grasset founded his publishing house, Éditions Grasset, in 1905. Today he is remembered essentially for two things: publishing the first volume of Marcel Proust's *À la recherche du temps perdu (In Search of Lost Time)* in 1913 at Proust's own expense; and being an unashamed collaborationist publisher during the Nazi occupation of France. Grasset had built himself a reputation in the 1920s for publishing contemporary authors, notably François Mauriac, Paul Morand, Jean Giraudoux and that well-known advocate of French fascism, Pierre Drieu La Rochelle. Grasset summarised France's wartime plight in *À la recherche de la France* (In Search of France), a collection of essays he published and prefaced during the occupation: 'The French find themselves', he wrote, 'entirely in the hands of a nation that has risen to the summit of unity and strength, and by the virtue of one man.' His fascist sympathies surfaced in the 1930s when he published the work of various extreme right-wing writers, including the anti-Semitic tracts of Céline. By the 1940s, Grasset, who was one of the most powerful publishers in France, was advising fellow publishers to comply with German demands.

Bernard Grasset

OSCAR WILDE

(1854–1900)

DIVISION 89

POET, DRAMATIST AND PHILOSOPHER

Ah, Robbie, when we are dead and buried in our porphyry tombs, and the trumpet of the Last Judgement is sounded, I shall turn and whisper to you, 'Robbie, Robbie, let us pretend we do not hear it.'

Oscar Wilde, to his friend and literary executor, Robbie Ross.

During the occupation the Germans imposed strict censorship on publishers. Censorship included: no Jewish employees, no publication of Jewish writers, Jewish publishers being renamed and Aryanised, and adherence to the Germans' so-called 'Otto List', a list of books forbidden by the German authorities. Any publisher's non-compliance would have meant the termination of their publishing house. Shamefully, 140 publishers signed self-censoring agreements with the Germans. The eager acceptance by French publishers of Nazi censorship may have guaranteed profits, but their integrity vanished.

Following the Liberation of France in 1944 there was a mass purge of German collaborators. Over 300,000 cases were investigated. Grasset, the most enthusiastic pro-German publisher, was arrested and jailed, but was released six weeks later. Éditions Grasset was subsequently banned from selling or publishing books. The ban was lifted in May 1946. Éditions Grasset still survives today on Paris's Rue des Saints-Pères.

See Also: Marcel Proust, Gaston Gallimard, Louis-Ferdinand Céline, Robert Brasillach.

Oscar Wilde died at the Hôtel d'Alsace on the Left Bank in the early afternoon of 30 November 1900. He was forty-seven years old. One of the greatest literary figures of his age, he died impoverished and shunned by those who had once feted him. The funeral left the hotel on 3 December at nine o'clock in the morning with the few mourners following the hearse on foot to the nearby church of Saint-Germain-des-Prés, where a low Mass was said. He was initially buried in a temporary concession at the Cimetière parisien de Bagneux in the south-west of the city. Doctors had advised that Wilde's body be buried in quicklime, which would absorb the flesh, leaving intact the skeleton, which afterwards could be easily removed to another coffin when the temporary concession expired.

In 1908 Wilde's literary executor, Robbie Ross, announced that a donor 'with cowardly generosity characteristic of anonymity' had sent him £2000 to erect a monument to Wilde at Père Lachaise, on the condition that it should be created by 'the brilliant young sculptor' Jacob Epstein. On 19 July 1909, Wilde's remains were transferred from Bagneux to

Jacob Epstein (1880–1959) in 1927 by William Orpen (1878–1931)

Père Lachaise, but before being placed in a fresh coffin the remains had to be officially identified. Contrary to what had been expected, however, the quicklime, instead of destroying the flesh, had actually preserved it. Wilde's face was discernible and his hair and beard had grown long.

Epstein found the 20-tonne block of stone he needed in Hopton Wood quarries in Derbyshire. The monument took three years to complete, and the end result, he said, 'was of course purely symbolical, the conception of a poet as a messenger.' On the back were hewn a few lines from *The Ballad of Reading Gaol*:

And alien tears will fill for him
Pity's long broken urn,
For his mourners will be outcast men,
And outcasts always mourn.

In 1912 the monument was transported from Epstein's London studio and erected over Wilde's grave. Shortly thereafter, Epstein arrived at the tomb to find a tarpaulin draped over it and a gendarme standing guard. He was informed the tomb was banned because the authorities considered the winged messenger's genitalia indecent. A surrogate fig leaf in the shape of a bronze plaque eventually covered the offending area, but the tomb remained covered until the outbreak of the First World War. A few years later students removed the plaque by force, and in 1961 someone actually chopped the genitals off. Legend has it that the culprits were two affronted English ladies, and that they donated the genitals to the cemetery conservateur who used them as a paperweight for many years. British architectural critic, Ian Nairn, wrote that Wilde 'was provided with a truly atrocious statue by Epstein, and one regrets the epigram he would have made out of it.'

See Also: Oscar Wilde (Hôtel d'Alsace).

Further Information: In 1950, on the fiftieth anniversary of Wilde's death, his tomb was opened and the ashes of his friend and former lover, Robbie Ross, were placed beside Wilde's remains. In 2011 a 'kiss proof' glass screen was erected around the tomb to end the vogue for kissing the tomb with lipstick-coated lips. Oscar would, no doubt, have been amused.

Further Reading: M. Pennington, *Angel for a Martyr: Jacob Epstein's Tomb of Oscar Wilde* (Pegasus Press, 1987).

Left: Detail of the 'poet as messenger'
Top: Oscar's tomb made from a 20-tonne block of stone and surrounded by its 'kiss proof' glass screen

503

EUGÈNE FRANÇOIS VIDOCQ
(1775–1857)

DIVISION 94

**FATHER OF MODERN CRIMINOLOGY
AND INSPIRATION FOR MANY FICTIONAL
CHARACTERS**

Eugène François Vidocq

*He had read Vidocq, and it is right to say
that if [Vidocq's] Mémoires had never been
published Poe would not have created his
amateur detective [Auguste Dupin], but one
should immediately add that Poe owed to
Vidocq only the inspiration that set light to
his imagination.*
Julian Symons, *Bloody Murder* (1972)

The English proverb 'Set a thief to catch a thief' was not inspired by Eugène François Vidocq, but a more fitting description of this great and masterful rogue's life would be difficult to find. All writers of detective fiction, including Poe, Gaboriau, Leblanc and Conan Doyle, owe a debt to Vidocq, and novelists Balzac, Dumas, Hugo, Dickens and Sue all created characters based on him. A former convict who became the father of modern criminology, Vidocq is credited with creating the first criminal records, introducing undercover agents and forensic ballistics, and remodelling the police force. In 1812 he became the founder and first chief of the crime detection unit, which evolved into the Sûreté nationale, an investigative bureau that would eventually become the inspiration for Scotland Yard and the FBI. In the early nineteenth century, when London only had the Bow Street Runners and New York a network of watchmen, the Sûreté was the most advanced police force in the world.

Vidocq, the second eldest of seven siblings, was the son of an Arras baker. Much of what is known of his childhood is based on his 1827 memoirs, where fact and fiction blur. He was, however, a thief from an early age, and amongst his first victims were his own family: at fourteen years of age he absconded with the contents of the bakery's cash box. A year later he enlisted in the army, but subsequently abandoned his military career at the age of eighteen. After a failed brief marriage he drifted into a life of crime, which resulted in several prison sentences. In prison he befriended some of the toughest characters of the underworld, and a life of crime seemed his unalterable destiny.

In 1809, in his early thirties, he was arrested in Lyons, but rather than face another lengthy prison sentence he offered his services as a police informer. 'I believe I might have become a perpetual spy', he wrote,

so far was every one from supposing that any connivance existed between the agents of the public authority and myself. Even the porters and keepers were in ignorance of my mission with which I was entrusted. Adored by the thieves, esteemed by the most determined bandits (for even these hardened wretches have a sentiment which they call esteem), I could always rely on their devotion to me.

After two years of spying he was released from prison, but continued as a secret agent in the Paris underworld. 'I frequented every house and street of ill fame,' he wrote, 'sometimes under one disguise and sometimes under another, assuming, indeed, all those rapid changes of dress and manner which indicated a person desirous of concealing himself from the observation of the police, till the rogues and thieves whom I daily met there firmly believed me to be one of themselves.'

While engaged in his undercover work Vidocq began perfecting his detective skills, and in so doing he laid the foundations of modern criminology. This included keeping files on criminals, producing plaster casts of footprints, and becoming a master of disguise. In 1811 he suggested to the police that he be allowed to form a new department – a plain-clothes bureau – for investigating crimes undercover. The following year the police adopted his idea and Vidocq became the leader of eight plain-clothes agents, all of them recruited from the underworld. 'It was with a troop so small as this', he wrote,

that I had to watch over more than twelve hundred pardoned convicts, freed, some from public prisons, others from solitary confinement: to put in execution, annually, from four to five hundred warrants, as well from the préfet as the judicial authorities; to procure information,

to undertake searches, and to obtain particulars of every description; to make nightly rounds, so perpetual and arduous during the winter season; to assist the commissaries of police in their searches, or in the execution of search warrants; to explore the various rendezvous in every part; to go to the theatres, the boulevards, the barriers, and all other public places, the haunts of thieves and pickpockets.

Although the Sûreté grew in size over the years Vidocq always had a thorny, often confrontational, relationship with the police, who suspected him of taking bribes and actually creating crimes to solve them, but nothing was ever proved. In 1834, aged fifty-eight, he created the world's first private detective agency, *Le Bureau des Renseignements*, a move which provoked the police even further. In 1842 he was found guilty of posing as a policeman and served ten months in prison, but despite continuing hostility from the authorities throughout the rest of his life, Vidocq is today considered to be the father of modern criminology. In 1827, with the help of ghostwriters, he wrote his autobiography, *Mémoires de Vidocq, chef de la police de Sûreté*, which became a bestseller. Vidocq died from a stroke in 1857 at the age of eighty-two, and he is buried in Père Lachaise in a grave that has long since ceased to be visible.

See Also: Émile Gaboriau, Victor Hugo, Honoré de Balzac, Edgar Allan Poe, Charles Dickens, Alexandre Dumas *père*, Maurice Leblanc, Eugène Sue.

Further Reading: J. Morton, *The First Detective* (Ebury Press, 2004); S. Edwards, *The Vidocq Dossier* (Houghton Mifflin, 1977); M. Capuzzo, *The Murder Room* (Penguin, 2011).

GERTRUDE STEIN
(1874–1946)
ALICE B. TOKLAS
(1877–1967)
DIVISION 94

THE TWENTIETH CENTURY'S MOST
FAMOUS LITERARY COUPLE

Gertrude and Alice made a strange-looking pair. In photographs they look like a double act of pontiff and acolyte ... a mountain and its shadow. Alice is always carrying the bags and umbrellas, or sitting in the lesser chair, or walking behind Gertrude, or is scarcely visible at all. But she fostered this image of the self-effacing maidservant, and it belied her force of character and true role in the relationship.
Diana Souhami, *Gertrude and Alice* (1991)

Gertrude Stein and Alice B. Toklas in 1934

For nearly forty years Gertrude Stein and Alice B. Toklas were devoted companions and lovers, and hosts of the world's most famous cultural salon. Together they welcomed some of the century's greatest artists and writers into their home, including Picasso, Matisse, Sherwood Anderson, Edith Sitwell, Ezra Pound, Thornton Wilder, Scott Fitzgerald, Ernest Hemingway, Sinclair Lewis and Paul Bowles. With Gertrude in charge and Alice in support they both became legends among legends.

Gertrude Stein died from stomach cancer at The American Hospital in Paris on 27 July (not 29 July as inscribed on her tombstone) 1946. The tombstone, designed by Francis Rose, also misspells Allegheny, her place of birth. For reasons unknown her body remained for nearly three months at the American Cathedral Church of the Holy Trinity, at 23 avenue George V, where 'special ceremonies' were performed and burial arrangements finalised. She was eventually buried on 22 October, at a ceremony attended by Alice B. Toklas, Gertrude's nephew Allan Stein and his wife, and a few friends.

Alice Babette Toklas died almost twenty-one years later on 7 March 1967, at her small apartment on Rue de la Convention. Her will decreed that she be buried 'in the same tomb as Gertrude Stein in Père Lachaise Cemetery', later stating that the tomb 'must be consecrated to the Holy Catholic Religion' and that its inscription 'with regard to name, birth date and date of death, must be placed on the back of the stone', a directive that consigned Alice B. Toklas to the eternal shadow of Gertrude Stein, which was exactly how she wanted it. 'I love my love with a b', Stein had written, 'because she is peculiar.'

See Also: The American Hospital in Paris, 27 rue de Fleurus, 5 rue Christine, The Luxembourg Gardens, Sherwood Anderson, Pablo Picasso, Ezra Pound, Thornton Wilder, Scott Fitzgerald, Ernest Hemingway, Sinclair Lewis, Paul Bowles.

Further Information: Gertrude and Alice were both Jewish, although Gertrude was a non-practising Jew, and Alice converted to Catholicism after Stein's death. Stones are often placed on their graves by visitors, a custom which has a special significance in Judaism. Explanations for the custom vary from it being a simple marker of a visit, to being an invocation to prevent the soul of the dead from rising from the grave.

Further Reading: D. Souhami, *Gertrude and Alice* (Pandora, 1991); J. Malcolm, *Two Lives: Gertrude and Alice* (Yale, 2007); O. Friedrich, *The Grave of Alice B. Toklas* (Holt, 1989).

The grave of Stein and Toklas

PAUL ÉLUARD
(1895–1952)
DIVISION 97

LYRIC POET AND ONE OF THE FOUNDERS OF THE SURREALIST MOVEMENT

Farewell sadness
Hello sadness
You are inscribed in the lines of the ceiling
You are inscribed in the eyes that I love.
Paul Éluard, from 'À peine défigurée' (Scarcely Disfigured) (1932)

One of the co-founders of the surrealist movement with André Breton and Louis Aragon, Paul Éluard was arguably France's leading twentieth-century love poet.

His often bewildering and sensuous poetry, with its evocative and dream-like images, is among the finest poetic gifts left to us by the surrealists.

Born in 1895 in Saint-Denis, one of the northern suburbs of Paris, he matured into a truly urban poet. A child of lower-middle-class parents, Éluard's chronic ill health and spells in sanatoriums drew him into writing poetry. His early pennings were strongly influenced by the surrealist movement, notably in the collections *Capital de la douleur (The Capital of Pain)* (1926) and *La Rose publique (The Public Rose)* (1934), possibly the best volumes of poetry to come out of the movement.

His great love and inspiration was his first wife, a young Russian girl named Elena Diakonova, known as Gala, whom he met in a Swiss sanatorium where he was being treated for tuberculosis. He was eighteen; she was nineteen. Their only child, Cécile, was born a year later in 1918. But although Gala was inspi-

Paul Éluard in 1911

rational, she was a very poor mother and she neglected her child. She later became the muse and model of artists Max Ernst, Picasso, and Salvador Dalí, whom she abandoned her family for in the early 1930s.

Provoked by the intensity of political events in 1930s Europe, Éluard parted from the surrealists in 1938 and became a staunch political activist, joining the Communist Party in 1942. During World War II he was active in the Resistance movement, and, along with Louis Aragon, became one of its leading poets. Many of his poems, which shored up the morale of the Resistance, were circulated secretly during the war in the volumes *Poésie et vérité (Poetry and Truth)* (1942) and *Au rendez-vous allemand* (To the German Rendezvous) (1944). Having the need to take refuge from the Nazis in the mental asylum of Saint-Alban in central France in 1943 provided the inspiration for one of his most poignant prose works, *Souvenirs de la maison des fous* (Memories of the Asylum) (1945).

Paul Éluard died from a heart attack on 18 November 1952 at his home in the south-eastern suburbs of Paris. The French government refused to arrange a state funeral on political grounds, so the French Communist Party organised the proceedings, at which thousands of mourners were present on the way to Père Lachaise. 'Ah, parents!', commented Éluard's daughter Cécile. 'I may not have had much of a mother, but at least I had a nice papa.'

See Also: André Breton, Louis Aragon, Salvador Dalí, Françoise Sagan.

Select Bibliography: *Thorns of Thunder* (1936); *Selected Writings of Paul Éluard* (1951); *Selected Poems* (1988); *Love, Poetry* (2007); *Last Love Poems* (1980); *Letters to Gala* (1989).

Further Reading: R. Nugent, *Paul Éluard* (Twayne, 1975); S. Roe, *In Montparnasse: The Emergence of Surrealism in Paris, from Duchamp to Dalí* (Penguin, 2019).

HENRI BARBUSSE

(1873–1935)

DIVISION 97

FRENCH NOVELIST, POET AND
JOURNALIST

WINNER OF THE PRIX GONCOURT
FOR HIS 1916 NOVEL *LE FEU*

*Crack! Crack! Boom! – rifle fire and cannon-
ade. Above us and all around, it crackles and
rolls, in long gusts or separate explosions.
The flaming and melancholy storm never,
never ends. For more than fifteen months, for
five hundred days in this part of the world
where we are, the rifles and the big guns
have gone on from morning to night and from
night to morning. We are buried deep in an
everlasting battlefield; but like the ticking of
the clocks at home in the days gone by – in
the now almost legendary Past – you only
hear the noise when you listen.*
Henri Barbusse, *Le Feu* (1916)

Henri Barbusse's *Le Feu: journal
d'une escouade (Under Fire: The
Story of a Squad)* is recognised today as
a classic of French war literature, and is
the most celebrated French war novel to
come out of World War I. Written with
an enduring and candid realism about
life in the trenches that had never been
described authentically before, it was
the first genuine eyewitness account of
the horrors of the Western Front. Although a work of fiction, it was based on
Barbusse's first-hand experiences with
the French infantry that he volunteered
for in 1914, aged forty-one and in poor
health. He fought in Artois, suffered
from acute dysentery, and eventually
became a stretcher-bearer. Twice commended for gallantry, he was discharged
because of his wounds in 1917.

Le Feu was first serialised in the periodical *L'Oeuvre* in the summer of 1916,
and that year won the Prix Goncourt,
France's most prestigious literary award.
By the 1920s Barbusse's writings were
turning more and more political and
radical and, having embraced pacifism,
he joined the French Communist Party
in 1923. His last work was a hero-wor-
shipping biography of Stalin, and it
was during the time he was writing
this in Moscow that Barbusse died of
pneumonia on 30 August 1935. He was
sixty-two years old.

See Also: Prix Goncourt, Erich Maria
Remarque.

Select Bibliography: *Under Fire* (Penguin
Modern Classics, 2003).

Further Reading: F. Field, *British and
French Writers of the First World War* (Cambridge University Press, 1991).

SUBURBS AND OUTLYING AREAS

NEUILLY-SUR-SEINE

THE AMERICAN AMBULANCE FIELD SERVICE
21 BOULEVARD D'INKERMANN

(Métro: Les Sablons)

THE LYCÉE PASTEUR
SITE OF THE AMERICAN AMBULANCE
FIELD SERVICE DURING WORLD WAR I

The night driving was the worst. We could not show the faintest light and the roads were pitted with shell holes. It was nerve-racking, crawling on low speed with a badly wounded man along those coal black devastated roads. Once I had a soldier die in my car – but I prefer to forget that. ... We were sorry for the poor devils but saw so many they were like shadows.
Robert Service, *Harper of Heaven* (1948)

W ith the outbreak of the First World War the American Hospital in Paris requisitioned the nearby high school, Lycée Pasteur, on Boulevard d'Inkermann, as an American military hospital, and the following year, in 1915, the transportation department of the hospital founded the American Ambulance Field Service, a volunteer-run ambulance

The Lycée Pasteur in 1918

service to transport the wounded from the front. There were several volunteer ambulance units during the First World War, but the AAFS became one of the most successful. Militarised in 1917 when the US joined the war, the AAFS carried more than 500,000 wounded from every major battle.

Many young American writers joined volunteer ambulance units as drivers. Among them were John Dos Passos, E.E. Cummings, Louis Bromfield, Ernest Hemingway, Harry Crosby, Malcolm Cowley, John Howard Lawson, Julien Green, Robert Hillyer, Sidney Howard, Archibald MacLeish, Ramon Guthrie and Charles Nordhoff. A large number of the wealthy and elite of American youth

An American Ambulance Field Service Ford Model T

were recruited from the Ivy League universities and prep schools of New England. Female American volunteers also joined the Ambulance Service, but as little written evidence remains concerning the part they played, they rarely receive the recognition they deserve. Gertrude Stein and Alice B. Toklas, as volunteer drivers for the American Fund for French Wounded, delivered supplies to hospitals, troops and 'devastated villages' in a truck they christened 'auntie'. For some the attraction of the ambulance service was the romance of war and a yearning for action. For others it was patriotism, altruism, pacifism, avoiding the draft, or, the fact that they were just not physically fit enough for the regular army. Ambulance duties usually fell into two camps: ferrying the wounded to and from trains and hospitals behind the front lines, or working close to the front

ferrying the wounded from dressing stations to evacuation hospitals. A few of the volunteers, literary and non-literary, wrote books about their experiences, notably Ernest Hemingway's *A Farewell to Arms*, E.E. Cummings's *The Enormous Room*, and John Dos Passos's *Three Soldiers*. But whatever their reasons for volunteering, many risked their lives, and for some it was a barbaric rite of passage.

'I saw the most gruesome sight I've ever seen,' wrote poet and publisher, Harry Crosby.

Lying on a bloodstained brancard [stretcher] was a man – not older than twenty I afterwards ascertained – suffering the agonies of hell. His whole right cheek was completely shot away so you could see all the insides of his face. He had no jaws, teeth, or lips left. His nose

The Lycée Pasteur dining hall during the First World War

was plastered in. Blood was streaming all over. Under his eyes the skin was just dead blue. ... It took us an hour drivibetween two or three miles per hour to get him to his destination. Of course he couldn't yell as his mouth or what was left of it was a mere mass of pulp. For a while I was afraid our ambulance was to be turned into a hearse, but he was still alive when we got him there.

Harry Crosby was posted to Verdun where he miraculously survived an artillery shell that blew his ambulance apart. 'There was a deafening explosion', he wrote, 'and then flying rocks, éclats, mud, everything in sight shot past us'. Nothing was left of the ambulance, but his body was unscathed. It was an experience that affected him for the rest of his short life, and no doubt contributed to his suicide at the age of thirty-one.

Ernest Hemingway signed up with the Italian Red Cross to serve as an ambulance driver early in 1918 during a Red Cross recruitment drive in Kansas City. Posted to the Italian Front, his active service lasted from 4 June to 8 July when he was seriously injured by a mortar shell while distributing supplies to the front line. According to Arlen Hansen in his book *Gentlemen Volunteers*, 'Ernest Hemingway, who received his wounds and consequently earned his medals as a canteen runner, became perhaps the most celebrated ambulance driver of World War I. The truth to tell, he had driven an ambulance only once or twice at the most.'

See Also: The American Hospital of Paris, E.E. Cummings, Robert Service, Ernest Hemingway, John Dos Passos, Harry Crosby, Gertrude Stein, Alice B. Toklas.

Further Reading: A. Hansen, *Gentlemen Volunteers: The Story of the American Ambulance Drivers in the First World War* (Skyhorse, 2011); E. Hemingway, *A Farewell to Arms* (Scribner, 1929); J. Rudd, *With the American Ambulance in France* (BCR, 2009).

THE AMERICAN HOSPITAL OF PARIS

63 BOULEVARD VICTOR HUGO

(Métro: Pont de Levallois–Bécon)

MEDICAL CENTRE FOR MANY WRITERS

FROM GERTRUDE STEIN

TO MARGUERITE DURAS

When, on 19 July 1946 ... [Gertrude Stein] suffered another attack of stomach pain, she was rushed to the American Hospital at Neuilly. There, as she lay in bed for the first few days of her collapse the room and its corridors outside gradually filled with hundreds of gifts of flowers from worried friends. Though the doctors refused to operate because the risks were too great, Gertrude insisted. Just before she was taken away to the operating theatre, she turned to Alice Toklas: 'What is the answer?' she said. Alice was silent. 'In that case What is the question?' Alice never saw her again. Gertrude died under anaesthetic at 6:30 that evening.
Janet Hobhouse, *Everybody Who Was Anybody* (1975)

A posed publicity shot of Sylvia Beach contemplating Hemingway's alcohol-inflicted head wound outside Shakespeare and Company in 1928

By the early twentieth century plans were afoot to create a hospital in Paris for American citizens in France, the numbers of whom were increasing dramatically, especially during the summer months. In 1910 the first American Hospital in Paris, with a mere twenty-four beds, opened its doors at 44 rue Chauveau, Neuilly-sur-Seine, in the city's western suburbs. By the early 1920s the American Hospital on Rue Chauveau had outgrown its facilities, and a new 120-bed hospital was built round the corner on Boulevard Victor Hugo.

Gertrude Stein died there from inoperable cancer. Henry Miller was given a clean bill of health there after fearing he had 'the pox'. And when Marguerite Duras's alcoholism reached its zenith, when she was diagnosed with cirrhosis of the liver, she was forced to dry out there, an experience that filled her with terror. But of all the American Hospital's stories of writers' medical woes, the most famous, and probably the most farcical, was that of Ernest Hemingway in 1928.

On the evening of 4 March at his apartment at 6 rue Férou, Hemingway had gone to the bathroom and pulled the lavatory chain – or so he thought. What he actually pulled was a cord for the skylight, which crashed down onto his forehead, leaving him with a horseshoe-shaped gash that would require nine stitches at the American Hospital. 'We stopped the hemmorage [sic]', he wrote to his editor, 'with thirty thicknesses of toilet paper – a magnificent absorbent which I've now used twice for that purpose.' The press got hold of the story, and his editor, Maxwell Perkins, demanded a publicity photo, hence the famous one of Hemingway standing outside the Shakespeare and Company bookshop taken shortly

The American Hospital of Paris

afterwards, with Sylvia Beach staring up at his bandaged head. Spotting the story in the press, Ezra Pound wired Hemingway: 'Haow the hellsufferin tomcats did you git drunk enough to fall upwards thru the blithering skylight!!!'

See Also: American Ambulance Field Service, Gertrude Stein, Alice B. Toklas, Ernest Hemingway, Harry Crosby, Henry Miller, Marguerite Duras, Ezra Pound, John Dos Passos, E.E. Cummings, Somerset Maugham, Robert Service, Sylvia Beach.

Further Information: The American Hospital of Paris was kept out of the hands of the Nazis during WWII, essentially through the conscientious efforts of its chief surgeon,

Dr Sumner Jackson, and the American-born Count Aldebert de Chambrun, who was married to the daughter of Vichy France's prime minister, Pierre Laval. A large number of writers volunteered as ambulance drivers during the First World War and wrote about their experiences. Writers working in other medical sectors included Gertrude Stein, John Masefield, E.M. Forster, Marjory Stoneman Douglas and Hugh Walpole.

Further Reading: D. Lagard, *American Hospital of Paris 1906–2006* (Le Cherche Midi, 2006); A. Hansen, *Gentlemen Volunteers: The Story of the American Ambulance Drivers in the Great War* (Skyhorse, 2011); C. Bove, D. Thomas, *A Paris Surgeon's Story* (Little Brown, 1956); E. Weeks, *My Green Age* (Little Brown, 1973).

ANAÏS NIN

7 RUE DU GÉNÉRAL HENRION BERTIER

(Métro: Pont de Neuilly)

BIRTHPLACE OF ANAÏS NIN

DIARIST, NOVELIST

AND WRITER OF EROTICA

I really believe that if I were not a writer, not a creator, not an experimenter, I might have been a very faithful wife.
Anaïs Nin, Diary entry (1931)

7 rue du Général Henrion Bertier

Anaïs Nin is not only remembered today for her literary works, but also for her celebrated lovers and erotic exploits. Her entire life was one of mystery and sexual turmoil, and it was no surprise she blossomed into the quintessential femme fatale, an image she encouraged throughout her life. Before her death in 1977, she had written over a hundred and fifty volumes of intimate diaries spanning most of her adult life. Her childhood was a tattered and unsettled experience, during which time her father frequently seduced her. Notable among the many lovers she had throughout her life was Henry Miller, who described her as 'forever ethereal, forever guileless, forever innocent', whereas Gore Vidal wrote that she 'gave self-love a bad name'. Nobody, it seemed, was more qualified to write female erotica than Anaïs Nin.

She was born in the Paris suburb of Neuilly in 1903 to Cuban parents Joaquin Nin, a composer and pianist, and singer Rosa Culmell. Their marriage collapsed when Anaïs was ten, and her mother eventually settled in New York City with her children in 1914. Ten years later, Anaïs returned to Paris with her new husband, banker Hugh Parker Guiler. It was here she penned her first book, a critique of D.H. Lawrence, published by Edward Titus's Black Manikin Press in 1932.

She met Henry Miller ('the only man who plucked the fruit at the right moment') in December 1931, at her house in Louveciennes. Miller, then still an unknown writer, had just begun writing *Tropic of Cancer*, and was brought along to the house by a family friend. Miller made quite an impression on her. 'I am singing, singing, … I've met Henry Miller', she wrote in her diary. Their affair began early in 1932 in Montparnasse's Hôtel Central, a liaison later complicated by Nin's affair with June Mansfield, Miller's bisexual wife. It's perhaps no coincidence that Nin began her early experiments in erotic writing that same year.

But erotica aside, Nin also published several novels, the first of which was *House of Incest* (1936), short story collections, notably *Under a Glass Bell* (1944), and essays. Nin was nothing, if not a controversial writer during her lifetime, and still remains so today. Some critics applauded her extraordinary expression of femininity and exploration of her innermost self. Others dismissed her as hedonistic and self-obsessed, with a pathological tendency to exaggerate and tell lies. Whatever one's standpoint, Anaïs Nin made her devoted readers and fiercest critics alike sit up and take notice, which was in itself a remarkable achievement.

Diagnosed with cervical cancer in 1974, Nin died three years later in Los Angeles, a feminist icon, at the age of seventy-three. Her ashes were scattered over Mermaid Cove in Santa Monica Bay. 'I must be a mermaid, Rango,' she wrote in *The Four-Chambered Heart*. 'I have no fear of depths and a great fear of shallow living.'

See Also: Henry Miller, Lawrence Durrell, D.H. Lawrence, Black Manikin Press.

Further Information: Louveciennes is a small village in the western suburbs of Paris. Nin and Guiler lived at 2 *bis* rue de Montbuisson, in a house connected to the manor house Villa des Filleuls. Hôtel Central is at 1 *bis* rue du Maine, Montparnasse. Nin and Miller's first sexual liaison took place in Room 401. Nin married twice: first to Hugh Parker Guiler in 1923, and in 1955 she bigamously married actor Rupert Pole while still married to Guiler. Fearing the legal consequences Nin had the marriage to Pole annulled in 1966. Guiler remained her husband until her death in 1977.

Select Bibliography: 7 volumes of diaries covering the years 1931–1974 (published 1966, 1967, 1969, 1971, 1974, 1976, 1980); *Henry and June: From the Unexpurgated Diary of Anaïs Nin* (Penguin, 1990). Fiction: *The House of Incest* (1936); *Winter of Artifice* (1939); *The Four-Chambered Heart* (1950); *A Spy in the House of Love* (1954). Nonfiction: *D.H. Lawrence: An Unprofessional Study* (1932).

Further Reading: N. Fitch, *Anaïs: The Erotic Life of Anaïs Nin* (Little, Brown & Co., 1993); D. Bair, *Anaïs Nin: A Biography* (Bloomsbury, 1995); G. Stuhlmann (ed.): *A Literate Passion: Letters of Anaïs Nin and Henry Miller, 1932–1953* (Harcourt Brace Jovanovich, 1987).

Top: Anaïs Nin dressed in one of her iconic cloaks
Above: Nin at the gates of her house at Louveciennes, her 'laboratory of the soul', where she lived from 1930 to 1936

AUVERS-SUR-OISE

(Approximately 33 km north-west of Paris.
No Métro. Reachable by train, bus or car)

THE ABSINTHE MUSEUM
44 RUE ALPHONSE CALLÉ

DECOR AND RELICS DEDICATED
TO FRENCH LITERATURE'S
MOST NOTORIOUS DRINK

The Absinthe Museum

'After the first glass [of absinthe], you see things as you wish they were. After the second, you see things as they are not. Finally you see things as they really are, and that is the most horrible thing in the world.' *'How do you mean?'* *[asked Leverson]* *'I mean disassociated. Take a top-hat! You think you see it as it really is. But you don't, because you associate it with other things and ideas. If you had never heard of one before, and suddenly saw it alone, you'd be frightened, or laugh. That is the effect absinthe has, and that is why it drives men mad.'* *He went on, 'Three nights I sat up all night drinking absinthe, and thinking that I was singularly clearheaded and sane. The waiter came in and began watering the sawdust. The most wonderful flowers, tulips, lilies, and roses sprang up and made a garden of the cafe. 'Don't you see them?' I said to him. 'Mais non, monsieur, il n'y a rien.'* *('But no, sir, there is nothing.')*
Oscar Wilde describing the effects of absinthe to his friend, the novelist Ada Leverson

Absinthe is often referred to as the cocaine of the nineteenth century, portrayed in the literature of that time as the mysterious green fairy, *la fée verte*, which, drunk from a demon's chalice, not only intoxicated, but destroyed the youth, wealth, talent and any shred of happiness the drinker ever possessed, leaving them a sunken-eyed, lifeless shadow of their former self. Although this is a fairly accurate description of a drink that wrecked many artists' lives, its beginnings were far removed from its nineteenth-century toxic reputation. *Artemisia absinthium*, or wormwood, was a popular medicinal herb dating back to the time of the ancient Egyptians, and was pretty much a cure-all for many ailments, including fevers, period pains, anaemia, rheumatism and digestive disorders. The Greeks called it *apsinthion* (undrinkable), due to its bitterness. Wormwood drinks were popular throughout history long before absinthe arrived, usually in the form of wormwood water, wine or beer. The absinthe of recent bohemian culture originated in Switzerland in the late eighteenth century, where a Major Dubied acquired a recipe consisting of wormwood, anise, fennel and herbs, which he began manufacturing as a medicinal tonic. In 1797 his daughter married Henri-Louis Pernod, with whom Dubied opened the first absinthe distillery. Shortly afterwards, they moved operations across the Swiss frontier to Pontarlier in France, to save on import duty, and the Pernod dynasty was born. A century later, in 1896, the distillery was producing 125,000 litres of the green fairy a day.

Absinthe as a national French tipple has its origins in the French colonial wars in North Africa in the early 1800s, where French soldiers were issued a daily absinthe ration to fend off fever and purify the drinking water. Soon the custom of an absinthe aperitif spread to civilian life in France, and the time for the pre-dinner glass of absinthe became known as *l'heure verte* (the green hour). Many brands of absinthe flooded the market, most of them at least twice the strength of whisky, and some containing up to 80 per cent pure alcohol. Mass production also made absinthe cheap, allowing artists, bohemians and the working classes to share its pleasures with the bourgeoisie, and, in so doing, turn a fashionable aperitif into the world's most infamous drink. Gustave Flaubert defined it in his *Dictionary of Received Ideas* as 'Extremely violent poison: a single glass and you're dead. Always drunk by journalists while writing their articles. Has killed more soldiers than the Bedouin.'

In the 1880s, due to the failure of the grape harvest, wine prices increased. As a consequence absinthe became cheaper than wine, escalating the national alcohol problem. And despite having the worst reputation by that time for any alcoholic drink, anywhere in the world, its popularity never waned, especially among bohemian writers and artists. 'If absinthe isn't banned,' wrote prohibitionist Georges Ohnet in 1907, 'our country will rapidly become an immense padded cell where half the Frenchmen will be occupied putting straightjackets on the other half.'

Absinthe was eventually banned by the French government in 1914, and remained illegal for almost a hundred years until the French Senate voted to repeal the prohibition in 2011.

See Also: Oscar Wilde, Gustave Flaubert.

Further Information: The Absinthe Museum opened in 1994 in Auvers-sur-Oise, a commune in the north-western suburbs of Paris. Auvers is also the town in which Vincent van Gogh committed suicide in 1890, and where he is buried, along with his brother Theo, in the town cemetery.

Further Reading: A. Leverson, *Letters to the Sphinx from Oscar Wilde* (Duckworth, 1930); P. Baker, *The Book of Absinthe, A Cultural History* (Dedalus, 2001).

Edgar Degas's *The Absinthe Drinker*, painted between 1875 and 1876 at Café de la Nouvelle-Athènes in Paris

VERSAILLES

(Approximately 25 km north of Paris.
No Métro. Reachable by train, bus or car)

EDITH WHARTON

19 RUE DE LA PORTE DE BUC

CIMETIÈRE DES GONARDS

GRAVE OF EDITH WHARTON (1862–1937)

AMERICAN NOVELIST

AND SHORT-STORY WRITER

[Edith Wharton's] tomb was covered with weeds, old bottles and a very ancient pot of dead flowers. Clearly no one had been there for a long time. It struck me as an unvisited and lonely tomb, of a person who died without close relatives nearby to look after it, the casualty of a disputed will. ... She herself was a dedicated visitor and keeper-up of the graves of her loved ones, and, as she said of herself, a very housekeeperish person. So this neglect seemed sad. In the rain, I weeded Edith, and planted a single white silk azalea, bought from the flower shop at the cemetery gate. She would probably have been scornful about the artificial flower, but would, I felt, have been glad to have her grave tidied up.
Hermione Lee, *Edith Wharton* (2007)

Following a heart attack and stroke, Edith Wharton died at six o'clock on the evening of 11 August 1937. Her last words were 'I want to go home'. One has to wonder, though, which home she was actually referring to, having had so many fabulous houses and apartments during her life in America and Europe. The house she died in was Le Pavillon Colombe in the village of Saint-Brice-sous-Forêt. On the day of her funeral, 14 August, her oak coffin, bearing the Latin inscription *O Crux Ave Spes Unica* (O Cross, Our Only Hope), had to be low-ered out of the window of her bedroom. A guard of honour, consisting of local firemen and WWI veterans, waited in the courtyard with a bugler playing the Last Post as the funeral cortège depart-ed for the Cimetière des Gonards. The guard of honour then followed behind the coffin. About thirty people gathered around the graveside where Dean Frederick Beekman, from the American Cathedral in Paris, read the prayers. There was no eulogy.

On 13 August, the day before the funeral, Wharton's friend Louis Gillet saw her for the last time in her bedroom lying in an open coffin. 'She had a lace bonnet covering her forehead,' he wrote to fellow art historian, Bernard Berenson, 'and it was the first time I hadn't been able to see her hair – that fiery abundance which refused to turn grey. ... Her mask-like features gave her a completely new severity, and she had her familiar regal air ... her silence appeared to be an expression of pride.'

See Also: Edith Wharton (Rue de Varenne).

Further Information: In 2012 the Edith Wharton Society collected funds to have the grave of Edith Wharton cleaned. From the main entrance take the second left sloping uphill. At the top, turn right. Wharton's grave is in Canton D, Allée E, first row on the right. The gravestone, as requested by Wharton, has the same Latin inscription as that on her coffin: *O Crux Ave Spes Unica.* The nearest train station to Cimetière des Gonards is Versailles-Chantiers.

Further Reading: H. Lee, *Edith Wharton* (Chatto & Windus, 2007); S. Benstock, *No Gifts from Chance: A Biography of Edith Wharton* (Penguin, 1994); E. Dwight, *Edith Wharton, an extraordinary life* (Abrams, 1994); R. and N. Lewis, *The Letters of Edith Wharton* (Simon & Schuster, 1988).

Above: Edith Wharton at her desk at the Pavillon Colombe, 1931
Below: Edith's grave, sparklingly restored by the Edith Wharton Society

AVON

(Approximately 57 km north of Paris.
No Métro. Reachable by train, bus or car)

KATHERINE MANSFIELD

RUE DU SOUVENIR

CIMETIÈRE D'AVON

GRAVE OF KATHERINE MANSFIELD
ONE OF THE GREAT MODERNIST
EXPONENTS OF THE SHORT STORY

Katherine Mansfield in 1916

All my manuscripts I leave entirely to you to do what you like with. Go through them one day, dear love, and destroy all you do not use. Please destroy all letters you do not wish to keep and all papers. You know my love of tidiness. Have a clean sweep, Bogey, and leave all fair – will you?

Katherine Mansfield, from a letter she instructed to be opened after her death, addressed to her husband, John Middleton Murry (7 August 1922)

Katherine Mansfield was one of the twentieth century's most original and unorthodox short-story writers, but by the time of her death in 1923 she had only published three volumes of stories. Her work, however, proved to be more abundant after her death, as copious books were later edited and published posthumously by her husband, John Middleton Murry, between her death in 1923 and 1959. According to New Zealand writer, Karl Stead, 'Murry published something like 700,000 words of those papers he was instructed to tidy and leave fair.' In the wake of these posthumous publications Murry turned Mansfield into a cult figure of his own making, and in so doing, turned himself into one of the most despised men in the world of English letters. Virginia Woolf wrote: 'He has been rolling in dung, and smells impure.' Lytton Strachey summed up the Mansfield myth as portrayed by Murry with the remark: 'Why that foul-mouthed, virulent, brazen-faced broomstick of a creature should have got herself up as a pad of rose-scented cotton wool is beyond me.' Katherine Mansfield Beauchamp was born as 'rose-scented' as she was ever going to be, in Wellington, New Zealand, in 1888, the third of six children of Harold Beauchamp, a wealthy businessman, and Annie Dyer. In 1903 she and her sisters were sent to London's Queen's College, the first institution in the world to award academic qualifications to women. After her schooling she returned to New Zealand; but weary of its provincial mores and her family's 'vulgar' materialism, she left for England at the age of nineteen to try to establish herself as a writer.

Her first year in London was miserable.

Embarking on a half-hearted love affair she became pregnant, then married a different man whom she deserted the same day. Her mother then took her to a Bavarian spa town where Mansfield had a miscarriage, an experience that inspired her first published collection of stories, *In a German Pension*. A few months later she was cut out of her mother's will, and by the end of that year she had managed to publish only one story. In 1911 she began a relationship with John Middleton Murry (1889–1957) whom she married in 1918. Murry was then editor of the short-lived literary magazine *Rhythm*, which had published Mansfield's stories. Murry also introduced her to the literati, including D.H. Lawrence, who portrayed Mansfield and Murry as Gudrun and Gerald in *Women in Love* (1921).

Mansfield's best work was achieved in the early 1920s with the collected stories in *Bliss* (1920) and *The Garden Party* (1922), many of which have New Zealand locations. Just as she was maturing as a writer her health began to decline, and in December 1917 she was diagnosed with tuberculosis. From then on she lived periodically abroad for her health, often experimenting with alternative cures. In October 1922 she booked herself in as a guest at Georges Gurdjieff's Institute for the Harmonious Development of Man at Le Prieuré in Avon, Fontainebleau. Gurdjieff (1872–1949) portrayed himself as a Russian mystic, his doctrines based on self-development and awakening the consciousness. With his shaved head, long drooping moustache and astrakhan hat, he resembled the archetypal Svengali. Many were mesmerised by him, while others deemed him a charlatan. One observer commented that his followers seemed 'like a hutchful of hypnotized rabbits under the gaze of a master conjuror'. Mansfield's brief stay at the Institute was a fairly miserable experience, consisting of poorly heated rooms, washing in ice-cold water, an inadequate diet, inhaling the breath of cows, and having her laundry stolen. On the evening of 9 January 1923, while running quickly up some stairs at the Institute she had a massive haemorrhage, and died. A few days later, a hearse pulled by two black-plumed horses carried her plain white coffin to the Cimetière d'Avon.

With her death Murry now had free rein to publish as he pleased, and the myth of Katherine Mansfield was begun in earnest. But 'When Murry's critical debris is cleared away,' wrote her biographer Jeffrey Meyers, 'the Katherine that emerges from the ruins is a darker and more earthly, a crueller and more capable figure than in the legend.'

Further Information: Katherine Mansfield's grave is located on the far left of the entrance to Cimetière d'Avon. The nearest train station is Fontainebleau-Avon.

Further Reading: C. Tomalin, *Katherine Mansfield* (Penguin, 2012).

Gurdjieff's former Institute at Le Prieuré, on Avon's Rue Bezout, built originally as a Carmelite monastery

BOUGIVAL

(Approximately 25 km west of Paris.
No Métro. Reachable by train, bus or car)

IVAN TURGENEV

PARC DE LA VILLA-VIARDOT

16 RUE YVAN-TOURGUENIEV

THE IVAN TURGENEV MUSEUM

FORMER HOME OF IVAN TURGENEV

RUSSIAN NOVELIST AND DRAMATIST

Turgenev, by Ilya Repin, 1874

Whereas I think: I'm lying here in a haystack ... The tiny space I occupy is so infinitesimal in comparison with the rest of space, which I don't occupy and which has no relation to me. And the period of time in which I'm fated to live is so insignificant beside the eternity in which I haven't existed and won't exist ... And yet in this atom, this mathematical point, blood is circulating, a brain is working, desiring something ... What chaos! What a farce!

Ivan Turgenev, *Fathers and Sons* (1862)

Ivan Sergeyevich Turgenev (1818–1883) was the first Russian writer to achieve international fame. This was partly because he lived for many years outside his native Russia, principally in Paris, making him one of the most westernised of Russian writers. He was the second child of a family that owned the vast Spasskoye estate, near Oryol in western Russia, which included twenty villages and five thousand serfs. His father was a womaniser, and his mother a tyrant to her family and her serfs alike. 'I was born and grew up in an atmosphere dominated by punches and pinches, blows, slaps, etc.,' he wrote. 'I acquired my early loathing of slavery and serfdom by observing the shameful environment in which I lived.' This experience in his formative years would make him a fervent campaigner for the emancipation of the Russian serf. Turgenev fled his home life and what it represented at the earliest opportunity, at first through university, and eventually through exile, but his mother's domination and obstinate personality still tormented him. His early days in Paris, interspersed with return trips to Spasskoye, were restricted by the meagre financial support his mother allowed him while he was trying to establish himself as a writer. In his *Literary Reminiscences and Autobiographical Fragments* he recalled his mother's attitude to his creative ambition: 'I cannot comprehend', she said, 'your desire to become a writer! Is that an activity for a gentleman?' Her feudal grip only ended with her death in 1850. The inheritance was divided between Turgenev and his brother, and overnight they both became very rich men.

In 1843, aged twenty-five, and while still struggling on the modest allowance he received from his mother, he met, and became infatuated with, the

524

acclaimed opera singer Pauline Viardot (1821–1910) in St Petersburg. Although Viardot was married, it did not stop Turgenev falling deeply in love with her, and for the rest of his days he was never far from her side. Whether their relationship was ever consummated is unknown, but he certainly lived with, or lived near, the Viardot family for the remainder of his life.

'The Viardots and I have bought a wonderful villa here [at Bougival],' Turgenev wrote to a friend in 1875. 'I am having a pavilion built … My main residence is [50] rue de Douai [the Viardot residence] in Paris, and I go to town three times a week.' The villa was called The Ashes and nearby stands Turgenev's 'pavilion', a Swiss-style chalet, gloriously reminiscent of a Russian dacha. By now he was a wealthy and established writer who had close ties with Gustave Flaubert, George Sand, Alphonse Daudet and Henry James. With the passing of time Dostoyevsky and Tolstoy have eroded his renown, but Turgenev still remains one of the great voices of the Russian people. 'His stories of peasant life', wrote Tolstoy, 'will forever remain a valuable contribution to Russian literature. I have always valued them highly. And in this respect none of us can stand comparison with him.'

He died following a long illness with cancer at his chalet in Bougival on 3 September 1883, aged sixty-five. A ceremony was held in Paris at the Russian Orthodox church on Rue Daru, which was attended by 'a whole little host of giant-sized persons,' wrote Edmond de Goncourt, 'flat-featured and bearded like God the Father, a whole little Russia whom no one had any idea was living in the capital.' From Paris, Turgenev's body was sent to his beloved Russia by train, and buried in St Petersburg's Volkovo cemetery, deep in the earth of the country he never forgot.

See Also: Pauline Viardot, Gustave Flaubert, George Sand, Alphonse Daudet, Henry James, Edmond de Goncourt.

Further Information: Turgenev never married, but he had a daughter by one of the family's serfs. In 1861 serfdom was abolished at the Tsar's imperial command. Bizet composed the opera *Carmen* at Turgenev's house in Bougival, and the area was also a popular painting location for Renoir, Monet, Morisot, Sisley and other Impressionists. The nearest train station is Bougival.

Select Bibliography: *A Sportsman's Sketches* (1852); *A Month in the Country* (1855); *Rudin* (1856); *The Diary of a Superfluous Man* (1850); *First Love* (1860); *Fathers and Sons* (1862); *Smoke* (1867); *Virgin Soil* (1877); *The Torrents of Spring* (1872).

Further Reading: B. Beaumont, *Flaubert and Turgenev: A Friendship in Letters* (Athlone, 1985); V. Pritchett, *The Gentle Barbarian* (Vintage, 1978).

Turgenev's chalet, reminiscent of a Russian dacha, at Bougival

LE PORT-MARLY
(Approximately 25 km west of Paris.
No Métro. Reachable by train, bus or car)

ALEXANDRE DUMAS
CHEMIN DU HAUT DES ORMES
CHÂTEAU DE MONTE-CRISTO

FORMER HOME OF ALEXANDRE DUMAS
NOVELIST AND PLAYWRIGHT

Dumas by Nadar, 1855

Better than any other novelist, Dumas knew how to share and satisfy the passions of the masses. Like them, he loved force, justice, and adventure; like them, he divided humanity into heroes and villains; like them, he fretted little over subtle distinctions. It has been said that he had no style. This is not so certain. He had charm, appeal, and movement. He knew how to tell a story like nobody else; under his pen the most banal factual account took on the look of an epic. Is not that a form of genius?
André Maurois, *Alexandre Dumas: A Great Life in Brief* (1954)

Alexandre Dumas began his writing life as a playwright before turning to the historical novels that made him internationally famous. Many of his novels were romances taken from incidents in French history, but they were not weighed down with psychology or even historical accuracy. Dumas's formula was simple: action, interlaced with love; it was a technique on which he built the foundations of his reputation. Like his hero D'Artagnan, Dumas made his way to Paris in his youth in search of fame and fortune. Fame he certainly achieved, but fortunes were gained and squandered during a life as dramatic and as colourful as his novels.

Dumas's grandfather was a minor aristocrat who settled in the Caribbean sugar colony of Saint-Domingue, where he fathered a son with a black slave named Marie-Cessette Dumas. Their son took his mother's name and became Alexandre Davy-Dumas, a legendary general in Napoleon's army. He married the daughter of a tavern keeper, Marie-Louise Labouret, at Villers-Cotterêts in northern France, and their union produced a son, the future novelist Alexandre Dumas, born at Villers-Cotterêts in 1802.

By the time he was twenty-one, Alexandre Dumas had settled in Paris where he began writing melodramas and comedies for the stage, and in 1829 his historical drama *Henri III et sa cour (The King's Gallant)* was produced at the Théâtre-Français. It was a great success, and Dumas was hailed as one of the innovators of the Romantic revolution in the theatre. In 1831 he had even more success with his society drama, *Antony*, and for the next twenty years he was one of the most celebrated dramatists in France. In 1844, now thoroughly weary of the theatre, he decided to devote his talents to writing historical novels. Dumas never offered any conclusive explanation for the shift, but he probably realised his career as a dramatist had reached its peak and bowed out while the going was good.

His series of romances, which he began writing in the 1840s, would prove a greater success than his plays. He regularly used collaborators, such as Auguste Maquet, who supplied the plots and settings. Dumas would breathe life into their rough drafts, creating triumphs like his outstandingly successful *Le Comte de Monte-Cristo* (1844–1846) and *Les Trois Mousquetaires* (1844). Most of his great works began life as *romans-feuilletons*, novels serialised in newspapers and periodicals that had to grip the reader's attention and make them eager for more. It was a technique in which Dumas became a master.

Although Dumas was a prodigious wordsmith who produced a vast output of works from novels to travel literature, his life fluctuated between states of poverty and enormous wealth. A reckless spendthrift and a notorious womaniser (his son Alexandre Dumas *fils* was the illegitimate child of a seamstress), he was bankrupted in 1852. He died after suffering a stroke in 1870, aged sixty-eight. Shortly before his death he is said to have reached out for two golden Louis that were on his bedside table. Holding them in his hand he said to his son: 'Alexandre, everybody says I have been prodigal … Well you see how wrong people can be. When I arrived in Paris for the first time, I had two golden Louis in my pocket … Look, I have them still.'

Alexandre Dumas was buried at his birthplace of Villers-Cotterêts; but in 2002, the bicentennial of Dumas's birth, his ashes were re-interred at the Panthéon, France's mausoleum for national heroes.

Château de Monte-Cristo

See Also: Alexandre Dumas *fils*, Alex Dumas (father of Alexandre), Auguste Maquet, D'Artagnan, *The Count of Monte Cristo, The Man in the Iron Mask*, Nadar, Gérard de Nerval, Panthéon.

Further Information: In the 1840s, when Dumas was at the height of his success, he built Château de Monte-Cristo along with its grottos, ornamental gardens, waterfalls and a miniature neo-Gothic castle surrounded by its own moat. It was, however, a paradise short-lived. Strapped for cash and overwhelmed by debts he sold the house and estate in 1849 for a pittance. After the sale he lived on as a tenant, but in 1851, fleeing his creditors, he left for Belgium. In 1970 work began on restoring the house and grounds to its former glory. Today it is a museum dedicated to the life, works, and sheer extravagance of Alexandre Dumas. The nearest train station is Marly le Roi.

Select Bibliography: *Les Frères Corses (The Corsican Brothers)* (1844); *Les Trois Mousquetaires (The Three Musketeers)* (1844); *Le Comte de Monte-Cristo (The Count of Monte Cristo)* (1844–1846); *La Reine Margot (Queen Margot)* (1845).

Further Reading: F. Hemmings, *The King of Romance* (Hamish Hamilton, 1979).

MÉDAN

(Approximateley 35 km north-west of Paris.
No Métro. Reachable by train, bus or car)

ÉMILE ZOLA

26 RUE PASTEUR

THE HOUSE WHERE ZOLA WROTE *NANA*,
GERMINAL AND *LA BÊTE HUMAINE*

Maison Zola

She alone was left standing, amid the accu-
mulated riches of her mansion, while a host of
men lay stricken at her feet. Like those mon-
sters of ancient times whose fearful domains
were covered with skeletons, she rested her
feet on human skulls and was surrounded by
catastrophes ... The fly that had come from the
dungheap of the slums, carrying the ferment
of social decay, had poisoned all these men
simply by alighting on them. It was fitting
and just. She had avenged the beggars and
outcasts of her world. And while, as it were,
her sex rose in a halo of glory and blazed
down on her prostrate victims like a rising
sun shining down on a field of carnage, she
remained as unconscious of her actions as a
splendid animal, ignorant of the havoc she
had wreaked, and as good-natured as ever.
Émile Zola, *Nana* (1880)

One of the major literary figures of
nineteenth-century France, Émile
Zola was first and foremost an author
of monumental influence and scope
who wrote over thirty novels as well
as collections of short stories, plays
and literary criticism. As a journalist
he is best remembered for his article
'J'accuse...!', an open letter to the
President of the Republic during the
Dreyfus Affair. He was also one of the
chief exponents of Naturalism, a literary
movement that portrayed reality through
science and the modern industrial world.
Zola was drawn to the characterisation
of the misery, vice, disease, poverty and
violence of nineteenth-century Paris,
where the salvation of mankind always
remained a scientific possibility. As
writer Jean-Albert Bédé observed, 'the
petite fleur bleue will never fail to blossom in the corner of even his darkest
novels'. Naturalism only lasted around
thirty years (1865–1895), but Zola was
its champion.

He was born in Paris in Rue Saint-Joseph
in 1840 to Émilie Aubert, and François
Zola (originally Francesco Zolla), an
Italian engineer. When he was three
years old the family moved to Aix-en-
Provence where his childhood friend
was Paul Cézanne. Four years later his
father died from pleurisy leaving his
mother to survive on a small pension.
In his late teens he settled with his
mother and grandfather in Paris, which
was, he recalled later in life, 'one of the
cruellest disappointments in my life.
I was expecting a row of palaces, but
for close on a league the heavy vehicle
passed between sinister looking buildings, taverns and thieves' dens, a whole

slum lining the road.' After continuing his schooling in Paris, which was also a miserable experience, he was found a situation as a copy clerk in the Excise Office; but this he soon relinquished, stating that his dream was 'to publish within two years from now two volumes, one of prose and one of verse. As for the future, who knows? If I definitely embark on a literary career, I shall be true to my motto: All or nothing.'

By good fortune his next job was with the publishing house Hachette. Initially it was in the dispatch office, but he was soon promoted to sales where he created advertising copy for Hachette's new titles. With his newly acquired knowledge of the ploys of the publishing world he was able to fast-track the publication of his first collection of tales, *Contes à Ninon (Stories for Ninon)*, which included writing his own blurb and reviews. His first novel, the autobiographical *La Confession de Claude (Claude's Confession)*, followed a year later in 1865. Some months later, after writing occasional articles for provincial newspapers, he left Hachette and plunged into the full-time treadmill of literary and political journalism.

Zola's early works received scant critical attention, but his first major novel, the one that still stands the test of time, was *Thérèse Raquin*, published in 1867, in which an adulterous couple hatch a plot to murder the woman's husband. The following year, Zola began his vast *Les Rougon-Macquart* series of twenty novels that would take him until 1893 to complete. The cycle was subtitled 'The Natural and Social History of a Family Under the Second Empire' seen through the lives of the Rougons and the Macquarts, containing 'all the natural and instinctive manifestations peculiar

Émile Zola in 1902

to humanity – whose outcome assumes the conventional name of virtue or vice'. The first novel in the series to achieve commercial success was *L'Assommoir* (1877), a study of alcoholism and poverty, but record-breaking sales were achieved by the ninth novel in the series, *Nana* (1880), which tells the story of the rise and fall of a Parisian prostitute: it sold a spectacular 55,000 copies on its first day of publication.

Zola had married in 1870 and, with the proceeds from *L'Assommoir*, he bought a villa in 1878 in the little hamlet of Médan on the banks of the Seine, which became his country retreat from the bustle of Paris. Here Zola gathered his friends and disciples of Naturalism around him at weekends. 'Le groupe de Médan', as it was known, included Guy de Maupassant, Alphonse Daudet, Edmond de Goncourt and Joris-Karl Huysmans. Six members of the group, including Zola, published a collection of Naturalist stories entitled *Les Soirées de Médan* in 1880. The anthology is recognised as launching the career of Guy de Maupassant with its inclusion of his masterpiece 'Boule de Suif'.

Zola died on 29 September 1902. His body was found lying on the bedroom floor of his Paris apartment at 21 *bis* rue de Bruxelles, while his wife lay unconscious, but still breathing, on the bed. An autopsy revealed that his death was due to carbon monoxide poisoning from a blocked chimney. A verdict of accidental death was entered onto the death certificate, but suspicion of foul play motivated by Zola's involvement in the Dreyfus Affair persists to this day. Zola's ashes were transferred to the Panthéon from the Cimetière de Montmartre (where the family grave still exists with his name on it) in 1908.

See Also: Émile Zola's birthplace, Cimetière de Montmartre, Panthéon, The Dreyfus Affair, La Morgue, Louis Hachette, Guy de Maupassant, Alphonse Daudet, Edmond de Goncourt, Joris-Karl Huysmans.

Further Information: Médan is a village in the north-western suburbs of Paris where Zola's house was inaugurated into a museum in 2016. It also incorporates a museum dedicated to the Dreyfus Affair. Zola's marriage was a childless one, but he did produce two children by Jeanne Rozerot, a twenty-one-year-old laundress who had been employed at Médan. The nearest train station is Poissy.

Select Bibliography: *La Confession de Claude* (1865); *Thérèse Raquin* (1867); *La Fortune des Rougon* (1871); *L'Assommoir* (1877); *Nana* (1880); *Germinal* (1885); *La Bête humaine* (1890).

Further Reading: F. W. J. Hemmings, *The Life and Times of Émile Zola* (Scribner, 1977); A. Wilson, *Émile Zola: An Introductory study of his novels* (Secker & Warburg, 1952); F. Brown: *Zola: A Life* (Papermac, 1997); A. Schom, *Émile Zola: A Biography* (Holt, 1988).

POISSY

(Approximately 31 km west of Paris.
No Métro. Reachable by train, bus or car)

CHRISTINE DE PIZAN
1 ENCLOS DE L'ABBAYE

REMAINS OF THE FOURTEENTH-CENTURY DOMINICAN PRIORY WHERE CHRISTINE DE PIZAN, FRANCE'S FIRST WOMAN OF LETTERS, TOOK REFUGE AND REMAINED UNTIL HER DEATH

Just as women's bodies are softer than men's, so their understanding is sharper.
Christine de Pizan

Christine de Pizan (*c.*1364–*c.*1430), France's first woman of letters, was a prolific writer who had a distinct feminist voice. She was a powerful and inspiring commentator at a time when women had no voice and no legal rights. 'How many women are there,' she wrote, 'who because of their husbands' harshness spend their weary lives in the bond of marriage in greater suffering than if they were slaves among the Saracens?' The book for which she is acclaimed is *Le Livre de la cité des*

The Porter's Lodge

dames (The Book of the City of Ladies) (1405). Written in celebration of women and defending their virtues and abilities, it strives to prove without a doubt that women are the moral and intellectual equals of men.

She was born in Venice *c.*1364, but while she was still a child her family moved to France where her father, Tommaso di Benvenuto da Pizzano, was appointed physician and astrologer at the court of King Charles V. At the age of fifteen she married Étienne du Castel, a young nobleman, with whom she had three children. When in 1380 Charles V died, her father lost his position at court and the family was left in straitened circumstances. Eight years later her father died, followed soon afterwards by her husband, who died from bubonic plague. Now a widow with children and a mother to provide for, and with her financial affairs in ruins, the only resource left to Christine in the face of these adversities was to try and earn a living by her pen. She began by writing both prose and verse, and, as was customary, she sent much of her work to members of the royal court who, in return, would send her money for her efforts. As her reputation grew, courtiers began to commission work from her and gradually she climbed her way out of debt. She became proficient writing about moral issues, public affairs and politics and, in particular, the cause of women. In *l'Épistre au Dieu d'amours* (1399) she explored the status of women in society and their portrayal in literature. With *Le ivre de la cité des dames* (1405) she once again championed the rights of women. The emphasis of much of her later work was on the wretched and moral decay of France endorsed by its unwavering commitment to war with England.

A 15th-century manuscript illustration of Christine de Pizan presenting a book to Louis I, Duke of Orléans

After France lost the Battle of Agincourt during the Hundred Years War, and with the outbreak of civil war that followed in its wake, Christine de Pizan took refuge in the convent of the Dominican Priory at Poissy in 1418, where her daughter was a nun. It was here that Christine died, *c.*1430, aged around sixty-five.

Further Information: All that remains today of the Priory is the Porter's Lodge (la Porterie), which was the former entrance. Since 1976 it has been a toy museum. Walking through the port will lead you into the former grounds, now a park, which is enclosed by the old walls of the Priory. The Priory was erected in the early fourteenth century in honour of Louis IX (1214–1270), the only French king to be declared a saint. It was generously subsidised by the royal family and contained houses for up to 120 nuns, 13 friar chaplains and a royal residence. The nearest train station is Poissy.

Further Reading: C. Willard (ed.), *The Writings of Christine de Pizan* (Norton, 2007); *Christine de Pizan: Her Life and Works* (Norton, 2013).

LE PETIT-CLAMART

(Approximately 20 km south-west of Paris.
No Métro. Reachable by train, bus or car)

THE DAY OF THE JACKAL

AVENUE DU CHARLES DE GAULLE

SITE OF THE ATTEMPTED ASSASSINATION
OF PRESIDENT CHARLES DE GAULLE
FEATURED IN FREDERICK FORSYTH'S
NOVEL *THE DAY OF THE JACKAL*

Bastien-Thiry had personally spent days
preparing the site of the assassination, meas-
uring angles of fire, speed and distance of the
moving vehicles, and the degree of firepower
necessary to stop them. ...
A mile up the road Bastien-Thiry was expe-
riencing the effects of his big mistake. He
would not learn of it until told by the police as
he sat months later in Death Row. Investigat-
ing the timetable of his assassination he had
consulted a calendar to discover that dusk
fell on 22nd August at 8.35, seemingly plenty
late enough even if De Gaulle was late on
his usual schedule, as indeed he was. But the
calendar the Air Force colonel had consulted
related to 1961. On 22nd August, 1962, dusk
fell at 8.10. Those twenty-five minutes were
to change the history of France.
Frederick Forsyth, *The Day of the Jackal*
(1971)

Several assassination attempts (a conservative estimate would be around
thirty) were made on President Charles
de Gaulle during his political life. Some,
like the plan to shoot him with cyanide
bullets from a gun designed to look like
a camera, were laughable. Others came
very close to succeeding, but de Gaulle
always seemed blessed with good luck
and always lived to fight another day.
One of the closest shaves he ever had

Top: Frederick Forsyth in 1994
Above: Arrow Books, 2011 edition

President de Gaulle in his iconic Citroën DS in 1963 driving through the village of Isles-sur-Suippe in the Marne, on his return from a visit to the Ardennes

was when he survived an ambush in the Paris suburb of Le Petit-Clamart in August 1962, when a volley of bullets fired from three directions sprayed the car he was riding in with his wife, at the crossroads of Avenue de la Libération (now Avenue du Général de Gaulle), Rue Charles Debry and Rue du Bois. Miraculously they both survived. Today a municipal sign marks the site of the attempted assassination.

Frederick Forsyth wove the event, including the execution of its architect, Jean Bastien-Thiry, into his fictional thriller, *The Day of the Jackal*. Bastien-Thiry was a colonel in the Armée de l'Air (the French Air Force) and a supporter of de Gaulle, but when de Gaulle championed a policy for Algerian independence, a move Bastien-Thiry strongly opposed, he abandoned his Gaullist sympathies and plotted revenge. After the failed assassination attempt, known as Opération Charlotte Corday, and Bastien-Thiry's execution by firing squad, the novel departs from fact and the plot turns to fiction, with the terrorists rethinking their approach, and deciding to hire a professional assassin to kill de Gaulle. An Englishman, whose name is never revealed, is contracted for the job and given the code name the Jackal.

Frederick Forsyth's own life has been as action packed as his books. The son of a furrier, he was born in Ashford, Kent, in 1938. At the age of nineteen, he became the youngest pilot in the Royal Air Force. Later he took up journalism and spent three years as a provincial reporter before moving to Europe as a correspondent for Reuters. In 1965 he joined the BBC and covered the Nigerian Civil War between Biafra and Nigeria. At the end of his six-month posting, frustrated by the BBC's indifference to the war and keen to continue reporting, Forsyth requested that his time there be extended. The BBC's response was that 'it is not our policy to cover this war'. Determined to counter what he perceived to be 'news management' and the BBC's 'lies and distortions', he resigned and returned to Biafra as a freelance reporter, where he wrote the highly controversial *The Biafra Story*. The year of its publication, 1969, he used his experience as a Reuters reporter in France to write *The Day of the Jackal*. Written in only thirty-five days, it has sold over 10 million copies. Many people confuse the anonymous Englishman known as the Jackal, in Forsyth's thriller, with the international terrorist known as Carlos the Jackal, who is now serving a life sentence in France for murder. The confusion stems back to the mid 1970s when Carlos was gaining notoriety. A boyfriend of an ex-girlfriend of Carlos's discovered a bag of weapons belonging to Carlos in her London flat. Curiously, the boyfriend phoned *The Guardian* newspaper, rather than the police, who sent a reporter to assess the situation. The reporter, spying a copy of *The Day of the Jackal* on a bookshelf, concluded it belonged to Carlos, and dubbed him Carlos the Jackal in his exclusive report the following day. Since then, this is the name the terrorist has been known by. Ironically, the book on the shelf actually belonged to the boyfriend.

Further Information: Jean Bastien-Thiry named his assassination plot Opération

Charlotte Corday after the French revolutionary who murdered the radical politician Jean-Paul Marat in 1793. Bastien-Thiry was the last person to be executed by firing squad in France. 'The French need martyrs,' said de Gaulle. 'They must choose them carefully ... I gave them Bastien-Thiry.' De Gaulle claimed he survived Bastien-Thiry's assassination attempt because of the superior qualities of his presidential car, the Citroën DS, which, after being peppered with bullets and with two of its armoured tyres punctured, still accelerated at speed away from the ambush. Now a classic car, the French celebrated the fiftieth anniversary of its launch in October 2005 when 1600 DS cars drove in procession past the Arc de Triomphe.

The French began slowly colonising Algeria in the 1830s and thousands of French people began to emigrate there, many of them settling on the confiscated lands of indigenous Algerians. In 1954 tensions exploded between the French and the Muslim population and thousands were killed on both sides. The Front de Libération Nationale (FLN), a pro-independence group, fought against the Organisation Armée secrète (OAS), an anti-independence group, and both led bloody terrorist attacks in France and Algeria. By 1962 the political will of the French to prolong the conflict was exhausted and the government pronounced Algeria an independent country.

Select Bibliography: *The Biafra Story* (1969); *The Day of the Jackal* (1971); *The Odessa File* (1972); *The Dogs of War* (1974); *The Devil's Alternative* (1979); *The Fourth Protocol* (1984); *The Cobra* (2010); *The Kill List* (2013).

Further Reading: A. Horne, *A Savage War of Peace: Algeria 1954–1962* (Viking, 1978); C. Williams, *The Last Great Frenchman – A Life of General de Gaulle* (Jossey Bass, 1997).

FONTENAY-SOUS-BOIS

(Approximately 18 km east of Paris.
No Métro. Reachable by train, bus or car)

BEAU GESTE

BOULEVARD DU 25 AOÛT 1944

FORT DE NOGENT

FOREIGN LEGION

RECRUITMENT CENTRE

> *Non, rien de rien!*
> *Non, je ne regrette rien!*
> *Ni le bien qu'on m'a fait,*
> *Ni le mal!*
> *Tout ça m'est bien égal!*
>
> *(No, nothing whatsoever!*
> *No, I regret nothing!*
> *Neither the good done to me,*
> *Nor the bad!)*

From the classic song, *Non, je ne regrette rien* (No Regrets) (1956). Composed by Charles Dumont, with lyrics by Michel Vaucaire, and made famous by Edith Piaf, who dedicated the song to the Légion étrangère (French Foreign Legion) in 1961.

LÉGION ÉTRANGÈRE

The most accomplished adventure stories depicting the exploits of the French Foreign Legion were not written by a Frenchman, but by Englishman Percy Wren (1875–1941). His books inspired a succession of Hollywood desert dramas, the most memorable being *Beau Geste*, set in the searing heat of the Sahara. Wren wrote over thirty novels, most of them about colonial soldiering, and although he maintained he served in the French Foreign Legion, the regiment has no record of him. His books helped shape the universal image of the glamorous, rugged Legionnaire in his white kepi, who dies for a forgotten cause in a remote, fly-blown outpost.

Top: A 1926 edition of *Beau Geste*
Centre: The Légion étrangère in 1852
Above: Entrance to Fort de Nogent

535

King Louis Philippe founded the Légion étrangère in 1831. Its objective was to remove the troublesome elements of society, both French and foreign, which included revolutionaries, out-of-work mercenaries, mischief-makers and general good-for-nothings. It would mould them into a regiment to fight the enemies of France, and if they died on the battlefield no one would shed a tear for these undesirables. A royal decree also stipulated that the Légion étrangère could only fight outside France; in other words, out of sight, out of mind: cannon fodder nobody would mourn.

Today France's colonial empire is on the wane, but the Légion étrangère is still a crack fighting force of around 8000 recruits, most of them enlisted from outside France. All recruits must still adopt a new name, a practice that upholds the old tradition of a fresh start through rebirth. All recruits must speak French, and after three years they can apply for French citizenship, although a Legionnaire wounded in battle can claim citizenship under the proviso '*Français par le sang versé*' ('French by spilled blood').

Criminals are no longer welcome, but a kepi blanc, a new identity, and the pride of the Legion still awaits new recruits.

See Also: Charles de Gaulle, Albert Camus, Blaise Cendrars.

Further Information: In 1961 during the Algerian War the 1er régiment étranger de parachutistes (an airborne unit of the Foreign Legion) was disbanded for taking part in a coup against the government of General de Gaulle. Two hundred officers involved in the coup, including those of 1er régiment étranger de parachutistes, were detained at Fort de Nogent for two months. The leadership of the regiment was arrested and tried, but the remaining Legionnaires were assigned to other units. The song *Non, je ne regrette rien* is now part of the Legion's heritage and is sung on parade.

Further Reading: P.C. Wren, *Beau Geste* (1924); *Beau Sabreur* (1926); *Beau Ideal* (1928); M. Windrow, *Our Friends Beneath the Sands: The Foreign Legion in France's Colonial Conquests 1870–1935* (Weidenfeld & Nicolson, 2010); S. Travers, *Tomorrow to Be Brave: A Memoir of the Only Woman Ever to Serve in the French Foreign Legion* (Free Press, 2001).

VINCENNES
(Métro: Château de Vincennes)

MARQUIS DE SADE
1 AVENUE DE PARIS
CHÂTEAU DE VINCENNES

STATE PRISON FROM THE SIXTEENTH TO
THE NINETEENTH CENTURY THAT ONCE
HOUSED THE MARQUIS DE SADE

[A] fascinating man who for twenty years brutally loved and hated women and then spent the rest of his life in jail writing about what he couldn't do any more. ... Next to him [Henry] Miller is a child and Genet an angel. Simone de Beauvoir, 'Must We Burn Sade?' (1955)

Top: A 19th-century engraving of Sade
Above: Title page of the first edition of *Justine, ou les malheurs de la vertu*

The Marquis de Sade spent around thirty-two years of his life in prison, eventually dying within the confines of an insane asylum aged seventy-four. Ten of these years were spent in the Bastille, and at least eight in the grim tower of the Château de Vincennes. Much of his work was written, and in many instances, destroyed, in prisons, where his licentious and obscene literature gave his name to the term 'sadism'.

Born in Paris in 1740, Sade was the only surviving child of diplomat Jean Baptiste François Joseph, Count de Sade, and noblewoman Marie Eléonore de Maillé de Carman. While Sade was a young child, his father abandoned his mother, who then took herself to the sanctuary of a convent, leaving her young son in the care of overindulgent servants. In his teens, Sade attended military academy. As a soldier, he rose though the ranks, becoming a colonel and fighting in the Seven Years War. He married in his early twenties – mainly for money – and thereafter led a life of debauchery and sexual perversion. In 1772 he was condemned to death, a sentence that was later commuted to imprisonment. In captivity he began to write his tales of sexual fantasy, including *Les 120 Journées de Sodom (The 120 Days of Sodom)* (1784), *La Philosophie dans le boudoir (The Bedroom Philosophers)* (1793), and *Justine, ou les malheurs de la vertu (Justine, or the Misfortunes of Virtue)* (1791).

During the nineteenth century his notoriety faded, but in the early twentieth century Apollinaire and other surrealists, including André Breton and Salvador Dalí, defended and were ultimately seduced by Sade's expressions of sexual emancipation and political liberty. In the 1950s Jean-Paul Sartre championed his works, and today his writings have acquired both literary and academic respectability having been published in Gallimard's esteemed Pléiade imprint, editions of outstanding classic literature. Following Sade's death in 1814 the French legal system did its best to eradicate his memory by banning all his works. Almost 150 years later, in 1957, the French courts still upheld the original 1814 ruling.

In today's more enlightened times, when Sade's works now qualify as classic literature, do they also qualify as *great* literature? Whatever your opinion, his overwhelming influence on celebrated writers, from Charles Baudelaire to Friedrich Nietzsche, guarantees him a place in world literature.

See Also: Bastille, Denis Diderot, Gallimard, André Breton, Salvador Dalí, Guillaume Apollinaire, François Rabelais, Marguerite Duras, Henry Miller, Jean Genet, Gaston Gallimard.

Further Information: Sade spent his last years confined as a lunatic in the Charenton Asylum, where he continued to write. He died in 1814 and was buried in the asylum cemetery. A few years after Sade's death his body was exhumed and his skull examined by enthusiasts of phrenology, believing its shape and size to be an indication of his character and mental abilities. It was subsequently lost and the findings are unknown.

Charenton Asylum, in the Paris commune of Saint-Maurice, was founded by the Brothers of Charity in 1645, and is remembered for its humanitarian treatment of patients. It is now a psychiatric hospital known as Hôpital Esquirol, named after the innovative French psychiatrist, Jean-Étienne Esquirol. Château de Vincennes was originally built as a hunting lodge for Louis VII at the end of the twelfth century. With the passage of time it has been rebuilt and remodelled to suit the tastes of generations of the French Royal household. Between the sixteenth and the seventeenth century the fortified tower standing 164 ft (50 m) was converted into a royal prison. French philosopher Denis Diderot was imprisoned for four months at the Château de Vincennes in 1749, following a government clampdown on writers and publishers of seditious literature. Located in the Bois de Vincennes, the Château is open to the public.

Hôpital Esquirol, formerly Charenton Asylum

Château de Vincennes

Select Bibliography: *Three Complete Novels: Justine, Philosophy in the Bedroom, and Other Writings* (Arrow, 1991); *120 Days of Sodom* (Penguin Classics, 2016).

Further Reading: R. Hayman, *Marquis de Sade: The Genius of Passion* (Constable, 1978); M. Lever, *Marquis de Sade: A Biography* (HarperCollins, 1993).

ACKNOWLEDGEMENTS

The writer may write the book, but it's the editor that polishes the text and makes it readable. The editorial contribution my wife Chris made to my work was so great I asked her to share its authorship, but she would have none of it. 'You're the author and I'm the editor,' she said emphatically. There was no arguing with her. All I can do, therefore, is make it known that this book would have been a much lesser achievement without the hundreds of hours she spent at her desk, untangling my sentences and making sense of my words, from Anna Akhmatova through to Émile Zola. For this I thank her with all my heart.

Thanks to my son, Kit, who designed the cover, and my daughter Lucy, for her cover artwork and 'editor at work' (below); also to Chloe Foster, Clare Hughes, Jack Foster, Dawn Greaves, Kath McDonald, Harry Winslow, Maureen and Arthur Still, the Sisters of Mercy (Maisie and Enid Still), Jason Patient, Jim Haynes, Isabelle Georges, Ron Morstyn, Melissa Arica-Cruz, Tamara Makarowa, Mark Wiederanders, and Bas Schuddeboom at *Lambiek Comiclopedia*.

Finally, I would like to quote Edward Dowden, who noted in the preface to his 1897 *History of French Literature*, 'My collaborators are on my shelves. Without them I could not have accomplished my task; here I give them credit for their assistance … I have accepted from each a gift.'

The author in the Bois de Boulogne

The editor at work

INDEX

Lightning Source UK Ltd.
Milton Keynes UK
UKHW021106180821
389055UK00012B/907